Beginning Android Games

Mario Zechner

Apress®

Beginning Android Games

ISBN-13 (pbk): 978-1-4302-3042-7

ISBN-13 (electronic): 978-1-4302-3043-4

President and Publisher: Paul Manning
Lead Editor: Steve Anglin
Development Editor: Matthew Moodie
Technical Reviewer: Robert Green
Editorial Board: Steve Anglin, Mark Beckner, Ewan Buckingham, Gary Cornell, Jonathan Gennick, Jonathan Hassell, Michelle Lowman, Matthew Moodie, Jeff Olson, Jeffrey Pepper, Frank Pohlmann, Douglas Pundick, Ben Renow-Clarke, Dominic Shakeshaft, Matt Wade, Tom Welsh
Coordinating Editor: Adam Heath
Copy Editors: Damon Larson, Jim Compton
Compositor: MacPS, LLC
Indexer: BIM Indexing & Proofreading Services
Artist: April Milne
Cover Designer: Anna Ishchenko

Distributed to the book trade worldwide by Springer Science+Business Media, LLC., 233 Spring Street, 6th Floor, New York, NY 10013. Phone 1-800-SPRINGER, fax (201) 348-4505, e-mail orders-ny@springer-sbm.com, or visit www.springeronline.com.

For information on translations, please e-mail rights@apress.com, or visit www.apress.com.

Apress and friends of ED books may be purchased in bulk for academic, corporate, or promotional use. eBook versions and licenses are also available for most titles. For more information, reference our Special Bulk Sales–eBook Licensing web page at www.apress.com/info/bulksales.

The source code for this book is available to readers at www.apress.com.

Dedicated to my idols, Mom and Dad, and to my love, Stefanie

Contents at a Glance

Contents

About the Author

Mario Zechner is a software engineer in R&D by day, and an enthusiastic game developer by night, publishing under the name of Badlogic Games. He developed the game Newton for Android, and Quantum for Windows, Linux, and Mac OSX, besides a ton of prototypes and small-scale games. He's currently working on an open source cross-platform solution for game development called libgdx. In addition to his coding activities, he actively writes tutorials and articles on game development, which are freely available on the Web and specifically his blog (`http://www.badlogicgames.com`).

About the Technical Reviewer

 Robert Green is an independent video game developer from Portland, Oregon, who publishes under the brand Battery Powered Games. He has developed six Android games, including Deadly Chambers, Antigen, Wixel, Light Racer, and Light Racer 3D. Before diving full-time into mobile video game development and publishing, Robert worked for software companies in Minneapolis and Chicago, including IBM Interactive. Robert's current focus is on cross-platform game development and high-performance mobile gaming.

Acknowledgments

I'd like to thank the Apress team that made this book possible in the first place. Specifically I'd like to thank Candace English and Adam Heath, my awesome coordinating editors, who never got tired answering all my silly questions; Matthew Moodie for helping me structure the sections and giving invaluable hints and suggestions to make this book a whole lot better; and Damon Larson and James Compton, for being the brave souls that had to correct all my grammar errors. Thanks guys, it's been a pleasure working with you.

Thanks to my dear friend Robert Green, who played the technical reviewer for this book. He made sure that my ramblings were technically correct. He'll also be my scapegoat in case people discover bugs and errors.

Special thanks to all my friends around the globe who gave me ideas, feedback, and comfort when I realized I was working at 3 a.m. again. This goes specifically to Nathan Sweet, Dave Clayton, Dave Fraska, Moritz Post, Christoph Widulle, and Tony Wang, the coding ninjas working with me on libgdx; John Phil and Ali Mosavian, my long-time coding buddies from Sweden; and Roman Kern and Markus Muhr, whom I have had the pleasure to work with at my day job.

Last but certainly not least I'd like to thank my love, Stefanie, who put up with all the long nights alone in bed, as well as my grumpiness. Luipo!

Introduction

Hi there, and welcome to the world of Android game development. My name is Mario; I'll be your guide for the next fourteen chapters. You came here to learn about game development on Android, and I hope to be the person who enables you to realize your ideas.

Together we'll cover quite a range of materials and topics: Android basics, audio and graphics programming, a little math and physics, and a scary thing called OpenGL ES. Based on all this knowledge we'll develop three different games, one even being 3D.

Game programming can be easy if you know what you're doing. Therefore I've tried to present the material in a way that not only gives you helpful code snippets to reuse, but actually shows you the big picture of game development. Understanding the underlying principles is the key to tackling ever more complex game ideas. You'll not only be able to write games similar to the ones developed over the course of this book, but you'll also be equipped with enough knowledge to go to the Web or the bookstore and take on new areas of game development on your own.

A Word About the Target Audience

This book is aimed first and foremost at complete beginners in game programming. You don't need any prior knowledge on the subject matter; I'll walk you through all the basics. However, I need to assume a little knowledge on your end about Java. If you feel rusty on the matter, I'd suggest refreshing your memory by reading the online edition of *Thinking in Java*, by Bruce Eckel (Prentice Hall, 2006), an excellent introductory text on the programming language. Other than that, there are no other requirements. No prior exposure to Android or Eclipse is necessary!

This book is also aimed at the intermediate-level game programmer that wants to get her hands dirty with Android. While some of the material may be old news for you, there are still a lot of tips and hints contained that should make reading this book worthwhile. Android is a strange beast at times, and this book should be considered your battle guide.

How This Book Is Organized

This book takes an iterative approach in that we'll slowly but surely work our way from the absolute basics to the esoteric heights of hardware-accelerated game programming goodness. Over the course of the chapters, we'll build up a reusable code base, so I'd suggest going through the chapters in sequence. More experienced readers can of course skip certain sections they feel confident with. Just make sure to read through the code listings of sections you skim over a little, so you will understand how the classes and interfaces are used in subsequent, more advanced sections.

Getting the Source Code

This book is fully self-contained; all the code necessary to run the examples and games is included. However, copying the listings from the book to Eclipse is error prone, and games do not consist of code alone, but also have assets that you can't easily copy out of the book. Also, the process of copying code from the book's text to Eclipse can introduce errors. Robert (the book's technical reviewer) and I took great care to ensure that all the listings in this book are error free, but the gremlins are always hard at work.

To make this a smooth ride, I created a Google Code project that offers you the following:

- The complete source code and assets, licensed under the GPL version 3, available from the project's Subversion repository.

- A quickstart guide showing you how to import the projects into Eclipse in textual form, and a video demonstration for the same.

- An issue tracker that allows you to report any errors you find, either in the book itself or in the code accompanying the book. Once you file an issue in the issue tracker, I can incorporate any fixes in the Subversion repository. This way you'll always have an up-to-date, (hopefully) error-free version of this book's code from which other readers can benefit as well.

- A discussion group that is free for everybody to join and discuss the contents of the book. I'll be on there as well of course.

For each chapter that contains code, there's an equivalent Eclipse project in the Subversion repository. The projects do not depend on each other, as we'll iteratively improve some of the framework classes over the course of the book. Each project therefore stands on its own. The code for both Chapters 5 and 6 is contained in the ch06-mrnom project.

The Google Code project can be found at http://code.google.com/p/beginning-android-games.

Chapter 1

Android, the New Kid on the Block

As a kid of the early nineties, I naturally grew up with my trusty Nintendo Game Boy. I spent countless hours helping Mario rescue the princess, getting the highest score in Tetris, and racing my friends in RC Pro-Am via link cable. I took this awesome piece of hardware with me everywhere and every time I could. My passion for games made me want to create my own worlds and share them with my friends. I started programming on the PC but soon found out that I couldn't transfer my little masterpieces to the Game Boy. I continued being an enthusiastic programmer, but over time my interest in actually playing video games faded. Also, my Game Boy broke . . .

Fast forward to 2010. Smartphones are becoming the new mobile gaming platforms of the era, competing with classic dedicated handheld systems such as the Nintendo DS or the Playstation Portable. That caught my interest again, and I started investigating which mobile platforms would be suitable for my development needs. Apple's iOS seemed like a good candidate to start coding games for. However, I quickly realized that the system was not open, that I'd be able to share my work with others only if Apple allowed it, and that I'd need a Mac to develop for the iOS. And then I found Android.

I immediately fell in love with Android. Its development environment works on all the major platforms, no strings attached. It has a vibrant developer community happy to help you with any problem you encounter as well as comprehensive documentation. I can share my games with anyone without having to pay a fee to do so, and if I want to monetize my work, I can easily publish my latest and greatest innovation to a global market with millions of users in a matter of minutes.

The only thing I was left with was actually figuring out how to write games for Android and how to transfer my PC game development knowledge to this new system. In the following chapters, I want to share my experience with you and get you started with Android game development. This is of course a rather selfish plan: I want to have more games to play on the go!

Let's start by getting to know our new friend: Android.

A Brief History of Android

Android was first publicly noticed in 2005 when Google acquired a small startup called Android, Inc. This fueled speculation that Google wanted to enter the mobile space. In 2008, the release of version 1.0 of Android put an end to all speculation, and Android became the new challenger on the mobile market. Since then, it's been battling it out with already established platforms such as iOS (then called iPhone OS) and BlackBerry, and its chances of winning look rather good.

Because Android is open source, handset manufacturers have a low barrier of entry when using the new platform. They can produce devices for all price segments, modifying Android itself to accommodate the processing power of a specific device. Android is therefore not limited to high-end devices but can also be deployed to low-budget devices, thus reaching a wider audience.

A crucial ingredient for Android's success was the formation of the Open Handset Alliance (OHA) in late 2007. The OHA includes companies such as HTC, Qualcomm, Motorola, and NVIDIA, which collaborate to develop open standards for mobile devices. Although Android's core is developed mainly by Google, all the OHA members contribute to its source in one form or another.

Android itself is a mobile operating system and platform based on the Linux kernel version 2.6 and is freely available for commercial and noncommercial use. Many members of the OHA build custom versions of Android for their devices with modified user interfaces (UIs)—for example, HTC's HTC Sense and Motorola's MOTOBLUR. The open source nature of Android also enables hobbyists to create and distribute their own versions of Android. These are usually called *mods*, *firmwares*, or *ROMs*. The most prominent ROM at the time of this writing was developed by a fellow known as Cyanogen and is aimed at bringing the latest and greatest improvements to all sorts of Android devices.

Since its release in 2008, Android has received seven version updates, all code-named after desserts (with the exception of Android 1.1, which is irrelevant nowadays). Each version has added new functionality to the Android platform that has relevance in one way or another for game developers. Version 1.5 (Cupcake) added support for including native libraries in Android applications, which were previously restricted to being written in pure Java. Native code can be very beneficial in situations where performance is of upmost concern. Version 1.6 (Donut) introduced support for different screen resolutions. We will revisit this fact a couple of times in this book because it has some impact on how we approach writing games for Android. With version 2.0 (Éclair) came support for multi-touch screens, and version 2.2 (Froyo) added just-in-time (JIT) compilation to the Dalvik virtual machine (VM), which powers all the Java applications on Android. The JIT speeds up the execution of Android applications considerably—depending on the scenario, up to a factor of five. At the time of this writing, the latest version is 2.3, called Gingerbread. It adds a new concurrent garbage collector to the Dalvik VM. If you haven't noticed yet: Android applications are written in Java.

A special version of Android, targeted at tablets, is also being released in 2011. It is called Honeycomb and represents version 3.0 of Android. Honeycomb is not meant to run on phones at this point. However, some features of Honeycomb will be ported to the main line of Android. At the time of this writing, Android 3.0 is not available to the public, and no devices on the market are running it. Android 2.3 can be installed on many devices using custom ROMs. The only handset using Gingerbread is the Nexus S, a developer phone sold by Google directly.

Fragmentation

The great flexibility of Android comes at a price: companies that opt to develop their own user interfaces have to play catch-up with the fast pace at which new versions of Android are released. This can lead to handsets not older than a few months becoming outdated really fast as carriers and handset manufacturers refuse to create updates that incorporate the improvements of new Android versions. The big bogeyman called *fragmentation* is a result of this process.

Fragmentation has many faces. For the end user, it means being unable to install and use certain applications and features because of being stuck on an old Android version. For developers, it means that some care has to be taken when creating applications that should work on all versions of Android. While applications written for earlier versions of Android will usually run fine on newer versions, the reverse is not true. Some features added in newer Android versions are of course not available on older versions, such as multi-touch support. Developers are thus forced to create separate code paths for different versions of Android.

But fear not. Although this sounds terrifying, it turns out that the measures that have to be taken are minimal. Most often, you can even completely forget about the whole issue and pretend there's only a single version of Android. As game developers, we're less concerned with differences in APIs and more concerned about hardware capabilities. This is a different form of fragmentation, which is also a problem for platforms such as iOS, albeit not as pronounced. Throughout this book, I will cover the relevant fragmentation issues that might get in your way while you develop your next game for Android.

The Role of Google

Although Android is officially the brainchild of the Open Handset Alliance, Google is the clear leader when it comes to implementing Android itself as well as providing the necessary ecosystem for Android to grow.

The Android Open Source Project

Google's efforts are summarized under the name *Android Open Source Project*. Most of the code is licensed under Apache License 2, a very open and nonrestrictive license compared to other open source licenses such as the GNU General Public License (GPL). Everyone is free to use this source code to build their own systems. However, systems that are claimed to be Android compatible first have to pass the Android Compatibility

Program, a process ensuring baseline compatibility with third-party applications written by developers like us. Compatible systems are allowed to participate in the Android ecosystem, which also includes the Android Market.

The Android Market

The *Android Market* was opened to the public in October 2008 by Google. It's an online software store that enables users to find and install third-party applications. The market is generally accessible only through the market application on a device. This situation will change in the near future, according to Google, which promises the deployment of a desktop-based online store accessible via the browser.

The market allows third-party developers to publish their applications either for free or as paid applications. Paid applications are available for purchase in only about 30 countries. Selling applications as a developer is possible in a slightly smaller number. Table 1–1 shows you the countries in which apps can be bought and sold.

Table 1–1. *Purchase and Selling Options per Country.*

Country	User Can Purchase Apps	Developer Can Sell Apps
Australia	Yes	Yes
Austria	Yes	Yes
Belgium	Yes	Yes
Brazil	Yes	Yes
Canada	Yes	Yes
Czech Republic	Yes	**No**
Denmark	Yes	Yes
Finland	Yes	Yes
France	Yes	Yes
Germany	Yes	Yes
Hong Kong	Yes	Yes
Hungary	Yes	Yes
India	Yes	Yes
Ireland	Yes	Yes

Country	User Can Purchase Apps	Developer Can Sell Apps
Israel	Yes	Yes
Italy	Yes	Yes
Japan	Yes	Yes
Mexico	Yes	Yes
Netherlands	Yes	Yes
New Zealand	Yes	Yes
Norway	Yes	Yes
Pakistan	Yes	**No**
Poland	Yes	**No**
Portugal	Yes	Yes
Russia	Yes	Yes
Singapore	Yes	Yes
South Korea	Yes	Yes
Spain	Yes	Yes
Sweden	Yes	Yes
Switzerland	Yes	Yes
Taiwan	Yes	Yes
United Kingdom	Yes	Yes
United States	Yes	Yes

Users get access to the market after setting up a Google account. Applications can be bought only via credit card at the moment. Buyers can decide to return an application within 15 minutes from the time of purchasing it and will receive a full refund. Previously, the refund time window was 24 hours. The recent change to 15 minutes has not been well received by end users.

Developers need to register an Android Developer account with Google for a one-time fee of $25 in order to be able to publish applications on the market. After successful registration, a developer can immediately start to publish a new application in a matter of minutes.

The Android Market has no approval process but relies on a permission system. A user is presented with a set of permissions needed by an application before the installation of the program. These permissions handle access to phone services, networking access, access to the Secure Digital (SD) card, and so on. Only after a user has approved these permissions is the application installed. The system relies on the user doing the right thing. On the PC, especially on Windows systems, this concept didn't work out too well. On Android, it seems to have worked so far; only a few of applications have been pulled from the market because of malicious behavior.

To sell applications, a developer has to additionally register a Google Checkout Merchant Account, which is free of charge. All financial business is handled through this account.

Challenges, Device Seeding, and Google I/O

In an ongoing effort to draw more developers to the Android platform, Google started to hold challenges. The first challenge, called the Android Developer Challenge (ADC) was launched in 2008, offering relatively high cash prices for the winning projects. The ADC was carried out in the subsequent year and was again a huge success in terms of developer participation. There was no ADC in 2010, which can probably be attributed to Android now having a considerable developer base and thus not needing any further actions to get new developers on board.

Google also started a device-seeding program in early 2010. Each developer who had one or more applications on the market with more than 5,000 downloads and an average user rating of 3.5 stars or above received a brand new Motorola Droid, Motorola Milestone, or Nexus One phone. This was a very well-received action within the developer community, although it was initially met with disbelief. Many considered the e-mail notifications that came out of the blue to be an elaborate hoax. Fortunately, the promotion turned out to be a reality, and thousands of devices were sent to developers across the planet—a great move by Google to keep its third-party developers happy and make them stick with the platform and to potentially attract new developers.

Google also provides the special Android Dev Phone (ADP) for developers. The first ADP was a version of the T-Mobile G1 (also known as HTC Dream). The next iteration, called ADP 2, was a variation of the HTC Magic. Google also released its own phone in the form of the Nexus One, available to end users. Although initially not released as an ADP, it was considered by many as the successor to the ADP 2. Google eventually stopped selling the Nexus One to end users, and it is now available for shipment only to partners and developers. At the end of 2010, the latest ADP was released; this Samsung device running Android 2.3 (Gingerbread) is called the Nexus S. ADPs can be bought via the Android Market, which requires you to have a developer account. The Nexus S can be bought via a separate Google site at www.google.com/phone.

The annual Google I/O conference is an event every Android developer looks forward to each year. At Google I/O, the latest and greatest Google technologies and projects are revealed, among which Android has gained a special place in recent years. Google I/O usually features multiple sessions on Android-related topics, which are also available as videos on YouTube's Google Developers channel.

Android's Features and Architecture

Android is not just another Linux distribution for mobile devices. While you develop for Android, you're not all that likely to meet the Linux kernel itself. The developer-facing side of Android is a platform that abstracts away the underlying Linux kernel and is programmed via Java. From a high-level view, Android possesses several nice features:

- An *application framework* providing a rich set of APIs to create various types of applications. It also allows the reuse and replacement of components provided by the platform and third-party applications.

- The *Dalvik virtual machine*, which is responsible for running applications on Android.

- A set of *graphics libraries* for 2D and 3D programming.

- *Media support* for common audio, video, and image formats such as Ogg Vorbis, MP3, MPEG-4, H.264, and PNG. There's even a specialized API for playing back sound effects, which will come in handy in our game development adventures.

- *APIs for accessing peripherals* such as the camera, Global Positioning System (GPS), compass, accelerometer, touch screen, trackball, and keyboard. Note that not all Android devices have all of these peripherals—hardware fragmentation in action.

There's of course a lot more to Android than the few features I just mentioned. For our game development needs, these features are the most relevant, though.

Android's architecture is composed of a stack of components, and each component builds on the components in the layer below it. Figure 1–1 gives an overview of Android's major components.

Figure 1–1. *Android architecture overview*

The Kernel

Starting from the bottom of the stack, you can see that the Linux kernel provides the basic drivers for the hardware components. Additionally, the kernel is responsible for such mundane things as memory and process management, networking, and so on.

The Runtime and Dalvik

The Android runtime is built on top of the kernel and is responsible for spawning and running Android applications. Each Android application is run in its own process with its own Dalvik virtual machine.

Dalvik runs programs in the DEX bytecode format. Usually you transform common Java .class files to the DEX format via a special tool called *dx* that is provided by the software development kit. The DEX format is designed to have a smaller memory footprint compared to classic Java .class files. This is achieved by heavy compression, tables, and merging of multiple .class files.

The Dalvik virtual machine interfaces with the core libraries, which provide the basic functionality exposed to Java programs. The core libraries provide some but not all of the classes available in Java SE through the use of a subset of the Apache Harmony Java implementation. This also means that there's no Swing or Abstract Window Toolkit (AWT) available, nor any classes that can be found in Java ME. However, with some care, you can still use many of the third-party libraries available for Java SE on Dalvik.

Before Android 2.2 (Froyo), all bytecode was interpreted. Froyo introduces a tracing JIT compiler, which compiles parts of the bytecode to machine code on the fly. This increases the performance of computationally intensive applications considerably. The JIT compiler can use CPU features specifically tailored for special computations such as a dedicated Floating Point Unit (FPU).

Dalvik also has an integrated garbage collector (GC). It's a mark-and-sweep nongenerational GC that has the tendency to drive developers a tad bit mad at times. With some attention to details, you can peacefully coexist with the GC in your day-to-day game development, though. The latest Android release (2.3) has an improved concurrent GC, which relieves some of the pain. We'll investigate GC issues in more detail later in the book.

Each application running in an instance of the Dalvik VM has a total of 16MB to 24MB of heap memory available. We'll have to keep that in mind as we juggle our image and audio resources.

System Libraries

Besides the core libraries, which provide some Java SE functionality, there's also a set of native C/C++ libraries that build the basis for the application framework (located in the next layer of Figure 1–1). These system libraries are mostly responsible for the computationally heavy tasks such as graphics rendering, audio playback, and database access, which would not be so well suited for the Dalvik virtual machine. The APIs are wrapped via Java classes in the application framework, which we'll exploit when we start writing our games. We'll abuse the following libraries in one form or another:

> *Skia Graphics Library (Skia)*: This software renderer for 2D graphics is used for rendering the UI of Android applications. We'll use it to draw our first 2D game.

> *OpenGL for Embedded Systems (OpenGL ES)*: This is the industry standard for hardware-accelerated graphics rendering. OpenGL ES 1.0 and 1.1 are exposed in Java on all versions of Android. OpenGL ES 2.0, which brings shaders to the table, is supported from only Android 2.2 (Froyo) onward. It should be mentioned that the Java bindings for OpenGL ES 2.0 are incomplete and lack a few vital methods. Also, the emulator and most of the older devices that still make up a considerable share of the market do not support OpenGL ES 2.0. We'll be concerned with OpenGL ES 1.0 and 1.1, to stay compatible as much as possible.

OpenCore: This is a media playback and recording library for audio and video. It supports a good mix of formats such as Ogg Vorbis, MP3, H.264, MPEG-4 and so on. We'll be mostly concerned with the audio portion, which is not directly exposed to the Java side but wrapped in a couple of classes and services.

FreeType: This is a library to load and render bitmap and vector fonts, most notably the TrueType format. FreeType supports the Unicode standard, including right-to-left glyph rendering for Arabic and similar peculiarities. Sadly, this is not entirely true for the Java side, which to this point does not support Arabic typography. As with OpenCore, FreeType is not directly exposed to the Java side but is wrapped in a couple of convenient classes.

These system libraries cover a lot of ground for game developers and perform most of the heavy lifting for us. They are the reason why we can write our games in plain old Java.

> Note: Although the capabilities of Dalvik are usually more than sufficient for our purposes, at times you might need more performance. This can be the case for very complex physics simulations or heavy 3D calculations—for which we would usually resort to writing native code. I do not cover this aspect in this book. A couple of open source libraries for Android already exist that can help you stay on the Java side of things. See `http://code.google.com/p/libgdx/` for an example. Also worth noting is the excellent book *Pro Android Games* by Vladimir Silva (Apress, 2009), which goes into depth about interfacing with native code in the context of game programming.

The Application Framework

The application framework ties together the system libraries and the runtime, creating the user side of Android. The framework manages applications and provides an elaborate framework within which applications operate. Developers create applications for this framework via a set of Java APIs that cover such areas as UI programming, background services, notifications, resource management, peripheral access, and so on. All core applications provided out of the box by Android, such as the mail client, are written with these APIs.

Applications, whether they are UIs or background services, can communicate their capabilities to other applications. This communication enables an application to reuse components of other applications. A simple example is an application that needs to take a photo and then perform some operations on it. The application queries the system for a component of another application that provides this service. The first application can then reuse the component (for example, a built-in camera application or photo gallery). This significantly lowers the burden on programmers and also enables you to customize a plethora of aspects of Android's behavior.

As game developers, we will create UI applications within this framework. As such, we will be interested in an application's architecture and life cycle as well as its interactions with the user. Background services usually play a small role in game development, which is why I will not go into details about them.

The Software Development Kit

To develop applications for Android, we will use the Android software development kit (SDK). The SDK is composed of a comprehensive set of tools, documentation, tutorials, and samples that will help you get started in no time. Also included are the Java libraries needed to create applications for Android. These contain the APIs of the application framework. All major desktop operating systems are supported as development environments.

Prominent features of the SDK are as follows:

- The *debugger*, capable of debugging applications running on a device or in the emulator

- A *memory and performance profile* to help you find memory leaks and identify slow code

- The *device emulator*, based on QEMU (an open source virtual machine to simulate different hardware platforms), which, although accurate, can be a bit slow at times

- *Command-line utilities* to communicate with devices

- *Build scripts* and tools to package and deploy applications

The SDK can be integrated with Eclipse, a popular and feature-rich open source Java integrated development environment (IDE). The integration is achieved through the Android Development Tools (ADT) plug-in, which adds a set of new capabilities to Eclipse to create Android projects; to execute, profile and debug applications in the emulator or on a device; and to package Android applications for their deployment to the Android Market. Note that the SDK can also be integrated into other IDEs such as NetBeans. There is, however, no official support for this.

> **NOTE:** Chapter 2 covers how to set up the development environment with the SDK and Eclipse.

The SDK and the ADT plug-in for Eclipse receive constant updates that add new features and capabilities. It's therefore a good idea to keep them updated.

Alongside any good SDK comes extensive documentation. Android's SDK does not fall short in this area and comes with a lot of sample applications. You can also find a developer guide and a full API reference for all the modules of the application framework at `http://developer.android.com/guide/index.html`.

The Developer Community

Part of the success of Android is its developer community, which gathers in various places around the Web. The most frequented site for developer exchange is the Android Developers group at `http://groups.google.com/group/android-developers`. This is the number one place to ask questions or seek help when you stumble across a seemingly unsolvable problem. The group is visited by all sorts of Android developers, from system programmers, to application developers, to game programmers. Occasionally, the Google engineers responsible for parts of Android also help out with valuable insights. Registration is free, and I highly recommend starting reading the group now! Apart from providing a place for you to ask questions, it's also a great place to search for already answered questions and solutions to problems. So, before asking a question, check whether it has been answered already.

Every developer community worth its salt has a mascot. Linux has Tux the penguin, GNU has its, well, gnu, and Mozilla Firefox has its trendy Web 2.0 fox. Android is no different and has selected a little green robot as its mascot of choice. Figure 1–2 shows you that little devil.

Figure 1–2. *Android's nameless mascot*

Although its choice of color may be disputable, this nameless little robot already starred in a couple of popular Android games. Its most notable appearance was in Replica Island, a free and open source platfom created by Google engineer Chris Pruett as a 20 percent project.

Devices, Devices, Devices!

Android is not locked into a single hardware ecosystem. Many prominent handset manufacturers such asHTC, Motorola, and Samsung have jumped onto the Android wagon and offer a wide range of devices running Android. Besides handsets, there's also a slew of tablet devices coming to the market that build upon Android. Some key concepts are shared by all devices, though, which makes our lives as game developers a little easier.

Hardware

There are no hard minimum requirements for an Android device. However, Google has recommended the following hardware specifications, which virtually all available Android devices fulfill and most often surpass significantly:

ARM-based CPU: At the time of writing this book, this requirement was relaxed. Android now also runs on the x86 architecture. The latest ARM-based devices are also starting to feature dual-core CPUs.

128MB RAM: This specification is a minimum. Current high-end devices already include 512MB RAM, and 1GB RAM devices are expected in the very near future.

256MB flash memory: This minimum amount of memory is for storing the system image and applications. For a long time, this lack of memory was the biggest gripe among Android users because third-party applications could be installed only to flash memory. This changed with the release of Froyo.

Mini or Micro SD card storage: Most devices come with a few gigabytes of SD card storage, which can be replaced with bigger SD cards by the user.

16-bit color Half-Size Video Graphics Array (HVGA) TFT LCD with touch screen: Before Android version 1.6, only HVGA screens (480×320 pixels) were supported by the operating system. Since version 1.6, lower- and higher-resolution screens are supported. The current high-end devices have Wide Video Graphis Array (WVGA) screens (800×480, 848×480, or 852×480 pixels), and some low-end devices sport Quarter-Size Video Graphics Array (QVGA) (320×280 pixels) screens. Touch screens are almost always capacitive and are only single-touch capable on most older devices.

Dedicated hardware keys: These keys are used for navigation. Most phones to date have at least a menu, search, home, and a back key. Some manufacturers have started to deviate from this and are including a subset of these keys or no keys at all.

Of course, there's a lot more hardware in actual Android devices. Almost all handsets have *GPS*, an *accelerometer*, and a *compass*. Many also feature *proximity and light sensors*. These peripherals offer game developers new ways to let the user interact – with the game, and we'll have a look at some of them later on. A few devices have a full *QWERTY keyboard* as well as a *trackball*. The latter is most often found in HTC devices.

Cameras are also available on almost all current devices. Some handsets and tablets have two cameras, one on the back and one on the front for video chat.

Especially crucial for game development are dedicated *graphics processor units (GPUs)*. The earliest handset to run Android already had an OpenGL ES 1.0compliant GPU. More-modern devices have GPUs comparable in performance to the Xbox or PlayStation 2 and support OpenGL ES 2.0. If no graphics processor is available, a fallback in the form of a software renderer called PixelFlinger is provided by the platform. Many low-budget handsets rely on the software renderer, which is often sufficiently fast for low-resolution screens.

Along with the graphics processor, any currently available Android device also has dedicated *audio hardware*. Many hardware platforms also have special circuitry to decode different media formats such as H.264 in hardware. Connectivity is provided via hardware components for mobile telephony, Wi-Fi, and Bluetooth. All these hardware modules of an Android device are most often integrated in a single *system on a chip (SoC)*, a system design also found in embedded hardware.

First Gen, Second Gen, Next Gen

Given the differences in capabilities, especially in terms of performance, Android developers usually group devices into first-, second-, and next-generation devices. This terminology comes up a lot, even more so when it comes to game development for Android. Let's try to define these terms.

Each generation has a specific set of characteristics, mostly a combination of the Android version(s) used, the CPU/GPU, and the screen resolution of the devices within a generation. Although the hardware specifications are static, this might not be the case for the Android version used on a device.

In the Beginning: First Generation

First-generation devices are the current baseline and are best described by examining one of their most prominent specimens, the HTC Hero, shown in Figure 1–3.

Figure 1–3. *The HTC Hero*

This was one of the first Android phones that was said to be an iPhone killer, released in October 2009. The Hero was first shipped with Android version 1.5 installed, which was the standard for most Android handsets for most of 2009. The last official update for the Hero was to Android version 2.1. Newer updates can be installed only if the phone is *rooted*, a process that grants full system access.

The Hero has a 3.2-inch HVGA capacitive LCD touch screen, a 528MHz Qualcomm MSM7201A CPU/GPU combination, an accelerometer, and a compass, as well as a 5-megapixel camera. It also has the typical set of navigational hardware keys that most first-generation devices exhibit, along with a trackball.

The Hero is a prime example of first-generation devices. The touch screen has only limited support for multi-touch gestures such as the pinch zoom and no true multi-touch capability. Note that multi-touch gestures are not officially supported by the device and are also not exposed through the APIs of the official Android version 1.5. In this regard, the Hero was a major diasppointment for game developers who had hoped for similar multi-touch capabilities as those found on the iPhone.

Another common trait of first-generation devices is the screen resolution of 480×320 pixels, the standard resolution up until Android version 1.6.

In the CPU/GPU department, the Hero employs the very common MSM7201A series by Qualcomm. This chip does not support hardware floating-point operations, another feature of high importance to game developers. The MSM7201A is OpenGL ES 1.0 compliant, which translates to a fixed-function pipeline as opposed to a programmable, shader-based pipeline. The GPU is reasonably fast but outperformed by the PowerVR MBX Lite chip found in the iPhone 3G, which was available at the same time. HTC used the same chip in a couple of other first-generation handsets, such as the famous HTC Dream (T-Mobile G1). The MSM7201A is considered the low end when it comes to hardware-accelerated 3D graphics and is thus your greatest enemy when you want to target all generations of Android devices.

First-generation devices can thus be identified by the following features:

- A CPU running at up to ~500MHz without hardware floating-point support
- A GPU, mostly in the form of the MSM7201A chip, supporting OpenGL ES 1.x
- A screen resolution of 480×320 pixels
- Limited multi-touch support
- Initially deployed with Android 1.5/1.6 or even earlier versions

This classification is of course not strict. Many low-budget devices just coming out share a similar feature set. Although they are not exactly first generation, we can still put them in the same category as the Hero and similar devices.

First-generation devices still have a considerable market share at the time of writing this book. If we want to reach the biggest possible audience, we have to consider their limitations and adapt our games accordingly.

More Power: Second Generation

At the end of 2009, a new generation of Android devices entered the scene. Spearheaded by the Motorola Droid and Nexus One (released in January 2010), this new generation of handsets demonstrated raw computational power previously unseen in mobile phones.

The Nexus One is powered by a 1GHz Qualcomm QSD8250, a member of the Snapdragon family of chips. The Motorola Droid uses a 550MHz Texas Instruments OMAP3430. Both CPUs support vector hardware floating-point operations via the Vector Floating Point (VFP) and NEON ARM extensions. The Nexus One has 512MB RAM, and the Motorola Droid has 256MB RAM. Figure 1–4 shows their designs.

Figure 1–4. *The Nexus One and Motorola Droid*

Both phones have a WVGA screen, an 800×480 pixel Active-Matrix Organic Light-Emiting Diode (AMOLED) screen (in the case of the Nexus One) or a 854×480 pixel LCD screen (in the case of the Motorola Droid). Both screens are capacitive multi-touch screens. Although both devices were advertised as multi-touch capable, they do not work as expected in a couple of situations. The most common problem is the reporting of false touch positions when two fingers are close on either the x- or y-axis on the screen.

The Nexus One was first shipped with Android version 2.1, and the Motorola Droid was shipped with version 2.0. Both phones have received updates to Android version 2.2.

Of special interest to game developers are the built-in GPUs. The PowerVR SGX530 is a very potent GPU also used in the iPhone 3GS. Note that the screen size of the iPhone 3GS is actually half that of the Motorola Droid, which gives the iPhone 3GS a slight performance advantage, because it has to draw fewer pixels per frame. The Adreno 200 chip used in the Nexus One is a Qualcomm product and slightly slower than the PowerVR SGX530. Depending on the rendered scene, both chips can be nearly a magnitude faster than the MSM7201A found in many first-generation devices.

Second-generation devices can be identified by the following features:

- A CPU running between 550MHz and 1GHz with hardware floating-point support

- A programmable GPU supporting OpenGL ES 1.*x* and 2.0

- A WVGA screen

- Multi-touch support

- Android version 2.0, 2.0.1, 2.1, or 2.2

Note that a few first-generation devices received updates to Android version 2.1, which has some positive impact on overall system performance but does not, of course, change the fact that their hardware specifications are inferior to second-generation devices. The distinction between first- and second-generation devices can thus be made only if all factors such as CPU, GPU, or screen resolution are taken into account.

Over the course of 2010, many more second-generation devices appeared, such as the HTC Evo or the Samsung i9200 Galaxy S. Although they feature some improvements over the Nexus One and Motorola Droid such as bigger screens and slightly faster CPUs/GPUs, they are still considered second-generation devices.

The Future: Next Generation

Device manufacturers try to keep their latest and greatest handsets a secret for as long as possible, but there are always some leaks of specifications.

General trends for all future devices are dual-core CPUs, more RAM, better GPUs, and higher screen resolutions. One such future device is the Samsung i9200 Galaxy S2, which is rumored to have a 1280×720 pixel AMOLED 2 display, a 2GHz dual-core CPU, and 1GB RAM. Not much is known about the GPU this handset will use. A possible candidate would be the new NVIDIA Tegra 2 family of chips, which promises a significant boost in graphics performance. The next generation is also expected to ship with the latest Android version (2.3).

Although mobile phones will probably remain the focus of Android for the immediate future, new form factors will also play a role in Android's evolution. Hardware manufacturers are creating tablet devices and netbooks, using Android as the operating system. Ports of Android for other architectures such as x86 are also already in the making, increasing the number of potential target platforms. And with Android 3.0, there's even a dedicated Android version for tablets available.

Whatever the future will bring, Android is here to stay!

Game Controllers

Given the differences of input methods available on various Android handsets, a few manufacturers produce special game controllers. Because there's no API in Android for such controllers, game developers have to integrate support separately by using the SDK provided by the game controller manufacturer.

One such game controller is called the Zeemote JS1, shown in Figure 1–5. It features an analog stick as well as a set of buttons.

Figure 1-5. *The Zeemote JS1 controller*

The controller is coupled with the device via Bluetooth. Game developers integrate support for the controller via a separate API provided by the Zeemote SDK. A couple of Android games already support this controller when available.

Users could in theory also couple the Nintendo Wii controller with their device via Bluetooth. A couple of prototypes exploiting the Wii controller exist, but there's no officially supported SDK—which makes integration a tad bit awkward.

The Game Gripper, shown in Figure 1-6, is an ingenious invention specifically designed for the Motorola Droid and Milestone. It is a simple rubber accessory that slides over the QWERTY keyboard of the phone and overlays a more or less standard game controller layout on top of the actual hardware keyboard. Game developers need only add keyboard controls to their game and don't have to integrate a special library to communicate with the Gripper. It's just a piece of rubber, after all.

Figure 1-6. *The Game Gripper in action*

Game controllers are still a bit esoteric in the realm of Android. However, some successful titles have integrated support for some controllers, a move generally well received by Android gamers. Integrating support for such peripherals should therefore be considered.

Mobile Gaming Is Different

Gaming was already huge way before the likes of the iPhone and Android started to conquer this market segment. However, with those new forms of hybrid devices, the landscape has started to change. Gaming is no longer something for nerdy kids. Serious businesspeople have been caught playing the latest trendy game on their mobile phones in public, newspapers pick up stories of successful small game developers making a fortune on mobile phone application markets, and established game publishers have a hard time keeping up with the developments in the mobile space. We game developers must recognize this change and adjust accordingly. Let's see what this new ecosystem has to offer.

A Gaming Machine in Every Pocket

Smartphones are ubiquitous. That's probably the key statement to take away from this section. From this, we can easily derive all the other facts about mobile gaming.

As hardware prices are constantly dropping and new cell phones have ever-increasing computational power, they also become ideal gaming devices. Mobile phones are a must-have nowadays, so market penetration is huge. Many people who are exchanging their old, classic mobile phones with the new generation of smartphones are discovering the new options available to them in the form of an incredibly wide range of applications.

Previously, people had to make the conscious decision to buy a video game system or a gaming PC in order to play video games. Now they get that functionality for free from their mobile phones. There's no additional cost involved (at least if you don't count the data plan you'll likely have), and your new gaming device is available to you at any time. Just grab it from your pocket or purse, and you are ready to go—no need to carry a second dedicated system with you, because everything's integrated in one package.

Apart from the benefit of having to carry only a single device for your telephony, Internet, and gaming needs, another factor makes gaming on mobile phones incredibly accessible to a much larger audience: you can fire up a dedicated market application on your phone, pick a game that looks interesting, and immediately start to play. There's no need to go to a store or download something via your PC only to find out, for example, that you lost the USB cable needed to transfer that game to your phone.

The increased processing power of current-generation smartphones also has an impact on what's possible for us as game developers. Even the middle class of devices is capable of generating gaming experiences similar to titles found on the older Xbox and PlayStation 2 systems. Given these capable hardware platforms, we can also start experimenting with more-elaborate games with physics simulations, an area offering great potential for innovation.

With new devices also come new input methods, which we have already discussed a little. A couple of games already exploit the GPS and/or compass available in most Android devices. The use of the accelerometer is already a mandatory feature of most games, and multi-touch screens offer new ways for the user to interact with the game world. Compared to classic gaming consoles (and ignoring the Wii for the moment), this is quite a change for game developers. A lot of ground has been covered already, but there are still new ways to use all this functionality in an innovative way.

Always Connected

Smartphones are usually bought along with data plans. They are not only used for pure telephony anymore but actually drive a lot of traffic to popular Internet sites. A user having a smartphone is very likely to be connected to the Web at any point in time (neglecting for a moment poor reception, for example, caused by hardware design failures).

Permanent connectivity opens up a completely new world for mobile gaming. People can challenge other people across the planet for a quick match of chess, explore virtual worlds together, or try fragging their best friend in another city in a fine death match of gentlemen. And all of this occurs on the go, on the bus or train or in their most beloved corner of the local park.

Apart from multiplayer functionality, social networks have also started to play a huge role in mobile gaming. Games provide functionality to tweet your latest high score directly to your Twitter account or to inform a friend of your latest achievements earned in that racing game you both love. Although growing social networks exist in the classical gaming world (for example, Xbox Live or the equivalent PlayStation service), the market penetration of services such as Facebook and Twitter is a lot higher, and so the user is relieved of the burden of managing multiple networks at once.

Casual and Hardcore

The huge user adaption of smartphones also means that people who have never even touched a NES controller suddenly discover the world of gaming. Their mental image of a good game often deviates quite a bit from the one a hardcore gamer might have.

Given the use cases for mobile phones, users tend to lean toward the more casual sort of games that they can fire up for a couple of minutes while on the bus or waiting in line at their preferred fast food restaurant. These games are equivalent toall those small flash games on the PC that are forcing many people in the workforce to Alt+Tab frantically each time they sense the presence of someone watching their back. Ask yourself this: how much time would you be willing to spend playing games on your mobile phone? Can you imagine playing a "quick" game of Civilization on such a device?

Surely there are people who would actually offer their firstborn if only they could play their beloved Advanced Dungeons & Dragons variant on a mobile phone. But this group is a small minority, as evidenced by the top-selling games on the iPhone and Android Markets. The top-selling games are usually extremely casual but have a nice trick under their sleeves: The average time taken to play a round of such a game is in the range of minutes, but the games make you come back by employing various evil schemes. The game might provide an elaborate online achievement system that lets you virtually brag about your skills. But it could also be an actual hardcore game in disguise. Offer users an easy way to save their progress, and you are set to sell them your hardcore game as a casual game!

Big Market, Small Developers

The low entry barrier is a main attractor for many hobbyists and independent developers. In the case of Android, this barrier is especially low: just get yourself the SDK and program away. You don't even need a device, just use the emulator (although I highly recommend having at least one development device). The open nature of Android also leads to a lot of activity on the Web. Information on all aspects of programming for the system can be found for free online. There's no need to sign an Non-Disclosure Agreement or wait for some authority to grant you access to their holy ecosystem.

At the time of this writing, the most successful games on the market were developed by one-person companies and small teams. Major publishers have not yet set foot in the market, at least not successfully. Gameloft serves as a prime example. Although big on the iPhone, Gameloft couldn't get a hold of the Android market and decided to sell their games on their own website instead. Gameloft might not have been happy with the missing Digital Rights Managment scheme (which is available on Android now)—a move that of course lowers the number of people who actually know about their games considerably.

The environment also allows for a lot of experimentation and innovation as bored people surfing the market are longing for little gems, including new ideas and game play mechanics. Experimentation on classic gaming platforms such as the PC or consoles are often met with failure. However, the Android Market enables you to reach a much larger audience that is willing to try experimental new ideas, and to reach them with a lot less effort.

This doesn't mean, of course, that you don't have to market your game. One way to do so is to inform various blogs and dedicated sites on the Web about your latest game. Many Android users are enthusiasts and regularly frequent such sites, checking in on the latest and greatest.

Another way to reach a large audience is to get featured in the Android Market. Once featured, your application will appear to users in a list immediately after they start the market application. Many developers have reported a tremendous increase in downloads directly correlated to getting featured on the market. How to get featured is a bit of a mystery, though. Having an awesome idea and executing it in the most polished way is your best bet, whether you are a big publisher or a small one-person shop.

Summary

Android is an exciting little beast. You have seen what it's made of and have gotten to know its developer ecosystem a little. It offers us a very interesting system in terms of software and hardware to develop for, and the barrier of entry is extremely low given the freely available SDK. The devices themselves are pretty powerful for handheld devices and will enable us to present visually rich gaming worlds to our users. The use of sensors such as the accelerometer let us create innovative game ideas with new user interactions. And after we have finished developing our games, we can deploy them to millions of potential gamers in a matter of minutes. Sounds exciting? Then let's get our hands dirty with some code!

Chapter 2

First Steps with the Android SDK

The Android SDK provides a set of tools that allows creating applications in no time. This chapter will guide you through the process of building a simple Android application with the SDK tools. This involves the following steps:

1. Setting up the development environment

2. Creating a new project in Eclipse and writing our code

3. Running the application on the emulator or on a device

4. Debugging and profiling the application

Let's start with setting up the development environment.

Setting Up the Development Environment

The Android SDK is pretty flexible and integrates well with a couple of development environments. Purists might choose to go all hard-core with command-line tools. We want things to be a little bit more comfortable, though, so we'll go for the simpler, more visual route using an IDE (integrated development environment).

Here's the grocery list of software you'll need to download and install in the given order:

- The Java Development Kit (JDK), version 5 or 6. I suggest going for 6.

- The Android Software Development Kit (Android SDK).

- Eclipse for Java Developers, version 3.4 or 3.5.

- The Android Development Tools (ADT) plug-in for Eclipse.

Let's go through the steps required to set everything up properly.

NOTE: As the Web is a moving target, I don't provide URLs here. Fire up your favorite search engine and find the appropriate places to get ahold of the above items.

Setting Up the JDK

Download the JDK with one of the specified versions for your operating system. On most systems it comes in the form of an installer or package, so there shouldn't be any hurdles. Once the JDK is installed, it is advisable to add a new environment variable called JDK_HOME pointing to the root directory of the JDK installation. Additionally, you should add the $JDK_HOME/bin (%JDK_HOME%\bin on Windows) directory to your PATH environment variable.

Setting Up the Android SDK

The Android SDK is also available for the three mainstream desktop operating systems. Choose the one fitting for your platform and download it. The SDK comes in the form of a ZIP or tar gzip file. Just uncompress it to a convenient folder (e.g., c:\android-sdk on Windows or /opt/android-sdk on Linux). The SDK comes with a couple of command-line utilities located in the tools/ folder. Create an environment variable called ANDROID_HOME pointing to the root directory of the SDK installation and add $ANDROID_HOME/tools (%ANDROID_HOME%\tools on Windows) to your PATH environment variable. This way you can easily invoke the command-line tools from a shell later on if the need arises.

After performing the preceding steps, you'll have a bare-bones installation that consists of the basic command-line tools needed to create, compile, and deploy Android projects, as well as the SDK and AVD manager, a tool for installing SDK components and creating virtual devices used by the emulator. These tools alone are not sufficient to start developing, so you need to install additional components. That's were the SDK and AVD manager comes in. The manager is a package manager, much like the package management tools you find on Linux. The manager allows you to install the following types of components:

Android platforms: For every official Android release there's a platform component for the SDK that includes the runtime libraries, a system image used by the emulator, and any version-specific tools.

SDK add-ons: Add-ons are usually external libraries and tools that are not specific to a platform. Some examples of these are the Google APIs that allow you to integrate Google maps in your application.

USB driver for Windows: These are necessary for running and debugging your application on a physical device on Windows. On Mac OS X and Linux you don't need a special driver.

Samples: For each platform there's also a set of platform-specific samples. These are great resources for seeing how to achieve specific goals with the Android runtime library.

Documentation: This is a local copy of the documentation for the latest Android framework API.

Being the greedy developers we are, we want to install all of these components to have the full set of functionality at our disposal. For this, we first have to start the SDK and AVD manager. On Windows there's an executable called SDK manager.exe in the root directory of the SDK. On Linux and Mac OS X you simply start the script android in the tools directory of the SDK.

Upon first startup, the SDK and AVD manager will connect to the package server and fetch a list of available packages. It will then present you with the dialog in Figure 2–1, which allows you to install individual packages. Simply check Accept All, click the Install button, and make yourself a nice cup of tea or coffee. The manager will take a while to install all the packages.

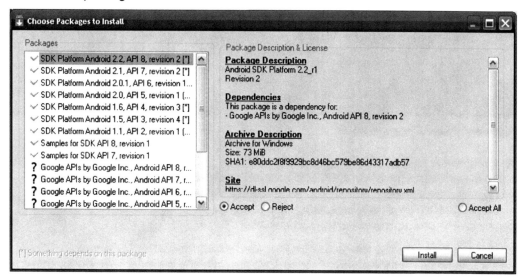

Figure 2–1. *First contact with the SDK and AVD manager*

You can use the SDK and AVD manager at any time to update components or install new ones. The manager is also used to create new AVDs, which will be necessary later on when we start running and debugging our applications on the emulator.

Once the installation process is finished, we can move on to the next step in setting up our development environment.

Installing Eclipse

Eclipse comes in a couple of different flavors. For Android developers, I suggest using Eclipse for Java Developers version 3.6, Like the Android SDK, Eclipse comes in the form of a ZIP or tar gzip package. Simply extract it to a folder of your choice. Once it's uncompressed, you can create a nice little shortcut on your desktop to the `eclipse` executable in the root directory of your Eclipse installation.

The first time you start Eclipse, you will be prompted to specify a workspace directory. Figure 2–2 shows you the dialog for this.

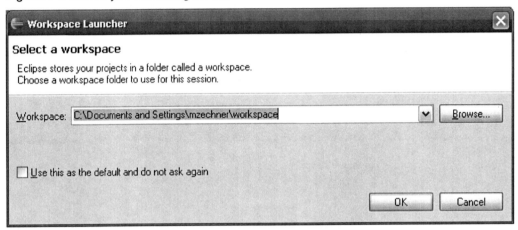

Figure 2–2. *Choosing a workspace*

A workspace is Eclipse's notion of a folder containing a set of projects. Whether you use a single workspace for all your projects or multiple workspaces that group just a few projects is completely up to you. The sample projects accompanying this book are all organized in a single workspace, which you could specify in this dialog. For now, we'll simply create an empty workspace somewhere.

Eclipse will then greet us with a welcome screen, which we can safely ignore and close. This will leave us with the default Eclipse Java perspective. We'll get to know Eclipse a little better in a later section. For now it suffices to have it running.

Installing the ADT Eclipse Plug-In

The last piece in our setup puzzle is installing the ADT Eclipse plug-in. Eclipse is based on a plug-in architecture that is used to extend its capabilities by third-party plug-ins. The ADT plug-in marries the tools found in the Android SDK with the powers of Eclipse. Given this combination, we can completely forget about invoking all the command-line Android SDK tools; the ADT plug-in integrates them transparently into our Eclipse workflow.

Installing plug-ins for Eclipse can be done either manually, by dropping the contents of a plug-in ZIP file into the plug-ins folder of Eclipse, or via the Eclipse plug-in manager integrated with Eclipse. Here we'll choose the second route.

1. To install a new plug-in, go to **Help ➤ Install New Software...**, which will open the installation dialog. In this dialog you can choose from which source to install what plug-in. First, you have to add the plug-in repository from which the ADT plug-in is fetched. Click the Add button, and you will be presented with the dialog depicted in Figure 2–3.

2. In the first text field, you can enter the name of the repository; something like "ADT repository" will do. The second text field specifies the URL of the repository. For the ADT plug-in, this field should be `https://dl-ssl.google.com/android/eclipse/`. Note that this URL might be different for newer versions, so check the ADT plug-in site for an up-to-date link.

Figure 2–3. *Adding a repository*

3. After you've confirmed the dialog, you'll be brought back to the installation dialog, which should now be fetching the list of available plug-ins in the repository. Check the Developer Tools check box and click the Next button.

4. Eclipse will now calculate all the necessary dependencies, and then present you a new dialog that lists all the plug-ins and dependencies that are going to be installed. Confirm that dialog with a click on the Next button.

5. Yet another dialog will pop up, prompting you to accept the licenses of each plug-in to be installed. You should of course accept those licenses, and finally initiate the installation with a click on the Finish button.

NOTE: During the installation you will be asked to confirm the installation of unsigned software. Don't worry, the plug-ins simply do not have a verified signature. Agree to the installation to continue the process.

6. Finally, Eclipse will ask you whether it should restart to apply the changes. You can opt for a full restart or for applying the changes without a restart. To play it safe, choose Restart Now, which will restart Eclipse as expected.

After all this dialog madness, you'll be presented with the same Eclipse window as before. The toolbar features a couple of new buttons specific to Android, which allow you to start the SDK and AVD manager directly from within Eclipse, as well as create new Android projects. Figure 2–4 shows these new shiny toolbar buttons.

Figure 2–4. *ADT toolbar buttons*

The first button on the left allows you to open the AVD and SDK Manager. The next button is a shortcut to creating a new Android project. The other two buttons will create a new unit test project or Android manifest file (functionality we won't use in this book).

As one last step in finishing the installation of the ADT plug-in, you have to tell the plug-in where the Android SDK is located.

1. Open **Window ➤ Preferences**, and select **Android** in the tree view in the upcoming dialog.

2. On the right side, click the Browse button to chose the root directory of your Android SDK installation.

3. Click the OK button to close the dialog, and you'll finally able to create your first Android application.

A Quick Tour of Eclipse

Eclipse is an open source IDE that you can use to develop applications written in various languages. Usually, Eclipse is used in connection with Java development. Given its plug-in architecture, a lot of extensions have been created, so it is also possible to develop pure C/C++, Scala, or Python projects as well. The possibilities are endless; there even exist plug-ins to write LaTeX projects, for example—something only slightly resembling your usual code development tasks.

An instance of Eclipse works with a workspace that holds one or more projects. We defined a workspace at startup earlier. All new projects we create will be stored in the workspace directory, along with configuration that defines the look of Eclipse when using the workspace, among other things.

The user interface (UI) of Eclipse revolves around two concepts:

- A *view*, which is a single UI component such as a source code editor, an output console, or a project explorer

- A *perspective*, which is a set of specific views that you'll most likely need for a specific development task, such as editing and browsing source code, debugging, profiling, synchronization with a version control repository, and so on.

Eclipse for Java Developers comes with a couple of predefined perspectives. The ones we are most interested in are called Java and Debug. The Java perspective is the one shown in Figure 2–5. It features the Package Explorer view on the left side, a source-editing view in the middle (it's empty as we didn't open a source file yet), a Task List view to the right, an Outline view, and a tabbed view that contains subviews called Problems view, Javadoc view, and Declaration view.

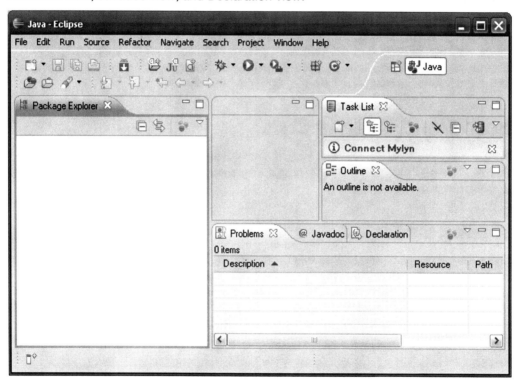

Figure 2–5. *Eclipse in action—the Java perspective*

You are free to rearrange the place of any view within a perspective via drag-and-drop. You can also resize views. Additionally, you can add and remove views to and from a perspective. To add a view, go to **Window ➤ Show View** and either select one from the list that is presented to you or choose **Other…** to get a list of all views that are available.

To switch to another perspective, you can go to **Window ➤ Open Perspective** and choose the one you want. A faster way to switch between already open perspectives is given to you in the top-left corner of Eclipse. There you will see which perspectives are already open and which perspective is the active one. In Figure 2–5, notice that the Java perspective is open and active. It's the only currently open perspective. Once you open additional perspectives, they will also show up in that part of the UI.

The toolbars shown in Figure 2–5 are also just views. Depending on the perspective you are in, the toolbars may change as well. Recall that a couple of new buttons appeared in the toolbar after we installed the ADT plug-in. This is common behavior of plug-ins: they will in general add new views and perspectives. In the case of the ADT plug-in, we can now also access a perspective called DDMS (which is specific to debugging and profiling Android applications) in addition to the standard Java Debug perspective. The ADT plug-in also adds a couple of new views, including the LogCat view, which displays the live logging information of any attached device or emulator.

Once you get comfortable with the perspective and view concepts, Eclipse is a lot less intimidating. In the following subsections, we will explore some of the perspectives and views we'll use to write Android games. I can't possibly cover all the details of developing with Eclipse, as it is such a huge beast. I therefore advise you to learn more about Eclipse via its extensive help system if the need arises.

Hello World, Android Style

With our development set up, we can now finally create our first Android project in Eclipse. The ADT plug-in installed a couple of wizards for us to make the creation of new Android projects really easy.

Creating the Project

There are two ways to create a new Android project. The first one works by right-clicking in the Package Explorer view (see Figure 2–4) and selecting **New ➤ Project...** from the pop-up menu. In the new dialog, select Android Project under the Android category. As you can see, there are a lot of other options for project creation in that dialog. This is the standard way to create a new project of any type in Eclipse. After confirming the dialog, the Android project wizard will open.

The second way is a lot easier: just click the button responsible for creating a new Android project (shown earlier in Figure 2–4).

Once you are in the Android project wizard dialog, you have to make a few choices.

1. First, you must define the project name. A usual convention is to keep it all lowercase. For this example, name the project "hello world."

2. Next, you have to specify the build target. For now, simply select the Android 1.5 build target, since this is the lowest common denominator and you don't need any fancy features like multitouch yet.

NOTE: In Chapter 1 you saw that each new release of Android adds new classes to the Android framework API. The build target specifies which version of this API you want to use in your application. For example, if you choose the Android 2.3 build target, you get access to the latest and greatest API features. This comes at a risk, though: if your application is run on a device that uses a lower API version (say, a device running Android version 1.5), then your application will crash if you access API features that are only available in version 2.3. In this case, you'd need to detect the supported SDK version during runtime and only access the 2.3 features when you're sure that the Android version on the device supports it. This may sound pretty nasty, but as you'll see in Chapter 5, given a good application architecture you can easily enable and disable certain version-specific features without running the risk of crashing.

3. Next, you have to specify the name of your application (e.g., Hello World), the name of the Java package in which all your source files will eventually be located (e.g., com.helloworld), and an activity name. An activity is similar to a window or dialog on a desktop operating system. Let's just name it HelloWorldActivity.

4. The Min SDK Version field allows you to specify what minimum Android version your application requires to run. This parameter is not required, but it's good practice to specify it. SDK versions are numbered starting from 1 (1.0) and increase with each release. Since 1.5 is the third release, specify 3 here. Remember that you had to specify a build target previously, which might be newer than the minimum SDK version. This allows you to work with a higher API level, but also deploy to older versions of Android (making sure that you only call the supported API methods for that version, of course).

5. Click Finish to create your first Android project.

NOTE: Setting the minimum SDK version has some implications. The application can only be run on devices with an Android version equal to or greater than the minimum SDK version you specify. When a user browses the Android Market via the Market application, only applications with a fitting minimum SDK version will be shown to her.

Exploring the Project

In the Package Explorer, you should now see a project called "hello world." If you expand it and all its children, you'll see something like Figure 2–6. This is the general structure of most Android projects. Let's explore it a little bit.

- `AndroidManifest.xml` describes your application. It defines what activities and services it is composed of, what minimum and target Android version it is supposed to run on, and what permissions it needs (e.g., access to the SD card or networking).

- `default.properties` holds various settings for the build system. We won't touch this, as the ADT plug-in will take care of modifying it when necessary.

- `src/` contains all your Java source files. Notice that the package has the same name as the one you specified in the Android project wizard.

- `gen/` contains Java source files generated by the Android build system. You shouldn't mess with them, as they get regenerated automatically in some cases.

- `assets/` is where you store file our application needs (e.g., configuration files or audio files and the like). These files get packaged with your Android application.

- `res/` holds resources your application needs, such as icons, strings for internationalization, and UI layouts defined via XML. Like assets, they also get packaged with your application.

- Android 1.5 tells us that we are building against an Android version 1.5 target. This is actually a dependency in the form of a standard JAR file that holds the classes of the Android 1.5 API.

The Package Explorer view hides another directory, called `bin/`, which holds the compiled code that is ready for deployment to a device or emulator. As with the gen/ folder, we usually don't care what happens in this folder.

Figure 2–6. *Hello World project structure*

We can easily add new source files, folders, and other resources in the Package Explorer view by right-clicking the folder we want to put the new resources in, and selecting New plus the corresponding resource type we want to create. For now, though, we'll leave everything as is. Next, let's modify the source code a little.

Writing the Application Code

We still haven't written a single line of code, so let's change that. The Android project wizard created a template activity class for us called HelloWorldActivity, which will get displayed when we run the application on the emulator or a device. Open the source of the class by double-clicking the file in the Package Explorer view. We'll replace that template code with the code in Listing 2–1.

Listing 2–1. *HelloWorldActivity.java*

```java
package com.helloworld;

import android.app.Activity;
import android.os.Bundle;
import android.view.View;
import android.widget.Button;

public class HelloWorldActivity extends Activity
```

```
                             implements View.OnClickListener {
    Button button;
    int touchCount;

    @Override
    public void onCreate(Bundle savedInstanceState) {
        super.onCreate(savedInstanceState);
        button = new Button(this);
        button.setText( "Touch me!" );
        button.setOnClickListener(this);
        setContentView(button);
    }

    public void onClick(View v) {
        touchCount++;
        button.setText("Touched me " + touchCount + " time(s)");
    }
}
```

Let's dissect Listing 2–1 so you can understand what it's doing. We'll leave the nitty-gritty details for later chapters. All we want is to get a sense of what's happening here.

The source code file starts off with the standard Java package declaration and a couple of imports. Most Android framework classes are located in the android package.

```
package com.helloworld;

import android.app.Activity;
import android.os.Bundle;
import android.view.View;
import android.widget.Button;
```

Next, we define our `HelloWorldActivity` and let it extend the base class `Activity`, which is provided by the Android framework API. An `Activity` is a lot like a window in classical desktop UIs, with the constraint that it always fills the complete screen (except for the notification bar at the top of the Android UI). Additionally, we let it implement the interface `OnClickListener`. If you have experience with other UI toolkits, you'll probably see what's coming next. More on that in a second.

```
public class HelloWorldActivity extends Activity
                             implements View.OnClickListener {
```

We let our `Activity` have two members: a `Button` and an integer that counts how often the `Button` was clicked.

```
    Button button;
    int touchCount;
```

Every `Activity` must implement the abstract method `Activity.onCreate()`, which gets called once by the Android system when the activity is first started. This replaces a constructor you'd normally expect to use to create an instance of a class. It is mandatory to call the base class `onCreate()` method as the first statement in the method body.

```
    @Override
    public void onCreate(Bundle savedInstanceState) {
        super.onCreate(savedInstanceState);
```

Next, we create a Button and set its initial text. Button is one of the many widgets that the Android framework API provides. Widgets are synonymous with so called Views on Android. Note that button is a member of our HelloWorldActivity class. We'll need a reference to it later on.

```
button = new Button(this);
button.setText( "Touch me!" );
```

The next line in onCreate() sets the OnClickListener of the Button. OnClickListener is a callback interface with a single method, OnClickListener.onClick(), that gets called when the Button is clicked. We want to be notified of clicks, so we let our HelloWorldActivity implement that interface and register it as the OnClickListener of the Button.

```
button.setOnClickListener(this);
```

The last line in the onCreate() method sets the Button as the so-called content View of our Activity. Views can be nested, and the content View of the Activity is the root of this hierarchy. In our case, we simply set the Button as the View to be displayed by the Activity. For simplicity's sake, we won't get into details on how the Activity will be laid out given this content View.

```
setContentView(button);
}
```

The next step is simply the implementation of the OnClickListener.onClick() method, which the interface requires of our Activity. This method gets called each time the Button is clicked. In it we increase the touchCount counter and set the Button's text to a new string.

```
public void onClick(View v) {
    touchCount++;
    button.setText("Touched me" + touchCount + "times");
}
```

So, to summarize our Hello World application, we construct an Activity with a Button. Each time the Button is clicked, we reflect this by setting its text accordingly. (This may not be the most exciting application on the planet, but it will do for further demonstration purposes.)

Note that we never had to manually compile anything. The ADT plug-in together with Eclipse will recompile the project every time we add, modify, or delete a source file or resource. The result of this compilation process is an APK file that is ready to be deployed to the emulator or an Android device. The APK file is located in the bin/ folder of the project.

You'll use this application in the following sections to learn how to run and debug Android applications on emulator instances as well as devices.

Running and Debugging Android Applications

Once we've written the first iteration of our application code, we want to run and test it to identify potential problems or just be amazed at its glory. We have two ways we can achieve this:

- We can run our application on a real device connected to the development PC via USB.

- We can fire up the emulator that is included in the SDK and test our application there.

In both cases we have to do a little bit of setup work before we can finally see our application in action.

Connecting a Device

Before we can connect our device for testing purposes, we have to make sure that it is recognized by the operating system. On Windows, this involves installing an appropriate driver, which is part of the SDK installation we installed earlier. Just connect your device and follow the standard driver installation project for Windows, pointing the process to the driver/ folder in your SDK installation's root directory. For some devices, you might have to get the driver from the manufacturer's web site.

On Linux and Mac OS X, you usually don't need to install any drivers, as these come with the operating system. Depending on your Linux flavor, you might have to fiddle with your USB device discovery a little bit, usually in the form of creating a new rules file for udev. This varies from device to device. A quick web search should bring up a solution for your device.

Creating an Android Virtual Device

The SDK comes with an emulator that will run so-called Android virtual devices (AVDs). A *virtual device* consists of a system image of a specific Android version, a skin, and a set of attributes, which include the screen resolution, SD-card size, and so on.

To create an AVD, you have to fire up the SDK and AVD manager. You can either do this as described previously in the SDK installation step, or directly from within Eclipse by clicking the SDK manager button in the toolbar.

1. Select Virtual Devices in the list on the left, and you will be presented with a list of currently available AVDs. Unless you've already messed around with the SDK manager, this list should be empty; let's change that.

2. To create a new AVD, click the New... button on the right, which will bring up the dialog shown in Figure 2–7.

Figure 2–7. *The AVD creation dialog of the SDK manager*

3. Each AVD has a name by which you can refer to it later on. The target specifies the Android version that the AVD should use. Additionally, you can specify the size of the SD card of the AVD, as well as the screen size. For our simple Hello World project, you can select an Android 1.5 target and leave everything else as it is. For real-life testing, you'd usually want to create multiple AVDs that cover all the Android versions and screen sizes you want your application to handle.

NOTE: Unless you have dozens of different devices with different Android versions and screen sizes, it is advisable to use the emulator for additional testing of Android version/screen size combinations.

Running an Application

Now that you've set up your devices and AVDs, you can finally run the Hello World application. You can easily do this in Eclipse by right-clicking the "hello world" project in the Package Explorer view, and then selecting **Run As ➤ Android Application** (or you can click the Run button on the toolbar). Eclipse will then perform the following steps for us in the background:

1. Compile the project to an APK file if any files have changed since the last compilation.

2. Create a new Run configuration for the Android project if one does not already exist. (We'll have a look into Run configurations in a minute.)

3. Install and run the application by starting or reusing an already running emulator instance with a fitting Android version, or by deploying and running the application on a connected device (which must also run at least the minimum Android version you specified as the Min SDK Level parameter when you created the project).

If you only created an Android 1.5 AVD, as suggested in the previous section, then the ADT Eclipse plug-in will fire up a new emulator instance running that AVD, deploy the Hello World APK file, and start the application. The output should look like Figure 2–8.

Figure 2–8. The awesome Hello World application in action!

The emulator works almost exactly like a real device, and you can interact with it via your mouse just as you would with your finger on a device. Here are a few differences between a real device and the emulator:

- The emulator only supports single-touch input. Simply use your mouse cursor and pretend it is your finger.

- The emulator is missing some applications, such as the Android Market.

- To change the orientation of the device on the screen, don't tilt your monitor! Instead, use the 7 key on your numpad to change it. For this, you have to first press the Num Lock key above the numpad to disable its number functionality.

- The emulator is really, really slow. Do not assess the performance of your application by running it on the emulator.

- The emulator currently only supports OpenGL ES 1.0 with a few extensions. We'll talk about OpenGL ES in Chapter 7. For our purposes this is fine, except that the OpenGL ES implementation on the emulator is buggy and will often give you different results from those you'll get on a real device. For now, just keep in mind that you should not test any OpenGL ES applications on the emulator.

Play around with it a little and get comfortable with it.

> **NOTE:** Starting a fresh emulator instance takes considerable time (up to minutes depending on your hardware). You can leave the emulator running for your whole development session so you don't have to restart it over and over again.

Sometimes when we run an Android application, the automatic emulator/device selection performed by the ADT plug-in is a hindrance. For example, we might have multiple devices/emulators connected, and want to test our application on a specific device/emulator. To deal with this, we can turn off the automatic device/emulator selection in the Run configuration of the Android project. So, what is a Run configuration?

A Run configuration provides a way to tell Eclipse how it should start your application when you tell it to run it. A Run configuration usually allows you to specify things like command-line arguments passed to the application, VM arguments (in the case of Java SE desktop applications), and so on. Eclipse and third-party plug-ins offer different Run configurations for specific project types. The ADT plug-in adds an Android Application Run configuration to the set of available Run configurations. When we first ran our application earlier in the chapter, Eclipse and ADT created a new Android Application Run configuration for us in the background with default parameters.

To get to the Run configuration of your Android project, do the following:

1. Right-click the project in the Package Explorer view and select **Run As ➤ Run Configurations**.

2. From the list on the left side, select the "hello world" project.

3. On the right side of the dialog, you can now modify the name of the Run configuration, and change other settings on the Android, Target, and Commons tabs.

4. To change automatic deployment to manual deployment, click the Target tab and select Manual.

When you run your application again, you'll be prompted to select a compatible emulator or device to run the application on. Figure 2–9 shows the dialog. In this figure, I added a couple more AVDs with different targets and also connected two devices.

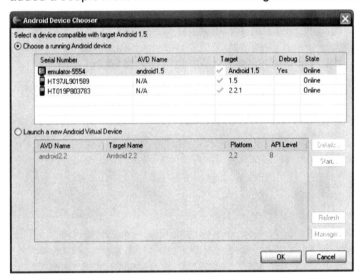

Figure 2–9. *Choosing an emulator/device to run the application on*

The dialog shows all the running emulators and currently connected devices, as well as all other AVDs that are not running at the moment. You can choose any emulator or device to run your application on.

Debugging an Application

Sometimes our application will behave in unsuspected ways or crash. To figure out what exactly is going wrong, we want to be able to debug our application.

Eclipse and ADT provide us with incredibly powerful debugging facilities for Android applications. We can set breakpoints in our source code, inspect variables and the current stack trace, and so forth.

Before we can debug our application, we have to modify its `AndroidManifest.xml` file first to enable debugging. This presents a bit of a chicken-and-egg problem, as we haven't looked into manifest files in detail yet. For now, it suffices to know that the manifest file specifies some attributes of our application. One of those attributes is whether the application is debuggable. This attribute is specified in the form of an `xml` attribute of the `<application>` tag in the manifest file. To enable debugging, we add the following attribute to the `<application>` in the manifest file:

```
android:debuggable="true"
```

While developing your application, you can safely leave that attribute in the manifest file. But don't forget to remove it before you deploy your application to the market.

Now that you've set up your application to be debuggable, you can debug it on an emulator or device. Usually, you will set breakpoints before debugging to inspect the program state at certain points in the program.

To set a breakpoint, simply open the source file in Eclipse and double-click the gray area in front of the line you want to set the breakpoint at. For demonstration purposes, do that for line 23 in the `HelloWorldActivity` class. This will make the debugger stop each time you click the button. The source code view should show you a small circle in front of that line after you double-click, as in Figure 2–10. You can remove breakpoints by again double-clicking them in the source code view.

```
    public void onClick(View v) {
        touchCount++;
        button.setText("Touched me "+touchCount+" time(s)");
    }
}
```

Figure 2–10. *Setting a breakpoint*

Starting the debugging is much like running the application, as described in the previous section. Right-click the project in the Package Explorer view and select **Debug As ➤ Android Application**. This will create a new Debug configuration for your project, just like in the case of simply running the application. You can change the default settings of that Debug configuration by choosing **Debug As ➤ Debug Configurations** from the context menu.

> **NOTE:** Instead of going through the context menu of the project in the Package Explorer view, you can use the **Run** menu to run and debug applications, as well as get access to the configurations.

If you start your first debugging session, Eclipse will ask you whether you want to switch to the Debug perspective, which you can happily confirm. Let's have a look at that perspective first. Figure 2–11 shows how it would look after starting debugging our Hello World application.

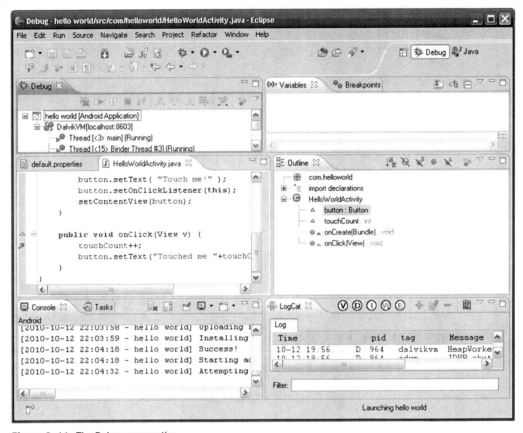

Figure 2–11. *The Debug perspective*

If you remember our quick tour of Eclipse, then you know that there are a couple of different perspectives, which consist of a set of views for a specific task. The Debug perspective looks a lot different from the Java perspective.

- The first new view to notice is the Debug view at the top left. It shows all currently running applications and the stack traces of all their threads if they are run in debug mode.

- Below the Debug view is the source-editing view we also used in the Java perspective.

- The Console view prints out messages from the ADT plug-in, telling us what it is doing.

- The LogCat view will be one of our best friends on our journey. It shows us logging output from the emulator/device that our application is running on. The logging output comes from system components, other applications, and our own application. It will show us a stack trace when our application crashes, and will also allow us to output our own logging messages at runtime. We'll have a closer look at LogCat in the next section.

- The Outline view is not very useful in the Debug perspective. You will usually be concerned with breakpoints and variables, and the current line that the program is suspended at while debugging. I often remove the Outline view from the Debug perspective to leave more space for the other views.

- The Variables view is especially useful for debugging purposes. When the debugger hits a breakpoint, we will be able to inspect and modify the variables in the current scope of the program.

- Finally, the Breakpoints view shows a list of breakpoints we've set so far.

If you are curious, you've probably already clicked the button in the running application to see how the debugger reacts. It will stop at line 23, as we instructed it by setting a breakpoint there. You will also have noticed that the Variables view now shows the variables in the current scope, which consist of the activity itself (this) and the parameter of the method (v). You can further drill down into the variables by expanding them.

The Debug view shows us the stack trace of the current stack down to the method we are currently in. Note that you might have multiple threads running and can pause them at any time in the Debug view.

Finally, notice that the line where we set the breakpoint is highlighted, indicating the position in the code where the program is currently paused.

You can instruct the debugger to execute the current statement (by pressing F6), step into any methods that get called in the current method (by pressing F5), or continue the program execution normally (by pressing F8). Alternatively, you can use the items on the Run menu to achieve the same. Also notice that there are more stepping options than the ones I've just mentioned. As with everything, I suggest you experiment to see what works for you and what doesn't.

NOTE: Curiosity is a building block for successfully developing Android games. You have to get really intimate with your development environment to get the most out of it. A book of this scope can't possible explain all the nitty-gritty details of Eclipse, so again I urge you to experiment.

LogCat and DDMS

The ADT Eclipse plug-in installs many new views and perspectives to be used in Eclipse. One of the most useful views—already briefly touched on in the last section—is the LogCat view.

LogCat is the Android event-logging system, which allows system components and applications to output logging information of various logging levels. Each log entry is composed of a time stamp, a logging level, the process ID the log came from, a tag defined by the logging application itself, and the actual logging message.

The LogCat view gathers and displays this information from a connected emulator or device. Figure 2–12 shows some sample output from the LogCat view.

Figure 2–12. *The LogCat view*

Notice that there are a number of buttons at the top right of the LogCat view.

■ The first five allow you to select the logging levels you want to see displayed.

■ The green plus button lets you define a filter based on the tag, the process ID, and the log level, which comes in handy if you want to show only the log output of your own application (which will probably use a specific tag for logging).

■ The rest of the buttons allow you to edit a filter, delete a filter, or clear the current output.

If several devices and emulators are currently connected, then the LogCat view will only output the logging data of one of these. To get finer-grained control and even more inspection options, you can switch to the DDMS perspective.

DDMS (Dalvik Debugging Monitor Server) provides a lot of in-depth information about the processes and Dalvik VMs running on all connected devices. You can switch to the DDMS perspective at any time via **Window ➤ Open Perspective ➤ Other ➤ DDMS**. Figure 2–13 shows what the DDMS perspective usually looks like.

As always, there are a couple of specific views that are suitable for our task at hand. In this case, we want to gather information about all the processes, their VMs and threads, the current state of the heap, LogCat information about a specific connected device, and so on.

■ The Devices view displays all currently connected emulators and devices, as well as all the processes running on them. Via the toolbar buttons of this view, you can perform various actions, including debugging a selected process, recording heap and thread information, and taking a screenshot.

■ The LogCat view is the same as in the previous perspective, with the difference that it will display the output of the device currently selected in the Devices view.

■ The Emulator Control view lets you alter the behavior of a running emulator instance. You can force the emulator to spoof GPS coordinates for testing, for example.

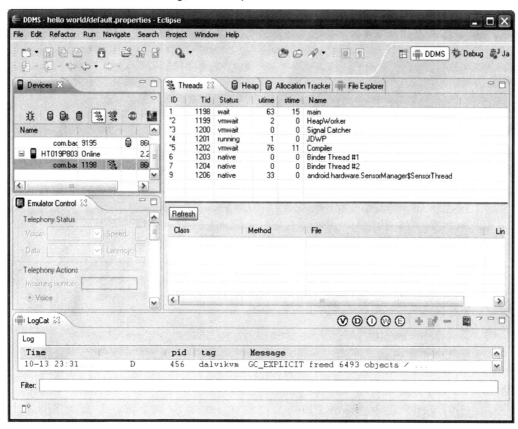

Figure 2–13. *DDMS in action*

■ The Threads view will display information about the threads running on the process currently selected in the Devices view. It will only show this information if you also enable thread tracking, which can be achieved by clicking the fifth button from the left in the Devices view.

■ The Heap view, which is not shown in Figure 2–13, gives information about the status of the heap on a device. As with the thread information, you have to explicitly enable heap tracking in the Devices view by clicking the second button from the left.

■ The Allocation Tracker view shows what classes have been allocated the most within the last few moments. It provides a great way to hunt down memory leaks.

■ Finally, there's the File Explorer view, which allows you to modify files on the connected Android device or emulator instance. You can drag and drop files into this view as you would with your standard operating system file explorer.

DDMS is actually a standalone tool that is integrated with Eclipse via the ADT plug-in. You can also start it as a standalone application from the $ANDROID_HOME/tools directory (%ANDROID_HOME%/tools on Windows). It does not directly connect to devices, but uses the Android Debug Bridge (ADB), another tool included in the SDK. Let's have a look at ADB to round off your knowledge about the Android development environment.

Using ADB

ADB lets you manage connected devices and emulator instances. It is actually a composite of three different components:

■ A client that runs on the development machine, which you can start from the command line by issuing the command adb (which should work if you set up your environment variables as described earlier). When we talk about ADB, we refer to this command-line program.

■ A server that also runs on your development machine. It is installed as a background service and is responsible for communication between an ADB program instance and any connected device or emulator instance.

■ The ADB daemon, which also runs as a background process on every emulator and device. The ADB server connects to this daemon for communication.

Usually, we use ADB via DDMS transparently and ignore its existence as a command-line tool. Sometimes it can come in handy for small tasks, so let's just go quickly over some of its functionality.

> **NOTE:** Check out the ADB documentation on the Android Developers site at `http://developer.android.com` for a full reference of the available commands.

A very useful task to perform with ADB is to query for all devices and emulators that are connected to the ADB server (and hence your development machine). To do this, execute the following command on the command line (note that > is not part of the command).

```
> adb devices
```

This will print a list of all connected devices and emulators with their respective serial numbers, and will resemble the following output:

```
List of devices attached
HT97JL901589   device
HT019P803783   device
```

The serial number of a device or emulator is used to target specific subsequent commands at it. The following command will install and APK file called `myapp.apk` located on the development machine on the device with the serial number HT019P803783.

```
> adb -s HT019P803783 install myapp.apk
```

The -s argument can be used with any ADB command that performs an action that is targeted at a specific device.

There also exist commands that will copy files to and from the device or emulator. The following command copies a local file called `myfile.txt` to the SD card of a device with the serial number HT019P803783.

```
> adb -s HT019P803783 push myfile.txt  /sdcard/myfile.txt
```

To pull a file called `myfile.txt` from the SD card, you could issue the following command:

```
> abd pull /sdcard/myfile.txt myfile.txt
```

If there's only a single device or emulator currently connected to the ADB server, you can omit the serial number. The adb tool will automatically target the connected device or emulator for you.

There are of course a lot more possibilities offered by the ADB tool. Most of them are exposed through DDMS, and we'll usually use that instead of going to the command line. For quick tasks, though, the command-line tool is ideal.

Summary

The Android development environment can be a little bit intimidating at times. Luckily, you only need a subset of the available options to get started, and the last couple of pages of this chapter should have given you enough information to get started with some basic coding.

The big lesson to take away from this chapter is how the pieces fit together. The JDK and the Android SDK provide the basis for all Android development. They offer the tools to compile, deploy, and run applications on emulator instances and devices. To speed up development, we use Eclipse along with the ADT plug-in, which abstracts away all the hard work we'd otherwise have to do on the command line with the JDK and SDK tools. Eclipse itself is built on a few core concepts: workspaces, which manage projects; views, which provide specific functionality, such as source editing or LogCat output; perspectives, which tie together views for specific tasks such as debugging; and Run and Debug configurations, which allow us to specify the startup settings used when we run or debug applications.

The secret to mastering all this is practice, as dull as it may sound. Throughout the book, we'll implement a couple of projects that should make you more comfortable with the Android development environment. At the end of the day, though, it is up to you to take it all one step further.

With all this information stuck in your head, you can move on to what you came here for in the first place: developing games.

Chapter 3

Game Development 101

Game development is hard. Not so much because it's rocket science, but because there's a huge amount of information to digest before you can actually start writing the game of your dreams. On the programming side, you have to worry about such mundane things as file input/output (I/O), input handling, audio and graphics programming, and networking code. And those are only the basics! On top of that, you will want to build your actual game mechanics. That code needs structure as well, and it is not always obvious how to create the architecture of your game. You'll have to decide how to actually make your game world move. Can you get away with not using a physics engine, but roll your own simple simulation code? What are the units and scale your game world is set in? How does it translate to the screen?

But there's actually another problem many beginners overlook: before you start hacking away, you actually have to have a game design first. Countless projects never see the light of day and get stuck in the tech-demo phase due to there being no clear idea of how the game should actually behave. And I'm not talking about the basic game mechanics of your average first-person shooter. That's the easy part: WASD plus mouse, and you're done. You should ask yourself questions like, Is there a splash screen? What does it transition to? What's on the main menu screen? What head-up display elements are available on the actual game screen? What happens if I press the pause button? What options should be offered on the settings screen? How will my UI design work out on different screen sizes and aspect ratios?

The fun part is that there's no silver bullet; there's no standard way to approach all these questions. I will not pretend to give you the be-all, end-all solution to developing games. Instead, I'll try to illustrate how I usually approach designing a game. You may decide to adapt it completely or modify it to better fit your needs. There are no rules—whatever works for you is OK. You should, however, always strive for an easy solution, in code and on paper.

Genres: To Each One's Taste

At the start of your project, you usually decide what genre your game will belong to. Unless you come up with something completely new and previously unseen, chances are high that your game idea fits into one of the broad genres currently popular. Most genres have established game mechanic standards (e.g., control schemes, specific goals, etc.). Deviating from these standards can make a game a great hit, as gamers always long for something new. It can also be a great risk, though, so consider carefully if your new platformer/first-person shooter/real-time strategy game actually has an audience.

Let's check out some examples for the more popular genres on the Android Market.

Causal Games

Probably the biggest segment of games on the Android Market consists of so-called *causal games*. So what exactly is a causal game? That question has no concrete answer, but causal games share a few common traits. Usually, they feature great accessibility, so even nongamers can pick them up easily, increasing the pool of potential players immensely. A game session is meant to take just a couple of minutes at most. However, the addictive nature of a causal game's simplicity often gets players hooked for hours. The actual game mechanics range from extremely simplistic puzzle games to one-button platformers to something as simple as tossing a paper ball into a basket. The possibilities are endless due to the causal genre having such a blurry definition.

Abduction and Abduction 2 (Figure 3–1), by the one-man shop Psym Mobile, is the perfect causal game. It belongs to the subgenre of jump-'em-up games (at least that's what I call them). The goal of the game is it to direct the always-jumping cow from platform to platform and reach the top of the level. On the way up you'll battle breaking platforms, spikes, and flying enemies. You can pick up power-ups that help you reach the top and so on. You control the cow by tilting the phone, thereby influencing the direction it is jumping/falling. Easy-to-understand controls, a clear goal, and cute graphics made this game one of the first hits on the Android Market.

Figure 3–1. *Abduction (left) and Abduction 2 (right), by Psym Mobile*

Antigen (Figure 3–2), by Battery Powered Games, is a completely different animal. You play an antibody that fights against different kinds of viruses. The game is actually a hybrid action puzzler. You control the antibody with the onscreen D-pad and rotation buttons at the top right. Your antibody has a set of connectors at each side that allow you to connect to viruses and thereby destroy them—a simple but highly addictive concept. While Abduction only features a single input mechanism via the accelerometer, the controls of Antigen are a little bit more involved. As some devices do not support multitouch, the developers came up with a couple of input schemes for all possible devices, Zeemote controls being one of them. To reach the largest possible audience, special care was taken to make the game work even on low-end devices with 320×240 pixel screens.

Figure 3–2. *Antigen, by Battery Powered Games*

Listing all the possible subgenres of the causal game category would probably fill up most of this book. Many more innovative game concepts can be found in this genre, and it is worth checking out the respective category in the market to get some inspiration.

Puzzle Games

Puzzle games need no introduction. We all know great games like Tetris and Bejeweled. They are a big part of the Android gaming market and highly popular with all segments of the demographic. In contrast to PC-based puzzle games, many puzzle games on Android deviate from the classic match-3 formula and use more elaborate, physics-based puzzles.

Super Tumble (Figure 3–3) is a superb example of a physics puzzler. The goal of the game is it to remove blocks by touching them, and get the star sitting on top of the blocks safely to the bottom platform. While this may sound fairly simple, it can get rather involved in later levels. The game is powered by Box2D, a 2D physics engine.

Figure 3–3. *Super Tumble, by Camel Games*

U Connect (Figure 3–4), by BitLogik, is a minimalistic but entertaining little brain-teaser. The goal is it to connect all the dots in the graph with a single line. Computer science students will probably recognize a familiar problem here.

Figure 3–4. *U Connect, by BitLogik*

Of course, you can also find all kinds of Tetris clones, match-3 games, and other standard formulas on the market. The preceding games demonstrate that a puzzle game can be more than yet another clone of a 20-year-old concept.

Action and Arcade Games

Action and arcade games usually unleash the full potential of the Android platform. Many of them feature stunning 3D visuals, demonstrating what is possible on the current generation of hardware. The genre has many subgenres, including racing games, shoot-'em-ups, first- and third-person shooters, and platformers. This segment of the Android Market is still a little underdeveloped, as big companies that have the resources to produce such titles are hesitant to jump on the Android wagon. Some indie developers have taken it upon themselves to fill that niche, though.

Replica Island (Figure 3–5) is probably the most successful platformer on Android to date. It was developed by Google engineer and game development advocate Chris Pruett in an attempt to show that one can write high-performance games in pure Java on Android. The game tries to accommodate all potential device configurations by offering a huge variety of input schemes. Special care was taken that the game performs well even on low-end devices. The game itself involves a robot that is instructed to retrieve a mysterious artifact. The game mechanics resemble the old SNES 16-bit platformers. In the standard configuration, the robot is moved via an accelerometer and two buttons, one for enabling its thruster to jump over obstacles, and the other to stomp enemies from above. The game is also open source, which is another plus.

Figure 3–5. *Replica Island, by Chris Pruett*

Exzeus (Figure 3–6), by HyperDevBox, is a classic rail shooter in the spirit of Starfox on the SNES, with high-fidelity 3D graphics. The game features it all: different weapons, power-ups, big boss fights, and a ton of things to shoot. As with many other 3D titles, the game is meant to be played on high-end devices only. The main character is controlled via tilt and onscreen buttons—a rather intuitive control scheme for this type of game.

Figure 3–6. *Exzeus, by HyperDevBox*

Deadly Chambers (Figure 3–7), by Battery Powered Games, is a third-person shooter in the style of such classics as Doom and Quake. The main character, Dr. Chambers, tries to get out of the dungeons of the evil wizard in the tower. Battery Powered Games also sticks to the standard of not having an elaborate backstory for their shooter. But who needs that if you can just mindlessly kill everything that gets in your way with a fine set of exquisite weapons? The main character is controlled via an onscreen analog stick. Additional buttons allow the player to switch into a first-person perspective for more fine-grained aiming, switching weapons, and so on. In contrast to Exzeus, the developer took great care to make the game run even on low-end devices. The game also offers a variety of input schemes, so you can even play the game on single-touch screens. Technically, the game is a major feat, especially considering that it was programmed by a single person over a period of roughly six months.

Figure 3–7. *Deadly Chambers, by Battery Powered Games*

Radiant (Figure 3–8), by Hexage, represents a brilliant evolutionary step from the old Space Invaders concept. Instead of offering a static playfield, the game presents side-scrolling levels, and has quite a bit of variety in level and enemy design. You control the ship by tilting the phone, and you can upgrade the ship's weapon systems by buying new weapons with points you've earned by shooting enemies. The semi-pixelated style of the graphics give this game a unique look and feel while bringing back memories of the old days.

Figure 3–8. *Radiant, by Hexage*

The action and arcade genre is still a bit underrepresented on the market. Players are longing for good action titles, so maybe that is your niche!

Tower-Defense Games

Given their immense success on the Android platform, I felt the need to discuss tower-defense games as their own genre. Tower-defense games became popular as a variant of PC real-time strategy games developed by the modding community. The concept was soon translated to standalone games. Tower-defense games currently represent the best-selling genre on Android.

In a typical tower-defense game, some mostly evil force is sending out critters in so-called waves to attack your castle/base/crystals/you name it. Your task is to defend that special place on the game map by placing defense turrets that shoot the incoming enemies. For each enemy you kill, you usually get some amount of money or points that you can invest in new turrets or upgrades.

The concept is extremely simple, but getting the balance of such a game right is quite difficult.

Robo Defense (Figure 3–9), by Lupis Labs Software, is the mother of all tower-defense games on Android. It has occupied the number-one paid game spot in the market for most of Android's lifetime. The game follows the standard tower-defense formula without any bells and whistles attached. It's a straightforward and dangerously addictive tower-defense implementation, with different pannable maps, achievements, and high scores. The presentation is sufficient to get the concept across, but not stellar, which offers more proof that a selling game doesn't necessarily need to feature cream-of-the-crop graphics and audio.

Figure 3–9. *Robo Defense, by Lupis Labs Software*

Innovation

Some games just can't be put into a category. They exploit the new capabilities and features of Android devices, such as the camera or the GPS, to create new sorts of experiences. This innovative crop of new games is social and location-aware, and even introduces some elements from the field of augmented reality.

SpecTrek (Figure 3–10) is one of the winners of the second Android Developer Challenge. The goal of the game is to roam around with GPS enabled to find ghosts and catch them with your camera. The ghosts are simply laid over a camera view, and it is the player's task to keep them in focus and press the Catch button to score points.

Figure 3–10. *SpecTrek, by SpecTrekking.com*

So, now that you know what's already available on Android, I suggest firing up the Market application and checking out some of the games presented previously. Pay attention to their structure (e.g., what screens lead to what other screens, what buttons do what, how game elements interact with each other, and so on). Getting a feeling for these things can actually be achieved by playing games with an analytic mindset. Push away the entertainment factor for a moment and concentrate on deconstructing the game. Once you're done, come back and read on. We are going to design a very simple game on paper.

Game Design: The Pen Is Mightier Than the Code

As I said earlier, it is rather tempting to fire up the IDE and just hack together a nice tech demo. This is OK if you want to prototype experimental game mechanics and see if those actually work. However, once you do that, throw away the prototype. Pick up a pen and some paper, sit down in a comfortable chair, and think through all high-level aspects of your game. Don't concentrate on technical details yet—you'll do that later on. Right now, you want to concentrate on designing the user experience of your game. For me, the best way to do this is by sketching up the following things:

- The core game mechanics

- A rough backstory with the main characters

- A rough sketch of the graphics style based on the backstory and characters

- Sketches of all the screens involved, as well as diagrams of transitions between screens, along with transition triggers (e.g., for the game-over state).

If you've peeked at the Table of Contents, you know that we are going to implement Snake on Android. Snake is one of the most popular games ever to hit the mobile market. If you don't know about Snake already, look it up on the Web before reading on. I'll wait here in the meantime . . .

Welcome back. So, now that you know what Snake is all about, let us pretend we just came up with the idea ourselves and start laying out the design for it. Let's begin with the game mechanics.

Core Game Mechanics

Before we start, here's a list of what we need:

- A pair of scissors

- Something to write with

- Plenty of paper

In this phase of our game design, everything's a moving target. Instead of carefully crafting nice images in Paint, Gimp, or Photoshop, I suggest creating basic building blocks out of paper and rearranging them on a table until they fit. We can easily change things physically, without having to cope with a silly mouse. Once we are OK with our paper design, we can take photos or scan the design in for future reference. Let's start by creating those basic blocks of our core game screen. Figure 3–11 shows you my version of what is needed for our core game mechanics.

Figure 3–11. *Game design building blocks*

The leftmost rectangle is our screen, roughly the size of my Nexus One's screen. That's where we'll place all the other elements on. The next building blocks are two buttons that we'll use to control the snake. Finally, there's the snake's head, a couple of tail parts, and a piece it can eat. I also wrote out some numbers and cut them out. Those will be used to display the score. Figure 3–12 illustrates my vision of the initial playing field.

Figure 3–12. *The initial playing field*

Let's define the game mechanics:

- The snake advances in the direction its head is pointed in, dragging along its tail. Head and tail are composed of equally sized parts that only differ in their visuals a little.

- If the snake goes outside the screen boundaries, it reenters the screen on the opposite side.

- If the right or left button is pressed, the snake takes a 90 degree clockwise (right) or counterclockwise (left) turn.

- If the snake hits itself (e.g., a part of its tail), the game is over.

- If the snake hits a piece with its head, the piece disappears, the score is increased by 10 points, and a new piece appears on the playing field in a location that is not occupied by the snake itself. The snake also grows by one tail part. That new tail part is attached to the end of the snake.

This is quite a big description for such a simple game. Note that I ordered the items by ascending complexity somewhat. The behavior of the game when the snake eats a piece on the playing field is probably the most complex one. More elaborate games can of course not be described in such a concise manner. Usually, you'd split these up into separate parts and design each part individually, connecting them in a final merge step at the end of the process.

The last game mechanics item has an implication: the game will end eventually, as all space on the screen will be used up by the snake.

Now that our totally original game mechanics idea looks good, let's try to come up with a backstory for it.

A Story and an Art Style

While an epic story with zombies, spaceships, dwarves, and lots of explosions would be fun, we have to realize that we are limited in resources. My drawing skills, as exemplified in Figure 3–12, are somewhat lacking. I couldn't draw a zombie if my life depended on it. So I do what any self-respecting indie game developer would do: I resort to the doodle style and adjust my settings accordingly.

Enter the world of Mr. Nom. Mr. Nom is a paper snake who's always eager to eat drops of ink that fall down from an unspecified source on his paper land. Mr. Nom is utterly selfish and has only a single, not-so-noble goal: becoming the biggest ink-filled paper snake in the world!

This little backstory allows us to define a few more things:

- The art style is doodly. We will actually scan in our building blocks later and use them in our game as graphical assets.

- As Mr. Nom is an individualist, we will modify his blocky nature a little and give him a proper snake face. And a hat.

- The digestible piece will be transformed into a set of ink stains.

- We'll trick out the audio aspect of the game by letting Mr. Nom grunt each time he eats an ink stain.

- Instead of going for a boring title like "Doodle Snake," let us call the game "Mr. Nom," a much more intriguing title.

Figure 3–13 shows Mr. Nom in his full glory along with some ink stains that will replace the original block. I also sketched a doodly Mr. Nom logo that we can reuse throughout the game.

Figure 3–13. *Mr. Nom, his hat, ink stains, and the logo*

Screens and Transitions

With the game mechanics, the backstory, the characters, and the art style fixed, we can now design our screens and the transitions between them. First, however, it's important to understand exactly what makes up a screen:

- A screen is an atomic unit that fills the entire display and is responsible for exactly one part of the game (e.g., the main menu, the settings menu, or the game screen where the action is happening).

- A screen can be composed of multiple components (e.g., buttons, controls, head-up displays, or the rendering of the game world).

- A screen allows the user to interact with the screen's elements. These interactions can trigger screen transitions (e.g., pressing a New Game button on the main menu could exchange the currently active main menu screen with the game screen or a level-selection screen).

With those definitions, we can put on our thinking caps and design all the screens of our Mr. Nom game.

The first thing our game will present to the player is the main menu screen. What makes a good main menu screen?

- Displaying the name of our game is a good idea in principle, so we'll put in the Mr. Nom logo.

- To make things look more consistent, we also need a background. We'll reuse the playing field background for this.

- Players will usually want to actually play the game, so let's throw in a Play button. This will be our first interactive component.

- Players want to keep track of their progress and awesomeness, so we'll also add a high-score button, another interactive component.

- There might be people out there that don't know Snake. Let's give them some help in the form of a Help button that will transition to a help screen.

- While our sound design will be lovely, some players might still prefer to play in silence. Giving them a symbolic toggle button to enable and disable the sound will do the trick.

How we actually lay out those components on our screen is a matter of taste. You could start studying a subfield of computer science called human computer interfaces (HCI) to get the latest scientific opinion on how to present your application to the user. For Mr. Nom, that might be a little overkill, though. I settled with the simplistic design in Figure 3–14.

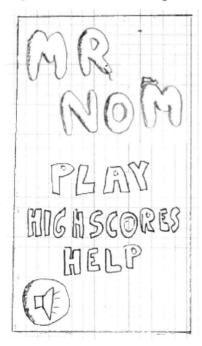

Figure 3–14. *The main menu screen*

Note that all those elements (the logo, the menu buttons, etc.) are all separate images.

Starting with the main menu screen has an immediate advantage: from the interactive components, we can directly derive more screens. In Mr. Nom's case we will need a game screen, a high-scores screen, and a help screen. We get away with not including a settings screen since the only setting (sound) is present on the main screen already.

Let's ignore the game screen for a moment and concentrate on the high-scores screen first. I decided that high scores will be stored locally in Mr. Nom, so we'll only keep track of a single player's achievements. I also decided that only the five highest scores will be recorded. The high-scores screen will therefore look like Figure 3–15, showing the "HIGHSCORES" text at the top, followed by the five top scores and a single button with an arrow on it indicating that you can transition back to something. We'll reuse the background of the playing field again because we like it cheap.

Figure 3–15. *The high-scores screen*

Next up is the help screen. It will inform the player of the backstory and the game mechanics. Now, all that information is a bit too much to be presented on a single screen. We'll therefore split up the help screen into multiple screens. Each of these screens will present one essential piece of information of the user: who Mr. Nom is and what he wants, how to control Mr. Nom to make him eat ink stains, and what Mr. Nom doesn't like (namely eating himself). That's a total of three screens, as shown in Figure 3–16. Note that I added a button to each screen indicating that there's more information to be read. We'll hook those screens up in a bit.

Figure 3–16. *The help screens*

Finally, there's our game screen, which we already saw in action. There are a few details we left out so far, though. First, the game shouldn't start immediately; we should give the player some time to get ready. The screen will thus start of with a request to touch the screen to start the munching. This does not warrant a separate screen; we will directly implement that initial pause in the game screen.

Speaking of pauses, we'll also add a button that allows pausing the game. Once it's paused, we also need to give the user a way to resume the game. We'll just display a big Resume button in that case. In the pause state, we'll also display another button that will allow the user to return to the main menu screen.

In case Mr. Nom bites his own tail, we need to inform the player that the game is over. We could implement a separate game-over screen, or we could stay within the game screen and just overlay a big "Game Over" message. In this case we'll opt for the latter. To round things out, we'll also display the score the player achieved along with a button to get back to the main menu.

Think of those different states of the game screen as subscreens. We have four subscreens: the initial get-ready state, the normal game-playing state, the paused state, and the game-over state. Figure 3–17 shows those.

Figure 3–17. *The game screen and its four different states*

Now it's time to hook up the screens with each other. Each screen has some interactive components that are made for transitioning to another screen.

- From the main menu screen, we can get to the game screen, the high-scores screen, and the help screen via the respective buttons.

- From the game screen we can get back to the main screen either via the button in the paused state or via the button in the game-over state.

- From the high-scores screen we can get back to the main screen.

- From the first help screen we can go to the second help screen, from the second to the third, and from the third to the fourth; from the fourth we'll return back to the main screen.

That's all of our transitions! Doesn't look so bad, does it? Figure 3–18 summarizes all the transitions visually with arrows from each interactive component to the target screen. I also put in all the elements our screens are composed of.

Figure 3–18. *All design elements and transitions*

With this we just finished our first full game design. What's left is the implementation. How do we actually make this design into an executable game?

> **NOTE:** The method we just used to create our game design is nice and dandy for smaller games. This book is called *Beginning Android Games*, so it's a fitting methodology. For larger projects you will most likely work on a team, with each team member specializing in one aspect. While you can still apply the preceding methodology in that context, you might need to tweak and tune it a little to accommodate the different environment. You will also work more iteratively, constantly refining your design.

Code: The Nitty-Gritty Details

Here's another chicken-and-egg situation: we only want to get to know the Android APIs relevant for game programming. But we still don't know how to actually program a game. We have an idea of how to design one, but transforming it into an executable is still voodoo magic to us. In the following subsections, I want to give you an overview of what a game is usually composed of. We'll look at some pseudocode for interfaces we'll later implement with what Android offers us. Interfaces are awesome for two reasons: they allow us to concentrate on the semantics without needing to know the implementation details, and they allow us to later exchange the implementation (e.g., instead of using 2D CPU rendering, we could exploit OpenGL ES to display Mr. Nom on the screen).

Every game needs some basic framework that abstracts away and eases the pain of communicating with the underlying operating system. Usually this is split up into modules, as follows:

Window management: This is responsible for creating a window and coping with things like closing the window or pausing/resuming the application on Android.

Input: This is related to the window management module, and keeps track of user input (e.g., touch events, keystrokes, and accelerometer readings).

File I/O: This allows us to get the bytes of our assets into our program from disk.

Graphics: This is probably the most complex module besides the actual game. It is responsible for loading graphics and drawing them on the screen.

Audio: This module is responsible for loading and playing everything that will hit our ears.

Game framework: This ties all the above together and provides an easy-to-use base to write our games.

Each of these modules is composed of one or more interfaces. Each interface will have at least one concrete implementation that implements the semantics of the interface based on what the underlying platform (in our case Android) provides us with.

NOTE: Yes, I deliberately left out networking from the preceding list. We will not implement multiplayer games in this book, I'm afraid. That is a rather advanced topic depending on the type of game. If you are interested in this topic, you can find a range of tutorials on the Web. (www.gamedev.net is a good place to start).

In the following discussion we will be as platform agnostic as possible. The concepts are the same on all platforms.

Application and Window Management

A game is just like any other computer program that has a UI. It is contained in some sort of window (if the underlying operating system's UI paradigm is window based, which is the case on all mainstream operating systems). The window serves as a container, and we basically think of it as a canvas that we draw our game content on.

Most operating systems allow the user to interact with the window in a special way besides touching the client area or pressing a key. On desktop systems you can usually drag the window around, resize it or minimize it to some sort of taskbar. On Android, resizing is replaced with accommodating an orientation change, and minimizing is similar to putting the application in the background via a press of the home button or as a reaction to an incoming call.

The application and window management module is also responsible for actually setting up the window and making sure it is filled by a single UI component that we can later render to and that receives input from the user in the form of touching or pressing keys. That UI component might be rendered to via the CPU or it can be hardware accelerated as it is the case with OpenGL ES.

The application and window management module does not have a concrete set of interfaces. We'll merge it with the game framework later on. What we have to remember are the application states and window events that we have to manage:

Create: Called once when the window (and thus the application) is started up.

Pause: Called when the application is paused by some mechanism.

Resume: Called when the application is resumed and the window is in the foreground again.

NOTE: Some Android aficionados might roll their eyes at this point. Why only use a single window (activity in Android speak)? Why not use more than one UI widget for the game—say, for implementing complex UIs that our game might need? The main reason is that we want complete control over the look and feel of our game. It also allows me to focus on Android game programming instead of Android UI programming, a topic for which better books exist—for example, Mark Murphy's excellent *Beginning Android 2* (Apress, 2010).

Input

The user will surely want to interact with our game in some way. That's where the input module comes in. On most operating systems, input events such as touching the screen or pressing a key are dispatched to the currently focused window. The window will then further dispatch the event to the UI component that has the focus. The dispatching process is usually transparent to us; all we need to care about is getting the events from the focused UI component. The UI APIs of the operating system provide a mechanism to hook into the event dispatching system so we can easily register and record the events. This hooking into and recording of events is the main task of the input module.

What can we do with the recorded information? There are two modi operandi:

Polling: With polling, we only check the current state of the input devices. Any states between the current check and the last check will be lost. This way of input handling is suitable for checking things like whether a user touches a specific button, for example. It is not suitable for tracking text input, as the order of key events is lost.

Event-based handling: This gives us a full chronological history of the events that have occurred since we last checked. It is a suitable mechanism to perform text input or any other task that relies on the order of events. It's also useful to detect when a finger first touched the screen or when it was lifted.

What input devices do we want to handle? On Android, we have three main input methods: touchscreen, keyboard/trackball, and accelerometer. The first two are suitable for both polling and event-based handling. The accelerometer is usually just polled. The touchscreen can generate three events:

Touch down: This happens when a finger is touched to the screen.

Touch drag: This happens when a finger is dragged across the screen. Before a drag there's always a down event.

Touch up: This happens when a finger is lifted from the screen.

Each touch event has additional information: the position relative to the UI components origin, and a pointer index used in multitouch environments to identify and track separate fingers.

The keyboard can generate two types of events:

Key down: This happens when a key is pressed down.

Key up: This happens when a key is lifted. This event is always preceded by a key-down event.

Key events also carry additional information. Key-down events store the pressed key's code. Key-up events store the key's code and an actual Unicode character. There's a difference between a key's code and the Unicode character generated by a key-up event. In the latter case, the state of other keys are also taken into account, such as the Shift key. This way, we can get upper- and lowercase letters in a key-up event, for the molecules to some sort of signal. How this signal is processed and stored is what makes the difference between analog and digital recording. We are working digitally, so let's just have a look at that case.

Recording audio digitally means that the state of the microphone membrane is measured and stored at discrete time steps. Depending on the pushing by the surrounding molecules, the membrane can be pushed inward or outward with regard to a neutral state. This process is called sampling, as we take membrane state samples at discrete points in time. The number of samples we take per time unit is called the *sampling rate*. Usually the time unit is given in seconds, and the unit is called Hertz (Hz). The more samples per second, the higher the quality of the audio. CDs play back at a sampling rate of 44,100 Hz, or 44.1 KHz. Lower sampling rates are found, for example, when transferring voice over the telephone line (8 KHz is common in this case).

The sampling rate is only one attribute responsible for a recording's quality. The way we store each membrane state sample also plays a role, and is also subject to digitalization. Let's recall what the membrane state actually is: it's the distance of the membrane from its neutral state. As it makes a difference whether the membrane is pushed inward or outward, we record the signed distance. Hence, the membrane state at a specific time step is a single negative or positive number. We can store such a signed number in a variety of ways: as a signed 8-, 16-, or 32-bit integer, as a 32-bit float, or even as a 64-bit float. Every data type has limited precision. An 8-bit signed integer can store 127 positive and 128 negative distance values. A 32-bit integer provides a lot more resolution. When stored as a float, the membrane state is usually normalized to a range between –1 and 1. The maximum positive and minimum negative values represent the farthest distance the membrane can have from its neutral state. The membrane state is also called the amplitude. It represents the loudness of the sound that it gets hit by.

With a single microphone we can only record mono sound, which loses all spatial information. With two microphones, we can measure sound at different locations in space, and thus get so-called *stereo sound*. You might achieve stereo sound, for example, by placing one microphone to the left and another to the right of an object emitting sound. When the sound is played back simultaniously through two speakers, we can sort of reproduce the spatial component of the audio. But this also means that we need to store twice the number of samples when storing stereo audio.

The playback is a simple matter in the end. Once we have our audio samples in digital form, with a specific sampling rate and data type we can throw that data at our audio processing unit, which will transform the information into a signal for an attached speaker. The speaker interprets this signal and translates it into the vibration of a membrane, which in turn will cause the surrounding air molecules to move and produce sound waves. It's exactly what is done for recording, only reversed!

Audio Quality and Compression

Wow, lots of theory. Why do we care? If you paid attention, you can now tell whether an audio file has a high quality or not depending on the sampling rate and the data type used to store each sample. The higher the sampling rate and the higher the data type precision, the better the quality of the audio. However, that also means that we need more storage room for our audio signal.

Imagine we record the same sound with a length of 60 seconds twice: once at a sampling rate of 8 KHz at 8 bits per sample, and once at a sampling rate of 44 KHz at 16-bit precision. How much memory would we need to store each sound? In the first case, we need 1 byte per sample. Multiply this by the sampling rate of 8,000 Hz, and we need 8,000 bytes per second. For our full 60 seconds of audio recording, that's 480,000 bytes, or roughly half a megabyte (MB). Our higher-quality recording needs quite a bit more memory: 2 bytes per sample, and 2 times 44,000 bytes per second. That's 88,000 bytes per second. Multiply this by 60 seconds, and we arrive at 5,280,000 bytes, or a little over 5 MB. Your usual 3–minute pop song would take up over 15 MB at that quality, and that's only a mono recording. For a stereo recording, we'd need twice that amount of memory. Quite a lot of bytes for a silly song!

Many smart people have come up with ways to reduce the number of bytes needed for an audio recording. They've invented rather complex psychoacoustic compression algorithms that analyze an uncompressed audio recording and output a smaller, compressed version. The compression is usually *lossy*, meaning that some minor parts of the original audio are omitted. When you play back MP3s or OGGs, you are actually listening to compressed lossy audio. So, using formats such as MP3 or OGG will help us reduce the amount of space needed to store our audio on disk.

What about playing back the audio from compressed files? While there exists dedicated decoding hardware for various compressed audio formats, common audio hardware can often only cope with uncompressed samples. Before actually feeding the audio card with samples, we have to first read them in and decompress them. We can do this once and store the all uncompressed audio samples in memory, or only stream in partitions from the audio file as needed.

In Practice

You have seen that even 3–minute songs can take up a lot of memory. When we play back our game's music, we will thus stream the audio samples in on the fly instead of preloading all audio samples to memory. Usually, we only have a single music stream playing, so we only have to access the disk once.

For short sound effects, such as explosions or gunshots, the situation is a little different. We often want to play a sound effect multiple times simultaneously. Streaming the audio samples from disk for each instance of the sound effect is not a good idea. We are lucky, though, as short sounds do not take up a lot of memory. We will therefore read in all samples of a sound effect to memory, from where we can directly and simultaneously play them back.

So, we have the following requirements:

- We need a way to load audio files for streaming playback and for playback from memory.

- We need a way to control the playback of streamed audio.

- We need a way to control the playback of fully loaded audio.

This directly translates into the Audio, Music, and Sound interfaces (shown in Listings 3–3 through 3–5, respectively).

Listing 3–3. *The Audio Interface*

```
package com.badlogic.androidgames.framework;

public interface Audio {
    public Music newMusic(String filename);

    public Sound newSound(String filename);
}
```

The Audio interface is our way to create new Music and Sound instances. A Music instance represents a streamed audio file. A Sound instance represents a short sound effect that we keep entirely in memory. The methods Audio.newMusic() and Audio.newSound() both take a filename as an argument and throw an IOException in case the loading process fails (e.g., when the specified file does not exist or is corrupt). The filenames refer to asset files in our application's APK file.

Listing 3–4. *The Music Interface*

```
package com.badlogic.androidgames.framework;

public interface Music {
    public void play();

    public void stop();

    public void pause();

    public void setLooping(boolean looping);

    public void setVolume(float volume);

    public boolean isPlaying();

    public boolean isStopped();

    public boolean isLooping();

    public void dispose();
}
```

The Music interface is a little bit more involved. It features methods to start playing the music stream, pausing and stopping it, and setting it to loop playback, which means it will start from the beginning automatically when it reaches the end of the audio file. Additionally, we can set the volume as a float in the range of 0 (silent) to 1 (maximum volume). There are also a couple of getter methods that allow us to poll the current state of the Music instance. Once we no longer need the Music instance, we have to dispose of it. This will close any system resources, such as the file the audio was streamed from.

Listing 3–5. *The Sound Interface*

```
package com.badlogic.androidgames.framework;

public interface Sound {
    public void play(float volume);

    public void dispose();
}
```

The Sound interface is simpler. All we need to do is call its play() method, which again takes a float parameter to specify the volume. We can call the play() method anytime we want (e.g., when a shot is fired or a player jumps). Once we no longer need the Sound instance, we have to dispose of it to free up the memory that the samples use, as well as other system resources potentially associated.

> **NOTE:** While we covered a lot of ground in this chapter, there's a lot more to learn about audio programming. I simplified some things to keep this section short and sweet. Usually you wouldn't specify the audio volume linearly, for example. In our context, it's OK to overlook this little detail. Just be aware that there's more to it!

Graphics

The last module close to the metal is the graphics module. As you might have guessed, it will be responsible for drawing images (also known as bitmaps) to our screen. That may sound easy, but if you want high-performance graphics, you have to know at least the basics of graphics programming. Let's start with the basics of 2D graphics.

The first question we need to ask goes like this: how on Earth are the images output to my display? The answer is rather involved, and we do not necessarily need to know all the details. We'll just quickly review what's happening inside our computer and the display.

Of Rasters, Pixels, and Framebuffers

Today's displays are raster based. A *raster* is a two-dimensional grid of so-called picture elements. You might know them as *pixels*, and we'll refer to them as such in the subsequent text. The raster grid has a limited width and height, which we usually express as the number of pixels per row and per column. If you feel brave, you can turn on your computer and try to make out individual pixels on your display. Note that I'm not responsible for any damage that does to your eyes, though.

A pixel has two attributes: a position within the grid and a color. A pixel's position is given as two-dimensional coordinates within a discrete coordinate system. *Discrete* means that a coordinate is always at an integer position. Coordinates are defined within a Euclidean coordinate system imposed on the grid. The origin of the coordinate system is the top-left corner of the grid. The positive x-axis points to the right and the y-axis points downward. The last item is what confuses people the most. We'll come back to it in a minute; there's a simple reason why this is the case.

Ignoring the silly y-axis, we can see that due to the discrete nature of our coordinates, the origin is coincident with the top-left pixel in the grid, which is located at (0,0). The pixel to the right of the origin pixel is located at (1,0), the pixel beneath the origin pixel is at (0,1), and so on (see the left side of Figure 3–20). The display's raster grid is finite, so there's a limited number of meaningful coordinates. Negative coordinates are outside the screen. Coordinates greater than or equal to the width or height of the raster are also outside the screen. Note that the biggest x-coordinate is the raster's width minus 1, and the biggest y-coordinate is the raster's height minus 1. That's due to the origin being coincident with the top-left pixel. Off-by-one errors are a common source of frustration in graphics programming.

The display receives a constant stream of information from the graphics processor. It encodes the color of each pixel in the display's raster as specified by the program or operating system in control of drawing to the screen. The display will refresh its state a few dozen times per second. The exact rate is called the refresh rate. It is expressed in Hertz. Liquid crystal displays (LCDs) usually have a refresh rate of 60 Hz per second; cathode ray tube (CRT) monitors and plasma monitors often have higher refresh rates.

The graphics processor has access to a special memory area known as video memory, or VRAM. Within VRAM there's a reserved area for storing each pixel to be displayed on the screen. This area is usually called the *framebuffer*. A complete screen image is therefore called a frame. For each pixel in the display's raster grid, there's a corresponding memory address in the framebuffer that holds the pixel's color. When we want to change what's displayed on the screen, we simply change the color values of the pixels in that memory area in VRAM.

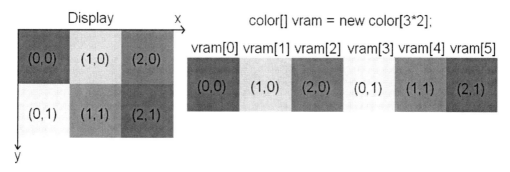

Figure 3–20. *Display raster grid and VRAM, oversimplified*

Time to explain why the y-axis in the display's coordinate system is pointing downward. Memory, be it VRAM or normal RAM, is linear and one dimensional. Think of it as a one-dimensional array. So how do we map the two-dimensional pixel coordinates to one-dimensional memory addresses? Figure 3–20 shows a rather small display raster grid of three-by-two pixels, as well as its representation in VRAM (we assume VRAM only consists of the framebuffer memory). From this we can easily derive the following formula to calculate the memory address of a pixel at (x,y):

```
int address = x + y * rasterWidth;
```

We can also go the other way around, from an address to the x- and y-coordinates of a pixel:

```
int x = address % rasterWidth;
int y = address / rasterWidth;
```

So, the y-axis is pointing downward because of the memory layout of the pixel colors in VRAM. This is actually a sort of legacy inherited from the early days of computer graphics. Monitors would update the color of each pixel on the screen starting at the top-left corner moving to the right, tracing back to the left on the next line, until they reached the bottom of the screen. It was convenient to have the VRAM contents laid out in a manner that eased the transfer of the color information to the monitor.

> **NOTE:** If we had full access to the framebuffer, we could use the preceding equation to write a full-fledged graphics library to draw pixels, lines, rectangles, images loaded to memory, and so on. Modern operating systems do not grant us direct access to the framebuffer for various reasons. Instead we usually draw to a memory area that is then copied to the actual framebuffer by the operating system. The general concepts hold true in this case as well, though! If you are interested in how to do these low-level things efficiently, search the Web for a guy called Bresenham and his line- and circle-drawing algorithms.

Vsync and Double-Buffering

Now, if you remember the paragraph about refresh rates, you might have noticed that those rates seem rather low, and that we might be able to write to the framebuffer faster than the display will refresh. That can happen. Even worse, we don't know when the display is grabbing its latest frame copy from VRAM, which could be a problem if we're in the middle of drawing something. In this case, the display will then show parts of the old framebuffer content and parts of the new state—an undesirable situation. You can see that effect in many PC games, where it expresses itself as tearing (in which the screen shows parts of the last frame and parts of the new frame simultaneously).

The first part of the solution to this problem is called *double-buffering*. Instead of having a single framebuffer, the graphics processing unit (GPU) actually manages two of them, a front buffer and a back buffer. The front buffer is available to the display to fetch the pixel colors from, and the back buffer is available to draw our next frame while the display happily feeds off the front buffer. When we finish drawing our current frame, we tell the GPU to switch the two buffers with each other, which usually means just swapping the address of the front and the back buffer. In graphics programming literature and API documentation, you may find the terms *page flip* and *buffer swap*, which refer to this process.

Double-buffering alone does not solve the problem entirely, though: the swap can still happen while the screen is in the middle of refreshing its content. That's where *vertical synchronization* (also known as *vsync*) comes into play. When we call the buffer swap method, the GPU will block until the display signals that it has finished its current refresh. If that happens, the GPU can safely swap the buffer addresses, and all will be well.

Luckily, we barely need to care about those pesky details nowadays. VRAM and the details of double-buffering and vsyncing are securely hidden from us so we cannot wreak havoc with them. Instead we are provided with a set of APIs that usually limit us to manipulating the contents of our application window. Some of these APIs, such as OpenGL ES, expose hardware acceleration, which basically does nothing more than manipulate VRAM with specialized circuits on the graphics chip. See, it's not magic! The reason you should be aware of the inner works, at least at a high level, is that it allows you to understand the performance characteristics of your application. When vsync is enabled, you can never go above the refresh rate of your screen, which might be puzzling if all you're doing is drawing a single pixel.

When we render with non-hardware-accelerated APIs, we don't directly deal with the display itself. Instead we draw to one of the UI components in our window. In our case we deal with a single UI component that is stretched over the whole window. Our coordinate system will therefore not stretch over the entire screen, but only our UI component. The UI component effectively becomes our display, with its own virtual framebuffer. The operating system will then manage compositing the contents of all the visible windows and make sure their contents are correctly transferred to the regions they cover in the real framebuffer.

What Is Color?

You will notice that I have conveniently ignored colors so far. I made up a type called `color` in Figure 3–20 and pretended all is well. Let's see what color really is.

Physically, color is the reaction of your retina and visual cortex to electromagnetic waves. Such a wave is characterized by its wavelength and its intensity. We can see waves with a wavelength between roughly 400 and 700 nm. That subband of the electromagnetic spectrum is also known as the visible light spectrum. A rainbow shows all the colors of this visible light spectrum, going from violet to blue to green to yellow, followed by orange and ending at red. All a monitor does is emit specific electromagnetic waves for each pixel, which we experience as the color of each pixel. Different types of displays use different methods to achieve that goal. A simplified version of this process goes like this: every pixel on the screen is made up of three different fluorescent particles that will emit light with one of the colors red, green, or blue. When the display refreshes, each pixel's fluorescent particles will emit light by some means (e.g., in the case of CRT displays, the pixel's particles get hit by a bunch of electrons). For each particle, the display can control how much light it emits. For example, if a pixel is entirely red, only the red particle will be hit with electrons at full intensity. If we want colors other than the three base colors, we can achieve that by mixing the base colors. Mixing is done by varying the intensity with which each particle emits its color. The electromagnetic waves will overlay each other on the way to our retina. Our brain interprets this mix as a specific color. A color can thus be specified by a mix of intensities of the base colors red, green, and blue.

Color Models

What we just discussed is called a color model, specifically the RGB color model. RGB stands for red, green, and blue, of course. There are many more color models we could use, such as YUV and CMYK. In most graphics programming APIs, the RGB color model is pretty much the standard, though, so we'll only discuss that here.

The RGB color model is called an additive color model, due to the fact that the final color is derived via mixing the additive primary colors red, green, and blue. You've probably experimented with mixing primary colors in school. Figure 3–21 shows you some examples for RGB color mixing to refresh your memory a little bit.

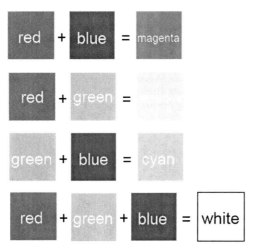

Figure 3–21. *Having fun with mixing the primary colors red, green, and blue*

We can of course generate a lot more colors than the ones shown in Figure 3–21 by varying the intensity of the red, green, and blue components. Each component can have an intensity value between 0 and some maximum value (say, 1). If we interpret each color component as a value on one of the three axes of a three-dimensional Euclidian space, we can plot a so-called *color cube*, as depicted in Figure 3–22. There are a lot more colors available to us if we vary the intensity of each component. A color is given as a triplet (red, green, blue) where each component is in the range between 0.0 and 1.0. 0.0 means no intensity for that color, and 1.0 means full intensity. The color black is at the origin (0,0,0), and the color white is at (1,1,1).

Figure 3–22. *The mighty RGB color cube*

Encoding Colors Digitally

How can we encode an RGB color triplet in computer memory? First we have to define what data type we want to use for the color components. We could use floating-point numbers and specify the valid range as being between 0.0 and 1.0. This would give us quite some resolution for each component and make a lot of different colors available to us. Sadly, this approach uses up a lot of space (3 times 4 or 8 bytes per pixel, depending on whether we use 32-bit or 64-bit floats).

We can do better at the expense of losing a few colors, which is totally OK, as displays usually have a limited range of colors they can emit. Instead of using a float for each component, we can use an unsigned integer. Now, if we use a 32-bit integer for each component, we haven't gained anything. Instead, we use an unsigned byte for each component. The intensity for each component then ranges from 0 to 255. For 1 pixel, we thus need 3 bytes, or 24 bits. That's 2 to the power of 24 (16,777,216) different colors. I'd say that's enough for our needs.

Can we get that down even more? Yes, we can. We can pack each component into a single 16-bit word, so each pixel needs 2 bytes of storage. Red uses 5 bits, green uses 6 bits, and blue uses the rest of 5 bits. The reason green gets 6 bits is that our eyes can see more shades of green than red and blue. All bits together make 2 to the power of 16 (65,536) different colors we can encode. Figure 3–23 shows how a color is encoded with the three encodings described previously.

float: (1.0, 0.5, 0.75)
24-bit: (255, 128, 196) = 0xFF80C4
16-bit: (31, 31, 45) = 0xFC0D

Figure 3–23. *Color encodings of a nice shade of pink (which will be gray in the print copy of this book, sorry)*

In the case of the float, we could use three 32-bit Java floats. In the 24-bit encoding case, we have a little problem: there's no 24-bit integer type in Java, so we could either store each component in a single byte or use a 32-bit integer with the upper 8 bits being unused. In case of the 16-bit encoding, we can again either use two separate bytes or store the components in a single short value. Note that Java does not have unsigned types. Due to the power of the two's complement, we can safely use signed integer types to store unsigned values, though.

For both 16- and 24-bit integer encodings, we need to also specify the order in which we store the three components in the short or integer value. There are usually two ways that are used: RGB and BGR. Figure 3–23 uses RGB encoding. The blue component is in the lowest 5 or 8 bits, the green component uses up the next 6 or 8 bits, and the red component uses the upper 5 or 8 bits. BGR encoding just reverses the order. The green bits stay where they are, and the red and blue bits swap places. We'll use the RGB order throughout this book, as Android's graphics APIs work with that order as well. Let's summarize the color encodings discussed so far:

- A 32-bit float RGB encoding has 12 bytes for each pixel, and intensities that vary between 0.0 and 1.0.

- A 24-bit integer RGB encoding has 3 or 4 bytes for each pixel, and intensities that vary between 0 and 255. The order of the components can be RGB or BGR. This is also known as RGB888 or BGR888 in some circles, where 8 specifies the number of bits per component.

- A 16-bit integer RGB encoding has 2 bytes for each pixel; red and blue have intensities between 0 and 31, and green has intensities between 0 and 63. The order of the components can be RGB or BGR. This is also known as RGB565 or BGR565 in some circles, where 5 and 6 specify the number of bits of the respective component.

The type of encoding we use is also called the color depth. Images we create and store on disk or in memory have a defined color depth, and so do the framebuffer of the actual graphics hardware and the display itself. Today's displays usually have a default color depth of 24 bit, and can be configured to use less in some cases. The framebuffer of the graphics hardware is also rather flexible, and can use many different color depths. Our own images can of course also have any color depth we like.

NOTE: There are a lot more ways to encode per-pixel color information. Apart from RGB colors, we could also have grayscale pixels, which only have a single component. As those are not used a lot, we'll ignore them at this point.

Image Formats and Compression

At some point in our game development process, our artist will provide us with images she created with some graphics software like Gimp, Paint.NET, or Photoshop. These images can be stored in a variety of formats on disk. Why is there a need for these formats in the first place? Can't we just store the raster as a blob of bytes on disk?

Well, we could, but let's check how much memory that would take up. Say we want the best quality, so we choose to encode our pixels in RGB888, at 24 bits per pixel. The image would be 1,024 × 1,024 in size. That's 3 MB for that single puny image alone! Using RGB565, we can get that down to roughly 2 MB.

As in the case of audio, there's been a lot of research on how to reduce the memory needed to store an image. As usual, compression algorithms are employed, specifically tailored for the needs of storing images and keeping as much of the original color information as possible. The two most popular formats are JPEG and PNG. JPEG is a lossy format. This means that some of the original information is thrown away in the process of compression. PNG is a lossless format, and will reproduce an image that's 100 percent true to the original. Lossy formats usually exhibit better compression characteristics and take up less space on disk. We can therefore chose what format to use depending on the disk memory constraints.

Similar to sound effects, we have to fully decompress an image when we load it into memory. So, even if your image is 20 KB compressed on disk, you still need the full width times height times color depth storage space in RAM.

Once loaded and decompressed, the image will be available in the form of an array of pixel colors, in exactly the same way the framebuffer is laid out in VRAM. The only difference is that the pixels are located in normal RAM and that the color depth might differ from the framebuffer's color depth. A loaded image also has a coordinate system like the framebuffer, with the origin being in its top-left corner, the x-axis pointing to the right, and the y-axis pointing downward.

Once an image is loaded, we can draw it in RAM to the framebuffer by simply transferring the pixel colors from the image to appropriate locations in the framebuffer. We don't do this by hand; instead we use an API that provides that functionality.

Alpha Compositing and Blending

Before we can start designing our graphics module interfaces, we have to tackle one more thing: image compositing. For the sake of this discussion, assume that we have a framebuffer we can render to, as well as a bunch of images loaded into RAM that we'll throw at the framebuffer. Figure 3–24 shows a simple background image, as well as Bob, a zombie-slaying ladies man.

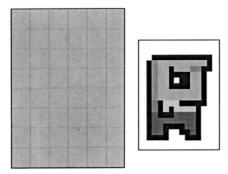

Figure 3–24. *A simple background, and Bob, master of the universe*

To draw Bob's world, we'd first draw the background image to the framebuffer, followed by Bob over the background image in the framebuffer. This process is called *compositing*, as we compose different images into a final image. The order in which we draw images is relevant, as any new draw call will overwrite the current contents in the framebuffer. So, what would be the final output of our compositing? Figure 3–25 shows it to you.

Figure 3–25. *Compositing the background and Bob into the framebuffer (not what we wanted)*

Ouch, that's not what we wanted. In Figure 3–24, notice that Bob is surrounded by white pixels. When we draw Bob on top of the background to the framebuffer, those white pixels also get drawn, effectively overwriting the background. How can we draw Bob's image so that only Bob's pixels are drawn, and the white background pixels are ignored?

Enter alpha blending. Well, in Bob's case it's technically called alpha masking, but that's just a subset of alpha blending. Graphics software usually lets us not only specify the RGB values of a pixel, but also its translucency. Think of it as yet another component of a pixel's color. We can encode it just like we encoded the red, green, and blue components.

I hinted earlier that we could store a 24-bit RGB triplet in a 32-bit integer. There are 8 unused bits in that 32-bit integer that we can grab and store our alpha value in. We can then specify the translucency of a pixel from 0 to 255, where 0 is fully transparent and 255 is opaque. This encoding is known as ARGB8888 or BGRA8888 depending on the order of the components. There are also RGBA8888 and ABGR8888 formats, of course.

In the case of 16-bit encoding, we have a little problem: all bits of our 16-bit short are taken up by the color components. Let's instead imitate the ARGB8888 format and define an ARGB4444 format analogously. That leaves 12 bits for our RGB values in total—4 bits per color component.

We can easily imagine how a rendering method for pixels that's fully translucent or opaque would work. In the first case, we'd just ignore pixels with an alpha component of zero. In the second case, we'd simply overwrite the destination pixel. When a pixel has neither a fully translucent nor fully opaque alpha component, however, things get a tiny bit more complicated.

When talking about blending in a formal way, we have to define a few things:

- Blending has two inputs and one output, each represented as an RGB triplet (C) plus an alpha value (α).

- The two inputs are called *source* and *destination*. The source is the pixel from the image we want to draw over the destination image (e.g., the framebuffer). The destination is the pixel we are going to (partially) overdraw with our source pixel.

- The output is again a color expressed as an RGB triplet and an alpha value. Usually we just ignore the alpha value, though. For simplicity we'll do that in this chapter.

- To simplify our math a little bit, we'll represent RGB and alpha values as floats in the range of 0.0 to 1.0.

Equipped with those definitions, we can create so-called blending equations. The simplest equation looks like this:

```
red = src.red * src.alpha + dst.red * (1 - src.alpha)
blue = src.green * src.alpha + dst.green * (1 - src.alpha)
green = src.blue * src.alpha + dst.blue * (1 - src.alpha)
```

src and dst are the pixels of the source and destination we want to blend with each other. We blend the two colors component-wise. Note the absence of the destination alpha value in these blending equations. Let's try an example and see what it does:

```
src = (1, 0.5, 0.5), src.alpha = 0.5, dst = (0, 1, 0)
red = 1 * 0.5 + 0 * (1 - 0.5) = 0.5
blue = 0.5 * 0.5 + 1 * (1 - 0.5) = 0.75
red = 0.5 * 0.5 + 0 * (1 - 0.5) = 0.25
```

Figure 3–26 illustrates the preceding equation. Our source color is a shade of pink, and the destination color is a shade of green. Both colors contribute equally to the final output color, resulting in a somewhat dirty shade of green or olive.

Figure 3–26. *Blending two pixels*

Two fine gentlemen called Porter and Duff came up with a slew of blending equations. We will stick with the preceding equation, though, as it covers most of our use cases. Try experimenting with it on paper or in your graphics software of choice to get a feeling for what blending will do to your composition.

> **NOTE:** Blending is a wide field. If you want to exploit it to its fullest potential, I suggest searching the Web for Porter and Duff's original work on the subject. For the games we will write, though, the preceding equation is sufficient.

Notice that there are a lot of multiplications involved in the preceding equations (six, to be precise). Multiplications are costly, and we should try to avoid them where possible. In the case of blending, we can get rid of three of those multiplications by premultiplying the RGB values of the source pixel color with the source alpha value. Most graphics software supports premultiplication of an image's RGB values with the respective alphas. If that is not supported, you can do it at load time in memory. However, when we use a graphics API to draw our image with blending, we have to make sure that we use the correct blending equation. Our image will still contain the alpha values, so the preceding equation would output incorrect results. The source alpha must not be multiplied with the source color. Luckily, all Android graphics APIs allow us to fully specify how we want to blend our images.

In Bob's case, we just set all the white pixels' alpha values to zero in our graphics software of choice, load the image in ARGB8888 or ARGB4444 format, maybe premultiply the alpha, and use a drawing method that does the actual alpha blending with the correct blending equation. The result would look like Figure 3–27.

Figure 3–27. *On the left is Bob blended; on the right is Bob in Paint.NET. The checkerboard illustrates that the alpha of the white background pixels is zero, so the background checkerboard shines through.*

NOTE: The JPEG format does not support storing alpha values per pixel. Use the PNG format in that case.

In Practice

With all this information, we can finally start to design the interfaces for our graphics module. Let's define the functionality of those interfaces. Note that when I refer to the framebuffer, I actually mean the virtual framebuffer of the UI component we draw to. We just pretend we directly draw to the real framebuffer. We'll need to be able to perform the following operations:

- Load images from disk and store them in memory for drawing them later on.

- Clear the framebuffer with a color so we can erase what's still there from the last frame.

- Set a pixel in the framebuffer at a specific location to a specific color.

- Draw lines and rectangles to the framebuffer.

- Draw previously loaded images to the framebuffer. We'd like to be able to either draw the complete image or portions of it. We also need to be able to draw images with and without blending.

- Get the dimensions of the framebuffer.

I propose two simple interfaces: Graphics and Pixmap. Let's start with the Graphics interface, shown in Listing 3–6.

Listing 3–6. *The Graphics Interface*

```java
package com.badlogic.androidgames.framework;

public interface Graphics {
    public static enum PixmapFormat {
        ARGB8888, ARGB4444, RGB565
    }

    public Pixmap newPixmap(String fileName, PixmapFormat format);

    public void clear(int color);

    public void drawPixel(int x, int y, int color);

    public void drawLine(int x, int y, int x2, int y2, int color);

    public void drawRect(int x, int y, int width, int height, int color);

    public void drawPixmap(Pixmap pixmap, int x, int y, int srcX, int srcY,
            int srcWidth, int srcHeight);

    public void drawPixmap(Pixmap pixmap, int x, int y);

    public int getWidth();

    public int getHeight();
}
```

We start with a public static enum called `PixmapFormat`. It encodes the different pixel formats we will support. Next we have the different methods of our Graphics interface:

- The `Graphics.newPixmap()` method will load an image given in either JPEG or PNG format. We specify a desired format for the resulting Pixmap, which is a hint for the loading mechanism. The resulting Pixmap might have a different format. We do this so we can somewhat control the memory footprint of our loaded images (e.g., by loading RGB888 or ARGB8888 images as RGB565 or ARGB4444 images). The filename specifies an asset in our application's APK file.

- The `Graphics.clear()` method clears the complete framebuffer with the given color. All colors in our little framework will be specified as 32-bit ARGB8888 values (Pixmaps might of course have a different format).

- The `Graphics.drawPixel()` method will set the pixel at (x,y) in the framebuffer to the given color. Coordinates outside the screen will be ignored. This is called *clipping*.

- The `Graphics.drawLine()` method is analogous to the `Graphics.drawPixel()` method. We specify the start point and endpoint of the line, along with a color. Any portion of the line that is outside the framebuffer's raster will be ignored.

The Game.getCurrentScreen() method returns the currently active Screen.

We'll use an abstract class called AndroidGame later on to implement the Game interface, which will implement all methods except the Game.getStartScreen() method. This method will be an abstract method. If we create the AndroidGame instance for our actual game, we'll derive from it and override the Game.getStartScreen() method, returning an instance to the first screen of our game.

To give you an impression of how easy it will be to set up our game, here's an example (assuming we have already implemented the AndroidGame class):

```java
public class MyAwesomeGame extends AndroidGame {
    public Screen getStartScreen () {
        return new MySuperAwesomeStartScreen(this);
    }
}
```

That is pretty awesome, isn't it? All we have to do is implement the screen we want our game to start with, and the AndroidGame class we'll derive from will do the rest for us. From that point onward, we'll have our MySuperAwesomeStartScreen be asked to update and render itself by the AndroidGame instance in the main loop thread. Note that we pass the MyAwesomeGame instance itself to the constructor of our Screen implementation.

> **NOTE:** If you're wondering what actually instantiates our MyAwesomeGame class, I'll give you a hint: AndroidGame will be derived from Activity, which will be automatically instantiated by the Android operating system when a user starts our game.

The last piece in the puzzle is the abstract class Screen. We make it an abstract class instead of an interface so we can already implement some bookkeeping. This way we have to write less boilerplate code in the actual implementations of the abstract Screen class. Listing 3–9 shows the abstract Screen class.

Listing 3–9. *The Screen Class*

```java
package com.badlogic.androidgames.framework;

public abstract class Screen {
    protected final Game game;

    public Screen(Game game) {
        this.game = game;
    }

    public abstract void update(float deltaTime);

    public abstract void present(float deltaTime);

    public abstract void pause();

    public abstract void resume();

    public abstract void dispose();
}
```

It turns out that the bookkeeping isn't so bad after all. The constructor receives the Game instance and stores it in a final member that's accessible to all subclasses. Via this mechanism we can achieve two things:

- We can get access to the low-level modules of the Game to play back audio, draw to the screen, get user input, and read and write files.

- We can set a new current Screen by invoking Game.setScreen() when appropriate (e.g., when a button is pressed that triggers a transition to a new screen).

The first point is pretty much obvious: our Screen implementation needs access to these modules so that it can actually do something meaningful, like rendering huge amounts of unicorns with rabies.

The second point allows us to implement our screen transitions easily within the Screen instances themselves. Each Screen can decide when to transition to which other Screen based on its state (e.g., when a menu button was pressed).

The methods Screen.update() and Screen.present() should be self-explanatory by now: they will update the screen state and present it accordingly. The Game instance will call them once in each iteration of the the main loop.

The methods Screen.pause() and Screen.resume() will be called when the game is paused or resumed. This is again done by the Game instance and applied to the currently active Screen.

The method Screen.dispose() will be called by the Game instance in case Game.setScreen() is called. The Game instance will dispose of the current Screen via this method and thereby give the Screen an opportunity to release all its system resources (e.g., graphical assets stored in Pixmaps) to make room for the new screen's resources in memory. The call to the Screen.dispose() method is also the last opportunity for a screen to make sure that any information that needs persistence is saved.

A Simple Example

Continuing with our MySuperAwesomeGame example, here is a very simple implementation of the MySuperAwesomeStartScreen class:

```java
public class MySuperAwesomeStartScreen extends Screen {
    Pixmap awesomePic;
    int x;

    public MySuperAwesomeStartScreen(Game game) {
        super(game);
        awesomePic = game.getGraphics().newPixmap("data/pic.png",
                PixmapFormat.RGB565);
    }

    @Override
    public void update(float deltaTime) {
        x += 1;
```

```
            if (x > 100)
                x = 0;
        }

        @Override
        public void present(float deltaTime) {
            game.getGraphics().clear(0);
            game.getGraphics().drawPixmap(awesomePic, x, 0, 0, 0,
                    awesomePic.getWidth(), awesomePic.getHeight());
        }

        @Override
        public void pause() {
            // nothing to do here
        }

        @Override
        public void resume() {
            // nothing to do here
        }

        @Override
        public void dispose() {
            awesomePic.dispose();
        }
    }
```

Let's see what this class in combination with the MySuperAwesomeGame class will do:

1. When the MySuperAwesomeGame class is created, it will set up the window, the UI component we render to and receive events from, the callbacks to receive window and input events, and the main loop thread. Finally, it will call its own MySuperAwesomeGame.getStartScreen() method, which will return an instance of the MySuperAwesomeStartScreen() class.

2. In the MySuperAwesomeStartScreen constructor, we load a bitmap from disk and store it in a member variable. This completes our screen setup, and the control is handed back to the MySuperAwesomeGame class.

3. The main loop thread will now constantly call the MySuperAwesomeStartScreen.update() and MySuperAwesomeStartScreen.render() methods of the instance we just created.

4. In the MySuperAwesomeStartScreen.update() method, we increase a member called x by one each frame. This member holds the x-coordinate of the image we want to render. When the x-coordinate is bigger than 100, we reset it to 0.

5. In the MySuperAwesomeStartScreen.render() method, we clear the framebuffer with the color black (0x00000000 = 0) and render our Pixmap at position (x,0).

6. The main loop thread will repeat steps 3 to 5 until the user quits the game by pressing the back button on his device. The Game instance will call then call the MySuperAwesomeStartScreen.dispose() method, which will dispose of the Pixmap.

And that's our first (not so) exciting game! All a user will see is that an image is moving from left to right on the screen. Not exactly a pleasant user experience, but we'll work on that later. Note that on Android, the game can be paused and resumed at any point in time. Our MyAwesomeGame implementation will then call the MySuperAwesomeStartScreen.pause() and MySuperAwesomeStartScreen.resume() methods. The main loop thread will be paused for as long as the application itself is paused.

There's one last problem we have to talk about: frame-rate independent movement.

Frame Rate–Independent Movement

Let's assume that the user's device can run our game from the last section at 60 FPS. Our Pixmap will advance 100 pixels in 100 frames as we increment the MySuperAwesomeStartScreen.x member by 1 pixel each frame. At a frame rate of 60 FPS, it will take roughly 1.66 seconds to reach position (100,0).

Now let's assume that a second user plays our game on a different device. That device is capable of running our game at 30 FPS. Each second, our Pixmap advances by 30 pixels, so it takes 3.33 seconds to reach position (100,0).

This is bad. It may not have an impact on the user experience our simple game generates. But replace the Pixmap with Super Mario and think about what it would mean to move him in a frame-dependent manner. Say we hold down the right D-pad button so that Mario runs to the right. In each frame, we advance him by 1 pixel, as we do in case of our Pixmap. On a device that can run the game at 60 FPS, Mario would run twice as fast as on a device that runs the game at 30 FPS! This would totally change the user experience depending on the performance of the device. We need to fix this.

The solution to this problem is called frame-independent movement. Instead of moving our Pixmap (or Mario) by a fixed amount each frame, we specify the movement speed in units per second. Say we want our Pixmap to advance 50 pixels per second. In addition to the 50-pixels-per-second value, we also need information on how much time has passed since we last moved the Pixmap. And this is where this strange delta time comes into play. It tells us exactly how much time has passed since the last update. So our MySuperAwesomeStartScreen.update() method should look like this:

```
@Override
public void update(float deltaTime) {
    x += 50 * deltaTime;
    if(x > 100)
        x = 0;
}
```

If our game runs at a constant 60 FPS, the delta time passed to the method will always be 1 / 60 ~ 0.016 seconds. In each frame we therefore advance by 50 × 0.016 ~ 0.83 pixels. At 60 FPS we advance 60 × 0.85 ~ 100 pixels! Let's test this with 30 FPS: 50 × 1 / 30 ~ 1.66. Multiplied by 30 FPS, we again move 100 pixels total each second. So, no matter how fast the device our game is running on can execute our game, our animation and movement will always be consistent with actual wall clock time.

If we actually tried this with our preceding code, our `Pixmap` wouldn't move at all at 60 FPS, though. This is because of a bug in our code. I'll give you some time to spot it. It's rather subtle, but a common pitfall in game development. The x member we increase each frame is actually an integer. Adding 0.83 to an integer will have no effect. To fix this we simply have to store x as a float instead of an int. This also means that we have to add a cast to int when we call `Graphics.drawPixmap()`.

> **NOTE:** While floating-point calculations are usually slower on Android than integer operations, the impact is mostly negligible, so we can get away with using more costly floating-point arithmetic.

And that is all there is to our game framework. We can directly translate the screens of our Mr. Nom design to our classes and interface of the framework. Of course, there are still some implementation details to tend to, but we'll leave that for a later chapter. For now you can be mighty proud of yourself that you kept on reading this chapter to the end: you are now ready to become a game developer for Android (and other platforms)!

Summary

Fifty highly condensed and informative pages later, you should have a good idea of what is involved in creating a game. We checked out some of the most popular genres on the Android Market and drew some conclusions. We designed a complete game from the ground up using only a scissor, a pen, and some paper. Finally, we explored the theoretical basis of game development, and even created a set of interfaces and abstract classes that we'll use throughout this book to implement our game designs based on those theoretical concepts. If you feel like you want to go beyond the basics covered here, then by all means consult the Web for more information. You are holding all the keywords in your hand. Understanding the principles is the key to developing stable and well-performing games. With that said, let's implement our game framework for Android!

Chapter 4

Android for Game Developers

Android's application framework is vast and confusing at times. For every possible task you could think of, there's an API you can use. Of course, you have to learn the APIs first. Luckily for us game developers, we only need an extremely limited set of these APIs. All we want is a window with a single UI component to draw to and receive input from, as well as the ability to play back audio. This covers all our needs to implement the game framework we designed in the last chapter in a rather platform-agnostic way.

In this chapter you'll learn the bare minimum of Android's APIs to make Mr. Nom a reality. You'll be surprised how little you actually need to know about those APIs to achieve that goal. Let's recall what ingredients we need:

> Window management
>
> Input
>
> File I/O
>
> Audio
>
> Graphics

For each of these modules, there's an equivalent in the application framework APIs. We'll pick and choose the APIs needed to handle those modules, discuss their internals, and finally implement the respective interfaces of the game framework we designed in the last chapter.

Before we can dive into window management on Android, however, we have to revisit something we only shortly discussed in Chapter 2: defining our application via the manifest file.

Defining an Android Application: The Manifest File

An Android application can consist of a multitude of different components:

Activities: These are user-facing components that present a UI to interact with.

Services: These are processes that work in the background and don't have a visible UI. A service might be responsible for polling a mail server for new e-mails, for example.

Content providers: These components make parts of your application data available to other applications.

Intents: These are messages created by the system or applications themselves, that are then passed on to any interested party. Intents might notify us of system events such as the SD card being removed or the USB cable being connected. Intents are also used by the system for starting components of our application, such as activities. We can also fire our own intents to ask other applications to perform an action, such as opening a photo gallery to display an image or starting the Camera application to take a photo.

Broadcast receivers: These react to specific intents, and might execute an action such as starting a specific activity or sending out another intent to the system.

An Android application has no single point of entry, as we are used to having on a desktop operating system (e.g., in the form of Java's main() method). Instead, components of an Android application are started up or asked to perform a certain action by specific intents.

What components our application is composed of and which intents these components react to are defined in the application's manifest file. The Android system uses this manifest file to get to know what our application is made of, such as the default activity to display when the application is started.

> **NOTE:** We are only concerned about activities in this book, so we'll only discuss the relevant portions of the manifest file for this type of component. If you want to get your head dizzy, you can learn more about the manifest file on the Android Developers site.

The manifest file serves many more purposes than just defining an application's components. The following list summarizes the relevant parts of a manifest file in the context of game development:

The version of our application as displayed and used on the Android Market

The Android versions our application can run on

Hardware profiles our application requires (e.g., multitouch, specific screen resolutions, or support for OpenGL ES 2.0)

Permissions for using specific components, such as for writing to the SD card or accessing the networking stack

We will create a template manifest in the following subsections that we can reuse in a slightly modified manner in all the projects we'll develop throughout this book. For this we'll go through all the relevant XML tags we need to define our application.

The <manifest> Element

The `<manifest>` tag is the root element of an `AndroidManifest.xml` file. Here's a basic example:

```
<manifest xmlns:android="http://schemas.android.com/apk/res/android"
    package="com.helloworld"
    android:versionCode="1"
    android:versionName="1.0"
    android:installLocation="preferExternal">
...
</manifest>
```

Assuming you have worked with XML before, you should be familiar with the first line. The `<manifest>` tag specifies a namespace called `android`, which is used throughout the rest of the manifest file. The `package` attribute defines the root package name of our application. Later on, we'll reference specific classes of our application relative to this package name.

The `versionCode` and `versionName` attributes specify the version of our application in two forms. The `versionCode` is an integer we have to increment each time we publish a new version of our application. It is used by the Android Market to track our application's version. The `versionName` is displayed to users of the Android Market when they browses our application. We can use any string we like here.

The `installLocation` attribute is only available to us if we set the build target of our Android project in Eclipse to Android 2.2 or newer. It specifies where our application should be installed. The string `preferExternal` tells the system that we'd like our application to be installed to the SD card. This will only work on Android 2.2 or newer, and is ignored by all earlier Android applications. On Android 2.2 or newer the application will always get installed to the internal storage if possible.

All attributes of the XML elements in a manifest file are generally prefixed with the `android` namespace, as shown previously. For brevity, I will not specify the namespace in the following sections when talking about a specific attribute.

Inside the `<manifest>` element, we then define the application's components, permissions, hardware profiles, and supported Android versions.

The <application> Element

As in the case of the `<manifest>` element, let's discuss the `<application>` element in the form of an example:

```
<application android:icon="@drawable/icon" android:label="@string/app_name"
android:debuggable="true">
...
</application>
```

Now this looks a little bit strange. What's up with the `@drawable/icon` and `@string/app_name` strings? When developing a standard Android application, we usually write a lot of XML files, each defining a specific portion of our application. To be able to fully define those portions, we must also be able to reference resources that are not defined in the XML file, such as images or internationalized strings. These resources are located in subfolders of the `res/` folder, as discussed in Chapter 2 when we dissected the Hello World project in Eclipse.

To reference resources, we use the preceding notation. The @ specifies that we want to reference a resource defined elsewhere. The following string identifies the type of the resource we want to reference, which directly maps to one of the folders or files in the `res/` directory. The final part specifies the name of the resource—in the preceding case an image called `icon` and a string called app_name. In the case of the image, it's the actual filename we specify, as found in the `res/drawable/` folder. Note that the image name does not have a suffix like `.png` or `.jpg`. Android will infer that automatically based on what's in the `res/drawable/` folder. The app_name string is defined in the `res/values/strings.xml` file, a file where all the strings used by the application will be stored. The name of the string was defined in the `strings.xml` file.

> **NOTE:** Resource handling on Android is an extremely flexible but also complex thing. For this book, I decided to skip most of it for two reasons: it's utter overkill for game development and we want to have full control over our resources. Android has the habit of modifying resources placed in the `res/` folder, especially images (called drawables). That's something we do not want as game developers. The only thing I'd suggest using the Android resource system for in game development is internationalizing strings. We won't get into that in this book; instead we'll use the more game development–friendly `assets/` folder, which leaves our resources untouched and allows us to specify our own folder hierarchy.

The meaning of the attributes of the `<application>` element should become a bit clearer now. The `icon` attribute specifies the image from the `res/drawable/` folder to be used as an icon for the application. This icon will be displayed in the Android Market as well as in the application launcher on the device. It is also the default icon for all the activities we define within the `<application>` element.

The `label` attribute specifies the string being displayed for our application in the application launcher. In the preceding example, this references a string in the `res/values/string.xml` file, which is what we specified when we created the Android project in Eclipse. We could also set this to a raw string, such as My Super Awesome Game. The label is also the default label for all the activities we define in the `<application>` element. The label will be shown in their title bar of our application.

The `debuggable` attribute specifies whether our application can be debugged or not. For development, we should usually set this to `true`. When you deploy your application to the market, just switch it to `false`. If you don't set this to `true`, you won't be able to debug the application in Eclipse.

We have only discussed a very small subset of the attributes you can specify for the
<application> element. However, these are sufficient for our game development needs.
If you want to know more, you can find the full documentation on the Android
Developers site.

The <application> element contains the definitions of all the application components,
including activities and services, as well as any additional libraries used.

The <activity> Element

Now it's getting interesting. Here's a hypothetical example for our Mr. Nom game:

```
<activity android:name=".MrNomActivity"
          android:label="Mr. Nom"
          android:screenOrientation="portrait">
          android:configChanges="keyboard|keyboardHidden|orientation">
    <intent-filter>
        <action android:name="android.intent.action.MAIN" />
        <category android:name="android.intent.category.LAUNCHER" />
    </intent-filter>
</activity>
```

Let's have a look at the attributes of the <activity> tag first.

name: This specifies the name of the activity's class relative to the package attribute
we specified in the <manifest> element. You can also specify a fully qualified class
name here.

label: We already specified the same attribute in the <application>. This label is
displayed in the title bar of the activity (if it has one).The label will also be used as
the text displayed in the application launcher if the activity we define is an entry
point to our application. If we don't specify it, the label from the <application>
element will be used instead. Note that I used a raw string here instead of a
reference to a string in the string.xml file.

screenOrientation: This attribute specifies what orientation the activity will use.
Here I specified portrait for our Mr. Nom game, which will only work in portrait
mode. Alternative, we could specify landscape if we wanted to run in landscape
mode. Both configurations will force the orientation of the activity to stay the same
over the activity's life cycle, no matter how the device is actually oriented. If we
leave out this attribute, then the activity will use whatever the current orientation of
the device is, usually based on accelerometer data. This also means that whenever
the device orientation changes, the activity will be destroyed and restarted—
something that's undesirable in the case of a game. Usually we fix the orientation of
our game's activity to either landscape or portrait mode.

configChanges: Reorienting the device or sliding out the keyboard is considered a configuration change. In the case of such a change, Android will destroy and restart our application to accommodate the change. That's not so good in the case of a game. The configChanges attribute of the <activity> element comes to the rescue. It allows us to specify which configuration changes we want to handle ourselves without destroying and recreating our activity. Multiple configuration changes can be specified by using the | character to concatenate them. In the preceding case, we handle the changes keyboard, keyboardHidden, and orientation ourselves.

As with the <application> element, there are of course more attributes that you can specify for an <activity> element. For game development, though, we get away with the four attributes just discussed.

Now, you might have noticed that the <activity> element isn't empty, but houses another element, which itself contains two more elements. What are those for?

As I pointed out earlier, there's no notion of a single main entry point to your application on Android. Instead, we can have multiple entry points in the form of activities and services that are started due to specific intents being sent out by the system or a third-party application. Somehow we need to communicate to Android which activities and services of our application will react (and in what ways) to specific intents. That's where the <intent-filter> element comes into play.

In the preceding example, we specify two types of intent filters: an <action> and a <category>. The <action> element tells Android that our activity is a main entry point to our application. The <category> element specifies that we want that activity to be added to the application launcher. Both elements together allow Android to infer that when the icon in the application launcher for the application is pressed, it should start that specific activity.

For both the <action> and <category> elements, all that gets specified is the name attribute, which identifies the intent the activity will react to. The intent android.intent.action.MAIN is a special intent that the Android system uses to start the main activity of an application. The intent android.intent.category.LAUNCHER is used to tell Android whether a specific activity of an application should have an entry in the application launcher.

Usually we'll only have one activity that specifies these two intent filters. However, a standard Android application will almost always have multiple activities, and these need to be defined in the manifest.xml file as well. Here's an example definition of such a subactivity:

```
<activity android:name=".MySubActivity"
          android:label="Sub Activity Title"
          android:screenOrientation="portrait">
          android:configChanges="keyboard|keyboardHidden|orientation"/>
```

Here, no intent filters are specified—only the four attributes of the activity we discussed earlier. When we define an activity like this, it is only available to our own application. We start such an activity programmatically with a special kind of intent, say, when a button is pressed in one activity to cause a new activity to open. We'll see in a later section how we can start an activity programmatically.

To summarize, we have one activity for which we specify two intent filter so that it becomes the main entry point of our application. For all other activities, we leave out the intent filter specification so that they are internal to our application. We'll start these programmatically.

> **NOTE:** As said earlier, we'll only ever have a single activity in our games. This activity will have exactly the same intent filter specification as shown previously. The reason I discussed how to specify multiple activities is that we are going to create a special sample application in a minute that will have multiple activities. Don't worry, it's going to be easy.

The <uses-permission> Element

We are leaving the `<application>` element now and coming back to elements we define as children of the `<manifest>` element. One of these elements is the `<uses-permission>` element.

Android has an elaborate security model. Each application is run in its own process and VM, with its own Linux user and group, and cannot influence other applications. Android also restricts the use of system resources, such as networking facilities, the SD card, and the audio-recording hardware. If our application wants to use any of these system resources, we have to ask for permission. This is done with the `<uses-permission>` element.

A permission always has the following form, where `string` specifies the name of the permission we want to be granted:

```
<uses-permission android:name="string"/>
```

Here are a few permission names that might come in handy:

> `android.permission.RECORD_AUDIO`: This grants us access to the audio-recording hardware.

> `android.permission.INTERNET`: This grants us access to all the networking APIs so we can, for example, fetch an image from the Net or upload high-scores.

> `android.permission.WRITE_EXTERNAL_STORAGE`: This allows us to read and write files on the external storage, usually the SD card of the device.

android.permission.WAKE_LOCK: This allows us to acquire a so-called *wake lock*. With this wake lock we can keep the device from going to sleep if the screen hasn't been touched for some time. This could happen in a game that is controlled only by the accelerometer, for example.

To get access to the networking APIs, we'd thus specify the following element as a child of the <manifest> element:

```
<uses-permission android:name="android.permission.INTERNET"/>
```

For any additional permissions, we simply add more <uses-permission> elements. There are many more permissions you can specify; I again refer you to the official Android documentation. We'll only need the set just discussed.

Forgetting to add a permission for something like accessing the SD card is a common error source that manifests itself as a message in LogCat, which might survive undetected due to all the clutter in LogCat. Think about the permissions your game will need and specify them when you create the project initially.

Another thing to notice is that when a user installs your application, she will first be asked to review all the permissions your application wants. Many users will just skip reading those and happily install whatever they can get ahold of. Some users are more conscious about their decisions and will review the permissions in detail. If you request suspicious permissions, like the ability to send out costly SMS messages or get a user's location, you may receive some nasty feedback from users in the Comments section for your application in the market. If you use one of those problematic permissions, then tell the user why you're using it in your application description. The best thing is to avoid those permissions in the first place, though.

The <uses-feature> Element

If you are an Android user yourself and possess an older device with an old Android version like 1.5, you will have noticed that some awesome applications won't show up in the Android Market application on the device. One reason for this can be the use of the <uses-feature> element in the manifest file of the application.

The Android Market application will filter all available applications by your hardware profile. With the <uses-feature> element, an application can specify which hardware features it needs—for example, multitouch or support for OpenGL ES 2.0. Any device that does not have the specified features will trigger that filter so that the end user isn't shown the application in the first place.

A <uses-feature> element has the following attributes:

```
<uses-feature android:name="string" android:required=["true" | "false"]
android:glEsVersion="integer" />
```

The name attribute specifies the feature itself. The required attribute tells the filter whether we really need the feature under all circumstances or if it's just nice to have.

The last attribute is optional and only used in conjunction with requiring a specific OpenGL ES version.

For game developers, the following features are most relevant:

android.hardware.touchscreen.multitouch: This requests that the device have a multitouch screen capable of basic multitouch interactions, such as pinch zooming and the like. These types of screens have problems with tracking multiple fingers independently, so you have to evaluate if those capabilities are sufficient for your game.

android.hardware.touchscreen.multitouch.distinct: This is the big brother of the last feature. This requests full multitouch capabilities suitable to implement things like onscreen virtual dual sticks for controls.

We'll look into multitouch in a later section of this chapter. For now it suffices to remember that when our game requires a multitouch screen, we can weed out all devices that don't support that feature by specifying a <uses-feature> element with one of the preceding feature names, like so:

```
<uses-feature android:name="android.hardware.touchscreen.multitouch"
android:required="true"/>
```

Another useful thing for game developers is to specify which OpenGL ES version is needed. Now, in this book we'll be concerned with OpenGL ES 1.0 and 1.1. For these, we usually don't specify a <uses-feature> element, as they aren't all that different from each other. However, any device that implements OpenGL ES 2.0 can be assumed to be a graphics powerhouse. If our game is visually complex and needs a lot of processing power, we can require OpenGL ES 2.0 so that the game only shows up for devices that are able to render our awesome visuals at an acceptable frame rate. Note that we don't use OpenGL ES 2.0, but just filter by hardware type so that our OpenGL ES 1.x code gets enough processing power. Here's how we can do this:

```
<uses-feature android:glEsVersion="0x00020000" required="true"/>
```

This will make our game only show up on devices that support OpenGL ES 2.0 and are thus assumed to have a fairly powerful graphics processor.

> **NOTE:** This feature is reported incorrectly by some devices out there, making your application invisible to otherwise perfectly fine devices. Use it with caution.

Now, every specific requirement you have in terms of hardware potentially decreases the amount of devices your game can be installed on, directly affecting your sales. Think twice before you specify any of the above. For example, if the standard mode of our game requires multitouch but we can also think of a way to make it work on single-touch devices, we should strive for having two code paths, one for each hardware profile, to be able to deploy to a bigger market.

The <uses-sdk> Element

The last element we'll put in our manifest file is the <uses-sdk> element. It is a child of the <manifest> element. We implicitly defined this element when we created our Hello World project in Chapter 2 when we specified the minimum SDK version in the New Android Project dialog. So what does this element do? Here's an example:

```
<uses-sdk android:minSdkVersion="3" android:targetSdkVersion="9"/>
```

As we discussed in Chapter 2, each Android version has an integer assigned, also known as an *SDK version*. The <uses-sdk> element specifies what minimum version our application supports and what the target version of our application is.

This element allows us to deploy an application that uses APIs that are only available in newer versions to devices that have a lower version installed. One prominent example would be the multitouch APIs, which are supported from SDK version 5 (Android 2.0) onward. When we set up our Android project in Eclipse, we use a build target that supports that API—for example, SDK version 5 or higher (I usually set it to the latest SDK version, which is 9 at the time of writing). If we want our game to run on devices with SDK version 3 (Android 1.5) as well, we specify the minSdkVersion as before in the manifest file. Of course we must be careful not to use any APIs that are not available on the lower version, at least on a 1.5 device. On a device with a higher version, we can use the newer APIs as well.

The preceding configuration is usually fine for most games (unless you can't provide a separate fallback code path for the higher-version APIs, in which case you will want to set the minSdkVersion attribute to the minimum SDK version you actually support).

Android Game Project Setup in Ten Easy Steps

Let's now combine all the preceding information and develop a simple step-by-step method to create a new Android game project in Eclipse. Here's what we want from our project:

> It should be able to use the latest SDK version's features while maintaining compatibility with the lowest SDK version that some devices still run. That means we want to support Android 1.5 and above.

> It should be installed to the SD card when possible so we don't fill up the internal storage of the device.

> It should be debuggable.

> It should have a single main activity that will handle all configuration changes itself so it doesn't get destroyed when the hardware keyboard is revealed or the orientation of the device is changed.

> The activity should be fixed to either portrait or landscape mode.

> It should allow us to access the SD card.

It should allow us to get ahold of a wake lock.

Those are some easy goals to achieve with the information you just acquired. So here are the steps:

1. Create a new Android project in Eclipse by opening the New Android Project dialog, as described in Chapter 2.

2. In the New Android Project dialog, specify your project's name and set the build target to the latest available SDK version.

3. In the same dialog, specify the name of your game, the package all your classes will be stored in, and the name of your main activity, Then set the minimum SDK version to 3. Press Finish to make the project a reality.

4. Open the `AndroidManifest.xml` file.

5. To make Android install the game on the SD card when available, add the `installLocation` attribute to the `<manifest>` element and set it to `preferExternal`.

6. To make the game debuggable, add the `debuggable` attribute to the `<application>` element and set it to `true`.

7. To fix the orientation of the activity, add the `screenOrientation` attribute to the `<activity>` element and specify the orientation you want (`portrait` or `landscape`).

   To tell Android that we want to handle the keyboard, keyboardHidden, and orientation configuration changes, set the `configChanges` attribute of the `<activity>` element to `keyboard|keyboardHidden|orientation`.

8. Add two `<uses-permission>` elements to the `<manifest>` element and specify the name attributes `android.permission.WRITE_EXTERNALSTORAGE` and `android.permission.WAKE_LOCK`.

9. Finally, add the `targetSdkVersion` attribute to the `<uses-sdk>` element and specify your target SDK. It should be the same as the one you specified for the build target in step 1.

And there you have it. Ten easy steps that will generate a fully defined application that will be installed to the SD card (on Android 2.2 and over), is debuggable, has a fixed orientation, will not explode on a configuration change, allows you to access the SD card and wake locks, and will work on all Android versions starting from 1.5 up to the latest version. Here's the final `AndroidManifest.xml` content after executing the preceding steps:

```xml
<?xml version="1.0" encoding="utf-8"?>
<manifest xmlns:android="http://schemas.android.com/apk/res/android"
```

```
        package="com.badlogic.awesomegame"
        android:versionCode="1"
        android:versionName="1.0"
        android:installLocation="preferExternal">
    <application android:icon="@drawable/icon"
             android:label="Awesomnium"
             android:debuggable="true">
       <activity android:name=".GameActivity"
             android:label="Awesomnium"
             android:screenOrientation="landscape"
             android:configChanges="keyboard|keyboardHidden|orientation">
          <intent-filter>
             <action android:name="android.intent.action.MAIN" />
             <category android:name="android.intent.category.LAUNCHER" />
          </intent-filter>
       </activity>
    </application>
    <uses-permission android:name="android.permission.WRITE_EXTERNAL_STORAGE"/>
    <uses-permission android:name="android.permission.WAKE_LOCK"/>
    <uses-sdk android:minSdkVersion="3" android:targetSdkVersion="9"/>
</manifest>
```

As you can see, I got rid of the @string/app_name in the label attributes of the
<application> and <activity> element. This is not really necessary, but I like having my
application definition in one place. From now on, it's all about the code! Or is it?

Defining the Icon of Your Game

When you deploy your game to a device and open the application launcher, you will see
that its entry has a nice but not really unique Android icon. The same icon would be
shown for your game in the market. How can we change it to a custom icon?

Have a closer look at the <application> element again. There we defined an attribute
called icon. It references an image in the res/drawable directory called icon. So it
should be obvious what to do: replace the icon image in the drawable folder with our
own icon image.

When you inspect the res/ folder, you'll see more than one drawable folder, as depicted
in Figure 4–1.

Figure 4-1. *What happened to my res/ folder?*

Now, this is again a classic chicken-and-egg problem. In Chapter 2 there was only a single res/drawable folder in our Hello World project. This was due to the fact that we specified SDK version 3 as our build target. That version only supported a single screen size. That changed with Android 1.6 (SDK version 4). We saw in Chapter 1 that devices can have different sizes, but we didn't talk about how Android handles those. It turns out that there's an elaborate mechanism that allows you to define your graphical assets for a set of so-called screen densities. *Screen density* is a combination of physical screen size and the number of pixels of the screen. We'll look into that topic in a later section in more detail. For now it suffices to know that Android defines three densities: ldpi for low-density screens, mdpi for standard-density screen and hdpi for high-density screens. For lower-density screens we usually use smaller images, and for higher-density screens we use high-resolution assets.

So, in the case of our icon we need to provide three versions, one for each density. But how big should those versions each be? Luckily, we already have default icons in the res/drawable folders from which we can reengineer the sizes our own icons should have. The icon in res/drawable-ldpi has a resolution of 36×36 pixels, the icon in res/drawable-mdpi has a resolution of 48×48 pixels, and the icon in res/drawable-hdpi has a resolution of 72×72 pixels. All we need to do is create versions of our custom icon with the same resolutions and replace the icon.png file in each of the folders with our own icon.png file. We can leave the manifest file unaltered as long as we call our icon image file icon.png. Note that file references in the manifest file are case sensitive. Always use all lowercase letters in resource files to play it safe.

For true Android 1.5 compatibility, we need to add a folder called res/drawable/ and place the icon image from the res/drawable-mdpi/ folder there. Android 1.5 does not know about the other drawable folders, so it might not find our icon.

Finally we are ready to get some Android coding done.

Android API Basics

In the rest of the chapter we'll concentrate on playing around with those Android APIs that are relevant to our game development needs. For this, we'll do something rather convenient: we'll set up a test project that will contain all our little test examples for the different APIs we are going to use. Let's get started.

Creating a Test Project

From the last section we already know how to set up all our projects. So the first thing we do is execute the ten steps outlined earlier. I followed these steps, creating a project named ch04-android-basics with a single main activity called AndroidBasicsStarter. We are going to use some older and some newer APIs, so I set the minimum SDK version to 3 (Android 1.5) and the build target as well as the target SDK version to 9 (Android 2.3). From here on, all we'll do is create new activity implementations, each demonstrating parts of the Android APIs.

But remember that we only have one main activity. So what does our main activity look like? We want a convenient way to add new activities as well as the ability to easily start a specific activity. With one main activity, it should be clear that that activity will somehow provide us with a means to start a specific test activity. The main activity will be specified as the main entry point in the manifest file, as discussed earlier. Each additional activity we add will be specified without the <intent-filter> child element. We'll start those programmatically from the main activity.

The AndroidBasicsStarter Activity

The Android API provides us with a special class called ListActivity, which derives from the Activity class we used in the Hello World project. The ListActivity is a special type of activity who's single purpose it is to display a list of things (e.g., strings). We use it to display the names of our test activities. When we touch one of the list items, we'll start the corresponding activity programmatically. Listing 4–1 shows the code for our AndroidBasicsStarter main activity.

Listing 4–1. *AndroidBasicsStarter.java, Our Main Activity Responsible for Listing and Starting All Our Tests*

```
package com.badlogic.androidgames;

import android.app.ListActivity;
import android.content.Intent;
import android.os.Bundle;
import android.view.View;
import android.widget.ArrayAdapter;
import android.widget.ListView;

public class AndroidBasicsStarter extends ListActivity {
    String tests[] = { "LifeCycleTest", "SingleTouchTest", "MultiTouchTest",
            "KeyTest", "AccelerometerTest", "AssetsTest",
            "ExternalStorageTest", "SoundPoolTest", "MediaPlayerTest",
```

```
              "FullScreenTest", "RenderViewTest", "ShapeTest", "BitmapTest",
              "FontTest", "SurfaceViewTest" };

    public void onCreate(Bundle savedInstanceState) {
        super.onCreate(savedInstanceState);
        setListAdapter(new ArrayAdapter<String>(this,
                android.R.layout.simple_list_item_1, tests));
    }

    @Override
    protected void onListItemClick(ListView list, View view, int position,
            long id) {
        super.onListItemClick(list, view, position, id);
        String testName = tests[position];
        try {
            Class clazz = Class
                    .forName("com.badlogic.androidgames." + testName);
            Intent intent = new Intent(this, clazz);
            startActivity(intent);
        } catch (ClassNotFoundException e) {
            e.printStackTrace();
        }
    }
}
```

The package name I chose is com.badlogic.androidgames. The imports should also be pretty self-explanatory; those are simply all the classes we are going to use in our code. Our AndroidBasicsStarter class derives from the ListActivity class—still nothing special. The field tests is a string array holding the names of all the test activities our starter application should display. Note that the names in that array are the exact Java class names of the activity classes we are going to implement later on.

The next piece of code should be familiar; it's the onCreate() method we have to implement for each of our activities, which will be called when the activity is created. Remember that we must call the onCreate() method of the base class of our activity. It's the first thing we must do in the onCreate() method of our own Activity implementation. If we don't, an exception will be thrown and the activity will not be displayed.

With that out of the way, the next thing we do is call a method called setListAdapter(). That method is provided to us by the ListActivity class we derived from. It lets us specify the list items we want the ListActivity to display for us. These need to be passed to the method in the form of a class instance that implements the ListAdapter interface. We use the convenient ArrayAdapter to do this. The constructor of this class takes three arguments: the first is our activity, the second one I'll explain in a bit, and the third is the array of items the ListActivity should display. We happily specify the tests array we defined earlier for the third argument, and that's all we need to do.

So what's this second argument to the ArrayAdapter constructor? To explain this, I'd have to go through all the Android UI API stuff, which we are not going to use in this book. So instead of wasting pages on something we are not going to need, I'll give you the quick-and-dirty explanation: each item in the list is displayed via a View. The argument defines the layout of each View, along with what type each View has. The value android.R.layout.simple_list_item_1 is a predefined constant provided by the UI API for getting up and running quickly. It stands for a standard list item View that will display text. Just as a quick refresher, a View is a UI widget on Android, such as a button, a text field, or a slider. We talked about that while dissecting the HelloWorld activity in Chapter 2.

If we start our activity with just this onCreate() method, we'll see something like in Figure 4–2.

Figure 4–2. *Our test starter activity, which looks fancy but doesn't do a lot yet*

Now let's make something happen when a list item is touched. We want to start the respective activity that is represented by the list item we touched.

Starting Activities Programmatically

The ListActivity class has a protected method called onListItemClick() that will be called when an item is clicked. All we need to do is to override that method in our AndroidBasicsStarter class. And that's exactly what we did in Listing 4–1.

The arguments to this method are the ListView that the ListActivity uses to display the items, the View that got touched and that's contained in that ListView, the position of the touched item in the list, and an ID, which doesn't interest us all that much. All we really care about is the position argument.

The onListItemClicked() method starts of by being a good citizen and calls the base class method first. This is always a good thing to do if we override methods of an activity. Next we fetch the class name from the tests array based on the position argument. That's the first piece of the puzzle.

We discussed earlier that we can start activities we defined in the manifest file programmatically via an Intent. The Intent class has a nice and simple constructor to do this, which takes two arguments: a Context instance and a Class instance, which represents the Java class of the activity we want to start.

The Context is an interface that provides us with global information about our application. It is implemented by the Activity class, so we simply pass the this reference to the Intent constructor.

To get the Class instance representing the activity we want to start, we use a little reflection, which you will probably familiar with if you've worked with Java. The static method Class.forName() takes a string containing the fully qualified name of a class we want to get a Class instance for. All the test activities we'll implement later will be contained in the com.badlogic.androidgames package. Concatenating the package name with the class name we fetched from the tests array will give us the fully qualified name of the activity class we want to start. We pass that name to Class.forName() and get a nice Class instance that we can pass to the Intent constructor.

Once the Intent is constructed, we can start it with a call to the startActivity() method. That method is also defined in the Context interface. Since our activity implements that interface, we just call its implementation of that method. And that's it!

So how will our application behave? First the starter activity will be displayed. Each time we touch an item on the list, the corresponding activity will be started. The starter activity will be paused and go into the background. The new activity will be created by the intent we send out and replace the starter activity on the screen. When we press the back button on the phone, the activity is destroyed and the starter activity is resumed, taking back the screen.

Creating the Test Activities

When we create a new test activity, we have to perform the following steps:

1. Create the corresponding Java class in the com.badlogic.androidgames package and implement its logic.

2. Add an entry for it in the manifest file, using whatever attributes it needs (e.g., android:configChanges or android:screenOrientation). Note that we won't specify an <intent-filter> element, as we'll start the activity programmatically.

3. Add the activity's class name to the tests array of the AndroidBasicsStarter class.

As long as we stick to this procedure, everything else will be taken care of by the logic we implemented in the `AndroidBasicsStarter` class. The new activity will automatically show up in the list and can be started by a simple touch.

One thing you might wonder is whether the test activity that gets started on a touch is running in its own process and VM. It is not. An application composed of activities has something called an *activity stack*. Each time we start a new activity, it gets pushed onto that stack. When we close the new activity, the last activity that got pushed to the stack will get popped and resumed, becoming the new active activity on the screen.

This also has some other implications. First, all the activities of the application (those on the stack that are paused and the one that is active) share the same VM. They also share the same memory heap. That can be a blessing and a curse. If you have static fields in your activities, they will get memory on the heap as soon as they are started. Being static fields, they will survive the destruction of the activity and the subsequent garbage collection of the activity instance. This can lead to some nice memory leaks if you carelessly use static fields. Think twice before using a static field.

As stated a couple of times already, though, we'll only ever have a single activity in our actual games. The preceding activity starter is an exception to this rule to make our lives a little easier. But don't worry, we'll have enough opportunities to get into trouble even with a single activity.

> **NOTE:** This is as deep as we'll get into Android UI programming. From here on we'll always use a single `View` in an activity to output things and receive input. If you want to learn about things like layouts, view groups, and all the bells and whistles the Android UI library offers, I suggest you check out Mark Murphy's book, *Beginning Android 2* (Apress, 2010), or the excellent developer guide on the Android Developers site.

The Activity Life Cycle

The first thing we have to figure out when programming for Android is how an activity behaves. On Android, this is called the *activity life cycle*. It describes the states and transitions between those states that an activity can live through. Let's start by discussing the theory behind this.

In Theory

An activity can be in three states:

> *Running*: In this state, it is the top-level activity that takes up the screen and directly interacts with the user.

> *Paused*: This happens when the activity is still visible on the screen but partially obscured by either a transparent activity or a dialog, or if the phone screen is locked. A paused activity can be killed by the Android system at any point in time

(e.g., due to low memory). Note that the activity instance itself is still alive and kicking in the VM heap and waiting to be brought back to a running state.

Stopped: This happens when the activity is completely obscured by another activity and thus is no longer visible on the screen. Our AndroidBasicsStarter activity will be in this state if we start one of the test activities, for example. It also happens when a user presses the home button to go to the home screen temporarily. The system can again decide to kill the activity completely and remove it from memory if memory gets low.

In both the paused and stopped states, the Android system can decide to kill the activity at any point in time. It can do so politely, by first informing the activity of that by calling its finished() method, or by being bad and silently killing its process.

The activity can be brought back to a running state from a paused or stopped state. Note again that when an activity is resumed from a paused or stopped state, it is still the same Java instance in memory, so all the state and member variables are the same as before the activity was paused or stopped.

An activity has some protected methods that we can override to get informed of state changes:

Activity.onCreate(): This is called when our activity is started up for the first time. Here we set up all the UI components and hook into the input system. This will only get called once in the life cycle of our activity.

Activity.onRestart(): This is called when the activity is resumed from a stopped state. It is preceded by a call to onStop().

Activity.onStart(): This is called after onCreate() or when the activity is resumed from a stopped state. In the latter case, it is preceded by a call to onRestart().

Activity.onResume(): This is called after onStart() or when the activity is resumed from a paused state (e.g., the screen is unlocked).

Activity.onPause(): This is called when the activity enters the paused state. It might be the last notification we receive, as the Android system might decide to silently kill our application. We should thus save all state we want to persist in this method!

Activity.onStop(): This is called when the activity enters the stopped state. It is preceded by a call to onPause(). This means that before an activity is stopped, it is paused first. As with onPause(), it might be the last thing we get notified of before the Android system silently kills the activity. We could also save persistent state here. However, the system might decide not to call this method and just kill the activity. As onPause() will always be called before onStop() and before the activity is silently killed, we'd rather save all our stuff in the onPause() method.

Activity.onDestroy(): This is called at the end of the activity life cycle when the activity is irrevocably destroyed. It's the last time we can persist any information we'd like to recover the next time our activity is created anew. Note that this method might actually never be called if the activity was destroyed silently after a call to onPause() or onStop() by the system.

Figure 4–3 illustrates the activity life cycle and the method call order.

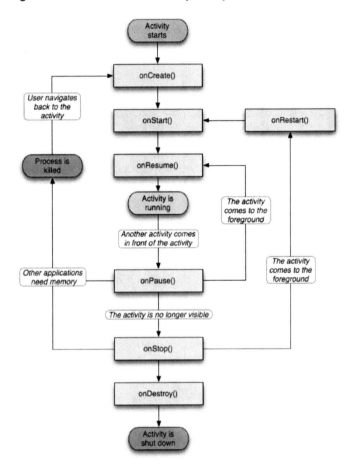

Figure 4–3. *The mighty, confusing activity life cycle*

Here are the three big lessons we should take away from this:

> Before our activity enters the running state, the onResume() method is always called, no matter whether we resume from a stopped state or from a paused state. We can thus safely ignore the onRestart() and onStart() methods. We don't care whether we resumed from a stopped or a paused state. For our games, it is only necessary to know that we are now actually running, and the onResume() method signals that to us.

The activity can be destroyed silently after onPause(). We should thus never assume that either onStop() or onDestroy() get called. We also know that onPause() will always be called before onStop(). We can thus safely ignore the onStop() and onDestroy() methods, and just override onPause(). In this method, we have to make sure that all the states we want to persist, like high-scores and level progress, get written to an external storage like the SD card. After onPause(), all bets are off, and we won't know whether our activity will ever get the chance to run again.

We know that onDestroy() might never be called if the system decides to kill the activity after onPause() or onStop(). However, sometimes we'd like to know whether the activity is actually going to be killed. So how do we do that if onDestroy() is not going to get called? The Activity class has a method called Activity.isFinishing() that we can call at any time to check whether our activity is going to get killed. We are guaranteed that at least the onPause() method is called before the activity is killed. All we need to do is call this isFinishing() method inside the onPause() method to decide whether the activity is going to die after the onPause() call.

This makes life a lot easier. We only override the onCreate(), onResume(), and onPause() methods.

In onCreate(), we set up our window and UI component that we render to and receive input from.

In onResume(), we (re)start our main loop thread (discussed in the last chapter).

In onPause(), we simply pause our main loop thread, and if Activity.isFinishing() returns true, we also save any state we want to persist to disk.

Many people struggle with the activity life cycle, but if we follow these simple rules, our game will be capable of handling pausing and resuming as well as cleaning up.

In Practice

Let's write our first test example that demonstrates the activity life cycle. We'll want to have some sort of output that displays which state changes have happened so far. We'll do this in two ways:

The sole UI component that the activity will display is a so-called TextView. It displays text—we've already used it implicitly for displaying each entry in our starter activity. Each time we enter a new state, we append a string to the TextView, which will display all the state changes that happened so far.

Since we won't be able to display the destruction event of our activity in the TextView, as it will vanish from the screen too fast, we also output all state changes to LogCat. We do this with the Log class, which provides a couple of static methods to append messages to LogCat.

Remember what we need to do to add a test activity to our test application. First, we define it in the manifest file in the form of an <activity> element, which is a child of the <application> element:

```
<activity android:label="Life Cycle Test"
        android:name=".LifeCycleTest"
        android:configChanges="keyboard|keyboardHidden|orientation" />
```

Next we add a new Java class called LifeCycleTest to our com.badlogic.androidgames package. Finally we add the class name to the tests member of the AndroidBasicsStarter class we defined earlier (of course, we already have that in there from when we wrote the class for demonstration purposes). We'll have to repeat all these steps for any test activity we create in the following sections. For brevity, I won't mention those steps again. Also note that I didn't specify an orientation for the LifeCycleTest activity. In this example we can thus be either in landscape or portrait mode depending on the device orientation. I did this so you can see the effect on an orientation change on the life cycle (none, due to how we set the configChanges attribute). Listing 4–2 shows you the code of the entire activity.

Listing 4–2. *LifeCycleTest.java,* Demonstrating the Activity Life Cycle

```java
package com.badlogic.androidgames;

import android.app.Activity;
import android.os.Bundle;
import android.util.Log;
import android.widget.TextView;

public class LifeCycleTest extends Activity {
    StringBuilder builder = new StringBuilder();
    TextView textView;

    private void log(String text) {
        Log.d("LifeCycleTest", text);
        builder.append(text);
        builder.append('\n');
        textView.setText(builder.toString());
    }

    @Override
    public void onCreate(Bundle savedInstanceState) {
        super.onCreate(savedInstanceState);
        textView = new TextView(this);
        textView.setText(builder.toString());
        setContentView(textView);
        log("created");
    }
```

```
    @Override
    protected void onResume() {
        super.onResume();
        log("resumed");
    }

    @Override
    protected void onPause() {
        super.onPause();
        log("paused");

        if (isFinishing()) {
            log("finishing");
        }
    }
}
```

Let's go through this code real quick. The class derives from Activity—not a big surprise. We define two members: a StringBuilder, which will hold all the messages we have produced so far, and the TextView, which we use to display those messages directly in the Activity.

Next we define a little private helper method that will log text to LogCat, append it to our StringBuilder, and update the TextView text. For the LogCat output, we use the static Log.d() method, which takes a tag as the first argument and the actual message as the second argument.

In the onCreate() method, we call the superclass method first as always. We create the TextView and set it as the content view of our activity. It will fill the complete space of the activity. Finally we log the message created to LogCat and update the TextView text with our previously defined helper method log().

Next we override the onResume() method of the activity. As with any activity methods we override, we first call the superclass method. All we do is call log() again with resumed as the argument.

The overridden onPause() method looks much like the onResume() method. We log the message as "paused" first. We also want to know whether the activity is going to be destroyed after the onPause() method call, so we check the Activity.isFinishing() method. If it returns true, we log the finishing event as well. Of course, we won't be able to see the updated TextView text, as the activity will be destroyed before the change is displayed on the screen. Thus, we also output everything to LogCat, as discussed earlier.

Run the application and play around with this test activity a little. Here's a sequence of actions you could execute:

1. Start up the test activity from the starter activity.

2. Lock the screen.

3. Unlock the screen.

4. Press the home button (which will get you back to the home screen).

5. On the home screen, hold the home button until you are presented with the currently running applications. Select the Android Basics Starter app to resume (which will bring the test activity back onscreen).

6. Press the back button (which will bring you back to the starter activity).

If your system didn't decide to kill the activity silently at any point it was paused, you will see the output in Figure 4–4 (of course, only if you haven't pressed the back button yet).

Figure 4–4. *Running the LifeCycleTest activity*

On startup, onCreate() is called, followed by onResume(). When we lock the screen, onPause() is called. When we unlock the screen, onResume() is called. When we press the home button, onPause() is called. Going back to the activity will call onResume() again. The same messages are of course shown in LogCat, which you can observe in Eclipse in the LogCat view. Figure 4–5 shows what we wrote to LogCat while executing the preceding sequence of actions (plus pressing the back button).

```
Log (32)  LifeCycleTest

Time                     pid    tag               Message
11-10 17:03...   D   2243   LifeCycleTest     created
11-10 17:03...   D   2243   LifeCycleTest     resumed
11-10 17:03...   D   2243   LifeCycleTest     paused
11-10 17:03...   D   2243   LifeCycleTest     resumed
11-10 17:03...   D   2243   LifeCycleTest     paused
11-10 17:03...   D   2243   LifeCycleTest     resumed
11-10 17:03...   D   2243   LifeCycleTest     paused
11-10 17:03...   D   2243   LifeCycleTest     finishing
```

Figure 4–5. *The LogCat output of LifeCycleTest*

Pressing the back button again invokes the onPause() method. As it also destroys the activity, the conditional in onPause() also gets triggered, informing us that this is the last we'll see from that activity.

And that was the activity life cycle, demystified and simplified four our game programming needs. We now can easily handle any pause and resume events, and are guaranteed to be notified when the activity is destroyed.

Input Device Handling

As discussed in previous chapters, there are many different input devices we can get information from on Android. In this section we'll discuss the three of the most relevant input devices on Android and how to work with them: the touchscreen, the keyboard, and the accelerometer.

Getting (Multi-)Touch Events

The touchscreen is probably the most important way to get input from the user. Until Android version 2.0, the API only supported processing single-finger touch events. Multitouch was introduced in Android 2.0 (SDK version 5). The multitouch event reporting was tagged onto the single-touch API, with some mixed results in usability. We'll first investigate handling single-touch events, which are available on all Android versions.

Processing Single-Touch Events

When we processed clicks on a button in Chapter 2, we saw that listener interfaces are the way Android reports events to us. Touch events are no different. Touch events are passed to an OnTouchListener interface implementation that we register with a View. The OnTouchListener interface has only a single method:

```
public abstract boolean onTouch (View v, MotionEvent event)
```

The first argument is the View that the touch events get dispatched to. The second argument is what we'll dissect to get the touch event.

An OnTouchListener can be registered with any View implementation via the View.setOnTouchListener() method. The OnTouchListener will be called before the MotionEvent is dispatched to the View itself. We can signal to the View in our implementation of the onTouch() method that we have already processed the event by returning true from the method. If we return false, the View itself will process the event.

The MotionEvent instance has three methods that are relevant to us:

> MotionEvent.getX() and MotionEvent.getY(): These methods report the x- and y-coordinate of the touch event relative to the View. The coordinate system is defined with the origin in the top left of the view, the x-axis points to the right, and the y-axis points downward. The coordinates are given in pixels. Note that the methods return floats, and thus the coordinates have subpixel accuracy.

> MotionEvent.getAction(): This returns the type of the touch event. It is an integer that takes on one of the values MotionEvent.ACTION_DOWN, MotionEvent.ACTION_MOVE, MotionEvent.ACTION_CANCEL, and MotionEvent.ACTION_UP.

Sounds simple, and it really is. The MotionEvent.ACTION_DOWN event happens when the finger touches the screen. When the finger moves, events with type MotionEvent.ACTION_MOVE are fired. Note that you will always get MotionEvent.ACTION_MOVE events, as you can't hold your finger still enough to avoid them. The touch sensor will recognize the slightest change. When the finger is lifted up again, the MotionEvent.ACTION_UP event is reported. MotionEvent.ACTION_CANCEL events are a bit of a mystery. The documentation says they will be fired when the current gesture is canceled. I have never come across that event in real life yet. However, we'll still process it and pretend it is a MotionEvent.ACTION_UP event when we start implementing our first game.

Let's write a simple test activity to see how this works in code. The activity should display the current position of the finger on the screen, as well as the event type. Listing 4–3 shows you what I came up with.

Listing 4–3. *SingleTouchTest.java; Testing Single-Touch Handling*

```
package com.badlogic.androidgames;

import android.app.Activity;
import android.os.Bundle;
import android.util.Log;
import android.view.MotionEvent;
import android.view.View;
import android.view.View.OnTouchListener;
import android.widget.TextView;

public class SingleTouchTest extends Activity implements OnTouchListener {
    StringBuilder builder = new StringBuilder();
    TextView textView;

    public void onCreate(Bundle savedInstanceState) {
```

```
        super.onCreate(savedInstanceState);
        textView = new TextView(this);
        textView.setText("Touch and drag (one finger only)!");
        textView.setOnTouchListener(this);
        setContentView(textView);
    }

    @Override
    public boolean onTouch(View v, MotionEvent event) {
        builder.setLength(0);
        switch (event.getAction()) {
        case MotionEvent.ACTION_DOWN:
            builder.append("down, ");
            break;
        case MotionEvent.ACTION_MOVE:
            builder.append("move, ");
            break;
        case MotionEvent.ACTION_CANCEL:
            builder.append("cancle, ");
            break;
        case MotionEvent.ACTION_UP:
            builder.append("up, ");
            break;
        }
        builder.append(event.getX());
        builder.append(", ");
        builder.append(event.getY());
        String text = builder.toString();
        Log.d("TouchTest", text);
        textView.setText(text);
        return true;
    }
}
```

We let our activity implement the OnTouchListener interface. We also have two members, one for the TextView, and a StringBuilder we'll use to construct our event strings.

The onCreate() method is pretty self-explanatory. The only novelty is the call to TextView.setOnTouchListener(), where we register our activity with the TextView so it receives MotionEvents.

What's left is the onTouch() method implementation itself. We ignore the view argument, as we know that it must be the TextView. All we are interested in is getting the touch event type, appending a string identifying it to our StringBuilder, appending the touch coordinates, and updating the TextView text. That's it. We also log the event to LogCat so we can see the order in which the events happen, as the TextView will only show the last event that we processed (we clear the StringBuilder every time onTouch() is called).

One subtle detail in the onTouch() method is the return statement, where we return true. Usually we'd stick to the listener concept and return false to not interfere with the event-dispatching process. If we do this in our example, we won't get any events other than the MotionEvent.ACTION_DOWN event. So we tell the TextView that we just consumed the event. That behavior might differ between different View implementations. Luckily we'll only need three other views in the rest of this book, and those will happily let us consume any event we want.

If we fire that application up on the emulator or a connected device, we can see how the TextView will always display the last event type and position reported to the onTouch() method. Additionally, you can see the same messages in LogCat.

I did not fix the orientation of the activity in the manifest file. If you rotate your device so that the activity is in landscape mode, the coordinate system of course changes. Figure 4–6 shows you the activity in portrait and landscape mode. In both cases I tried to touch the middle of the View. Note how the x- and y-coordinates seem to get swapped. The figure also shows you the x- and y-axes in both cases (the yellow lines) along with the point on the screen that I roughly touched (the green circle). In both cases the origin is in the upper-left corner of the TextView, with the x-axis pointing to the right and the y-axis pointing downward.

Figure 4–6. *Touching the screen in portrait and landscape modes*

Depending on the orientation, our maximum x and y values change, of course. The preceding images were taken on a Nexus One, which has a screen resolution of 480×800 pixels in portrait mode (800×480 in landscape mode). Since the touch coordinates are given relative to the View, and since the view doesn't fill the complete screen, our maximum y value will be smaller than the resolution height. We'll later see how we can enable full-screen mode so the title bar and notification bar don't get in our way.

Sadly there are a few issues with touch events on older Android versions and first-generation devices:

Touch event flood: The driver will report as many touch events as possible when a finger is down on the touchscreen—on some devices hundreds per second. We can fix this issue by putting a `Thread.sleep(16)` call into our `onTouch()` method, which will put the UI thread on which those events are dispatched to sleep for 16 milliseconds. With this we'll get 60 events per second at most, which is more than enough to have a responsive game. This is only a problem on devices with Android version 1.5.

Touching the screen eats the CPU: Even if we sleep in our `onTouch()` method, the system has to process the events in the kernel as reported by the driver. On old devices such as the Hero or G1, this can use up to 50 percent of the CPU, which leaves a lot less processing power for our main loop thread. As a consequence, our perfectly fine frame rate will drop considerably, sometimes to the point where the game becomes unplayable. On second-generation devices, the problem is a lot less pronounced and can usually be neglected. Sadly, there's no solution for this on older devices.

In general you will want to put `Thread.sleep(16)` in all your `onTouch()` methods just to make sure. On newer devices it will have no effect; on older devices it at least prevents the touch event flooding.

With the first generation of devices slowly dying out, this becomes less of a problem the more time passes. It still causes major grief among game developers, though. Try to explain to your users that your game runs like molasses cause something in the driver is using up all the CPU. Yeah, nobody will care.

Processing Multitouch Events

Warning, major pain ahead. The multitouch API has been tagged onto the `MotionEvent` class, which originally only handled single touches. This makes for some major confusion when trying to decode multitouch events. Let's try to make some sense of it.

> **NOTE:** The multitouch API is apparently also confusing for the Android engineers that created it. It received a major overhaul in SDK version 8 (Android 2.2) with new methods, new constants, and even renamed constants. These changes should make working with multitouch a little bit easier. However, they are only available from SDK version 8 onward. To support all multitouch-capable Android versions (2.0 through 2.2.1), we have to use the API of SDK version 5.

Handling multitouch is very similar to handling single-touch events. We still implement the same `OnTouchListener` interface we implemented for single-touch events. We also get a `MotionEvent` instance to read the data from. We also process the event types we processed before, like `MotionEvent.ACTION_UP`, plus a couple of new ones that aren't too big of a deal.

Pointer IDs and Indices

The differences start when we want to access the coordinates of a touch event. MotionEvent.getX() and MotionEvent.getY() return the coordinates of a single finger on the screen. When we process multitouch events, we use overloaded variants of these methods that take a so-called *pointer index*. This might look as follows:

```
event.getX(pointerIndex);
event.getY(pointerIndex);
```

Now, one would expect that pointerIndex directly corresponds to one of the fingers touching the screen (e.g., the first finger that went down has pointerIndex 0, the next finger that went down has pointerIndex 1, etc.). Sadly this is not the case.

The pointerIndex is an index into internal arrays of the MotionEvent that hold the coordinates of the event for a specific finger that is touching the screen. The real identifier of a finger on the screen is called the *pointer identifier*. There's a separate method called MotionEvent.getPointerIdentifier(int pointerIndex) that returns the pointer identifier based on a pointer index. A pointer identifier will stay the same for a single finger as long as it touches the screen. This is not necessarily true for the pointer index.

Let's start by examining how we can get to the pointer index of an event. We'll ignore the event type for now.

```
int pointerIndex = (event.getAction() & MotionEvent.ACTION_POINTER_ID_MASK) >>
MotionEvent.ACTION_POINTER_ID_SHIFT;
```

You probably have the same thoughts as I had when I first implemented this. Before we lose all faith in humanity, let's try to decipher what's happening here. We fetch the event type from the MotionEvent via MotionEvent.getAction(). Good, we've done that before. Next we perform a bitwise AND operation, using the integer we get from the MotionEvent.getAction() method and a constant called MotionEvent.ACTION_POINTER_ID_MASK. Now the fun begins.

That constant has a value of 0xff00, so we essentially make all bits 0, other than bits 8 to 15, which hold the pointer index of the event. The lower eight bits of the integer returned by event.getAction() hold the value of the event type, such as MotionEvent.ACTION_DOWN and its siblings. We essentially throw away the event type by this bitwise operation. The shift should make a bit more sense now. We shift by MotionEvent.ACTION_POINTER_ID_SHIFT, which has a value of 8, so we basically move bits 8 through 15 to bits 0 through 7, arriving at the actual pointer index of the event. With this, we can then get the coordinates of the event as well as the pointer identifier.

Notice that our magic constants are called XXX_POINTER_ID_XXX instead of XXX_POINTER_INDEX_XXX (which would make more sense, as we actually want to extract the pointer index, not the pointer identifier). Well, the Android engineers must have been confused as well. In SDK version 8, they deprecated those constants and introduced new constants called XXX_POINTER_INDEX_XXX, which have the exact same values as the deprecated ones. In order for legacy applications that are written against SDK version 5 to continue working on newer Android versions, the old constants are of course still made available.

So we now know how to get that mysterious pointer index with which we can query for the coordinates and the pointer identifier of the event.

The Action Mask and More Event Types

Next we have to get the pure event type minus the additional pointer index that is encoded in the integer returned by MotionEvent.getAction(). We just need to mask the pointer index out:

```
int action = event.getAction() & MotionEvent.ACTION_MASK;
```

OK, that was easy. Sadly you'll only understand it if you know what that pointer index is and that it is actually encoded in the action.

What's left is to decode the event type as we did before. I already said that there are a few new event types, so let's go through them:

> MotionEvent.ACTION_POINTER_DOWN: This event happens for any additional finger that touches the screen after the first finger touches. The first finger will still produce a MotionEvent.ACTION_DOWN event.

> MotionEvent.ACTION_POINTER_UP: This is analogous the previous action. This gets fired when a finger is lifted up from the screen and more than one finger is touching the screen. The last finger on the screen to go up will produce a MotionEvent.ACTION_UP event. This finger doesn't necessarily have to be the first finger that touched the screen.

Luckily we can just pretend that those two new event types are the same as the old MotionEvent.ACTION_UP and MotionEvent.ACTION_DOWN events.

The last difference is the fact that a single MotionEvent can have data for multiple events. Yes, you read that right. For this to happen, the merged events have to have the same type. In reality this will only happen for the MotionEvent.ACTION_MOVE event, so we only have to deal with this fact when processing said event type. To check how many events are contained in a single MotionEvent, we use the MotionEvent.getPointerCount() method, which tells us for how many fingers the MotionEvent contains coordinates for. We then can fetch the pointer identifier and coordinates for the pointer indices 0 to MotionEvent.getPointerCount() - 1 via the MotionEvent.getX(), MotionEvent.getY(), and MotionEvent.getPointerId() methods.

In Practice

Let's write an example for this fine API. We want to keep track of ten fingers at most (there's no device yet that can track more, so we are on the safe side here). Android will assign pointer identifiers from 0 to 9 to these fingers in the sequence they touch the screen. So we keep track of each pointer identifier's coordinates and touch state (touching or not), and output this information to the screen via a TextView. Let's call our test activity MultiTouchTest. Listing 4–4 shows the complete code.

Listing 4–4. *MultiTouchTest.java; Testing the Multitouch API*

```java
package com.badlogic.androidgames;

import android.app.Activity;
import android.os.Bundle;
import android.view.MotionEvent;
import android.view.View;
import android.view.View.OnTouchListener;
import android.widget.TextView;

public class MultiTouchTest extends Activity implements OnTouchListener {
    StringBuilder builder = new StringBuilder();
    TextView textView;
    float[] x = new float[10];
    float[] y = new float[10];
    boolean[] touched = new boolean[10];

    private void updateTextView() {
        builder.setLength(0);
        for(int i = 0; i < 10; i++) {
            builder.append(touched[i]);
            builder.append(", ");
            builder.append(x[i]);
            builder.append(", ");
            builder.append(y[i]);
            builder.append("\n");
        }
        textView.setText(builder.toString());
    }

    public void onCreate(Bundle savedInstanceState) {
        super.onCreate(savedInstanceState);
        textView = new TextView(this);
        textView.setText("Touch and drag (multiple fingers supported)!");
        textView.setOnTouchListener(this);
        setContentView(textView);
    }

    @Override
    public boolean onTouch(View v, MotionEvent event) {
        int action = event.getAction() & MotionEvent.ACTION_MASK;
        int pointerIndex = (event.getAction() & MotionEvent.ACTION_POINTER_ID_MASK) >>
MotionEvent.ACTION_POINTER_ID_SHIFT;
        int pointerId = event.getPointerId(pointerIndex);

        switch (action) {
        case MotionEvent.ACTION_DOWN:
        case MotionEvent.ACTION_POINTER_DOWN:
            touched[pointerId] = true;
            x[pointerId] = (int)event.getX(pointerIndex);
            y[pointerId] = (int)event.getY(pointerIndex);
            break;
```

```
        case MotionEvent.ACTION_UP:
        case MotionEvent.ACTION_POINTER_UP:
        case MotionEvent.ACTION_CANCEL:
            touched[pointerId] = false;
            x[pointerId] = (int)event.getX(pointerIndex);
            y[pointerId] = (int)event.getY(pointerIndex);
            break;

        case MotionEvent.ACTION_MOVE:
            int pointerCount = event.getPointerCount();
            for (int i = 0; i < pointerCount; i++) {
                pointerIndex = i;
                pointerId = event.getPointerId(pointerIndex);
                x[pointerId] = (int)event.getX(pointerIndex);
                y[pointerId] = (int)event.getY(pointerIndex);
            }
            break;
        }

        updateTextView();
        return true;
    }
}
```

We implement the OnTouchListener interface as before. To keep track of the coordinates and touch state of the ten fingers, we add three new member arrays that will hold that information for us. The arrays x and y hold the coordinates for each pointer ID, and the array touched stores whether the finger with that pointer ID is down or not.

Next, I took the freedom to create a little helper method that will output the current state of the fingers to the TextView. It simply iterates through all the ten finger states and concatenates them via a StringBuilder. The final text is set to the TextView.

The onCreate() method sets up our activity and registers it as an OnTouchListener with the TextView. We already know that part by heart.

Now for the scary part: the onTouch() method. We start off by getting the event type by masking the integer returned by event.getAction(). Next we extract the pointer index and fetch the corresponding pointer identifier from the MotionEvent, as discussed earlier.

The heart of the onTouch() method is that big nasty switch statement, which we already used in a reduced form to process single-touch events. We group all the events into three categories on a high level:

A touch-down event happened (MotionEvent.ACTION_DOWN, MotionEvent.ACTION_PONTER_DOWN). We set the touch state for the pointer identifier to true, and also save the current coordinates of that pointer.

A touch-up event happened (MotionEvent.ACTION_UP, MotionEvent.ACTION_POINTER_UP, MotionEvent.CANCEL). We set the touch state to false for that pointer identifier and save its last known coordinates.

One or more fingers were dragged across the screen (MotionEvent.ACTION_MOVE). We check how many events are contained in the MotionEvent and then update the coordinates for the pointer indices 0 to MotionEvent.getPointerCount() - 1. For each event, we fetch the corresponding pointer identifier and update the coordinates.

Once the event is processed, we update the TextView via a call to the updateView() method we defined earlier. Finally we return true, indicating that we processed the touch event.

Figure 4–7 shows the output of the activity after I touch two fingers on my Nexus One and drag them around a little.

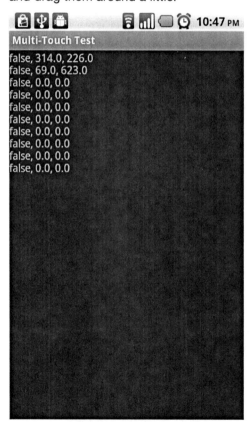

Figure 4–7. *Fun with multitouch*

There are a few things we can observe when we run this example:

> If we start it on a device or emulator with an Android version lower than 2.0, we get a nasty exception, as we're use an API that is not available on those earlier versions. We can work around that by determining which Android version the application is running on, using the single-touch code on devices with Android 1.5 and 1.6, and using the multitouch code on devices with Android 2.0 or newer. We'll get back to that in the next chapter.

> There's no multitouch on the emulator. The API is there if we create an emulator running Android version 2.0 or higher, but we only have a single mouse. And even if we had two mice, it wouldn't make a difference.

> Touch two fingers down, lift the first one, and touch it down again. The second finger will keep its pointer identifier after the first finger is lifted. When the first finger is touched down for the second time, it gets the first free pointer identifier, which is 0 in this case. Any new finger that touches the screen will get the first free pointer identifier. That's a rule to remember.

> If you try this on a Nexus One or a Droid, you will notice some strange behavior when your cross two fingers on one axis. This is due to the fact that the screens of those devices do not fully support the tracking of individual fingers. It's a big problem, but we can work around it somewhat by designing our UIs with some care. We'll have another look at the issue in a later chapter. The phrase to keep in mind is *don't cross the streams!*

And that's how multitouch processing works on Android. It is a pain in the buttocks, but once you untangle all the terminology and come to peace with the bit twiddling, it becomes somewhat OK to use.

> **NOTE:** I'm sorry if this made your head explode. This section was rather heavy duty. Sadly, the official documentation for the API is extremely lacking, and most people "learn" the API by simply hacking away at it. I suggest you play around with the preceding code example until you fully grasp what's going on.

Processing Key Events

After the insanity of the last section, we deserve something dead simple. Welcome to processing key events.

To catch key events, we implement another listener interface, called OnKeyListener. It has a single method called onKey(), with the following signature:

```
public boolean onKey(View view, int keyCode, KeyEvent event)
```

The View specifies the view that received the key event, the keyCode argument is one of the constants defined in the KeyEvent class, and the final argument is the key event itself, which has some additional information.

What is a key code? Each key on the (onscreen) keyboard and each of the system keys has a unique number assigned to it. These key codes are defined in the KeyEvent class as static public final integers. One such key code is KeyCode.KEYCODE_A, which is the code for the A key. This has nothing to do with the character that is generated in a text field when a key is pressed. It really just identifies the key itself.

The KeyEvent class is similar to the MotionEvent class. It has two methods that are relevant for us:

> KeyEvent.getAction(): This method returns KeyEvent.ACTION_DOWN, KeyEvent.ACTION_UP, and KeyEvent.ACTION_MULTIPLE. For our purposes we can ignore the last key event type. The other two will be sent when a key is either pressed or released.

> KeyEvent.getUnicodeChar(): This returns the Unicode character the key would produce in a text field. Say we hold down the Shift key and press the A key. This would be reported as an event with a key code of KeyEvent.KEYCODE_A, but with a Unicode character A. We can use this method if we want to do text input ourselves.

To receive keyboard events, a View must have the focus. This can be forced with the following method calls:

```
View.setFocusableInTouchMode(true);
View.requestFocus();
```

The first method will guarantee that the View can be focused. The second method requests that the specific view gets the focus.

Let's implement a simple test activity to see how this works in combination. We want to get key events and display the last one we received in a TextView. The information we'll display is the key event type, along with the key code and the Unicode character, if one would be produced. Note that some keys do not produce a Unicode character on their own, but only in combination with other characters. Listing 4–5 demonstrates how we can achieve all this in a couple of code lines.

Listing 4–5. *KeyTest.Java; Testing the Key Event API*

```java
package com.badlogic.androidgames;

import android.app.Activity;
import android.os.Bundle;
import android.util.Log;
import android.view.KeyEvent;
import android.view.View;
import android.view.View.OnKeyListener;
import android.widget.TextView;

public class KeyTest extends Activity implements OnKeyListener {
    StringBuilder builder = new StringBuilder();
    TextView textView;
```

```java
public void onCreate(Bundle savedInstanceState) {
    super.onCreate(savedInstanceState);
    textView = new TextView(this);
    textView.setText("Press keys (if you have some)!");
    textView.setOnKeyListener(this);
    textView.setFocusableInTouchMode(true);
    textView.requestFocus();
    setContentView(textView);
}

@Override
public boolean onKey(View view, int keyCode, KeyEvent event) {
    builder.setLength(0);
    switch (event.getAction()) {
    case KeyEvent.ACTION_DOWN:
        builder.append("down, ");
        break;
    case KeyEvent.ACTION_UP:
        builder.append("up, ");
        break;
    }
    builder.append(event.getKeyCode());
    builder.append(", ");
    builder.append((char) event.getUnicodeChar());
    String text = builder.toString();
    Log.d("KeyTest", text);
    textView.setText(text);

    if (event.getKeyCode() == KeyEvent.KEYCODE_BACK)
        return false;
    else
        return true;
}
}
```

We start off by declaring that the activity implements the OnKeyListener interface. Next we define two members we are already familiar with: a StringBuilder to construct the text to be displayed and a TextView to display the text.

In the onCreate() method we make sure the TextView has the focus so it can receive key events. We also register the activity as the OnKeyListener via the TextView.setOnKeyListener() method.

The onKey() method is also pretty straightforward. We process the two event types in the switch statement, appending a proper string to the StringBuilder. Next we append the key code as well as the Unicode character from the KeyEvent itself and output it to LogCat as well as the TextView.

The last if statement is interesting: in case the back key is pressed, we return false from the onKey() method, making the TextView process the event. Otherwise we return true. Why differentiate here?

If we were to return true in the case of the back key, we'd mess with the activity life cycle a little. The activity would not be closed, as we decided to consume the back key ourselves. Of course, there are scenarios where we'd actually want to catch the back key so that our activity does not get closed. However, it is strongly advised not to do this unless absolutely necessary.

Figure 4–8 illustrates the output of the activity while I hold down the Shift and A keys on the keyboard of my Droid.

Figure 4–8. *Pressing the Shift and A keys simultaneously*

There are couple of things to note here:

> When you look at the LogCat output, notice that we can easily process simultaneous key events. Holding down multiple keys is not a problem.

> Pressing the D-pad and rolling the trackball are both reported as key events.

> As with touch events, key events can eat up considerable CPU resources on old Android versions and first-generation devices. However, they will not produce a flood of events.

That was pretty relaxing compared to the previous section, wasn't it?

> **NOTE:** The key processing API is a bit more complex than what I have shown here. For our game programming projects, the information contained here is more than sufficient, though. If you need something a bit more complex, refer to the official documentation on the Android Developers site.

Reading the Accelerometer State

A very interesting input option for games is the accelerometer. All Android devices are required to contain a three-axis accelerometer. We talked about accelerometers in the last chapter a little bit. We'll generally only poll the state of the accelerometer.

So how do we get that accelerometer information? You guessed correctly, by registering a listener. The interface we need to implement is called SensorEventListener, which has two methods:

```
public void onSensorChanged(SensorEvent event);
public void onAccuracyChanged(Sensor sensor, int accuracy);
```

The first method is called when a new accelerometer event arrives. The second method is called when the accuracy of the accelerometer changes. We can safely ignore the second method for our purposes.

So where do we register our SensorEventListener? For this we have to do a little bit of work. First we need to check whether there actually is an accelerometer installed in the device. Now, I just told you that all Android devices must contain an accelerometer. This is still true, but might change in the future. We therefore want to make 100 percent sure that that input method is available to us.

The first thing we need to do is get an instance of the so-called SensorManager. That guy will tell us whether an accelerometer is installed, and is also where we register our listener. To get the SensorManager we use a method of the Context interface:

```
SensorManager manager = (SensorManager)context.getSystemService(Context.SENSOR_SERVICE);
```

The SensorManager is a so-called *system service* that is provided by the Android system. Android is composed of multiple system services, each serving different pieces of system information to anyone who asks nicely.

Once we have the manager, we can check whether the accelerometer is available:

```
boolean hasAccel = manager.getSensorList(Sensor.TYPE_ACCELEROMETER).size() > 0;
```

With this bit of code we poll the manager for all the installed sensors that have the type accelerometer. While this implies that a device can have multiple accelerometers, in reality this will only ever return one accelerometer sensor, though.

If an accelerometer is installed, we can fetch it from the SensorManager and register the SensorEventListener with it as follows:

```
Sensor sensor = manager.getSensorList(Sensor.TYPE_ACCELEROMETER).get(0);
boolean success = manager.registerListener(listener, sensor,
SensorManager.SENSOR_DELAY_GAME);
```

The argument SensorManager.SENSOR_DELAY_GAME specifies how often the listener should be updated with the latest state of the accelerometer. This is a special constant that is specifically designed for games, so we happily use that. Notice that the SensorManager.registerListener() method returns a boolean indicating whether the registration process worked or not. That means we have to check the boolean afterward to make sure we'll actually get any events from the sensor.

Once we have registered the listener, we'll receive SensorEvents in the SensorEventListener.onSensorChanged() method. The method name implies that it is only called when the sensor state has changed. This is a little bit confusing, as the accelerometer state is changed constantly. When we register the listener, we actually specify the frequency with which we want to get sensor state updates.

So how do we process the SensorEvent? That's rather easy. The SensorEvent has a public float array member called SensorEvent.values that holds the current acceleration values of each of the three axes of the accelerometer. SensorEvent.values[0] holds the value of the x-axis, SensorEvent.values[1] holds the value of the y-axis, and SensorEvent.values[2] holds the value of the z-axis. We discussed what these values mean in Chapter 3, so if you forgot that, go and check out the "Input" section again.

With this information we can write a simple test activity. All we want to do is output the accelerometer values for each accelerometer axis in a TextView. Listing 4–6 shows you how to do this.

Listing 4–6. *AccelerometerTest.java; Testing the Accelerometer API*

```
package com.badlogic.androidgames;

import android.app.Activity;
import android.content.Context;
import android.hardware.Sensor;
import android.hardware.SensorEvent;
import android.hardware.SensorEventListener;
import android.hardware.SensorManager;
import android.os.Bundle;
import android.widget.TextView;

public class AccelerometerTest extends Activity implements SensorEventListener {
    TextView textView;
    StringBuilder builder = new StringBuilder();

    @Override
    public void onCreate(Bundle savedInstanceState) {
        super.onCreate(savedInstanceState);
        textView = new TextView(this);
        setContentView(textView);

        SensorManager manager = (SensorManager)
getSystemService(Context.SENSOR_SERVICE);
        if (manager.getSensorList(Sensor.TYPE_ACCELEROMETER).size() == 0) {
            textView.setText("No accelerometer installed");
        } else {
            Sensor accelerometer = manager.getSensorList(
                    Sensor.TYPE_ACCELEROMETER).get(0);
            if (!manager.registerListener(this, accelerometer,
                    SensorManager.SENSOR_DELAY_GAME)) {
                textView.setText("Couldn't register sensor listener");
            }
        }
    }
}
```

```
@Override
public void onSensorChanged(SensorEvent event) {
    builder.setLength(0);
    builder.append("x: ");
    builder.append(event.values[0]);
    builder.append(", y: ");
    builder.append(event.values[1]);
    builder.append(", z: ");
    builder.append(event.values[2]);
    textView.setText(builder.toString());
}

@Override
public void onAccuracyChanged(Sensor sensor, int accuracy) {
    // nothing to do here
}
}
```

We start with checking whether an accelerometer sensor is available. If it is, we fetch it from the SensorManager and try to register our activity, which implements the SensorEventListener interface. If any of this fails, we set the TextView to display a proper error message.

The onSensorChanged() method simply reads the axis values from the SensorEvent it gets passed and updates the TextView text accordingly.

The onAccuracyChanged() method is just there so that we fully implement the SensorEventListener interface. It serves no real other purpose.

Figure 4–9 shows you what values the axes take on in portrait mode and landscape modes when the device is held perpendicular to the ground.

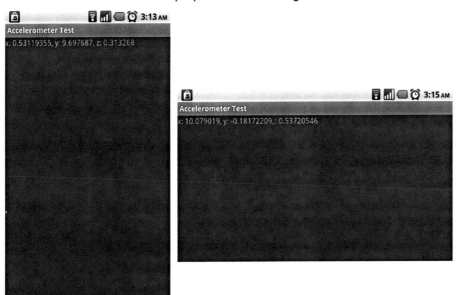

Figure 4–9. *Accelerometer axis values in portrait mode (left) and landscape mode (right) when the device is held perpendicular to the ground*

Here are a few closing comments on accelerometers:

As you can see in the right screenshot in Figure 4–9, the accelerometer values might sometimes get over their specified range. This is due to small inaccuracies in the sensor, so you have to adjust for that if you need those values to be as exact as possible.

The accelerometer axes always get reported in the same order, no matter what orientation our activity is displayed in.

With this, we have discussed all the input processing–related classes of the Android API we'll need for game development.

NOTE: As the name implies, the `SensorManager` class grants you access to other sensors as well. This includes the compass and light sensors. If you wanted to be creative, you could come up with a game idea that uses these sensors. Processing their events is similar to how we processed the data of the accelerometer. The documentation over at the Android Developers site will give you more information.

File Handling

Android offers us a couple of ways to read and write files. In this section we'll check out assets and accessing the external storage, mostly implemented as an SD card. Let's start with assets.

Reading Assets

In Chapter 2 we had a brief look at all the folders an Android project has. We identified the `assets/` and `res/` folders to be the ones we can put files in that should get distributed with our application. When we discussed the manifest file, I told you that we're not going to make use of the `res/` folder, as it implies restrictions on how we structure our file set. The `assets/` directory is the place to put all our files, in whatever folder hierarchy we want.

The files in the `assets/` folder are exposed via a class called `AssetManager`. We can get a reference to that manager for our application as follows:

```
AssetManager assetManager = context.getAssets();
```

We already saw the `Context` interface earlier; it is implemented by the `Activity` class. In real life we'd fetch the `AssetManager` from our activity.

Once we have the `AssetManager`, we can start opening files like crazy:

```
InputStream inputStream = assetManager.open("dir/dir2/filename.txt");
```

This method will return a plain-old Java `InputStream`, which we can use to read-in any sort of file. The only argument to the `AssetManager.open()` method is the filename relative to the asset directory. In the preceding example we have two directories in the assets/ folder, where the second one (dir2/) is a child of the first one (dir/). In our Eclipse project the file would be located in assets/dir/dir2/.

Let's write a simple test activity testing out this functionality. We want to load a text file named myawesometext.txt from a subdirectory of the assets/ directory called texts. The content of the text file will be displayed in a TextView. Listing 4–7 shows the source for this awe-inspiring activity.

Listing 4–7. *AssetsTest.java, Demonstrating How to Read Asset Files*

```java
package com.badlogic.androidgames;

import java.io.ByteArrayOutputStream;
import java.io.IOException;
import java.io.InputStream;

import android.app.Activity;
import android.content.res.AssetManager;
import android.os.Bundle;
import android.widget.TextView;

public class AssetsTest extends Activity {
    @Override
    public void onCreate(Bundle savedInstanceState) {
        super.onCreate(savedInstanceState);
        TextView textView = new TextView(this);
        setContentView(textView);

        AssetManager assetManager = getAssets();
        InputStream inputStream = null;
        try {
            inputStream = assetManager.open("texts/myawesometext.txt");
            String text = loadTextFile(inputStream);
            textView.setText(text);
        } catch (IOException e) {
            textView.setText("Couldn't load file");
        } finally {
            if (inputStream != null)
                try {
                    inputStream.close();
                } catch (IOException e) {
                    textView.setText("Couldn't close file");
                }
        }
    }

    public String loadTextFile(InputStream inputStream) throws IOException {
        ByteArrayOutputStream byteStream = new ByteArrayOutputStream();
        byte[] bytes = new byte[4096];
        int len = 0;
        while ((len = inputStream.read(bytes)) > 0)
            byteStream.write(bytes, 0, len);
        return new String(byteStream.toByteArray(), "UTF8");
    }
}
```

No big surprises, other than that loading simple text from an `InputStream` is rather verbose in Java. I wrote a little method called `loadTextFile()` that will squeeze all the bytes out of the `InputStream` and return the bytes in the form of a string. I assume that the text file is encoded as UTF-8. The rest is just catching and handling various exceptions. Figure 4–10 shows you the output of this little activity.

Figure 4–10. *The text output*

You should take away the following from this section:

> Loading a text file from an `InputStream` in Java is a mess! Usually we'd do that with something like Apache IOUtils. I'll leave that up for you as an excercise.

> We can only read assets, not write them.

> We could easily modify the `loadTextFile()` method to load binary data instead. We would just need to return the byte array instead of the string.

Accessing the External Storage

While assets are superb for shipping all our images and sounds with our application, there are times when we need to be able to persist some information and reload it later on. A common example would be with high-scores.

Android offers many different ways of doing this: you can use local shared preferences of an application, a small SQLite database, and so on. All these options have one thing in common: they don't handle large binary files all that gracefully. Why would we need that anyway? While we can tell Android to install our application on the external storage, and thus not waste memory on the internal storage, this will only work on Android version 2.2 and above. For earlier versions all our application data would get installed on the internal storage. In theory we could only include the code of our application in the APK file and download all the asset files from a server to the SD card the first time our application is started. Many of the high-profile games on Android do this.

There are also other scenarios where we'd want to have access to the SD card (which is pretty much synonymous with the term *external storage* on all currently available devices). We could allow our users to create their own levels with an in-game editor. We'd need to store them somewhere, and the SD card is just perfect for that purpose.

So, now that I've convinced you not to use the fancy mechanisms Android offers us to store application preferences, let's have a look at how to read and write files on the SD card.

The first thing we have to do is request the permission to actually access the external storage. This is done in the manifest file with the `<uses-permission>` element as discussed earlier in this chapter.

The next thing we have to do is to check whether there is actually an external storage available on the device we run. For example, if you create an AVD, you have the option of not having it simulate an SD card, so you couldn't write to it in your application. Another reason for not getting access to the SD card could be that the external storage is currently in use by something else (e.g., the user may be exploring it via USB on a desktop PC). So here's how we get the state of the external storage:

```
String state = Environment.getExternalStorageState();
```

Hmm, we get a string. The `Environment` class defines a couple of constants. One of these is called `Environment.MEDIA_MOUNTED`. It is also a string. If the string returned by the preceding method equals this constant, we have full read/write access to the external storage. Note that you really have to use the `equals()` method to compare the two strings; reference equality won't work in every case.

Once we have determined that we can actually access the external storage, we need to get its root directory name. If we then want to access a specific file, we need to specify it relative to this directory. To get that root directory, we use another `Environment` static method:

```
File externalDir = Environment.getExternalStorageDirectory();
```

From here on we can use the standard Java I/O classes to read and write files.

Let's write a quick example that writes a file to the SD card, reads it back in, displays its content in a `TextView`, and then deletes the file from the SD card again. Listing 4–8 shows the source code for that.

Listing 4–8. *The ExternalStorageTest Activity*

```java
package com.badlogic.androidgames;

import java.io.BufferedReader;
import java.io.BufferedWriter;
import java.io.File;
import java.io.FileReader;
import java.io.FileWriter;
import java.io.IOException;

import android.app.Activity;
import android.os.Bundle;
import android.os.Environment;
import android.widget.TextView;

public class ExternalStorageTest extends Activity {
    @Override
    public void onCreate(Bundle savedInstanceState) {
        super.onCreate(savedInstanceState);
        TextView textView = new TextView(this);
        setContentView(textView);

        String state = Environment.getExternalStorageState();
        if (!state.equals(Environment.MEDIA_MOUNTED)) {
            textView.setText("No external storage mounted");
        } else {
            File externalDir = Environment.getExternalStorageDirectory();
            File textFile = new File(externalDir.getAbsolutePath()
                    + File.separator + "text.txt");
            try {
                writeTextFile(textFile, "This is a test. Roger");
                String text = readTextFile(textFile);
                textView.setText(text);
                if (!textFile.delete()) {
                    textView.setText("Couldn't remove temporary file");
                }
            } catch (IOException e) {
                textView.setText("something went wrong! " + e.getMessage());
            }
        }
    }

    private void writeTextFile(File file, String text) throws IOException {
        BufferedWriter writer = new BufferedWriter(new FileWriter(file));
        writer.write(text);
        writer.close();
    }

    private String readTextFile(File file) throws IOException {
        BufferedReader reader = new BufferedReader(new FileReader(file));
        StringBuilder text = new StringBuilder();
        String line;
        while ((line = reader.readLine()) != null) {
            text.append(line);
            text.append("\n");
        }
```

```
        }
        reader.close();
        return text.toString();
    }
}
```

First we check whether the SD card is actually mounted. If not we bail out early. Next we get the external storage directory and construct a new `File` instance that points to the file we are going to create in the next statement. The `writeTextFile()` method uses standard Java I/O classes to do its magic. If the file doesn't exist yet, this method will create it; otherwise it will overwrite an already existing file. After we successfully dump our test text to the file on the external storage, we read it in again and set it as the text of the `TextView`. As a final step we delete the file from the external storage again. All this is done with standard safety measures in place that will report if something went goes by outputting an error message to the `TextView`. Figure 4–11 shows the output of the activity.

Figure 4–11. *Roger!*

Here are the lessons to take away from this section:

> Don't mess with any files that don't belong to you. Your users will be angry if you delete the photos of their last holiday.

> Always check whether the external storage is mounted.

> Do not mess with any of the files on the external storage! I mean it!

Seeing how easy it is to delete all the files on the external storage, you might think twice before you install your next app from the market that requests permissions to the SD card. The app has full control over your files once it's installed.

Audio Programming

Android offers a couple of easy-to-use APIs for playing back sound effects and music files—just perfect for our game programming needs. Let's have a look at those APIs.

Setting the Volume Controls

If you possess an Android device, you will have noticed that when you press the volume up and down buttons, you control different volume settings depending on what application you are currently in. In a call you control the volume of the incoming voice stream. In the YouTube application you control the volume of the video's audio. On the home screen you control the volume of the ringer.

Android has different audio streams for different purposes. When we play back audio in our game, we use classes that output sound effects and music to a specific stream called the *music stream*. Before we think about playing back sound effects or music, though, we have to first make sure that the volume buttons will control the correct audio stream. For this we use another method of the Context interface:

```
context.setVolumeControlStream(AudioManager.STREAM_MUSIC);
```

As always, the Context implementation of our choice will be our activity. After this call, the volume buttons will control the music stream, to which we'll later output our sound effects and music. We need to call this method only once in our activity life cycle. The Activity.onCreate() method is the best place to do this.

Writing an example that only contains a single line of code is a bit of overkill. I'll thus refrain from doing that at this point. Just remember to use this method in all the activities that output sound.

Playing Sound Effects

In Chapter 3 we discussed the difference between streaming music and playing back sound effects. The latter are stored in memory and are usually no longer than a few seconds. Android provides us with a class called SoundPool that makes playing back sound effects really easy.

We can simply instantiate a new SoundPool instances as follows:

```
SoundPool soundPool = new SoundPool(20, AudioManager.STREAM_MUSIC, 0);
```

The first parameter defines how many sound effects we can play simultaneously at most. This does not mean that we can't have more sound effects loaded, it only restricts how many sound effects can be played concurrently. The second parameter defines which audio stream the SoundPool will output the audio to. We choose the music stream that we have set the volume controls for as well. The final parameter is currently unused and should default to 0.

To load a sound effect from an audio file into heap memory, we can use the SoundPool.load() method. We store all our files in the assets/ directory, so we need to use the overloaded SoundPool.load() method, which takes an AssetFileDescriptor. How do you we get that AssetFileDescriptor? Easy, via the AssetManager we worked with before. Here's how we'd load an OGG file called explosion.ogg from the assets/ directory via the SoundPool:

```
AssetFileDescriptor descriptor = assetManager.openFd("explosion.ogg");
int explosionId = soundPool.load(descriptor, 1);
```

Getting the AssetFileDescriptor is straightforward via the AssetManager.openFd() method. Loading the sound effect via the SoundPool is just as easy. The first argument of the SoundPool.load() method is our AssetFileDescriptor, and the second argument specifies the priority of the sound effect. This is currently not used, and should be set to 1 for future compatibility.

The SoundPool.load() method returns an integer, which serves as a handle to the loaded sound effect. When we want to play the sound effect, we specify this handle so the SoundPool knows what effect to play.

Playing the sound effect is again very easy:

```
soundPool.play(explosionId, 1.0f, 1.0f, 0, 0, 1);
```

The first argument is the handle we received from the SoundPool.load() method. The next two parameters specify the volume to be used for the left and right channels. These values should be in a range between 0 (silent) and 1 (ears explode). Next come two arguments we'll rarely use. The first one is the priority, which is currently unused and should be set to 0. The other argument specifies how often the sound effect should be looped. I wouldn't recommend looping sound effects, so you should generally use 0 here. The final argument is the playback rate. Setting it to something higher than 1 will play back the sound effect faster than it was recorded, and setting it to something lower than 1 will play back the sound effect slower.

When we don't need a sound effect anymore and want to free some memory, we can use the SoundPool.unload() method:

```
soundPool.unload(explosionId);
```

We simply pass in the handle we received from the SoundPool.load() method for that sound effect and it will get unloaded from memory.

Generally we'll have a single SoundPool instance in our game, which we'll use to load, play, and unload sound effects as needed. When we are done with all our audio output and don't need the SoundPool anymore, we should always call the SoundPool.release() method, which will release all resources the SoundPool uses up. After the release you can't use the SoundPool anymore, of course. Also, all sound effects loaded by that SoundPool will be gone.

Let's write a simple test activity that will play back an explosion sound effect each time we tap the screen. We already know everything we need to know to implement this, so Listing 4–9 shouldn't hold any big surprises.

Listing 4–9. *SoundPoolTest.java; Playing Back Sound Effects*

```java
package com.badlogic.androidgames;

import java.io.IOException;

import android.app.Activity;
import android.content.res.AssetFileDescriptor;
import android.content.res.AssetManager;
import android.media.AudioManager;
import android.media.SoundPool;
import android.os.Bundle;
import android.view.MotionEvent;
import android.view.View;
import android.view.View.OnTouchListener;
import android.widget.TextView;

public class SoundPoolTest extends Activity implements OnTouchListener {
    SoundPool soundPool;
    int explosionId = -1;

    @Override
    public void onCreate(Bundle savedInstanceState) {
        super.onCreate(savedInstanceState);
        TextView textView = new TextView(this);
        textView.setOnTouchListener(this);
        setContentView(textView);

        setVolumeControlStream(AudioManager.STREAM_MUSIC);
        soundPool = new SoundPool(20, AudioManager.STREAM_MUSIC, 0);

        try {
            AssetManager assetManager = getAssets();
            AssetFileDescriptor descriptor = assetManager
                    .openFd("explosion.ogg");
            explosionId = soundPool.load(descriptor, 1);
        } catch (IOException e) {
            textView.setText("Couldn't load sound effect from asset, "
                    + e.getMessage());
        }
    }

    @Override
    public boolean onTouch(View v, MotionEvent event) {
        if (event.getAction() == MotionEvent.ACTION_UP) {
            if (explosionId != -1) {
                soundPool.play(explosionId, 1, 1, 0, 0, 1);
            }
        }
        return true;
    }
}
```

We start off by deriving our class from `Activity` and letting it implement the OnTouchListener interface so we can later process taps on the screen. Our class has two members: the SoundPool, and the handle to the sound effect we are going to load and play back. We set that to –1 initially, indicating that the sound effect has not yet been loaded.

In the `onCreate()` method, we do what we've done a couple of times before: create a TextView, register the activity as an OnTouchListener, and set the TextView as the content view.

The next line sets the volume controls to control the music stream, as discussed before. We then create the SoundPool and configure it so it can play 20 concurrent effects at once. That should suffice for the majority of games.

Finally we get an `AssetFileDescriptor` for the `explosion.ogg` file I put in the assets/ directory from the `AssetManager`. To load the sound, we simply pass that descriptor to the `SoundPool.load()` method and store the returned handle. The `SoundPool.load()` method throws an exception in the case something goes wrong while loading, in which case we catch that and display an error message.

In the onTouch() method we simply check whether a finger went up, which indicates that the screen was tapped. If that's the case and the explosion sound effect was loaded successfully (indicated by the handle not being –1), we simply play back that sound effect.

When you execute that little activity, simply touch the screen to make the world explode. If you touch the screen in rapid succession, you'll notice that the sound effect is played multiple times in an overlapping manner. It would be pretty hard to exceed the 20 playbacks maximum we configured the SoundPool with. However, if that happened, one of the currently playing sounds would just be stopped to make room for the new requested playback.

Notice that we didn't unload the sound or released the SoundPool in the preceding example. This is for brevity. Usually you'd release the SoundPool in the onPause() method when the activity is going to be destroyed. Just remember to always release or unload anything you no longer need.

While the SoundPool class is very easy to use, there are a couple of caveats you have to be aware of:

> The SoundPool.load() method executes the actual loading asynchronously. This means that you have to wait for a little bit before you call the SoundPool.play() method with that sound effect, as the loading might not be finished yet. Sadly there's no way to check when the sound effect is done loading. That's only possible with the SDK version 8 of SoundPool, and we want to support all Android versions. Usually it's not a big deal, though, as you will most likely load other assets as well before the sound effect is played for the first time.

SoundPool is known to have problems with MP3 files and long sound files, where *long* is defined as "longer than 5 to 6 seconds." Both problems are undocumented, so there are no strict rules for deciding whether your sound effect will be troublesome or not. As a general rule I'd suggest sticking to OGG audio files instead of MP3s, and trying for the lowest possible sampling rate and duration you can get away with before the audio quality becomes poor.

> **NOTE:** As with any API we discuss, there's more functionality in SoundPool. I briefly told you that you can make sound effects loop. For this you get an ID from the `SoundPool.play()` method that you can use to pause or stop a looped sound effect. Check out the `SoundPool` documentation on the Android Developers site if you need that functionality.

Streaming Music

Small sound effects fit into the limited heap memory an Android application gets from the operating system. Bigger audio files containing longer music pieces don't. For this reason we need to stream the music to the audio hardware, which means that we only read-in a small chunk at a time, enough to decode it to raw PCM data and throw that at the audio chip.

That sounds intimidating. Luckily there's the `MediaPlayer` class, which handles all that business for us. All we need to do is point it at the audio file and tell it to play it back.

Instantiating the `MediaPlayer` class is dead simple:

```
MediaPlayer mediaPlayer = new MediaPlayer();
```

Next we need to tell the `MediaPlayer` what file to play back. That's again done via an `AssetFileDescriptor`:

```
AssetFileDescriptor descriptor = assetManager.openFd("music.ogg");
mediaPlayer.setDataSource(descriptor.getFileDescriptor(), descriptor.getStartOffset(),
descriptor.getLength());
```

There's a little bit more going on here than in the SoundPool case. The `MediaPlayer.setDataSource()` method does not directly take an `AssetFileDescriptor`. Instead it wants a `FileDescriptor`, which we get via the `AssetFileDescriptor.getFileDescriptor()` method. Additionally we have to specify the offset and the length of the audio file. Why the offset? Assets are all stored in a single file in reality. For the `MediaPlayer` to get to the start of the file we have to provide it with the offset of the file within the containing asset file.

Before we can start playing back the music file, we have to call one more method that prepares the `MediaPlayer` for playback:

```
mediaPlayer.prepare();
```

This will actually open the file and check whether it can be read and played back by the `MediaPlayer` instance. From here on we are free to play the audio file, pause it, stop it, set it to be looped, and change the volume.

To start the play back we simply call the following method:

```
mediaPlayer.start();
```

Note that this can only be called after the `MediaPlayer.prepare()` method has been called successfully (you'll notice if it throws a runtime exception).

We can pause the playback after having started it with a call to the `pause()` method:

```
mediaPlayer.pause();
```

Calling this method is again only valid if we have successfully prepared the `MediaPlayer` and started playback already. To resume a paused `MediaPlayer`, we can call the `MediaPlayer.start()` method again without any preparation.

To stop the playback we call the following method:

```
mediaPlayer.stop();
```

Note that when we want to start a stopped `MediaPlayer`, we have to first call the `MediaPlayer.prepare()` method again.

We can set the `MediaPlayer` to loop the playback with the following method:

```
mediaPlayer.setLooping(true);
```

To adjust the volume of the music playback, we can use this method:

```
mediaPlayer.setVolume(1, 1);
```

This will set the volume of the left and right channels. The documentation does not specify what range these two arguments have to be in. From experimentation, the valid range seems to be 0 to 1.

Finally, we need a way to check whether the playback has finished. We can do this in two ways. For one, we can register an `OnCompletionListener` with the `MediaPlayer` that will be called when the playback has finished:

```
mediaPlayer.setOnCompletionListener(listener);
```

If we want to poll for the state of the `MediaPlayer`, we can use the following method instead:

```
boolean isPlaying = mediaPlayer.isPlaying();
```

Note that if the `MediaPlayer` is set to loop, none of the preceding methods will indicate that the `MediaPlayer` has stopped.

Finally, if we are done with that `MediaPlayer` instance, we make sure all the resources it takes up are released by calling the following method:

```
mediaPlayer.release();
```

It's considered good practice to always do this before throwing away the instance.

In case we didn't set the MediaPlayer to be looped and the playback has finished, we can restart the MediaPlayer by calling the MediaPlayer.prepare() and MediaPlayer.start() methods again.

Most of these methods work asynchronously, so even if you called MediaPlayer.stop() the MediaPlayer.isPlaying() method might return for a short period after that. It's usually nothing we worry about too much. In most games we set the MediaPlayer to be looped and stop it when the need arises (e.g., when we switch to a different screen that we want other music to be played on).

Let's write a small test activity where we play back a sound file from the assets/ directory in looping mode. This sound effect will be paused and resumed according to the activity life cycle; when our activity gets paused, so should the music, and when the activity is resumed, the music playback should pick up from where it left off. Listing 4–10 shows you how that's done.

Listing 4–10. *MediaPlayerTest.java; Playing Back Audio Streams*

```java
package com.badlogic.androidgames;

import java.io.IOException;

import android.app.Activity;
import android.content.res.AssetFileDescriptor;
import android.content.res.AssetManager;
import android.media.AudioManager;
import android.media.MediaPlayer;
import android.os.Bundle;
import android.widget.TextView;

public class MediaPlayerTest extends Activity {
    MediaPlayer mediaPlayer;

    @Override
    public void onCreate(Bundle savedInstanceState) {
        super.onCreate(savedInstanceState);
        TextView textView = new TextView(this);
        setContentView(textView);

        setVolumeControlStream(AudioManager.STREAM_MUSIC);
        mediaPlayer = new MediaPlayer();
        try {
            AssetManager assetManager = getAssets();
            AssetFileDescriptor descriptor = assetManager.openFd("music.ogg");
            mediaPlayer.setDataSource(descriptor.getFileDescriptor(),
                    descriptor.getStartOffset(), descriptor.getLength());
            mediaPlayer.prepare();
            mediaPlayer.setLooping(true);
        } catch (IOException e) {
            textView.setText("Couldn't load music file, " + e.getMessage());
            mediaPlayer = null;
        }
    }

    @Override
```

```
    protected void onResume() {
        super.onResume();
        if (mediaPlayer != null) {
            mediaPlayer.start();
        }
    }

    protected void onPause() {
        super.onPause();
        if (mediaPlayer != null) {
            mediaPlayer.pause();
            if (isFinishing()) {
                mediaPlayer.stop();
                mediaPlayer.release();
            }
        }
    }
}
```

We keep a reference to the MediaPlayer in the form of a member of our activity. In the onCreate() method we simply create a TextView for outputting any error messages, as always.

Before we start playing around with the MediaPlayer, we make sure the volume controls actually control the music stream. Having that set up, we instantiate the MediaPlayer. We fetch the AssetFileDescriptor from the AssetManager for a file called music.ogg located in the assets/ directory, and set it as the data source of the MediaPlayer. All that's left is preparing the MediaPlayer instance and setting it to loop the stream. In case anything goes wrong, we set the mediaPlayer member to null so we can later determine whether loading was successful or not. Additionally we output some error text to the TextView.

In the onResume() method we simply start the MediaPlayer (if creating it was successful). The onResume() method is the perfect place to do this, as it is called after onCreate() and after onPause(). In the first case it will start the playback for the first time; in the second case it will simply resume the paused MediaPlayer.

The onResume() method pauses the MediaPlayer. If the activity is going to be killed, we stop the MediaPlayer and then release all its resources.

If you play around with this, make sure to also test out how it reacts to pausing and resuming the activity by either locking the screen or temporarily switching to the home screen. When resumed, the MediaPlayer will pick up from where it left when it was paused.

Here are couple of things to remember:

> The methods MediaPlayer.start(), MediaPlayer.pause(), and
> MediaPlayer.resume() can only be called in certain states as just
> discussed. Never try to call them when you haven't prepared the
> MediaPlayer yet. Call MediaPlayer.start() only after preparing the
> MediaPlayer or when you want to resume it after you've explicitly
> paused it via a call to MediaPlayer.pause().

MediaPlayer instances are pretty heavyweight. Having many of them instanced will take up considerable resources. We should always try to have only one for music playback. Sound effects are better handled with the SoundPool class.

Remember to set the volume controls to handle the music stream, or else your players won't be able to adjust the volume of your game.

We are almost done with this chapter, but one big topic still lies ahead of us: 2D graphics.

Basic Graphics Programming

Android offers us two big APIs for drawing to the screen. One is mainly used for simple 2D graphics programming, and the other is used for hardware-accelerated 3D graphics programming. This and the next chapter will focus on 2D graphics programming with the Canvas API, which is a nice wrapper around the Skia library and suitable for modestly complex 2D graphics. Before we get to that, though, there are two things we need to talk about first: going full-screen and wake locks.

Using Wake Locks

If you leave the tests we wrote so far alone for a few seconds, the screen of your phone will dim. Only if you touch the screen or hit a button will the screen go back to its full brightness. To keep our screen awake at all times, we can use a so-called *wake lock*.

The first thing we need to do is add a proper <uses-permission> tag in the manifest file with the name android.permission.WAKE_LOCK. This will allow us to actually use the WakeLock class.

We can get a WakeLock instance from the PowerManager like this:

```
PowerManager powerManager =
(PowerManager)context.getSystemService(Context.POWER_SERVICE);
WakeLock wakeLock = powerManager.newWakeLock(PowerManager.FULL_WAKE_LOCK, "My Lock");
```

Like all other system services, we acquire the PowerManager from a Context instance. The PowerManager.newWakeLock() method takes two arguments: the type of the lock and a tag we can freely define. There are a couple of different wake lock types; for our purposes the PowerManager.FULL_WAKE_LOCK type is the correct one. It will make sure that the screen will stay on, the CPU will work at full speed, and] the keyboard will stay enabled.

To enable the wake lock we have to call its acquire() method:

```
wakeLock.acquire();
```

The phone will be kept awake from this point on, no matter how much time passes without user interaction. When our application is paused or destroyed, we have to disable or release the wake lock again:

```
wakeLock.release();
```

Usually we instantiate the WakeLock instance on the Activity.onCreate() method, call WakeLock.acquire() in the Activity.onResume() method, and call the WakeLock.release() method in the Activity.onPause() method. This way we guarantee that our application still performs well in the case of being paused or resumed. Given that there are only four lines of code to add, we're not going to write a full-fledged example. Instead I suggest you simply add it to the full-screen example of the next section and observe the effects.

Going Full-Screen

Before we dive headfirst into drawing our first shapes with the Android APIs, let's fix something else. Up until this point, all our activities have shown their title bars. The notification bar was visible as well. We'd like to immerse our players a little bit more by getting rid of those. We can do that with two simple calls:

```
requestWindowFeature(Window.FEATURE_NO_TITLE);
getWindow().setFlags(WindowManager.LayoutParams.FLAG_FULLSCREEN,
WindowManager.LayoutParams.FLAG_FULLSCREEN);
```

The first call gets rid of the activity's title bar. To make the activity go full-screen and thus eliminate the notification bar as well, we call the second method. Note that we have to call these methods before we set the content view of our activity.

Listing 4–11 shows you a very simple test activity that demonstrates how to go full-screen.

Listing 4–11. *FullScreenTest.java; Making Our Activity Go Full-Screen*

```
package com.badlogic.androidgames;

import android.os.Bundle;
import android.view.Window;
import android.view.WindowManager;

public class FullScreenTest extends SingleTouchTest {

    @Override
    public void onCreate(Bundle savedInstanceState) {
        requestWindowFeature(Window.FEATURE_NO_TITLE);
        getWindow().setFlags(WindowManager.LayoutParams.FLAG_FULLSCREEN,
                WindowManager.LayoutParams.FLAG_FULLSCREEN);
        super.onCreate(savedInstanceState);
    }
}
```

What's happening here? We simply derive from the TouchTest class we created earlier and override the onCreate() method. In the onCreate() method, we enable full-screen mode and then call the onCreate() method of the superclass (in this case the TouchTest activity), which will set up all the rest of the activity. Note again that we have to call those two methods before we set the content view. Hence, the superclass onCreate() method is called after we execute these two methods.

We also fixed the orientation of the activity to portrait mode in the manifest file. You didn't forget to add <activity> elements in the manifest file for each test we wrote, right? From now on we'll always fix it to either portrait or landscape mode, since we don't want a changing coordinate system all the time.

By deriving from TouchTest, we have a fully working example with which we can explore the coordinate system we are going to draw in. The activity will show you the coordinates at which you touch the screen, as in the old TouchTest example. The difference is that this time we are full-screen, which means that the maximum coordinates of our touch events are equal to the screen resolution (minus one in each dimension, as we start at [0,0]). For a Nexus One, the coordinate system would span the coordinates (0,0) to (479,799) in portrait mode (for a total of 480×800 pixels).

While it may seem that the screen is redrawn continuously, it actually is not. Remember from our TouchTest class that we update the TextView every time a touch event is processed. This in turn makes the TextView redraw itself. If we don't touch the screen, the TextView will not redraw itself. For a game, we need to be able to redraw the screen as often as possible, preferably within our main loop thread. We'll start off easy, though, and begin with continuous rendering in the UI thread.

Continuous Rendering in the UI Thread

All we've done up until now is set the text of a TextView when needed. The actual rendering has been performed by the TextView itself. Let's create our own custom View whose sole purpose it is to let us draw stuff to the screen. We also want it to redraw itself as often as possible, and we want a simple way to perform our own drawing in that mysterious redraw method.

Although this may sound complicated, in reality Android makes it really easy for us to create such a thing. All we have to do is create a class that derives from the View class, and override a method called View.onDraw(). This method is called by the Android system every time it needs our View to redraw itself. Here's what that could look like:

```
class RenderView extends View {
    public RenderView(Context context) {
        super(context);
    }

    protected void onDraw(Canvas canvas) {
        // to be implemented
    }
}
```

Not exactly rocket science, is it? We get an instance of a class called Canvas passed to the onDraw() method. This will be our workhorse in the following sections. It lets us draw shapes and bitmaps to either another bitmap or a View (or a surface, which we'll talk about that in a bit).

We can use this RenderView as we'd use a TextView. We just set it as the content view of our activity and hook up any input listeners we need. However, it's not all that useful yet, for two reasons: it doesn't actually draw anything, and even if it did, it would only do so when the activity needed to be redrawn (i.e., when it is created or resumed, or when a dialog that overlaps it becomes invisible). How can we make it redraw itself?

Easy, like this:

```
protected void onDraw(Canvas canvas) {
    // all drawing goes here
    invalidate();
}
```

The call to the `View.invalidate()` method at the end of `onDraw()` will tell the Android system to redraw the `RenderView` as soon as it finds time to do that again. All this still happens on the UI thread, which is a bit of a lazy horse. But we actually have continuous rendering with the `onDraw()` method, albeit relatively slow continuous rendering. We'll fix that later; for now it suffices for our needs.

So let's get back to the mysterious `Canvas` class again. It is a pretty powerful class that wraps a custom low-level graphics library called Skia, specifically tailored to perform 2D rendering on the CPU. The `Canvas` class provides us with many drawing methods for various shapes, bitmaps, and even text.

Where do the draw methods draw to? That depends. A `Canvas` can render to a `Bitmap` instance; `Bitmap` is another class provided by the Android's 2D API, which we'll look into later on. In this case, it is drawing to the area on the screen that the `View` is taking up. Of course, this is an insane oversimplification. Under the hood, it will not directly draw to the screen, but to some sort of bitmap that the system will later use in combination with the bitmaps of all other `View`s of the activity to composite the final output image. That image will then be handed over to the GPU, which will display it on the screen through another set of mysterious paths.

We don't really need to care about the details. From our perspective, our `View` seems to stretch over the whole screen, so it may as well be drawing to the framebuffer of the system. For the rest of this discussion, we'll pretend that we directly draw to the framebuffer, with the system doing all the nifty things like vertical retrace and double-buffering for us.

The `onDraw()` method will be called as often as the system permits. For us, it is very similar to the body of our theoretical game main loop. If we were to implement a game with this method, we'd place all our game logic into this method. We won't do that for various reasons, though, performance being one of them.

So let's do something interesting. Every time I get access to a new drawing API, I write a little test that checks if the screen is really redrawn frequently. It's a sort of a poor man's light show. All I do in each call to the redraw method is fill the screen with a new random color. That way I only need to find the method of that API that allows me to fill the screen, without needing to know a lot about the nitty-gritty details. Let's write such a test with our own custom `RenderView` implementation.

The method of the `Canvas` to fill its rendering target with a specific color is called `Canvas.drawRGB()`:

```
Canvas.drawRGB(int r, int g, int b);
```

The r, g, and b arguments each stand for one component of the color we want to fill the "screen" with. Each of them has to be in the range 0 to 255, so we actually specify a color in the RGB888 format here. If you don't remember the details regarding colors, take a look at the "Encoding Colors Digitally" section of Chapter 3 again, as we'll be using that info throughout the rest of this chapter.

Listing 4–12 shows you the code for our little light show.

> **CAUTION:** Running this code will rapidly fill the screen with a random color. If you have epilepsy or are otherwise light-sensitive in any way, don't run it.

Listing 4–12. *The RenderViewTest Activity*

```
package com.badlogic.androidgames;

import java.util.Random;

import android.app.Activity;
import android.content.Context;
import android.graphics.Canvas;
import android.os.Bundle;
import android.view.View;
import android.view.Window;
import android.view.WindowManager;

public class RenderViewTest extends Activity {
    class RenderView extends View {
        Random rand = new Random();

        public RenderView(Context context) {
            super(context);
        }

        protected void onDraw(Canvas canvas) {
            canvas.drawRGB(rand.nextInt(256), rand.nextInt(256),
                    rand.nextInt(256));
            invalidate();
        }
    }

    @Override
    public void onCreate(Bundle savedInstanceState) {
        super.onCreate(savedInstanceState);
        requestWindowFeature(Window.FEATURE_NO_TITLE);
        getWindow().setFlags(WindowManager.LayoutParams.FLAG_FULLSCREEN,
                WindowManager.LayoutParams.FLAG_FULLSCREEN);
        setContentView(new RenderView(this));
    }
}
```

For our first graphics demo, this is pretty concise. We define the RenderView class as an inner class of the RenderViewTest activity. The RenderView class derives from the View class, as discussed earlier, and has a mandatory constructor, as well as the overridden onDraw() method. It also has an instance of the Random class as a member; we'll use that to generate our random colors.

The onDraw() method is dead simple. We first tell the Canvas to fill the whole view with a random color. For each color component, we simply specify a random number between 0 and 255 (Random.nextInt() is exclusive). After that we tell the system that we want the onDraw() method to be called again as soon as possible.

The onCreate() method of the activity enables full-screen mode and sets an instance of our RenderView class as the content view. To keep the example short, we're leaving out the wake lock for now.

Taking a screenshot of this example is a little bit pointless. All it does is fill the screen with a random color as fast as the system allows on the UI thread. It's nothing to write home about. Let's do something more interesting instead: draw some shapes.

> **NOTE:** While the preceding method of continuous rendering works, I strongly recommend not to use it! We should do as little work on the UI thread as possible. We'll discuss in a minute how to do it properly in a separate thread, where we can also implement our game logic later on.

Getting the Screen Resolution (and Coordinate Systems)

In Chapter 2 we talked a lot about the framebuffer and its properties. Remember that a framebuffer holds the colors of the pixels that get displayed on the screen. The number of pixels available to us is defined by the screen resolution, which is given by its width and height in pixels.

Now, with our custom View implementation, we don't actually render directly to the framebuffer. But since our View spans the complete screen, we can pretend it does. In order to know where we can render our game elements to, we need to know how many pixels there are on the x-axis and on the y-axis, or the width and height of the screen.

The Canvas class has two methods that provide us with that information:

```
int width = canvas.getWidth();
int height = canvas.getHeight();
```

This returns the width and height in pixels of the target the Canvas renders to. Note that, depending on what orientation our activity has, the width might be smaller or larger than the height. My Nexus One, for example, has a resolution of 480×800 pixels in portrait mode, so the Canvas.getWidth() method would return 480 and the Canvas.getHeight() method would return 800. In landscape mode, the two values are simply swapped: Canvas.getWidth() would return 800 and Canvas.getHeight() would return 480.

The second piece of information we need to know is how the coordinate system we render to is organized. First of all, only integer pixel coordinates make sense (there is a concept called subpixels, but we will ignore it). We also already know that the origin of that coordinate system at (0,0) is always at the top-left corner of the display, be it in portrait or landscape mode. The positive x-axis is always pointing to the right, and the y-axis is always pointing downward. Figure 4–12 shows a hypothetical screen with a resolution of 48×32 pixels, in landscape mode.

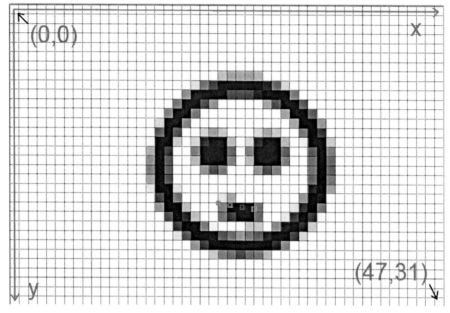

Figure 4–12. *The coordinate system of a 48×32-pixel-wide screen*

Note how the origin of the coordinate system in Figure 4–12 coincides with the top-left pixel of the screen. The bottom-left pixel of the screen is thus not at (48,32), as we'd expect, but at (47,31). In general, (width – 1, height – 1) is always the position of the bottom-right pixel of the screen.

Figure 4–12 shows you a hypothetical screen coordinate system in landscape mode. By now you should be able to image how the coordinate system would look in portrait mode.

All the drawing methods of Canvas operate within such a coordinate system. Usually we can address a lot more pixels than in our 48x32-pixel example (e.g., 800×480). That said, let's finally draw some pixels, lines, circles, and rectangles.

> **NOTE:** You may have noticed that different devices can have difference screen resolutions. We'll look into that problem in the next chapter. For now let's just concentrate on finally getting something on the screen ourselves.

Drawing Simple Shapes

One hundred fifty pages later and we are finally on our way to drawing our first pixel. We'll quickly go over some of the drawing methods provided to us by the Canvas class.

There's another method that will come in handy, as well:

```
Canvas.drawBitmap(Bitmap bitmap, Rect src, Rect dst, Paint paint);
```

This method is super-awesome. It allows us to specify a portion of the `Bitmap` to draw via the second parameter. The `Rect` class holds the top-left and bottom-right corner coordinates of a rectangle. When we specify a portion of the `Bitmap` via the `src`, we do it in the `Bitmap`'s coordinate system. If we specify `null`, the complete `Bitmap` will be used.

The third parameter defines where the portion of the the `Bitmap` should be drawn to, again in the form of a `Rect` instance. This time the corner coordinates are given in the coordinate system of the target of the `Canvas`, though (either a `View` or another `Bitmap`). The big surprise is that the two rectangles do not have to be the same size. If we specify the destination rectangle to be smaller in size than the source rectangle, then the `Canvas` will automatically scale for us. The same is true for specifying a larger destination rectangle, of course. The last parameter we'll usually set to `null` again. Note, however, that this scaling operation is very expensive. We should only use it when absolutely necessary.

So, you might wonder, if we have `Bitmap` instances with different color formats, do we need to convert them to some kind of standard format before we can draw them via a `Canvas`? The answer is no. The `Canvas` will do this for us automatically. Of course, it will be a bit faster if we use color formats that are equal to the native framebuffer format. Usually we just ignore this, though.

Blending is also enabled by default, so if our images contain an alpha component per pixel, it is actually interpreted.

Putting It All Together

With all this information, we can finally load and render some Bobs. Listing 4–14 shows you the source of the `BitmapTest` activity I wrote for demonstration purposes.

Listing 4–14. *The BitmapTest Activity*

```java
package com.badlogic.androidgames;

import java.io.IOException;
import java.io.InputStream;

import android.app.Activity;
import android.content.Context;
import android.content.res.AssetManager;
import android.graphics.Bitmap;
import android.graphics.BitmapFactory;
import android.graphics.Canvas;
import android.graphics.Rect;
import android.os.Bundle;
import android.util.Log;
import android.view.View;
import android.view.Window;
import android.view.WindowManager;
```

```java
public class BitmapTest extends Activity {
    class RenderView extends View {
        Bitmap bob565;
        Bitmap bob4444;
        Rect dst = new Rect();

        public RenderView(Context context) {
            super(context);

            try {
                AssetManager assetManager = context.getAssets();
                InputStream inputStream = assetManager.open("bobrgb888.png");
                bob565 = BitmapFactory.decodeStream(inputStream);
                inputStream.close();
                Log.d("BitmapText",
                        "bobrgb888.png format: " + bob565.getConfig());

                inputStream = assetManager.open("bobargb8888.png");
                BitmapFactory.Options options = new BitmapFactory.Options();
                options.inPreferredConfig = Bitmap.Config.ARGB_4444;
                bob4444 = BitmapFactory
                        .decodeStream(inputStream, null, options);
                inputStream.close();
                Log.d("BitmapText",
                        "bobargb8888.png format: " + bob4444.getConfig());

            } catch (IOException e) {
                // silently ignored, bad coder monkey, baaad!
            } finally {
                // we should really close our input streams here.
            }
        }

        protected void onDraw(Canvas canvas) {
            dst.set(50, 50, 350, 350);
            canvas.drawBitmap(bob565, null, dst, null);
            canvas.drawBitmap(bob4444, 100, 100, null);
            invalidate();
        }
    }

    @Override
    public void onCreate(Bundle savedInstanceState) {
        super.onCreate(savedInstanceState);
        requestWindowFeature(Window.FEATURE_NO_TITLE);
        getWindow().setFlags(WindowManager.LayoutParams.FLAG_FULLSCREEN,
                WindowManager.LayoutParams.FLAG_FULLSCREEN);
        setContentView(new RenderView(this));
    }
}
```

The onCreate() method of our activity is old hat, so let's move on to our custom View.

It has two Bitmap members, one storing an image of Bob (introduced in Chapter 3) in RGB565 format, and another storing Bob in ARGB4444 format. We also have a Rect member where we store the destination rectangle for rendering.

In the constructor of the RenderView class, we first load Bob into the bob565 member of the View. Note that the image is loaded from an RGB888 PNG file, and that the BitmapFactory will automatically convert this to an RGB565 image. To prove this, we also output the Bitmap.Config of the Bitmap to LogCat. The RGB888 version of Bob has an opaque white background, so no blending needs to be performed.

Next we load Bob from an ARGB8888 PNG file stored in the assets/ directory. To save some memory, we also tell the BitmapFactory to convert this image of Bob to an ARGB4444 bitmap. The factory may not obey this request (for unknown reasons). To see whether it was nice to us, we ouput the Bitmap.Config file of this Bitmap to LogCat as well.

The onDraw() method is puny. All we do is draw bob565 scaled to 250×250 pixels (from his original size of 160×183 pixels) and draw bob4444 on top of him, unscaled but blended (which is done automagically by the Canvas). Figure 4–14 shows you the two Bobs in all their glory.

Figure 4–14. *Two Bobs on top of each other (at 480×800-pixel resolution)*

LogCat reports that bob565 indeed has the color format Config.RGB_565, and that bob4444 was converted to Config.ARGB_4444. The BitmapFactory did not fail us!

Here are some things you should take away from this section:

> Use the minimum color format you can get away with to conserve memory. This might, however, come at the price of less visual quality and slightly reduced rendering speed.

Unless absolutely necessary, refrain from drawing bitmaps scaled. If you know their scaled size, prescale them offline or during loading time.

Always make sure you call the `Bitmap.recycle()` method if you no longer need a `Bitmap`. Otherwise you'll get some memory leaks or run low on memory.

Using LogCat all this time for text output is a bit tedious. Let's see how we can render text via the `Canvas`.

> **NOTE:** As with other classes, there's more to `Bitmap` than what I could describe in this couple of pages. I covered the bare minimum we need to write Mr. Nom. If you want more, check out the documentation on the Android Developers site.

Rendering Text

While the text we'll output in the Mr. Nom game will be drawn by hand, it doesn't hurt to know how to draw text via TrueType fonts. Let's start by loading a custom TrueType font file from the `assets/` directory.

Loading Fonts

The Android API provides us with a class called `Typeface` that encapsulates a TrueType font. It provides a simple static method to load such a font file from the `assets/` directory:

```
Typeface font = Typeface.createFromAsset(context.getAssets(), "font.ttf");
```

Interestingly enough, this method does not throw any kind of `Exception` if the font file can't be loaded. Instead a `RuntimeException` is thrown. Why no explicit exception is thrown for this method is a bit of a mystery to me.

Drawing Text with a Font

Once we have our font, we set it as the `Typeface` of a `Paint` instance:

```
paint.setTypeFace(font);
```

Via the `Paint` instance, we also specify the size we want to render the font at:

```
paint.setTextSize(30);
```

The documentation of this method is again a little sparse. It doesn't tell whether the text size is given in points or pixels. We just assume the latter.

Finally, we can draw text with this font via the following `Canvas` method:

```
canvas.drawText("This is a test!", 100, 100, paint);
```

The first parameter is the text to draw. The next two parameters are the coordinates where the text should be drawn to. The last argument is familiar to us: it's the `Paint` instance that specifies the color, font, and size of the text to be drawn. By setting the color of the `Paint`, you also set the color of the text to be drawn.

Text Alignment and Boundaries

Now, you might wonder how the coordinates of the preceding method relate to the rectangle the text string fills. Do they specify the top-left corner of the rectangle the text is contained in? The answer is a bit more complicated. The `Paint` instance has an attribute called the *align setting*. It can be set via this method of the `Paint` class:

```
Paint.setTextAlign(Paint.Align align);
```

The `Paint.Align` enumeration has three values: `Paint.Align.LEFT`, `Paint.Align.CENTER`, and `Paint.Align.RIGHT`. Depending on what alignment is set, the coordinates passed to the `Canvas.drawText()` method are interpreted as either the top-left corner of the rectangle, the top-center pixel of the rectangle, or the top-right corner of the rectangle. The standard alignment is `Paint.Align.LEFT`.

Sometimes it's also useful to know the bounds of a specific string in pixels. For this, the `Paint` class offers the following method:

```
Paint.getTextBounds(String text, int start, int end, Rect bounds);
```

The first argument is the string we want to get the bounds for. The second and third arguments specify the start character and the end character within the string that should be measured. The end argument is exclusive. The final argument, bounds, is a `Rect` instance we allocate ourselves and pass into the method. The method will write the width and height of the bounding rectangle into the `Rect.right` and `Rect.bottom` fields. For convenience we can call `Rect.width()` and `Rect.height()` to get the same values.

Note that all these methods work on a single line of text only. If we want to render multiple lines, we have to do the layout ourselves.

Putting It All Together

Enough talk, let's do some more coding. Listing 4–15 shows you text rendering in action.

Listing 4–15. *The FontTest Activity*

```
package com.badlogic.androidgames;

import android.app.Activity;
import android.content.Context;
import android.graphics.Canvas;
import android.graphics.Color;
import android.graphics.Paint;
import android.graphics.Rect;
import android.graphics.Typeface;
import android.os.Bundle;
```

```
import android.view.View;
import android.view.Window;
import android.view.WindowManager;

public class FontTest extends Activity {
    class RenderView extends View {
        Paint paint;
        Typeface font;
        Rect bounds = new Rect();

        public RenderView(Context context) {
            super(context);
            paint = new Paint();
            font = Typeface.createFromAsset(context.getAssets(), "font.ttf");
        }

        protected void onDraw(Canvas canvas) {
            paint.setColor(Color.YELLOW);
            paint.setTypeface(font);
            paint.setTextSize(28);
            paint.setTextAlign(Paint.Align.CENTER);
            canvas.drawText("This is a test!", canvas.getWidth() / 2, 100,
                    paint);

            String text = "This is another test o_0";
            paint.setColor(Color.WHITE);
            paint.setTextSize(18);
            paint.setTextAlign(Paint.Align.LEFT);
            paint.getTextBounds(text, 0, text.length(), bounds);
            canvas.drawText(text, canvas.getWidth() - bounds.width(), 140,
                    paint);
            invalidate();
        }
    }

    @Override
    public void onCreate(Bundle savedInstanceState) {
        super.onCreate(savedInstanceState);
        requestWindowFeature(Window.FEATURE_NO_TITLE);
        getWindow().setFlags(WindowManager.LayoutParams.FLAG_FULLSCREEN,
                WindowManager.LayoutParams.FLAG_FULLSCREEN);
        setContentView(new RenderView(this));
    }
}
```

We won't discuss the onCreate() method of the activity, since we've seen it before.

Our RenderView implementation has three members: a Paint, a Typeface, and a Rect, where we'll store the bounds of a text string later on.

In the constructor we create a new Paint instance and load a font from the file font.ttf in the assets/ directory.

In the onDraw() method, we set the Paint to the color yellow, set the font and its size, and specify the text alignment to be used when interpreting the coordinates in the call to

Canvas.drawText(). The actual drawing call renders the string This is a test!, centered horizontally at coordinate 100 on the y-axis.

For the second text-rendering call, we do something else: we want the text to be right-aligned with the right edge of the screen. We could do this by using Paint.Align.RIGHT and an x-coordinate of Canvas.getWidth() – 1. Instead we do it the hard way by using the bounds of the string to practice very basic text layout a little. We also change the color and the size of the font for rendering. Figure 4–15 shows the output of this activity.

Figure 4–15. *Fun with text (480×800-pixel resolution)*

Another mystery of the Typeface class is that it does not allow us to explicitly release all its resources. We have to rely on the garbage collector to do the dirty work for us.

NOTE: We only scratched the surface of text rendering here. If you want to know more . . . well, I guess by now you know where to look.

Continuous Rendering with SurfaceView

This is the section where we become real women and men. It involves threading and all the pain that is associated with it. We'll get through it alive. I promise!

Motivation

When we first tried to do continuous rendering, we did it the wrong way. Hogging the UI thread is unacceptable; we need a solution that does all the dirty work in a separate thread. Enter SurfaceView.

As the name gives away, the SurfaceView class is a View that handles a Surface, another class of the Android API. What is a Surface? It's an abstraction of a raw buffer that is used by the screen compositor for rendering that specific View. The screen compositor is the mastermind behind all rendering on Android, and is ultimately responsible for pushing all pixels to the GPU. The Surface can be hardware accelerated in some cases. We don't care that much about that fact, though. All we need to know is that it is a more direct way to render things to the screen.

Our goal is it to perform our rendering in a separate thread so that we do not hog the UI thread, which is busy with other things. The SurfaceView class provides us with a way to render to it from a thread other than the UI thread.

SurfaceHolder and Locking

In order to render to a SurfaceView from a different thread than the UI thread, we need to acquire an instance of the SurfaceHolder class, like this:

```
SurfaceHolder holder = surfaceView.getHolder();
```

The SurfaceHolder is a wrapper around the Surface, and does some bookkeeping for us. It provides us with two methods:

```
Canvas SurfaceHolder.lockCanvas();
SurfaceHolder.unlockAndPost(Canvas canvas);
```

The first method locks the Surface for rendering and returns a nice Canvas instance we can use. The second method unlocks the Surface again and makes sure that what we've drawn via the Canvas gets displayed on the screen. We will use these two methods in our rendering thread to acquire the Canvas, render with it, and finally make the image we just rendered visible on the screen. The Canvas we have to pass to the SurfaceHolder.unlockAndPost() method must be the one we received from the SurfaceHolder.lockCanvas() method.

The Surface is not immediately created when the SurfaceView is instantiated. Instead it is created asynchronously. The surface will be destroyed each time the activity is paused and recreated when the activity is resumed again.

Surface Creation and Validity

We cannot acquire the Canvas from the SurfaceHolder as long as the Surface is not yet valid. However, we can check whether the Surface has been created or not via the following statement:

```
boolean isCreated = surfaceHolder.getSurface().isValid();
```

If this method returns true, we can safely lock the surface and draw to it via the Canvas we receive. We have to make absolutely sure that we unlock the Surface again after a call to SurfaceHolder.lockCanvas(), or else our activity might lock up the phone!

Putting It All Together

So how do we integrate all this with a separate rendering thread, as well as with the activity life cycle? The best way to figure this out is to look at some actual code. Listing 4–16 shows you a complete example that performs the rendering in a separate thread on a SurfaceView.

Listing 4–16. *The SurfaceViewTest Activity*

```
package com.badlogic.androidgames;
import android.app.Activity;
import android.content.Context;
import android.graphics.Canvas;
import android.os.Bundle;
import android.view.SurfaceHolder;
import android.view.SurfaceView;
import android.view.Window;
import android.view.WindowManager;

public class SurfaceViewTest extends Activity {
    FastRenderView renderView;

    public void onCreate(Bundle savedInstanceState) {
        super.onCreate(savedInstanceState);
        requestWindowFeature(Window.FEATURE_NO_TITLE);
        getWindow().setFlags(WindowManager.LayoutParams.FLAG_FULLSCREEN,
                             WindowManager.LayoutParams.FLAG_FULLSCREEN);
        renderView = new FastRenderView(this);
        setContentView(renderView);
    }

    protected void onResume() {
        super.onResume();
        renderView.resume();
    }

    protected void onPause() {
        super.onPause();
        renderView.pause();
    }

    class FastRenderView extends SurfaceView implements Runnable {
        Thread renderThread = null;
        SurfaceHolder holder;
        volatile boolean running = false;

        public FastRenderView(Context context) {
            super(context);
            holder = getHolder();
        }
```

```java
    public void resume() {
        running = true;
        renderThread = new Thread(this);
        renderThread.start();
    }

    public void run() {
        while(running) {
            if(!holder.getSurface().isValid())
                continue;

            Canvas canvas = holder.lockCanvas();
            canvas.drawRGB(255, 0, 0);
            holder.unlockCanvasAndPost(canvas);
        }
    }

    public void pause() {
        running = false;
        while(true) {
            try {
                renderThread.join();
            } catch (InterruptedException e) {
                // retry
            }
        }
    }
}
```

This doesn't look all that intimidating, does it? Our activity holds a FastRenderView instance as a member. This is a custom SurfaceView subclass that will handle all the thread business and surface locking for us. To the activity, it looks like a plain-old View.

In the onCreate() method we enable full-screen mode, create the FastRenderView instance, and set it as the content view of the activity.

We also override the onResume() method this time. In this method we will start our rendering thread indirectly by calling the FastRenderView.resume() method, which does all the magic internally. This means that the thread will get started when the activity is initially created (because onCreate() is always followed by a call to onResume()). It will also get restarted when the activity is resumed from a paused state.

This of course implies that we have to stop the thread somewhere; otherwise we'd create a new thread every time onResume() was called. That's where onPause() comes in. It calls the FastRenderView.pause() method, which will completely stop the thread. The method will not return before the thread is completely stopped.

So let's look at the core class of this example: FastRenderView. It's similar to the RenderView classes we implemented in the last couple of examples in that it derives from another View class. In this case we directly derive it from the SurfaceView class. It also implements the Runnable interface so that we can pass it to the rendering thread in order for it to run the render thread logic.

The `FastRenderView` class has three members. The `renderThread` member is simply a reference to the `Thread` instance that will be responsible for executing our rendering thread logic. The `holder` member is a reference to the `SurfaceHolder` instance we get from the `SurfaceView` superclass we derive from. Finally, the `running` member is a simple boolean flag we will use to signal the rendering thread that it should stop execution. The `volatile` modifier has a special meaning we'll get to in a minute.

All we do in the constructor is call the superclass constructor and store the reference to the `SurfaceHolder` in the `holder` member.

Next comes the `FastRenderView.resume()` method. It is responsible for starting up the rendering thread. Notice that we create a new `Thread` each time this method is called. This is in line with what we discussed when we talked about the activity's `onResume()` and `onPause()` methods. We also set the `running` flag to `true`. You'll see how that's used in the rendering thread in a bit. The final piece to take away is that we set the `FastRenderView` instance itself as the `Runnable` of the thread. This will execute the next method of the `FastRenderView` in that new thread.

The `FastRenderView.run()` method is the workhorse of our custom `View` class. Its body is executed in the rendering thread. As you can see, it's merely composed of a loop that will stop executing as soon as the `running` flag is set to `false`. If that happens, the thread will also be stopped and die. Inside the `while` loop, we first check whether the `Surface` is valid, and if it is we lock it, render to it, and unlock it again, as discussed earlier. In this example we simply fill the `Surface` with the color red.

The `FastRenderView.pause()` method looks a little strange. First we set the `running` flag to `false`. If you look up a little, you will see that the `while` loop in the `FastRenderView.run()` method will eventually terminate due to this, and hence stop the rendering thread. In the next couple of lines we simply wait for the thread to completely die by invoking `Thread.join()`. This method will wait for the thread to die, but might throw an `InterruptedException` before the thread actually dies. Since we have to make absolutely sure that the thread is dead before we return from that method, we perform the join in an endless loop until it is successful.

Let's come back to the `volatile` modifier of the `running` flag. Why do we need it? The reason is delicate: the compiler might decide to reorder the statements in the `FastRenderView.pause()` method if it recognizes that there are no dependencies between the first line in that method and the `while` block. It is allowed to do this if it thinks it will make the code execute faster. However, we depend on the order of execution that we specified in that method. Imagine if the `running` flag were set after we tried to join the thread. We'd go into an endless loop, as the thread would never terminate.

The `volatile` modifier prevents this from happening. Any statements where this member is referenced will be executed in order. This saves us from a nasty heisenbug, a bug that comes and goes without the ability to be consistently reproduced.

There's one more thing you might think will make this code explode. What if the surface is destroyed between the calls to `SurfaceHolder.getSurface().isValid()` and

SurfaceHolder.lock()? Well, we are lucky—this can never happen. To understand why, we have to take a step back and see how the life cycle of the Surface works.

We know that the Surface is created asynchronously. It is likely that our rendering thread will execute before the Surface is valid. We safeguard against this by not locking the Surface unless it is valid. So that covers the surface creation case.

The reason the rendering thread code does not explode from the Surface being destroyed between the validity check and the locking has to with the point in time the Surface gets destroyed. The Surface is always destroyed after we return from the activity's onPause() method. And since we wait for the thread to die in that method via the call to FastRenderView.pause(), the rendering thread will not be alive anymore when the Surface is actually destroyed. Sexy, isn't it? But it's also confusing.

We now perform our continuous rendering the right way. We do not hog the UI thread anymore, but use a separate rendering thread instead. We made it respect the activity life cycle as well, so that it does not run in the background, eating the battery while the activity is paused. The whole world is a happy place again. Of course, we'll need to synchronize the processing of input events in the UI thread with our rendering thread. But that will turn out to be really easy, which you'll see in the next chapter when we implement our game framework based on all the information you digested in this chapter.

Best Practices

Android (or rather Dalvik) has some strange performance characteristics at times. To round of this chapter, I'll present to you some of the most important best practices you should follow to make your games as smooth as silk.

The garbage collector is your biggest enemy. Once it gets CPU time to do its dirty work, it will stop the world for up to 600 ms. That's half a second that our game will not update or render. The user will complain. Avoid object creation as much as possible, especially in your inner loops.

Objects can get created in some not-so-obvious places, which you'll want to avoid. Don't use iterators, as they create new objects. Don't use any of the standard Set or Map collection classes, as they create new objects on each insertion; use the SparseArray class provided by the Android API instead. Use StringBuffers instead of concatenating strings with the + operator. That will create a new StringBuffer each time. And for the love of all that's good in this world, don't use boxed primitives!

Method calls have a larger associated cost in Dalvik than in other VMs. Use static methods if you can, as those perform best. Static methods are generally regarded as evil, much like static variables, as they promote bad design. So try to keep your design as clean as possible. You should maybe avoid getters and setters as well. Direct field access is about three times faster than method invocations without the JIT, and about seven times faster with the JIT. Again, think of your design before removing all your getters and setters, though.

Floating-point operations are implemented in software on older devices and Dalvik versions without a JIT (anything before Android version 2.2). Old-school game developers would immediately fall back to fixed-point math. Don't do that either, since integer divisions are slow as well. Most of the time you can get away with floats, though, and newer devices sport floating-point units (FPUs), which speed things up quite a bit once the JIT kicks in.

Try to cram frequently accessed values into local variables inside a method. Accessing local variables is faster than accessing members or calling getters.

There are of course more things we should be careful with. I'll sprinkle the rest of the book with some performance hints when the context allows it. If you follow the preceding recommendations, you should be on the safe side. Just don't let the garbage collector win!

Summary

This chapter covered everything we need to write a decent little 2D game for Android. We looked at how easy it is to set up a new game project with some defaults. We discussed the mysterious activity life cycle and how to live with it. We battled with touch (and more importantly, multitouch) events, processed key events, and checked the orientation of our device via the accelerometer. We explored how to read and write files. Outputting audio on Android turns out to be child's play, and apart from the threading issues with the SurfaceView, drawing stuff to the screen isn't that hard either. Mr. Nom can now become a reality—a terrible, hungry reality!

Chapter 5

An Android Game Development Framework

We've been through four chapters already and haven't written a single line of game code. The reason I've put you through all this boring theory and let you implement silly little test programs is simple: if you want to write games, you have to know exactly what's going on. You can't just copy and paste together code from all over the Web and hope that it will magically form the next first-person shooter hit. You should now have a firm grasp on how to design a simple game from the ground up, how to structure a nice API for 2D game development, and which Android APIs provide the functionality to implement your ideas.

To make Mr. Nom a reality, we have to do two things: implement the game framework interfaces and classes we designed in Chapter 3, and based on that, code up the game mechanics of Mr. Nom. Let's start with the game framework by merging what we designed in Chapter 3 with what we discussed in Chapter 4. Ninety percent of the code should be familiar to you already, since we did most of it in the tests in the last chapter.

Plan of Attack

In Chapter 3 we laid out a very minimal and clean design for a game framework that abstracts away all the platform specifics and let's us concentrate on what we are here for: game development. We'll implement all these interfaces and abstract classes now, in a bottom-up fashion, from easiest to hardest. The interfaces of Chapter 3 are located in the package com.badlogic.androidgames.framework. We'll put our implementation in the package com.badlogic.androidgames.framework.impl, indicating that this holds the actual implementation of the framework for Android. We'll prefix all our interface implementations with Android so that we can distinguish them from the interfaces. Let's start off with the easiest part: file I/O.

The code of this and the next chapter will be merged into a single Eclipse project. For now, just create a new Android project in Eclipse following the steps in the last chapter. How you name your default activity at this point doesn't matter for now.

The AndroidFileIO Class

The original FileIO interface was lean and mean. It only contained three methods: one to get an InputStream for an asset, another to get an InputStream for a file on the external storage, and a third that returns an OutputStream for a file on the external storage. In Chapter 4 you learned how we can open assets and files on the external storage with the Android APIs. Listing 5–1 shows you the implementation of the FileIO interface we'll use based on the knowledge from Chapter 4.

Listing 5–1. *AndroidFileIO.java; Implementing the FileIO Interface*

```java
package com.badlogic.androidgames.framework.impl;

import java.io.File;
import java.io.FileInputStream;
import java.io.FileOutputStream;
import java.io.IOException;
import java.io.InputStream;
import java.io.OutputStream;

import android.content.res.AssetManager;
import android.os.Environment;

import com.badlogic.androidgames.framework.FileIO;

public class AndroidFileIO implements FileIO {
    AssetManager assets;
    String externalStoragePath;

    public AndroidFileIO(AssetManager assets) {
        this.assets = assets;
        this.externalStoragePath = Environment.getExternalStorageDirectory()
                .getAbsolutePath() + File.separator;
    }

    @Override
    public InputStream readAsset(String fileName) throws IOException {
        return assets.open(fileName);
    }

    @Override
    public InputStream readFile(String fileName) throws IOException {
        return new FileInputStream(externalStoragePath + fileName);
    }

    @Override
    public OutputStream writeFile(String fileName) throws IOException {
        return new FileOutputStream(externalStoragePath + fileName);
    }
}
```

Everything's straightforward. We implement the `FileIO` interface, store an `AssetManager` along with the path of the external storage, and implement the three methods based on this. We pass through any `IOExceptions` that get thrown so we'll know if anything is fishy on the calling side.

Our `Game` interface implementation will hold an instance of this class and return it via `Game.getFileIO()`. This also means that our `Game` implementation will need to pass in the `AssetManager` later on for the `AndroidFileIO` instance to work.

Note that we do not check for the external storage to be available. If it's not available, or if we forgot to add the proper permission to the manifest file, we'll get an exception, so error checking is done implicitly. So we can move on to the next pieces of our framework: audio.

AndroidAudio, AndroidSound, and AndroidMusic: Crash, Bang, Boom!

We designed three interfaces in Chapter 3 for all our audio needs: Audio, Sound, and Music. Audio is responsible for creating Sound and Music instances from asset files. Sound let's us playback sound effects completely stored in RAM, and Music streams bigger music files from disk to the audio card. In Chapter 4 you learned what Android APIs we need to implement this. We start off with the implementation of AndroidAudio, as shown in Listing 5–2.

Listing 5–2. *AndroidAudio.java; Implementing the Audio Interface*

```java
package com.badlogic.androidgames.framework.impl;

import java.io.IOException;

import android.app.Activity;
import android.content.res.AssetFileDescriptor;
import android.content.res.AssetManager;
import android.media.AudioManager;
import android.media.SoundPool;

import com.badlogic.androidgames.framework.Audio;
import com.badlogic.androidgames.framework.Music;
import com.badlogic.androidgames.framework.Sound;

public class AndroidAudio implements Audio {
    AssetManager assets;
    SoundPool soundPool;
```

The AndroidAudio implementation has an AssetManager and a SoundPool instance. The AssetManager is needed so that we can load sound effects from asset files into the SoundPool on a call to AndroidAudio.newSound(). The SoundPool itself is also managed by the AndroidAudio instance.

```java
    public AndroidAudio(Activity activity) {
        activity.setVolumeControlStream(AudioManager.STREAM_MUSIC);
```

```
        this.assets = activity.getAssets();
        this.soundPool = new SoundPool(20, AudioManager.STREAM_MUSIC, 0);
    }
```

In the constructor we pass in the Activity of our game for two reasons: it allows us to set the volume control to the media stream (remember we always want to do that), and it gives us an AssetManager instance, which we happily store in the corresponding member of the class. The SoundPool is configured to be able to play back 20 sound effects in parallel—enough for our needs.

```
    @Override
    public Music newMusic(String filename) {
        try {
            AssetFileDescriptor assetDescriptor = assets.openFd(filename);
            return new AndroidMusic(assetDescriptor);
        } catch (IOException e) {
            throw new RuntimeException("Couldn't load music '" + filename + "'");
        }
    }
```

The newMusic() method creates a new AndroidMusic instance. The constructor of that class takes an AssetFileDescriptor, from which it creates a MediaPlayer internally (more on that in a bit). The AssetManager.openFd() method throws an IOException in case something goes wrong. We catch it and rethrow it as a RuntimeException. Why not hand the IOException to the caller? First, it would clutter the calling code considerably, so we would rather throw a RuntimeException, which does not have to be caught explicitly. Second, we load the music from an asset file. It will only fail if we actually forget to add the music file to the assets/ directory or if our music file contains bogus bytes. These would constitute unrecoverable errors, as we need that Music instance for our game to function properly. To avoid that, we'll employ the strategy of throwing a RuntimeException instead of checked exceptions in a few more places in our game framework.

```
    @Override
    public Sound newSound(String filename) {
        try {
            AssetFileDescriptor assetDescriptor = assets.openFd(filename);
            int soundId = soundPool.load(assetDescriptor, 0);
            return new AndroidSound(soundPool, soundId);
        } catch (IOException e) {
            throw new RuntimeException("Couldn't load sound '" + filename + "'");
        }
    }
}
```

Finally, the newSound() method loads a sound effect from an asset into the SoundPool and returns an AndroidSound instance. The constructor of that instance takes a SoundPool and the ID of the sound effect the SoundPool assigned to it. We again throw any checked exception and rethrow it as an unchecked RuntimeException.

NOTE: We do not release the SoundPool in any of the methods. The reason for this is that there will always be a single Game instance holding a single Audio instance that holds a single SoundPool instance. The SoundPool instance will thus be alive as long as the activity (and with it our game) is alive. It will be destroyed automatically as soon as the activity drops dead.

Next up is the AndroidSound class, which implements the Sound interface. Listing 5–3 shows you its implementation.

Listing 5–3. *AndroidSound.java; Implementing the Sound Interface*

```java
package com.badlogic.androidgames.framework.impl;

import android.media.SoundPool;

import com.badlogic.androidgames.framework.Sound;

public class AndroidSound implements Sound {
    int soundId;
    SoundPool soundPool;

    public AndroidSound(SoundPool soundPool, int soundId) {
        this.soundId = soundId;
        this.soundPool = soundPool;
    }

    @Override
    public void play(float volume) {
        soundPool.play(soundId, volume, volume, 0, 0, 1);
    }

    @Override
    public void dispose() {
        soundPool.unload(soundId);
    }
}
```

No surprises here. We simply store the SoundPool and the ID of the loaded sound effect for later playback and disposal via the play() and dispose() methods. It doesn't get any easier. All hail to the Android API.

Finally we have to implement the AndroidMusic class returned by AndroidAudio.newMusic(). Listing 5–4 shows the code for that class. It looks a little more complex than before. That's due to the state machine that the MediaPlayer really uses, which will throw exceptions like mad if we call methods in certain states.

Listing 5–4. *AndroidMusic.java; Implementing the Music Interface*

```java
package com.badlogic.androidgames.framework.impl;

import java.io.IOException;

import android.content.res.AssetFileDescriptor;
import android.media.MediaPlayer;
```

```
import android.media.MediaPlayer.OnCompletionListener;

import com.badlogic.androidgames.framework.Music;

public class AndroidMusic implements Music, OnCompletionListener {
    MediaPlayer mediaPlayer;
    boolean isPrepared = false; package com.badlogic.androidgames.framework.impl;

import java.io.IOException;

import android.content.res.AssetFileDescriptor;
import android.media.MediaPlayer;
import android.media.MediaPlayer.OnCompletionListener;

import com.badlogic.androidgames.framework.Music;

public class AndroidMusic implements Music, OnCompletionListener {
    MediaPlayer mediaPlayer;
    boolean isPrepared = false;
```

The AndroidMusic class stores a MediaPlayer instance along with a boolean called
isPrepared. Remember, we can only call MediaPlayer.start()/stop()/pause() when the
MediaPlayer is prepared. This member helps us keep track of the MediaPlayer's state.

The AndroidMusic class implements not only the Music interface, but also the
OnCompletionListener interface. In Chapter 3 we briefly defined this interface as a
means to get informed about when a MediaPlayer has stopped playing back a music
file. If this happens, then the MediaPlayer needs to be prepared again before we can
invoke any of the other methods on it. The method
OnCompletionListener.onCompletion() might be called in a separate thread, and since
we set the isPrepared member in this method, we have to make sure that it is safe from
concurrent modifications.

```
    public AndroidMusic(AssetFileDescriptor assetDescriptor) {
        mediaPlayer = new MediaPlayer();
        try {
            mediaPlayer.setDataSource(assetDescriptor.getFileDescriptor(),
                    assetDescriptor.getStartOffset(),
                    assetDescriptor.getLength());
            mediaPlayer.prepare();
            isPrepared = true;
            mediaPlayer.setOnCompletionListener(this);
        } catch (Exception e) {
            throw new RuntimeException("Couldn't load music");
        }
    }
```

In the constructor we create and prepare the MediaPlayer from the AssetFileDescriptor
that gets passed in, and we set the isPrepared flag, along with registering the
AndroidMusic instance as an OnCompletionListener with the MediaPlayer. If anything
goes wrong, we again throw an unchecked RuntimeException.

```
    @Override
    public void dispose() {
```

```
        if (mediaPlayer.isPlaying())
            mediaPlayer.stop();
        mediaPlayer.release();
    }
```

The dispose() method first checks if the MediaPlayer is still playing, and if so, stops it. Otherwise the call to MediaPlayer.release() would throw a runtime exception.

```
    @Override
    public boolean isLooping() {
        return mediaPlayer.isLooping();
    }

    @Override
    public boolean isPlaying() {
        return mediaPlayer.isPlaying();
    }

    @Override
    public boolean isStopped() {
        return !isPrepared;
    }
```

The methods isLooping(), isPlaying(), and isStopped() are straightforward. The first two use methods provided by the MediaPlayer; the last one uses the isPrepared flag, which indicates if the MediaPlayer is stopped—something MediaPlayer.isPlaying() does not necessarily tell us, as it returns false in case the MediaPlayer is paused but not stopped.

```
    @Override
    public void play() {
        if (mediaPlayer.isPlaying())
            return;

        try {
            synchronized (this) {
                if (!isPrepared)
                    mediaPlayer.prepare();
                mediaPlayer.start();
            }
        } catch (IllegalStateException e) {
            e.printStackTrace();
        } catch (IOException e) {
            e.printStackTrace();
        }
    }
```

The play() method is a little involved. If we are already playing, we simply return from the function. Next we have a mighty try...catch block within which we first check if the MediaPlayer is already prepared based on our flag, and prepare it if needed. If all goes well, we call the MediaPlayer.start() method, which will start the playback. All this is done in a synchronized block, as we use the isPrepared flag, which might get set on a separate thread due to our implementing the `OnCompletionListener` interface. In case something goes wrong, we again throw an unchecked `RuntimeException`.

```
@Override
    public void setLooping(boolean isLooping) {
        mediaPlayer.setLooping(isLooping);
    }

    @Override
    public void setVolume(float volume) {
        mediaPlayer.setVolume(volume, volume);
    }
```

The `setLooping()` and `setVolume()` methods can be called in any state of the `MediaPlayer`, and just delegate to the respective `MediaPlayer` methods.

```
@Override
    public void stop() {
        mediaPlayer.stop();
        synchronized (this) {
            isPrepared = false;
        }
    }
```

The `stop()` method stops the `MediaPlayer` and sets the `isPrepared` flag in a synchronized block again.

```
@Override
    public void onCompletion(MediaPlayer player) {
        synchronized (this) {
            isPrepared = false;
        }
    }
}
```

Finally there's the `OnCompletionListener.onCompletion()` method that the `AndroidMusic` class implements. All it does is set the `isPrepared` flag in a synchronized block so the other methods don't start throwing exceptions out of the blue.

Next we'll move on to our input-related classes.

AndroidInput and AccelerometerHandler

The Input interface we designed in Chapter 3 grants us access to the accelerometer, the touchscreen and the keyboard in polling and event modes via a couple of convenient methods. Putting all the code for an implementation of that interface into a single file is a bit nasty, though, so we will outsource all the input event handling into handler classes. The Input implementation will then use those handlers to pretend that it is actually performing all the work.

AccelerometerHandler: Which Side Is Up?

Let's start with the easiest of all handlers: the `AccelerometerHandler`. Listing 5–5 shows you its code.

Listing 5–5. *AccelerometerHandler.java; Performing All the Accelerometer Handling*

```java
package com.badlogic.androidgames.framework.impl;

import android.content.Context;
import android.hardware.Sensor;
import android.hardware.SensorEvent;
import android.hardware.SensorEventListener;
import android.hardware.SensorManager;

public class AccelerometerHandler implements SensorEventListener {
    float accelX;
    float accelY;
    float accelZ;

    public AccelerometerHandler(Context context) {
        SensorManager manager = (SensorManager) context
                .getSystemService(Context.SENSOR_SERVICE);
        if (manager.getSensorList(Sensor.TYPE_ACCELEROMETER).size() != 0) {
            Sensor accelerometer = manager.getSensorList(
                    Sensor.TYPE_ACCELEROMETER).get(0);
            manager.registerListener(this, accelerometer,
                    SensorManager.SENSOR_DELAY_GAME);
        }
    }

    @Override
    public void onAccuracyChanged(Sensor sensor, int accuracy) {
        // nothing to do here
    }

    @Override
    public void onSensorChanged(SensorEvent event) {
        accelX = event.values[0];
        accelY = event.values[1];
        accelZ = event.values[2];
    }

    public float getAccelX() {
        return accelX;
    }

    public float getAccelY() {
        return accelY;
    }

    public float getAccelZ() {
        return accelZ;
    }
}
```

Unsurprisingly, the class implements the SensorEventListener interface, which we used in Chapter 4. The class stores three members, holding the acceleration on each of the three accelerometer axes.

The constructor takes a Context, from which it gets a SensorManager instance to set up the event listening. The rest of the code is equivalent to what we did in the last chapter. Note that if no accelerometer is installed, the handler will happily return zero acceleration on all axes throughout its life. We thus don't need any extra error-checking or exception-throwing code.

The next two methods, onAccuracyChanged() and onSensorChanged(), should also be familiar. In the first we don't do anything, as there's nothing much to report. In the second one we fetch the accelerometer values from the provided SensorEvent and store them in the handler's members.

The final three methods simply return the current acceleration for each axis.

Note that we do not need to perform any synchronization here, even though the onSensorChanged() method might be called in a different thread. The Java memory model guarantees that writes and reads to and from primitive types such as boolean, int, or byte are atomic. In this case it's OK to rely on this fact, as we don't do anything more complex than assigning a new value. We'd need to have proper synchronization if this were not the case (e.g., if we did something with the member variables in the onSensorChanged() method.

The Pool Class: Because Reuse is Good for You!

What's the worst thing that can happen to us as Android developers? World-stopping garbage collection! If you look at the Input interface definition in Chapter 3, you'll find the methods getTouchEvents() and getKeyEvents(). These return lists of TouchEvents and KeyEvents. In our keyboard and touch event handlers, we'll constantly create instances of these two classes and store them in lists internal to the handlers. The Android input system fires a lot of those events when a key is pressed or a finger is touching the screen, so we'd constantly create new instances that will get collected by the garbage collector in short intervals. In order to avoid this, we will implement a concept known as *instance pooling*. Instead of creating new instances of a class frequently, we'll simply reuse previously created instances. The Pool class is a convenient way to implement that behavior. Let's have a look at its code in Listing 5–6.

Listing 5–6. *Pool.java; Playing Well with the Garbage Collector*

```
package com.badlogic.androidgames.framework;

import java.util.ArrayList;
import java.util.List;

public class Pool<T> {
```

Here come generics: the first thing to recognize is that this class is a generically typed class, much like collection classes, such as ArrayList or HashMap. Generics allow us to store any type of object in our Pool without having to cast like mad. So what does the Pool class do?

```
public interface PoolObjectFactory<T> {
    public T createObject();
}
```

The first thing that's defined is an interface called PoolObjectFactory, which is again generic. It has a single method, createObject(), which will return a shiny new object that has the generic type of the Pool/PoolObjectFactory instance.

```
private final List<T> freeObjects;
private final PoolObjectFactory<T> factory;
private final int maxSize;
```

The Pool class has three members: an ArrayList to store pooled objects, a PoolObjectFactory that is used to generate new instances of the type the class holds, and a member that stores the maximum number of objects the Pool can hold. The last bit is needed so that our Pool does not grow indefinitely; otherwise we might run into an out-of-memory exception.

```
public Pool(PoolObjectFactory<T> factory, int maxSize) {
    this.factory = factory;
    this.maxSize = maxSize;
    this.freeObjects = new ArrayList<T>(maxSize);
}
```

The constructor of the Pool class takes a PoolObjectFactory and the maximum number of objects it should store. We store both parameters in the respective members and instantiate a new ArrayList with the capacity set to the maximum number of objects.

```
public T newObject() {
    T object = null;

    if (freeObjects.size() == 0)
        object = factory.createObject();
    else
        object = freeObjects.remove(freeObjects.size() - 1);

    return object;
}
```

The newObject() method is responsible for either handing us a brand-new instance of the type that the Pool holds via the PoolObjectFactory.newObject() method, or returning a pooled instance in case there's one in the freeObjects ArrayList. If we use this method, we'll get recycled objects as long as the Pool has some stored in the freeObjects list. Otherwise the method will create a new one via the factory.

```
public void free(T object) {
    if (freeObjects.size() < maxSize)
        freeObjects.add(object);
}
}
```

The free() method lets us reinsert objects we no longer use. All it does is insert the object into the freeObjects list if it is not filled to capacity yet. If the list is full, the object is not added, and is likely to be consumed by the garbage collector the next time it executes.

So how can we use that class? Let's look at some pseudocode usage of the Pool class in conjunction with touch events:

```
PoolObjectFactory<TouchEvent> factory = new PoolObjectFactory<TouchEvent>() {
    @Override
    public TouchEvent createObject() {
        return new TouchEvent();
    }
};
Pool<TouchEvent> touchEventPool = new Pool<TouchEvent>(factory, 50);
TouchEvent touchEvent = touchEventPool.newObject();
… do something here …
touchEventPool.free(touchEvent);
```

We first define a PoolObjectFactory that creates TouchEvent instances. Next we instantiate the Pool, telling it to use our factory and that it should maximally store 50 TouchEvents. When we want a new TouchEvent from the Pool, we call the Pool's newObject() method. Initially the Pool is empty, so it will ask the factory to create a brand-new TouchEvent instance. When we no longer need the TouchEvent, we can reinsert it into the Pool by calling the Pool's free() method. The next time we call the newObject() method, we will get the same TouchEvent instance again, recycling it so the garbage collector doesn't get mad at us. That class will come in handy in a couple of places. Just note that you have to take care if you reuse objects: it's easy to not fully reinitialize them when they're fetched from the Pool.

KeyboardHandler: Up, Up, Down, Down, Left, Right . . .

The KeyboardHandler has to fulfill a couple of tasks. First it must hook up with the View from which keyboard events are to be received. Next it must store the current state of each key for polling. It must also keep a list of KeyEvent instances, which we designed in Chapter 3 for event-based input handling. Finally it must properly synchronize all this, as it will receive events on the UI thread while being polled from our main game loop, which is executed on a different thread. Quite a lot of work. As a little refresher, let me show you the KeyEvent class again, which we defined in Chapter 3 as part of the Input interface:

```
public static class KeyEvent {
    public static final int KEY_DOWN = 0;
    public static final int KEY_UP = 1;

    public int type;
    public int keyCode;
    public char keyChar;
}
```

It simply defines two constants encoding the key event type along with three members, holding the type, key code, and Unicode character of the event. With this we can implement our handler.

Listing 5–7 shows the implementation of the handler with the Android APIs discussed earlier and our new Pool class.

Listing 5–7. *KeyboardHandler.java: Handling Keys Since 2010*

```java
package com.badlogic.androidgames.framework.impl;

import java.util.ArrayList;
import java.util.List;

import android.view.View;
import android.view.View.OnKeyListener;

import com.badlogic.androidgames.framework.Input.KeyEvent;
import com.badlogic.androidgames.framework.Pool;
import com.badlogic.androidgames.framework.Pool.PoolObjectFactory;

public class KeyboardHandler implements OnKeyListener {
    boolean[] pressedKeys = new boolean[128];
    Pool<KeyEvent> keyEventPool;
    List<KeyEvent> keyEventsBuffer = new ArrayList<KeyEvent>();
    List<KeyEvent> keyEvents = new ArrayList<KeyEvent>();
```

The KeyboardHandler class implements the OnKeyListener interface so that it can receive key events from a View. Next up are the members.

The first member is an array holding 128 booleans. We'll store the current state (pressed or not) of each key in this array. It is indexed by the key code of a key. Luckily for us, the android.view.KeyEvent.KEYCODE_XXX constants (which encode the key codes) are all in the range between 0 and 127, so we can store them in this garbage collector–friendly form. Note that by an unlucky accident our KeyEvent class shares its name with the Android KeyEvent class, instances of which get passed to our OnKeyEventListener.onKeyEvent() method. This slight confusion is limited to this handler code only. As there's hardly a better name for a key event than KeyEvent, we chose to live with this short-lived confusion.

The next member is a Pool that holds instances of our KeyEvent class. We don't want to make the garbage collector angry, so we recycle all the KeyEvent objects we create.

The third member stores the KeyEvents that have not yet been consumed by our game. Each time we get a new key event on the UI thread we'll add it to this list.

The last member stores the KeyEvents we'll return upon a call to KeyboardHandler.getKeyEvents(). We'll see why we have to double-buffer the key events in a minute.

```java
    public KeyboardHandler(View view) {
        PoolObjectFactory<KeyEvent> factory = new PoolObjectFactory<KeyEvent>() {
            @Override
            public KeyEvent createObject() {
```

```
            return new KeyEvent();
        }
    };
    keyEventPool = new Pool<KeyEvent>(factory, 100);
    view.setOnKeyListener(this);
    view.setFocusableInTouchMode(true);
    view.requestFocus();
}
```

The constructor has a single parameter consisting of the View we want to receive key events from. We create the Pool instance with a proper PoolObjectFactory, register the handler as an OnKeyListener with the View, and finally make sure that the View will receive key events by making it the focused View.

```
@Override
public boolean onKey(View v, int keyCode, android.view.KeyEvent event) {
    if (event.getAction() == android.view.KeyEvent.ACTION_MULTIPLE)
        return false;

    synchronized (this) {
        KeyEvent keyEvent = keyEventPool.newObject();
        keyEvent.keyCode = keyCode;
        keyEvent.keyChar = (char) event.getUnicodeChar();
        if (event.getAction() == android.view.KeyEvent.ACTION_DOWN) {
            keyEvent.type = KeyEvent.KEY_DOWN;
            if(keyCode > 0 && keyCode < 127)
                pressedKeys[keyCode] = true;
        }
        if (event.getAction() == android.view.KeyEvent.ACTION_UP) {
            keyEvent.type = KeyEvent.KEY_UP;
            if(keyCode > 0 && keyCode < 127)
                pressedKeys[keyCode] = false;
        }
        keyEventsBuffer.add(keyEvent);
    }
    return false;
}
```

Next up is our implementation of the OnKeyListener.onKey() interface method, which gets called each time the View receives a new key event. We start by ignoring any (Android) key events that encode a KeyEvent.ACTION_MULTIPLE event. These are not relevant in our context. We follow that up with a tasty synchronized block. Remember that the events are received on the UI thread and read on the main loop thread, so we have to make sure none of our members are accessed in parallel.

Within the synchronized block we first fetch a KeyEvent instance (of our KeyEvent implementation) from the Pool. This will either get us a recycled instance or a brand-new one, depending on the state of the Pool. Next we set the KeyEvent's keyCode and keyChar members based on the contents of the Android KeyEvent that got passed to the method. We then decode the type of the Android KeyEvent and set the type of our KeyEvent as well as the element in the pressedKey array accordingly. Finally we add our KeyEvent to the keyEventBuffer list we defined earlier.

```
    public boolean isKeyPressed(int keyCode) {
        if (keyCode < 0 || keyCode > 127)
            return false;
        return pressedKeys[keyCode];
    }
```

Next we have the isKeyPressed() method, which basically implements the semantics of Input.isKeyPressed(). We pass in an integer specifying the key code (one of the Android KeyEvent.KEYCODE_XXX constants) and return whether that key is pressed or not. We do so by looking up the state of the key in the pressedKey array after some range checking. Remember that we set the elements of this array in the previous method, which gets called on the UI thread. As we are again working with primitive types, there's no need for synchronization.

```
    public List<KeyEvent> getKeyEvents() {
        synchronized (this) {
            int len = keyEvents.size();
            for (int i = 0; i < len; i++)
                keyEventPool.free(keyEvents.get(i));
            keyEvents.clear();
            keyEvents.addAll(keyEventsBuffer);
            keyEventsBuffer.clear();
            return keyEvents;
        }
    }
}
```

The last method of our handler is called getKeyEvents(), and implements the semantics of the Input.getKeyEvents() method. We start off with a juicy synchronized block again, remembering that this method will be called from a different thread.

Next we do something very mysterious. We loop through the keyEvents array and insert all the KeyEvents stored in it into our Pool. Remember that we fetch instances from the Pool in the onKey() method on the UI thread. Here we reinsert them into the Pool. But isn't the keyEvents list empty? Yes, but only the first time we invoke that method. To understand why that is, you have to grasp the rest of the method first.

After our mysterious Pool insertion loop, we clear the keyEvents list and fill it with the events in our keyEventsBuffer list. Finally we clear the keyEventsBuffer list and return the newly filled keyEvents list to the caller. What is happening here?

Let me illustrate it by giving you a simple example. We'll examine what happens to the keyEvents and keyEventsBuffer lists, as well as our Pool each time a new event arrives on the UI thread or the game is fetching the events in the main thread:

```
UI thread: onKey() ->
        keyEvents = { }, keyEventsBuffer = {KeyEvent1}, pool = { }
Main thread: getKeyEvents() ->
        keyEvents = {KeyEvent1}, keyEventsBuffer = { }, pool { }
UI thread: onKey() ->
        keyEvents = {KeyEvent1}, keyEventsBuffer = {KeyEvent2}, pool { }
Main thread: getKeyEvents() ->
        keyEvents = {KeyEvent2}, keyEventsBuffer = { }, pool = {KeyEvent1}
UI thread: onKey() ->
```

```
keyEvents = {KeyEvent2}, keyEventsBuffer = {KeyEvent1}, pool = { }
```

1. First we get a new event in the UI thread. There's nothing in the Pool yet, so a new KeyEvent instance (KeyEvent1) is created and inserted into the keyEventsBuffer list.

2. Next we call getKeyEvents() on the main thread. It takes KeyEvent1 from the keyEventsBuffer list and puts it into the keyEvents list it returns to the caller.

3. We get another event on the UI thread. We still have nothing in the Pool, so a new KeyEvent instance (KeyEvent2) is created and inserted into the keyEventsBuffer list.

4. The main thread calls getKeyEvents() again. Now something interesting happens. Upon entry into the method, the keyEvents list still holds KeyEvent1. The mysterious insertion loop will place that event into our Pool. It then clears the keyEvents list and inserts any KeyEvent into the keyEventsBuffer, in this case KeyEvent2. We just recycled a key event.

5. Finally another key event arrives on the UI thread. This time we have a free KeyEvent in our Pool, which we'll happily reuse. Look mom, no garbage collection!

This mechanism comes with one caveat, though: we have to call KeyboardHandler.getKeyEvents() frequently or else the keyEvents list will fill up quickly, and no objects will be returned to the Pool. As long as we remember this, all is well.

Touch Handlers

And now fragmentation hits us. In the last chapter we talked a little about the fact that multitouch is supported on Android versions greater than 1.6 only. All the nice constants we used in our multitouch code (e.g., MotionEvent.ACTION_POINTER_ID_MASK) are not available to us on Android 1.5 or 1.6. While we can use them in our code just fine if we set the build target of our project to an Android version that has this API, the application will crash on any device running Android 1.5 or 1.6. We want our games to run on all currently available Android versions, so how do we solve this problem?

We employ a simple trick. We write two handlers, one using the single-touch API of Android 1.5 and another using the multitouch API of Android 2.0 and above. As long as we don't execute the code of the multitouch handler on a device with a lower Android version than 2.0, we are safe. The code won't get loaded by the VM, and it won't throw exceptions like crazy. All we need to do is to find out which Android version the device is running and instantiate the proper handler. You'll see how that works when we discuss the AndroidInput class. For now let's concentrate on the two handlers.

The TouchHandler Interface

In order to be able to use our two handler classes interchangeably, we need to define a common interface. Listing 5–8 shows this interface, called TouchHandler.

Listing 5–8. *TouchHandler.java, to Be Implemented for Android 1.5 and 1.6.*

```java
package com.badlogic.androidgames.framework.impl;

import java.util.List;

import android.view.View.OnTouchListener;

import com.badlogic.androidgames.framework.Input.TouchEvent;

public interface TouchHandler extends OnTouchListener {
    public boolean isTouchDown(int pointer);

    public int getTouchX(int pointer);

    public int getTouchY(int pointer);

    public List<TouchEvent> getTouchEvents();
}
```

All TouchHandlers must also implement the OnTouchListener interface, which we use to register the handler with a View. The methods of the interface correspond to the respective methods in the Input interface defined in Chapter 3. The first three are for polling the state of a specific pointer, and the last one is for getting TouchEvents so we can do event-based input handling. Note that the polling methods take a pointer ID.

The SingleTouchHandler Class

In the case of our single-touch handler, we'll ignore any IDs other than zero. As a refresher, let's recall the TouchEvent class defined in Chapter 3 as part of the Input interface:

```java
public static class TouchEvent {
    public static final int TOUCH_DOWN = 0;
    public static final int TOUCH_UP = 1;
    public static final int TOUCH_DRAGGED = 2;

    public int type;
    public int x, y;
    public int pointer;
}
```

Like the KeyEvent class, it defines a couple of constants encoding the touch event's type, along with the x- and y-coordinates in the coordinate system of the View and the pointer ID.

Listing 5–9 shows the implementation of the TouchHandler interface for Android 1.5 and 1.6.

Listing 5–9. *SingleTouchHandler.java; Good with Single Touch, Not So Good with Multitouch*

```java
package com.badlogic.androidgames.framework.impl;

import java.util.ArrayList;
import java.util.List;

import android.view.MotionEvent;
import android.view.View;

import com.badlogic.androidgames.framework.Pool;
import com.badlogic.androidgames.framework.Input.TouchEvent;
import com.badlogic.androidgames.framework.Pool.PoolObjectFactory;

public class SingleTouchHandler implements TouchHandler {
    boolean isTouched;
    int touchX;
    int touchY;
    Pool<TouchEvent> touchEventPool;
    List<TouchEvent> touchEvents = new ArrayList<TouchEvent>();
    List<TouchEvent> touchEventsBuffer = new ArrayList<TouchEvent>();
    float scaleX;
    float scaleY;
```

We start off by letting the class implement the TouchHandler interface, which also means that we have to implement the OnTouchListener interface. Next are a couple of members that should look familiar. We have three members storing the current state of the touchscreen for one finger, followed by a Pool and two lists holding TouchEvents. This is exactly the same thing we had in the KeyboardHandler. We also have two members, scaleX and scaleY. We'll talk about those in a minute. We'll use these to cope with different screen resolutions.

> **NOTE:** Of course, we could have made that more elegant by letting the KeyboardHandler and SingleTouchHandler derive from a base class that handles all this pooling and synchronization stuff. It would have complicated the explanation even more, though, so instead we'll just write a few more lines of code.

```java
public SingleTouchHandler(View view, float scaleX, float scaleY) {
        PoolObjectFactory<TouchEvent> factory = new PoolObjectFactory<TouchEvent>() {
            @Override
            public TouchEvent createObject() {
                return new TouchEvent();
            }
        };
        touchEventPool = new Pool<TouchEvent>(factory, 100);
        view.setOnTouchListener(this);

        this.scaleX = scaleX;
        this.scaleY = scaleY;
    }
```

In the constructor we register the handler as an OnTouchListener and set up the Pool we use to recycle TouchEvents. We also store the scaleX and scaleY parameters that are passed to the constructor (and ignore them for now).

```java
@Override
    public boolean onTouch(View v, MotionEvent event) {
        synchronized(this) {
            TouchEvent touchEvent = touchEventPool.newObject();
            switch (event.getAction()) {
            case MotionEvent.ACTION_DOWN:
                touchEvent.type = TouchEvent.TOUCH_DOWN;
                isTouched = true;
                break;
            case MotionEvent.ACTION_MOVE:
                touchEvent.type = TouchEvent.TOUCH_DRAGGED;
                isTouched = true;
                break;
            case MotionEvent.ACTION_CANCEL:
            case MotionEvent.ACTION_UP:
                touchEvent.type = TouchEvent.TOUCH_UP;
                isTouched = false;
                break;
            }

            touchEvent.x = touchX = (int)(event.getX() * scaleX);
            touchEvent.y = touchY = (int)(event.getY() * scaleY);
            touchEventsBuffer.add(touchEvent);

            return true;
        }
    }
}
```

The onTouch() method does the same thing as the onKey() method of our KeyboardHandler, the only difference being that we now handle TouchEvents, not KeyEvents. All the synchronization, pooling, and MotionEvent handling are already known to us. The only interesting thing is that we actually multiply the reported x- and y-coordinates of a touch event by scaleX and scaleY. Remember this, as we'll take a look at it again later on.

```java
@Override
    public boolean isTouchDown(int pointer) {
        synchronized(this) {
            if(pointer == 0)
                return isTouched;
            else
                return false;
        }
    }

    @Override
    public int getTouchX(int pointer) {
        synchronized(this) {
            return touchX;
        }
    }
```

```
        @Override
        public int getTouchY(int pointer) {
            synchronized(this) {
                return touchY;
            }
        }
    }
```

The methods isTouchDown(), getTouchX(), and getTouchY() allow us to poll the touchscreen state based on the members that we set in the onTouch() method. The only noticeable thing about them is that they'll only return useful data for a pointer ID with a value zero, as we only support single-touch screens with this class.

```
    @Override
        public List<TouchEvent> getTouchEvents() {
            synchronized(this) {
                int len = touchEvents.size();
                for( int i = 0; i < len; i++ )
                    touchEventPool.free(touchEvents.get(i));
                touchEvents.clear();
                touchEvents.addAll(touchEventsBuffer);
                touchEventsBuffer.clear();
                return touchEvents;
            }
        }
    }
```

The final method, SingleTouchHandler.getTouchEvents(), should be familiar to you, and works similarly to the KeyboardHandler.getKeyEvents() methods. Remember that we need to call this method frequently so that the touchEvents list doesn't get filled up.

The MultiTouchHandler

For multitouch handling, we have a class called MultiTouchHandler, as shown in Listing 5–10.

Listing 5–10. *MultiTouchHandler.java (More of the Same)*

```
package com.badlogic.androidgames.framework.impl;

import java.util.ArrayList;
import java.util.List;

import android.view.MotionEvent;
import android.view.View;

import com.badlogic.androidgames.framework.Input.TouchEvent;
import com.badlogic.androidgames.framework.Pool;
import com.badlogic.androidgames.framework.Pool.PoolObjectFactory;

public class MultiTouchHandler implements TouchHandler {
    boolean[] isTouched = new boolean[20];
    int[] touchX = new int[20];
    int[] touchY = new int[20];
    Pool<TouchEvent> touchEventPool;
```

```
List<TouchEvent> touchEvents = new ArrayList<TouchEvent>();
List<TouchEvent> touchEventsBuffer = new ArrayList<TouchEvent>();
float scaleX;
float scaleY;
```

We again let the class implement the TouchHandler interface and have a couple of members to store the current state and events. Instead of storing the state for a single pointer, we simply store the state of 20 pointers. We also have those mysterious scaleX and scaleY members again.

```
public MultiTouchHandler(View view, float scaleX, float scaleY) {
    PoolObjectFactory<TouchEvent> factory = new PoolObjectFactory<TouchEvent>() {
        @Override
        public TouchEvent createObject() {
            return new TouchEvent();
        }
    };
    touchEventPool = new Pool<TouchEvent>(factory, 100);
    view.setOnTouchListener(this);

    this.scaleX = scaleX;
    this.scaleY = scaleY;
}
```

The constructor is exactly the same as the constructor of the SingleTouchHandler: we create a Pool for TouchEvent instances register the handler as an OnTouchListener, and store the scaling values.

```
@Override
    public boolean onTouch(View v, MotionEvent event) {
        synchronized (this) {
            int action = event.getAction() & MotionEvent.ACTION_MASK;
            int pointerIndex = (event.getAction() & MotionEvent.ACTION_POINTER_ID_MASK)
>> MotionEvent.ACTION_POINTER_ID_SHIFT;
            int pointerId = event.getPointerId(pointerIndex);
            TouchEvent touchEvent;

            switch (action) {
            case MotionEvent.ACTION_DOWN:
            case MotionEvent.ACTION_POINTER_DOWN:
                touchEvent = touchEventPool.newObject();
                touchEvent.type = TouchEvent.TOUCH_DOWN;
                touchEvent.pointer = pointerId;
                touchEvent.x = touchX[pointerId] = (int) (event
                        .getX(pointerIndex) * scaleX);
                touchEvent.y = touchY[pointerId] = (int) (event
                        .getY(pointerIndex) * scaleY);
                isTouched[pointerId] = true;
                touchEventsBuffer.add(touchEvent);
                break;

            case MotionEvent.ACTION_UP:
            case MotionEvent.ACTION_POINTER_UP:
            case MotionEvent.ACTION_CANCEL:
                touchEvent = touchEventPool.newObject();
```

```
                    touchEvent.type = TouchEvent.TOUCH_UP;
                    touchEvent.pointer = pointerId;
                    touchEvent.x = touchX[pointerId] = (int) (event
                            .getX(pointerIndex) * scaleX);
                    touchEvent.y = touchY[pointerId] = (int) (event
                            .getY(pointerIndex) * scaleY);
                    isTouched[pointerId] = false;
                    touchEventsBuffer.add(touchEvent);
                    break;

            case MotionEvent.ACTION_MOVE:
                int pointerCount = event.getPointerCount();
                for (int i = 0; i < pointerCount; i++) {
                    pointerIndex = i;
                    pointerId = event.getPointerId(pointerIndex);

                    touchEvent = touchEventPool.newObject();
                    touchEvent.type = TouchEvent.TOUCH_DRAGGED;
                    touchEvent.pointer = pointerId;
                    touchEvent.x = touchX[pointerId] = (int) (event
                            .getX(pointerIndex) * scaleX);
                    touchEvent.y = touchY[pointerId] = (int) (event
                            .getY(pointerIndex) * scaleY);
                    touchEventsBuffer.add(touchEvent);
                }
                break;
            }

            return true;
        }
    }
```

The onTouch() method looks as intimidating as in our test example in the last chapter.
All we do is marry that test code with our event pooling and synchronization here (things
we've already talked about in detail). The only real difference to the
SingleTouchHandler.onTouch() method is that we handle multiple pointers and set the
TouchEvent.pointer member accordingly (instead of just to zero).

```
@Override
    public boolean isTouchDown(int pointer) {
        synchronized (this) {
            if (pointer < 0 || pointer >= 20)
                return false;
            else
                return isTouched[pointer];
        }
    }

    @Override
    public int getTouchX(int pointer) {
        synchronized (this) {
            if (pointer < 0 || pointer >= 20)
                return 0;
            else
                return touchX[pointer];
```

```
        }
    }

    @Override
    public int getTouchY(int pointer) {
        synchronized (this) {
            if (pointer < 0 || pointer >= 20)
                return 0;
            else
                return touchY[pointer];
        }
    }
```

The polling methods isTouchDown(), getTouchX(), and getTouchY() should look familiar as well. We perform some error checking and then fetch the corresponding pointer state from one of the member arrays that we fill in the onTouch() method.

```
@Override
    public List<TouchEvent> getTouchEvents() {
        synchronized (this) {
            int len = touchEvents.size();
            for (int i = 0; i < len; i++)
                touchEventPool.free(touchEvents.get(i));
            touchEvents.clear();
            touchEvents.addAll(touchEventsBuffer);
            touchEventsBuffer.clear();
            return touchEvents;
        }
    }
}
```

The final method, getTouchEvents(), is again exactly the same as the corresponding method of SingleTouchHandler.getTouchEvents().

Equipped with all those handlers, we can now implement the Input interface.

AndroidInput: The Great Coordinator

The Input implementation of our game framework ties together all the handlers we just developed. Any method calls will be delegated to the corresponding handler. The only interesting part of this implementation is where we choose which TouchHandler implementation we use based on the Android version the device is running. Listing 5–11 shows you the implementation, called AndroidInput.

Listing 5–11. *AndroidInput.java; Handling the Handlers with Style*

```
package com.badlogic.androidgames.framework.impl;

import java.util.List;

import android.content.Context;
import android.os.Build.VERSION;
import android.view.View;

import com.badlogic.androidgames.framework.Input;
```

```
public class AndroidInput implements Input {
    AccelerometerHandler accelHandler;
    KeyboardHandler keyHandler;
    TouchHandler touchHandler;
```

We start off by letting the class implement the Input interface we defined in Chapter 3.
Next we find three members: an AccelerometerHandler, a KeyboardHandler, and a
TouchHandler.

```
public AndroidInput(Context context, View view, float scaleX, float scaleY) {
        accelHandler = new AccelerometerHandler(context);
        keyHandler = new KeyboardHandler(view);
        if(Integer.parseInt(VERSION.SDK) < 5)
            touchHandler = new SingleTouchHandler(view, scaleX, scaleY);
        else
            touchHandler = new MultiTouchHandler(view, scaleX, scaleY);
    }
```

These members get initialized in the constructor, which takes a Context, a View, and
those scaleX and scaleY parameters that we can happily ignore again. The
AccelerometerHandler gets instantiated via the Context parameter, and the
KeyboardHandler needs the View that gets passed in.

To decide which TouchHandler to use, we simply check the Android version the
application runs on. This can be done via the VERSION.SDK string, a constant provided by
the Android API. Why it is a string is unclear, as it directly encodes the SDK version
numbers we use in our manifest file. We therefore need to make it an integer to do some
comparisons. The first Android version to support the multitouch API was version 2.0,
which corresponds to SDK version 5. If the current device runs an Android version
below that, we instantiate the SingleTouchHandler; otherwise we use the
MultiTouchHandler. And that's all the fragmentation we have to care about at an API
level. When we start doing OpenGL rendering, we'll hit a few more of these
fragmentation issues—but don't worry, they can be as easily resolved as the touch API
problems.

```
@Override
    public boolean isKeyPressed(int keyCode) {
        return keyHandler.isKeyPressed(keyCode);
    }

    @Override
    public boolean isTouchDown(int pointer) {
        return touchHandler.isTouchDown(pointer);
    }

    @Override
    public int getTouchX(int pointer) {
        return touchHandler.getTouchX(pointer);
    }

    @Override
    public int getTouchY(int pointer) {
        return touchHandler.getTouchY(pointer);
```

```
    }

    @Override
    public float getAccelX() {
        return accelHandler.getAccelX();
    }

    @Override
    public float getAccelY() {
        return accelHandler.getAccelY();
    }

    @Override
    public float getAccelZ() {
        return accelHandler.getAccelZ();
    }

    @Override
    public List<TouchEvent> getTouchEvents() {
        return touchHandler.getTouchEvents();
    }

    @Override
    public List<KeyEvent> getKeyEvents() {
        return keyHandler.getKeyEvents();
    }
}
```

The rest of this class is more than self-explanatory. Each method call is delegated to the appropriate handler, which does the actual work. And with this, we have finished the input API of our little game framework. Next we'll move on to graphics.

AndroidGraphics and AndroidPixmap: Double Rainbow

It's time to get back to our most beloved topic: graphics programming. In Chapter 3 we defined two interfaces, Graphics and Pixmap; we are now going to implement them based on what you learned in Chapter 4. But there's one thing we have postponed until now: how to handle different screen sizes and resolutions.

Handling Different Screen Sizes and Resolutions

Android has supported different screen resolutions since version 1.6; it can handle resolutions ranging from 240! 320 pixels to a much beefier 480! 854 pixels on some new devices (in portrait mode; for landscape mode, just swap the values). In the last chapter we already saw the effect of these different screen resolutions and physical screen sizes: drawing with absolute coordinates and sizes given in pixels will produce unexpected results. Figure 5–1 shows you once more what happens when we render a 100! 100-pixel rectangle with the upper-left corner at (219,379) on 480! 800 and 320! 480 screens.

Figure 5–1. *A 100×100-pixel rectangle drawn at (219,379) on a 480×800 screen (left) and a 320×480 screen (right)*

This difference is bad for two reasons. First, we can't just draw our game assuming a fixed resolution. The second reason is subtler ,however. In Figure 5–1, I silently assumed that both screens have the same density (i.e., that each pixel has the same physical size on both devices), but this is hardly the case in reality.

Density

Density is usually specified in pixels per inch or pixels per centimeter (you'll sometimes also hear dots per inch, which is not technically exact). The Nexus One has a 480! 800-pixel screen with a physical size of 8! 4.8 centimeters. The HTC Hero has a 320! 480-pixel screen with a physical size of 6.5! 4.5 centimeters. That's 100 pixels per centimeter on both axes on the Nexus One, and roughly 71 pixels per centimeter on both axes on the Hero. We can calculate the pixels per centimeter easily like this:

```
pixels per centimeter (on x-axis) = width in pixels / width in centimeters
```

or this:

```
pixels per centimeter (on y-axis) = height in pixels / height in centimeters
```

Usually we only need to calculate this on a single axis, as the physical pixels are square (well, they're actually three pixels, but we'll just ignore that here).

How big would our 100! 100-pixel rectangle be in centimeters? On the Nexus One we'd have a 1! 1-centimeter rectangle, while on the Hero we'd have a 1.4! 1.4-centimeter rectangle. That's something we would need to account for if we had, for example, things like buttons that should be big enough for the average thumb on all screen sizes. However, while this example makes it look like this issue could present a huge problem, it usually doesn't. We just need to make sure that our buttons have a good size on high-density screens (e.g., the Nexus One). They will automatically be big enough on lower-density screens.

Aspect Ratio

There's also another problem we have to cope with, though: aspect ratio. The aspect ratio of a screen is the ratio between the width and height, either in pixels or centimeters. We can calculate that like this:

```
pixel aspect ratio = width in pixels / height in pixels
```

or this:

```
physical aspect ratio = width in centimeters / height in centimeters
```

When we use *width* and *height* here, we usually mean the width and height in landscape mode. The Nexus One has a pixel and physical aspect ratio of ~1.66. The Hero has a pixel and physical aspect ratio of 1.5. What does this mean? On the Nexus One we have more pixels available on the x-axis in landscape mode relative to the height than we have on the Hero. Figure 5–2 illustrates what this means with screenshots from Replica Island on both devices.

> **NOTE:** In this book we'll use the metric system. I know that it might be a bit hard to get comfortable with if you are used to inches and pounds. However, as we will also do a little physics later on, which is usually defined in the metric system, it's best get used to it now. Just remember that 1 inch is roughly 2.54 centimeters.

Figure 5–2. *Replica Island on the Nexus One (top) and the HTC Hero (bottom)*

The Nexus One displays a tiny bit more of the world on the x-axis. Everything stays the same on the y-axis though. Hmm, what did the creator of Replica Island do here?

Coping with Different Aspect Ratios

Replica Island performs a cheap but very useful magic trick in order to deal with the aspect ratio problem. The game was originally designed for everything to fit on a 480! 320-pixel screen, including all the sprites (e.g., the robot and the doctor), the tiles of the world, and the UI elements (e.g., the buttons at the bottom left and the status info at the top of the screen). When the game is rendered on a Hero, each pixel in the sprite bitmaps maps to exactly one pixel on the screen. On a Nexus One, everything is scaled up while rendering, so 1 pixel of a sprite actually takes up 1.5 pixels on the screen. In other words, a 32! 32-pixel sprite will be 48! 48 pixels big on the screen. This scaling factor can be easily calculated by

```
scaling factor (on x-axis) = screen width in pixels / target width in pixels
```

and

```
scaling factor (on y-axis) = screen height in pixels / target height in pixels
```

The target width and height equal the screen resolution that the graphical assets were designed for; in Replica Island, that's 480! 320 pixels. For the Nexus One, this means that we have a scaling factor of 1.66 on the x-axis and a scaling factor of 1.5 on the y-axis. But why are the scaling factors on the two axes different?

This is due to the two screen resolutions having different aspect ratios. If we simply stretch a 480! 320-pixel image to an 800! 480-pixel image, the original image will be stretched on the x-axis. For most games, this won't make too big of an impact, so we can simply draw our graphical assets for a specific target resolution and stretch them to the actual screen resolution on the fly while rendering (remember the Bitmap.drawBitmap() method).

For some games, however, you might want to get a little fancier. Figure 5–3 shows Replica Island simply scaled up from 480! 320 to 800! 480 pixels, and overlaid with a faint image of how it actually looks.

Figure 5–3. *Replica Island stretched from 480×320 to 800×480 pixels, overlaid with a faint image of how it is actually rendered on a 800×480-pixel display*

Replica Island does something very intelligent here: it performs normal stretching on the y-axis with the scaling factor we just calculated (1.5). But instead of using the x-axis scaling factor (1.66), which would make the image look squished, it uses the y-axis scaling factor. This neat little trick allows all objects on the screen keep their aspect ratio. A 32! 32-pixel sprite becomes 48! 48 pixels instead of 53! 48 pixels. However, this also means that our coordinate system is no longer bounded between (0,0) and (479,319). Instead it now goes from (0,0) to (533,319). And this is why we see more of the world of Replica Island on a Nexus One than on an HTC Hero.

Note, however, that using this fancy method might not be appropriate for some games. For example, having the world size depend on the screen aspect ratio could give an unfair advantage to players with wider screens. This would be the case in a game like Starcraft 2. Also, if you want the entire game world to fit onto a single screen (like in Mr. Nom), it would be better to use the simpler, stretching method. With the fancier version, we'd have blank space left over on wider screens.

A Simpler Solution

Replica Island has one advantage: it does all this stretching and scaling via OpenGL ES, which is hardware accelerated. So far we've only discussed how to draw to a `Bitmap` and a `View` via the `Canvas` class, which doesn't involve hardware acceleration on the GPU, but slow number-crunching on the CPU.

We'll therefore perform a simple trick: we'll create a framebuffer in the form of a `Bitmap` instance that has our target resolution. This way we don't have to worry about the actual screen resolution when designing our graphical assets or when rendering them via code. We just pretend that the screen resolution is the same on all devices. All our draw calls will target this "virtual" framebuffer `Bitmap` via a `Canvas` instance. When we're done rendering a frame of our game, we'll simply draw this framebuffer `Bitmap` to our `SurfaceView` via a call to the `Canvas.drawBitmap()` method, which allows us to draw a `Bitmap` stretched.

If we want to use the same technique as Replica Island, we just need to adjust the size of our framebuffer on the bigger axis (i.e., on the x-axis in landscape mode, and on the y-axis in portrait mode). We also have to make sure that we fill the extra pixels we get so there's no blank space.

The Implementation

So let's summarize all this by forming a simple plan of attack:

- We design all our graphic assets for a fixed target resolution (320! 480 in Mr. Nom's case).

- We create a `Bitmap` the same size as our target resolution and direct all our drawing calls to it, effectively working in a fixed-coordinate system.

- When we are done drawing a frame of our game, we draw our framebuffer `Bitmap` stretched to the `SurfaceView`. On devices with a lower screen resolution the image will be scaled down, and on devices with a higher resolution it will be scaled up.

- We have to make sure that all the UI elements the user interacts with are big enough at all screen densities when we do our scaling trick. This is something we can do in the graphic asset–design phase using the sizes of actual devices in combination with the formulas shown previously.

Now that we know how we will handle different screen resolutions and densities, I can also explain the scaleX and scaleY variables we met when we implemented the SingleTouchHandler and MultiTouchHandler a few pages earlier.

All our game code will be tuned to work with our fixed target resolution (320! 480 pixels). If we receive touch events on a device that has a higher or lower resolution, the x- and y-coordinates of those events will be defined in the View's coordinate system, not in our target resolution coordinate system. Thus we have to transform the coordinates from their original system to our system based on the scaling factors. Here's how we do that:

```
transformed touch x = real touch x * (target pixels on x axis / real pixels on x axis)
transformed touch y = real touch y * (target pixels on y axis / real pixels on y axis)
```

Let's calculate a simple example for a target resolution of 320! 480 pixels and a device with a resolution of 480! 800 pixels. If we touch the middle of the screen, we'll receive an event with the coordinates (240,400). Using the two preceding formulas, we arrive at the following, which is exactly in the middle of our target coordinate system:

```
transformed touch x = 240 * (320 / 480) = 160
transformed touch y = 400 * (480 / 800) = 240
```

Let's do another one, assuming a real resolution of 240! 320, again touching the middle of the screen, at (120,160):

```
transformed touch x = 120 * (320 / 240) = 160
transformed touch y = 160 * (480 / 320) = 240
```

Hurray, it works in both directions. If we multiply the real touch event coordinates by the target factor divided by the real factor, we don't have to care about all this transforming in our actual game code. All the touch coordinates will be expressed in our fixed–target coordinate system.

With that out of our way, let's implement the last few classes of our game framework.

AndroidPixmap: Pixels for the People

According to the design of our Pixmap interface from Chapter 3, there's not much to implement. Listing 5–12 shows the code.

Listing 5–12. *AndroidPixmap.java, a Pixmap Implementation Wrapping a Bitmap*

```java
package com.badlogic.androidgames.framework.impl;

import android.graphics.Bitmap;

import com.badlogic.androidgames.framework.Graphics.PixmapFormat;
import com.badlogic.androidgames.framework.Pixmap;

public class AndroidPixmap implements Pixmap {
    Bitmap bitmap;
    PixmapFormat format;

    public AndroidPixmap(Bitmap bitmap, PixmapFormat format) {
        this.bitmap = bitmap;
```

```
        this.format = format;
    }

    @Override
    public int getWidth() {
        return bitmap.getWidth();
    }

    @Override
    public int getHeight() {
        return bitmap.getHeight();
    }

    @Override
    public PixmapFormat getFormat() {
        return format;
    }

    @Override
    public void dispose() {
        bitmap.recycle();
    }
}
```

All we do is store the `Bitmap` instance that we wrap, along with its format, which is stored as a `PixmapFormat` enumeration value, as defined in Chapter 3. Additionally we implement the required methods of the `Pixmap` interface so we can query the width and height of the `Pixmap` and its format, and also ensure that the pixels can get dumped from RAM. Note that the `bitmap` member is package private, so we can access it in AndroidGraphics, which we'll implement now.

AndroidGraphics: Serving Our Drawing Needs

The `Graphics` interface we designed in Chapter 3 is also pretty lean and mean. It will draw pixels, lines, rectangles, and `Pixmap`s to the framebuffer. As discussed, we'll use a `Bitmap` as our framebuffer and direct all drawing calls to it via a `Canvas`. It is also responsible for creating `Pixmap` instances from asset files. We'll thus also need an `AssetManager` again. Listing 5–13 shows the code for our implementation of that interface, AndroidGraphics.

Listing 5–12. *AndroidGraphics.java; Implementing the Graphics Interface*

```
package com.badlogic.androidgames.framework.impl;

import java.io.IOException;
import java.io.InputStream;

import android.content.res.AssetManager;
import android.graphics.Bitmap;
import android.graphics.Bitmap.Config;
import android.graphics.BitmapFactory;
import android.graphics.BitmapFactory.Options;
import android.graphics.Canvas;
```

```
import android.graphics.Paint;
import android.graphics.Paint.Style;
import android.graphics.Rect;

import com.badlogic.androidgames.framework.Graphics;
import com.badlogic.androidgames.framework.Pixmap;

public class AndroidGraphics implements Graphics {
    AssetManager assets;
    Bitmap frameBuffer;
    Canvas canvas;
    Paint paint;
    Rect srcRect = new Rect();
    Rect dstRect = new Rect();
```

The class implements the Graphics interface. It has an AssetManager member that we'll
use to load Bitmap instances, a Bitmap member that represents our artificial framebuffer,
a Canvas member that we'll use to draw to the artificial framebuffer, a Paint we need for
drawing, and two Rect members we'll need for implementing the
AndroidGraphics.drawPixmap() methods. These last three members are there so that we
don't have to create new instances of these classes on every draw call. That would
make the garbage collector run wild.

```
    public AndroidGraphics(AssetManager assets, Bitmap frameBuffer) {
        this.assets = assets;
        this.frameBuffer = frameBuffer;
        this.canvas = new Canvas(frameBuffer);
        this.paint = new Paint();
    }
```

In the constructor we get an AssetManager and Bitmap representing our artificial
framebuffer from the outside. We store these in the respective members and additionally
create the Canvas instance that will draw to the artificial framebuffer, as well as the
Paint, which we'll use for some of the drawing methods.

```
    @Override
    public Pixmap newPixmap(String fileName, PixmapFormat format) {
        Config config = null;
        if (format == PixmapFormat.RGB565)
            config = Config.RGB_565;
        else if (format == PixmapFormat.ARGB4444)
            config = Config.ARGB_4444;
        else
            config = Config.ARGB_8888;

        Options options = new Options();
        options.inPreferredConfig = config;

        InputStream in = null;
        Bitmap bitmap = null;
        try {
            in = assets.open(fileName);
            bitmap = BitmapFactory.decodeStream(in);
            if (bitmap == null)
```

```
                throw new RuntimeException("Couldn't load bitmap from asset '"
                        + fileName + "'");
        } catch (IOException e) {
            throw new RuntimeException("Couldn't load bitmap from asset '"
                    + fileName + "'");
        } finally {
            if (in != null) {
                try {
                    in.close();
                } catch (IOException e) {
                }
            }
        }
    }

    if (bitmap.getConfig() == Config.RGB_565)
        format = PixmapFormat.RGB565;
    else if (bitmap.getConfig() == Config.ARGB_4444)
        format = PixmapFormat.ARGB4444;
    else
        format = PixmapFormat.ARGB8888;

    return new AndroidPixmap(bitmap, format);
}
```

The newPixmap() method tries to load a Bitmap from an asset file, using the
PixmapFormat specified. We start off by translating the PixmapFormat into one of the
constants of the Android Config class we used in Chapter 4. Next we create a new
Options instance and set our preferred color format. We then try to load the Bitmap from
the asset via the BitmapFactory. We throw a RuntimeException if something goes wrong.
Otherwise we check what format the BitmapFactory decided to load the Bitmap with and
translate that into a PixmapFormat enumeration value. Remember that the BitmapFactory
might decide to ignore our desired color format, so we have to check afterward what it
decoded the image to. Finally we construct a new AndroidBitmap instance based on the
Bitmap we loaded and its PixmapFormat, and return it to the caller.

```
@Override
public void clear(int color) {
    canvas.drawRGB((color & 0xff0000) >> 16, (color & 0xff00) >> 8,
            (color & 0xff));
}
```

The clear() method simply extracts the red, green, and blue components of the
specified 32-bit ARGB color parameter and calls the Canvas.drawRGB() method, which
will clear our artificial framebuffer with that color. This method ignores any alpha value of
the specified color, so we don't have to extract it.

```
@Override
public void drawPixel(int x, int y, int color) {
    paint.setColor(color);
    canvas.drawPoint(x, y, paint);
}
```

The drawPixel() method draws a pixel to our artificial framebuffer via the Canvas.drawPoint() method. We first set the color of our paint member variable and pass that to the drawing method in addition to the x- and y-coordinates of the pixel.

```
@Override
public void drawLine(int x, int y, int x2, int y2, int color) {
    paint.setColor(color);
    canvas.drawLine(x, y, x2, y2, paint);
}
```

The drawLine() method draws the given line to the artificial framebuffer, again using the paint member to specify the color when calling the Canvas.drawLine() method.

```
@Override
public void drawRect(int x, int y, int width, int height, int color) {
    paint.setColor(color);
    paint.setStyle(Style.FILL);
    canvas.drawRect(x, y, x + width - 1, y + width - 1, paint);
}
```

The drawRect() method first sets the Paint member's color and style attributes so that we can draw a filled, colored rectangle. In the actual Canvas.drawRect() call, we then have to transform the x, y, width, and height parameters to the coordinates of the top-left and bottom-right corners of the rectangle. For the top-left corner we simply use the x and y parameters. For the bottom-right-corner coordinates, we add the width and height to x and y and subtract 1. For example, imagine if we were to render a rectangle with an x and y of (10,10) and a width and height of 2 and 2. If we don't subtract 1, the resulting rectangle on the screen would be 3! 3 pixels in size.

```
@Override
public void drawPixmap(Pixmap pixmap, int x, int y, int srcX, int srcY,
        int srcWidth, int srcHeight) {
    srcRect.left = srcX;
    srcRect.top = srcY;
    srcRect.right = srcX + srcWidth - 1;
    srcRect.bottom = srcY + srcHeight - 1;

    dstRect.left = x;
    dstRect.top = y;
    dstRect.right = x + srcWidth - 1;
    dstRect.bottom = y + srcHeight - 1;

    canvas.drawBitmap(((AndroidPixmap) pixmap).bitmap, srcRect, dstRect,
            null);
}
```

The drawPixmap() method, which allows drawing a portion of a Pixmap, first sets up the source and destination Rect members that get used in the actual drawing call. As with drawing a rectangle, we have to translate the x- and y-coordinates together with the width and height to the top-left and bottom-right corners. We again have to subtract 1, or else we'll overshoot by 1 pixel. Next we perform the actual drawing via the Canvas.drawBitmap() method, which will automatically do blending as well if the Pixmap we draw has a PixmapFormat.ARGB4444 or PixmapFormat.ARGB8888 color depth. Note that we have to cast the Pixmap parameter to an AndroidPixmap in order to be able to fetch the `bitmap` member for drawing with the `Canvas`. That's a little bit nasty, but we can be sure that the `Pixmap` instance passed in is actually an `AndroidPixmap`.

```java
@Override
    public void drawPixmap(Pixmap pixmap, int x, int y) {
        canvas.drawBitmap(((AndroidPixmap)pixmap).bitmap, x, y, null);
    }
```

The second `drawPixmap()` method just draws the complete `Pixmap` to the artificial framebuffer at the given coordinates. We again do some casting to get to the `Bitmap` member of the `AndroidPixmap`.

```java
@Override
    public int getWidth() {
        return frameBuffer.getWidth();
    }

    @Override
    public int getHeight() {
        return frameBuffer.getHeight();
    }
}
```

Finally we have the methods `getWidth()` and `getHeight()`, which simply return the size of the artificial framebuffer the `AndroidGraphics` instance stores and renders to internally.

There's one more class we need to implement related to graphics: `AndroidFastRenderView`.

AndroidFastRenderView: Loop, Strech, Loop, Stretch

The name of this class should already give away what lies ahead. In the last chapter we discussed using a `SurfaceView` to perform continuous rendering in a separate thread that could also house our game's main loop. We developed a very simple class called `FastRenderView`, which derived from the `SurfaceView` class, we made sure we play nice with the activity life cycle, and we set up a thread in which we constantly rendered to the `SurfaceView` via a `Canvas`.

We'll reuse this `FastRenderView` class and augment it to do a few more things:

- It will keep a reference to a `Game` instance from which it can get the active `Screen`. We will constantly call the `Screen.update()` and `Screen.present()` methods from within the `FastRenderView` thread.

- It will keep track of the delta time between frames that gets passed to the active `Screen`.

- It will take the artificial framebuffer that the `AndroidGraphics` instance draws to and draw it to the `SurfaceView`, scaled if necessary.

Listing 5–13 shows the implementation of the `AndroidFastRenderView` class.

Listing 5–13. *AndroidFastRenderView.java, a Threaded SurfaceView Executing Our Game Code*

```
package com.badlogic.androidgames.framework.impl;

import android.graphics.Bitmap;
import android.graphics.Canvas;
import android.graphics.Rect;
import android.view.SurfaceHolder;
import android.view.SurfaceView;

public class AndroidFastRenderView extends SurfaceView implements Runnable {
    AndroidGame game;
    Bitmap framebuffer;
    Thread renderThread = null;
    SurfaceHolder holder;
    volatile boolean running = false;
```

This should look very familiar. We just need to add two more members: an `AndroidGame` instance and a `Bitmap` instance representing our artificial framebuffer. The other members are the same as in our `FastRenderView` from Chapter 3.

```
    public AndroidFastRenderView(AndroidGame game, Bitmap framebuffer) {
        super(game);
        this.game = game;
        this.framebuffer = framebuffer;
        this.holder = getHolder();
    }
```

In the constructor we simply call the base class's constructor with the `AndroidGame` parameter (which is an `Activity`; more on that in a bit) and store the parameters in the respective members. We also get a `SurfaceHolder` again, as we did previously.

```
    public void resume() {
        running = true;
        renderThread = new Thread(this);
        renderThread.start();
    }
```

The `resume()` method is an exact copy of the `FastRenderView.resume()` method, so we don't need to go over that again. It just makes sure that our thread plays nice with the activity life cycle.

```
    public void run() {
        Rect dstRect = new Rect();
        long startTime = System.nanoTime();
        while(running) {
            if(!holder.getSurface().isValid())
                continue;

            float deltaTime = (System.nanoTime()-startTime) / 1000000000.0f;
```

```
        startTime = System.nanoTime();

        game.getCurrentScreen().update(deltaTime);
        game.getCurrentScreen().present(deltaTime);

        Canvas canvas = holder.lockCanvas();
        canvas.getClipBounds(dstRect);
        canvas.drawBitmap(framebuffer, null, dstRect, null);
        holder.unlockCanvasAndPost(canvas);
    }
}
```

The run() method has a few more bells and whistles. The first addition is the tracking of the delta time between each frame. We use System.nanoTime() for this, which returns the current time in nanoseconds as a long.

NOTE: A nanosecond is one-billionth of a second.

In each loop iteration, we start off by taking the difference between the last loop iteration's start time and the current time. To make working with that delta time easier, we convert it to seconds. Next we save the current time stamp, which we'll use in the next loop iteration to calculate the next delta time. With the delta time at hand, we call the current Screen's update() and present() methods, which will update the game logic and render things to the artificial framebuffer. Finally we get ahold of the Canvas for the SurfaceView and draw the artificial framebuffer. The scaling is performed automatically in case the destination rectangle we pass to the Canvas.drawBitmap() method is smaller or bigger than the framebuffer.

Note that we've used a shortcut here to get a destination rectangle that stretches over the whole SurfaceView via the Canvas.getClipBounds() method. It will set the top and left members of dstRect to 0 and 0, and the bottom and right members to the actual screen dimensions (480! 800 in portrait mode on a Nexus One). The rest of the method is exactly the same as what we had in our FastRenderView test. It just makes sure that the thread stops when the activity is paused or destroyed.

```
public void pause() {
    running = false;
    while(true) {
        try {
            renderThread.join();
            break;
        } catch (InterruptedException e) {
            // retry
        }
    }
}
```

The last method of this class, pause(), is again exactly the same as the FastRenderView.pause() method. It simply terminates the rendering/main loop thread and waits for it to completely die before returning.

We are nearly done with our framework. The last piece of the puzzle is the implementation of the Game interface.

AndroidGame: Tying Everything Together

Our little game development framework is nearly complete. All we need to do is tie together the loose ends by implementating the Game interface we designed in Chapter 3, using the classes we created in the previous sections of this chapter. Here's a list of responsibilities:

- Perform window management. In our context, that means setting up an activity and an AndroidFastRenderView, and handling the activity life cycle in a clean way.

- Use and manage a WakeLock so that the screen does not get dimmed.

- Instantiate and hand out references to Graphics, Audio, FileIO, and Input to interested parties.

- Manage Screens and integrate them with the activity life cycle.

Our general goal is it to have a single class called AndroidGame from which we can derive. All we want to do is implement the Game.getStartScreen() method later on to start off our game, like this:

```java
public class MrNom extends AndroidGame {
    @Override
    public Screen getStartScreen() {
        return new MainMenu(this);
    }
}
```

I hope you can see why it pays off to design a nice little framework before diving headfirst into programming the actual game. We can reuse this framework for all future games that are not to graphically intensive. So let's discuss Listing 5–14, which shows the AndroidGame class.

Listing 5–14. *AndroidGame.java; Tying Everything Together*

```java
package com.badlogic.androidgames.framework.impl;

import android.app.Activity;
import android.content.Context;
import android.content.res.Configuration;
import android.graphics.Bitmap;
import android.graphics.Bitmap.Config;
import android.os.Bundle;
import android.os.PowerManager;
import android.os.PowerManager.WakeLock;
import android.view.Window;
import android.view.WindowManager;

import com.badlogic.androidgames.framework.Audio;
import com.badlogic.androidgames.framework.FileIO;
import com.badlogic.androidgames.framework.Game;
```

```
import com.badlogic.androidgames.framework.Graphics;
import com.badlogic.androidgames.framework.Input;
import com.badlogic.androidgames.framework.Screen;

public abstract class AndroidGame extends Activity implements Game {
    AndroidFastRenderView renderView;
    Graphics graphics;
    Audio audio;
    Input input;
    FileIO fileIO;
    Screen screen;
    WakeLock wakeLock;
```

The class definition starts off by letting AndroidGame extend the Activity class and implement the Game interface. Next we define a couple of members that should be familiar. The first member is the AndroidFastRenderView, which we'll draw to, and which will manage our main loop thread for us. The Graphics, Audio, Input, and FileIO members will be set to instances of AndroidGraphics, AndroidAudio, AndroidInput, and AndroidFileIO—no big surprise there. The next member holds the currently active Screen. Finally there's a member that holds a WakeLock, which we'll use to keep the screen from dimming.

```
@Override
    public void onCreate(Bundle savedInstanceState) {
        super.onCreate(savedInstanceState);

        requestWindowFeature(Window.FEATURE_NO_TITLE);
        getWindow().setFlags(WindowManager.LayoutParams.FLAG_FULLSCREEN,
                WindowManager.LayoutParams.FLAG_FULLSCREEN);

        boolean isLandscape = getResources().getConfiguration().orientation ==
Configuration.ORIENTATION_LANDSCAPE;
        int frameBufferWidth = isLandscape ? 480 : 320;
        int frameBufferHeight = isLandscape ? 320 : 480;
        Bitmap frameBuffer = Bitmap.createBitmap(frameBufferWidth,
                frameBufferHeight, Config.RGB_565);

        float scaleX = (float) frameBufferWidth
                / getWindowManager().getDefaultDisplay().getWidth();
        float scaleY = (float) frameBufferHeight
                / getWindowManager().getDefaultDisplay().getHeight();

        renderView = new AndroidFastRenderView(this, frameBuffer);
        graphics = new AndroidGraphics(getAssets(), frameBuffer);
        fileIO = new AndroidFileIO(getAssets());
        audio = new AndroidAudio(this);
        input = new AndroidInput(this, renderView, scaleX, scaleY);
        screen = getStartScreen();
        setContentView(renderView);

        PowerManager powerManager = (PowerManager)
getSystemService(Context.POWER_SERVICE);
        wakeLock = powerManager.newWakeLock(PowerManager.FULL_WAKE_LOCK, "GLGame");
    }
```

The onCreate() method, which is the familiar startup method of the Activity class, starts off by calling the base class's onCreate() method, as it is required. Next we make the Activity full-screen, as we did in a couple of tests in the previous chapter already. In the next few lines we set up our artificial framebuffer. Depending on the orientation of the activity, we either want to use a 320! 480 framebuffer (portrait mode) or a 480! 320 framebuffer (landscape mode). To determine what screen orientation the Activity uses, we fetch the orientation member from a class called Configuration, which we get via a call to getResources().getConfiguration(). Based on the value of that member, we then set the framebuffer size and instantiate a Bitmap, which we'll hand to the AndroidFastRenderView and AndroidGraphics instances a little later.

> **NOTE:** The Bitmap instance has an RGB565 color format. This way we don't waste memory, and all our drawing is a little faster.

We also calculate the scaleX and scaleY values that the SingleTouchHandler and MultiTouchHandler classes will use to transform the touch event coordinates to our fixed-coordinate system.

Next we instantiate the AndroidFastRenderView, AndroidGraphics, AndroidAudio, AndroidInput, and AndroidFileIO with the necessary constructor arguments. Finally we call the getStartScreen() method, which our actual game will implement, and set the AndroidFastRenderView as the content view of the Activity. All these helper classes we just instantiated will do some more work in the background, of course. The AndroidInput class will tell the touch handler it selected to hook up with the AndroidFastRenderView, for example.

```
@Override
public void onResume() {
    super.onResume();
    wakeLock.acquire();
    screen.resume();
    renderView.resume();
}
```

Next up is the onResume() method of the Activity class, which we override. As usual, the first thing we do is call the superclass method because we are good citizens in Android land. Next we acquire the WakeLock and make sure the current Screen gets informed of the fact that the game (and thereby the activity) has just been resumed. Finally we tell the AndroidFastRenderView to resume the rendering thread, which will also kick off our game's main loop, in which we tell the current Screen to update and present itself in each iteration.

```
@Override
public void onPause() {
    super.onPause();
    wakeLock.release();
    renderView.pause();
    screen.pause();

    if (isFinishing())
```

```
            screen.dispose();
    }
```

The onPause() method first calls the superclass method again. Next it releases the WakeLock and makes sure that the rendering thread is terminated. If we didn't terminate the thread before calling the current Screen's onPause(), we could run into concurrency issues since the UI thread and the main loop thread would both access the Screen at the same time. Once we are sure the main loop thread is no longer alive, we tell the current Screen that it should pause itself. In case the Activity is going to be destroyed, we also inform the Screen of that event so it can do any cleanup work necessary.

```
    @Override
    public Input getInput() {
        return input;
    }

    @Override
    public FileIO getFileIO() {
        return fileIO;
    }

    @Override
    public Graphics getGraphics() {
        return graphics;
    }

    @Override
    public Audio getAudio() {
        return audio;
    }
```

The getInput(), getFileIO(), getGraphics(), and getAudio() methods should need no explanation. We simply return the respective instances to the caller. The caller will always be one of our Screen implementations of our game later on.

```
    @Override
    public void setScreen(Screen screen) {
        if (screen == null)
            throw new IllegalArgumentException("Screen must not be null");

        this.screen.pause();
        this.screen.dispose();
        screen.resume();
        screen.update(0);
        this.screen = screen;
    }
```

The setScreen() method we inherit from the Game interface looks simple at first glance. We start off with some old-school null-checking, as we can't allow a null Screen. Next we tell the current Screen to pause and dispose of itself so it can make room for the new Screen. The new Screen is asked to resume itself and update itself once with a delta time of zero. Finally we set the Screen member to the new Screen.

Let's think about who will call this method, and when. When we designed Mr. Nom, we identified all the transitions between various `Screen` instances. We'll usually call the `AndroidGame.setScreen()` method in the `update()` method of one of these `Screen` instances.

Say we have a main menu `Screen` where we check if the Play button is pressed in the `update()` method. If that is the case, we'll want to transition to the next `Screen`, and we can do so by calling the `AndroidGame.setScreen()` method from within the `MainMenu.update()` method with a brand-new instance of that next `Screen`. The `MainMenu` screen will get back control after the call to `AndroidGame.setScreen()`, and should immediately return to the caller, as it is no longer the active `Screen`. In this case the caller is the `AndroidFastRenderView` in the main loop thread. If you check the portion of the main loop responsible for updating and rendering the active `Screen`, you'll see that the `update()` method would be called on the `MainMenu` class, but the `present()` method would be called on the new current `Screen`. This would be bad, as we defined the `Screen` interface in a way that guarantees that the `resume()` and `update()` methods will be called at least once before the `Screen` is asked to present itself. And that's why we call these two methods in the `AndroidGame.setScreen()` method on the new `Screen`. All is taken care of for us by the mighty `AndroidGame` class.

```
public Screen getCurrentScreen() {
        return screen;
    }
}
```

The last method is called `getCurrentScreen()`. It simply returns the currently active `Screen`.

We've now created an easy-to-use Android game development framework. All we need to do now is implement the `Screens` of our game. We can also reuse the framework for any future games we can think of, as long as they do not need immense graphics power. If we need that, we have to start using OpenGL ES. However, we only need to replace the graphics part of our framework for that. All the other classes for audio, input, and file I/O can be reused.

Summary

In this chapter, we implemented a full-fledged 2D Android game development framework from scratch that we can reuse for all our future games (as long as they are graphically modest). Great care was taken to achieve a good, extensible design. We could take this code we have and replace the rendering portions with OpenGL ES, making Mr. Nom go 3D.

With all this boilerplate code in place, let's concentrate on what we are here for: writing games!

Chapter **6**

Mr. Nom Invades Android

In Chapter 3 we churned out a full design for Mr. Nom, consisting of the game mechanics, a simple background story, handcrafted graphical assets, and definitions for all the screens based on some paper cutouts. In the last chapter we developed a full-fledged game-development framework that allows us to easily transfer our design screens to code. But enough talking; let's start writing our first game!

Creating the Assets

We have two types of assets in Mr. Nom: audio assets and graphical assets. I recorded the audio assets via a nice open source application called Audacity and a bad netbook microphone. I created a sound effect for when a button is pressed or a menu item is chosen, one for when Mr. Nom eats a stain, and one for when he eats himself. I saved them as OGGs to the assets/ folder, under the names click.ogg, eat.ogg, and bitten.ogg, respectively.

Earlier, I mentioned that we'll want to reuse those paper cutouts from the design phase as our real game graphics. For this, we have to first make them fit with our target resolution.

I chose a fixed target resolution of 320! 480 (portrait mode) for which we'll design all our graphical assets. I scanned in all the paper cutouts and resized them a little. I saved most of the assets in separate files and merged some of them into a single file. All images are saved in PNG format. The background is the only image that is RGB888; all others are ARGB8888. Figure 6–1 shows you what I ended up with.

Figure 6–1. *All the graphical assets of Mr. Nom, with their respective filenames and sizes in pixels*

Let's break down those images a little:

background.png: This is our background image, which will be the first thing we'll draw to the framebuffer. It has the same size as our target resolution for obvious reasons.

buttons.png: This contains all the buttons we'll need in our game. I put them into a single file, as we can easily draw them via the Graphics.drawPixmap() method, which allows drawing portions of an image. We'll use that technique more often when we start drawing with OpenGL ES, so we better get used to it now. Merging several images into a single image is often called *atlasing*, and the image itself is called an *image atlas* (or texture atlas, or sprite sheet). Each button has a size of 64! 64 pixels, which will come in handy when we have to decide whether a touch event has hit a button on the screen.

help1.png, help2.png, help3.png: These are the images we'll display on the three help screens of Mr. Nom. They all have the same size, which makes placing them on the screen easier.

logo.png: This is the logo we'll display on the main menu screen.

mainmenu.png: This contains the three options that we'll present to the player on the main menu. Selecting one of these will trigger a transition to the respective screen. Each option has a height of roughly 42 pixels, something we can use to easily detect which option was touched.

ready.png, pause.png, gameover.png: We'll draw these when the game is about to be started, when it is paused, and when it is over, respectively.

numbers.png: This holds all the digits we need to render our high scores later on. What's to remember about this image is that each digit has the same width and height, 20! 32 pixels, except for the dot at the end, which is 10! 32 pixels in size. We can later use this fact to easily render any number that is thrown at us.

tail.png: This is the tail of Mr. Nom, or rather one part of his tail. It's 32! 32 pixels in size, which has some implications we'll discuss in a minute.

headdown.png, headleft.png, headright.png, headup.png: These images are for the head of Mr. Nom; there's one for each direction he can be moving in. Because of his hat, we have to make these images a little bigger than the tail image. Each head image is 42! 42 pixels in size.

stain1.png, stain2.png, stain3.png: These are the three types of stains we can render. Having three types will make the game screen a little more diverse. They are 32! 32 pixels in size, just like the tail image.

Great, now let's start implementing the screens!

Setting Up the Project

As mentioned in the last chapter, we will merge the code for Mr. Nom with our framework code. All the classes related to Mr. Nom will be placed in the package com.badlogic.androidgames.mrnom. Additionally we have to modify the manifest file, as outlined in Chapter 4. Our default activity will be called MrNomGame. Just follow the ten steps outlined in the section "Android Game Project Setup in Ten Easy Steps " in Chapter 4 to set the <activity> attributes properly (e.g., so that the game is fixed in portrait mode and configuration changes are handled by application) and to give our application the proper permissions (writing to external storage, using a wake lock, etc.).

All the assets from the previous sections are located in the assets/ folder of the project. Additionally we have to put icon.png files into the res/drawable, res/drawable-ldpi, res/drawable-mdpi, and res/drawable-hdpi folders. I just took the headright.png of Mr. Nom, renamed it icon.png, and put a properly resized version of it in each of the folders.

All that's left is putting our into the com.badlogic.androidgames.mrnom package of the Eclipse project!

MrNomGame: The Main Activity

Our application needs a main entry point, also known as default Activity on Android. We will call this default Activity MrNomGame and let it derive from AndroidGame, the class we implemented in Chapter 5 to run our game. It will be responsible for creating and running our first screen later on. Listing 6–1 shows you our MrNomGame class.

Listing 6–1. *MrNomGame.java, Our Main Activity/Game Hybrid*

```
package com.badlogic.androidgames.mrnom;

import com.badlogic.androidgames.framework.Screen;
import com.badlogic.androidgames.framework.impl.AndroidGame;

public class MrNomGame extends AndroidGame {
    @Override
    public Screen getStartScreen() {
        return new LoadingScreen(this);
    }
}
```

All we need to do is derive from AndroidGame and implement the getStartScreen() method, which will return an instance of the LoadingScreen class (which we'll implement in a minute). Remember, this will get us started with all the things we need for our game, from setting up the different modules for audio, graphics, input, and file I/O to starting the main loop thread. Pretty easy, huh?

Assets: A Convenient Asset Store

The loading screen will load all the assets of our game. But where do we store them? To store them, we'll do something that is not seen very often in Java land: we'll create a class that has a ton of static public members that hold all the Pixmaps and Sounds that we've loaded from the assets. Listing 6–2 shows you that class.

Listing 6–2. *Assets.java, Holding All Our Pixmaps and Sounds for Easy Access*

```java
package com.badlogic.androidgames.mrnom;

import com.badlogic.androidgames.framework.Pixmap;
import com.badlogic.androidgames.framework.Sound;

public class Assets {
    public static Pixmap background;
    public static Pixmap logo;
    public static Pixmap mainMenu;
    public static Pixmap buttons;
    public static Pixmap help1;
    public static Pixmap help2;
    public static Pixmap help3;
    public static Pixmap numbers;
    public static Pixmap ready;
    public static Pixmap pause;
    public static Pixmap gameOver;
    public static Pixmap headUp;
    public static Pixmap headLeft;
    public static Pixmap headDown;
    public static Pixmap headRight;
    public static Pixmap tail;
    public static Pixmap stain1;
    public static Pixmap stain2;
    public static Pixmap stain3;

    public static Sound click;
    public static Sound eat;
    public static Sound bitten;
}
```

We have a static member for every image and sound we load from the assets. If we want to use one of these assets, we can do something like this:

```java
game.getGraphics().drawPixmap(Assets.background, 0, 0)
```

or something like this:

```java
Assets.click.play(1);
```

Now, that's convenient. However, note that nothing is keeping us from overwriting those static members, as they are not final. But as long as we don't overwrite them, we are safe. These public, non-final members make this "design pattern" an antipattern, actually. For our game it's OK to be a little lazy, though. A cleaner solution would hide the assets behind setters and getters in a so-called *singleton class*. We'll stick to our poor-man's asset manager, though.

Settings: Keeping Track of User Choices and High Scores

There are two other things that we need to load in the loading screen: the user settings and the high scores. If you look back at the main menu and high-scores screens in Chapter 3, you'll see that we allow the user to toggle the sounds, and that we store the top five high scores. We'll save these settings to the external storage so that we can reload them the next time the game starts. For this, we'll implement another simple class, called Settings, as shown in Listing 6–3.

Listing 6–3. *Settings.java, Which Stores Our Settings and Loads/Saves Them*

```java
package com.badlogic.androidgames.mrnom;

import java.io.BufferedReader;
import java.io.BufferedWriter;
import java.io.IOException;
import java.io.InputStreamReader;
import java.io.OutputStreamWriter;

import com.badlogic.androidgames.framework.FileIO;

public class Settings {
    public static boolean soundEnabled = true;
    public static int[] highscores = new int[] { 100, 80, 50, 30, 10 };
```

Whether sound effects are played back is determined by a public static boolean called soundEnabled. The high scores are stored in a five-element integer array, sorted from highest to lowest. We define sensible defaults for both settings. We can access these two members the same way we access the members of the Assets class.

```java
    public static void load(FileIO files) {
        BufferedReader in = null;
        try {
            in = new BufferedReader(new InputStreamReader(
                    files.readFile(".mrnom")));
            soundEnabled = Boolean.parseBoolean(in.readLine());
            for (int i = 0; i < 5; i++) {
                highscores[i] = Integer.parseInt(in.readLine());
            }
        } catch (IOException e) {
            // :( It's ok we have defaults
        } catch (NumberFormatException e) {
            // :/ It's ok, defaults save our day
        } finally {
            try {
                if (in != null)
                    in.close();
            } catch (IOException e) {
            }
        }
    }
}
```

The static load() method tries to load the settings from a file called .mrnom from the external storage. It needs a FileIO instance for that, which we pass to the method. It assumes that the sound setting and each high-score entry is stored on a separate line and simple reads them in. If anything goes wrong (e.g., if the external storage is not available or there is no settings file yet), we simply fall back to our defaults and ignore the failure.

```java
public static void save(FileIO files) {
    BufferedWriter out = null;
    try {
        out = new BufferedWriter(new OutputStreamWriter(
                files.writeFile(".mrnom")));
        out.write(Boolean.toString(soundEnabled));
        for (int i = 0; i < 5; i++) {
            out.write(Integer.toString(highscores[i]));
        }

    } catch (IOException e) {
    } finally {
        try {
            if (out != null)
                out.close();
        } catch (IOException e) {
        }
    }
}
```

Next up is a method called save(). It takes the current settings and serializes them to the .mrnom file on the external storage (e.g., /sdcard/.mrnom).The sound setting and each high-score entry is stored as a separate line in that file, as expected by the load() method. If something goes wrong, we just ignore the failure and use the default values defined earlier. In an AAA title, you might want to inform the user about this loading error.

```java
public static void addScore(int score) {
    for (int i = 0; i < 5; i++) {
        if (highscores[i] < score) {
            for (int j = 4; j > i; j--)
                highscores[j] = highscores[j - 1];
            highscores[i] = score;
            break;
        }
    }
}

}
```

The final method, addScore(), is a convenience method. We will use it to add a new score to the high scores, automatically resorting them depending on the value we want to insert.

LoadingScreen: Fetching the Assets from Disk

With those classes at hand, we can now easily implement the loading screen. Listing 6–4 shows you the code.

Listing 6–4. *LoadingScreen.java, Which Loads All Assets and the Settings*

```java
package com.badlogic.androidgames.mrnom;

import com.badlogic.androidgames.framework.Game;
import com.badlogic.androidgames.framework.Graphics;
import com.badlogic.androidgames.framework.Screen;
import com.badlogic.androidgames.framework.Graphics.PixmapFormat;

public class LoadingScreen extends Screen {
    public LoadingScreen(Game game) {
        super(game);
    }
```

We let the LoadingScreen class derive from the Screen class we defined in Chapter 3. This requires that we implement a constructor that takes a Game instance, which we hand to the superclass constructor. Note that this constructor will be called in the MrNomGame.getStartScreen() method we defined earlier.

```java
    @Override
    public void update(float deltaTime) {
        Graphics g = game.getGraphics();
        Assets.background = g.newPixmap("background.png", PixmapFormat.RGB565);
        Assets.logo = g.newPixmap("logo.png", PixmapFormat.ARGB4444);
        Assets.mainMenu = g.newPixmap("mainmenu.png", PixmapFormat.ARGB4444);
        Assets.buttons = g.newPixmap("buttons.png", PixmapFormat.ARGB4444);
        Assets.help1 = g.newPixmap("help1.png", PixmapFormat.ARGB4444);
        Assets.help2 = g.newPixmap("help2.png", PixmapFormat.ARGB4444);
        Assets.help3 = g.newPixmap("help3.png", PixmapFormat.ARGB4444);
        Assets.numbers = g.newPixmap("numbers.png", PixmapFormat.ARGB4444);
        Assets.ready = g.newPixmap("ready.png", PixmapFormat.ARGB4444);
        Assets.pause = g.newPixmap("pausemenu.png", PixmapFormat.ARGB4444);
        Assets.gameOver = g.newPixmap("gameover.png", PixmapFormat.ARGB4444);
        Assets.headUp = g.newPixmap("headup.png", PixmapFormat.ARGB4444);
        Assets.headLeft = g.newPixmap("headleft.png", PixmapFormat.ARGB4444);
        Assets.headDown = g.newPixmap("headdown.png", PixmapFormat.ARGB4444);
        Assets.headRight = g.newPixmap("headright.png", PixmapFormat.ARGB4444);
        Assets.tail = g.newPixmap("tail.png", PixmapFormat.ARGB4444);
        Assets.stain1 = g.newPixmap("stain1.png", PixmapFormat.ARGB4444);
        Assets.stain2 = g.newPixmap("stain2.png", PixmapFormat.ARGB4444);
        Assets.stain3 = g.newPixmap("stain3.png", PixmapFormat.ARGB4444);
        Assets.click = game.getAudio().newSound("click.ogg");
        Assets.eat = game.getAudio().newSound("eat.ogg");
        Assets.bitten = game.getAudio().newSound("bitten.ogg");
        Settings.load(game.getFileIO());
        game.setScreen(new MainMenuScreen(game));
    }
```

Next up is our implementation of the update() method, where we load the assets and settings. For the image assets, we simply create new Pixmaps via the Graphics.newPixmap() method. Note that we specify which color format the Pixmaps should have. The background has an RGB565 format, and all other images have an ARGB4444 format (if the BitmapFactory respects our hint). We do this conserve memory and increase our rendering speed a little later on. Our original images are stored in RGB888 and ARGB8888 format as PNGs. We also load in the three sound effects and store them in the respective members of the Assets class. Next we load the settings from the external storage via the Settings.load() method. Finally we initiate a screen transition to a Screen called MainMenuScreen, which will take over execution from that point on.

```
    @Override
    public void present(float deltaTime) {

    }

    @Override
    public void pause() {

    }

    @Override
    public void resume() {

    }

    @Override
    public void dispose() {

    }
}
```

The other methods are just stubs and do not perform any actions. Since the update() method will immediatly trigger a screen transition after all assets are loaded, there's nothing more to do on this screen.

The Main Menu Screen

The main menu screen is pretty dumb. It just renders the logo, the main menu options, and the sound setting in the form of a toggle button. All it does is react to touches on either the main menu options or the sound setting toggle button. To implement this behaviour we need to know two things: where on the screen we render the images and what the touch areas are that will either trigger a screen transition or toggle the sound setting. Figure 6–2 shows where we'll render the different images on the screen. From that we can directly derive the touch areas.

Figure 6–2. *The main menu screen. The coordinates specify where we'll render the different images, and the outlines show the touch areas.*

The x-coordinates of the logo and main menu option images are calculated so that they are centered on the x-axis.

Next, let's implement the Screen. Listing 6–5 shows the code.

Listing 6–5. *MainMenuScreen.java, the Main Menu Screen*

```
package com.badlogic.androidgames.mrnom;

import java.util.List;

import com.badlogic.androidgames.framework.Game;
import com.badlogic.androidgames.framework.Graphics;
import com.badlogic.androidgames.framework.Input.TouchEvent;
import com.badlogic.androidgames.framework.Screen;

public class MainMenuScreen extends Screen {
    public MainMenuScreen(Game game) {
        super(game);
    }
```

We let the class derive from Screen again and implement an adequate constructor for it.

```
    @Override
    public void update(float deltaTime) {
        Graphics g = game.getGraphics();
        List<TouchEvent> touchEvents = game.getInput().getTouchEvents();
        game.getInput().getKeyEvents();

        int len = touchEvents.size();
```

```
        for(int i = 0; i < len; i++) {
            TouchEvent event = touchEvents.get(i);
            if(event.type == TouchEvent.TOUCH_UP) {
                if(inBounds(event, 0, g.getHeight() - 64, 64, 64)) {
                    Settings.soundEnabled = !Settings.soundEnabled;
                    if(Settings.soundEnabled)
                        Assets.click.play(1);
                }
                if(inBounds(event, 64, 220, 192, 42) ) {
                    game.setScreen(new GameScreen(game));
                    if(Settings.soundEnabled)
                        Assets.click.play(1);
                    return;
                }
                if(inBounds(event, 64, 220 + 42, 192, 42) ) {
                    game.setScreen(new HighscoreScreen(game));
                    if(Settings.soundEnabled)
                        Assets.click.play(1);
                    return;
                }
                if(inBounds(event, 64, 220 + 84, 192, 42) ) {
                    game.setScreen(new HelpScreen(game));
                    if(Settings.soundEnabled)
                        Assets.click.play(1);
                    return;
                }
            }
        }
    }
}
```

Next we have the update() method, in which we'll do all our touch event checking. We first fetch the TouchEvents and KeyEvents from the Input instance the Game provides to us. Note that we do not use the KeyEvents, but we fetch them anyway in order to clear the internal buffer (yes, that's a tad bit nasty, but let's make it a habit). We then loop over all the TouchEvents until we find one with the type TouchEvent.TOUCH_UP. (We could alternatively look for TouchEvent.TOUCH_DOWN events, but in most UIs the up event is used to indicate that a UI component was pressed).

Once we have a fitting event, we check whether it either hit the sound toggle button or one of the menu entries. To make that code a little cleaner, I wrote a method called inBounds(), which takes a touch event, x- and y-coordinates, and a width and height. The method checks whether the touch event is inside the rectangle defined by those parameters, and returns either true or false.

If the sound toggle button is hit, we simply invert the Settings.soundEnabled boolean value. In case any of the main menu entries are hit, we transition to the appropriate screen by instancing it and setting it via Game.setScreen(). We can immediately return in that case, as the MainMenuScreen doesn't have anything to do anymore. We also play the click sounds if either the toggle button or a main menu entry is hit and sound is enabled.

Remember that all the touch events will be reported relative to our target resolution of 320! 480 pixels, thanks to the scaling magic we perform in the touch event handlers discussed in Chapter 5:

```java
private boolean inBounds(TouchEvent event, int x, int y, int width, int height) {
    if(event.x > x && event.x < x + width - 1 &&
       event.y > y && event.y < y + height - 1)
        return true;
    else
        return false;
}
```

The inBounds() method works as just discussed: put in a TouchEvent and a rectangle, and it tells you whether the touch event's coordinates are inside that rectangle.

```java
@Override
    public void present(float deltaTime) {
        Graphics g = game.getGraphics();

        g.drawPixmap(Assets.background, 0, 0);
        g.drawPixmap(Assets.logo, 32, 20);
        g.drawPixmap(Assets.mainMenu, 64, 220);
        if(Settings.soundEnabled)
            g.drawPixmap(Assets.buttons, 0, 416, 0, 0, 64, 64);
        else
            g.drawPixmap(Assets.buttons, 0, 416, 64, 0, 64, 64);
    }
```

The present() method is probably the one you've been waiting for most, but I'm afraid it isn't all that exciting. Out little game framework makes it really simple to render our main menu screen. All we do is render the background at (0,0), which will basically erase our framebuffer, so no call to Graphics.clear() is needed. Next we draw the logo and main menu entries at the coordinates shown in Figure 6–2. We end that method by drawing the sound toggle button based on the current setting. As you can see, we use the same Pixmap, but only draw the appropriate portion of it (the sound toggle button; see Figure 6–1). Now that was easy.

```java
@Override
    public void pause() {
        Settings.save(game.getFileIO());
    }
```

The final piece we need to discuss is the pause() method. Since we can change one of the settings on that screen, we have to make sure that it gets persisted to the external storage. With our Settings class that's pretty easy!

```java
    @Override
    public void resume() {

    }

    @Override
    public void dispose() {

    }
}
```

The resume() and dispose() methods don't have anything to do in this Screen.

The HelpScreen Class(es)

Next, let's implement the HelpScreen, HighscoreScreen, and GameScreen classes we used previously in the update() method.

We defined three help screens in Chapter 3, each more or less explaining one aspect of the game play. We now directly translate those to Screen implementations called HelpScreen, HelpScreen2, and HelpScreen3. They all have a single button that will initiate a screen transition. The HelpScreen3 screen will transition back to the MainMenuScreen. Figure 6–3 shows the three help screens with the drawing coordinates and touch areas.

Figure 6–3. *The three help screens, drawing coordinates, and touch areas*

Now that seems simple enough to implement. Let's start with the HelpScreen class, shown in Listing 6–6.

Listing 6–6. *HelpScreen.java, the First Help Screen*

```
package com.badlogic.androidgames.mrnom;

import java.util.List;

import com.badlogic.androidgames.framework.Game;
import com.badlogic.androidgames.framework.Graphics;
import com.badlogic.androidgames.framework.Input.TouchEvent;
import com.badlogic.androidgames.framework.Screen;

public class HelpScreen extends Screen {
    public HelpScreen(Game game) {
        super(game);
    }

    @Override
    public void update(float deltaTime) {
        List<TouchEvent> touchEvents = game.getInput().getTouchEvents();
```

```
            game.getInput().getKeyEvents();

            int len = touchEvents.size();
            for(int i = 0; i < len; i++) {
                TouchEvent event = touchEvents.get(i);
                if(event.type == TouchEvent.TOUCH_UP) {
                    if(event.x > 256 && event.y > 416 ) {
                        game.setScreen(new HelpScreen2(game));
                        if(Settings.soundEnabled)
                            Assets.click.play(1);
                        return;
                    }
                }
            }
        }

        @Override
        public void present(float deltaTime) {
            Graphics g = game.getGraphics();
            g.drawPixmap(Assets.background, 0, 0);
            g.drawPixmap(Assets.help1, 64, 100);
            g.drawPixmap(Assets.buttons, 256, 416, 0, 64, 64, 64);
        }

        @Override
        public void pause() {

        }

        @Override
        public void resume() {

        }

        @Override
        public void dispose() {

        }
    }
```

Again, very simple. We derive from Screen and implement a proper constructor. Next we have our familiar update() method, which simply checks if the button at the bottom was pressed. If that's the case, we play the click sound and transition to HelpScreen2.

The present() method just renders the background again, followed by the help image and the button.

The HelpScreen2 and HelpScreen3 classes look the same; the only difference is the help image they draw and the screen they transition to. I guess we can agree that we don't have to look at their code. On to the high-scores screen!

The High-Scores Screen

The high-scores screen simply draws the top five high scores we store in the Settings class, plus a fancy header telling the player that she is on the high-scores screen, and a button at the bottom left that will transition back to the main menu when pressed. The interesting part is how we render the high scores. Let's first have a look at where we render the images, which is shown in Figure 6–4.

Figure 6–4. *The high-scores screen, without high scores*

That looks as easy as the other screens we have implemented. But how can we draw the dynamic scores?

Rendering Numbers: An Excursion

We have an asset image called numbers.png that contains all digits from 0 to 9 plus a dot. Each digit is 20! 32 pixels, and the dot is 10! 32 pixels in size. The digits are arranged from left to right in ascending order. The high-scores screen should display five lines, each line showing one of the five high scores. One such line would start with the high score's position (e.g., "1." or "5."), followed by a space, followed by the actual score. How can we do that?

We have two things at our disposal: the numbers.png image and Graphics.drawPixmap(), which allows us to draw portions of an image to the screen. Say we want the first line of the default high scores (with the string "1. 100") to be rendered at (20, 100) so that the top-left corner of the digit 1 coincides with those coordinates. We call `Graphics.drawPixmap()` like this:

```
game.getGraphics().drawPixmap(Assets.numbers, 20, 100, 20, 0, 20, 32);
```

We know that the digit 1 has a width of 20 pixels. The next character of our string would have to be rendered at (20+20,100). In the case of the string "1. 100," this character is the dot, which has a width of 10 pixels in the numbers.png image:

```
game.getGraphics().drawPixmap(Assets.numbers, 40, 100, 200, 0, 10, 32);
```

The next character in the string needs to be rendered at (20+20+10,100). That character is a space, which we don't need to draw. All we need to do is advance on the x-axis by 20 pixels again, as we assume that's the width of the space character. The next character, 1, would therefore be rendered at (20+20+10+20,100). See a pattern here?

Given the coordinates of the upper-left corner of our first character in the string, we can loop through each character of the string, draw it, and increment the x-coordinate for the next character to be drawn by either 20 or 10 pixels, depending on the character we just drew.

We also need to figure out which portion of the numbers.png image we should draw given the current character. For that we need the x- and y-coordinates of the upper-left corner of that portion, as well as its width and height. The y-coordinate will always be zero, which should be obvious when looking at Figure 6–1. The height is also a constant; 32 in our case. The width is either 20 pixels (if the character of the string is a digit) or 10 pixels (if it is a dot). The only thing that we need to calculate is the x-coordinate of the portion in the numbers.png image. We can do that by using a neat little trick.

The characters in a string can be interpreted as Unicode characters or as 16–bit integers. This means that we can actually do calculations with those character codes. By a lucky coincidence, the characters 0 to 9 have ascending integer representations. We can use that fact to calculate the x-coordinate of the portion of the number.png image for a digit like this:

```
char character = string.charAt(index);
int x = (character - '0') * 20;
```

That will give us 0 for the character 0, 3 ! 20 = 60 for the character 3, and so on. That's exactly the x-coordinate of the portion of each digit. Of course, this won't work for the dot character, so we need to treat that specially. Let's summarize this in a method that can render one of our high-score lines given the string of the line and the x- and y-coordinates that the rendering should start at.

```
public void drawText(Graphics g, String line, int x, int y) {
    int len = line.length();
    for (int i = 0; i < len; i++) {
        char character = line.charAt(i);

        if (character == ' ') {
            x += 20;
            continue;
```

```
        }

        int srcX = 0;
        int srcWidth = 0;
        if (character == '.') {
            srcX = 200;
            srcWidth = 10;
        } else {
            srcX = (character - '0') * 20;
            srcWidth = 20;
        }

        g.drawPixmap(Assets.numbers, x, y, srcX, 0, srcWidth, 32);
        x += srcWidth;
    }
}
```

We iterate over each character of the string. If the current character is a space, we just advance the x-coordinate by 20 pixels. Otherwise we calculate the x-coordinate and width of the current character's region in the numbers.png image. The character is either a digit or a dot. We then render the current character and advance the rendering x-coordinate by the width of the character we've just drawn. This method will of course blow up if our string contains anything other than spaces, digits, and dots. Can you think of a way to make it work with any string?

Implementing the Screen

Equipped with this new knowledge, we can now easily implement the HighscoreScreen class, as shown in Listing 6–7.

Listing 6–7. *HighscoreScreen.java, Showing Us Our Best Achievements So Far*

```java
package com.badlogic.androidgames.mrnom;

import java.util.List;

import com.badlogic.androidgames.framework.Game;
import com.badlogic.androidgames.framework.Graphics;
import com.badlogic.androidgames.framework.Screen;
import com.badlogic.androidgames.framework.Input.TouchEvent;

public class HighscoreScreen extends Screen {
    String lines[] = new String[5];

    public HighscoreScreen(Game game) {
        super(game);

        for (int i = 0; i < 5; i++) {
            lines[i] = "" + (i + 1) + ". " + Settings.highscores[i];
        }
    }
```

As we want to stay friends with the garbage collector, we store the strings of the five high-score lines in a string array member. We construct the strings based on the Settings.highscores array in the constructor.

```
@Override
public void update(float deltaTime) {
    List<TouchEvent> touchEvents = game.getInput().getTouchEvents();
    game.getInput().getKeyEvents();

    int len = touchEvents.size();
    for (int i = 0; i < len; i++) {
        TouchEvent event = touchEvents.get(i);
        if (event.type == TouchEvent.TOUCH_UP) {
            if (event.x < 64 && event.y > 416) {
                if(Settings.soundEnabled)
                    Assets.click.play(1);
                game.setScreen(new MainMenuScreen(game));
                return;
            }
        }
    }
}
```

Next we define the update() method, which is unsurprisingly boring. All we do is check for whether a touch-up event hit the button in the bottom-left corner. If that's the case, we play the click sound and transition back to the MainMenuScreen.

```
@Override
public void present(float deltaTime) {
    Graphics g = game.getGraphics();

    g.drawPixmap(Assets.background, 0, 0);
    g.drawPixmap(Assets.mainMenu, 64, 20, 0, 42, 196, 42);

    int y = 100;
    for (int i = 0; i < 5; i++) {
        drawText(g, lines[i], 20, y);
        y += 50;
    }

    g.drawPixmap(Assets.buttons, 0, 416, 64, 64, 64, 64);
}
```

The present() method is pretty simple with the help of the mighty drawText() method we just defined. We render the background image first as usual, followed by the "HIGHSCORES" portion of the Assets.mainmenu image. We could have stored that in a separate file, but we reuse it to free up more memory.

Next we loop through the five strings for each high-score line we created in the constructor. We draw each line with the drawText() method. The first line starts at (20,100), the next line is rendered at (20,150), and so on. We just increase the y-coordinate for text rendering by 50 pixels for each line so that we have a nice vertical spacing between the lines. We finish the method off by drawing our button.

```java
public void drawText(Graphics g, String line, int x, int y) {
        int len = line.length();
        for (int i = 0; i < len; i++) {
            char character = line.charAt(i);

            if (character == ' ') {
                x += 20;
                continue;
            }

            int srcX = 0;
            int srcWidth = 0;
            if (character == '.') {
                srcX = 200;
                srcWidth = 10;
            } else {
                srcX = (character - '0') * 20;
                srcWidth = 20;
            }

            g.drawPixmap(Assets.numbers, x, y, srcX, 0, srcWidth, 32);
            x += srcWidth;
        }
    }

    @Override
    public void pause() {

    }

    @Override
    public void resume() {

    }

    @Override
    public void dispose() {

    }
}
```

The remaining methods should be self-explanatory. Let's get to the last missing piece of our Mr. Nom game: the game screen.

Abstracting...

So far we've only implemented boring UI stuff and some housekeeping code for our assets and settings. We'll now abstract the world of Mr. Nom and all the objects in it. We'll also free Mr. Nom from the screen resolution and let him live in his own little world with his own little coordinate system.

Abstracting the World of Mr. Nom: Model, View, Controller

If you are a long-time coder, you've probably heard about design patterns. They are more or less strategies to design your code given a scenario. Some of them are academic, and some have uses in the real world. For game development we can borrow some ideas from the *Model-View-Controller (MVC)* design pattern. It's often used by the database and web community to separate the data model from the presentation layer and the data manipulation layer. We won't strictly follow this design pattern, but rather adapt it in a simpler form.

So what does this mean for Mr. Nom? First of all we need an abstract representation of our world that is independent of any bitmaps, sounds, framebuffers, or input events. Instead we'll model Mr. Nom's world with a few simple classes in an object-oriented manner. We'll have a class for the stains in the world and a class for Mr. Nom himself. Mr. Nom is composed of a head and tail parts, which we'll also represent by a separate class. To tie everything together, we'll have an all-knowing class representing the complete world of Mr. Nom, including the stains and Mr. Nom himself. All this represents the *model* part of MVC.

The *view* in MVC will be the code that is responsible for rendering the world of Mr. Nom. We'll have a class or a method that takes the class for the world, reads its current state, and renders it to the screen. *How* it is rendered does not concern the model classes, though, and this is the most important lesson to take away from MVC. The model classes are independent of everything, but the view classes and methods depend on the model classes.

Finally we have the *controller* in MVC. It tells the model classes to change their state based on things like user input or the time ticking away. The model classes provide methods to the controller (e.g., with instructions like "Turn Mr. Nom to the left."), which the controller can then use to modify the state of the model. We don't have any code in the model classes that directly accesses things like the touchscreen or the accelerometer. This way we can keep the model classes clear of any external dependencies.

This may sound complicated, and you may be wondering why we do things this way. However, there are a lot of benefits to this approach. We can implement all our game logic without having to know about graphics, audio, or input devices. We can modify the rendering of the game world without having to change the model classes themselves. We could even go so far as to exchange a 2D world renderer with a 3D world renderer. We can easily add support for new input devices by using a controller. All it does is translate input events to method calls of the model classes. Want to turn Mr. Nom via the accelerometer? No problem—read the accelerometer values in the controller and translate them to a "turn Mr. Nom left" or "turn Mr. Nom right" method call on the model of Mr. Nom. Want to add support for the Zeemote? No problem, just do the same as in the case of the accelerometer! The best thing about using controllers is that we don't have to touch a single line of Mr. Nom's code to make all this happen.

Let's start by defining Mr. Nom's world. To do this we'll break away from the strict MVC pattern a little and use our graphical assets to illustrate the basic ideas. This will also help us to implement the view component later on (rendering Mr. Nom's abstract world in pixels).

Figure 6–5 shows the game screen with the world of Mr. Nom superimposed on it, in the form of a grid.

Figure 6–5. Mr. Nom's world superimposed onto our game screen

Notice that Mr. Nom's world is confined to a grid of 10! 13 cells. We address cells in a coordinate system with the origin in the upper-left corner at (0,0) spanning to the bottom-right corner at (9,12). Any part of Mr. Nom must be in one of these cells, and thus must have integer x- and y-coordinates within this world. The same is true for the stains in this world. Each part of Mr. Nom fits into exactly one cell of 1! 1 units. Note that the type of units doesn't matter—this is our own fantasy world free from the shackles of the SI system or pixels!

Mr. Nom can't travel outside this small world. If he passes an edge he'll just come out the other end, and all his parts will follow. (We have the same problem here on earth by the way—go in any direction for long enough and you'll come back to your starting point). Mr. Nom can also only advance cell by cell. All his parts will always be at integer coordinates. He'll never, for example, occupy two and a half cells.

NOTE: As stated earlier, what we use here is not a strict MVC pattern. If you are interested in the real definition of an MVC pattern, I suggest taking reading *Design Patterns: Elements of Reusable Object-Oriented Software*, by Erich Gamm, Richard Helm, Ralph Johnson, and John M. Vlissides (aka the Gang of Four) (Addison-Wesley, 1994). In their book, the MVC pattern is knows as the Observer pattern.

The Stain Class

The simplest object in Mr. Nom's world is a stain. It just sits in a cell of the world, waiting to be eaten. When we designed Mr. Nom, we created three different visual representations of a stain. The type of a stain does not make a difference in Mr. Nom's world, but we'll include it in our Stain class anyway. Listing 6–8 shows the Stain class.

Listing 6–8. *Stain.java*

```java
package com.badlogic.androidgames.mrnom;

public class Stain {
    public static final int TYPE_1 = 0;
    public static final int TYPE_2 = 1;
    public static final int TYPE_3 = 2;
    public int x, y;
    public int type;

    public Stain(int x, int y, int type) {
        this.x = x;
        this.y = y;
        this.type = type;
    }
}
```

The Stain class defines three public static constants that encode the type of a stain. Each Stain has three members, x- and y-coordinates in Mr. Nom's world, and a type, which is one of the constants defined earlier. To make our code simple, we don't include getters and setters, as is common practice. We finish the class off with a nice constructor that allows us to instantiate a Stain instance easily.

One thing to notice is the lack of any connection to graphics, sound, or other classes. The Stain class stands on its own, proudly encoding the attributes of a stain in Mr. Nom's world.

The Snake and SnakePart Classes

Mr. Nom is like a moving chain, composed of interconnected parts that will move along when we pick one part and drag it somewhere. Each part occupies a single cell in Mr. Nom's world, much like a stain. In our model, we do not distinguish between the head and tail parts, so we can have a single class that represents both types of parts of Mr.

Nom. Listing 6–9 shows called SnakePart class, which is used to define both parts of Mr. Nom.

Listing 6–9. *SnakePart.java*

```
package com.badlogic.androidgames.mrnom;

public class SnakePart {
    public int x, y;

    public SnakePart(int x, int y) {
        this.x = x;
        this.y = y;
    }
}
```

This is essentially the same as the Stain class—we just removed the type member. The first really interesting class of our model of Mr. Nom's world is the Snake class. Let's think about what it has to be able to do:

> It must store the head and tail parts.
>
> It must know which way Mr. Nom is currently heading.
>
> It must be able to grow a new tail part when Mr. Nom eats a stain.
>
> It must be able to move by one cell in the current direction.

The first and second items are easy. We just need a list of SnakePart instances—the first part in that list being the head and the other parts making up the tail. Mr. Nom can move up, down, left, and right. We can encode that with some constants and store his current direction in a member of the Snake class.

The third item isn't all that complicated either. We just add another SnakePart to the list of parts we already have. The question is, at what position we should add that part? It may sound surprising, but we give it the same position as the last part in the list. The reason for this becomes clearer when we look at how we can implement the last item on the preceding list: moving Mr. Nom.

Figure 6–6 shows Mr. Nom in his initial configuration. He is composed of three parts, the head, at (5,6), and two tail parts, at (5,7) and (5,8).

Figure 6–6. *Mr. Nom in his initial configuration*

The parts in the list are ordered beginning with the head and ending at the last tail part. When Mr. Nom advances by one cell, all the parts behind his head have to follow. However, Mr. Nom's parts might not be laid out in a straight line, as in Figure 6–6, so simply shifting all the parts in the direction Mr. Nom advances is not enough. We have to do something a little more sophisticated.

We need to start at the last part in the list, as counterintuitive as that may sound. We move it to the position of the part before it, and we repeat this for all other parts in the list except for the head, as there's no part before it. In the case of the head, we check which direction Mr. Nom is currently heading and modify the head's position accordingly. Figure 6–7 illustrates this with a bit more complicated configuration of Mr. Nom.

Figure 6–7. *Mr. Nom advancing and taking his tail with him*

This movement strategy works well with our eating strategy. When we add a new part to Mr. Nom, it will stay at the same position as the part before it the next time Mr. Nom moves. Also note that this will allow us to easily implement wrapping Mr. Nom to the other side of the world if he passes one of the edges. We just set the head's position accordingly, and the rest is done automatically.

With all this information we can now implement the Snake class representing Mr. Nom. Listing 6–10 shows the code.

Listing 6–10. *Snake.java; Mr. Nom in Code*

```java
package com.badlogic.androidgames.mrnom;

import java.util.ArrayList;
import java.util.List;

public class Snake {
    public static final int UP = 0;
    public static final int LEFT = 1;
    public static final int DOWN = 2;
    public static final int RIGHT = 3;

    public List<SnakePart> parts = new ArrayList<SnakePart>();
    public int direction;
```

We start off by defining a couple of constants that encode the direction of Mr. Nom. Remember that Mr. Nom can only turn left and right, so the way we define the constants' values is critical. It will later allow us to easily rotate the direction by plus and minus 90 degrees by just incrementing and decrementing the current direction constant by one.

Next we define a list called parts that holds all the parts of Mr. Nom. The first item in that list is the head, and the other items are the tail parts. The second member of the Snake class holds the direction Mr. Nom is currently heading in.

```java
public Snake() {
        direction = UP;
        parts.add(new SnakePart(5, 6));
        parts.add(new SnakePart(5, 7));
        parts.add(new SnakePart(5, 8));
    }
```

In the constructor, we set up Mr. Nom to be composed of his head and two additional tail parts, positioned more or less in the middle of the world, as shown previously in Figure 6–6. We also set the direction to Snake.UP so that Mr. Nom will advance upward by one cell the next time he's asked to advance.

```java
public void turnLeft() {
        direction += 1;
        if(direction > RIGHT)
            direction = UP;
    }

    public void turnRight() {
```

```
        direction -= 1;
        if(direction < UP)
            direction = RIGHT;
    }
```

The methods turnLeft() and turnRight() just modify the direction member of the Snake class. For a turn left we increment it by one, and for a turn right we decrement it. We also have to make sure that we wrap around if the direction value gets outside the range of the constants we defined earlier.

```
public void eat() {
        SnakePart end = parts.get(parts.size()-1);
        parts.add(new SnakePart(end.x, end.y));
    }
```

Next up is the eat() method. All it does is add a new SnakePart to the end of the list; this new part will have the same position as the current end part. Next time Mr. Nom advances, those to overlapping parts will move apart, as discussed earlier.

```
public void advance() {
        SnakePart head = parts.get(0);

        int len = parts.size() - 1;
        for(int i = len; i > 0; i--) {
            SnakePart before = parts.get(i-1);
            SnakePart part = parts.get(i);
            part.x = before.x;
            part.y = before.y;
        }

        if(direction == UP)
            head.y -= 1;
        if(direction == LEFT)
            head.x -= 1;
        if(direction == DOWN)
            head.y += 1;
        if(direction == RIGHT)
            head.x += 1;

        if(head.x < 0)
            head.x = 9;
        if(head.x > 9)
            head.x = 0;
        if(head.y < 0)
            head.y = 12;
        if(head.y > 12)
            head.y = 0;
    }
```

The next method, advance(),implements the logic illustrated in Figure 6–7. First we move each part to the position of the part before it, starting with the last part. We exclude the head from this mechanism. Then we move the head according to Mr. Nom's current direction. Finally we perform some checks to make sure Mr. Nom doesn't go outside his world. If that's the case we just wrap him around so that he comes out at the other side of the world.

```
public boolean checkBitten() {
        int len = parts.size();
        SnakePart head = parts.get(0);
        for(int i = 1; i < len; i++) {
            SnakePart part = parts.get(i);
            if(part.x == head.x && part.y == head.y)
                return true;
        }
        return false;
    }
}
```

The final method, checkBitten(), is a little helper method that checks if Mr. Nom has bitten his tail. All it does is check that no tail part is at the same position as the head. If that's the case, Mr. Nom will die and the game will end.

The World Class

The last of our model classes is called World. The World class has a couple of tasks to fulfill:

Keeping track of Mr. Nom (in the form of a Snake instance) as well as the Stain that dropped on the World. There will only ever be a single stain in our world.

Providing a method that will update Mr. Nom in a time-based manner (e.g., he should advance by one cell every 0.5 seconds). This method will also check if Mr. Nom has eaten a stain or has bitten himself.

Keeping track of the score, which is basically just the number of stains eaten so far times 10.

Increasing the speed of Mr. Nom after every ten stains he's eaten. That will make the game a little bit more challenging.

Keeping track of whether Mr. Nom is still alive. We'll use this to determine whether the game is over later on.

Creating a new stain after Mr. Nom eats the current one (a subtle but important and surprisingly complex task).

There are only two items on this task list that we haven't discussed yet: updating the world in a time-based manner and placing a new stain.

Time-Based Movement of Mr. Nom

In Chapter 3 we talked about time-based movement. This basically means that we define velocities of all our game objects, measure the time that has passed since the last update (aka the delta time), and advance the objects by multiplying their velocity by the delta time. In the example given in Chapter 3, we used floating-point values to achieve this. Mr. Nom's parts have integer positions, though, so we need to figure out how to advance the objects in this scenario.

Let's first define the velocity of Mr. Nom. The world of Mr. Nom has time, and we measure it in seconds. Initially Mr. Nom should advance by one cell every 0.5 seconds. All we need to do is keep track of how much time has passed since we last advanced Mr. Nom. If that accumulated time goes over our 0.5-second threshold, we call the Snake.advance() method and reset our time accumulator. Where do we get those delta times from? Remember the Screen.update() method. It gets the frame delta time. We just pass that on to the update method of our World class, which will do the accumulation. To make the game more challenging, we will decrease that threshold by 0.05 seconds each time Mr. Nom eats another ten stains. We have to make sure, of course, that we don't reach a threshold of 0, or else Mr. Nom would travel at infinite speed—something Einstein wouldn't take to kindly.

Placing Stains

The second issue we have to solve is how to place a new stain when Mr. Nom has eaten the current one. It should appear in a random cell of the world. So, we could just instantiate a new Stain with a random position, right? Sadly it's not that easy.

Imagine Mr. Nom taking up a considerable number of cells. The probability that the stain would be placed in a cell that's already occupied by Mr. Nom will increase the bigger Mr. Nom gets. We thus have to find a cell that is currently not occupied by Mr. Nom. Easy again, right? Just iterate over all cells and use the first one that is not occupied by Mr. Nom.

Well, again, that's a little suboptimal. If we started our search at the same position, the stain wouldn't be placed randomly. Instead we'll start at a random position in the world, scan all cells until we reach the end of the world, and then scan all cells above the start position if we haven't found a free cell yet.

How do we check whether a cell is free? The naïve solution would be to go over all cells, take each cell's x- and y-coordinates, and check all the parts of Mr. Nom against those coordinates. We have 10 ! 13 = 130 cells, and Mr. Nom can take up 55 cells. That would be 130 ! 55 = 7,150 checks! Granted, most devices could handle that, but we can do better.

We'll create a two-dimensional array of booleans where each array element represents a cell in the world. When we have to place a new stain, we first go through all parts of Mr. Nom and set those elements that are occupied by a part in the array to true. We then simply choose a random position from which we start scanning until we find a free cell that we can place the new stain in. With Mr. Nom being composed of 55 parts, that would take 130 + 55 = 185 checks. That's a lot better!

Determining When the Game Is Over

There's one last thing we have to think of: what if all cells are taken up by Mr. Nom? In that case, the game would be over, as Mr. Nom would officially become the whole world. Given that we add 10 to the score each time Mr. Nom eats a stain, the maximally achievable score is (10 ! 13 – 3) ! 10 = 1,000 points (remember, Mr. Nom starts off with three parts already).

Implementing the World Class

Phew, we have a lot of stuff to implement, so let's get going. Listing 6–11 shows the code of the World class.

Listing 6–11. *World.java*

```java
package com.badlogic.androidgames.mrnom;

import java.util.Random;

public class World {
    static final int WORLD_WIDTH = 10;
    static final int WORLD_HEIGHT = 13;
    static final int SCORE_INCREMENT = 10;
    static final float TICK_INITIAL = 0.5f;
    static final float TICK_DECREMENT = 0.05f;

    public Snake snake;
    public Stain stain;
    public boolean gameOver = false;;
    public int score = 0;

    boolean fields[][] = new boolean[WORLD_WIDTH][WORLD_HEIGHT];
    Random random = new Random();
    float tickTime = 0;
    static float tick = TICK_INITIAL;
```

As always, we start off by defining a couple of constants—in this case, the world's width and height in cells, the value we increment the score with each time Mr. Nom eats a stain, the initial time interval used to advance Mr. Nom (called a *tick*), and the value we decrement the tick each time Mr. Nom has eaten ten stains in order to speed up things a little.

Next we have some public members that hold a Snake instance, a Stain instance, a boolean that stores whether the game is over, and the current score.

We define another four package private members: the 2D array we'll use to place a new stain; an instance of the Random class, through which we'll produce random numbers to place the stain and generate its type; the time accumulator variable, tickTime, to which we'll add the frame delta time; and the current duration of a tick, which defines how often we advance Mr. Nom.

```java
public World() {
        snake = new Snake();
        placeStain();
    }
```

In the constructor we create an instance of the Snake class, which will have the initial configuration shown in Figure 6–6. We also place the first random stain via the placeStain() method.

```java
private void placeStain() {
        for (int x = 0; x < WORLD_WIDTH; x++) {
            for (int y = 0; y < WORLD_HEIGHT; y++) {
                fields[x][y] = false;
            }
        }

        int len = snake.parts.size();
        for (int i = 0; i < len; i++) {
            SnakePart part = snake.parts.get(i);
            fields[part.x][part.y] = true;
        }

        int stainX = random.nextInt(WORLD_WIDTH);
        int stainY = random.nextInt(WORLD_HEIGHT);
        while (true) {
            if (fields[stainX][stainY] == false)
                break;
            stainX += 1;
            if (stainX >= WORLD_WIDTH) {
                stainX = 0;
                stainY += 1;
                if (stainY >= WORLD_HEIGHT) {
                    stainY = 0;
                }
            }
        }
        stain = new Stain(stainX, stainY, random.nextInt(3));
    }
```

The placeStain() method implements the placement strategy discussed earlier. We start off by clearing the cell array. Next we set all the cells occupied by parts of the snake to true. Finally we scan the array for a free cell starting at a random position. Once we have found a free cell, we create a Stain with a random type. Note that if all cells are occupied by Mr. Nom, then the loop will never terminate. We'll make sure that will never happen in the next method.

```java
public void update(float deltaTime) {
        if (gameOver)
            return;

        tickTime += deltaTime;

        while (tickTime > tick) {
            tickTime -= tick;
            snake.advance();
            if (snake.checkBitten()) {
                gameOver = true;
                return;
            }
```

```
        SnakePart head = snake.parts.get(0);
        if (head.x == stain.x && head.y == stain.y) {
            score += SCORE_INCREMENT;
            snake.eat();
            if (snake.parts.size() == WORLD_WIDTH * WORLD_HEIGHT) {
                gameOver = true;
                return;
            } else {
                placeStain();
            }

            if (score % 100 == 0 && tick - TICK_DECREMENT > 0) {
                tick -= TICK_DECREMENT;
            }
        }
    }
  }
}
```

The `update()` method is responsible for updating the `World` and all the objects in it based on the delta time we pass to it. This method will be called each frame in the game screen so that the `World` is updated constantly. We start off by checking whether the game is over. If that's the case, then we don't need to update anything, of course. Next we add the delta time to our accumulator. The `while` loop will use up as many ticks as have been accumulated (e.g., when `tickTime` is 1.2 and one tick should take 0.5 seconds, we can update the world twice, leaving 0.2 seconds in the accumulator). This is called a *fixed-time-step simulation*.

In each iteration we first subtract the tick interval from the accumulator. Next we tell Mr. Nom to advance. We check if he has bitten himself afterward, and set the game-over flag if that's the case. Finally we check whether Mr. Nom's head is in the same cell as the stain. If that's the case we increment the score and tell Mr. Nom to grow. Next we check whether Mr. Nom is composed of as many parts as there are cells in the world. If that's the case, the game is over and we return from the function. Otherwise we place a new stain with the `placeStain()` method. The last thing we do is check whether Mr. Nom has just eaten ten more stains. If that's the case and our threshold is above zero, we decrease it by 0.05 seconds. The tick will be shorter and thus make Mr. Nom move faster.

This completes our set of model classes. The last thing we need to implement is the game screen!

The GameScreen Class

There's only one more screen to implement. Let's see what that screen does:

> As defined in Mr. Nom's design in Chapter 3, it can be in one of three states: waiting for the user to confirm that he's ready, running the game, waiting in a paused state, and waiting for the user to click a button in the game-over state.

In the ready state we simply ask the user to touch the screen to start the game.

In the running state we update the world, render it, and also tell Mr. Nom to turn left and right when the player presses one of the buttons at the bottom of the screen.

In the paused state we simply show two options: one to resume the game and one to quit it.

In the game-over state we tell the user that the game is over and provide him with a button to touch so that he can get back to the main menu.

For each state we have different update and present methods to implement, as each state does different things and shows a different UI.

Once the game is over we have to make sure that we store the score if it is a high score.

That's quite a bit of responsibility, which translates to more code than usual. We'll therefore split up the source listing of this class. Before we dive into the code, let's lay out how we arrange the different UI elements in each state. Figure 6–8 shows the four different states.

Figure 6–8. *The game screen in its four states: ready, running, paused, and game-over*

Note that we also render the score at the bottom of the screen, along with a line that separates Mr. Nom's world from the buttons at the bottom. The score is rendered with the same routine that we used in the HighscoreScreen. We additionally center it horizontally based on the score string width.

The last missing bit of information is how to render Mr. Nom's world based on its model. That's actually pretty easy. Take a look at Figure 6–1 and 6–5 again. Each cell is exactly 32! 32 pixels in size. The stain images are also 32! 32 pixels in size, and so are the tail parts of Mr. Nom. The head images of Mr. Nom for all directions are 42! 42 pixels, so they don't fit entirely into a single cell. That's not a problem, though. All we need to do to render Mr. Nom's world is take each stain and snake part, and multiply its world coordinates by 32 to arrive at the object's center in pixels on the screen—for example, a stain at (3,2) in world coordinates would have its center at 96! 64 on the screen. Based on these centers, all that's left to do is take the appropriate asset and render it centered around those coordinates. Let's get coding. Listing 6–12 shows the GameScreen class.

Listing 6–12. *GameScreen.java*

```java
package com.badlogic.androidgames.mrnom;

import java.util.List;

import android.graphics.Color;

import com.badlogic.androidgames.framework.Game;
import com.badlogic.androidgames.framework.Graphics;
import com.badlogic.androidgames.framework.Input.TouchEvent;
import com.badlogic.androidgames.framework.Pixmap;
import com.badlogic.androidgames.framework.Screen;

public class GameScreen extends Screen {
    enum GameState {
        Ready,
        Running,
        Paused,
        GameOver
    }

    GameState state = GameState.Ready;
    World world;
    int oldScore = 0;
    String score = "0";
```

We start off by defining an enumeration called GameState that encodes our four states (ready, running, paused, and game-over). Next we define a member that holds the current state of the screen, another member that holds the World instance, and two more members that hold the currently displayed score in the form of an integer and as a string. The reason we have the last two members is that we don't want to constantly create new strings from the World.score member each time we draw the score. Instead we'll cache the string and only create a new one when the score changes. That way we play nice with the garbage collector.

```java
    public GameScreen(Game game) {
        super(game);
        world = new World();
    }
```

The constructor just calls the superclass constructor and creates a new World instance. The game screen will be in the ready state after the constructor returns to the caller.

```java
@Override
    public void update(float deltaTime) {
        List<TouchEvent> touchEvents = game.getInput().getTouchEvents();
        game.getInput().getKeyEvents();
```

```
        if(state == GameState.Ready)
            updateReady(touchEvents);
        if(state == GameState.Running)
            updateRunning(touchEvents, deltaTime);
        if(state == GameState.Paused)
            updatePaused(touchEvents);
        if(state == GameState.GameOver)
            updateGameOver(touchEvents);
    }
```

Next comes the screen's update() method. All it does is fetch the TouchEvents and
KeyEvents from the input module and then delegate the update to one of the four update
methods that we implement for each state based on the current state.

```
private void updateReady(List<TouchEvent> touchEvents) {
        if(touchEvents.size() > 0)
            state = GameState.Running;
    }
```

The next method is called updateReady(). It will be called when the screen is in the
ready state. All it does is check if the screen was touched. If that's the case, it changes
the state to running.

```
private void updateRunning(List<TouchEvent> touchEvents, float deltaTime) {
        int len = touchEvents.size();
        for(int i = 0; i < len; i++) {
            TouchEvent event = touchEvents.get(i);
            if(event.type == TouchEvent.TOUCH_UP) {
                if(event.x < 64 && event.y < 64) {
                    if(Settings.soundEnabled)
                        Assets.click.play(1);
                    state = GameState.Paused;
                    return;
                }
            }
            if(event.type == TouchEvent.TOUCH_DOWN) {
                if(event.x < 64 && event.y > 416) {
                    world.snake.turnLeft();
                }
                if(event.x > 256 && event.y > 416) {
                    world.snake.turnRight();
                }
            }
        }

        world.update(deltaTime);
        if(world.gameOver) {
            if(Settings.soundEnabled)
                Assets.bitten.play(1);
            state = GameState.GameOver;
        }
        if(oldScore != world.score) {
            oldScore = world.score;
            score = "" + oldScore;
            if(Settings.soundEnabled)
```

```
            Assets.eat.play(1);
        }
    }
```

The updateRunning()method first checks whether the pause button in the top-left corner of the screen was pressed. If that's the case, it sets the state to paused. It then checks whether one of the controller buttons at the bottom of the screen was pressed. Note that we don't check for touch-up events here, but for touch-down events. If either of the buttons was pressed, we tell the Snake instance of the World to turn left or right. That's right, the updateRunning() method contains the controller code of our MVC schema! After all the touch events have been checked, we tell the world to update itself with the given delta time. If the World signals that the game is over, we change the state accordingly, and also play the bitten.ogg sound. Next we check if the old score we have cached is different from the score that the World stores. If it is, then we know two things: Mr. Nom has eaten a stain, and the score string must be changed. In that case, we play the eat.ogg sound. And that's all there is to the running state update.

```java
private void updatePaused(List<TouchEvent> touchEvents) {
    int len = touchEvents.size();
    for(int i = 0; i < len; i++) {
        TouchEvent event = touchEvents.get(i);
        if(event.type == TouchEvent.TOUCH_UP) {
            if(event.x > 80 && event.x <= 240) {
                if(event.y > 100 && event.y <= 148) {
                    if(Settings.soundEnabled)
                        Assets.click.play(1);
                    state = GameState.Running;
                    return;
                }
                if(event.y > 148 && event.y < 196) {
                    if(Settings.soundEnabled)
                        Assets.click.play(1);
                    game.setScreen(new MainMenuScreen(game));
                    return;
                }
            }
        }
    }
}
```

The updatePaused() method again just checks whether one of the menu options was touched and changes state accordingly.

```java
private void updateGameOver(List<TouchEvent> touchEvents) {
    int len = touchEvents.size();
    for(int i = 0; i < len; i++) {
        TouchEvent event = touchEvents.get(i);
        if(event.type == TouchEvent.TOUCH_UP) {
            if(event.x >= 128 && event.x <= 192 &&
                event.y >= 200 && event.y <= 264) {
                if(Settings.soundEnabled)
                    Assets.click.play(1);
                game.setScreen(new MainMenuScreen(game));
                return;
```

```
                }
            }
        }
    }
```

The updateGameOver() method also just checks if the button in the middle of the screen was pressed. If it has, then we initiate a screen transition back to the main menu screen.

```
@Override
    public void present(float deltaTime) {
        Graphics g = game.getGraphics();

        g.drawPixmap(Assets.background, 0, 0);
        drawWorld(world);
        if(state == GameState.Ready)
            drawReadyUI();
        if(state == GameState.Running)
            drawRunningUI();
        if(state == GameState.Paused)
            drawPausedUI();
        if(state == GameState.GameOver)
            drawGameOverUI();

        drawText(g, score, g.getWidth() / 2 - score.length()*20 / 2, g.getHeight() -
42);
    }
```

Next up are the rendering methods. The present() method first draws the background image, as that is needed in all states. Next it calls the respective drawing method for the state we are in. Finally it renders Mr. Nom's world and draws the score at the bottom-center of the screen.

```
private void drawWorld(World world) {
        Graphics g = game.getGraphics();
        Snake snake = world.snake;
        SnakePart head = snake.parts.get(0);
        Stain stain = world.stain;


        Pixmap stainPixmap = null;
        if(stain.type == Stain.TYPE_1)
            stainPixmap = Assets.stain1;
        if(stain.type == Stain.TYPE_2)
            stainPixmap = Assets.stain2;
        if(stain.type == Stain.TYPE_3)
            stainPixmap = Assets.stain3;
        int x = stain.x * 32;
        int y = stain.y * 32;
        g.drawPixmap(stainPixmap, x, y);

        int len = snake.parts.size();
        for(int i = 1; i < len; i++) {
            SnakePart part = snake.parts.get(i);
            x = part.x * 32;
            y = part.y * 32;
            g.drawPixmap(Assets.tail, x, y);
        }
```

```
        Pixmap headPixmap = null;
        if(snake.direction == Snake.UP)
            headPixmap = Assets.headUp;
        if(snake.direction == Snake.LEFT)
            headPixmap = Assets.headLeft;
        if(snake.direction == Snake.DOWN)
            headPixmap = Assets.headDown;
        if(snake.direction == Snake.RIGHT)
            headPixmap = Assets.headRight;
        x = head.x * 32 + 16;
        y = head.y * 32 + 16;
        g.drawPixmap(headPixmap, x - headPixmap.getWidth() / 2, y -
headPixmap.getHeight() / 2);
    }
```

The drawWorld() method draws the world, as we just discussed. It starts off by choosing the Pixmap to use for rendering the stain, and then draws it and centers it horizontally at its screen position. Next we render all the tail parts of Mr. Nom, which is pretty simple. Finally we choose which Pixmap of the head to use based on Mr. Nom's direction, and draw that Pixmap at the position of the head in screen coordinates. As with the other objects, we also center the image around that position. And that's the code of the view in MVC.

```
private void drawReadyUI() {
        Graphics g = game.getGraphics();

        g.drawPixmap(Assets.ready, 47, 100);
        g.drawLine(0, 416, 480, 416, Color.BLACK);
    }

    private void drawRunningUI() {
        Graphics g = game.getGraphics();

        g.drawPixmap(Assets.buttons, 0, 0, 64, 128, 64, 64);
        g.drawLine(0, 416, 480, 416, Color.BLACK);
        g.drawPixmap(Assets.buttons, 0, 416, 64, 64, 64, 64);
        g.drawPixmap(Assets.buttons, 256, 416, 0, 64, 64, 64);
    }

    private void drawPausedUI() {
        Graphics g = game.getGraphics();

        g.drawPixmap(Assets.pause, 80, 100);
        g.drawLine(0, 416, 480, 416, Color.BLACK);
    }

    private void drawGameOverUI() {
        Graphics g = game.getGraphics();

        g.drawPixmap(Assets.gameOver, 62, 100);
        g.drawPixmap(Assets.buttons, 128, 200, 0, 128, 64, 64);
        g.drawLine(0, 416, 480, 416, Color.BLACK);
    }

    public void drawText(Graphics g, String line, int x, int y) {
```

```
            int len = line.length();
            for (int i = 0; i < len; i++) {
                char character = line.charAt(i);

                if (character == ' ') {
                    x += 20;
                    continue;
                }

                int srcX = 0;
                int srcWidth = 0;
                if (character == '.') {
                    srcX = 200;
                    srcWidth = 10;
                } else {
                    srcX = (character - '0') * 20;
                    srcWidth = 20;
                }

                g.drawPixmap(Assets.numbers, x, y, srcX, 0, srcWidth, 32);
                x += srcWidth;
            }
        }
```

The methods drawReadUI(), drawRunningUI(), drawPausedUI(), and drawGameOverUI()
are nothing new. They perform the same old UI rendering as always, based on the
coordinates shown Figure 6–8. The drawText() method is the same as the one in
HighscoreScreen, so we won't discuss that one either.

```
        @Override
        public void pause() {
            if(state == GameState.Running)
                state = GameState.Paused;

            if(world.gameOver) {
                Settings.addScore(world.score);
                Settings.save(game.getFileIO());
            }
        }

        @Override
        public void resume() {

        }

        @Override
        public void dispose() {

        }
    }
```

Finally there's one last vital method, pause(), which gets called when the activity is
paused or the game screen is replaced by another screen. That's the perfect place to
save our settings. First we set the state of the game to paused. If the paused() method
got called due to the activity being paused, this will guarantee that the user will be asked

to resume the game when she returns to it. That's good behavior, as it would be stressful to immediately pick up from where one left the game. Next we check whether the game screen is in a game-over state. If that's the case, we add the score the player achieved to the high scores (or not, depending on its value) and save all the settings to the external storage.

And that's it. We've written a full-fledged game for Android from scratch! We can be proud of ourselves, as we've conquered all the necessary topics to create almost any game we like. From here on, it's mostly just cosmetics.

Summary

In this chapter, we implemented a complete game on top of our framework with all the bells and whistles (minus music). You learned why it makes sense to separate the model from the view and the controller, and you learned that we don't need to define our game world in terms of pixels. We could take this code and replace the rendering portions with OpenGL ES, making Mr. Nom go 3D. We could also spice up the current renderer by adding animations to Mr. Nom, adding in some color, adding new game mechanics, and so on. We have just scratched the surface of the possibilities, however.

Before continuing with the book, I suggest taking the game code and playing around with it. Add some new game modes, power-ups, and enemies—anything you can think of.

Once you come back, in the next chapter we'll beef up our knowledge of graphics programming to make our games look a bit fancier, and we'll also take the first steps into the third dimension!

Chapter 7

OpenGL ES: A Gentle Introduction

Mr. Nom was a great success. Due to our good initial design and the game framework we wrote, actually implementing Mr. Nom was a breeze. Best of all, the game runs smoothly even on low-end devices. Of course, Mr. Nom is not a very complex or graphically intense game, so using the Canvas API for rendering was a good idea.

However, once you want to do something more complex—say, something like Replica Island—you will hit a wall: Canvas just can't keep up with the visual complexity of such a game. And if you want to go fancy-pants 3D, Canvas won't help you either. So what can we do?

This is where OpenGL ES comes to the rescue. In this chapter we'll first briefly look at what OpenGL ES actually is and does. We'll then focus on using OpenGL ES for 2D graphics, without having to dive into the more mathematically complex realms of using the API for 3D graphics (we'll get to that in a later chapter). We'll take baby steps at first, as OpenGL ES can get quite involved. So, let's get to know OpenGL ES.

What Is OpenGL ES and Why Should I Care?

OpenGL ES is an industry standard for (3D) graphics programming. It is especially targeted at mobile and embedded devices. It is maintained by the Khronos Group, which is a conglomerate of companies including ATI, NVIDIA, and Intel, who together define and extend the standard.

Speaking of standards, there are currently three incremental versions of OpenGL ES: 1.0, 1.1, and 2.0. The first two are the ones we are concerned with in this book. All Android devices support OpenGL ES 1.0, and most also support 1.1, which adds some new features to the 1.0 specification. OpenGL ES 2.0, however, breaks compatibility with the 1.x versions. You can use either 1.x or 2.0, but not both at the same time. The reason for this is that the 1.x versions use a programming model called *fixed-function pipeline*, while 2.0 lets you programmatically define parts of the rendering pipeline via *so-called* shaders.

Many of the second-generation devices already support OpenGL ES 2.0; however, the Java bindings are currently not in a usable state (unless you target the new Android 2.3). OpenGL ES 1.x is more than good enough for most games, though, so we will stick to it here.

> **NOTE:** The emulator only supports OpenGL ES 1.0. The implementation is a little shoddy, though, so never rely on the emulator for testing. Use a real device.

OpenGL ES is an API that comes in the form of a set of C header files provided by the Khronos group, along with a very detailed specification of how the API defined in those headers should behave. This includes things such as how pixels and lines have to be rendered. Hardware manufacturers then take this specification and implement it for their GPU on top of the GPU driver. The quality of these implementations varies a little; some companies strictly adhere to the standard (PowerVR) while others seem to have difficulty sticking to the standard. This can sometimes result in GPU-dependent bugs in the implementation that have nothing to do with Android itself, but with the hardware drivers provided by the manufacturers. I'll point out any device-specific issues along our way into OpenGL ES land.

> **NOTE:** OpenGL ES is more or less a sibling of the more feature-rich desktop OpenGL standard. It deviates from the latter in that some of the functionality is reduced or completely removed. Nevertheless, it is possible to write an application that can run with both specifications, which is great if you want to port your game to the desktop as well.

So what does OpenGL ES actually do? The short answer is that's it's a lean and mean triangle-rendering machine. The long answer is a little bit more involved.

The Programming Model: An Analogy

OpenGL ES is in general a 3D graphics programming API. As such it has a pretty nice and (hopefully) easy-to-understand programming model that we can illustrate with a simple analogy.

Think of OpenGL ES as working like a camera. To take a picture you have to first go to the scene you want to photograph. Your scene is composed of objects—say, a table with more objects on it. They all have a position and orientation relative to your camera, as well as different materials and textures. Glass is translucent and a little reflective, a table is probably made out of wood, a magazine has the latest photo of some politician on it, and so on. Some of the objects might even move around (e.g., a fruit fly you can't get rid of). Your camera also has some properties, such as focal length, field of view, image resolution and size the photo will be taken at, and its own position and orientation within the world (relative to some origin). Even if both objects and the camera are moving, when you press the button to take the photo you catch a still image of the scene (for now we'll neglect the shutter speed, which might cause a blurry image). For that infinitely small moment everything stands still and is well defined, and the picture reflects exactly all those configurations of positions, orientations, textures, materials, and lighting. Figure 7–1 shows an abstract scene with a camera, a light, and three objects with different materials.

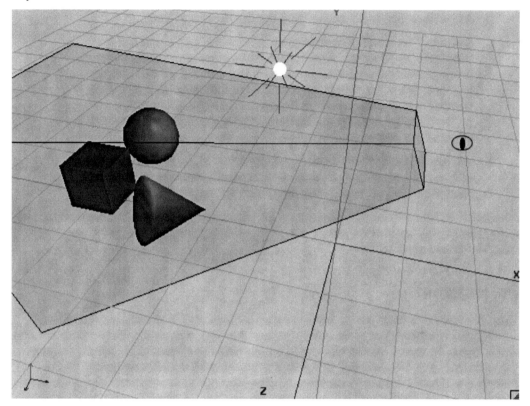

Figure 7–1. *An abstract scene*

Each object has a position and orientation relative to the scene's origin. The camera, indicated by the eye, also has a position in relation to the scene's origin. The pyramid in Figure 7–1 is the so-called *view volume* or *view frustum*, which shows how much of the scene the camera captures and how the camera is oriented. The little white ball with the rays is our light source in the scene, which also has a position relative to the origin.

We can directly map this scene to OpenGL ES, but to do so we need to define a couple of things:

▪ *Objects (aka models)*: These are generally composed of two four: their geometry, as well as their color, texture, and material. The geometry is specified as a set of triangles. Each triangle is composed of three points in 3D space, so we have x-, y-, and z coordinates defined relative to the coordinate system origin, as in Figure 7–1. Note that the z-axis points toward us. The color is usually specified as an RGB triple, as we are already used to. Textures and materials are little bit more involved. We'll get to those later on.

- *Lights*: OpenGL ES offers us a couple of different light types with various attributes. They are just mathematical objects with a position and/or direction in 3D space, plus attributes such as color.

- *Camera*: This is also a mathematical object that has a position and orientation in 3D space. Additionally it has parameters that govern how much of the image we see, similar to a real camera. All this things together define a view volume, or view frustum (indicated as the pyramid with the top cut off in Figure 7–1). Anything inside this pyramid can be seen by the camera; anything outside will not make it into the final picture.

- *Viewport*: This defines the size and resolution of the final image. Think of it as the type of film you put into your analog camera or the image resolution you get for pictures taken with your digital camera.

Given all this, OpenGL ES can construct a 2D bitmap of our scene from the point of view of the camera. Notice that we define everything in 3D space. So how can OpenGL ES map that to two dimensions?

Projections

This 2D mapping is done via something called *projection*. We already mentioned that OpenGL ES is mainly concerned with triangles. A single triangle has three points defined in 3D space. To render such a triangle to the framebuffer, OpenGL ES needs to know the coordinates of these 3D points within the pixel-based coordinate system of the framebuffer. Once it knows those three corner-point coordinates, it can simply draw the pixels in the framebuffer that are inside the triangle. We could even write our own little OpenGL ES implementation by projecting 3D points to 2D, and simply draw lines between them via the Canvas.

There are two kinds of projections that are commonly used in 3D graphics. :

- *Parallel, or orthographic, projection*: If you have ever played with a CAD application you might already know about these. A parallel projection doesn't care how far an object is away from the camera; the object will always have the same size in the final image. This type of projection is typically used for rendering 2D graphics in OpenGL ES.

- *Perspective projections*: These are what we are used to when using our eyes. Objects further away from us will appear smaller on our retina. This type of projection is typically used when we do 3D graphics with OpenGL ES.

In both cases we need something called a *projection plane*. This is nearly exactly the same as the retina of our eyes. It's where the light is actually registered to form the final image. While a mathematical plane is infinite, our retina is limited in area. Our OpenGL

ES "retina" is equal to the rectangle at the top of the view frustum in Figure 7–1. This part of the view frustum is where OpenGL ES will project the points to. It is called the *near clipping plane* and has its own little 2D coordinate system. Figure 7–2 shows that near clipping plane again, from the point of view of the camera, with the coordinate system superimposed.

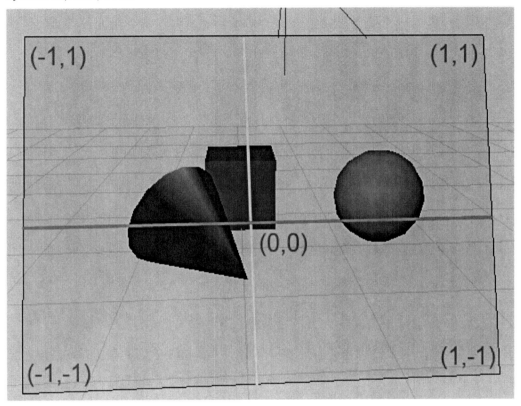

Figure 7–2. *The near clipping plane (also known as the projection plane) and its coordinate system.*

Note that the coordinate system is by no means fixed. We can manipulate it so that we can work in any projected coordinate system we like (e.g., we could instruct OpenGL ESto let the origin be in the bottom-left corner, and let the visible area of the "retina" be 480 units on the x-axis and 320 units on the y-axis). Sounds familiar? Yes, OpenGL ES allows us to specify any coordinate system we want for the projected points.

Once we specify our view frustum, OpenGL ES then takes each point of a triangle and shoots a ray from it through the projection plane. The difference between a parallel and a perspective projection is how the direction of those rays is constructed. Figure 7–3 shows the difference between the two, viewed from above.

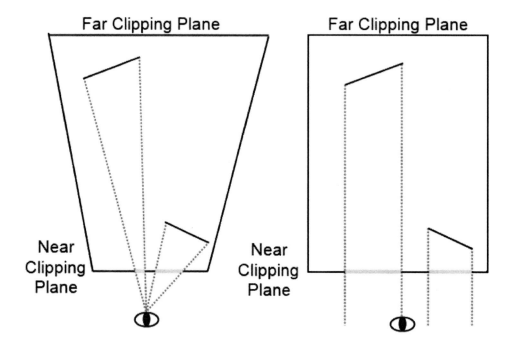

Figure 7–3. *A perspective projection (left) and a parallel projection (right)*

A perspective projection shoots the rays from the triangle points through the camera (or eye, in this case). Objects further away will thus appear smaller on the projection plane. When we use a parallel projection, the rays are shot perpendicular to the projection plane. In this case an object will keep its size on the projection plane no matter how far away it is.

Our projection plane is called a near clipping plane in OpenGL ES lingo, as pointed out earlier. All of the sides of the view frustum have similar names. The one furthest away from the camera is called the far clipping plane. The others are called the left, right, top, and bottom clipping planes. Anything outside or behind those planes will not be rendered. Objects that are partially within the view frustum will be clipped from these planes, meaning that the parts outside the view frustum get cut away. That's where the name *clipping plane* comes from.

You might be wondering why the view frustum of the parallel projection case in Figure 7–3 is rectangular. It turns out that the projection is actually governed by how we define our clipping planes. In the case of a perspective projection, the left, right, top, and bottom clipping planes are not perpendicular to the near and far planes (see Figure 7–3, which only shows the left and right clipping planes. In the case of the parallel projection, these planes are perpendicular, which tells OpenGL ES to render everything at the same size no matter how far away it is from the camera.

Normalized Device Space and the Viewport

Once OpenGL ES has figured out the projected points of a triangle on the near clipping plane, it can finally translate them to pixel coordinates in the framebuffer. For this, it must first transform the points to so-called *normalized device space*. This equals the coordinate system depicted in Figure 7–2. Based on these normalized device space coordinates OpenGL ES calculates the final framebuffer pixel coordinates via the following simple formulas:

```
pixelX = (norX + 1) / (viewportWidth + 1) + norX
pixelY = (norY + 1) / (viewportHeight +1) + norY
```

where norX and norY are the normalized device coordinates of a 3D point, and viewportWidth and viewportHeight are the size of the viewport in pixels on the x- and y-axes. We don't have to worry about the normalized device coordinates all that much, as OpenGL will do the transformation for us automagically. What we do care about, though, are the viewport and the view frustum.

Matrices

Later you will see how to specify a view frustum, and thus a projection. OpenGL ES expresses projections in the form of so-called *matrices*. For our purposes we don't need to know the internals of matrices. We only need to know what they do to the points we define in our scene. Here's the executive summary of matrices:

■ A matrix encodes transformations to be applied to a point. A transformation can be a projection, a translation (in which the point is moved around), a rotation around another point and axis, or a scale, among other thing.

■ By multiplying such a matrix with a point, we apply the transformation to the point. For example, multiplying a point with a matrix that encodes a translation by 10 units on the x-axis will move the point 10 units on the x-axis and thereby modify its coordinates.

■ We can concatenate transformations stored in separate matrices into a single matrix by multiplying the matrices. When we multiply this single concatenated matrix with a point, all the transformations stored in that matrix will be applied to that point. The order in which the transformations are applied is dependent on the order in which we multiplied the matrices with each other.

- There's a special matrix called an *identity matrix*. If we multiply a matrix or a point with it, nothing will happen. Think of multiplying a point or matrix by an identity matrix as multiplying a number by 1. It simply has no effect. The relevance of the identity matrix will become clear once we learn how OpenGL ES handles matrices (see the section "Matrix Modes and Active Matrices"). A classic hen and egg problem.

> **NOTE:** When I talk about points in this context, I actually mean 3D vectors.

OpenGL ES has three different matrices that it applies to the points of our models:

- *Model-view matrix*: We can use this matrix to move, rotate, or scale the points of our triangles around (this is the *model* part of the model-view matrix). This matrix is also used to specify the position and orientation of our camera (this is the *view* part).

- *Projection matrix*: The name says it all—this matrix encodes a projection, and thus the view frustum of our camera.

- *Texture matrix*: This matrix allow us to manipulate so-called texture coordinates (which we'll discuss later). However, we'll avoid using this matrix in this book since this part of OpenGL ES is broken on a couple of devices thanks to buggy drivers.

The Rendering Pipeline

OpenGL ES keeps track of these three matrices. Each time we set one of the matrices, it will remember it until we change the matrix again. In OpenGL ES speak, this is called a state. OpenGL keeps track of more than just the matrix states, though; it also keeps track of whether we want it to alpha-blend triangles, whether we want lighting to be taken into account, which texture should be applied to our geometry, and so on. In fact, OpenGL ES is one huge state machine. We set its current state, feed it the geometries of our objects, and tell it to render an image for us. Let's see how a triangle passes through this mighty triangle-rendering machine. Figure 7–4 shows a very high-level, simplified view of the OpenGL ES pipeline:

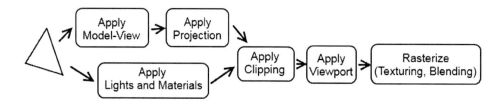

Figure 7–4. *The way of the triangle*

The way of the a triangle through this pipeline looks as follows:

1. Our brave triangle is first transformed by the model-view matrix. This means that all its points are multiplied with this matrix. This multiplication will effectively move the triangle's points around in the world.

2. The output of this is then multiplied by the projection matrix, effectively transforming the 3D points onto the 2D projection plane.

3. In between these two steps (or parallel to them), the currently set lights and materials are also applied to our triangle, giving it its color.

4. Once all that is done, the projected triangle is clipped to our "retina" and transformed to framebuffer coordinates.

5. As a final step, OpenGL fills in the pixels of the triangle based on the colors from the lighting stage, textures to be applied to the triangle, and the blending state, in which each pixel of the triangle might or might not be combined with the pixel in the framebuffer.

All we need to learn is how to throw geometry and textures at OpenGL ES, and set the states used by each of the preceding steps. Before we can do that, though, we need to check out how Android grants us access to OpenGL ES.

NOTE: While the high-level description of the OpenGL ES pipeline is mostly correct, it is heavily simplified and leaves out some details that will become important in a later chapter. Another thing to note is that when OpenGL ES performs projections, it doesn't actually project onto a 2D coordinate system. Instead it projects into something called a *homogenous coordinate system*, which is actually four dimensional. This is a very involved mathematical topic, so for the sake of simplicity, we'll just stick to the simplified belief that OpenGL ES projects to 2D coordinates.

Before We Begin

In the rest of this chapter, we'll write a lot of small examples, as we did in Chapter 4 when discussing the Android API basics. We'll use the same starter class as we did in Chapter 4, which shows us a list of test Activitys we can start. The only things that will change are the names of the Activitys we instantiate via reflection, and the package they are located in. All the examples of the rest of this chapter will be in the package com.badlogic.androidgames.glbasics. The rest of the code will stay the same. Our new starter Activity will be called GLBasicsStarter. We will also copy over all the source code from Chapter 5, which contains our framework classes, as we of course want to reuse those. Finally, we will write some new framework and helper classes, which will go in the com.badlogic.androidgames.framework package and subpackages.

We also have a manifest file again. As each of the following little examples will be an Activity, we also have to make sure it has an entry in the manifest. All the examples will use a fixed orientation (either portrait or landscape, depending on the example), and will tell Android that they can handle keyboard, keyboardHidden, and orientationChange events.

With that out of our way, let the fun begin!

GLSurfaceView: Making Things Easy Since 2008

The first thing we need is some type of View that will allow us to draw via OpenGL ES. Luckily there's such a View in the Android API. It's called GLSurfaceView, and it's a descendent of the SurfaceView class, which we already used for drawing the world of Mr. Nom.

We also need a separate main loop thread again so that we don't bog down the UI thread. Surprise: GLSurfaceView already sets up such a thread for us! All we need to do is implement a listener interface called GLSurfaceView.Renderer and register it with the GLSurfaceView. The interface has three methods:

```
interface Renderer {
    public void onSurfaceCreated(GL10 gl, EGLConfig config);

    public void onSurfaceChanged(GL10 gl, int width, int height);

    public void onDrawFrame(GL10 gl);
}
```

The onSurfaceCreated() method is called each time the GLSurfaceView surface is created. This happens the first time we fire up the Activity and each time we come back to the Activity from a paused state. The method takes two parameters, a GL10 instance and an EGLConfig. The GL10 instance allows us to issue commands to OpenGL ES. The EGLConfig just tells us about the attributes of the surface, such as the color depth and so on. We usually ignore it. We will set up our geometries and textures in the onSurfaceCreated() method.

The onSurfaceChanged() method is called each time the surface is resized. We get the new width and height of the surface in pixels as parameters, along with a GL10 instance if we want to issue OpenGL ES commands.

The onDrawFrame() method is where the fun happens. It is similar in spirit to our Screen.render() method, which gets called as often as possible by the rendering thread that the GLSurfaceView sets up for us. In this method we perform all our rendering.

Besides registering a Renderer listener, we also have to call GLSurfaceView.onPause()/onResume() in our Activity's onPause()/onResume() methods. The reason for this is simple. The GLSurfaceView will start up the rendering thread in its onResume() method and tear it down in its onPause() method. This means that our listener will not be called while our Activity is paused, since the rendering thread which calls our listener will also be paused.

And here comes the only bummer: each time our Activity is paused, the surface of the GLSurfaceView will be destroyed. When the Activity is resumed again (and GLSurfaceView.onResume() is called by us), the GLSurfaceView instantiates a new OpenGL ES rendering surface for us, and informs us of this by calling our listener's onSurfaceCreated() method. This would all be well if not for a single problem: all the OpenGL ES states we set so far will be lost. This also includes things such as textures and so on, which we'll have to reload in that case. This problem is known as a *context loss*. The word *context* stems from the fact that OpenGL ES associates a so-called context with each surface we create, which holds the current states. When we destroy that surface, the context is lost as well. It's not all that bad, though, given that we design our games properly to handle this context loss.

> **NOTE:** Actually, it's EGL that is responsible for the context and surface creation and destruction. EGL is another Khronos Group standard; it defines how an operating system's UI works together with OpenGL ES, and how the operating system grants OpenGL ES access to the underlying graphics hardware. This includes surface creation as well as context management. Since GLSurfaceView handles all the EGL stuff for us, we can safely ignore it in almost all cases.

Following tradition, let's write a small example that will clear the screen with a random color each frame. Listing 7–1 shows the code.

Listing 7–1. *GLSurfaceViewTest.java; Screen-Clearing Madness*

```java
package com.badlogic.androidgames.glbasics;

import java.util.Random;

import javax.microedition.khronos.egl.EGLConfig;
import javax.microedition.khronos.opengles.GL10;

import android.app.Activity;
import android.opengl.GLSurfaceView;
import android.opengl.GLSurfaceView.Renderer;
import android.os.Bundle;
import android.util.Log;
import android.view.Window;
import android.view.WindowManager;

public class GLSurfaceViewTest extends Activity {
    GLSurfaceView glView;

    public void onCreate(Bundle savedInstanceState) {
        super.onCreate(savedInstanceState);
        requestWindowFeature(Window.FEATURE_NO_TITLE);
        getWindow().setFlags(WindowManager.LayoutParams.FLAG_FULLSCREEN,
                WindowManager.LayoutParams.FLAG_FULLSCREEN);
        glView = new GLSurfaceView(this);
        glView.setRenderer(new SimpleRenderer());
        setContentView(glView);
    }
```

We keep a reference to a GLSurfaceView instance as a member of the class. In the onCreate() method, we make our application go full-screen, create the GLSurfaceView, set our Renderer implementation, and make the GLSurfaceView the content view of our Activity.

```
@Override
public void onResume() {
    super.onPause();
    glView.onResume();
}

@Override
public void onPause() {
    super.onPause();
    glView.onPause();
}
```

In the onResume() and onPause() methods, we call the supermethods as well as the respective GLSurfaceView methods. These will start up and tear down the rendering thread of the GLSurfaceView, which in turn will trigger the callback methods of our Renderer implementation at appropriate times.

```
static class SimpleRenderer implements Renderer {
    Random rand = new Random();

    @Override
    public void onSurfaceCreated(GL10 gl, EGLConfig config) {
        Log.d("GLSurfaceViewTest", "surface created");
    }

    @Override
    public void onSurfaceChanged(GL10 gl, int width, int height) {
        Log.d("GLSurfaceViewTest", "surface changed: " + width + "x"
                + height);
    }

    @Override
    public void onDrawFrame(GL10 gl) {
        gl.glClearColor(rand.nextFloat(), rand.nextFloat(),
                rand.nextFloat(), 1);
        gl.glClear(GL10.GL_COLOR_BUFFER_BIT);
    }
}
```

The final piece of the code is our Renderer implementation. It's just logs some information in the onSurfaceCreated() and onSurfaceChanged() methods. The really interesting part is the onDrawFrame() method.

As said earlier, the GL10 instance gives us access to the OpenGL ES API. The 10 in GL10 indicates that it offers us all the functions defined in the OpenGL ES 1.0 standard. For now we can be happy with that. All the methods of that class map to a corresponding C function, as defined in the standard. Each method begins with the prefix gl, an old tradition of OpenGL ES.

The first OpenGL ES method we call is glClearColor(). You probably already know what that will do. It sets the color to be used when we issue a command to clear the screen. Colors in OpenGL ES are almost always RGBA colors where each component has a range between 0 and 1. There are ways to define a color in, say, RGB565, but for now let's stick to the floating-point representation. We could set the color used for clearing only once and OpenGL ES would remember it. The color we set with glClearColor() is one of OpenGL ES's states.

The next call actually clears the screen with the clear color we just specified. The method glClear() takes a single argument that specifies which buffer to clear. OpenGL ES does not only have the notation of a framebuffer that holds pixels, but also other types of buffers. We'll get to know them in Chapter 10, but for now all we care about is the framebuffer that holds our pixels. OpenGL ES calls that the *color buffer*. To tell OpenGL ES that we want to clear that exact buffer, we specify the constant GL10.GL_COLOR_BUFFER_BIT.

OpenGL ES has a lot of constants, which are all defined as static public members of the GL10 interface. Like the methods, each constant has the prefix GL_.

And that was our first OpenGL ES application. I'll spare you the impressive screenshot, since you probably know what it looks like.

> **NOTE:** Thou shall never call OpenGL ES from another thread! First and last commandment! The reason is that OpenGL ES is designed to be used in single threaded environments only and is not thread-safe. It can be made to somewhat work on multiple threads, but many drivers have problems with this and there's no real benefit to doing so.

GLGame: Implementing the Game Interface

In the previous chapter, we implemented the AndroidGame class, which ties together all the submodules for audio, file I/O, graphics, and user input handling. We want to reuse most of this for our upcoming 2D OpenGL ES game, so let's implement a new class called GLGame that implements the Game interface we defined earlier.

The first thing you will notice is that we can't possibly implement the Graphics interface with our current knowledge of OpenGL ES. Here's a surprise: we won't implement it. OpenGL does not lend itself well to the programming model of our Graphics interface. Instead we'll implement a new class, GLGraphics, which will keep track of the GL10 instance we get from the GLSurfaceView. Listing 7–2 shows the code.

Listing 7–2. *GLGraphics.java; Keeping Track of the GLSurfaceView and the GL10 Instance*

```
package com.badlogic.androidgames.framework.impl;

import javax.microedition.khronos.opengles.GL10;

import android.opengl.GLSurfaceView;
```

```java
public class GLGraphics {
    GLSurfaceView glView;
    GL10 gl;

    GLGraphics(GLSurfaceView glView) {
        this.glView = glView;
    }

    public GL10 getGL() {
        return gl;
    }

    void setGL(GL10 gl) {
        this.gl = gl;
    }

    public int getWidth() {
        return glView.getWidth();
    }

    public int getHeight() {
        return glView.getHeight();
    }
}
```

This class has just a few getters and setters. Note that we will use this class in the rendering thread set up by the GLSurfaceView. As such, it might be problematic to call methods of a View, which lives mostly on the UI thread. In this case it's OK, though, as we only query for the GLSurfaceView's width and height, so we get away with it.

The GLGame class is a bit more involved. It borrows most of its code from the AndroidGame class. The only thing that is a little bit more complex is the synchronization between the rendering and UI threads. Let's have a look at it in Listing 7–3.

Listing 7–3. *GLGame.java, the Mighty OpenGL ES Game Implementation*

```java
package com.badlogic.androidgames.framework.impl;

import javax.microedition.khronos.egl.EGLConfig;
import javax.microedition.khronos.opengles.GL10;

import android.app.Activity;
import android.content.Context;
import android.opengl.GLSurfaceView;
import android.opengl.GLSurfaceView.Renderer;
import android.os.Bundle;
import android.os.PowerManager;
import android.os.PowerManager.WakeLock;
import android.view.Window;
import android.view.WindowManager;

import com.badlogic.androidgames.framework.Audio;
import com.badlogic.androidgames.framework.FileIO;
import com.badlogic.androidgames.framework.Game;
import com.badlogic.androidgames.framework.Graphics;
```

```
import com.badlogic.androidgames.framework.Input;
import com.badlogic.androidgames.framework.Screen;

public abstract class GLGame extends Activity implements Game, Renderer {
    enum GLGameState {
        Initialized,
        Running,
        Paused,
        Finished,
        Idle
    }

    GLSurfaceView glView;
    GLGraphics glGraphics;
    Audio audio;
    Input input;
    FileIO fileIO;
    Screen screen;
    GLGameState state = GLGameState.Initialized;
    Object stateChanged = new Object();
    long startTime = System.nanoTime();
    WakeLock wakeLock;
```

The class extends the Activity class and implements the Game and
GLSurfaceView.Renderer interface. It has an enum called GLGameState that keeps track
of the state the GLGame instance is currently in. We'll see how those are used in a bit.

The members of the class consist of a GLSurfaceView and GLGraphics instance. The
class also has Audio, Input, FileIO, and Screen instances, which we need for writing our
game, just as in the AndroidGame class. The state member keeps track of the state via
one of the GLGameState enums. The stateChanged member is an object we'll use to
synchronize the UI thread and the rendering thread. Finally we have a member to keep
track of the delta time and a WakeLock we'll use to keep the screen from dimming.

```
    @Override
    public void onCreate(Bundle savedInstanceState) {
        super.onCreate(savedInstanceState);
        requestWindowFeature(Window.FEATURE_NO_TITLE);
        getWindow().setFlags(WindowManager.LayoutParams.FLAG_FULLSCREEN,
                            WindowManager.LayoutParams.FLAG_FULLSCREEN);
        glView = new GLSurfaceView(this);
        glView.setRenderer(this);
        setContentView(glView);

        glGraphics = new GLGraphics(glView);
        fileIO = new AndroidFileIO(getAssets());
        audio = new AndroidAudio(this);
        input = new AndroidInput(this, glView, 1, 1);
        PowerManager powerManager = (PowerManager)
getSystemService(Context.POWER_SERVICE);
        wakeLock = powerManager.newWakeLock(PowerManager.FULL_WAKE_LOCK, "GLGame");
    }
```

In the onCreate() we perform the usual setup routine. We make the Activity go full-
screen and instantiate the GLSurfaceView, setting it as the content View. We also

instantiate all the other classes that implement framework interfaces, such as the `AndroidFileIO` or `AndroidInput` classes. Note that we reuse the classes we used in the `AndroidGame` class, except for `AndroidGraphics`. Another important point is that we no longer let the `AndroidInput` class scale the touch coordinates to a target resolution, as in `AndroidGame`. The scale values are both 1, so we will get the real touch coordinates. It will become clear later on why we do that. The last thing we do is create the `WakeLock` instance.

```
public void onResume() {
    super.onResume();
    glView.onResume();
    wakeLock.acquire();
}
```

In the `onResume()` method we let the `GLSurfaceView` start the rendering thread with a call to its `onResume()` method. We also acquire the `WakeLock`.

```
@Override
public void onSurfaceCreated(GL10 gl, EGLConfig config) {
    glGraphics.setGL(gl);

    synchronized(stateChanged) {
        if(state == GLGameState.Initialized)
            screen = getStartScreen();
        state = GLGameState.Running;
        screen.resume();
        startTime = System.nanoTime();
    }
}
```

The next thing that will be called is the `onSurfaceCreate()` method. The method is invoked on the rendering thread, of course. Here we can see how the state enums are used. If the application is started for the first time, the state will be `GLGameState.Initialized`. In this case we call the `getStartScreen()` method to return the starting screen of the game. If the game is not in an initialized state, but was already been running, we know that we have just resumed from a paused state. In any case we set the state to `GLGameState.Running` and call the current Screen's `resume()` method. We also keep track of the current time so we can calculate the delta time later on.

The synchronization is necessary, since the members we manipulate within the synchronized block could be manipulated in the `onPause()` method on the UI thread. That's something we have to prevent, so we use an object as a lock. We could have also used the `GLGame` instance itself here, or a proper lock.

```
@Override
public void onSurfaceChanged(GL10 gl, int width, int height) {
}
```

The `onSurfaceChanged()` method is basically just a stub. There's nothing for us to do here.

```
@Override
public void onDrawFrame(GL10 gl) {
    GLGameState state = null;
```

```
        synchronized(stateChanged) {
            state = this.state;
        }

        if(state == GLGameState.Running) {
            float deltaTime = (System.nanoTime()-startTime) / 1000000000.0f;
            startTime = System.nanoTime();

            screen.update(deltaTime);
            screen.present(deltaTime);
        }

        if(state == GLGameState.Paused) {
            screen.pause();
            synchronized(stateChanged) {
                this.state = GLGameState.Idle;
                stateChanged.notifyAll();
            }
        }

        if(state == GLGameState.Finished) {
            screen.pause();
            screen.dispose();
            synchronized(stateChanged) {
                this.state = GLGameState.Idle;
                stateChanged.notifyAll();
            }
        }
    }
}
```

The onDrawFrame() method is were the bulk of all the work is performed. It is called by
the rendering thread as often as possible. Here we check which state our game is
currently in and react accordingly. As the state can be set on the onPause() method on
the UI thread, we have to synchronize the access to it.

If the game is running we calculate the delta time and tell the current Screen to update
and present itself.

If the game is paused we tell the current Screen to pause itself as well. We then change
the state to GLGameState.Idle, indicating that we have received the pause request from
the UI thread. Since we wait for this to happen in the onPause() method in the UI thread,
we notify the UI thread that it can now really pause the application. This notification is
necessary, as we have to make sure that the rendering thread is paused/shut down
properly in case our Activity is paused or closed on the UI thread.

If the Activity is being closed (and not paused), we react to GLGameState.Finished. In
this case we tell the current Screen to pause and dispose of itself, and then send
another notification to the UI thread, which waits for the rendering thread to properly
shut things down.

```
    @Override
    public void onPause() {
        synchronized(stateChanged) {
            if(isFinishing())
```

```
                    state = GLGameState.Finished;
                else
                    state = GLGameState.Paused;
                while(true) {
                    try {
                        stateChanged.wait();
                        break;
                    } catch(InterruptedException e) {
                    }
                }
            }
        wakeLock.release();
        glView.onPause();
        super.onPause();
    }
```

The onPause() method is our usual Activity notificaton method that's called on the UI thread when the Activity is paused. Depending on whether the application is closed or paused, we set the state accordingly and wait for the rendering thread to process the new state. This is achieved with the standard Java wait/notify mechanism.

Finally we release the WakeLock and tell the GLSurfaceView and the Activity to pause themselves, effectivley shutting down the rendering thread and destroying the OpenGL ES surface, which triggers the dreaded OpenGL ES context loss mentioned earlier.

```
    public GLGraphics getGLGraphics() {
        return glGraphics;
    }
```

The getGLGraphics() method is a new method that is only accessible via the GLGame class. It returns the instance of GLGraphics we store so that we can get access to the GL10 interface in our Screen implementations later on.

```
    @Override
    public Input getInput() {
        return input;
    }

    @Override
    public FileIO getFileIO() {
        return fileIO;
    }

    @Override
    public Graphics getGraphics() {
        throw new IllegalStateException("We are using OpenGL!");
    }

    @Override
    public Audio getAudio() {
        return audio;
    }

    @Override
    public void setScreen(Screen screen) {
        if (screen == null)
```

```
                throw new IllegalArgumentException("Screen must not be null");

            this.screen.pause();
            this.screen.dispose();
            screen.resume();
            screen.update(0);
            this.screen = screen;
        }

        @Override
        public Screen getCurrentScreen() {
            return screen;
        }
    }
```

The rest of the class works as before. In case we accidentally try to access the standard Graphics instance, we throw an exception, though, as it is not supported by GLGame. Instead we'll work with the GLGraphics method we get via the GLGame.getGLGraphics() method.

Why did we go through all the pain of synchronizing with the rendering thread? Well, it will make our Screen implementations live entirely on the rendering thread. All the methods of Screen will be executed there, which is necessary if we want to access OpenGL ES functionaility. Remeber, we can only access OpenGL ES on the rendering thread.

Let's round this out with an example. Listing 7–4 shows how our first example in this chapter looks when using GLGame and Screen.

Listing 7–4. *GLGameTest.java; More Screen Clearing, Now with 100 Percent More GLGame*

```
package com.badlogic.androidgames.glbasics;

import java.util.Random;

import javax.microedition.khronos.opengles.GL10;

import com.badlogic.androidgames.framework.Game;
import com.badlogic.androidgames.framework.Screen;
import com.badlogic.androidgames.framework.impl.GLGame;
import com.badlogic.androidgames.framework.impl.GLGraphics;

public class GLGameTest extends GLGame {
    @Override
    public Screen getStartScreen() {
        return new TestScreen(this);
    }

    class TestScreen extends Screen {
        GLGraphics glGraphics;
        Random rand = new Random();

        public TestScreen(Game game) {
            super(game);
            glGraphics = ((GLGame) game).getGLGraphics();
```

```
        }

        @Override
        public void present(float deltaTime) {
            GL10 gl = glGraphics.getGL();
            gl.glClearColor(rand.nextFloat(), rand.nextFloat(),
                    rand.nextFloat(), 1);
            gl.glClear(GL10.GL_COLOR_BUFFER_BIT);
        }

        @Override
        public void update(float deltaTime) {
        }

        @Override
        public void pause() {
        }

        @Override
        public void resume() {
        }

        @Override
        public void dispose() {
        }
    }
}
```

This is the same program as in our last example, except that we now derive from GLGame instead of Activity, and we provide a Screen implementation instead of a GLSurfaceView.Renderer implementation.

In the following examples, we'll only have a look at the relevant parts of each example's Screen implementation. The overall structure of our examples will stay the same. Of course, we have to add the example GLGame implementations to our starter Activity, as well as to the manifest file.

With that out of our way, let's render our first triangle.

Look Mom, I Got a Red Triangle!

You already learned that OpenGL ES needs a couple of things set before we can tell it to draw some geometry. The two things we are most concerned about are the projection matrix (and with it our view frustum) and the viewport, which governs the size of our output image and the position of our rendering output in the framebuffer.

Defining the Viewport

OpenGL ES uses the viewport as a way to translate the coordinates of points projected to the near clipping plane to framebuffer pixel coordinates. We can tell OpenGL ES to use only a portion of our framebuffer, or all of it, with the following method:

```
GL10.glViewport(int x, int y, int width, int height)
```

The x- and y-coordinates specify the top-left corner of the viewport in the framebuffer, and width and height specify the viewport's size in pixels. Note that OpenGL ES assumes the framebuffer coordinate system to have its origin in the lower left of the screen. Usually we set x and y to zero and width and height to our screen resolution, as we are using full-screen mode. We could instruct OpenGL ES to only use a portion of the framebuffer with this method. It would then take the rendering output and automatically stretch it to that portion.

> **NOTE:** While this method looks like it sets up a 2D coordinate system for us to render to, it actually does not. It only defines the portion of the framebuffer OpenGL ES uses to output the final image. Our coordinate system is defined via the projection and model-view matrices.

Defining the Projection Matrix

The next thing we need to define is the projection matrix. As we are only concerned with 2D graphics in this chapter, we want to use a parallel projection. How do we do that?

Matrix Modes and Active Matrices

We already discussed that OpenGL ES keeps track of three matrices: the projection matrix, the model-view matrix, and the texture matrix (which we'll continue to ignore). OpenGL ES offers us a couple of specific methods to modify these matrices. Before we can use these methods, however, we have to tell OpenGL ES which matrix we want to manipulate. This is done with the following method:

```
GL10.glMatrixMode(int mode)
```

The mode parameter can be GL10.GL_PROJECTION, GL10.GL_MODELVIEW, or GL10.GL_TEXTURE. It should be clear which of these constants will make which matrix active. Any subsequent calls to the matrix manipulation methods will target the matrix we set with this method until we change the active matrix again via another call to this method. This matrix mode is one of OpenGL ES's states (which will get lost when we lose the context if our application is paused and resumed). To manipulate the projection matrix with any subsequent calls, we can call the method like this:

```
gl.glMatrixMode(GL10.GL_PROJECTION);
```

Orthographic Projection with glOrthof

OpenGL ES offers us the following method for setting the active matrix to an orthographic (parallel) projection matrix:

```
GL10.glOrthof(int left, int right, int bottom, int top, int near, int far)
```

Hey, that looks a lot like it has something to do with our view frustum's clipping planes. And indeed it does. So what values do we specify here?

OpenGL ES has a standard coordinate system, as depicted in Figure 7–4. The positive x-axis points to the right, the positive y-axis points upward, and the positive z-axis points toward us. With glOrthof() we define the view frustum of our parallel projection in this coordinate system. If you look back at Figure 7–3, you can see that the view frustum of a parallel projection is a box. We can interpret the parameters for glOrthof() as specifying two of these corners of our view frustum box. Figure 7–5 illustrates this.

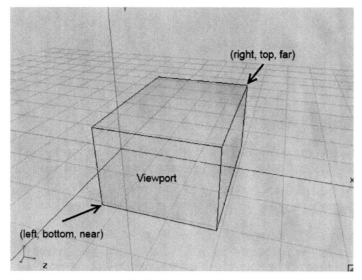

Figure 7–5. *An orthographic view frustum*

The front side of our view frustum will be directly mapped to our viewport. In the case of a full-screen viewport from, say, (0,0) to (480,320) (e.g., landscape mode on a Hero), the bottom-left corner of the front side would map to the bottom-left corner of our screen, and the top-right corner of the front side would map to the top-left corner of our screen. OpenGL will perform the stretching automatically for us.

Since we want to do 2D graphics, we will specify the corner points (left, bottom, near) and (right, top, far) (see figure 7–5) in a way that allows us to work in a sort of pixel coordinate system, as we did with the Canvas and Mr. Nom. Here's how we could set up such a coordinate system:

```
gl.glOrthof(0, 480, 0, 320, 1, -1);
```

Figure 7–6 shows the view frustum.

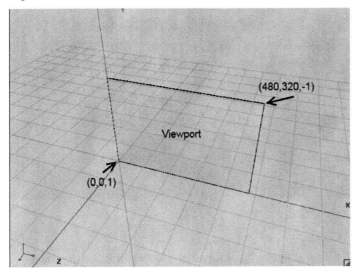

Figure 7–6. *Our parallel projection view frustum for 2D rendering with OpenGL ES*

Our view frustum is pretty thin, but that's OK because we'll only be working in 2D. The visible part of our coordinate system goes from (0,0,1) to (480,320,–1). Any points we specify within this box will be visible on the screen as well. The points will be projected onto the front side of this box, which is our beloved near clipping plane. The projection will then get stretched out onto the viewport, whatever dimensions it has. Say we have a Nexus One with a resolution of 800×480 pixels in landscape mode. When we specify our view frustum as just mentioned, we can work in a 480×320 coordinate system, and OpenGL will stretch it to the 800×480 framebuffer (if we specified that the viewport covers the complete framebuffer). Best of all, there's nothing keeping us from using crazier view frustums. We could also use one with the corners (–1,–1,100) and (2,2,–100). Everything we specify that falls inside this box will be visible and get stretched automatically. Pretty nifty.

Note that we also set the near and far clipping planes. Since we are going to neglect the z-coordinate completely in this chapter, you might be tempted to use zero for both near and far. However, that's a bad idea for various reasons. To play it safe, we grant the view frustum a little buffer in the z-axis. All our geometries' points will be defined in the x-y plane with z set to zero, though—2D all the way.

> **NOTE:** You might have noticed that the y-axis is pointing upward now, and the origin is in the lower-left corner of our screen. While the Canvas, the UI framework, and many other 2D-rendering APIs use the y-down, origin-top-left convention, it is actually more convenient to use this "new" coordinate system for game programming. For example, if Super Mario is jumping, wouldn't you expect his y-coordinate to increase instead of decrease while he's on his way up? Want to work in the other coordinate system? Fine, just swap the bottom and top parameters of glOrthof(). Also, while the illustration of the view frustum is mostly correct from a geometric point of view, the near and far clipping planes are actually interpreted a little differently by glOrthof(). Since that is a little involved, we'll just pretend the preceding illustrations are correct, though.

A Helpful Snippet

Here's a small snippet that will be used in all of our examples in this chapter. It clears the screen with black, sets the viewport to span the whole framebuffer, and sets up the projection matrix (and thereby the view frustum) so we can work in a comfortable coordinate system with the origin in the lower-left corner of the screen and the y-axis pointing upward:

```
gl.glClearColor(0,0,0,1);
gl.glClear(GL10.GL_COLOR_BUFFER_BIT);
gl.glViewport(0, 0, glGraphics.getWidth(), glGraphics.getHeight());
gl.glMatrixMode(GL10.GL_PROJECTION);
gl.glLoadIdentity();
gl.glOrthof(0, 320, 0, 480, 1, -1);
```

Wait, what does glLoadIdentity() do in there? Well, most of the methods OpenGL ES offers us to manipulate the active matrix don't actually set the matrix. Instead they construct a temporary matrix from whatever parameters they take and multiply it with the current matrix. The glOrthof() method is no exception. For example, if we called glOrthof() each frame, we'd multiply the projection matrix to death with itself. So instead of doing that, we make sure we have a clean identity matrix in place before we multiply the projection matrix. Remember, multiplying a matrix by the identity matrix will output the matrix itself again. And that's what glLoadIdentity() is for. Think of it as first loading the value 1 and then multiplying it with whatever we have (in our case, the projection matrix produced by glOrthof()).

Note that our coordinate system now goes from (0,0,1) to (320,480,–1)—that's for portrait mode rendering.

Specifying Triangles

Next up we have to figure out how we can tell OpenGL ES about the triangles we want it to render. First let's define what a triangle is made of:

- A triangle is made of three points.

- Each point is called a vertex.

- A vertex has a position in 3D space.

- A position in 3D space is given as three floats, specifying the x-, y-, and z-coordinates.

- A vertex can have additional attributes, such as a color or texture coordinates (which we'll talk about later). These can be represented as floats as well.

OpenGL ES expects to send our triangle definitions in the form of arrays. However, given that OpenGL ES is actually a C API, we can't just use standard Java arrays. Instead we have to use Java NIO buffers, which are just memory blocks of consecutive bytes.

A Small NIO Buffer Digression

To be totally exact, we need to use *direct* NIO buffers. This means that the memory is not allocated in the virtual machine's heap memory, but in native heap memory. To construct such a direct NIO buffer, we can use the following code snippet:

```
ByteBuffer buffer = ByteBuffer.allocateDirect(NUMBER_OF_BYTES);
buffer.order(ByteOrder.nativeOrder());
```

This will allocate a ByteBuffer that can hold NUMBER_OF_BYTES bytes in total, and make sure that the byte order is equal to the byte order used by the underlying CPU. A NIO buffer has three attributes:

- Capacity: The number of elements the buffer can hold in total

- Position: The current position to which the next element would be written to or read from

- Limit: The index of the last element that has been defined plus one

The capacity of a buffer is actually its size. In the case of a ByteBuffer, it is given in bytes. The position and limit attributes can be thought of as defining a segment within the buffer starting at position and ending at limit (exclusive).

Since we want to specify our vertices as floats, it would be nice not to have to cope with bytes. Luckily we can convert the ByteBuffer instance to a FloatBuffer instance which allows us just that: working with floats.

```
FloatBuffer floatBuffer = buffer.asFloatBuffer();
```

Capacity, position, and limit are given in floats in the case of a FloatBuffer. Our usage pattern of these buffers will be pretty limited—it goes like this:

```
float[] vertices = { ... definitions of vertex positions etc  ...;
floatBuffer.clear();
floatBuffer.put(vertices);
floatBuffer.flip();
```

We first define our data in a standard Java float array. Before we put that float array into the buffer, we tell the buffer to clear itself via the `clear()` method. This doesn't actually erase any data, but sets the position to zero and the limit to the capacity. Next we use the `FloatBuffer.put(float[] array)` method to copy the content of the complete array to the buffer, beginning at the buffer's current position. After the copying, the position of the buffer will be increased by the length of the array. Next, the call to the `put()` method then appends the additional data to the data of the last array we copied to the buffer. The final call to `FloatBuffer.flip()` just swaps the position and limit.

For this example, let's assume that our vertices array is five floats in size and that our `FloatBuffer` has enough capacity to store those five floats. After the call to `FloatBuffer.put()`, the position of the buffer will be 5 (indices 0 to 4 are taken up by the five floats from our array). The limit will still be equal to whatever the capacity of the buffer is. After the call to `FloatBuffer.flip()`, the position will be set to 0 and the limit will be set to 5. Any party interested in reading the data from the buffer will then know that it should read the floats from index 0 to 4 (remember that the limit is exclusive). And that's exactly what OpenGL ES needs to know as well. Note, however, that it will happily ignore the limit. Usually we have to tell it the number of elements to read in addition to passing the buffer to it. There's no error checking done, so watch out.

Sometimes it is useful to set the position of the buffer manually after we have filled it. This can be done via a call to the following method:

```
FloatBuffer.position(int position)
```

This will come in handy later on, when we temporarily set the position of a filled buffer to something other than zero for OpenGL ES to start reading at a specific position.

Sending Vertices to OpenGL ES

So how do we define the positions of the three vertices of our first triangle? Easy—assuming our coordinate system is (0,0,1) to (320,480,–1), as we defined it in the preceding code snippet, we can do the following:

```
ByteBuffer byteBuffer = ByteBuffer.allocateDirect(3 * 2 * 4);
byteBuffer.order(ByteOrder.nativeOrder());
FloatBuffer vertices = byteBuffer.asFloatBuffer();
vertices.put(new float[] {    0.0f,   0.0f,
                            319.0f,   0.0f,
                            160.0f, 479.0f  });
vertices.flip();
```

The first three lines should be familiar already. The only interesting part is how many bytes we allocate. We have three vertices, each composed of a position given as x- and y-coordinates. Each coordinate is a float, and thus takes up 4 bytes. That's three vertices times two coordinates times four bytes, for a total of 24 bytes for our triangle.

> **NOTE:** We can specify vertices with x- and y-coordinates only, and OpenGL ES will automatically set the z-coordinate to zero for us.

Next we put a float array holding our vertex positions into the buffer. Our triangle starts at the bottom-left corner (0,0), goes to the right edge of the view frustum/screen (319,0), and then goes to the middle of the top edge of the view frustum/screen. Being the good NIO buffer users we are, we also call the flip() method on our buffer. Thus, the position will be 0 and the limit will be 6 (remember, FloatBuffer limits and positions are given in floats, not bytes).

Once we have our NIO buffer ready, we can tell OpenGL ES to draw it with its current state (e.g., viewport and projection matrix). This can be done with the following snippet:

```
gl.glEnableClientState(GL10.GL_VERTEX_ARRAY);
gl.glVertexPointer( 2, GL10.GL_FLOAT, 0, vertices);
gl.glDrawArrays(GL10.GL_TRIANGLES, 0, 3);
```

The call to glEnableClientState() is a bit of a relic. It tells OpenGL ES that the vertices we are going to draw have a position. This is a bit silly for two reasons:

- The constant is called GL10.GL_VERTEX_ARRAY, which is a bit confusing. It would make more sense if it were called GL10.GL_POSITION_ARRAY.

- There's no way to draw anything that has no position, so the call to this method is a little bit superfluous. We do it anyway, though, to make OpenGL ES happy.

In the call to glVertexPointer() we tell OpenGL ES where it can find the vertex positions, and give it some additional information. The first parameter tells OpenGL ES that each vertex position is composed of two coordinates, x and y. If we would have specified x, y, and z, we would have passed 3 to the method. The second parameter tells OpenGL ES the data type we used to store each coordinate. In this case it's GL10.GL_FLOAT, indicating that we used floats encoded as 4 bytes each. The third parameter, stride, tells OpenGL how far apart each of our vertex positions are from each other in bytes. In the preceding case, stride is zero, as the positions are tightly packed (vertex 1 (x,y), vertex 2(x,y), etc.). The final parameter is our FloatBuffer, for which there are two things to remember:

- The FloatBuffer represents a memory block in the native heap, and thus has a starting address.

- The position of the FloatBuffer is an offset from that starting address.

OpenGL ES will take the buffer's starting address and add the buffer's positions to arrive at the float in the buffer that it will start reading the vertices from when we tell it to draw the contents of the buffer. The vertex pointer (which again should be called the position pointer) is a state of OpenGL ES. As long as we don't change it (and the context isn't lost), OpenGL ES will remember and use it for all subsequent calls that need vertex positions.

Finally there's the call to glDrawArrays(). It will draw our triangle. The first parameter specifies what type of primitive we are going to draw. In this case we say that we want to render a list of triangles, which is specified via GL10.GL_TRIANGLES. The next parameter is an offset relative to the first vertex the vertex pointer points to. The offset is measured in vertices, not bytes or floats. If we'd have specified more than one triangle, we could use this offset to render only a subset of our triangle list. The final argument tells OpenGL ES how many vertices it should use for rendering. In our case that's three vertices. Note that we always have to specify a multiple of 3 if we draw GL10.GL_TRIANGLES. Each triangle is composed of three vertices, so that makes sense. For other primitive types the rules are a little different.

Once we issue the glVertexPointer() command, OpenGL ES will transfer the vertex positions to the GPU and store them there for all subsequent rendering commands. Each time we tell OpenGL ES to render vertices, it takes their positions from the data we last specified via glVertexPointer().

Each of our vertices might have more attributes than just its position. One other attribute might be a vertex's color. We usually refer to those attributes as *vertex attributes*.

You might wonder how OpenGL ES knows what color our triangle should have, as we have only specified positions. It turns out that OpenGL ES has sensible defaults for any vertex attribute that we don't specify. Most of these defaults can be set directly. For example, if we want to set a default color for all vertices that we draw, we can use the following method:

```
GL10.glColor4f(float r, float g, float b, float a)
```

This method will set the default color to be used for all vertices for which we didn't specify a color. The color is given as RGBA values in the range 0.0 to 1.0, as was the case for the clear color earlier. The default color OpenGL ES starts with is (1,1,1,1)—that is, fully opaque white.

And that is all the code we need to render a triangle with a custom parallel projection with OpenGL ES. That's a mere 16 lines of code for clearing the screen, setting the viewport and projection matrix, creating an NIO buffer that we store our vertex positions in, and drawing the triangle. Now compare that to the six pages it took me to explain this to you. I could have of course left out the details and used coarser language. The problem is that OpenGL ES is a pretty complex beast at times, and to avoid getting an empty screen, it's best to learn what it is all about rather than just copying and pasting code.

Putting It Together

To round this section out, let's put all this together via a nice GLGame and Screen implementation. Listing 7–5 shows the complete example.

Listing 7–5. *FirstTriangleTest.java*

```java
package com.badlogic.androidgames.glbasics;

import java.nio.ByteBuffer;
import java.nio.ByteOrder;
import java.nio.FloatBuffer;

import javax.microedition.khronos.opengles.GL10;

import com.badlogic.androidgames.framework.Game;
import com.badlogic.androidgames.framework.Screen;
```

```
import com.badlogic.androidgames.framework.impl.GLGame;
import com.badlogic.androidgames.framework.impl.GLGraphics;

public class FirstTriangleTest extends GLGame {
    @Override
    public Screen getStartScreen() {
        return new FirstTriangleScreen(this);
    }
```

The FirstTriangleTest class derives from GLGame, and thus has to implement the Game.getStartScreen() method. In that method we create a new FirstTriangleScreen, which will then be frequently called to update and present itself by the GLGame. Note that when this method is called, we are already in the main loop—or rather the GLSurfaceView rendering thread—so we can use OpenGL ES methods in the constructor of the FirstTriangleScreen class. Let's have a closer look at that Screen implementation:

```
class FirstTriangleScreen extends Screen {
    GLGraphics glGraphics;
    FloatBuffer vertices;

    public FirstTriangleScreen(Game game) {
        super(game);
        glGraphics = ((GLGame)game).getGLGraphics();

        ByteBuffer byteBuffer = ByteBuffer.allocateDirect(3 * 2 * 4);
        byteBuffer.order(ByteOrder.nativeOrder());
        vertices = byteBuffer.asFloatBuffer();
        vertices.put( new float[] {    0.0f,   0.0f,
                                     319.0f,   0.0f,
                                     160.0f, 479.0f});
        vertices.flip();
    }
```

The FirstTriangleScreen class holds two members: a GLGraphics instance and our trusty FloatBuffer, which stores the 2D positions of the three vertices of our triangle. In the constructor we fetch the GLGraphics instance from the GLGame and create and fill the FloatBuffer according to our previous code snippet. Since the Screen constructor gets a Game instance, we have to cast it to a GLGame instance so we can use the GLGame.getGLGraphics() method.

```
    @Override
    public void present(float deltaTime) {
        GL10 gl = glGraphics.getGL();
        gl.glViewport(0, 0, glGraphics.getWidth(), glGraphics.getHeight());
        gl.glClear(GL10.GL_COLOR_BUFFER_BIT);
        gl.glMatrixMode(GL10.GL_PROJECTION);
        gl.glLoadIdentity();
        gl.glOrthof(0, 320, 0, 480, 1, -1);

        gl.glColor4f(1, 0, 0, 1);
        gl.glEnableClientState(GL10.GL_VERTEX_ARRAY);
        gl.glVertexPointer( 2, GL10.GL_FLOAT, 0, vertices);
        gl.glDrawArrays(GL10.GL_TRIANGLES, 0, 3);
    }
```

The present() method then reflects what we just discussed: we set the viewport, clear the screen, set the projection matrix so that we can work in our custom coordinate system, set the default vertex color (red in this case), specify that our vertices will have positions, tell OpenGL ES where it can find those vertex positions, and finally render our awesome little red triangle.

```java
    @Override
    public void update(float deltaTime) {
        game.getInput().getTouchEvents();
        game.getInput().getKeyEvents();
    }

    @Override
    public void pause() {

    }

    @Override
    public void resume() {

    }

    @Override
    public void dispose() {

    }
  }
}
```

The rest of the class is just boilerplate code. In the update() method we make sure that our event buffers don't get filled up. The rest of the code does nothing.

> **NOTE:** From here on we'll only focus on the Screen classes themselves, as the enclosing GLGame derivatives, such as FirstTriangleTest, will always be the same. We'll also reduce the code size a little by leaving out any empty or boilerplate methods of the Screen class. The following examples will all just differ in terms of members, constructors, and present methods.

Figure 7–7 shows the output of the preceding example.

Figure 7–7. *Our first sexy triangle*

So here's what we did wrong in this example in terms of OpenGL ES best practices:

- We set the same states to the same values over and over again without any need. State changes in OpenGL ES are expensive—some a little bit more, some a little bit less. We should always try to reduce the number of state changes we make in a single frame.

- The viewport and projection matrix will never change once we set them. We could move that code to the resume() method, which is only called once each time the OpenGL ES surface gets (re)-created, thus also handling OpenGL ES context loss.

- We could also move setting the color used for clearing and setting the default vertex color to the resume() method. These two colors won't change either.

- We could move the glEnableClientState() and glVertexPointer() methods to the resume() method.

- The only things that we need to call each frame are glClear() and glDrawArrays(). Both use the current OpenGL ES states, which will stay the same as long as we don't change them and as long as we don't lose the context due to the Activity being paused and resumed.

If we had put these optimizations into practice, we would have only two OpenGL ES calls in our main loop. For the sake of clarity, we'll refrain from using these kind of minimal state change optimizations for now. When we start writing our first OpenGL ES game, though, we'll have to follow those practices as best as we can to guarantee good performance.

Let's add some more attributes to our triangle's vertices, starting with color.

> **NOTE:** Very, very alert readers might have noticed that the triangle in Figure 7–7 is actually missing a pixel in the bottom-right corner. This may look like a typical off-by-one error, but it's actually due to the way OpenGL ES rasterizes (draws the pixels of) the triangle. There's a specific triangle rasterization rule that is responsible for that artifact. Worry not—we are mostly concerned with rendering 2D rectangles (composed of two triangles), where this effect will vanish.

Specifying Per Vertex Color

In the last example we set a global default color for all vertices we draw via `glColor4f()`. Sometimes we want to have more granular control (e.g., we want to set a color per vertex). OpenGL ES offers us this functionality, and it's really easy to use. All we have to do is add RGBA float components to each vertex and tell OpenGL ES where it can find the color for each vertex, similar to how we told it where it can find the position for each vertex. Let's start by adding the colors to each vertex:

```
int VERTEX_SIZE = (2 + 4) * 4;
ByteBuffer byteBuffer = ByteBuffer.allocateDirect(3 * VERTEX_SIZE);
byteBuffer.order(ByteOrder.nativeOrder());
FloatBuffer vertices = byteBuffer.asFloatBuffer();
vertices.put( new float[] {   0.0f,   0.0f, 1, 0, 0, 1,
                            319.0f,   0.0f, 0, 1, 0, 1,
                            160.0f, 479.0f, 0, 0, 1, 1});
vertices.flip();
```

We first have to allocate a `ByteBuffer` for our three vertices. How big should that `ByteBuffer` be? We have two coordinates and four (RGBA) color components per vertex, so that's six floats in total. Each float value takes up 4 bytes, so a single vertex uses 24 bytes. We store this information in `VERTEX_SIZE`. When we call `ByteBuffer.allocateDirect()`, we just multiply `VERTEX_SIZE` by the number of vertices we want to store in the `ByteBuffer`. The rest is pretty self-explanatory. We get a `FloatBuffer` view to our `ByteBuffer` and `put()` the vertices into the `ByteBuffer`. Each row of the float array holds the x- and y-coordinates, and the R, G, B, and A components of a vertex, in that order.

If we want to render this, we have to tell OpenGL ES that our vertices not only have a position, but also a color attribute. We start off, as before, by calling `glEnableClientState()`:

```
gl.glEnableClientState(GL10.GL_VERTEX_ARRAY);
gl.glEnableClientState(GL10.GL_COLOR_ARRAY);
```

Now that OpenGL ES knows that it can expect position and color information for each vertex, we have to tell it where it can find that information:

```
vertices.position(0);
gl.glVertexPointer(2, GL10.GL_FLOAT, VERTEX_SIZE, vertices);
vertices.position(2);
gl.glColorPointer(4, GL10.GL_FLOAT, VERTEX_SIZE, vertices);
```

We start of by setting the position of our FloatBuffer, which holds our vertices to 0. The position thus points to the x-coordinate of our first vertex in the buffer. Next we call glVertexPointer(). The only difference from the previous example is that we now also specify the vertex size (remember, it's given in bytes). OpenGL ES will then start reading in vertex positions from the position in the buffer we told it to start from. For the second vertex position it will add VERTEX_SIZE bytes to the first position's address, and so on.

Next we set the position of the buffer to the R component of the first vertex and call glColorPointer(), which tells OpenGL ES where it can find the colors of our vertices. The first argument is the number of components per color. This is always four, as OpenGL ES demands an R, G, B, and A component per vertex from us. The second parameter specifies the type of each component. As with the vertex coordinates, we use GL10.GL_FLOAT again to indicate that each color component is a float in the range between 0 and 1. The third parameter is the stride between vertex colors. It's of course the same as the stride between vertex positions. The final parameter is our vertices buffer again.

Since we called vertices.position(2) before the glColorPointer() call, OpenGL ES knows that the first vertex color can be found starting from the third float in the buffer. If we wouldn't have set the position of the buffer to 2, OpenGL ES would have started reading in the colors from position 0. That would have been bad, as that's where the x-coordinate of our first vertex is. Figure 7–8 shows where OpenGL ES will read our vertex attributes from, and how it jumps from one vertex to the next for each attribute.

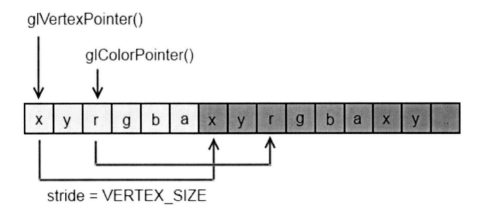

Figure 7–8. *Our vertices FloatBuffer, start addresses for OpenGL ES to read position/color from, and stride to be used to jump to the next position/color.*

To draw our triangle, we again call glDrawElements(), which tells OpenGL ES to draw a triangle using the first three vertices of our FloatBuffer:

```
gl.glDrawElements(GL10.GL_TRIANGLES, 0, 3);
```

Since we enabled the GL10.GL_VERTEX_ARRAY and GL10.GL_COLOR_ARRAY, OpenGL ES knows that it should use the attributes specified by glVertexPointer() and glColorPointer(). It will ignore the default color, as we provide our own per-vertex colors.

> **NOTE:** The way we just specified our vertices' positions and colors is called *interleaving*. This means that we pack the attributes of a vertex in one continuous memory block. There's another way we could have achieved this: *noninterleaved vertex arrays*. We'd have used two FloatBuffers, one for the positions and one for the colors. However, interleaving performs a lot better due to memory locality, so we won't discuss noninterleaved vertex arrays here.

Putting it all together into a new GLGame and Screen implementation should be a breeze by now. Listing 7–6 shows an excerpt from the file ColoredTriangleTest.java. I left out the boilerplate code.

Listing 7–6. *Excerpt from ColoredTriangleTest.java; Interleaving Position and Color Attributes*

```
class ColoredTriangleScreen extends Screen {
    final int VERTEX_SIZE = (2 + 4) * 4;
    GLGraphics glGraphics;
    FloatBuffer vertices;

    public ColoredTriangleScreen(Game game) {
        super(game);
        glGraphics = ((GLGame) game).getGLGraphics();

        ByteBuffer byteBuffer = ByteBuffer.allocateDirect(3 * VERTEX_SIZE);
        byteBuffer.order(ByteOrder.nativeOrder());
        vertices = byteBuffer.asFloatBuffer();
        vertices.put( new float[] {   0.0f,   0.0f, 1, 0, 0, 1,
                                    319.0f,   0.0f, 0, 1, 0, 1,
                                    160.0f, 479.0f, 0, 0, 1, 1});
        vertices.flip();
    }

    @Override
    public void present(float deltaTime) {
        GL10 gl = glGraphics.getGL();
        gl.glViewport(0, 0, glGraphics.getWidth(), glGraphics.getHeight());
        gl.glClear(GL10.GL_COLOR_BUFFER_BIT);
        gl.glMatrixMode(GL10.GL_PROJECTION);
        gl.glLoadIdentity();
        gl.glOrthof(0, 320, 0, 480, 1, -1);

        gl.glEnableClientState(GL10.GL_VERTEX_ARRAY);
        gl.glEnableClientState(GL10.GL_COLOR_ARRAY);

        vertices.position(0);
```

```
        gl.glVertexPointer(2, GL10.GL_FLOAT, VERTEX_SIZE, vertices);
        vertices.position(2);
        gl.glColorPointer(4, GL10.GL_FLOAT, VERTEX_SIZE, vertices);

        gl.glDrawArrays(GL10.GL_TRIANGLES, 0, 3);
    }
```

Cool, that still looks pretty straightforward. All we changed compared to the previous example is adding the four color components to each vertex in our FloatBuffer and enabling the GL10.GL_COLOR_ARRAY. The best thing about it is that any additional vertex attributes we add in the subsequent examples will work the same way. We just tell OpenGL ES to not use the default value for that specific attribute but instead look up the attributes in our FloatBuffer, starting at a specific position and moving from vertex to vertex by VERTEX_SIZE bytes.

Now, we could also turn off the GL10.GL_COLOR_ARRAY so that OpenGL ES uses the default vertex color again, which we can specify via glColor4f() as we did previously. For this we can call

```
gl.glDisableClientState(GL10.GL_COLOR_ARRAY);
```

OpenGL ES will just turn off the feature to read the colors from our FloatBuffer. If we already set a color pointer via glColorPointer(), OpenGL ES will remember the pointer, though. We just told it to not use it.

To round this example out, let's have a look at the output of the preceding program. Figure 7–9 shows a screenshot.

Figure 7–9. *Per-vertex colored triangle*

Woah, this is pretty neat. We didn't make any assumptions about how OpenGL ES will use the three colors we specified (red for the bottom-left vertex, green for the bottom-right vertex, and blue for the top vertex). It turns out that it will interpolate the colors between the vertices for us. With this we can easily create nice gradients. However, colors alone will not make us happy for very long. We want to draw images with OpenGL ES. And that's where so-called texture mapping comes into play.

Texture Mapping: Wallpapering Made Easy

When we wrote Mr. Nom we loaded some bitmaps and directly drew them to the framebuffer—no rotation involved, just a little bit of scaling, which is pretty easy to achieve. In OpenGL ES we are mostly concerned with triangles, which can have any orientation or scale we want them to have. So how can we render bitmaps with OpenGL ES?

Easy, just load up the bitmap to OpenGL ES (and for that matter to the GPU, which has its own dedicated RAM), add a new attribute to each of our triangle's vertices, and tell OpenGL ES to render our triangle and apply the bitmap (also known as *texture* in OpenGL ES speak) to the triangle. Let's first look at what these new vertex attributes actually specify.

Texture Coordinates

To map a bitmap to a triangle we need to add so-called *texture coordinates* to each vertex of the triangle. What is a texture coordinate? It specifies a point within the texture (our uploaded bitmap) to be mapped to one of the triangle's vertices. Texture coordinates are usually 2D.

While we call our positional coordinates x, y, and z, texture coordinates are usually called u and v or s and t, depending on the circle of graphics programmers you are a part of. OpenGL ES calls them s and t, so that's what we'll stick to. If you read resources on the Web that use the u/v nomenclature, don't get confused: it's the same as s and t. So what does the coordinate system look like? Figure 7–10 shows Bob in the texture coordinate system after we uploaded him to OpenGL ES.

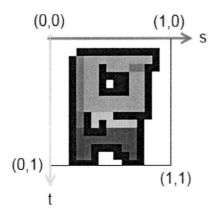

Figure 7–10. *Bob, uploaded to OpenGL ES, shown in the texture coordinate system*

There are a couple of interesting things going on here. First of all, s equals the x-coordinate in a standard coordinate system, and t is equal to the y-coordinate. The s-axis points to the right, and the t-axis points downward. The origin of the coordinate system coincides with the top-left corner of Bob's image. The bottom-right corner of the image maps to (1,1).

So, what happened to pixel coordinates? It turns out that OpenGL ES doesn't like them a lot. Instead, any image we upload, no matter its width and height in pixels, will be embedded into this coordinate system. The top-left corner of the image will always be at (0,0), the bottom-right corner will always be at (1,1)—even if, say, the width is twice as large as the height. We call these *normalized coordinates*, and they actually makes our lives easier at times. So how can we map Bob to our triangle? Easy, we just give each vertex of the triangle a texture coordinate pair in Bob's coordinate system. Figure 7–11 shows a few configurations.

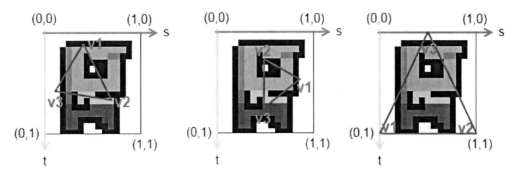

Figure 7–11. *Three different triangles mapped to Bob. The names v1, v2, and v3 each specify a vertex of the triangle.*

We can map our triangle's vertices to the texture coordinate system however we want. Note that the orientation of the triangle in the positional coordinate system does not have to be the same as in the texture coordinate system. The coordinate systems are completely decoupled. So let's see how we can add those texture coordinates to our vertices:

```
Int VERTEX_SIZE = (2 + 2) * 4;
ByteBuffer byteBuffer = ByteBuffer.allocateDirect(3 * VERTEX_SIZE);
byteBuffer.order(ByteOrder.nativeOrder());
vertices = byteBuffer.asFloatBuffer();
vertices.put( new float[] {     0.0f,   0.0f, 0.0f, 1.0f,
                              319.0f,   0.0f, 1.0f, 1.0f,
                              160.0f, 479.0f, 0.5f, 0.0f});
vertices.flip();
```

That was easy. All we have to do is to make sure that we have enough room in our buffer, and then append the texture coordinates to each vertex. The preceding code corresponds to the rightmost mapping in Figure 7–10. Note that our vertex positions are still given in the usual coordinate system we defined via our projection. If we wanted to, we could also add the color attributes to each vertex, as in the previous example. OpenGL ES would then mix the interpolated vertex colors with the colors from the pixels of the texture that the triangle maps to on the fly. Of course, we'd need to adjust the size of our buffer, as well as the VERTEX_SIZE constant, accordingly (e.g., (2 + 4 + 2) × 4). To tell OpenGL ES that our vertices have texture coordinates, we again use glEnableClientState() together with the glTexCoordPointer()method, which behaves exactly the same as glVertexPointer() and glColorPointer() (can you see a pattern here?).

```
gl.glEnableClientState(GL10.GL_VERTEX_ARRAY);
gl.glEnableClientState(GL10.GL_TEXTURE_COORD_ARRAY);

vertices.position(0);
gl.glVertexPointer(2, GL10.GL_FLOAT, VERTEX_SIZE, vertices);
vertices.position(2);
gl.glTexCoordPointer(2, GL10.GL_FLOAT, VERTEX_SIZE, vertices);
```

Nice, that looks very familiar. So, the remaining question is how we can upload the texture to OpenGL ES and tell it to map it to our triangle. Naturally that's a little bit more involved. But fear not, it's still pretty easy.

Uploading Bitmaps

First we have to load our bitmap. We already know how to do that on Android:

```
Bitmap bitmap = BitmapFactory.decodeStream(game.getFileIO().readAsset("bobrgb888.png"));
```

Here we load Bob in an RGB888 configuration. The next thing we need to do is tell OpenGL ES that we want to create a new texture. OpenGL ES has the notion of objects for a couple of things, such as textures. To create a texture object, we can call the following method:

```
GL10.glGenTextures(int numTextures, int[] ids, int offset)
```

The first parameter specifies how many texture objects we want to create. Usually we only want to create one. The next parameter is an int array to which OpenGL ES will write the IDs of the generated texture objects. The final parameter just tells OpenGL ES where in the array it should start writing the IDs to.

You already learned that OpenGL ES is a C API. Naturally it can't return a Java object to us for a new texture. Instead it gives us an ID, or handle, to that texture. Each time we want OpenGL ES to do something with that specific texture, we specify its ID. So here's a more complete code snippet showing how to generate a single new texture object and get its ID:

```
int textureIds[] = new int[1];
gl.glGenTextures(1, textureIds, 0);
int textureId = textureIds[0];
```

The texture object is still empty, which means it doesn't have any image data yet. Let's upload our bitmap. For this we have to first bind the texture. To bind something in OpenGL ES means that we want OpenGL ES to use that specific object for all subsequent calls until we change the binding again. Here we want to bind a texture object for which the method glBindTexture() is available. Once we have bound a texture, we can manipulate its attributes, such as its image data. Here's how we can upload Bob to our new texture object:

```
gl.glBindTexture(GL10.GL_TEXTURE_2D, textureId);
GLUtils.texImage2D(GL10.GL_TEXTURE_2D, 0, bitmap, 0);
```

First we bind the texture object with glBindTexture(). The first parameter specifies the type of texture we want to bind. Our image of Bob is 2D, so we use GL10.GL_TEXTURE_2D. There are other texture types, but we don't have a need for them in this book. We'll always specify GL10.GL_TEXTURE_2D for the methods that need to know the texture type we want to work with. The second parameter of that method is our texture ID. Once the method returns, all subsequent methods that work with a 2D texture will work with our texture object.

The next method call invokes a method of the GLUtils class, a class provided by the Android framework. Usually the task of uploading a texture image is pretty involved; this little helper class eases the pain for us a lot. All we need to do is specify the texture type (GL10.GL_TEXTURE_2D) the mip mapping level (we'll look at that in Chapter 11; it defaults to zero), the bitmap we want to upload, and another argument, which has to be set to zero in all cases. After this call our texture object has image data attached to it.

> **NOTE:** The texture object and its image data are actually held in video RAM, not in our usual RAM. The texture object (and the image data) will get lost when the OpenGL ES context is destroyed (e.g., when our activity is paused and resumed). This means that we have to re-create the texture object and reupload our image data every time the OpenGL ES context is (re)-created. If we don't do this, all we'll see is a white triangle.

Texture Filtering

There's one last thing we need to define before we can use the texture object. It has to do with the fact that our triangle might take up more or fewer pixels on the screen than there are pixels in the mapped region of the texture. For example, the image of Bob in Figure 7–10 has a size of 128×128 pixels. Our triangle maps to half that image, so uses (128×128) / 2 pixels from the texture (which are also called *texels*). When we draw the triangle to the screen with the coordinates we defined in the preceding snippet, it will take up (320×480) / 2 pixels. That's a lot more pixels we use on the screen than we fetch from the texture map. It can of course also be the other way around: we use fewer pixels on the screen than from the mapped region of the texture. The first case is called *magnification*, and the second *minification*. For each case we need to tell OpenGL ES how it should upscale or downscale the texture. The up- and downscaling are also referd to as minification and magnification filters in OpenGL ES lingo. These filters are attributes of our texture object, much like the image data itself. To set them we have to first make sure that the texture object is bound via a call to glBindTexture(). If that's the case, we can set them like this:

```
gl.glTexParameterf(GL10.GL_TEXTURE_2D, GL10.GL_TEXTURE_MIN_FILTER, GL10.GL_NEAREST);
gl.glTexParameterf(GL10.GL_TEXTURE_2D, GL10.GL_TEXTURE_MAG_FILTER, GL10.GL_NEAREST);
```

Both times we use the method GL10.glTexParameterf(), which sets an attribute of the texture. In the first call we specify the minification filter; in the second we call the magnification filter. The first parameter to that method is the texture type, which defaults to GL10.GL_TEXTURE_2D for us. The second argument tells the method which attributes we want to set—in our case, the GL10.GL_TEXTURE_MIN_FILTER and the GL10.GL_TEXTURE_MAG_FILTER. The last parameter specifies the type of filter that should be used. We have two options here: GL10.GL_NEAREST and GL10.GL_LINEAR.

The first filter type will always choose the nearest texel in the texture map to be mapped to a pixel. The second filter type will sample the four nearest texels for a pixel of the triangle and average them to arrive at the final color. We use the first type of filter if we want to have a pixelated look and the second if we want a smoothed look. Figure 7–12 shows the difference between the two types of filters.

Figure 7–12. *GL10.GL_NEAREST vs. GL10.GL_LINEAR. The first filter type makes for a pixelated look; the second one smoothes things out a little.*

Our texture object is now fully defined: we created an ID, set the image data, and specified the filters to be used in case our rendering is not pixel perfect. It is a common practice to unbind the texture once we are done defining it. We should also recycle the Bitmap we loaded, as we no longer need it. Why waste memory? That can be achieved with the following snippet:

```
gl.glBindTexture(GL10.GL_TEXTURE_2D, 0);
bitmap.recycle();
```

0 is a special ID that tells OpenGL ES that it should unbind the currently bound object. If we want to use the texture for drawing our triangles, we need to bind it again, of course.

Disposing of Textures

It is also useful to know how to delete a texture object from video RAM if we no longer need it (like we use Bitmap.recycle() to release the memory of a bitmap). This can be achieved with the following snippet:

```
gl.glBindTexture(GL10.GL_TEXTURE_2D, 0);
int textureIds = { textureid };
gl.glDeleteTextures(1, textureIds, 0);
```

Note that we first have to make sure that the texture object is not currently bound before we can delete it. The rest is similar to how we used glGenTextures() to create a texture object.

A Helpful Snippet

For reference, here's the complete snippet to create a texture object, load image data, and set the filters on Android:

```
Bitmap bitmap = BitmapFactory.decodeStream(game.getFileIO().readAsset("bobrgb888.png"));
int textureIds[] = new int[1];
gl.glGenTextures(1, textureIds, 0);
int textureId = textureIds[0];
gl.glBindTexture(GL10.GL_TEXTURE_2D, textureId);
GLUtils.texImage2D(GL10.GL_TEXTURE_2D, 0, bitmap, 0);
gl.glTexParameterf(GL10.GL_TEXTURE_2D, GL10.GL_TEXTURE_MIN_FILTER, GL10.GL_NEAREST);
gl.glTexParameterf(GL10.GL_TEXTURE_2D, GL10.GL_TEXTURE_MAG_FILTER, GL10.GL_NEAREST);
gl.glBindTexture(GL10.GL_TEXTURE_2D, 0);
bitmap.recycle();
```

Not so bad after all. The most important part of all this is to actually recycle the Bitmap once we are done. Otherwise we'd waste memory. Our image data is safely stored in video RAM in the texture object (until the context is lost and we need to reload it again).

Enabling Texturing

There's one more thing before we can draw our triangle with the texture. We need to bind the texture, and we need to tell OpenGL ES that it should actually apply the texture to all triangles we render. Whether texture mapping is performed or not is another state of OpenGL ES, which we can enable and disable with the following methods:

```
GL10.glEnable(GL10.GL_TEXTURE_2D);
GL10.glDisable(GL10.GL_TEXTURE_2D);
```

These look vaguely familiar. When we enabled/disabled vertex attributes in the previous sections, we used glEnableClientState()/glDisableClientState(). As I said earlier, those are relics from the infancy of OpenGL itself. There's a reason why those are not merged with glEnable()/glDisable(), but we won't go into that here. Just remember to use glEnableClientState()/glDisableClientState() to enable and disable vertex attributes, and use glEnable()/glDisable() for any other states of OpenGL, such as texturing.

Putting It Together

With that out of our way, we can now write a small example that puts all of this together. Listing 7–7 shows an excerpt of the TexturedTriangleTest.java source file, listing only the relevant parts of the TexturedTriangleScreen class contained in it.

Listing 7–7. *Excerpt from TexturedTriangleTest.java; Texturing a Triangle*

```
class TexturedTriangleScreen extends Screen {
    final int VERTEX_SIZE = (2 + 2) * 4;
    GLGraphics glGraphics;
    FloatBuffer vertices;
    int textureId;
```

```java
    public TexturedTriangleScreen(Game game) {
        super(game);
        glGraphics = ((GLGame) game).getGLGraphics();

        ByteBuffer byteBuffer = ByteBuffer.allocateDirect(3 * VERTEX_SIZE);
        byteBuffer.order(ByteOrder.nativeOrder());
        vertices = byteBuffer.asFloatBuffer();
        vertices.put( new float[] {     0.0f,    0.0f, 0.0f, 1.0f,
                                      319.0f,    0.0f, 1.0f, 1.0f,
                                      160.0f, 479.0f, 0.5f, 0.0f});
        vertices.flip();
        textureId = loadTexture("bobrgb888.png");
    }

    public int loadTexture(String fileName) {
        try {
            Bitmap bitmap =
BitmapFactory.decodeStream(game.getFileIO().readAsset(fileName));
            GL10 gl = glGraphics.getGL();
            int textureIds[] = new int[1];
            gl.glGenTextures(1, textureIds, 0);
            int textureId = textureIds[0];
            gl.glBindTexture(GL10.GL_TEXTURE_2D, textureId);
            GLUtils.texImage2D(GL10.GL_TEXTURE_2D, 0, bitmap, 0);
            gl.glTexParameterf(GL10.GL_TEXTURE_2D, GL10.GL_TEXTURE_MIN_FILTER,
GL10.GL_NEAREST);
            gl.glTexParameterf(GL10.GL_TEXTURE_2D, GL10.GL_TEXTURE_MAG_FILTER,
GL10.GL_NEAREST);
            gl.glBindTexture(GL10.GL_TEXTURE_2D, 0);
            bitmap.recycle();
            return textureId;
        } catch(IOException e) {
            Log.d("TexturedTriangleTest", "couldn't load asset 'bobrgb888.png'!");
            throw new RuntimeException("couldn't load asset '" + fileName + "'");
        }
    }

    @Override
    public void present(float deltaTime) {
        GL10 gl = glGraphics.getGL();
        gl.glViewport(0, 0, glGraphics.getWidth(), glGraphics.getHeight());
        gl.glClear(GL10.GL_COLOR_BUFFER_BIT);
        gl.glMatrixMode(GL10.GL_PROJECTION);
        gl.glLoadIdentity();
        gl.glOrthof(0, 320, 0, 480, 1, -1);

        gl.glEnable(GL10.GL_TEXTURE_2D);
        gl.glBindTexture(GL10.GL_TEXTURE_2D, textureId);

        gl.glEnableClientState(GL10.GL_VERTEX_ARRAY);
        gl.glEnableClientState(GL10.GL_TEXTURE_COORD_ARRAY);

        vertices.position(0);
        gl.glVertexPointer(2, GL10.GL_FLOAT, VERTEX_SIZE, vertices);
        vertices.position(2);
        gl.glTexCoordPointer(2, GL10.GL_FLOAT, VERTEX_SIZE, vertices);
```

```
    gl.glDrawArrays(GL10.GL_TRIANGLES, 0, 3);
}
```

I took the freedom to put the texture loading into a method called loadTexture(), which simply takes the filename of a bitmap to be loaded. The method returns the texture object ID generated by OpenGL ES, which we'll use in the present() method to bind the texture.

The definition of our triangle shouldn't be a big surprise; we just added texture coordinates to each vertex.

The present() method does what it always does: it clears the screen and sets the projection matrix. Next we enable texture mapping via a call to glEnable() and bind our texture object. The rest is just what we did before: enabling the vertex attributes we want to use, telling OpenGL ES where it can find them and what strides to use, and finally drawing the triangle with a call to glDrawArrays(). Figure 7–13 shows the output of the preceding code.

Figure 7–13. *Texture mapping Bob onto our triangle*

There's one last thing I haven't mentioned yet, and it's of great importance:

All bitmaps we load must have a width and height that is a power of two.

Stick to it or else things will explode.

So what does this actually mean? The image of Bob that we used in our example has a size of 128×128 pixels. The value 128 is 2 to the power of 7 (2×2×2×2×2×2×2). Other valid image sizes would be 2×8, 32×16, 128×256, and so on. There's also a limit to how big our images can be. Sadly, it varies depending on the hardware our application is running on. The OpenGL ES 1.x standard doesn't specify a minimally supported texture size to my knowledge. However, from my experience it seems that 512×512-pixel textures work on all current Android devices (and most likely will work on all future devices as well). I'd even go so far to say that 1024×1024 is OK as well.

Another issue that we have pretty much ignored so far is the color depth of our textures. Luckily the method `GLUtils.texImage2D()`, which we used to upload our image data to the GPU, handles this for us pretty well. OpenGL ES can cope with color depths like RGBA8888, RGB565, and so on. We should always strive to use the lowest possible color depth to decrease bandwidth. For this we can employ the `BitmapFactory.Options` class, as in previous chapters, to load a RGB888 `Bitmap` to a RGB565 `Bitmap` in memory, for example. Once we have loaded our `Bitmap` instance with the color depth we want it to have, `GLUtils.texImage2D()` takes over and makes sure that OpenGL ES gets the image data in the correct format. Of course, you should always check whether the reduction in color depth has a negative impact on the visual fidelity of your game.

A Texture Class

To reduce the code needed for subsequent examples, I wrote a little helper class called Texture. It will load a bitmap from an asset and create a texture object from it. It also has a few convenience methods to bind the texture and dispose of it. Listing 7–8 shows the code.

Listing 7–8. *Texture.java, a Little OpenGL ES Texture Class*

```
package com.badlogic.androidgames.framework.gl;

import java.io.IOException;
import java.io.InputStream;

import javax.microedition.khronos.opengles.GL10;

import android.graphics.Bitmap;
import android.graphics.BitmapFactory;
import android.opengl.GLUtils;

import com.badlogic.androidgames.framework.FileIO;
import com.badlogic.androidgames.framework.impl.GLGame;
import com.badlogic.androidgames.framework.impl.GLGraphics;

public class Texture {
    GLGraphics glGraphics;
    FileIO fileIO;
    String fileName;
    int textureId;
    int minFilter;
    int magFilter;
```

```java
    public Texture(GLGame glGame, String fileName) {
        this.glGraphics = glGame.getGLGraphics();
        this.fileIO = glGame.getFileIO();
        this.fileName = fileName;
        load();
    }

    private void load() {
        GL10 gl = glGraphics.getGL();
        int[] textureIds = new int[1];
        gl.glGenTextures(1, textureIds, 0);
        textureId = textureIds[0];

        InputStream in = null;
        try {
            in = fileIO.readAsset(fileName);
            Bitmap bitmap = BitmapFactory.decodeStream(in);
            gl.glBindTexture(GL10.GL_TEXTURE_2D, textureId);
            GLUtils.texImage2D(GL10.GL_TEXTURE_2D, 0, bitmap, 0);
            setFilters(GL10.GL_NEAREST, GL10.GL_NEAREST);
            gl.glBindTexture(GL10.GL_TEXTURE_2D, 0);
        } catch(IOException e) {
            throw new RuntimeException("Couldn't load texture '" + fileName +"'", e);
        } finally {
            if(in != null)
                try { in.close(); } catch (IOException e) { }
        }
    }

    public void reload() {
        load();
        bind();
        setFilters(minFilter, magFilter);
        glGraphics.getGL().glBindTexture(GL10.GL_TEXTURE_2D, 0);
    }

    public void setFilters(int minFilter, int magFilter) {
        this.minFilter = minFilter;
        this.magFilter = magFilter;
        GL10 gl = glGraphics.getGL();
        gl.glTexParameterf(GL10.GL_TEXTURE_2D, GL10.GL_TEXTURE_MIN_FILTER, minFilter);
        gl.glTexParameterf(GL10.GL_TEXTURE_2D, GL10.GL_TEXTURE_MAG_FILTER, magFilter);
    }

    public void bind() {
        GL10 gl = glGraphics.getGL();
        gl.glBindTexture(GL10.GL_TEXTURE_2D, textureId);
    }

    public void dispose() {
        GL10 gl = glGraphics.getGL();
        gl.glBindTexture(GL10.GL_TEXTURE_2D, textureId);
        int[] textureIds = { textureId };
        gl.glDeleteTextures(1, textureIds, 0);
    }
}
```

The only interesting thing about this class is the `reload()` method, which we can use when the OpenGL ES context is lost. Also note that the `setFilters()` method will only work if the `Texture` is actually bound. Otherwise it will set the filters of the currently bound texture.

We could also write a little helper method for our vertices buffer. But before we can do this we have to discuss one more thing: indexed vertices.

Indexed Vertices: Because Reuse Is Good for You

Up until this point, we have always defined lists of triangles, where each triangle has its own set of vertices. We have actually only ever drawn a single triangle, but adding more would not have been a big deal.

There are cases, however, where two or more triangles can share some vertices. Let's think about how we'd render a rectangle with our current knowledge. We'd simply define two triangles that would have two vertices with the same positions, colors, and texture coordinates. We can do better. Figure 7–14 shows the old way and the new way of rendering a rectangle.

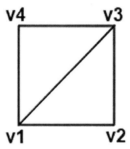

Figure 7–14. *Rendering a rectangle as two triangles with six vertices (left), and rendering it with four vertices (right)*

Instead of duplicating vertex v1 and v2 with vertex v4 and v6, we only define these vertices once. We still render two triangles in this case, but we tell OpenGL ES explicitly which vertices to use for each triangle (e.g., use v1, v2, and v3 for the first triangle and v3, v4, and v1 for the second one). Which vertices to use for each triangle is defined via indices into our vertices array. The first vertex in our array has index 0, the second vertex has index 1, and so on. For the preceding rectangle, we'd have a list of indices like this:

```
short[] indices = { 0, 1, 2,
                    2, 3, 0  };
```

Incidentally, OpenGL ES wants us to specify the indices as shorts (which is not entirely correct; we could also use bytes). However, as with the vertex data, we can't just pass a short array to OpenGL ES. It wants a direct `ShortBuffer`. We already know how to handle that:

```
ByteBuffer byteBuffer = ByteBuffer.allocate(indices.length * 2);
```

```
byteBuffer.order(ByteOrder.nativeOrder());
ShortBuffer shortBuffer = byteBuffer.asShortBuffer();
shortBuffer.put(indices);
shortBuffer.flip();
```

A short needs 2 bytes of memory, so we allocate indices.length × 2 bytes for our ShortBuffer. We set the order to native again and get a ShortBuffer view so we can handle the underlying ByteBuffer more easily. All that's left is putting our indices into the ShortBuffer and flipping it so the limit and position are set correctly.

If we wanted to draw Bob as a rectangle with two indexed triangles, we could define our vertices like this:

```
ByteBuffer byteBuffer = ByteBuffer.allocateDirect(4 * VERTEX_SIZE);
byteBuffer.order(ByteOrder.nativeOrder());
vertices = byteBuffer.asFloatBuffer();
vertices.put(new float[] {  100.0f, 100.0f, 0.0f, 1.0f,
                            228.0f, 100.0f, 1.0f, 1.0f,
                            228.0f, 229.0f, 1.0f, 0.0f,
                            100.0f, 228.0f, 0.0f, 0.0f });
vertices.flip();
```

The order of the vertices is exactly the same as in the right part of Figure 7–13. We tell OpenGL ES that we have positions and texture coordinates for our vertices and where it can find these vertex attributes via the usual calls to glEnableClientState() and glVertexPointer()/glTexCoordPointer(). The only thing that is different is the method we call to actually draw the two triangles:

```
gl.glDrawElements(GL10.GL_TRIANGLES, 6, GL10.GL_UNSIGNED_SHORT, indices);
```

It is very similar to glDrawArrays(), actually. The first parameter specifies the type of primitive we want to render—in this case a list of triangles. The next parameter specifies how many vertices we want to use, which equals six in our case. The third parameter specifies what type the indices have—we specify unsigned short. Note that Java has no unsigned types, though. However, given the one-complement encoding of signed numbers, it's OK to use a ShortBuffer that actually holds signed shorts. The last parameter is our ShortBuffer holding the six indices.

So, what will OpenGL ES do? It knows that we want to render triangles. It knows that we want to render two triangles, as we specified six vertices to be rendered. But instead of fetching six vertices sequentially from the vertices array, it goes sequentially through the index buffer and uses the vertices indexed by it.

Putting It Together

When we put it all together, we arrive at the code in Listing 7–9.

Listing 7–9. *Excerpt from IndexedTest.java; Drawing Two Indexed Triangles*

```
class IndexedScreen extends Screen {
    final int VERTEX_SIZE = (2 + 2) * 4;
    GLGraphics glGraphics;
    FloatBuffer vertices;
    ShortBuffer indices;
```

```java
Texture texture;

public IndexedScreen(Game game) {
    super(game);
    glGraphics = ((GLGame) game).getGLGraphics();

    ByteBuffer byteBuffer = ByteBuffer.allocateDirect(4 * VERTEX_SIZE);
    byteBuffer.order(ByteOrder.nativeOrder());
    vertices = byteBuffer.asFloatBuffer();
    vertices.put(new float[] {  100.0f, 100.0f, 0.0f, 1.0f,
                                228.0f, 100.0f, 1.0f, 1.0f,
                                228.0f, 228.0f, 1.0f, 0.0f,
                                100.0f, 228.0f, 0.0f, 0.0f });
    vertices.flip();

    byteBuffer = ByteBuffer.allocateDirect(6 * 2);
    byteBuffer.order(ByteOrder.nativeOrder());
    indices = byteBuffer.asShortBuffer();
    indices.put(new short[] { 0, 1, 2,
                              2, 3, 0 });
    indices.flip();

    texture = new Texture((GLGame)game, "bobrgb888.png");
}

@Override
public void present(float deltaTime) {
    GL10 gl = glGraphics.getGL();
    gl.glViewport(0, 0, glGraphics.getWidth(), glGraphics.getHeight());
    gl.glClear(GL10.GL_COLOR_BUFFER_BIT);
    gl.glMatrixMode(GL10.GL_PROJECTION);
    gl.glLoadIdentity();
    gl.glOrthof(0, 320, 0, 480, 1, -1);

    gl.glEnable(GL10.GL_TEXTURE_2D);
    texture.bind();

    gl.glEnableClientState(GL10.GL_TEXTURE_COORD_ARRAY);
    gl.glEnableClientState(GL10.GL_VERTEX_ARRAY);

    vertices.position(0);
    gl.glVertexPointer(2, GL10.GL_FLOAT, VERTEX_SIZE, vertices);
    vertices.position(2);
    gl.glTexCoordPointer(2, GL10.GL_FLOAT, VERTEX_SIZE, vertices);

    gl.glDrawElements(GL10.GL_TRIANGLES, 6, GL10.GL_UNSIGNED_SHORT, indices);
}
```

Note the use of our awesome Texture class, which brings down the code size considerably. Figure 7–15 shows the output, and Bob in all his glory.

Figure 7–15. *Bob, indexed*

Now, this is pretty close already to how we worked with Canvas. We have a lot more flexibility as well, since we are not limited to axis-aligned rectangles anymore.

This example has covered all we need to know about vertices for now. We saw that every vertex must have at least a position, and can have additional attributes, such as a color given as four RGBA float values and texture coordinates. We also saw that we can reuse vertices via indexing in case we want to avoid duplication. This gives us a little performance boost, since OpenGL ES does not have to multiply more vertices by the projection and model-view matrices than absolutely necessary (which is again not entirely correct, but let's stick to this interpretation).

A Vertices Class

Let's make our code easier to write by creating a Vertices class that can hold a maximum number of vertices and, optionally, indices to be used for rendering. It should also take care of enabling all the states needed for rendering, as well as cleaning up the states after rendering has finished, so that other code can rely on a clean set of OpenGL ES states. Listing 7–10 shows our easy-to-use Vertices class.

Listing 7–10. *Vertices.java; Encapsulating (Indexed) Vertices*

```
package com.badlogic.androidgames.framework.gl;

import java.nio.ByteBuffer;
import java.nio.ByteOrder;
import java.nio.FloatBuffer;
```

```java
import java.nio.ShortBuffer;

import javax.microedition.khronos.opengles.GL10;

import com.badlogic.androidgames.framework.impl.GLGraphics;

public class Vertices {
    final GLGraphics glGraphics;
    final boolean hasColor;
    final boolean hasTexCoords;
    final int vertexSize;
    final FloatBuffer vertices;
    final ShortBuffer indices;
```

The Vertices class has a reference to the GLGraphics instance, so we can get ahold of the GL10 instance when we need it. We also store whether the vertices have colors and texture coordinates. This gives us great flexibility, as we can choose the minimal set of attributes we need for rendering. We also store a FloatBuffer that holds our vertices and a ShortBuffer that holds the optional indices.

```java
    public Vertices(GLGraphics glGraphics, int maxVertices, int maxIndices, boolean
hasColor, boolean hasTexCoords) {
        this.glGraphics = glGraphics;
        this.hasColor = hasColor;
        this.hasTexCoords = hasTexCoords;
        this.vertexSize = (2 + (hasColor?4:0) + (hasTexCoords?2:0)) * 4;

        ByteBuffer buffer = ByteBuffer.allocateDirect(maxVertices * vertexSize);
        buffer.order(ByteOrder.nativeOrder());
        vertices = buffer.asFloatBuffer();

        if(maxIndices > 0) {
            buffer = ByteBuffer.allocateDirect(maxIndices * Short.SIZE / 8);
            buffer.order(ByteOrder.nativeOrder());
            indices = buffer.asShortBuffer();
        } else {
            indices = null;
        }
    }
```

In the constructor, we specify how many vertices and indices our Vertices instance can hold maximally, as well as whether the vertices have colors or texture coordinates. Inside the constructor, we then set the members accordingly, and instantiate the buffers. Note that the ShortBuffer will be set to null if maxIndices is zero. Our rendering will be performed nonindexed in that case.

```java
    public void setVertices(float[] vertices, int offset, int length) {
        this.vertices.clear();
        this.vertices.put(vertices, offset, length);
        this.vertices.flip();
    }

    public void setIndices(short[] indices, int offset, int length) {
        this.indices.clear();
        this.indices.put(indices, offset, length);
```

```
        this.indices.flip();
    }
```

Next up are the setVertices() and setIndices() methods. The latter will throw a NullPointerException in case the Vertices instance does not store indices. All we do is clear the buffers and copy the contents of the arrays.

```java
    public void draw(int primitiveType, int offset, int numVertices) {
        GL10 gl = glGraphics.getGL();

        gl.glEnableClientState(GL10.GL_VERTEX_ARRAY);
        vertices.position(0);
        gl.glVertexPointer(2, GL10.GL_FLOAT, vertexSize, vertices);

        if(hasColor) {
            gl.glEnableClientState(GL10.GL_COLOR_ARRAY);
            vertices.position(2);
            gl.glColorPointer(4, GL10.GL_FLOAT, vertexSize, vertices);
        }

        if(hasTexCoords) {
            gl.glEnableClientState(GL10.GL_TEXTURE_COORD_ARRAY);
            vertices.position(hasColor?6:2);
            gl.glTexCoordPointer(2, GL10.GL_FLOAT, vertexSize, vertices);
        }

        if(indices!=null) {
            indices.position(offset);
            gl.glDrawElements(primitiveType, numVertices, GL10.GL_UNSIGNED_SHORT, indices);
        } else {
            gl.glDrawArrays(primitiveType, offset, numVertices);
        }

        if(hasTexCoords)
            gl.glDisableClientState(GL10.GL_TEXTURE_COORD_ARRAY);

        if(hasColor)
            gl.glDisableClientState(GL10.GL_COLOR_ARRAY);
    }
}
```

The final method of the Vertices class is draw(). It takes the type of the primitive (e.g., GL10.GL_TRIANGLES), the offset into the vertices buffer (or the indices buffer if we use indices), and the number of vertices to use for rendering. Depending on whether the vertices have colors and texture coordinates, we enable the relevant OpenGL ES states and tell OpenGL ES where to find the data. We do the same for the vertex positions, of course, which are always needed. Depending on whether indices are used or not, we either call glDrawElements() or glDrawArrays() with the parameters passed to the method. Note that the offset parameter can also be used in case of indexed rendering: we simply set the position of the indices buffer accordingly so that OpenGL ES starts reading the indices from that offset instead of the first index of the indices buffer. The last thing we do in the draw() method is clean up the OpenGL ES state a little. We call glDisableClientState() with either GL10.GL_COLOR_ARRAY or

GL10.GL_TEXTURE_COORD_ARRAY in case our vertices have these attributes. We need to do this, as another instance of Vertices might not use those attributes. If we rendered that other Vertices instance, OpenGL ES would still look for colors and/or texture coordinates.

We could replace all the tedious code in the constructor of our preceding example with the following snippet:

```
Vertices vertices = new Vertices(glGraphics, 4, 6, false, true);
vertices.setVertices(new float[] { 100.0f, 100.0f, 0.0f, 1.0f,
                                   228.0f, 100.0f, 1.0f, 1.0f,
                                   228.0f, 228.0f, 1.0f, 0.0f,
                                   100.0f, 228.0f, 0.0f, 0.0f }, 0, 16);
vertices.setIndices(new short[] { 0, 1, 2, 2, 3, 0 }, 0, 6);
```

Likewise, we could replace all the calls for setting up our vertex attribute arrays and rendering with a single call to the following:

```
vertices.draw(GL10.GL_TRIANGLES, 0, 6);
```

Together with our Texture class we have a pretty nice basis for all our 2D OpenGL ES rendering now. One of the things we are still missing to be able to completely reproduce all our Canvas rendering abilities is, though, blending. Let's have a look at that.

Alpha Blending: I Can See Through You

Alpha blending in OpenGL ES is pretty easy to enable. We only need two method calls:

```
gl.glEnable(GL10.GL_BLEND);
gl.glBlendFunc(GL10.GL_SRC_ALPHA, GL10.GL_ONE_MINUS_SRC_ALPHA);
```

The first method call should be familiar: it just tells OpenGL ES that it should apply alpha blending to all triangles we render from this point on. The second method is a little bit more involved. It specifies how the source and destination color should be combined. If you remember what we discussed in Chapter 3, the way a source color and a destination color are combined is governed by a simple blending equation. The method glBlendFunc() just tells OpenGL ES which kind of equation to use. The preceding parameters specify that we want the source color to be mixed with the destination color exactly as specified in the blending equation in Chapter 3. This is equal to how the Canvas blended Bitmaps for us.

Blending in OpenGL ES is pretty powerful and complex, and there's a lot more to it. For our purposes, we can ignore all those details, though, and just use the preceding blending function whenever we want to blend our triangles with the framebuffer—the same way we blended Bitmaps with the Canvas.

The second question is where the source and destination colors come from. The latter is easy to explain: it's the color of the pixel in the framebuffer we are going to overwrite with the triangle we draw. The source color is actually a combination of two colors:

The vertex color: This is the color we either specify via glColor4f() for all vertices or on a per-vertex basis by adding a color attribute to each vertex.

The texel color: As mentioned before, a texel is a pixel from a texture. When our triangle is rendered with a texture mapped to it, OpenGL ES will mix the texel colors with the vertex colors for each pixel of a triangle.

So if our triangle is not texture mapped, the source color for blending is equal to the vertex color. If the triangle is texture mapped, the source color for each of the triangle's pixels is a mixture of the vertex color and the texel color. We could specify how the vertex and texel colors are combined by using the glTexEnv() method. The default is to *modulate* the vertex color by the texel color, which basically means that the two colors are multiplied with each other component-wise (vertex r × texel r, and so on). For all our use cases in this book, this is exactly what we want, so we won't go into glTexEnv(). There are also some very specialized cases where you might want to change how the vertex and texel colors are combined. As with glBlendFunc(), we'll ignore the details and just use the default.

When we load a texture image that doesn't have an alpha channel, OpenGL ES will automatically assume an alpha value of 1 for each pixel. If we load an image in RGBA8888 format, OpenGL ES will happily use the supplied alpha values for blending.

For vertex colors we always have to specify an alpha component, either by using glColor4f(), where the last argument is the alpha value, or by specifying the four components per vertex, where again the last component is the alpha value.

Let's put this into practice with a little example. We want to draw Bob twice: once by using the image bobrgb888.png, which does not have an alpha channel per pixel, and a second time by using the image bobargb8888.png, which has alpha information. Note that the PNG image actually stores the pixels in ARGB8888 format instead of RGBA8888. Luckily the GLUtils.texImage2D() method we use to upload the image data for a texture will do the conversion for us automatically. Listing 7–11 shows the code of our little experiment, using the Texture and Vertices classes.

Listing 7–11. *Excerpt from BlendingTest.java; Blending in Action*

```java
class BlendingScreen extends Screen {
    GLGraphics glGraphics;
    Vertices vertices;
    Texture textureRgb;
    Texture textureRgba;

    public BlendingScreen(Game game) {
        super(game);
        glGraphics = ((GLGame)game).getGLGraphics();

        textureRgb = new Texture((GLGame)game, "bobrgb888.png");
        textureRgba = new Texture((GLGame)game, "bobargb8888.png");

        vertices = new Vertices(glGraphics, 8, 12, true, true);
        float[] rects = new float[] {
                100, 100, 1, 1, 1, 0.5f, 0, 1,
                228, 100, 1, 1, 1, 0.5f, 1, 1,
                228, 228, 1, 1, 1, 0.5f, 1, 0,
                100, 228, 1, 1, 1, 0.5f, 0, 0,
```

```
          100, 300, 1, 1, 1, 1, 0, 1,
          228, 300, 1, 1, 1, 1, 1, 1,
          228, 428, 1, 1, 1, 1, 1, 0,
          100, 428, 1, 1, 1, 1, 0, 0
      };
      vertices.setVertices(rects, 0, rects.length);
      vertices.setIndices(new short[] {0, 1, 2, 2, 3, 0,
                                       4, 5, 6, 6, 7, 4 }, 0, 12);
  }
```

Our little BlendingScreen implementation holds a single Vertices instance where we'll store the two rectangles, as well as two Texture instances—one holding the RGBA8888 image of Bob and the other one storing the RGB888 version of Bob. In the constructor we load both textures from the files bobrgb888.png and bobargb8888.png, and rely on the Texture class and GLUtils.texImag2D() to convert the ARGB8888 PNG to RGBA8888, as needed by OpenGL ES. Next up, we define our vertices and indices. The first rectangle, consisting of four vertices, maps to the RGB888 texture of Bob. The second rectangle maps to the RGBA8888 version of Bob and is rendered 200 units above the RGB888 Bob rectangle. Note that the vertices of the first rectangle all have the color (1,1,1,0.5f) while the vertices of the second rectangle have the color (1,1,1,1).

```
  @Override
  public void present(float deltaTime) {
      GL10 gl = glGraphics.getGL();
      gl.glViewport(0, 0, glGraphics.getWidth(), glGraphics.getHeight());
      gl.glClearColor(1,0,0,1);
      gl.glClear(GL10.GL_COLOR_BUFFER_BIT);
      gl.glMatrixMode(GL10.GL_PROJECTION);
      gl.glLoadIdentity();
      gl.glOrthof(0, 320, 0, 480, 1, -1);

      gl.glEnable(GL10.GL_BLEND);
      gl.glBlendFunc(GL10.GL_SRC_ALPHA, GL10.GL_ONE_MINUS_SRC_ALPHA);

      gl.glEnable(GL10.GL_TEXTURE_2D);
      textureRgb.bind();
      vertices.draw(GL10.GL_TRIANGLES, 0, 6 );

      textureRgba.bind();
      vertices.draw(GL10.GL_TRIANGLES, 6, 6 );
  }
```

In our present() method we clear the screen with red and set the projection matrix, as we are used to doing. Next we enable alpha blending and set the correct blend equation. Finally we enable texture mapping and render the two rectangles. The first rectangle is rendered with the RGB888 texture bound, and the second rectangle is rendered with the RGBA8888 texture bound. We store both rectangles in the same Vertices instance and thus use offsets with the vertices.draw() methods. Figure 7–16 shows the output of this little gem.

Figure 7–16. *Bob, vertex color blended (bottom) and texture blended (top)*

In the case of RGB888 Bob, the blending is performed via the alpha values in the per-vertex colors. Since we set those to 0.5f, Bob is 50 percent translucent.

In the case of RGBA8888 Bob, the per-vertex colors all have an alpha value of 1. However, since the background pixels of that texture have alpha values of 0, and since the vertex colors and the texel colors are modulated, the background of this version of Bob disappears. If we'd have set the per-vertex colors' alpha values to 0.5f as well, then Bob himself would also have been 50 percent as translucent as his clone in the bottom of the screen. Figure 7–17 shows what that would have looked like.

Figure 7–17. *An alternative version of RGBA8888 Bob using per-vertex alpha of 0.5f (top of the screen)*

And that's basically all we need to know about blending with OpenGL ES in 2D.

However, there is one more very important thing I'd like to point out: *Blending is expensive!* Seriously, don't overuse it. Current mobile GPUs are not all that good at blending massive amounts of pixels. You should only use blending if absolutely necessary.

More Primitives: Points, Lines, Strips, and Fans

When I told you that OpenGL ES was a big, nasty triangle-rendering machine, I was not being 100 percent honest. In fact, OpenGL ES can also render points and lines. Best of all: these are also defined via vertices, and thus all of the above also applies to them (texturing, per-vertex colors, etc.). All we need to do to render these primitives is use something other than GL10.GL_TRIANGLES when we call glDrawArrays()/glDrawElements(). We can also perform indexed rendering with these primitives, although that's a bit redundant (in the case of points at least). Figure 7–18 shows a list of all the primitive types OpenGL ES offers us.

Figure 7–18. *All the primitives OpenGL ES can render*

Let's go through all of these primitives really quickly:

Point: With a point, each vertex is its own primitive.

Line: A line is made up of two vertices. As with triangles, we can just have $2 \times n$ vertices to define n lines.

Line strip: All the vertices are interpreted as belonging to one long line.

Line loop: This is similar to a line strip, with the difference that OpenGL ES will automatically draw an additional line from the last vertex to the first vertex.

Triangle: This we already know. Each triangle is made up of three vertices.

Triangle strip: Instead of specifying three vertices, we just specify *number of triangles* + 1 vertices. OpenGL ES will then construct the first triangle from vertices (v1,v2,v3), the next triangle from vertices (v2,v3,v4), and so on.

Triangle fan: This has one base vertex (v1) that is shared by all triangles. The first triangle will be (v1,v2,v3), the next triangle (v1,v3,v4), and so on.

Triangle strips and fans are a little bit less flexible than pure triangle lists. But they can give a little performance boost, as fewer vertices have to be multiplied by the projection and model-view matrices. We'll stick to triangle lists in all our code, though, as they are easier to use and can be made to achieve similar performance by using indices.

Points and lines are a little bit strange in OpenGL ES. When we use a pixel-perfect orthographic projection (e.g., our screen resolution is 320×480 pixels and our glOrthof() call uses those exact values), we still don't get pixel-perfect rendering in all cases. The positions of the point and line vertices have to be offset by 0.375f due to something called the diamond exit rule. Keep that in mind if you want to render pixel-perfect points and lines. We already saw that something similar applies to triangles. However, given that we usually draw rectangles in 2D, we don't run into that problem.

Given that all you have to do to render primitives other than GL10.GL_TRIANGLES is to use one of the other constants in Figure 7–17, I'll spare you an example program. We'll stick to triangle lists for the most part, especially when doing 2D graphics programming.

Let's now dive into one more thing OpenGL ES offers us: the almighty model-view matrix.

2D Transformations: Fun with the Model-View Matrix

All we have done so far is define static geometries in the form of triangle lists. There was nothing moving, rotating, or scaling. Also, even when the vertex data itself stayed the same (e.g., the width and height of a rectangle composed of two triangles along with texture coordinates and color), we still had to duplicate the vertices if we wanted to draw the same rectangle at different places. Look back at Listing 7–11 and ignore the color attributes of the vertices for now. The two rectangles only differ in their y-coordinates by 200 units. If we had a way to move those vertices without actually changing their values we could get away with defining the rectangle of Bob only once, and simply drawing him at different locations. And that's exactly what we can use the model-view matrix for.

World and Model Space

To understand how this works we have to literally think outside of our little orthographic view frustum box. Our view frustum is in a special coordinate system called the *world space*. This is the space where all our vertices are going to end up eventually.

Up until now we have specified all vertex positions in absolute coordinates relative to the origin of this world space (compare with Figure 7–5). What we really want is to make the definition of the positions of our vertices independent from this world space coordinate system. We can achieve this by giving each of our models (e.g., Bob's rectangle, a spaceship, etc.) its own coordinate system.

This is what we usually call *model space*, the coordinate system within which we define the positions of our model's vertices. Figure 7–19 illustrates this concept in 2D, and the same rules apply to 3D as well (just add a z-axis).

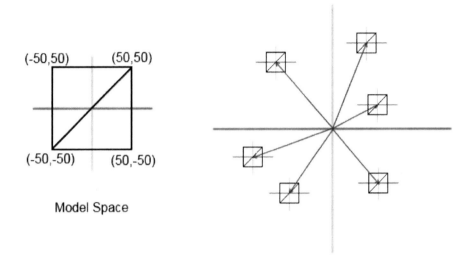

Model Space

Eye/World Space

Figure 7–19. *Defining our model in model space, reusing it, and rendering it at different locations in the world space*

In Figure 7–19 we have a single model, defined via a `Vertices` instance—for example, like this:

```
Vertices vertices = new Vertices(glGraphics, 4, 12, false, false);
vertices.setVertices(new float[] { -50, -50,
                                     50, -50,
                                     50,  50,
                                    -50,  50 }, 0, 8);
vertices.setIndices(new short[] {0, 1, 2, 2, 3, 0}, 0, 6);
```

For our discussion we just leave out any vertex colors or texture coordinates. Now, when we render this model without any further modifications, it will be placed around the origin in the world space in our final image. If we want to render it at a different position—say, its center being at (200,300) in world space—we could redefine the vertex positions like this:

```
vertices.setVertices(new float[] { -50 + 200, -50 + 300,
                                     50 + 200, -50 + 300,
                                     50 + 200,  50 + 300,
                                    -50 + 200,  50 + 300 }, 0, 8);
```

On the next call to vertices.draw(), the model would be rendered with its center at (200,300). But this is a tad bit tedious isn't it?

Matrices Again

Remember when we briefly talked about matrices earlier? We discussed how matrices can encode transformations such as translations (moving stuff around), rotations, and scaling. The projection matrix we use to project our vertices onto the projection plane encodes a special type of transformation: a projection.

Matrices are the key to solving our previous problem more elegantly. Instead of manually moving our vertex positions around by redefining them, we simply set a matrix that encodes a translation. Since the projection matrix of OpenGL ES is already occupied by our orthographics projection matrix we specified via glOrthof(), we use a different OpenGL ES matrix: the model-view matrix. Here's how we could render our model with its origin moved to a specific location in eye/world space:

```
gl.glMatrixMode(GL10.GL_MODELVIEW);
gl.glLoadIdentity();
gl.glTranslatef(200, 300, 0);
vertices.draw(GL10.GL_TRIANGLES, 0, 6);
```

We have to first tell OpenGL ES which matrix we want to manipulate. In our case that's the model-view matrix, which is specified by the constant GL10.GL_MODELVIEW. Next we make sure that the model-view matrix is set to an identity matrix. Basically we just overwrite anything that was in there already—we sort of clear the matrix. The next call is where the magic happens.

The method glTranslatef() takes three arguments: the translation on the x-, y-, and z-axes. Since we want the origin of our model to be placed at (200,300) in eye/world space, we specify a translation by 200 units on the x-axis and a translation by 300 units on the y-axis. As we are working in 2D, we simply ignore the z-axis and set the translation component to zero. We didn't specify a z-coordinate for our vertices, so these will default to zero. Adding zero to zero equals zero, so our vertices will stay in the x-y plane.

From this point on, the model-view matrix of OpenGL ES encodes a translation by (200,300,0), which will be applied to all vertices that pass through the OpenGL ES pipeline. If you refer back to Figure 7–4, you'll see that OpenGL ES will multiply each vertex with the model-view matrix first and then apply the projection matrix. Up until this point, the model-view matrix was set to an identity matrix (the default of OpenGL ES). It therefore did not have an effect on our vertices. Our little glTranslatef() call changes this, and will move all vertices first before they are projected.

Of course, this is done on the fly; the values in our `Vertices` instance do not change at all. We would have noticed any permanent change to your `Vertices` instance as by that logic the projection matrix would have changed it already.

An First Example Using Translation

What can we use this for? Say we want to render 100 Bobs at different positions in our world. Additionally we want them to move around on the screen and change direction each time they hit an edge of the screen (or rather a plane of our parallel projection view frustum, which coincides with the extents of our screen). We could do this by having one large `Vertices` instance that holds the vertices of the 100 rectangles—one for each Bob—and recalculate the vertex positions each frame. The easier method is to have one small `Vertices` instance that only holds a single rectangle (the model of Bob) and reuse it by translating it with the model-view matrix on the fly. Let's define our Bob model:

```
Vertices bobModel = new Vertices(glGraphics, 4, 12, false, true);
bobModel.setVertices(new float[] { -16, -16, 0, 1,
                                    16, -16, 1, 1,
                                    16,  16, 1, 0,
                                   -16,  16, 0, 0, }, 0, 8);
bobModel.setIndices(new short[] {0, 1, 2, 2, 3, 0}, 0, 6);
```

So, each Bob is 32×32 units in size. We also texture map him (we'll use `bobrgb888.png` to see the extents of each Bob).

Bob Becomes a Class

Let's define a simple `Bob` class. It will be responsible for holding a Bob's position and advancing his position in his current direction based on the delta time, just like we advanced Mr. Nom (with the difference that we don't move in a grid anymore). The `update()` method will also make sure that Bob doesn't escape our view volume bounds. Listing 7–12 shows the `Bob` class.

Listing 7–12. *Bob.java*

```java
package com.badlogic.androidgames.glbasics;

import java.util.Random;

class Bob {
    static final Random rand = new Random();
    public float x, y;
    float dirX, dirY;

    public Bob() {
        x = rand.nextFloat() * 320;
        y = rand.nextFloat() * 480;
        dirX = 50;
        dirY = 50;
    }

    public void update(float deltaTime) {
```

```
            x = x + dirX * deltaTime;
            y = y + dirY * deltaTime;

            if (x < 0) {
                dirX = -dirX;
                x = 0;
            }

            if (x > 320) {
                dirX = -dirX;
                x = 320;
            }

            if (y < 0) {
                dirY = -dirY;
                y = 0;
            }

            if (y > 480) {
                dirY = -dirY;
                y = 480;
            }
        }
    }
}
```

Every Bob will place himself at a random location in the world when we construct him. All the Bobs will initially move in the same direction: 50 units to the right and 50 units upward per second (as we multiply by the deltaTime). In the update() method we simply advance Bob in his current direction in a time-based manner, and then check if he left the view frustum bounds. If that's the case we invert his direction and make sure he's still in the view frustum.

Now let's assume we are instantiating 100 Bobs, like this:

```
Bob[] bobs = new Bob[100];
for(int i = 0; i < 100; i++) {
    bobs[i] = new Bob();
}
```

To render each of these Bobs, we'd do something like this (assuming we've already cleared the screen, set the projection matrix, and bound the texture):

```
gl.glMatrixMode(GL10.GL_MODELVIEW);
for(int i = 0; i < 100; i++) {
    bob.update(deltaTime);
    gl.glLoadIdentity();
    gl.glTranslatef(bobs[i].x, bobs[i].y, 0);
    bobModel.render(GL10.GL_TRIANGLES, 0, 6);
}
```

That is pretty sweet, isn't it? For each Bob, we call his update() method, which will advance his position and make sure he stays within the bounds of our little world. Next we load an identity matrix into the model-view matrix of OpenGL ES so we have a clean slate. We then use the current Bob's x- and y-coordinates in a call to glTransltef(). When we then render the Bob model in the next call, all the vertices will be offset by the current Bob's position—exactly what we wanted.

Putting It Together

Let's make this a full-blown example. Listing 7–13 shows the code.

Listing 7–13. *BobTest.java; 100 Moving Bobs!*

```java
package com.badlogic.androidgames.glbasics;

import javax.microedition.khronos.opengles.GL10;

import com.badlogic.androidgames.framework.Game;
import com.badlogic.androidgames.framework.Screen;
import com.badlogic.androidgames.framework.gl.FPSCounter;
import com.badlogic.androidgames.framework.gl.Texture;
import com.badlogic.androidgames.framework.gl.Vertices;
import com.badlogic.androidgames.framework.impl.GLGame;
import com.badlogic.androidgames.framework.impl.GLGraphics;

public class BobTest extends GLGame {

    @Override
    public Screen getStartScreen() {
        return new BobScreen(this);
    }

    class BobScreen extends Screen {
        static final int NUM_BOBS = 100;
        GLGraphics glGraphics;
        Texture bobTexture;
        Vertices bobModel;
        Bob[] bobs;
```

Our BobScreen class holds a Texture (loaded from bobrbg888.png), a Vertices instance holding the model of Bob (a simple textured rectangle), and an array of Bob instances. We also define a little constant named NUM_BOBS so we can modify the number of Bobs we want to have on the screen.

```java
        public BobScreen(Game game) {
            super(game);
            glGraphics = ((GLGame)game).getGLGraphics();

            bobTexture = new Texture((GLGame)game, "bobrgb888.png");

            bobModel = new Vertices(glGraphics, 4, 12, false, true);
            bobModel.setVertices(new float[] { -16, -16, 0, 1,
                                                16, -16, 1, 1,
                                                16,  16, 1, 0,
                                               -16,  16, 0, 0, }, 0, 16);
            bobModel.setIndices(new short[] {0, 1, 2, 2, 3, 0}, 0, 6);


            bobs = new Bob[100];
            for(int i = 0; i < 100; i++) {
                bobs[i] = new Bob();
            }
        }
```

The constructor just loads the texture, creates the model, and instantiates NUM_BOBS Bob instances.

```java
@Override
    public void update(float deltaTime) {
        game.getInput().getTouchEvents();
        game.getInput().getKeyEvents();

        for(int i = 0; i < NUM_BOBS; i++) {
            bobs[i].update(deltaTime);
        }
    }
```

The update() method is where we let our Bobs update themselves. We also make sure our input event buffers are emptied.

```java
@Override
    public void present(float deltaTime) {
        GL10 gl = glGraphics.getGL();
        gl.glClearColor(1,0,0,1);
        gl.glClear(GL10.GL_COLOR_BUFFER_BIT);
        gl.glMatrixMode(GL10.GL_PROJECTION);
        gl.glLoadIdentity();
        gl.glOrthof(0, 320, 0, 480, 1, -1);

        gl.glEnable(GL10.GL_TEXTURE_2D);
        bobTexture.bind();

        gl.glMatrixMode(GL10.GL_MODELVIEW);
        for(int i = 0; i < NUM_BOBS; i++) {
            gl.glLoadIdentity();
            gl.glTranslatef(bobs[i].x, bobs[i].y, 0);
            gl.glRotatef(45, 0, 0, 1);
            gl.glScalef(2, 0.5f, 0);
            bobModel.draw(GL10.GL_TRIANGLES, 0, 6);
        }
    }
```

In the render() method we clear the screen, set the projection matrix, enable texturing, and bind the texture of Bob. The last couple of lines are responsible for actually rendering each Bob instance. Since OpenGL ES remembers its states, we have to set the active matrix only once (in this case we are going to modify the model-view matrix in the rest of the code). We then loop through all the Bobs, set the model-view matrix to a translation matrix based on the position of the current Bob, and render the model, which will be translated by the model view-matrix automatically.

```java
@Override
public void pause() {
}

@Override
public void resume() {
}

@Override
```

```
        public void dispose() {
        }
    }
}
```

That's it. Best of all, we employed the MVC pattern we used in Mr. Nom again. It really lends itself well to game programming. The logical side of Bob is completely decoupled from his appearance, which is nice, as we can easily replace his appearance with something more complex. Figure 7–20 shows the output of our little program after running for a few seconds.

Figure 7–20. *That's a lot of Bobs.*

That's not the end of all our fun with transformations yet. If you remember what I said a couple of pages ago, you'll know what's coming: rotations and scaling.

More Transformations

Besides the glTranslatef() method, OpenGL ES also offers us two methods for transformations: glRotatef() and glScalef().

Rotation

Here's the signature of glRotatef():

```
GL10.glRotatef(float angle, float axisX, float axisY, float axisZ);
```

The first parameter is the angle in degrees we want to rotate our vertices by. But what do the rest of the parameters mean?

When we rotate something, we rotate it around an axis. What is an axis? Well, we already know three axes: the x-axis, the y-axis, and the z-axis. We can express these three axes as so-called *vectors*. The positive x-axis would be described as (1,0,0), the positive y-axis would be (0,1,0) and the positive z-axis would be (0,0,1). As you can see, a vector actually encodes a direction, in our case in 3D space. Bob's direction is also a vector, but in 2D space. Vectors can also encode positions, like Bob's position in 2D space.

To define the axis around which we want to rotate the model of Bob, we need to go back to 3D space, actually. Figure 7–21 shows the model of Bob (with a texture applied for orientation) as defined in the previous code in 3D space.

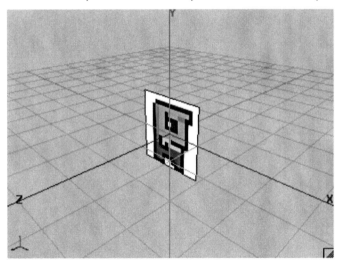

Figure 7–21. *Bob in 3D*

Since we haven't defined z-coordinates for Bob's vertices, he is embedded in the x-y plane of our 3D space (which is actually the model space, remember?). If we want to rotate Bob, we can do it around any axis we can think of: the x-, y-, or z-axis, or even a totally crazy axis like (0.75,0.75,0.75). However, for our 2D graphics programming needs, it makes sense to rotate Bob in the x-y plane. Hence, we'll use the positive z-axis as our rotation axis, which can be defined as (0,0,1). The rotation will be counterclockwise around the z-axis. A call to glRotatef(), like this, would cause the vertices of Bob's model to be rotated as shown in Figure 7–22:

```
gl.glRotatef(45, 0, 0, 1);
```

Figure 7–22. *Bob, rotated around the z-axis by 45 degrees*

Scaling

We can also scale Bob's model with glScalef(), like this:

```
glScalef(2, 0.5f, 1);
```

which, given Bob's original model pose, would result in the new orientation depicted in Figure 7–23.

Figure 7–23. *Bob, scaled by a factor of 2 on the x-axis and a factor of 0.5 on the y-axis. Ouch.*

Combining Transformations

Now, we also discussed that we can combine the effect of multiple matrices by multiplying them together to form a new matrix. All the methods—glTranslatef(), glScalef(), glRotatef(), and glOrthof()—actually do just that. They multiply the current active matrix by the temporary matrix they create internally based on the parameters we pass to them. So let's combine the rotation and scaling of Bob:

```
gl.glRotatef(45, 0, 0, 1);
gl.glScalef(2, 0.5f, 1);
```

This would make Bob's model look like Figure 7–24 (remember, we are still in model space).

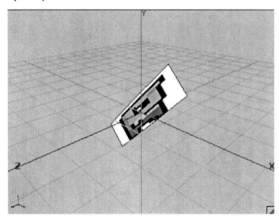

Figure 7–24. *Bob, first scaled and then rotated (still not looking happy)*

What would happen if we applied the transformations the other way around, like this:

```
gl.glScalef(2, 0.5, 0);
gl.glRotatef(45, 0, 0, 1)
```

Figure 7–25 gives you the answer.

Figure 7–25. *Bob, first rotated, and then scaled*

Wow, this is not the Bob we used to know. What happened here? If you look at the code snippets, you'd actually expect Figure 7–24 to look like Figure 7–25, and Figure 7–25 to look like Figure 7–24. In the first snippet we apply the rotation first, and then scale Bob, right?

Wrong. The way OpenGL ES multiplies matrices with each other dictates the order in which the transformations the matrices encode are applied to a model. The last matrix we multiply the currently active matrix with will be the first that gets applied to the vertices. So if we want to scale, rotate, and translate Bob, in that exact order, we have to call the methods like this:

```
glTranslatef(bobs[i].x, bobs[i].y, 0);
glRotatef(45, 0, 0, 1);
glScalef(2, 0.5f, 1);
```

If we changed the loop in our `BobScreen.present()` method to the following code:

```
gl.glMatrixMode(GL10.GL_MODELVIEW);
for(int i = 0; i < NUM_BOBS; i++) {
    gl.glLoadIdentity();
    gl.glTranslatef(bobs[i].x, bobs[i].y, 0);
    gl.glRotatef(45, 0, 0, 1);
    gl.glScalef(2, 0.5f, 0);
    bobModel.draw(GL10.GL_TRIANGLES, 0, 6);
}
```

the output would look like Figure 7–25.

Figure 7–26. *A hundred Bobs, scaled, rotated, and translated (in that order) to their positions in world space*

I always mixed up the order of these matrix operations when I started out with OpenGL on the desktop. To remember how to do it correctly, I eventually arrived at a mnemonic device called it the LASFIA principle: last specified, first applied. (Yeah, my mnemonics aren't all that great huh?)

The easiest way to get comfortable with model-view transformations is to use them heavily. I suggest you take the `BobTest.java` source file, modify the inner loop for some time, and observe the effects. Note that you can specify as many transformations as you want for rendering each model. Add more rotations, translations, and scaling. Go crazy.

With this last example we basically know everything we need to know about OpenGL ES to write 2D games. Or do we?

Optimizing for Performance

When we run this example on a beefy second-generation device like a Droid or a Nexus One, everything will run smooth as silk. If we run it on a Hero, everything will start to stutter and look pretty unpleasant. But hey, didn't I say OpenGL ES was the silver bullet for fast graphics rendering? Well, yes it is. But only if we do things the way OpenGL ES wants us to do them.

Measuring Frame Rate

BobTest provides a perfect example to start with some optimizations. Before we can do that, though, we need a way to assess performance. Manual visual inspection ("doh, it looks like it stutters a little") is not precise enough. A better way to measure how fast our program performs is to count the number of frames we render per second. If you remember Chapter 3, we talked about something called the vertical synchronization, or vsync for short. This is enabled on all Android devices that are on the market so far, and limits the maximum frames per second (FPS) we can achieve to 60. We know our code is good enough when we run at that frame rate.

> **NOTE:** While 60 FPS would be nice to have, in reality it is pretty hard to achieve such performance. Devices like the Nexus One and the Droid have a lot of pixels to fill, even if we're just clearing the screen. We'll be happy if our game renders the world at more than 30 FPS in general. More frames don't hurt, though.

Let's write a little helper class that counts the FPS and outputs that value periodically. Listing 7–14 shows the code of a class called FPSCounter.

Listing 7–14. *FPSCounter.java; Counting Frames and Logging Them to LogCat Each Second*

```java
package com.badlogic.androidgames.framework.gl;

import android.util.Log;

public class FPSCounter {
    long startTime = System.nanoTime();
    int frames = 0;

    public void logFrame() {
        frames++;
        if(System.nanoTime() - startTime >= 1000000000) {
            Log.d("FPSCounter", "fps: " + frames);
```

```
            frames = 0;
            startTime = System.nanoTime();
        }
    }
}
```

We can put an instance of this class in our BobScreen class and call the logFrame() method once in the BobScreen.present() method. I just did this, and here is the output for a Hero (running Android 1.5), a Droid (running Android 2.2), and a Nexus One (running Android 2.2.1).

```
Hero:
12-10 03:27:05.230: DEBUG/FPSCounter(17883): fps: 22
12-10 03:27:06.250: DEBUG/FPSCounter(17883): fps: 22
12-10 03:27:06.820: DEBUG/dalvikvm(17883): GC freed 21818 objects / 524280 bytes in
132ms
12-10 03:27:07.270: DEBUG/FPSCounter(17883): fps: 20
12-10 03:27:08.290: DEBUG/FPSCounter(17883): fps: 23

Droid:
12-10 03:29:44.825: DEBUG/FPSCounter(8725): fps: 39
12-10 03:29:45.864: DEBUG/FPSCounter(8725): fps: 38
12-10 03:29:46.879: DEBUG/FPSCounter(8725): fps: 38
12-10 03:29:47.879: DEBUG/FPSCounter(8725): fps: 39
12-10 03:29:48.887: DEBUG/FPSCounter(8725): fps: 40

Nexus One:
12-10 03:28:05.923: DEBUG/FPSCounter(930): fps: 43
12-10 03:28:06.933: DEBUG/FPSCounter(930): fps: 43
12-10 03:28:07.943: DEBUG/FPSCounter(930): fps: 44
12-10 03:28:08.963: DEBUG/FPSCounter(930): fps: 44
12-10 03:28:09.973: DEBUG/FPSCounter(930): fps: 44
12-10 03:28:11.003: DEBUG/FPSCounter(930): fps: 43
12-10 03:28:12.013: DEBUG/FPSCounter(930): fps: 44
```

Upon first inspection we can see the following:

- The Hero is twice as slow as the Droid and the Nexus One.

- The Nexus One is slightly faster than the Droid.

- We generate garbage on the Hero in our process (17883).

Now, the last item on that list is somewhat puzzling. We run the same code on all three devices. And upon further inspection, we do not allocate any temporary objects in either the present() or update() method. So what's happening on the Hero?

The Curious Case of the Hero on Android 1.5

It turns out that there is a bug in Android 1.5. Well, it's not a bug, it's just some extremely sloppy programming. Remember that we use direct NIO buffers for our vertices and indices. These are actually memory blocks in native heap memory. Each time we call glVertexPointer(), glColorPointer(), or any other of the glXXXPointer() methods, OpenGL ES will try to fetch the native heap memory address of that buffer to look up the vertices to transfer the data to video RAM. The problem on Android 1.5 is that each time we request the memory address from a direct NIO buffer, it will generate a temporary object called PlatformAddress. Since we have a lot of calls to the glXXXPointer() and glDrawElements() methods (remember, the latter fetches the address from a direct ShortBuffer), Android allocates a metric ton of temporary PlatformAdress instances, and there's nothing we can do about it. (Well, there's actually a workaround, but for now we won't discuss it). Let's just accept the fact that using NIO buffers on Android 1.5 is horribly broken and move on.

What's Making My OpenGL ES Rendering So Slow?

That the Hero is slower than the second-generation devices is no big surprise. However, the PowerVR chip in the Droid is slightly faster than the Adreno chip in the Nexus One, so the preceding results are a little bit strange at first sight. On further inspection we can probably attribute the difference not to the GPU power but to the fact that we call many OpenGL ES methods each frame, which are costly Java Native Interface methods. This means that they actually call into C code, which costs more than calling a Java method on Dalvik. The Nexus One has a JIT compiler and can optimize a little bit there. So let's just assume that the difference stems from the JIT compiler (which is probably not entirely correct).

Now let's examine what's bad for OpenGL ES:

- Changing states a lot per frame (e.g., blending, enabling/disabling texture mapping, etc.)
- Changing matrices a lot per frame.
- Binding textures a lot per frame.
- Changing the vertex, color, and texture coordinate pointers a lot per frame.

It all boils down to changing state really. Why is this costly? GPUs work like an assembly line in a factory. While the front of the line processes new incoming pieces, the end of the line finishes off pieces already processed by previous stages of the line. Let's try it with a little car factory analogy.

The production line has a few states, such as the tools that are available to factory workers, the type of bolts that are used to assemble parts of the cars, the color the cars get painted with, and so on. Yes, real car factories have multiple assembly lines, but let's just pretend there's only one. Now, each stage of the line will be busy as long as we don't change any of the states. As soon as we change a single state, however, the line will stall until all the cars currently being assembled are finished off. Only then can we actually change the state and assemble cars with the new paint/bolts/whatever.

The key insight is that a call to glDrawElements() or glDrawArrays() is not immediately executed. Instead the command is put into a buffer that is processed asynchronously by the GPU. This means that the calls to the drawing methods will not block. It's therefore a bad idea to measure the time a call to glDrawElements() takes, as the actual work might be performed in the future. That's why we measure FPS instead. When the framebuffer is swapped (yes, we use double-buffering with OpenGL ES as well), OpenGL ES will make sure that all pending operations will be executed.

So translating the car factory analogy to OpenGL ES means the following. While new triangles enter the command buffer via a call to glDrawElements() or glDrawArrays(), the GPU pipeline might finish off the rendering of currently processed triangles from earlier calls to the render methods (e.g., a triangle can be currently processed in the rasterization state of the pipeline). This has the following implications:

- Changing the currently bound texture is expensive. Any triangles in the command buffer that have not been processed yet and that use the texture must be rendered first. The pipeline will stall.

- Changing the vertex, color, and texture coordinate pointers is expensive. Any triangles in the command buffer that haven't been rendered yet and use the old pointers must be rendered first. The pipeline will stall.

- Changing blending state is expensive. Any triangles in the command buffer that need/don't need blending and haven't been rendered yet must be rendered first. The pipeline will stall.

- Changing the model-view or projection matrix is expensive. Any triangles in the command buffer that haven't been processed yet and to which the old matrices should be applied must be rendered first. The pipeline will stall.

The quintessence of all this is *reduce your state changes*—all of them.

Removing Unnecessary State Changes

So let's look at the present() method of BobTest and see what we can change. Here's the snippet for reference (I added the FPSCounter in, and we also use glRotatef() and glScalef()):

```
@Override
public void present(float deltaTime) {
    GL10 gl = glGraphics.getGL();
    gl.glViewport(0, 0, glGraphics.getWidth(), glGraphics.getHeight());
    gl.glClearColor(1,0,0,1);
    gl.glClear(GL10.GL_COLOR_BUFFER_BIT);
    gl.glMatrixMode(GL10.GL_PROJECTION);
    gl.glLoadIdentity();
    gl.glOrthof(0, 320, 0, 480, 1, -1);

    gl.glEnable(GL10.GL_TEXTURE_2D);
    bobTexture.bind();

    gl.glMatrixMode(GL10.GL_MODELVIEW);
    for(int i = 0; i < NUM_BOBS; i++) {
        gl.glLoadIdentity();
```

```
            gl.glTranslatef(bobs[i].x, bobs[i].y, 0);
            gl.glRotatef(45, 0, 0, 1);
            gl.glScalef(2, 0.5f, 1);
            bobModel.draw(GL10.GL_TRIANGLES, 0, 6);
        }
        fpsCounter.logFrame();
    }
```

The first thing we could do is to move the calls to glViewport() and glClearColor(), as well as the method calls that set the projection matrix to the BobScreen.resume() method. The clear color will never change, the viewport and the projection matrix won't change either. Why not put the code to setup all persistent OpenGL states like the viewport or projection matrix in the constructor of BobScreen? Well, we need to battle context loss. All OpenGL ES state modifications we perform will get lost, and when our screen's resume() method is called, we know that the context has been recreated and is thus missing all the states we might have set before. We can also put the call the glEnable() and the texture-binding call into the resume() method. After all, we want texturing to be enabled all the time, and we also only want to use that single Bob texture. For good measure we also call texture.reload() in the resume() method so that our texture image data is also reloaded in the case of a context loss. So here are our modified present() and resume() methods:

```
@Override
public void resume() {
    GL10 gl = glGraphics.getGL();
    gl.glViewport(0, 0, glGraphics.getWidth(), glGraphics.getHeight());
    gl.glClearColor(1, 0, 0, 1);
    gl.glMatrixMode(GL10.GL_PROJECTION);
    gl.glLoadIdentity();
    gl.glOrthof(0, 320, 0, 480, 1, -1);

    bobTexture.reload();
    gl.glEnable(GL10.GL_TEXTURE_2D);
    bobTexture.bind();
}

@Override
public void present(float deltaTime) {
    GL10 gl = glGraphics.getGL();
    gl.glClear(GL10.GL_COLOR_BUFFER_BIT);

    gl.glMatrixMode(GL10.GL_MODELVIEW);
    for(int i = 0; i < NUM_BOBS; i++) {
        gl.glLoadIdentity();
        gl.glTranslatef(bobs[i].x, bobs[i].y, 0);
        gl.glRotatef(45, 0, 0, 1);
        gl.glScalef(2, 0.5f, 0);
        bobModel.draw(GL10.GL_TRIANGLES, 0, 6);
    }

    fpsCounter.logFrame();
}
```

Running this "improved" version gives the following performance on the three devices:

```
Hero:
12-10 04:41:56.750: DEBUG/FPSCounter(467): fps: 23
12-10 04:41:57.770: DEBUG/FPSCounter(467): fps: 23
12-10 04:41:58.500: DEBUG/dalvikvm(467): GC freed 21821 objects / 524288 bytes in 133ms
12-10 04:41:58.790: DEBUG/FPSCounter(467): fps: 19
12-10 04:41:59.830: DEBUG/FPSCounter(467): fps: 23

Droid:
12-10 04:45:26.906: DEBUG/FPSCounter(9116): fps: 39
12-10 04:45:27.914: DEBUG/FPSCounter(9116): fps: 41
12-10 04:45:28.922: DEBUG/FPSCounter(9116): fps: 41
12-10 04:45:29.937: DEBUG/FPSCounter(9116): fps: 40

Nexus One:
12-10 04:37:46.097: DEBUG/FPSCounter(2168): fps: 43
12-10 04:37:47.127: DEBUG/FPSCounter(2168): fps: 45
12-10 04:37:48.147: DEBUG/FPSCounter(2168): fps: 44
12-10 04:37:49.157: DEBUG/FPSCounter(2168): fps: 44
12-10 04:37:50.167: DEBUG/FPSCounter(2168): fps: 44
```

So all the devices have already benefited a tiny bit by our optimizations. Of course, the effect is not exactly huge. This can be attributed to the fact that when we originally called all those methods at the beginning of the frame, there were no triangles in the pipeline yet.

Reducing Texture Size Means Fewer Pixels to Be Fetched

So what else could be changed? Something that is not all that obvious. Our Bob instances are 32×32 units in size. We use a projection plane that is 320×480 units in size. On a Hero, that will give us pixel-perfect rendering. On a Nexus One or a Droid, a single unit in our coordinate system would take up a little under a pixel. In any case our texture is actually 128×128 pixels in size. We don't need that much resolution, so let's resize the texture image bobrgb888.png to 32×32 pixels. We'll call the new image bobrgb888-32x32.png. Using this smaller texture, we get the following FPS for each device:

```
Hero:
12-10 04:48:03.940: DEBUG/FPSCounter(629): fps: 23
12-10 04:48:04.950: DEBUG/FPSCounter(629): fps: 23
12-10 04:48:05.860: DEBUG/dalvikvm(629): GC freed 21812 objects / 524256 bytes in 134ms
12-10 04:48:05.990: DEBUG/FPSCounter(629): fps: 21
12-10 04:48:07.030: DEBUG/FPSCounter(629): fps: 24

Droid:
12-10 04:51:11.601: DEBUG/FPSCounter(9191): fps: 56
12-10 04:51:12.609: DEBUG/FPSCounter(9191): fps: 56
12-10 04:51:13.625: DEBUG/FPSCounter(9191): fps: 55
12-10 04:51:14.641: DEBUG/FPSCounter(9191): fps: 55

Nexus One:
12-10 04:48:18.067: DEBUG/FPSCounter(2238): fps: 53
12-10 04:48:19.077: DEBUG/FPSCounter(2238): fps: 56
12-10 04:48:20.077: DEBUG/FPSCounter(2238): fps: 53
12-10 04:48:21.097: DEBUG/FPSCounter(2238): fps: 54
```

Wow, that makes a huge difference on the second-generation devices. It turns out that the GPUs of those devices hate nothing more than having to scan over a large amount of pixels. This is true for fetching texels from a texture as well as actually rendering triangles to the screen. The rate at which those GPUs can fetch texels and render pixels to the framebuffer is called the *fill rate*. All the second-generation GPUs are heavily fill-rate limited, so we should try to use textures that are as small as possible (or map our triangles only to a small portion of them), and not render extremely huge triangles to the screen. We should also look out for overlap: the fewer overlapping triangles, the better.

> **NOTE:** Actually, overlap is not an extremely big problem with GPUs such as the PowerVR SGX 350 on the Droid. These GPUs have a special mechanism, called *tile-based deferred rendering*, that can eliminate a lot of that overlap under certain conditions. We should still care about pixels that will never be seen on the screen, though.

The Hero did only slightly benefit from the decrease in texture image size. So what could be the culprit here?

Reducing Calls to OpenGL ES/JNI Methods

The first suspects are the many OpenGL ES calls we issue per frame when we render the model for each Bob. First of all, we have four matrix operations per Bob. If we don't need rotation or scaling, we can bring that down to two calls. Here are the FPS numbers for each device when we only use `glLoadIdentity()` and `glTranslatef()` in the inner loop:

```
Hero:
12-10 04:57:49.610: DEBUG/FPSCounter(766): fps: 27
12-10 04:57:49.610: DEBUG/FPSCounter(766): fps: 27
12-10 04:57:50.650: DEBUG/FPSCounter(766): fps: 28
12-10 04:57:50.650: DEBUG/FPSCounter(766): fps: 28
12-10 04:57:51.530: DEBUG/dalvikvm(766): GC freed 22910 objects / 568904 bytes in 128ms

Droid:
12-10 05:08:38.604: DEBUG/FPSCounter(1702): fps: 56
12-10 05:08:39.620: DEBUG/FPSCounter(1702): fps: 57
12-10 05:08:40.628: DEBUG/FPSCounter(1702): fps: 58
12-10 05:08:41.644: DEBUG/FPSCounter(1702): fps: 57

Nexus One:
12-10 04:58:01.277: DEBUG/FPSCounter(2509): fps: 54
12-10 04:58:02.287: DEBUG/FPSCounter(2509): fps: 54
12-10 04:58:03.307: DEBUG/FPSCounter(2509): fps: 55
12-10 04:58:04.317: DEBUG/FPSCounter(2509): fps: 55
```

Well, it improved the performance on the Hero quite a bit, and the Droid and Nexus One also benefited a little from removing the two matrix operations. Of course, there's a little bit of cheating involved: if we need to rotate and scale our Bobs, there's no way around issuing those two additional calls. However, when all we do is 2D rendering, there's a neat little trick we can use that will get rid of all matrix operations (we'll look into this in the next chapter).

OpenGL ES is a C API provided to Java via a JNI wrapper. This means that any OpenGL ES method we call has to cross that JNI wrapper to call the actual C native function. This is somewhat costly on earlier Android versions, but has gotten better with more recent versions. As shown, the impact is not all that huge, especially if the actual operations take up more time than issuing the call itself.

The Concept of Binding Vertices

So is there anything else we can improve? Let's look at our current present() method one more time (with removed glRotatef() and glScalef()):

```java
public void present(float deltaTime) {
    GL10 gl = glGraphics.getGL();
    gl.glClear(GL10.GL_COLOR_BUFFER_BIT);

    gl.glMatrixMode(GL10.GL_MODELVIEW);
    for(int i = 0; i < NUM_BOBS; i++) {
        gl.glLoadIdentity();
        gl.glTranslatef(bobs[i].x, bobs[i].y, 0);
        bobModel.draw(GL10.GL_TRIANGLES, 0, 6);
    }

    fpsCounter.logFrame();
}
```

That looks pretty much optimal, doesn't it? Well, in fact it is not optimal. First, we can also move the gl.glMatrixMode() call to the resume() method. But that won't have a huge impact on performance, as we already saw. The second thing that can be optimized is a little subtler.

We use the Vertices class to store and render the model of our Bobs. Remember the Vertices.draw() method? Here it is one more time:

```java
public void draw(int primitiveType, int offset, int numVertices) {
    GL10 gl = glGraphics.getGL();

    gl.glEnableClientState(GL10.GL_VERTEX_ARRAY);
    vertices.position(0);
    gl.glVertexPointer(2, GL10.GL_FLOAT, vertexSize, vertices);

    if(hasColor) {
        gl.glEnableClientState(GL10.GL_COLOR_ARRAY);
        vertices.position(2);
        gl.glColorPointer(4, GL10.GL_FLOAT, vertexSize, vertices);
    }

    if(hasTexCoords) {
        gl.glEnableClientState(GL10.GL_TEXTURE_COORD_ARRAY);
        vertices.position(hasColor?6:2);
        gl.glTexCoordPointer(2, GL10.GL_FLOAT, vertexSize, vertices);
    }
```

```
        if(indices!=null) {
            indices.position(offset);
            gl.glDrawElements(primitiveType, numVertices, GL10.GL_UNSIGNED_SHORT, indices);
        } else {
            gl.glDrawArrays(primitiveType, offset, numVertices);
        }

        if(hasTexCoords)
            gl.glDisableClientState(GL10.GL_TEXTURE_COORD_ARRAY);

        if(hasColor)
            gl.glDisableClientState(GL10.GL_COLOR_ARRAY);
    }
```

Now look at preceding the loop again. Notice something? For each Bob, we enable the same vertex attributes over and over again via glEnableClientState(). We actually only need to set those once, as each Bob uses the same model, which always uses the same vertex attributes. The next big problems are the calls to glXXXPointer() for each Bob. Since those pointers are also OpenGL ES states, we only need to set them once as well, as they will never change once set. So how can we fix that? Let's rewrite the Vertices.draw() method a little:

```
public void bind() {
    GL10 gl = glGraphics.getGL();

    gl.glEnableClientState(GL10.GL_VERTEX_ARRAY);
    vertices.position(0);
    gl.glVertexPointer(2, GL10.GL_FLOAT, vertexSize, vertices);

    if(hasColor) {
        gl.glEnableClientState(GL10.GL_COLOR_ARRAY);
        vertices.position(2);
        gl.glColorPointer(4, GL10.GL_FLOAT, vertexSize, vertices);
    }

    if(hasTexCoords) {
        gl.glEnableClientState(GL10.GL_TEXTURE_COORD_ARRAY);
        vertices.position(hasColor?6:2);
        gl.glTexCoordPointer(2, GL10.GL_FLOAT, vertexSize, vertices);
    }
}

public void draw(int primitiveType, int offset, int numVertices) {
    GL10 gl = glGraphics.getGL();

    if(indices!=null) {
        indices.position(offset);
        gl.glDrawElements(primitiveType, numVertices, GL10.GL_UNSIGNED_SHORT, indices);
    } else {
        gl.glDrawArrays(primitiveType, offset, numVertices);
    }
}

public void unbind() {
    GL10 gl = glGraphics.getGL();
```

```
    if(hasTexCoords)
        gl.glDisableClientState(GL10.GL_TEXTURE_COORD_ARRAY);

    if(hasColor)
        gl.glDisableClientState(GL10.GL_COLOR_ARRAY);
}
```

Can you see what we've done here? We can treat our vertices and all those pointers just like we treat a texture. We "bind" the vertex pointers via a single call to Vertices.bind(). From this point onward every Vertices.draw() call will work with those "bound" vertices, just like the draw call will also use the currently bound texture. Once we are done rendering stuff with that Vertices instance, we call Vertices.unbind() to disable any vertex attributes that another Vertices instance might not need. Keeping our OpenGL ES state clean is a good thing. Here's how our present() method looks now (I moved the glMatrixMode(GL10.GL_MODELVIEW) call to resume() as well):

```
@Override
public void present(float deltaTime) {
    GL10 gl = glGraphics.getGL();
    gl.glClear(GL10.GL_COLOR_BUFFER_BIT);

    bobModel.bind();
    for(int i = 0; i < NUM_BOBS; i++) {
        gl.glLoadIdentity();
        gl.glTranslatef(bobs[i].x, bobs[i].y, 0);
        bobModel.draw(GL10.GL_TRIANGLES, 0, 6);
    }
    bobModel.unbind();

    fpsCounter.logFrame();
}
```

This effectively calls the glXXXPointer() and glEnableClientState() methods only once per frame. We thus save nearly 100 × 6 calls to OpenGL ES. That should have a huge impact on performance, right? Right.

```
Hero:
12-10 05:16:59.710: DEBUG/FPSCounter(865): fps: 51
12-10 05:17:00.720: DEBUG/FPSCounter(865): fps: 46
12-10 05:17:01.720: DEBUG/FPSCounter(865): fps: 47
12-10 05:17:02.610: DEBUG/dalvikvm(865): GC freed 21815 objects / 524272 bytes in 131ms
12-10 05:17:02.740: DEBUG/FPSCounter(865): fps: 44
12-10 05:17:03.750: DEBUG/FPSCounter(865): fps: 50

Droid:
12-10 05:22:27.519: DEBUG/FPSCounter(2040): fps: 57
12-10 05:22:28.519: DEBUG/FPSCounter(2040): fps: 57
12-10 05:22:29.526: DEBUG/FPSCounter(2040): fps: 57
12-10 05:22:30.526: DEBUG/FPSCounter(2040): fps: 55

Nexus One:
12-10 05:18:31.915: DEBUG/FPSCounter(2509): fps: 56
12-10 05:18:32.935: DEBUG/FPSCounter(2509): fps: 56
12-10 05:18:33.935: DEBUG/FPSCounter(2509): fps: 55
12-10 05:18:34.965: DEBUG/FPSCounter(2509): fps: 54
```

All three devices are nearly on par now. The Droid performs the best, followed by the Nexus One. Our little Hero performs great as well. We are up to 50 FPS from 22 FPS in the nonoptimized case. That's an increase in performance by 100 percent. We can be proud of ourselves. Our optimized Bob test is pretty much optimal.

Our new bindable `Vertices` class has of course a few restrictions now:

- We can only set the vertex and index data when the `Vertices` instance is not bound, as the upload of that information is performed in `Vertices.bind()`.

- We can't bind two `Vertices` instances at once. This means that we can only render with a single `Vertices` instance at any point in time. That's usually not a big problem, though, and given the impressive increase in performance, we will live with it.

In Closing

There's one more optimization we can apply that is suited for 2D graphics programming with flat geometry, such as with rectangles. We'll look into that in the next chapter. The keyword to search for is *batching*, which means reducing the number of `glDrawElements()`/`glDrawArrays()` calls. An equivalent for 3D graphics exists as well, called *instancing*, but that's not possible to do with OpenGL ES 1.x.

I want to mention two more things before we close this chapter. First of all, when you run either `BobText` or `OptimizedBobTest` (which contains the superoptimized code we just developed), notice that the Bobs wobble around the screen somewhat. This is due to the fact that their positions are passed to `glTranslatef()` as floats. The problem with pixel-perfect rendering is that OpenGL ES is really sensitive to vertex positions with fractional parts in their coordinates. We can't really work around this problem; the effect will be less pronounced or even nonexistent in a real game, as we'll see when we implement our next game. We can hide the effect to some extent by using a more diverse background, among other things.

The second thing I want to point out is how we interpret the FPS measurements. As you can see from the preceding output, the FPS fluctuate a little. This can be attributed to background processes that run alongside our application. We will never have all of the system resources for our game, so we have to learn to live with this issue. When you are optimizing your program, don't fake the environment by killing all background processes. Run the application on a phone that is in a normal state, as you'd use it yourself during the day. This will reflect the same experience that a user will have.

Our nice achievement concludes this chapter. As a word of warning, only start optimizing your rendering code after you have it working, and only then after you actually have a performance problem. Premature optimization is often a cause for having to rewrite your entire rendering code, as it may become unmaintainable.

Summary

OpenGL ES is a huge beast. We managed to boil all that down to a size that makes it easily usable for our game programming needs. We discussed what OpenGL ES is (a lean, mean triangle-rendering machine) and how it works. We then explored how to make use of OpenGL ES functionality by specifying vertices, how to create textures, and how to use states such as blending for some nice effects. We also looked a little bit into projections and how they are connected to matrices. While we didn't discuss what a matrix does internally, we explored how to use them to rotate, scale, and translate reusable models from model space to world space. When we use OpenGL ES for 3D programming later, you'll notice that you've already learned 90 percent of what you need to know. All we'll do is change the projection and add a z-coordinate to our vertices. (Well, there are a few more things, but on a high level that's actually it). Before that, though, we'll write a nice 2D game with OpenGL ES. In the next chapter, you'll get to know some of the 2D programming techniques we might need for that.

Chapter 8

2D Game Programming Tricks

Chapter 7 demonstrated that OpenGL ES offers us quite a lot of features to exploit for 2D graphics programming, such as easy rotation and scaling, and automatic stretching of our view frustum to the viewport. It also offers performance benefits over using the Canvas.

Now it's time to look at some of the more advanced topics of 2D game programming. Some of these concepts we used intuitively when we wrote Mr. Nom, including time-based state updates and image atlases. A lot of what's to come is indeed very intuitive as well, and chances are high that you'd have come up with the same solution sooner or later. But it doesn't hurt to learn about these things explicitly.

We will look at a handful of crucial concepts for 2D game programming. Some of them will be graphics related, and others will deal with how we represent and simulate our game world. All of these have one thing in common: they rely on a little linear algebra and trigonometry. Fear not, the level of math we need to write games like Super Mario Brothers is not exactly mind blowing. Let's begin by reviewing some concepts of 2D linear algebra and trigonometry.

Before We Begin

As with the previous "theoretical" chapters, we are going to create a couple of examples to get a feel for what's happening. For this chapter we'll reuse what we developed in the last chapter, mainly the GLGame, GLGraphics, Texture, and Vertices classes, along with the rest of the framework classes.

Our demo project consists of a starter called GameDev2DStarter, which presents a list of tests to run. We can reuse the code of the GLBasicsStarter and simply replace the class names of the tests. We also have to add each of the tests to the manifest in the form of <activity> elements.

Each of the tests is again an instance of the Game interface, and the actual test logic is implemented in the form of a Screen contained in the Game implementation of the test, as in the previous chapter. I will only present the relevant portions of the Screen to conserve some pages. The naming conventions are again XXXTest and XXXScreen for the GLGame and Screen implementation of each test.

With that out of our way, let's talk about vectors.

In the Beginning There Was the Vector

In the last chapter I told you that vectors shouldn't be mixed up with positions. This is not entirely true, as we can (and will) represent a position in some space via a vector. A vector can actually have many interpretations:

- *Position*: We already used this in the previous chapters to encode the coordinates of our entities relative to the origin of the coordinate system.

- *Velocity and acceleration*: These are physical quantities we'll talk about in the next section. While we are used to thinking about velocity and acceleration as being a single value, they should actually be represented as 2D or 3D vectors. They encode not only the speed of an entity (e.g., a car driving at 100 kilometers per hour), but also the direction the entity is traveling in. Note that this kind of vector interpretation does not state that the vector is given relative to the origin. This makes sense since the velocity and direction of a car is independent of its position. Think of a car traveling northwest on a straight highway at 100 kilometers per hour. As long as its speed and direction don't change, the velocity vector won't change either.

- *Directions and distances*: Directions are similar to velocities but lack physical quantities in general. We can use such a vector interpretation to encode states such as *this entity is pointing southeast*. Distances just tell us the how far away and in what direction a position is from another position.

Figure 8–1 shows these interpretations in action.

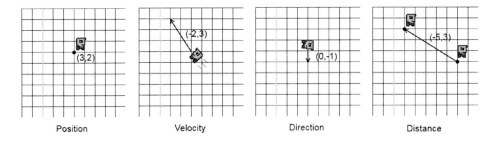

Position   Velocity   Direction   Distance

Figure 8–1. *Bob, with position, velocity, direction, and distance expressed as vectors*

Figure 8–1 is of course not exhaustive. Vectors can have a lot more interpretations. For our game development needs, however, these four basic interpretations suffice.

One thing that's left out from Figure 8–1 is what units the vector components have. We always have to make sure that those are sensible (e.g., Bob's velocity could be in meters per second, so he travels 2 meters to the left and 3 meters up in 1 second). The same is true for positions and distances, which we could also express in meters, for example. The direction of Bob is a special case, though—it is unitless. This will come in handy if we want to specify the general direction of an object while keeping the direction's physical features separate. We could do this for the velocity of Bob, storing the direction of his velocity as a direction vector and his speed as a single value. Single values are also known as *scalars*. For this, the direction vector must be of length 1, as we'll discuss later on.

Working with Vectors

The power of vectors stems from the fact that we can easily manipulate and combine them. Before we can do that, though, we need to define how we represent vectors:

$v = (x,y)$

Now, that wasn't a big surprise; we've done that a gazillion times already. Every vector has an x and a y component in our 2D space (yes, we'll be staying in two dimensions in this chapter). We can also add two vectors:

$c = a + b = (a.x, a.y) + (b.x, b.y) = (a.x + b.x, a.y + b.y)$

All we need to do is add the components together to arrive at the final vector. Try it out with the vectors given in Figure 8–1. Say we take Bob's position, $p = (3,2)$, and add his velocity, $v = (-2,3)$. We arrive at a new position, $p' = (3 + -2, 2 + 3) = (1,5)$. Don't get confused by the apostrophe behind the *p* here, it's just there to denote that we have a new vector *p*. Of course, this little operation only makes sense when the units of the position and velocity fit together. In this case we assume the position is given in meters (m) and the velocity is given in meters per second (m/s), which fits perfectly fine.

Of course, we can also subtract vectors:

$c = a - b = (a.x, a.y) - (b.x, b.y) = (a.x - b.x, a.y - b.y)$

Again, all we do is combine the components of the two vectors. Note, however, that the order in which we subtract one vector from the other is important. Take the rightmost image in Figure 8–1, for example. We have a green Bob at pg = (1,4) and a red Bob at pr = (6,1), where pg and pr stand for position green and red respectively.. When we take the distance vector from green Bob to red Bob, we calculate the following:

$d = pg - pr = (1, 4) - (6, 1) = (-5, 3)$

Now that is strange. That vector is actually pointing from red Bob to green Bob! To get the direction vector from green Bob to red Bob, we have to reverse the order of subtraction:

$d = pr - pg = (6, 1) - (1, 4) = (5, -3)$

If we want to find the distance vector from a position *a* to a position *b*, we use the following general formula:

```
d = b - a
```

In other words, we always subtract the start position from the end position. That's a little confusing at first, but if you think about it, it makes absolute sense. Try it out on some graph paper!

We can also multiply a vector by a scalar (remember, a scalar is just a single value):

```
a' = a * scalar = (a.x * scalar, a.y * scalar)
```

We multiply each of the components of the vector by the scalar. This allows us to scale the length of a vector. Take the direction vector in Figure 8–1 as an example. It's specified as $d = (0,-1)$. If we multiply it with the scalar $s = 2$, we effectively double its length: $d \times s = (0,-1 \times 2) = (0,-2)$. We can of course make it smaller as well, by using a scalar less than 1—for example, *d* multiplied by $s = 0.5$ creates a new vector $d' = (0,-0.5)$.

Speaking of length, we can also calculate the length of a vector (in the units it's given in):

```
|a| = sqrt(a.x*a.x + a.y*a.y)
```

The |a| notation just tells us that this represents the length of the vector. If you didn't sleep through your linear algebra class at school, you might recognize the formula for the vector length. It's the Pythagorean theorem applied to our fancy 2D vector. The x and y components of the vector form two sides of a right triangle, and the third side is the length of the vector. Figure 8–2 illustrates this.

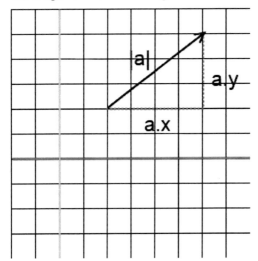

Figure 8–2. *Pythagoras would love vectors too*

The vector length is always positive or zero, given the properties of the square root. If we apply this to the distance vector between the red and green Bob, we can figure out that they are

```
|pr - pg| = sqrt(5*5 + -3*-3) = sqrt(25 + 9) = sqrt(34) ~= 5.83m
```

apart from each other (if their positions are given in meters). Note that if we calculated |*pg* – *pr*|, we'd arrive at the same value, as the length is independent of the direction of the vector. This new knowledge also has another implication: when we multiply a vector with a scalar, its length changes accordingly. Given a vector d = (0,–1) with an original length of 1 unit, we can multiply it by 2.5 and arrive at a new vector with a length of 2.5 units.

We discussed that direction vectors usually don't have any units associated with them. We can make them have a unit by multiplying them with a scalar—for example, we can multiply a direction vector d = (0,1) with a speed constant s = 100 m/s to get a velocity vector v = (0 × 100,1 × 100) = (0,100). It's therefore always a good idea to let our direction vectors have a length of 1. Vectors with a length of 1 are called *unit vectors*. We can make any vector a unit vector by dividing each of its components by its length:

```
d' = (d.x/|d|, d.y/|d|)
```

Remember that |*d*| just means the length of the vector *d*. Let's try it out. Say we want a direction vector that points exactly northeast: d = (1,1). It might seem that this vector is already unit length, as both components are 1, right? Wrong:

```
|d| = sqrt(1*1 + 1*1) = sqrt(2) ~= 1.44
```

We can easily fix that by making the vector a unit vector:

```
d' = (d.x/|d|, d.y/|d|) = (1/|d|, 1/|d|) ~= (1/1.44, 1/1.44) = (0.69, 0.69)
```

This is also called *normalizing* a vector, which just means that we make it have a length of 1. With this little trick we can create a unit-length direction vector out of a distance vector, for example. Of course, we have to watch out for zero-length vectors, as we'd have division by zero in that case!

A Little Trigonometry

Let's turn to trigonometry for a minute. There are two essential functions in trigonometry: *cosine* and *sine*. Each takes a single argument: an *angle*. We are used to specifying angles in degrees (e.g., 45° or 360°). In most math libraries, trigonometry functions expect the angle in radians, though. We can easily convert between degrees and radians with the following equations:

```
degreesToRadians(angleInDegrees) = angleInDegrees / 180 * pi
radiansToDegrees(angle) = angleInRadians / pi * 180
```

Here, pi is our beloved superconstant, with an approximate value of 3.14159265. pi radians equal 180 degrees, so that's how the preceding functions come to be.

So what do cosine and sine actually calculate given an angle? They calculate the x and y components of a unit-length vector relative to the origin. Figure 8–3 illustrates this.

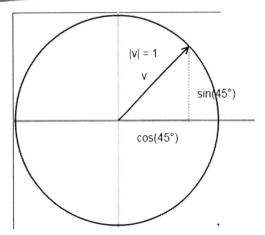

Figure 8–3. *Cosine and sine produce a unit vector with its endpoint lying on the unit circle*

Given an angle, we can therefore easily create a unit-length direction vector like this:

```
v = (cos(angle), sin(angle))
```

We can go the other way around as well, and calculate the angle of a vector with respect to the x-axis:

```
angle = atan2(v.y, v.x)
```

The atan2 function is actually an artificial construct. It uses the arcus tangent function (which is the inverse of the tangent function, which is another fundamental function in trigonometry) to construct an angle in the range of –180 degrees to 180 degrees (or –pi to pi, if the angle is returned in radians). The internals are a little involved and do not matter all that much for our discussion. The arguments are the y and x components of our vector. Note that the vector does not have to be a unit vector for the atan2 function to work. Also note that the y component is most often given first, and then the x component—but this depends on the math library we use. This is a common source for errors.

Let's try a few examples. Given a vector v = (cos(97°),sin(97°)), the result of atan2(sin(97°),cos(97°)) is 97°. Great, that was easy. Using a vector v = (1,–1), we get atan2(–1,1) = –45°. So if our vector's y component is negative, we'll get a negative angle in the range 0° to –180°. We can fix this by adding 360° (or 2pi) if the output of atan2 is negative. In the preceding example, we'd then get 315°.

The final operation we want to be able to apply to our vectors is rotating them by some angle. The derivation of the equations that follow are again a little involved. Luckily we can just use them as is without knowing about orthogonal base vectors (hint: that's the key phrase to search for on the Web if you want to know what's going on under the hood). Here's the magical pseudocode:

```
v.x' = cos(angle) * v.x - sin(angle) * v.y
v.y' = sin(angle) * v.x + cos(angle) * v.y
```

Woah, that was less complicated then expected. This will rotate any vector counterclockwise around the origin, no matter what interpretation we have of the vector.

Together with vector addition, subtraction, and multiplication by a scalar, we can actually implement all the OpenGL matrix operations ourselves. This is one part of the solution to further increase the performance of our BobTest in the last chapter. We'll talk about this in one of the following sections. For now, let's concentrate on what we discussed and transfer it to code.

Implementing a Vector Class

We want to create an easy-to-use vector class for 2D vectors. Let's call it Vector2. It should have two members, for holding the x and y components of the vector. Additionally it should have a couple of nice methods that allow us to the following:

- Add and subtract vectors
- Multiply the vector components with a scalar
- Measure the length of a vector
- Normalize a vector
- Calculate the angle between a vector and the x-axis
- Rotate the vector

Java lacks operator overloading, so we have to come up with a mechanism that makes working with the Vector2 class less cumbersome. Ideally we should have something like the following:

```
Vector2 v = new Vector2();
v.add(10,5).mul(10).rotate(54);
```

We can easily achieve this by letting each of the Vector2 methods return a reference to the vector itself. Of course, we also want to overload methods like Vector2.add() so that we can either pass in two floats or an instance of another Vector2. Listing 8–1 shows our Vector2 class in its full glory.

Listing 8–1. *Vector2.java: Implementing Some Nice 2D Vector Functionality*

```java
package com.badlogic.androidgames.framework.math;

import android.util.FloatMath;

public class Vector2 {
    public static float TO_RADIANS = (1 / 180.0f) * (float) Math.PI;
    public static float TO_DEGREES = (1 / (float) Math.PI) * 180;
    public float x, y;

    public Vector2() {
    }

    public Vector2(float x, float y) {
        this.x = x;
        this.y = y;
    }
```

```java
    public Vector2(Vector2 other) {
        this.x = other.x;
        this.y = other.y;
    }
```

We put that class in the package com.badlogic.androidgames.framework.math, where we'll house any other math-related classes as well.

We start off by defining two static constants, TO_RADIANS and TO_DEGREES. To convert an angle given in radians, we just need to multiply it by TO_DEGREES; to convert an angle given in degrees to radians, we multiply it by TO_RADIANS. You can double-check this by looking at the two previously defined equations that govern degree-to-radian conversion. With this little trick we can shave off a division to speed things up a little.

Next we define the two members x and y that store the components of the vector and a couple of constructors—nothing too complex:

```java
    public Vector2 cpy() {
        return new Vector2(x, y);
    }
```

We also have a cpy() method that will create a duplicate instance of the current vector and return it. This might come in handy if we want to manipulate a copy of a vector, preserving the value of the original vector.

```java
    public Vector2 set(float x, float y) {
        this.x = x;
        this.y = y;
        return this;
    }

    public Vector2 set(Vector2 other) {
        this.x = other.x;
        this.y = other.y;
        return this;
    }
```

The set() methods allow us to set the x and y components of a vector, based on either two float arguments or another vector. The methods return a reference to this vector, so we can chain operations as discussed previously.

```java
    public Vector2 add(float x, float y) {
        this.x += x;
        this.y += y;
        return this;
    }

    public Vector2 add(Vector2 other) {
        this.x += other.x;
        this.y += other.y;
        return this;
    }

    public Vector2 sub(float x, float y) {
        this.x -= x;
```

```
        this.y -= y;
        return this;
    }

    public Vector2 sub(Vector2 other) {
        this.x -= other.x;
        this.y -= other.y;
        return this;
    }
```

The add() and sub() methods come in two flavors: in once case they work with two float arguments, and in the other case they take another Vector2 instance. All four methods return a reference to this vector so we can chain operations.

```
    public Vector2 mul(float scalar) {
        this.x *= scalar;
        this.y *= scalar;
        return this;
    }
```

The mul() method just multiplies the x and y components of the vector with the given scalar value, and again returns a reference to the vector itself for chaining.

```
    public float len() {
        return FloatMath.sqrt(x * x + y * y);
    }
```

The len() method calculates the length of the vector exactly like we defined it previously. Note that we use the FastMath class instead of the usual Math class that Java SE provides. This is a special Android API class that works with floats instead of doubles, and is a little bit faster than the Math equivalent.

```
    public Vector2 nor() {
        float len = len();
        if (len != 0) {
            this.x /= len;
            this.y /= len;
        }
        return this;
    }
```

The nor() method normalizes the vector to unit length. We use the len() method internally to calculate the length first. If it is zero, we can bail out early and avoid a division by zero. Otherwise we divide each component of the vector by its length to arrive at a unit-length vector. For chaining we return the reference to this vector again.

```
    public float angle() {
        float angle = (float) Math.atan2(y, x) * TO_DEGREES;
        if (angle < 0)
            angle += 360;
        return angle;
    }
```

The angle() method calculates the angle between the vector and the x-axis using the atan2() method, as discussed previously. We have to use the Math.atan2() method, as the FastMath class doesn't have that method. The returned angle is given in radians, so we convert it to degrees by multiplying it by TO_DEGREES. If the angle is less than zero, we add 360 degrees to it so we can return a value in the range 0 to 360 degrees.

```java
public Vector2 rotate(float angle) {
    float rad = angle * TO_RADIANS;
    float cos = FloatMath.cos(rad);
    float sin = FloatMath.sin(rad);

    float newX = this.x * cos - this.y * sin;
    float newY = this.x * sin + this.y * cos;

    this.x = newX;
    this.y = newY;

    return this;
}
```

The rotate() method simply rotates the vector around the origin by the give angle. Since the FastMath.cos() and FastMath.sin() methods expect the angle to be given in radians, we first convert from degrees to radians. Next we use the previously defined equations to calculate the new x and y components of the vector, and finally return the vector itself again for chaining.

```java
public float dist(Vector2 other) {
    float distX = this.x - other.x;
    float distY = this.y - other.y;
    return FloatMath.sqrt(distX * distX + distY * distY);
}

public float dist(float x, float y) {
    float distX = this.x - x;
    float distY = this.y - y;
    return FloatMath.sqrt(distX * distX + distY * distY);
}
}
```

Finally we have two methods that calculate the distance between this and another vector.

And that's our shiny Vector2 class, which we'll use to represent positions, velocities, distances, and directions in the code that follows. To get a feeling for our new class, let's use it in a simple example.

A Simple Usage Example

Here's my proposal for a simple test:

- We'll create a sort of cannon represented by a triangle that has a fixed position in our world. The center of the triangle will be at (2.4,0.5).

- Each time we touch the screen, we want to rotate the triangle to face the touch point.

- Our view frustum will show us the region of our world between (0,0) and (4.8,3.2). We do not operate in pixel coordinates, but instead define our own coordinate system, were one unit equals one meter. Also, we'll be working in landscape mode.

There are a couple of things we need to think about. We already know how to define a triangle in model space—we can use a `Vertices` instance for this. Our cannon should point to the right at an angle of 0 degrees in its default orientation. Figure 8–4 shows the cannon triangle in model space.

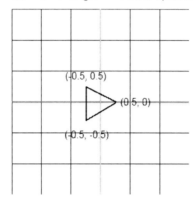

Figure 8–4. *The cannon triangle in model space*

When we render that triangle, we simply use `glTranslatef()` to move it to its place in the world at (2.4,0.5).

We also want to rotate the cannon so that its tip points in the direction of the point on the screen that we last touched. For this we need to figure out where the last touch event was touching our world. The `GLGame.getInput().getTouchX()` and `getTouchY()` methods will return the touch point in screen coordinates, with the origin in the top-left corner. We also said that the `Input` instance will not scale the events to a fixed coordinate system, as it did in Mr. Nom. Instead we will get the coordinates (479,319) when touching the bottom-right corner of the (landscape-oriented) screen on a Hero, and (799,479) on a Nexus One. We need to convert these touch coordinates to our world coordinates. We already did that in the touch handlers in Mr. Nom and the `Canvas`-based game framework; the only difference this time is that our coordinate system extents are a little smaller and our world's y-axis is pointing upward. Here's the pseudocode showing how we can achieve the conversion in the general case, which is nearly the same as in the touch handlers of Chapter 5:

```
worldX = (touchX / Graphics.getWidth()) * viewFrustmWidth
worldY = (1 - touchY / Graphics.getHeight()) * viewFrustumHeight
```

We normalize the touch coordinates to the range (0,1) by dividing them by the screen resolution. In the case of the y-coordinate, we subtract the normalized y-coordinate of the touch event from 1 to flip the y-axis. All that's left is scaling the x- and y-coordinates by the view frustum's width and height—in our case that's 4.8 and 3.2. From worldX and worldY we can then construct a Vector2 that stores the position of the touch point in our world's coordinates.

The last thing we need to do is calculate the angle to rotate the canon with. Let's look at Figure 8–5, which shows our cannon and a touch point in world coordinates.

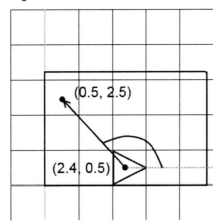

Figure 8–5. *Our cannon in its default state, pointing to the right (angle = 0°), a touch point, and the angle we need to rotate the cannon by. The rectangle is the area of the world that our view frustum will show on the screen: (0,0) to (4.8,3.2).*

All we need to do is create a distance vector from the cannon's center at (2.4,0.5) to the touch point (and remember, we have to subtract the cannon's center from the touch point, not the other way around). Once we have that distance vector we can calculate the angle with the Vector2.angle() method. This angle can then be used to rotate our model via glRotatef().

Let's code that. Listing 8–2 shows the relevant portion of our CannonScreen, part of the CannonTest class.

Listing 8–2. *Excerpt from CannonTest.java; Touching the Screen Will Rotate the Cannon*

```
class CannonScreen extends Screen {
    float FRUSTUM_WIDTH = 4.8f;
    float FRUSTUM_HEIGHT = 3.2f;
    GLGraphics glGraphics;
    Vertices vertices;
    Vector2 cannonPos = new Vector2(2.4f, 0.5f);
    float cannonAngle = 0;
    Vector2 touchPos = new Vector2();
```

We start off with two constants that define our frustum's width and height, as discussed earlier. Next we have a GLGraphics instance, as well as a Vertices instance. We also store the cannon's position in a Vector2 and its angle in a float. Finally we have another Vector2, which we'll use to calculate the angle between a vector from the origin to the touch point and the x-axis.

Why do we store the Vector2 instances as class members? We could instantiate them every time we need them, but that would make the garbage collector angry. In general we should try to instantiate all the Vector2 instances once and reuse them as often as possible.

```java
public CannonScreen(Game game) {
    super(game);
    glGraphics = ((GLGame) game).getGLGraphics();
    vertices = new Vertices(glGraphics, 3, 0, false, false);
    vertices.setVertices(new float[] { -0.5f, -0.5f,
                                        0.5f, 0.0f,
                                       -0.5f, 0.5f }, 0, 6);
}
```

In the constructor, we fetch the GLGraphics instance and create the triangle according to Figure 8–4.

```java
@Override
public void update(float deltaTime) {
    List<TouchEvent> touchEvents = game.getInput().getTouchEvents();
    game.getInput().getKeyEvents();

    int len = touchEvents.size();
    for (int i = 0; i < len; i++) {
        TouchEvent event = touchEvents.get(i);

        touchPos.x = (event.x / (float) glGraphics.getWidth())
                * FRUSTUM_WIDTH;
        touchPos.y = (1 - event.y / (float) glGraphics.getHeight())
                * FRUSTUM_HEIGHT;
        cannonAngle = touchPos.sub(cannonPos).angle();
    }
}
```

Next up is the update() method. We simply loop over all TouchEvents and calculate the angle for the cannon. This is done in a couple of steps. First we transform the screen coordinates of the touch event to the world coordinate system, as discussed earlier. We store the world coordinates of the touch event in the touchPoint member. We then subtract the position of the cannon from the touchPoint vector, which will result in the vector depicted in Figure 8–5. We then calculate the angle between this vector and the x-axis. And that's all there is to it!

```java
@Override
public void present(float deltaTime) {

    GL10 gl = glGraphics.getGL();
    gl.glViewport(0, 0, glGraphics.getWidth(), glGraphics.getHeight());
    gl.glClear(GL10.GL_COLOR_BUFFER_BIT);
    gl.glMatrixMode(GL10.GL_PROJECTION);
    gl.glLoadIdentity();
    gl.glOrthof(0, FRUSTUM_WIDTH, 0, FRUSTUM_HEIGHT, 1, -1);
    gl.glMatrixMode(GL10.GL_MODELVIEW);
    gl.glLoadIdentity();

    gl.glTranslatef(cannonPos.x, cannonPos.y, 0);
    gl.glRotatef(cannonAngle, 0, 0, 1);
    vertices.bind();
    vertices.draw(GL10.GL_TRIANGLES, 0, 3);
```

```
            vertices.unbind();
    }
```

The present() method does the same boring things it did before. We set the viewport, clear the screen, set up the orthographic projection matrix using our frustum's width and height, and tell OpenGL ES that all subsequent matrix operations will work on the model-view matrix. We also load an identity matrix to the model-view matrix to "clear" it. Next we multiply the (identity) model-view matrix with a translation matrix, which will move the vertices of our triangle from model space to world space. We also call glRotatef() with the angle we calculated in the update() method so that our triangle gets rotated in model space before it is translated. Remember, transformations are applied in reverse order—the last specified transform is applied first. Finally we bind the vertices of the triangle, render it, and unbind it.

```
    @Override
    public void pause() {

    }

    @Override
    public void resume() {

    }

    @Override
    public void dispose() {

    }
}
```

Now we have a triangle that will follow our every touch. Figure 8–6 shows the output after touching the upper-left corner of the screen.

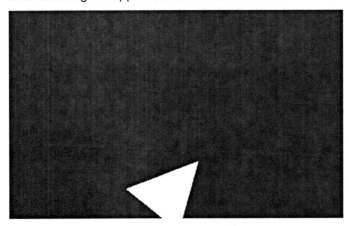

Figure 8–6. *Our triangle cannon reacting to a touch event in the upper-left corner*

Note that it doesn't really matter whether we render a triangle at the cannon position or a rectangle texture mapped to an image of a cannon—OpenGL ES doesn't really care. We also have all the matrix operations in the present() method again. The truth of the matter is that it is easier to keep track of OpenGL ES states this way, and often we will use multiple view frustums in one present() call (e.g., one setting up a world in meters for rendering our world and another setting up a world in pixels for rendering UI elements). The impact on performance is not all that big, as described in the last chapter, so it's OK to do it this way most of the time. Just remember that we could optimize this if the need arises.

Vectors will be our best friends from now on. We'll use them to specify virtually everything in our world. We will also do some very basic physics with vectors. What's a cannon good for if it can't shoot, right?

A Little Physics in 2D

In this section we'll use a very simple and limited version of physics. Games are all about being good fakes. They cheat wherever possible to get rid of potentially heavy calculations. The behavior of objects in a game need not be 100 percent physically accurate, it just needs to be good enough to look believable. Sometimes we don't event want physically accurate behavior (e.g., one set of objects should fall downward and another, crazier, set of objects should fall upward).

Even a game like the original Super Mario Brothers uses at least some basic principles of Newtonian physics. These principles are really simple and easy to implement. We will only talk about the absolute minimum required to implement a very simple physics model for our game objects.

Newton and Euler, Best Friends Forever

We are mostly concerned with motion physics of so-called *point masses*, which refers to the change in position, velocity, and acceleration of an object over time. Point mass means that we approximate all our objects with an infinitesimally small point that has an associated mass. We do not deal with things like torque—the rotational velocity of an object around its center of mass—because that is a rather complex problem domain about which more than one complete book has been written. Let's just look at these three properties of an object:

- The position of an object is simply a vector in some space—in our case a 2D space. We represent it as a vector. Usually the position is given in meters.

- The velocity of an object is its change in position per second. Velocity is given as a 2D velocity vector, which is a combination of the unit-length direction vector the object is heading in and the speed that the object will move at, given in meters per seconds. Note that the speed just governs the length of the velocity vector; if we normalize the velocity vector by the speed, we get a nice unit-length direction vector.

- The acceleration of an object is its change in velocity per second. We can either represent this as a scalar that only affects the speed of the velocity (the length of the velocity vector), or as a 2D vector, so that we can have different acceleration in the x- and y-axes. Here we'll choose the latter, as it allows us to use things such as ballistics more easily. Acceleration is usually given in meters per second per second (m/s^2). No, that's not a typo—we change the velocity by some amount given in meters per second, each second.

When we know these properties of an object for a given point in time, we can integrate them to simulate the object's path through the world over time. This may sound scary, but we already did this with Mr. Nom and our Bob test. In those cases we just didn't use acceleration; we set the velocity to a fixed vector. Here's how we can integrate the acceleration, velocity and position of an object in general:

```
Vector2 position = new Vector2();
Vector2 velocity = new Vector2();
Vector2 acceleration = new Vector2(0, -10);
while(simulationRuns) {
    float deltaTime = getDeltaTime();
    velocity.add(acceleration.x * deltaTime, acceleration.y * deltaTime);
    position.add(velocity.x * deltaTime, velocity.y * deltaTime);
}
```

This is called *numerical Euler integration*, and is the most intuitive of the integration methods used in games. We start off with a position at (0,0), a velocity given as (0,0), and an acceleration of (0,−10), which means that the velocity will increase by 1 meter per second on the y-axis. There will be no movement on the x-axis. Before we enter the integration loop, our object is standing still. Within the loop we first update the velocity based on the acceleration multiplied by the delta time, and then update the position based on the velocity times the delta time. That's all there is to the big, scary word *integration*.

> **NOTE:** As usual, that's not even half of the story. Euler integration is an "unstable" integration method and should be avoided when possible. Usually one would employ a variant of the so-called *verlet integration*, which is just a bit more complex. For our purposes, the easier Euler integration is sufficient though.

Force and Mass

You might wonder where the acceleration comes from. That's a good question with many answers. The acceleration of a car comes from its engine. The engine applies a force to the car that causes it to accelerate. But that's not all. Our car will also accelerate toward the center of earth due to gravity. The only thing that keeps it from falling through the center of the earth is the ground it can't pass through. The ground cancels out this gravitational force. The general idea is this:

```
force = mass x acceleration
```

We can rearrange this to the following equation:

```
acceleration = force / mass
```

Force is given in the SI unit *Newton* (guess who came up with this). If we specify acceleration as a vector, then we also have to specify the force as a vector. A force can thus have a direction. For example, the gravitational force pulls downward in the direction (0,–1). The acceleration is also dependent on the mass of an object. The more mass an object has, the more force we need to apply to make it accelerate as fast as an object of less weight. This is a direct consequence of the preceding equations.

For simple games we can, however, ignore the mass and force, and just work with velocity and acceleration directly. In the preceding pseudocode, we set the acceleration to (0,–10) m/s per second (again, not a typo), which is roughly the acceleration an object will experience when it is falling toward earth, no matter its mass (ignoring things like air resistance). It's true, ask Galileo!

Playing Around, Theoretically

So let's use our preceding example to play with an object falling toward earth. Let's assume that we let the loop iterate ten times and that `getDeltaTime()` will always return 0.1 seconds. We'll get the following positions and velocities for each iteration:

```
time=0.1, position=(0.0,-0.1), velocity=(0.0,-1.0)
time=0.2, position=(0.0,-0.3), velocity=(0.0,-2.0)
time=0.3, position=(0.0,-0.6), velocity=(0.0,-3.0)
time=0.4, position=(0.0,-1.0), velocity=(0.0,-4.0)
time=0.5, position=(0.0,-1.5), velocity=(0.0,-5.0)
time=0.6, position=(0.0,-2.1), velocity=(0.0,-6.0)
time=0.7, position=(0.0,-2.8), velocity=(0.0,-7.0)
time=0.8, position=(0.0,-3.6), velocity=(0.0,-8.0)
time=0.9, position=(0.0,-4.5), velocity=(0.0,-9.0)
time=1.0, position=(0.0,-5.5), velocity=(0.0,-10.0)
```

After 1 second, our object falls 5.5 meters and has a velocity of (0,–10) m/s, straight down to the core of the earth (until it hits the ground, of course).

Our object will increase its downward speed without end, as we don't factor in air resistance. (As I said before, we can easily cheat our own system.) We can just enforce a maximum velocity by checking the current velocity length, which equals the speed of our object.

All-knowing Wikipedia tells us that a human in free fall can have a maximum, or terminal, velocity of roughly 125 miles per hour. Converting that to meters per second (125 × 1.6 × 1000 / 3600), we get 55.5 m/s. To make our simulation more realistic, we can modify the loop as follows:

```
while(simulationRuns) {
    float deltaTime = getDeltaTime();
    if(velocity.len() < 55.5)
        velocity.add(acceleration.x * deltaTime, acceleration.y * deltaTime);
    position.add(velocity.x * deltaTime, velocity.y * deltaTime);

}
```

As long as the speed of our object (the length of the velocity vector) is smaller than 55.5 m/s, we increase the velocity by the acceleration. When we've reached the terminal velocity, we simply don't increase it by the acceleration anymore. That simple capping of velocities is a trick used heavily in many games.

We could add some wind to the equation by adding another acceleration in the x direction, say (–1,0) m/s². For this we just need to add up the gravitational acceleration and the wind acceleration before we add it to the velocity:

```
Vector2 gravity = new Vector2(0,-10);
Vector2 wind = new Vector2(-1,0);
while(simulationRuns) {
    float deltaTime = getDeltaTime();
    acceleration.set(gravity).add(wind);
    if(velocity.len() < 55.5)
        velocity.add(acceleration.x * deltaTime, acceleration.y * deltaTime);
    position.add(velocity.x * deltaTime, velocity.y * deltaTime);
}
```

We can also ignore acceleration altogether and let our objects have a fixed velocity. We did exactly this in the BobTest earlier. We changed the velocity of each Bob only if he hit an edge, and we did so instantly.

Playing Around, Practically

The possibilities, even with this simple model, are endless. Let's extend our little CannonTest so we can actually shoot a cannonball. Here's what we want to do:

- As long as the user drags his finger over the screen, the canon will follow it. That's how we'll specify the angle at which we'll shoot the ball.

- As soon as we receive a touch-up event, we'll fire a cannonball in the direction the cannon is pointing. The initial velocity of the cannonball will be a combination of the cannon's direction and the speed the cannonball will have from the start. The speed is equal to the distance between the cannon and the touch point. The further away we touch, the faster the cannonball will fly.

- The cannonball will fly for as long as there's no new touch-up event.

- We'll double the size of our view frustum to (0,0) to (9.6, 6.4) so that we can see more of our world. Additionally we'll place the cannon at (0,0). Note that all units of our world are now given in meters.

- We'll render the cannonball as a red rectangle of the size 0.2×0.2 meters, or 20x20 centimeters. Close enough to a real cannonball, I guess. The pirates among you may choose a more realistic size, of course.

Initially the position of the cannonball will be (0,0)—the same as the cannon's position. The velocity will also be (0,0). Since we apply gravity in each update, the cannonball will just fall straight downward.

Once a touch-up event is received, we set the ball's position back to (0,0) and its initial velocity to (Math.cos(cannonAngle),Math.sin(cannonAngle)). This will ensure that our cannonball flies in the direction the cannon is pointing. We also set the speed by simply multiplying the velocity by the distance between the touch point and the cannon. The closer the touch point to the cannon, the more slowly the cannonball will fly.

Sounds easy enough, so let's implement it. I copied over the code from the CannonTest to a new file, called CannonGravityTest.java. I renamed the classes contained in that file to CannonGravityTest and CannonGravityScreen. Listing 8–3 shows the CannonGravityScreen.

Listing 8–3. *Excerpt from CannonGravityTest*

```
class CannonGravityScreen extends Screen {
    float FRUSTUM_WIDTH = 9.6f;
    float FRUSTUM_HEIGHT = 6.4f;
    GLGraphics glGraphics;
    Vertices cannonVertices;
    Vertices ballVertices;
    Vector2 cannonPos = new Vector2();
    float cannonAngle = 0;
    Vector2 touchPos = new Vector2();
    Vector2 ballPos = new Vector2(0,0);
    Vector2 ballVelocity = new Vector2(0,0);
    Vector2 gravity = new Vector2(0,-10);
```

Not a lot has changed. We simply double the size of the view frustum, and reflect that by setting FRUSTUM_WIDTH and FRUSTUM_HEIGHT to 9.6 and 6.2, respectively. This means that we can see a rectangle of 9.2×6.2 meters of our world. Since we also want to draw the cannonball, I added another Vertices instance, called ballVertices, that will hold the four vertices and six indices of the rectangle of the cannonball. The new members ballPos and ballVelocity store the position and velocity of the cannonball, and the member gravity is the gravitational acceleration, which will stay at a constant (0,–10) m/s² over the lifetime of our program.

```
    public CannonGravityScreen(Game game) {
        super(game);
        glGraphics = ((GLGame) game).getGLGraphics();
        cannonVertices = new Vertices(glGraphics, 3, 0, false, false);
        cannonVertices.setVertices(new float[] { -0.5f, -0.5f,
                                                  0.5f, 0.0f,
                                                 -0.5f, 0.5f }, 0, 6);
        ballVertices = new Vertices(glGraphics, 4, 6, false, false);
        ballVertices.setVertices(new float[] { -0.1f, -0.1f,
                                                0.1f, -0.1f,
                                                0.1f,  0.1f,
                                               -0.1f,  0.1f }, 0, 8);
        ballVertices.setIndices(new short[] {0, 1, 2, 2, 3, 0}, 0, 6);
    }
```

In the constructor we simply create the additional `Vertices` instance for the rectangle of the cannonball. We again define it in model space with the vertices (–0.1,–0.1), (0.1,–0.1), (0.1,0.1), and (–0.1,0.1). We use indexed drawing, so we also specify six vertices in this case.

```
@Override
public void update(float deltaTime) {
    List<TouchEvent> touchEvents = game.getInput().getTouchEvents();
    game.getInput().getKeyEvents();

    int len = touchEvents.size();
    for (int i = 0; i < len; i++) {
        TouchEvent event = touchEvents.get(i);

        touchPos.x = (event.x / (float) glGraphics.getWidth())
                * FRUSTUM_WIDTH;
        touchPos.y = (1 - event.y / (float) glGraphics.getHeight())
                * FRUSTUM_HEIGHT;
        cannonAngle = touchPos.sub(cannonPos).angle();

        if(event.type == TouchEvent.TOUCH_UP) {
            float radians = cannonAngle * Vector2.TO_RADIANS;
            float ballSpeed = touchPos.len();
            ballPos.set(cannonPos);
            ballVelocity.x = FloatMath.cos(radians) * ballSpeed;
            ballVelocity.y = FloatMath.sin(radians) * ballSpeed;
        }
    }

    ballVelocity.add(gravity.x * deltaTime, gravity.y * deltaTime);
    ballPos.add(ballVelocity.x * deltaTime, ballVelocity.y * deltaTime);
}
```

The `update()` method has also only changed slightly. The calculation of the touch point in world coordinates and the angle of the cannon are still the same. The first addition is the `if` statement inside the event-processing loop. In case we get a touch-up event, we prepare our cannonball to be shot. We first transform the cannon's aiming angle to radians, as we'll use `FastMath.cos()` and `FastMath.sin()` later on. Next we calculate the distance between the cannon and the touch point. This will be the speed of our cannonball. We then set the ball's position to the cannon's position. Finally we calculate the initial velocity of the cannonball. We use sine and cosine, as discussed in the previous section, to construct a direction vector from the cannon's angle. We multiply this direction vector by the cannonball's speed to arrive at our final cannonball velocity. This is interesting, as the cannonball will have this velocity from the start. In the real world, the cannonball would of course accelerate from 0 m/s to whatever it can reach given air resistance, gravity, and the force applied to it by the cannon. We can cheat here, though, as that acceleration would happen in a very tiny time window (a couple hundred milliseconds). The last thing we do in the `update()` method is update the velocity of the cannonball, and based on that, adjust its position.

```
@Override
    public void present(float deltaTime) {

        GL10 gl = glGraphics.getGL();
        gl.glViewport(0, 0, glGraphics.getWidth(), glGraphics.getHeight());
        gl.glClear(GL10.GL_COLOR_BUFFER_BIT);
        gl.glMatrixMode(GL10.GL_PROJECTION);
        gl.glLoadIdentity();
        gl.glOrthof(0, FRUSTUM_WIDTH, 0, FRUSTUM_HEIGHT, 1, -1);
        gl.glMatrixMode(GL10.GL_MODELVIEW);

        gl.glLoadIdentity();
        gl.glTranslatef(cannonPos.x, cannonPos.y, 0);
        gl.glRotatef(cannonAngle, 0, 0, 1);
        gl.glColor4f(1,1,1,1);
        cannonVertices.bind();
        cannonVertices.draw(GL10.GL_TRIANGLES, 0, 3);
        cannonVertices.unbind();

        gl.glLoadIdentity();
        gl.glTranslatef(ballPos.x, ballPos.y, 0);
        gl.glColor4f(1,0,0,1);
        ballVertices.bind();
        ballVertices.draw(GL10.GL_TRIANGLES, 0, 6);
        ballVertices.unbind();
    }
```

In the present() method, we simply add the rendering of the cannonball rectangle. We do this after rendering the cannon's triangle, which means that we have to "clean" the model-view matrix before we can render the rectangle. We do this with glLoadIdentity(), and then use glTranslatef() to convert the cannonball's rectangle from model space to world space at the ball's current position.

```
@Override
    public void pause() {

    }

    @Override
    public void resume() {

    }

    @Override
    public void dispose() {

    }
}
```

If you run the example and touch the screen a couple of times, you'll get a pretty good feel for how the cannonball will fly. Figure 8–7 shows the output (which is not all that impressive, since it is a still image).

Figure 8–7. *A triangle cannon that shoots red rectangles. Impressive!*

That's enough physics for our purposes. With this simple model, we can simulate much more than cannonballs. Super Mario, for example, could be simulated much in the same way. If you have ever played Super Mario Brothers, then you will notice that Mario takes a little bit of time before he reaches his maximum velocity when running. This can be implemented with a very fast acceleration and velocity capping, as in the preceding pseudocode. Jumping can be implemented in much the same way as we shot the cannonball. Mario's current velocity would be adjusted by an initial jump velocity on the y-axis (remember that we can add velocities like any other vectors). If there were no ground beneath his feet, we would apply gravitational acceleration so that he would actually fall back to the ground. The velocity in the x direction is not influenced by what's happening on the y-axis. We could still press left and right to change the velocity on the x-axis. The beauty of this simple model is that it allows us to implement very complex behavior with very little code. We'll actually use a similar this type of physics when we write our next game.

Just shooting a cannonball is not a lot of fun. We want to be able to hit objects with the cannonball. For this we need something called collision detection, which we'll investigate in the next section.

Collision Detection and Object Representation in 2D

Once we have moving objects in our world, we want them to interact as well. One such mode of interaction is simple collision detection. Two objects are said to be colliding when they overlap in some way. We already did a little bit of collision detection in Mr. Nom when we checked whether Mr. Nom bit himself or ate an ink stain.

Collision detection is accompanied by collision response: once we determine that two objects have collided, we need to respond to that collision by adjusting the position and/or movement of our objects in a sensible manner. For example, when Super Mario jumps on a Goomba, the Goomba goes to Goomba heaven and Mario performs another little jump. A more elaborate example is the collision and response of two or more billiard balls. We won't go into this kind of collision response, as it is overkill for our purposes. Our collision responses will usually only consist of changing the state of an object (e.g., letting an object explode or die, collecting a coin and setting the score, etc.). This type of response is game dependent, so we won't talk about it in this section.

So how do we figure out whether two objects have collided? First we need to think about when to check for collisions. If our objects follow some sort of simple physics model, as discussed in the last section, we could check for collisions after we move all our objects for the current frame and time step.

Bounding Shapes

Once we have the final positions for our objects, we can perform the collision tests, which boil down to testing for overlap. But what overlaps? Each of our objects needs to have some mathematically defined form or shape that bounds it. The correct term in this case is *bounding shape*. Figure 8–8 shows a couple of choices we have for bounding shapes.

Triangle Mesh   Axis Aligned Bounding Box   Bounding Circle

Figure 8–8. *Various bounding shapes around Bob*

The properties of the three types of bounding shapes in Figure 8–8 are as follows:

■ *Triangle mesh*: This bounds the object as tightly as possible by approximating its silhouette with a couple of triangles. It requires the most storage space, and it's hard to construct and expensive to test against. It gives the most precise results, though. We won't necessarily use the same triangles for rendering, but instead just store them for collision detection. The mesh can be stored as a list of vertices, where each subsequent three vertices form a triangle. To conserve memory, we could also use indexed vertex lists.

- *Axis-aligned bounding box*: This bounds the object via a rectangle that is axis aligned, which means that the bottom and top edges are always aligned with the x-axis, and the left and right edges are aligned with the y-axis. This is also fast to test against, but less precise than a triangle mesh. A bounding box is usually stored in the form of the position of its lower-left corner plus its width and height. (In the case of 2D, these are also referred to as *bounding rectangles*).

- *Bounding circle*: This bounds the object with the smallest circle that can contain the object. It's very fast to test against, but it is the least precise bounding shape of them all. The circle is usually stored in the form of its center position and its radius.

Every object in our game gets a bounding shape that encloses it, in addition to its position, scale, and orientation. Of course, we need to adjust the bounding shape's position, scale, and orientation according to the object's position, scale, and orientation when we move the object, say, in a physics integration step.

Adjusting for position changes is easy: we simple move the bounding shape accordingly. In the case of the triangle mesh we just move each vertex, in the case of the bounding rectangle we move the lower-left corner, and in the case of the bounding circle we just move the center.

Scaling a bound shape is a little harder. We need to define the point around which we scale. Usually this is the object's position, which is often given as the center of the object. If we use this convention, then scaling is easy as well. For the triangle mesh we scale the coordinates of each vertex; for the bounding rectangle we scale its width, height, and lower-left corner position; and for the bounding circle we scale its radius (the circle center is equal to the object's center).

Rotating a bounding shape is also dependent on the definition of a point around which to rotate. Using the convention just mentioned (where the object center is the rotation point), rotation becomes easy as well. In the case of the triangle mesh, we simple rotate all vertices around the object's center. In the case of the bounding circle, we do not have to do anything, as the radius will stay the same no matter how we rotate our object. The bounding rectangle is a little bit more involved. We need to construct all four corner points, rotate them, and then find the axis-aligned bounding rectangle that encloses those four points. Figure 8–9 shows the three bounding shapes after rotation.

Figure 8–9. *Rotated bounding shapes with the center of the object as the rotation point*

While rotating a triangle mesh or a bounding circle is rather easy, the results for the axis-aligned bounding box are not all that satisfying. Notice that the bounding box of the original object fits tighter than its rotated version. This leads us to the question of how we got our bounding shapes for Bob in the first place.

Constructing Bounding Shapes

In this example, I simply constructed the bounding shapes by hand based on Bob's image. But Bob's image is given in pixels, and our world might operate in, say, meters. The solutions to this problem involve normalization and model space. Imagine the two triangles we'd use for Bob in model space when we'd render him with OpenGL. The rectangle is centered at the origin in model space and has the same aspect ratio (width/height) as Bob's texture image (e.g., 32×32 pixels in the texture map as compared to 2×2 meters in model space). Now we can apply Bob's texture and figure out where in model space the points of the bounding shape are. Figure 8–10 shows how we can construct the bounding shapes around Bob in model space.

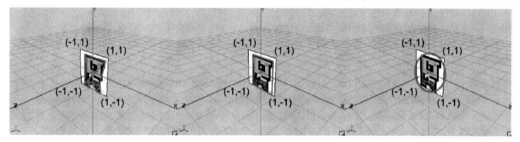

Figure 8–10. *Bounding shapes around Bob in model space*

This process may seem a little cumbersome, but the steps involved are not all that hard. The first thing we have to remember is how texture mapping works. We specify the texture coordinates for each vertex of Bob's rectangle (which is composed of two triangles) in texture space. The upper-left corner of the texture image in texture space is at (0,0), and the lower-left corner is at (1,1), no matter the actual width and height of the image in pixels. To convert from the pixel space of our image to texture space, we can thus use this simple transformation:

```
u = x / imageWidth
v = y / imageHeight
```

where u and v are the texture coordinates of the pixel given by x and y in image space. The imageWidth and imageHeight are set to the image's dimensions in pixels (32×32 in Bob's case). Figure 8–11 shows how the center of Bob's image maps to texture space.

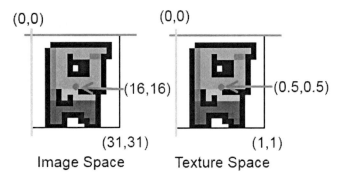

Figure 8–11. *Mapping a pixel from image space to texture space*

The texture is applied to a rectangle that we define in model space. In Figure 8–10 we have an example with the upper-left corner at (–1,1) and the lower-right corner at (1,–1). We use meters as the units in our world, so the rectangle has a width and height of 2 meters each. Additionally we know that the upper-left corner has the texture coordinates (0,0) and the lower-right corner has the texture coordinates (1,1), so we map the complete texture to Bob. This won't always be the case, as you'll see in one of the next sections.

So let's come up with a generic way to map from texture to model space. We can make our lives a little easier by constraining our mapping to only axis-aligned rectangles in texture and model space. This means we assume that an axis-aligned rectangular region in texture space is mapped to an axis-aligned rectangle in model space. For the transformation we need to know the width and height of the rectangle in model space and the width and height of the rectangle in texture space. In our Bob example we have a 2×2 rectangle in model space and a 1×1 rectangle in texture space (since we map the complete texture to the rectangle). We also need to know the coordinates of the upper-left corner of each rectangle in its respective space. For the model space rectangle, that's (–1,1), and for the texture space rectangle it's (0,0) (again, since we map the complete texture, not just a portion). With this information and the u- and v-coordinates of the pixel we want to map to model space, we can do the transformation with these two equations:

```
mx = (u - minU) / (tWidth) × mWidth + minX
my = (1 - ((v - minV) / (tHeight)) × mHeight - minY
```

The variables u and v are the coordinates we calculated in the last transformation from pixel to texture space. The variables `minU` and `minV` are the coordinates of the top-left corner of the region we map from texture space. The variables `tWidth` and `tHeight` are the width and height of our texture space region. The variables `mWidth` and `mHeight` are the width and height of our model space rectangle. The variables `minX` and `minY` are— you guessed it—the coordinates of the top-left corner of the rectangle in model space. Finally we have `mx` and `my`, which are the transformed coordinates in model space.

These equations take the u- and v-coordinates, map them to the range 0 to 1, and then scale and position them in model space. Figure 8–12 shows a texel in texture space and how it is mapped to a rectangle in model space. On the sides you see tWidth and tHeight, and mWidth and mHeight, respectively. The top-left corner of each rectangle corresponds to (minU, minV) in texture space and (minX, minY) in model space.

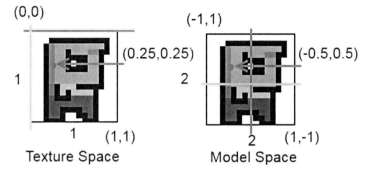

Figure 8–12. *Mapping from texture space to model space*

Substituting the first two equations we can directly go from pixel space to model space:

```
mx = ((x/imageWidth) - minU) / (tWidth) * mWidth + minX
my = (1 - (((y/imageHeight) - minV) / (tHeight)) * mHeight - minY
```

We can use these two equations to calculate the bounding shapes of our objects based on the image we map to their rectangles via texture mapping. In the case of the triangle mesh, this can get a little tedious; the bounding rectangle and bounding circle cases are a lot easier. Usually we don't go this hard route, but instead try to create our textures so that at least the bounding rectangles have the same aspect ratio as the rectangle we render for the object via OpenGL ES. This way we can construct the bounding rectangle from the object's image dimension directly. The same is true for the bounding circle. I just wanted to show you how you can construct an arbitrary bounding shape given an image that gets mapped to a rectangle in model space.

You should now know how to construct a nicely fitting bounding shape for your 2D objects. But remember, we define those bounding shape sizes manually, when we create our graphical assets and define the units and sizes of our objects in the game world. We then use these sizes in our code to collide objects with each other.

Game Object Attributes

Bob just got fatter. In addition to the mesh we use for rendering (the rectangle mapping to Bob's image texture), we now have a second data structure holding his bounds in some form. It is crucial to realize that while we model the bounds after the mapped version of Bob in model space, the actual bounds are independent of the texture region we map Bob's rectangle to. Of course, we try to have as close a match to the outline of Bob's image in the texture as possible when we create the bounding shape. It does not matter, however, whether the texture image is 32×32 or 128×128 pixels. An object in our world thus has three attribute groups:

- Its position, orientation, scale, velocity, and acceleration. With these we can apply our physics model from the previous section. Of course, some objects might be static, and thus will only have position, orientation, and scale. Often we can even leave out orientation and scale. The position of the object usually coincides with the origin in model space, as in Figure 8–10. This makes some calculations easier.

- Its bounding shape (usually constructed in model space around the object's center), which coincides with its position and is aligned with the object's orientation and scale, as shown in Figure 8–10. This gives our object a boundary and defines its size in the world. We can make this shape as complex as we want. We could, for example, make it a composite of several bounding shapes.

- Its graphical representation. As shown in Figure 8–12, we still use two triangles to form a rectangle for Bob and texture-map his image onto the rectangle. The rectangle is defined in model space but does not necessarily equal the bounding shape, as shown in Figure 8–10. The graphical rectangle of Bob that we send to OpenGL ES is slightly larger than Bob's bounding rectangle.

This separation of attributes allows us to apply our Model-View-Controller (MVC) pattern again.

- On the model side we simply have Bob's physical attributes, composed of his position, scale, rotation, velocity, acceleration, and bounding shape. Bob's position, scale, and orientation govern where his bounding shape is located in world space.

- The view just takes Bob's graphical representation (e.g., the two texture-mapped triangles defined in model space) and renders them at their world space position according to Bob's position, rotation, and scale. Here we can use the OpenGL ES matrix operations as we did previously.

- The controller is responsible for updating Bob's physical attributes according to user input (e.g., a left button press could move him to the left), and according to physical forces, such as gravitational acceleration (like we applied to the cannonball in the previous section).

Of course, there's some correspondence between Bob's bounding shape and his graphical representation in the texture, as we base the bounding shape on that graphical representation. Our MVC pattern is thus not entirely clean, but we can live with that.

Broad-Phase and Narrow-Phase Collision Detection

We still don't know how to check for collisions between our objects and their bounding shapes. There are two phases of collision detection:

Broad phase: In this phase we try to figure out which objects can potentially collide. Imagine having 100 objects that could each collide with each other. We'd need to perform 100 × 100 / 2 overlap tests if we chose to naively test each object against each other object. This naïve overlap testing approach is of $O(n^2)$ asymptotic complexity, meaning it would take n^2 steps to complete (it actually finished in half that many steps, but the asymptotic complexity leaves out any constants). In a good, non-brute-force broad phase, we try to figure out which pairs of objects are actually in danger of colliding. Other pairs (e.g., two objects that are too far apart for a collision to happen) will not be checked. We can reduce the computational load this way, as narrow-phase testing is usually pretty expensive.

Narrow phase: Once we know which pairs of objects can potentially collide, we test whether they really collide or not by doing an overlap test of their bounding shapes.

Let's focus on the narrow phase first and leave the broad phase for later.

Narrow Phase

Once we are done with the broad phase, we have to check whether the bounding shapes of the potentially colliding objects overlap. I mentioned earlier that we have a couple of options for bounding shapes. Triangle meshes are the most computationally expensive and cumbersome to create. It turns out that we can get away with bounding rectangles and bounding circles in most 2D games, so that's what we'll concentrate on here.

Circle Collision

Bounding circles are the cheapest way to check whether two objects collide. Let's define a simple `Circle` class. Listing 8–4 shows the code.

Listing 8–4. *Circle.java, a Simple Circle Class*

```
package com.badlogic.androidgames.framework.math;

public class Circle {
    public final Vector2 center = new Vector2();
    public float radius;

    public Circle(float x, float y, float radius) {
        this.center.set(x,y);
        this.radius = radius;
    }
}
```

We just store the center as a `Vector2` and the radius as a simple float. How can we check whether two circles overlap? Look at Figure 8–13.

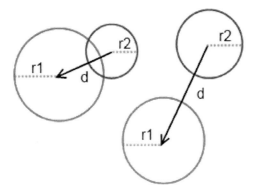

Figure 8–13. *Two circles overlapping (left), and two circles not overlapping (right)*

It's really simple and computationally efficient. All we need to do is figure out the distance between the two centers. If the distance is greater then the sum of the two radii, then we know the two circles do not overlap. In code this will look as follows:

```
public boolean overlapCircles(Circle c1, Circle c2) {
    float distance = c1.center.dist(c2.center);
    return distance <= c1.radius + c2.radius;
}
```

We first measure the distance between the two centers and then check if the distance is smaller or equal to the sum of the radii.

We have to take a square root in the `Vector2.dist()` method. That's unfortunate, as taking the square root is a costly operation. Can we make this faster? Yes we can—all we need to do is reformulate our condition:

```
sqrt(dist.x × dist.x + dist.y × dist.y) <= radius1 + radius2
```

We can get rid of the square root by exponentiating both sides of the inequality, as follows:

```
dist.x × dist.x + dist.y × dist.y <= (radius1 + radius2) × (radius1 + radius2)
```

We trade the square root for an additional addition and multiplication on the right side. That's a lot better. Let's create a `Vector2.distSquared()` function that will return the squared distance between two vectors:

```
public float distSquared(Vector2 other) {
    float distX = this.x - other.x;
    float distY = this.y - other.y;
    return distX*distX + distY*distY;
}
```

The `overlapCircles()` method then becomes the following:

```
public boolean overlapCircles(Circle c1, Circle c2) {
    float distance = c1.center.distSquared(c2.center);
    float radiusSum = c1.radius + c2.radius;
    return distance <= radiusSum * radiusSum;
}
```

Rectangle Collision

Let's move on to rectangles. First we need a class that can represent a rectangle. We previously said we want a rectangle to be defined by its lower-left corner position plus its width and height. We do just that in Listing 8–5.

Listing 8–5. *Rectangle.java, a Rectangle Class*

```java
package com.badlogic.androidgames.framework.math;

public class Rectangle {
    public final Vector2 lowerLeft;
    public float width, height;

    public Rectangle(float x, float y, float width, float height) {
        this.lowerLeft = new Vector2(x,y);
        this.width = width;
        this.height = height;
    }
}
```

We store the lower-left corner's position in a Vector2 and the width and height in two floats. How can we check whether two rectangles overlap? Figure 8–14 should give you a hint.

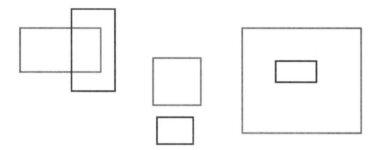

Figure 8–14. *Lots of overlapping and nonoverlapping rectangles*

The first two cases of partial overlap and nonoverlap are easy. The last one is a surprise. A rectangle can of course be completely contained in another rectangle. That can happen in the case of circles as well. However, our circle overlap test will return the correct result if one circle is contained in the other circle.

Checking for overlap in the rectangle case looks complex at first. However, we can create a very simple test if we invoke a little logic. Here's the simplest method to check for overlap between two rectangles:

```java
public boolean overlapRectangles(Rectangle r1, Rectangle r2) {
    if(r1.lowerLeft.x < r2.lowerLeft.x + r2.width &&
       r1.lowerLeft.x + r1.width > r2.lowerLeft.x &&
       r1.lowerLeft.y < r2.lowerLeft.y + r2.height &&
       r1.lowerLeft.y + r1.height > r2.lowerLeft.y)
        return true;
```

```
    else
        return false;
}
```

This looks a little bit confusing at first sight, so let's go over each condition. The first condition states that the left edge of the first rectangle must be to the left of the right edge of the second rectangle. The next condition states that the right edge of the first rectangle must be to the right of the left edge of the second rectangle. The other two conditions state the same for the top and bottom edges of the rectangles. If all these conditions are met, then the two rectangles overlap. Double-check this with Figure 8–14. It also covers the containment case.

Circle/Rectangle Collision

Can we check for overlap between a circle and a rectangle? Yes we can. However, it is a little more involved. Take a look at Figure 8–15.

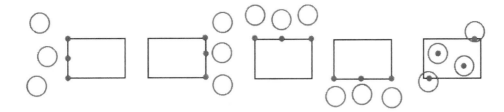

Figure 8–15. *Overlap-testing a circle and a rectangle by finding the closest point on/in the rectangle to the circle*

The overall strategy for testing for overlap between a circle and a rectangle goes like this:

- Find the closest x-coordinate on or in the rectangle to the circle's center. This coordinate can either be a point on the left or right edge of the rectangle, unless the circle center is contained in the rectangle, in which case the closest x-coordinate is the circle center's x-coordinate.

- Find the closest y-coordinate on or in the rectangle to the circle's center. This coordinate can either be a point on the top or bottom edge of the rectangle, unless the circle center is contained in the rectangle, in which case the closest y-coordinate is the circle center's y-coordinate.

- If the point composed of the closest x- and y-coordinates is within the circle, the circle and rectangle overlap.

While not depicted in Figure 8–15, this method also works for circles that completely contain the rectangle. Let's code it up:

```
public boolean overlapCircleRectangle(Circle c, Rectangle r) {
    float closestX = c.center.x;
    float closestY = c.center.y;
```

```
        if(c.center.x < r.lowerLeft.x) {
            closestX = r.lowerLeft.x;
        }
        else if(c.center.x > r.lowerLeft.x + r.width) {
            closestX = r.lowerLeft.x + r.width;
        }

        if(c.center.y < r.lowerLeft.y) {
            closestY = r.lowerLeft.y;
        }
        else if(c.center.y > r.lowerLeft.y + r.height) {
            closestY = r.lowerLeft.y + r.height;
        }

        return c.center.distSquared(closestX, closestY) < c.radius * c.radius;
}
```

The description looked a lot scarier than the implementation. We determine the closest point on the rectangle to the circle, and then simply check whether the point lies inside the circle. If that's the case, there is an overlap between the circle and the rectangle.

Note that I added an overloaded distSquared() method to Vector2 that takes two float arguments instead of another Vector2. I did the same for the dist() function.

Putting It All Together

Checking whether a point lies inside a circle or rectangle can be useful too. Let's code up two more methods and put them into a class called OverlapTester, together with the other three methods we just defined. Listing 8–6 shows the code.

Listing 8–6. *OverlapTester.java; Testing Overlap Between Circles, Rectangles, and Points*

```java
package com.badlogic.androidgames.framework.math;

public class OverlapTester {
    public static boolean overlapCircles(Circle c1, Circle c2) {
        float distance = c1.center.distSquared(c2.center);
        float radiusSum = c1.radius + c2.radius;
        return distance <= radiusSum * radiusSum;
    }

    public static boolean overlapRectangles(Rectangle r1, Rectangle r2) {
        if(r1.lowerLeft.x < r2.lowerLeft.x + r2.width &&
           r1.lowerLeft.x + r1.width > r2.lowerLeft.x &&
           r1.lowerLeft.y < r2.lowerLeft.y + r2.height &&
           r1.lowerLeft.y + r1.height > r2.lowerLeft.y)
            return true;
        else
            return false;
    }

    public static boolean overlapCircleRectangle(Circle c, Rectangle r) {
        float closestX = c.center.x;
        float closestY = c.center.y;
```

```
            if(c.center.x < r.lowerLeft.x) {
                closestX = r.lowerLeft.x;
            }
            else if(c.center.x > r.lowerLeft.x + r.width) {
                closestX = r.lowerLeft.x + r.width;
            }

            if(c.center.y < r.lowerLeft.y) {
                closestY = r.lowerLeft.y;
            }
            else if(c.center.y > r.lowerLeft.y + r.height) {
                closestY = r.lowerLeft.y + r.height;
            }

            return c.center.distSquared(closestX, closestY) < c.radius * c.radius;
        }

    public static boolean pointInCircle(Circle c, Vector2 p) {
        return c.center.distSquared(p) < c.radius * c.radius;
    }

    public static boolean pointInCircle(Circle c, float x, float y) {
        return c.center.distSquared(x, y) < c.radius * c.radius;
    }

    public static boolean pointInRectangle(Rectangle r, Vector2 p) {
        return r.lowerLeft.x <= p.x && r.lowerLeft.x + r.width >= p.x &&
                r.lowerLeft.y <= p.y && r.lowerLeft.y + r.height >= p.y;
    }

    public static boolean pointInRectangle(Rectangle r, float x, float y) {
        return r.lowerLeft.x <= x && r.lowerLeft.x + r.width >= x &&
                r.lowerLeft.y <= y && r.lowerLeft.y + r.height >= y;
    }
}
```

Sweet, now we have a fully functional 2D math library we can use for all our little physics models and collision detection. Let's talk about the broad phase in a little more detail now.

Broad Phase

So how can we achieve the magic that the broad phase promises us? Look at Figure 8–16, which shows a typical Super Mario Brothers scene.

Figure 8–16. *Super Mario and his enemies. Boxes around objects are their bounding rectangles; the big boxes make up a grid imposed on the world.*

Can you already guess what we could do to eliminate some checks? The blue grid in Figure 8–16 represents cells we partition our world with. Each cell has the exact same size, and the whole world is covered in cells. Mario is currently in two of those cells, and the other objects Mario could potentially collide with are in different cells. We thus don't need to check for any collisions, as Mario is not in the same cells as any of the other objects in the scene. All we need to do is the following:

- Update all objects in the world based on our physics and controller step.

- Update the position of each bounding shape of each object according to the object's position. We can of course also include the orientation and scale as well here.

- Figure out which cell or cells each object is contained in based on its bounding shape, and add it to the list of objects contained in those cells.

- Check for collisions, but only between object pairs that can collide (e.g., Goombas don't collide with other Goombas) and are in the same cell.

This is called a *spatial hash grid* broad phase, and it is very easy to implement. The first thing we have to define is the size of each cell. This is highly dependent on the scale and units we use for our game's world.

An Elaborate Example

Let's develop the spatial hash grid broad phase based on our last cannonball example. We will completely rework it to incorporate everything covered in this section so far. In addition to the cannon and the ball, we also want to have targets to fire at. We'll make our lives easy and just use squares of size 0.5×0.5 meters as targets. These squares don't move; they're static. Our cannon is static as well. The only thing that moves is the cannonball itself. We can generally categorize objects in our game world as static objects or dynamic objects. So let's devise a class that can represent such objects.

GameObject, DynamicGameObject, and Cannon

Let's start with the static case, or base case, in Listing 8–7.

Listing 8–7. *GameObject.java, a Static Game Object with a Position and Bounds*

```java
package com.badlogic.androidgames.gamedev2d;

import com.badlogic.androidgames.framework.math.Rectangle;
import com.badlogic.androidgames.framework.math.Vector2;

public class GameObject {
    public final Vector2 position;
    public final Rectangle bounds;

    public GameObject(float x, float y, float width, float height) {
        this.position = new Vector2(x,y);
        this.bounds = new Rectangle(x-width/2, y-height/2, width, height);
    }
}
```

Every object in our game has a position that coincides with its center. Additionally we let each object have a single bounding shape—a rectangle in this case. In our constructor we set the position and bounding rectangle (which is centered around the center of the object) according to the parameters.

For dynamic objects, that is, objects which move, we also need to keep track of their velocity and acceleration (if they're actually accelerated by themselves—e.g., via an engine or thruster). Listing 8–8 shows the code for the DynamicGameObject class.

Listing 8–8. *DynamicGameObject.java: Extending the GameObject with a Velocity and Acceleration Vector*

```java
package com.badlogic.androidgames.gamedev2d;

import com.badlogic.androidgames.framework.math.Vector2;

public class DynamicGameObject extends GameObject {
    public final Vector2 velocity;
    public final Vector2 accel;

    public DynamicGameObject(float x, float y, float width, float height) {
        super(x, y, width, height);
        velocity = new Vector2();
```

```
        accel = new Vector2();
    }
}
```

We just extend the GameObject class to inherit the position and bounds members. Additionally we create vectors for the velocity and acceleration. A new dynamic game object will have zero velocity and acceleration after it has been initialized.

In our cannonball example we have the cannon, the cannonball, and the targets. The cannonball is a DynamicGameObject, as it moves according to our simple physics model. The targets are static and can be implemented by using the standard GameObject. The cannon itself can also be implemented via the GameObject class. We will derrive a Cannon class from the GameObject class and add a field storing the cannon's current angle. Listing 8–9 shows the code.

Listing 8–9. *Cannon.java: Extending the GameObject with an Angle*

```java
package com.badlogic.androidgames.gamedev2d;

public class Cannon extends GameObject {
    public float angle;

    public Cannon(float x, float y, float width, float height) {
        super(x, y, width, height);
        angle = 0;
    }
}
```

That nicely encapsulates all the data needed to represent an object in our cannon world. Every time we need a special kind of object, like the cannon, we can simply derive from GameObject if it is a static object, or DynamicGameObject if it has a velocity and acceleration.

> **NOTE:** The overuse of inheritance can lead to severe headaches and very ugly code architecture. Do not use it just for the sake of using it. The simple class hierarchy just used is OK, but we shouldn't let it go a lot deeper (e.g., by extending Cannon). There are alternative representations of game objects that do away with all inheritance by composition. For our purposes, simple inheritance is more than enough, though. If you are interested in other representations, search for "composites" or "mixins" on the Web.

The Spatial Hash Grid

Our cannon will be bounded by a rectangle of 1×1 meters, the cannonball will have a bounding rectangle of 0.2×0.2 meters, and the targets will each have a bounding rectangle of 0.5×0.5 meters. The bounding rectangles are centered around each object's positions to make our lives a little easier.

When our cannon example starts up, we'll simply place a number of targets at random positions. Here's how we could set up the objects in our world:

```
Cannon cannon = new Cannon(0, 0, 1, 1);
DynamicGameObject ball = new DynamicGameObject(0, 0, 0.2f, 0.2f);
GameObject[] targets = new GameObject[NUM_TARGETS];
for(int i = 0; i < NUM_TARGETS; i++) {
    targets[i] = new GameObject((float)Math.random() * WORLD_WIDTH,
                                (float)Math.random() * WORLD_HEIGHT,
                                0.5f, 0.5f);
}
```

The constants WORLD_WIDTH and WORLD_HEIGHT define the size of our game world.
Everything should happen inside the rectangle bounded by (0,0) and
(WORLD_WIDTH,WORLD_HEIGHT). Figure 8–17 shows a little mock-up of our game world so
far.

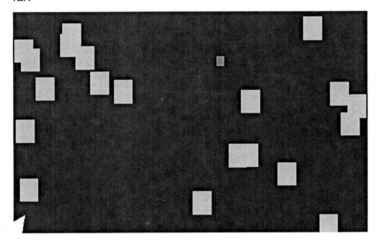

Figure 8–17. *A mock-up of our game world*

Our world will look like this later on, but for now, let's overlay a spatial hash grid. How
big should the cells of the hash grid be? There's no silver bullet, but I tend to choose it
to be five times bigger than the biggest object in the scene. In our example, the biggest
object is the cannon, but we do not collide anything with the cannon. So let's base the
grid size on the next biggest objects in our scene, the targets. These are 0.5×0.5 meters
in size. A grid cell should thus have a size of 2.5×2.5 meters. Figure 8–18 shows the grid
overlaid onto our world.

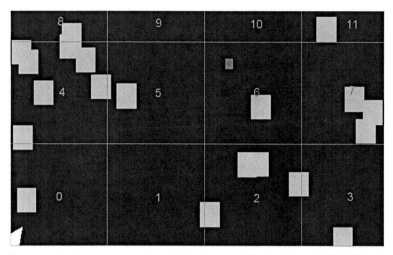

Figure 8–18. *Our cannon world overlaid with a spatial hash grid consisting of 12 cells*

We have a fixed number of cells—in the case of the cannon world, 12 cells to be exact. We give each cell a unique number, starting at the bottom-left cell, which gets the ID 0. Note that the top cells actually extend outside of our world. This is not a problem; we just need to make sure all our objects stay inside the boundaries of our world.

What we want to do is figure out which cell(s) an object belongs to. Ideally we want to calculate the IDs of the cells the object is contained in. This allows us to use the following simple data structure to store our cells:

```
List<GameObject>[] cells;
```

That's right, we represent each cell as a list of `GameObject`s. The spatial hash grid itself is then just composed of an array of lists of `GameObject`s.

Let's think about how we can figure out the IDs of the cells an object is contained in. Figure 8–18 shows a couple of targets that span two cells. In fact, a small object can span up to four cells, and an object bigger than a grid cell can span even more than four cells. We can make sure this never happens by choosing our grid cell size to be a multiple of the size of the biggest object in our game. That leaves us with the possibility of one object being contained in at most four cells.

To calculate the cell IDs for an object, we can simply take the four corner points of its bounding rectangle and check which cell each corner point is in. Determining the cell that a point is in is easy—we just need to divide its coordinates by the cell width first. Say we have a point at (3,4) and a cell size of 2.5×2.5 meters. The point would be in the cell with ID 5 in Figure 8–18.

We can divide each the point's coordinates by the cell size to get 2D integer coordinates , as follows:

```
cellX = floor(point.x / cellSize) = floor(3 / 2.5) = 1
cellY = floor(point.y / cellSize) = floor(4 / 2.5) = 1
```

And from these cell coordinates, we can easily get the cell ID:

cellId = cellX + cellY × cellsPerRow = 1 + 1 × 4 = 5

The constant `cellsPerRow` is simply the number of cells we need to cover our world with cells on the x-axis:

cellsPerRow = ceil(worldWidth / cellSize) = ceil(9.6 / 2.5) = 4

We can calculate the number of cells needed per column like this:

cellsPerColumn = ceil(worldHeight / cellSize) = ceil(6.4 / 2.5) = 3

Based on this we can implement the spatial hash grid rather easily. We set up it up by giving it the world's size and the desired cell size. We assume that all the action is happening in the positive quadrant of the world. This means that all x- and y-coordinates of points in the world will be positive. That's a constraint we can accept.

From the parameters, the spatial hash grid can figure out how many cells it needs (cellsPerRow × cellsPerColumn). We can also add a simple method to insert an object into the grid that will use the object's boundaries to determine the cells it is contained in. The object will then be added to each cell's list of objects that it contains. In case one of the corner points of the bounding shape of the object is outside of the grid, we'll just ignore that corner point.

We will reinsert every object into the spatial hash grid each frame after we update its position. However, there are objects in our cannon world that don't move, so inserting them anew each frame is very wasteful. We'll thus make a distinction between dynamic objects and static objects by storing two lists per cell. One will be updated each frame and only hold moving objects, and the other will be static and only modified when a new static object is inserted.

Finally we need a method that returns a list of objects in the cells of an object we'd like to collide with other objects. All this method will do is check which cells the object in question is in, retrieve the list of dynamic and static objects in those cells, and return them to the caller. We'll of course have to make sure that we don't return any duplicates, which can happen if an object is in multiple cells.

Listing 8–10 shows the code (well, most of it). We'll discuss the `SpatialHashGrid.getCellIds()` method in a minute, as it is a little involved.

Listing 8–10. *Excerpt from SpatialHashGrid.java: A Spatial Hash Grid Implementation*

```
package com.badlogic.androidgames.framework.gl;

import java.util.ArrayList;
import java.util.List;

import com.badlogic.androidgames.gamedev2d.GameObject;

import android.util.FloatMath;

public class SpatialHashGrid {
    List<GameObject>[] dynamicCells;
    List<GameObject>[] staticCells;
    int cellsPerRow;
    int cellsPerCol;
```

```
    float cellSize;
    int[] cellIds = new int[4];
    List<GameObject> foundObjects;
```

As discussed we store two cell lists, one for dynamic and one for static objects. We also store the cells per row and column so we can later decide whether a point we check is inside or outside of the world. The cell size needs to be stored as well. The `cellIds` array is a working array that we'll use to temporarily store the four cell IDs a `GameObject` is contained in. If it is only contained in one cell, then only the first element of the array will be set to the cell ID of the cell that contains the object entirely. If the object is contained in two cells, then the first two elements of that array will hold the cell ID, and so on. To indicate the number of cell IDs we set all "empty" elements of the array to −1. The `foundObjects` list is also a working list, which we'll return upon a call to `getPotentialColliders()`. Why do keep those two members instead of instantiating a new array and list each time one is needed? Remember the garbage collector monster.

```
    @SuppressWarnings("unchecked")
    public SpatialHashGrid(float worldWidth, float worldHeight, float cellSize) {
        this.cellSize = cellSize;
        this.cellsPerRow = (int)FloatMath.ceil(worldWidth/cellSize);
        this.cellsPerCol = (int)FloatMath.ceil(worldHeight/cellSize);
        int numCells = cellsPerRow * cellsPerCol;
        dynamicCells = new List[numCells];
        staticCells = new List[numCells];
        for(int i = 0; i < numCells; i++) {
            dynamicCells[i] = new ArrayList<GameObject>(10);
            staticCells[i] = new ArrayList<GameObject>(10);
        }
        foundObjects = new ArrayList<GameObject>(10);
    }
```

The constructor of that class takes the world's size and the desired cell size. From those arguments we calculate how many cells are needed, and instantiate the cell arrays and the lists holding the objects contained in each cell. We also initialize the `foundObjects` list here. All the `ArrayLists` we instantiate will have an initial capacity of ten `GameObjects`. We do this to avoid memory allocations. The assumption is that it is unlikely that one single cell will contain more than ten `GameObjects`. As long as that is true, the arrays don't need to be resized.

```
    public void insertStaticObject(GameObject obj) {
        int[] cellIds = getCellIds(obj);
        int i = 0;
        int cellId = -1;
        while(i <= 3 && (cellId = cellIds[i++]) != -1) {
            staticCells[cellId].add(obj);
        }
    }

    public void insertDynamicObject(GameObject obj) {
        int[] cellIds = getCellIds(obj);
        int i = 0;
        int cellId = -1;
        while(i <= 3 && (cellId = cellIds[i++]) != -1) {
```

```
        dynamicCells[cellId].add(obj);
    }
}
```

Next up are the methods insertStaticObject() and insertDynamicObject(). They calculate the IDs of the cells that the object is contained in via a call to getCellIds(), and insert the object into the appropriate lists accordingly. The getCellIds() method will actually fill the cellIds member array.

```
public void removeObject(GameObject obj) {
    int[] cellIds = getCellIds(obj);
    int i = 0;
    int cellId = -1;
    while(i <= 3 && (cellId = cellIds[i++]) != -1) {
        dynamicCells[cellId].remove(obj);
        staticCells[cellId].remove(obj);
    }
}
```

We also have a removeObject() method, which we'll use to figure out what cells the object is in and then delete it from the dynamic and static lists accordingly. This will be needed when a game object dies, for example.

```
public void clearDynamicCells(GameObject obj) {
    int len = dynamicCells.length;
    for(int i = 0; i < len; i++) {
        dynamicCells[i].clear();
    }
}
```

The clearDynamicCells() method will be used to clear all dynamic cell lists. We need to call this each frame before we reinsert the dynamic objects, as discussed earlier.

```
public List<GameObject> getPotentialColliders(GameObject obj) {
    foundObjects.clear();
    int[] cellIds = getCellIds(obj);
    int i = 0;
    int cellId = -1;
    while(i <= 3 && (cellId = cellIds[i++]) != -1) {
        int len = dynamicCells[cellId].size();
        for(int j = 0; j < len; j++) {
            GameObject collider = dynamicCells[cellId].get(j);
            if(!foundObjects.contains(collider))
                foundObjects.add(collider);
        }

        len = staticCells[cellId].size();
        for(int j = 0; j < len; j++) {
            GameObject collider = staticCells[cellId].get(j);
            if(!foundObjects.contains(collider))
                foundObjects.add(collider);
        }
    }
    return foundObjects;
}
```

Finally there's the getPotentialColliders() method. It takes an object and returns a list of neighboring objects that are contained in the same cells as that object. We use the working list foundObjects to store the list of found objects. Again, we do not want to instantiate a new list each time this method is called. All we do is figure out which cells the object passed to the method is in. We then simply add all dynamic and static objects found in those cells to the foundObjects list and make sure that there are no duplicates. Using foundObjects.contains() to check for duplicates is of course a little suboptimal. But given that the number of found objects will never be large, it is OK to use it in this case. If you run into performance problems, then this is your number one candidate to optimize. Sadly, that's not trivial, however. We could use a Set, of course, but that allocates new objects internally each time we add an object to it. For now, we'll just leave it as it is, knowing that we can come back to it should anything go wrong performance-wise.

The method I left out is SpatialHashGrid.getCellIds(). Listing 8–11 shows its code. Don't be afraid, it just looks menacing.

Listing 8–11. *The Rest of SpatialHashGrid.java: Implementing getCellIds()*

```java
    public int[] getCellIds(GameObject obj) {
        int x1 = (int)FloatMath.floor(obj.bounds.lowerLeft.x / cellSize);
        int y1 = (int)FloatMath.floor(obj.bounds.lowerLeft.y / cellSize);
        int x2 = (int)FloatMath.floor((obj.bounds.lowerLeft.x + obj.bounds.width) /
cellSize);
        int y2 = (int)FloatMath.floor((obj.bounds.lowerLeft.y + obj.bounds.height) /
cellSize);

        if(x1 == x2 && y1 == y2) {
            if(x1 >= 0 && x1 < cellsPerRow && y1 >= 0 && y1 < cellsPerCol)
                cellIds[0] = x1 + y1 * cellsPerRow;
            else
                cellIds[0] = -1;
            cellIds[1] = -1;
            cellIds[2] = -1;
            cellIds[3] = -1;
        }
        else if(x1 == x2) {
            int i = 0;
            if(x1 >= 0 && x1 < cellsPerRow) {
                if(y1 >= 0 && y1 < cellsPerCol)
                    cellIds[i++] = x1 + y1 * cellsPerRow;
                if(y2 >= 0 && y2 < cellsPerCol)
                    cellIds[i++] = x1 + y2 * cellsPerRow;
            }
            while(i <= 3) cellIds[i++] = -1;
        }
        else if(y1 == y2) {
            int i = 0;
            if(y1 >= 0 && y1 < cellsPerCol) {
                if(x1 >= 0 && x1 < cellsPerRow)
                    cellIds[i++] = x1 + y1 * cellsPerRow;
                if(x2 >= 0 && x2 < cellsPerRow)
                    cellIds[i++] = x2 + y1 * cellsPerRow;
            }
```

```
            while(i <= 3) cellIds[i++] = -1;
        }
        else {
            int i = 0;
            int y1CellsPerRow = y1 * cellsPerRow;
            int y2CellsPerRow = y2 * cellsPerRow;
            if(x1 >= 0 && x1 < cellsPerRow && y1 >= 0 && y1 < cellsPerCol)
                cellIds[i++] = x1 + y1CellsPerRow;
            if(x2 >= 0 && x2 < cellsPerRow && y1 >= 0 && y1 < cellsPerCol)
                cellIds[i++] = x2 + y1CellsPerRow;
            if(x2 >= 0 && x2 < cellsPerRow && y2 >= 0 && y2 < cellsPerCol)
                cellIds[i++] = x2 + y2CellsPerRow;
            if(x1 >= 0 && x1 < cellsPerRow && y2 >= 0 && y2 < cellsPerCol)
                cellIds[i++] = x1 + y2CellsPerRow;
            while(i <= 3) cellIds[i++] = -1;
        }
        return cellIds;
    }

}
```

The first four lines of this method just calculate the cell coordinates of the bottom-left and top-right corners of the object's bounding rectangle. We already discussed this calculation earlier. To understand the rest of this method, we have to think about how an object can overlap grid cells. There are four possibilities:

- The object is contained in a single cell. The bottom-left and top-right corners of the bounding rectangle thus both have the same cell coordinates.

- The object overlaps two cells horizontally. The bottom-left corner is in one cell and the top-right corner is in the cell to the right.

- The object overlaps two cells vertically. The bottom-left corner is in one cell and the top-right corner is in the cell above.

- The object overlaps four cells. The bottom-left corner is in one cell, the bottom-right corner is in the cell to the right, the top-right corner is in the cell above that, and the top-left corner is in the cell above the first cell.

All this method does is make a special case for each of these possibilities. The first if statement checks for the single-cell case, the second if statement checks for the horizontal double-cell case, the third if statement checks for the vertical double-cell case, and the else block handles the case of the object overlapping four grid cells. In each of the four blocks we make sure that we only set the cell ID if the corresponding cell coordinates are within the world. And that's all there is to this method.

Now, the method looks like it would take a lot of computational power. And indeed it does, but less than its size would suggest. The most common case will be the first one, and processing that is pretty cheap. Can you see opportunities to optimize this method further?

Putting It All Together

Let's put all the knowledge we gathered in this section together to form a nice little example. We'll extend the cannon example of the last section as discussed a few pages back. We'll use a Cannon object for the cannon, a DynamicGameObject for the cannonball, and a number of GameObjects for the targets. Each target will have a size of 0.5×0.5 meters and be placed randomly in the world.

We want to be able to shoot those targets. For this we need collision detection. We could just loop over all targets and check them against the cannonball, but that would be boring. We'll use our fancy new SpatialHashGrid class to speed up finding the potentially colliding targets for the current ball position. We won't insert the ball or the cannon into the grid, though, as that wouldn't really gain us anything.

Since this example is already pretty big, we'll split it up into multiple listings. We'll call the test CollisionTest and the corresponding screen CollisionScreen. As always, we'll only look at the screen. Let's start with the members and the constructor, in Listing 8–12.

Listing 8–12. *Excerpt from CollisionTest.java: Members and Constructor*

```
class CollisionScreen extends Screen {
    final int NUM_TARGETS = 20;
    final float WORLD_WIDTH = 9.6f;
    final float WORLD_HEIGHT = 4.8f;
    GLGraphics glGraphics;
    Cannon cannon;
    DynamicGameObject ball;
    List<GameObject> targets;
    SpatialHashGrid grid;

    Vertices cannonVertices;
    Vertices ballVertices;
    Vertices targetVertices;

    Vector2 touchPos = new Vector2();
    Vector2 gravity = new Vector2(0,-10);

    public CollisionScreen(Game game) {
        super(game);
        glGraphics = ((GLGame)game).getGLGraphics();

        cannon = new Cannon(0, 0, 1, 1);
        ball = new DynamicGameObject(0, 0, 0.2f, 0.2f);
        targets = new ArrayList<GameObject>(NUM_TARGETS);
        grid = new SpatialHashGrid(WORLD_WIDTH, WORLD_HEIGHT, 2.5f);
        for(int i = 0; i < NUM_TARGETS; i++) {
            GameObject target = new GameObject((float)Math.random() * WORLD_WIDTH,
                                               (float)Math.random() * WORLD_HEIGHT,
                                               0.5f, 0.5f);
            grid.insertStaticObject(target);
            targets.add(target);
        }
```

```
            cannonVertices = new Vertices(glGraphics, 3, 0, false, false);
            cannonVertices.setVertices(new float[] { -0.5f, -0.5f,
                                                      0.5f, 0.0f,
                                                     -0.5f, 0.5f }, 0, 6);

            ballVertices = new Vertices(glGraphics, 4, 6, false, false);
            ballVertices.setVertices(new float[] { -0.1f, -0.1f,
                                                    0.1f, -0.1f,
                                                    0.1f,  0.1f,
                                                   -0.1f,  0.1f }, 0, 8);
            ballVertices.setIndices(new short[] {0, 1, 2, 2, 3, 0}, 0, 6);

            targetVertices = new Vertices(glGraphics, 4, 6, false, false);
            targetVertices.setVertices(new float[] { -0.25f, -0.25f,
                                                      0.25f, -0.25f,
                                                      0.25f,  0.25f,
                                                     -0.25f,  0.25f }, 0, 8);
            targetVertices.setIndices(new short[] {0, 1, 2, 2, 3, 0}, 0, 6);
    }
```

We brought over a lot from the CannonGravityScreen. We start off with a couple of constant definitions, governing the number of targets and our world's size. Next we have the GLGraphics instance, as well as the objects for the cannon, the ball, and the targets, which we store in a list. We also have a SpatialHashGrid, of course. For rendering our world we need a few meshes: one for the cannon, one for the ball, and one we'll use to render each target. Remember that we only had a single rectangle in BobTest to render the 100 Bobs to the screen. We'll reuse that principle here as well, instead of having a single Vertices instance holding the triangles (rectangles) of our targets. The last two members are the same as in the CannonGravityTest. We use them to shoot the ball and apply gravity when the user touches the screen.

The constructor just does all the things we discussed already. We instantiate our world objects and meshes. The only interesting thing is that we also add the targets as static objects to the spatial hash grid.

Let's check out the next method of the CollisionTest class, in Listing 8–13.

Listing 8–13. *Excerpt from CollisionTest.java: The update() Method*

```
@Override
public void update(float deltaTime) {
    List<TouchEvent> touchEvents = game.getInput().getTouchEvents();
    game.getInput().getKeyEvents();

    int len = touchEvents.size();
    for (int i = 0; i < len; i++) {
        TouchEvent event = touchEvents.get(i);

        touchPos.x = (event.x / (float) glGraphics.getWidth())* WORLD_WIDTH;
        touchPos.y = (1 - event.y / (float) glGraphics.getHeight()) * WORLD_HEIGHT;

        cannon.angle = touchPos.sub(cannon.position).angle();

        if(event.type == TouchEvent.TOUCH_UP) {
            float radians = cannon.angle * Vector2.TO_RADIANS;
```

```
                float ballSpeed = touchPos.len() * 2;
                ball.position.set(cannon.position);
                ball.velocity.x = FloatMath.cos(radians) * ballSpeed;
                ball.velocity.y = FloatMath.sin(radians) * ballSpeed;
                ball.bounds.lowerLeft.set(ball.position.x - 0.1f, ball.position.y - 0.1f);
            }
        }

        ball.velocity.add(gravity.x * deltaTime, gravity.y * deltaTime);
        ball.position.add(ball.velocity.x * deltaTime, ball.velocity.y * deltaTime);
        ball.bounds.lowerLeft.add(ball.velocity.x * deltaTime, ball.velocity.y * deltaTime);

        List<GameObject> colliders = grid.getPotentialColliders(ball);
        len = colliders.size();
        for(int i = 0; i < len; i++) {
            GameObject collider = colliders.get(i);
            if(OverlapTester.overlapRectangles(ball.bounds, collider.bounds)) {
                grid.removeObject(collider);
                targets.remove(collider);
            }
        }
    }
}
```

As always, we first fetch the touch and key events, and only iterate over the touch events. The handling of touch events is nearly the same as in the CannonGravityTest. The only difference is that we use the Cannon object instead of the vectors we had in the old example, and we also reset the ball's bounding rectangle when the cannon is made ready to shoot on a touch-up event.

The next change is how we update the ball. Instead of straight vectors, we use the members of the DynamicGameObject that we instantiated for the ball. We neglect the DynamicGameObject.acceleration member and instead add our gravity to the ball's velocity. We also multiply the ball's speed by 2 so that the cannonball flies a little faster. The interesting thing is that we update not only the ball's position, but also the bounding rectangle's lower-left corner's position. This is crucial, as otherwise our ball would move but its bounding rectangle wouldn't. Why don't we just use the ball's bounding rectangle to store the ball's position? We might want to have multiple bounding shapes attached to an object. Which bounding shape would then hold the actual position of the object? Separating these two things is thus beneficial, and introduces only a little computational overhead. We could of course optimize this a little by only multiplying the velocity with the delta time once. The overhead would then boil down to two more additions—a small price to pay for the flexibility we gain.

The final portion of this method is our collision detection code. All we do is find the targets in the spatial hash grid that are in the same cells as our cannonball. We use the SpatialHashGrid.getPotentialColliders() method for this. Since the cells the ball is contained in are evaluated in that method directly, we do not need to insert the ball into the grid. Next we loop through all the potential colliders and check if there really is an overlap between the ball's bounding rectangle and a potential collider's bounding rectangle. If there is, we simply remove the target from the target list. Remember, we only added targets as static objects to the grid.

And those are our complete game mechanics. The last piece of the puzzle is the actual rendering, which shouldn't really surprise you. See the code in Listing 8–14.

Listing 8–14. *Excerpt from CollisionTest.java: The present() Method*

```java
@Override
public void present(float deltaTime) {
    GL10 gl = glGraphics.getGL();
    gl.glViewport(0, 0, glGraphics.getWidth(), glGraphics.getHeight());
    gl.glClear(GL10.GL_COLOR_BUFFER_BIT);
    gl.glMatrixMode(GL10.GL_PROJECTION);
    gl.glLoadIdentity();
    gl.glOrthof(0, WORLD_WIDTH, 0, WORLD_HEIGHT, 1, -1);
    gl.glMatrixMode(GL10.GL_MODELVIEW);

    gl.glColor4f(0, 1, 0, 1);
    targetVertices.bind();
    int len = targets.size();
    for(int i = 0; i < len; i++) {
        GameObject target = targets.get(i);
        gl.glLoadIdentity();
        gl.glTranslatef(target.position.x, target.position.y, 0);
        targetVertices.draw(GL10.GL_TRIANGLES, 0, 6);
    }
    targetVertices.unbind();

    gl.glLoadIdentity();
    gl.glTranslatef(ball.position.x, ball.position.y, 0);
    gl.glColor4f(1,0,0,1);
    ballVertices.bind();
    ballVertices.draw(GL10.GL_TRIANGLES, 0, 6);
    ballVertices.unbind();

    gl.glLoadIdentity();
    gl.glTranslatef(cannon.position.x, cannon.position.y, 0);
    gl.glRotatef(cannon.angle, 0, 0, 1);
    gl.glColor4f(1,1,1,1);
    cannonVertices.bind();
    cannonVertices.draw(GL10.GL_TRIANGLES, 0, 3);
    cannonVertices.unbind();
}
```

Nothing new here. As always, we set the projection matrix and viewport, and clear the screen first. Next we render all targets, reusing the rectangular model stored in targetVertices. This is essentially the same thing we did in BobTest, but this time we render targets instead. Next we render the ball and the cannon, as we did in the CollisionGravityTest.

The only thing to note here is that I changed the drawing order so that the ball will always be above the targets and the cannon will always be above the ball. I also colored the targets green with a call to glColor4f().

The output of this little test is exactly the same as in Figure 8–17, so I'll spare you the repetition. When you fire the cannonball, it will plow through the field of targets. Any target that gets hit by the ball will be removed from the world.

This example could actually be a nice game if we polish it up a little and add some motivating game mechanics. Can you think of additions? I suggest you play around with the example a little to get a feeling for all the new tools we have developed over the course of the last couple of pages.

There are a few more things I'd like to discuss in this chapter: cameras, texture atlases, and sprites. These use graphics-related tricks that are independent of our model of the game world. Let's get going!

A Camera in 2D

Up until now, we haven't had the concept of a camera in our code; we've only had the definition of our view frustum via glOrthof(), like this:

```
gl.glMatrixMode(GL10.GL_PROJECTION);
gl.glLoadIdentity();
gl.glOrthof(0, FRUSTUM_WIDTH, 0, FRUSTUM_HEIGHT, 1, -1);
```

From Chapter 6 we know that the first two parameters define the x-coordinates of the left and right edges of our frustum in the world, the next two parameters define the y-coordinates of the bottom and top edges of the frustum, and the last two parameters define the near and far clipping planes. Figure 8–19 shows that frustum again.

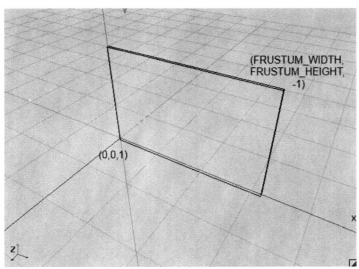

Figure 8–19. *The view frustum for our 2D world, again*

So we only see the region (0,0,1) to (FRUSTUM_WIDTH, FRUSTUM_HEIGHT,–1) of our world. Wouldn't it be nice if we could move the frustum? Say, to the left? Of course that would be nice, and it is dead simple as well:

```
gl.glOrthof(x, x + FRUSTUM_WIDTH, 0, FRUSTUM_HEIGHT, 1, -1);
```

In this case, x is just some offset we can define. We can of course also move on the x- and y-axes:

```
gl.glOrthof(x, x + FRUSTUM_WIDTH, y, y + FRUSTUM_HEIGHT, 1, -1);
```

Figure 8–20 shows what that means.

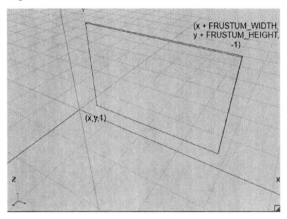

Figure 8–20. *Moving the frustum around*

By this we simply specify the bottom-left corner of our view frustum in the world space. This is already sufficient to implement a freely movable 2D camera. But we can do better. What about not specifying the bottom-left corner of the view frustum with x and y, but instead specifying the center of the view frustum? That way we could easily center our view frustum on an object at a specific location—say, the cannonball from our preceding example:

```
gl.glOrthof(x - FRUSTUM_WIDTH / 2, x + FRUSTUM_WIDTH / 2, y - FRUSTUM_HEIGHT / 2, y +
FRUSTUM_HEIGHT / 2, 1, -1);
```

Figure 8–21 shows what this looks like.

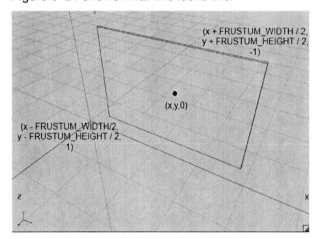

Figure 8–21. *Specifying the view frustum in terms of its center*

That's still not all we can do with glOrthof(). What about zooming? Let's think about this for a little while. We know that via glViewportf() we can tell OpenGL ES what portion of our screen to render the contents of our view frustum to. OpenGL ES will automatically stretch and scale the output to align with the viewport. Now, if we make the width and height of our view frustum smaller, we will simply show a smaller region of our world on the screen. That's zooming in. If we make the frustum bigger, we'll show more of our world—that's zooming out. We can therefore introduce a zoom factor and multiply it by our frustum's width and height to zoom in an out. A factor of 1 will show us the world as in Figure 8–21, using the normal frustum width and height. A factor smaller than 1 will zoom in on the center of our view frustum. And a factor bigger than 1 will zoom out, showing us more of our world (e.g., setting the zoom factor to 2 will show us twice as much of our world). Here's how we can use glOrthof() to do that for us:

```
gl.glOrthof(x - FRUSTUM_WIDTH / 2 * zoom, x + FRUSTUM_WIDTH / 2 * zoom, y -
FRUSTUM_HEIGHT / 2 * zoom, y + FRUSTUM_HEIGHT / 2 * zoom, 1, -1);
```

Dead simple! We can now create a camera class that has a position it is looking at (the center of the view frustum), a standard frustum width and height, and a zoom factor that makes the frustum smaller or bigger, thereby showing us either less of our world (zooming in) or more of our world (zooming out). Figure 8–22 shows a view frustum with a zoom factor of 0.5 (the inner gray box), and one with a zoom factor of 1 (the outer, transparent box).

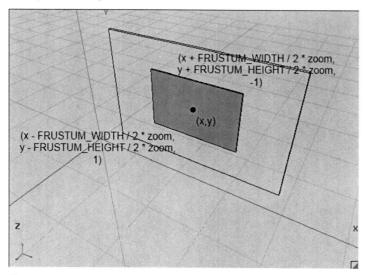

Figure 8–22. *Zooming by manipulating the frustum size*

To make our lives complete we should add one more thing. Imagine that we touch the screen and want to figure out what point in our 2D world we touched. We already did this a couple of times in our iteratively improving cannon examples. With a view frustum configuration that does not factor in the camera's position and zoom, as in Figure 8–19, we had the following equations (see the update() method of our cannon examples):

```
worldX = (touchX / Graphics.getWidth()) × FRUSTUM_WIDTH;
worldY = (1 - touchY / Graphics.getHeight()) × FRUSTUM_HEIGHT;
```

We first normalize the touch x- and y-coordinates to the range 0 to 1 by dividing by the screen's width and height, and then we scale them so that they are expressed in terms of our world space by multiplying them with the frustum's width and height. All we need to do is factor in the position of the view frustum as well as the zoom factor. Here's how we do that:

```
worldX = (touchX / Graphics.getWidth()) x FRUSTUM_WIDTH + x - FRUSTUM_WIDTH / 2;
worldY = (1 - touchY / Graphics.getHeight()) x FRUSTUM_HEIGHT + y - FRUSTUM_HEIGHT / 2;
```

Here, x and y are our camera's position in world space.

The Camera2D Class

Let's put all this together into a single class. We want it to store the camera's position, the standard frustum width and height, and the zoom factor. We also want a convenience method that sets the viewport (always use the whole screen) and projection matrix correctly. Additionally we want a method that can translate touch coordinates to world coordinates. Listing 8–15 shows our new Camera2D class.

Listing 8–15. *Camera2D.java, Our Shiny New Camera Class for 2D Rendering*

```java
package com.badlogic.androidgames.framework.gl;

import javax.microedition.khronos.opengles.GL10;

import com.badlogic.androidgames.framework.impl.GLGraphics;
import com.badlogic.androidgames.framework.math.Vector2;

public class Camera2D {
    public final Vector2 position;
    public float zoom;
    public final float frustumWidth;
    public final float frustumHeight;
    final GLGraphics glGraphics;
```

As discussed, we store the camera's position, frustum width and height, and zoom factor as members. The position and zoom factor are public, so we can easily manipulate them. We also need a reference to GLGraphics so we can get the up-to-date width and height of the screen in pixels for transforming touch coordinates to world coordinates.

```java
    public Camera2D(GLGraphics glGraphics, float frustumWidth, float frustumHeight) {
        this.glGraphics = glGraphics;
        this.frustumWidth = frustumWidth;
        this.frustumHeight = frustumHeight;
        this.position = new Vector2(frustumWidth / 2, frustumHeight / 2);
        this.zoom = 1.0f;
    }
```

In the constructor we take a GLGraphics instance and the frustum's width and height at the zoom factor 1 as parameters. We store them and initialize the position of the camera to look at the center of the box bounded by (0,0,1) and (frustumWidth, frustumHeight,–1), as in Figure 8–19. The initial zoom factor is set to 1.

```
        public void setViewportAndMatrices() {
            GL10 gl = glGraphics.getGL();
            gl.glViewport(0, 0, glGraphics.getWidth(), glGraphics.getHeight());
            gl.glMatrixMode(GL10.GL_PROJECTION);
            gl.glLoadIdentity();
            gl.glOrthof(position.x - frustumWidth * zoom / 2,
                        position.x + frustumWidth * zoom/ 2,
                        position.y - frustumHeight * zoom / 2,
                        position.y + frustumHeight * zoom/ 2,
                        1, -1);
            gl.glMatrixMode(GL10.GL_MODELVIEW);
            gl.glLoadIdentity();
        }
```

The setViewportAndMatrices() method sets the viewport to span the whole screen, and sets the projection matrix in accordance with our camera's parameters, as discussed previously. At the end of the method we tell OpenGL ES that all further matrix operations are targeting the model view matrix and load an identity matrix. We will call this method each frame so we can start from a clean slate. No more direct OpenGL ES calls to set up our viewport and projection matrix.

```
        public void touchToWorld(Vector2 touch) {
            touch.x = (touch.x / (float) glGraphics.getWidth()) * frustumWidth * zoom;
            touch.y = (1 - touch.y / (float) glGraphics.getHeight()) * frustumHeight * zoom;
            touch.add(position).sub(frustumWidth * zoom / 2, frustumHeight * zoom / 2);
        }
    }
```

The touchToWorld() method takes a Vector2 instance containing touch coordinates and transforms the vector to world space. This is the same thing we just discussed; the only difference is that we use our fancy Vector2 class.

An Example

Let's use the Camera2D class in our cannon example. I copied the CollisionTest file and renamed it Camera2DTest. I also renamed the GLGame class inside the file Camera2DTest, and renamed the CollisionScreen class Camera2DScreen. We'll just discuss the little changes we have to make to use our new Camera2D class.

The first thing we do is add a new member to the Camera2DScreen class:

Camera2D camera;

We initialize this member in the constructor as follows:

camera = new Camera2D(glGraphics, WORLD_WIDTH, WORLD_HEIGHT);

We just pass in our GLGraphics instance and the world's width and height, which we previously used as the frustum's width and height in our call to glOrthof(). All we need to do now is replace our direct OpenGL ES calls in the present() method, which looked like this:

```
gl.glViewport(0, 0, glGraphics.getWidth(), glGraphics.getHeight());
gl.glClear(GL10.GL_COLOR_BUFFER_BIT);
gl.glMatrixMode(GL10.GL_PROJECTION);
```

```
gl.glLoadIdentity();
gl.glOrthof(0, WORLD_WIDTH, 0, WORLD_HEIGHT, 1, -1);
gl.glMatrixMode(GL10.GL_MODELVIEW);
```

We replace them with this:

```
gl.glClear(GL10.GL_COLOR_BUFFER_BIT);
camera.setViewportAndMatrices();
```

We still have to clear the framebuffer, of course, but all the other direct OpenGL ES calls are nicely hidden inside the `Camera2D.setViewportAndMatrices()` method. If you run that code, you'll see that nothing has changed. Everything works like before—all we did was make things a little nicer and more flexible.

We can also simplify the `update()` method of the test a little. Since we added the `Camera2D.touchToWorld()` method to the camera class, we might as well use it. We can replace this snippet from the update method:

```
touchPos.x = (event.x / (float) glGraphics.getWidth())* WORLD_WIDTH;
touchPos.y = (1 - event.y / (float) glGraphics.getHeight()) * WORLD_HEIGHT;
```

with this:

```
camera.touchToWorld(touchPos.set(event.x, event.y));
```

Neat, everything is nicely encapsulated now. But it would be very boring if we didn't use the features of our camera class to their full extent. Here's the plan: we want to have the camera look at the world in the "normal" way as long as the cannonball does not fly. That's easy; we're already doing that. We can determine whether the cannonball flies or not by checking whether the y-coordinate of its position is less than or equal to zero. Since we always apply gravity to the cannonball, it will of course fall even if we don't shoot it, so that's a cheap way to check matters.

Our new addition will come into effect when the cannonball is flying (when the y-coordinate is greater than zero). We want the camera to follow the cannonball. We can achieve this by simply setting the camera's position to the cannonball's position. That will always keep the cannonball in the center of the screen. We also want to try out our zooming functionality. Therefore well increase the zoom factor depending on the y-coordinate of the cannonball. The further away from zero, the higher the zoom factor. This will make the camera zoom out if the cannonball has a higher y-coordinate. Here's what we need to add at the end of the `update()` method in our test's screen:

```
if(ball.position.y > 0) {
    camera.position.set(ball.position);
    camera.zoom = 1 + ball.position.y / WORLD_HEIGHT;
} else {
    camera.position.set(WORLD_WIDTH / 2, WORLD_HEIGHT / 2);
    camera.zoom = 1;
}
```

As long as the y-coordinate of our ball is greater then zero, the camera will follow it and zoom out. We just add a value to the standard zoom factor of 1. That value is just the relation between the ball's y-position and the world's height. If the ball's y-coordinate is at `WORLD_HEIGHT`, the zoom factor will be 2, so we we'll see more of our world. The way I did this is really arbitrary; you could come up with any formula that you want here—

there's nothing magical about it. In case the ball's position is less than or equal to zero, we show the world normally, as we did in the previous examples.

Texture Atlas: Because Sharing Is Caring

Up until this point we have only ever used a single texture in our programs. What if we not only want to render Bob, but other superheroes or enemies or explosions or coins as well? We could have multiple textures, each holding the image of one object type. But OpenGL ES wouldn't like that much, since we'd need to switch textures for every object type we render (e.g., bind Bob's texture, render Bobs, bind the coin texture, render coins, etc.). We can do better by putting multiple images into a single texture. And that's a texture atlas: a single texture containing multiple images. We only need to bind that texture once, and we can then render any entity types for which there is an image in the atlas. That saves some state change overhead and increases our performance. Figure 8–23 shows such a texture atlas.

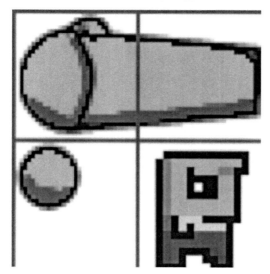

Figure 8–23. *A texture atlas*

There are three objects in Figure 8–23: a cannon, a cannonball, and Bob. The grid is not part of the texture; it's only there to illustrate how I usually create my texture atlases.

The texture atlas is 64×64 pixels in size, and each grid is 32×32 pixels. The cannon takes up two cells, the cannonball a little less than one-quarter of a cell, and Bob a single cell. Now, if you look back at how we defined the bounds (and graphical rectangles) of the cannon, cannonball, and targets, you will notice that the relation of their sizes to each other is very similar to what we have in the grid here. The target is 0.5×0.5 meters in our world, and the cannon is 0.2×0.2 meters. In our texture atlas, Bob takes up 32×32 pixels and the cannonball a little under 16×16 pixels. The relationship between the texture atlas and the object sizes in our world should be clear: 32 pixels in the atlas equals 0.5 meters in our world. Now, the cannon was 1×1 meters in our original example, but we can of course change that. According to our texture atlas, in which the cannon takes up 64×32 pixels, we should let our cannon have a size of 1×0.5 meters in our world. Wow, that is exceptionally easy isn't it?

So why did I choose 32 pixels to match 1 meter in our world? Remember that textures must have power-of-two widths and heights. Using a power-of-two pixel unit like 32 to map to 0.5 meters in our world is a convenient way for the artist to cope with the restriction on texture sizes. It also makes it easier to get the size relations of different objects in our world right in the pixel art as well.

Note that there's nothing keeping you from using more pixels per world unit. You could choose 64 pixels or 50 pixels to match 0.5 meters in our world just fine. So what's a good pixel-to-meters size, then? That again depends on the screen resolution our game will run at. Let's do some calculations.

Our cannon world is bounded by (0,0) in the bottom-left corner and (9.6,4.8) in the top-left corner. This is mapped to our screen. Let's figure out how many pixels per world unit we have on the screen of a Hero (480×320 pixels in landscape mode):

```
pixelsPerUnitX = screenWidth / worldWidth = 480 / 9.6 =  50 pixels / meter
pixelsPerUnitY = screenHeight / worldHeight = 320 / 6.4 = 50 pixels / meter
```

Our cannon, which will now take up 1×0.5 meters in the world, will thus use 50x25 pixels on the screen. We'd use a 64×32-pixel region from our texture, so we'd actually downscale the texture image a little when rendering the cannon. That's totally fine— OpenGL ES will do this automatically for us. Depending on the minification filter we set for the texture, the result will either be crisp and pixelated (GL_NEAREST) or a little smoothed out (GL_LINEAR). If we wanted a pixel-perfect rendering on the Hero, we'd need to scale our texture images a little. We could use a grid size of 25×25 pixels instead of 32×32. However, if we just resized the atlas image (or rather redraw everything by hand), we'd have a 50×50-pixel image—a no-go with OpenGL ES. We'd have to add padding to the left and bottom to obtain a 64×64 image (since OpenGL ES requires power-of-two widths and heights). I'd say we are totally fine with OpenGL ES scaling our texture image down on the Hero.

How's the situation on higher-resolution devices like the Nexus One (800×480 in landscape mode)? Let's perform the calculations for this screen configuration via the following equations:

```
pixelsPerUnitX = screenWidth / worldWidth = 800 / 9.6 =  83 pixels / meter
pixelsPerUnitY = screenHeight / worldHeight = 480 / 6.4 = 75 pixels / meter
```

We have different pixels per unit on the x- and y-axes because the aspect ratio of our view frustum (9.6 / 6.4 = 1.5) is different from the screen's aspect ratio (800 / 480 = 1.66). We already talked about this in Chapter 4 when we outlined a couple of solutions. Back then we targeted a fixed pixel size and aspect ratio; now we'll adopt that scheme and target a fixed frustum width and height for our example. In the case of the Nexus One, the cannon, the cannonball, and Bob would get scaled up a little and stretched, due to the higher resolution and different aspect ratio. We accept this fact since we want all players to see the same region of our world. Otherwise, players with higher aspect ratios could have the advantage of being able to see more of the world.

So, how do we use such a texture atlas? We just remap our rectangles. Instead of using all of the texture, we just use portions of it. To figure out the texture coordinates of the corners of the images contained in the texture atlas, we can reuse the equations from one of the last examples. Here's a quick refresher:

```
u = x / imageWidth
v = y / imageHeight
```

Here, u and v are the texture coordinates and x and y are the pixel coordinates. Bob's top-left corner in pixel coordinates is at (32,32). If we plug that into the preceding equation, we get (0.5,0.5) as texture coordinates. We can do the same for any other corners we need, and based on this set the correct texture coordinates for the vertices of our rectangles.

An Example

Let's add this texture atlas to our previous example to make it look more beautiful. Bob will be out target.

We just copy the Camera2DTest and modify it a little. I placed the copy in a file called TextureAtlasTest.java and renamed the two classes contained in it accordingly (TextureAtlasTest and TextureAtlasScreen).

The first thing we do is add a new member to the TextureAtlasScreen:

```
Texture texture;
```

Instead of creating a Texture in the constructor, we create it in the resume() method. Remember that textures will get lost when our application comes back from a paused state, so we have to re-create them in the resume() method:

```
@Override
public void resume() {
    texture = new Texture(((GLGame)game), "atlas.png");
}
```

I just put the image in Figure 8–23 in the assets/ folder of our project and named it atlas.png. (It of course doesn't contain the gridlines shown in the figure.)

Next we need to change the definitions of the vertices. We have one Vertices instance for each entity type (cannon, cannonball, and Bob) holding a single rectangle of four vertices and six indices, making up three triangles. All we need to do is add texture coordinates to each of the vertices in accordance with the texture atlas. We also change the cannon from being represented as a triangle to being represented by a rectangle of size 1×0.5 meters. Here's what we replace the old vertex creation code in the constructor with:

```
cannonVertices = new Vertices(glGraphics, 4, 6, false, true);
cannonVertices.setVertices(new float[] { -0.5f, -0.25f, 0.0f, 0.5f,
                                          0.5f, -0.25f, 1.0f, 0.5f,
                                          0.5f,  0.25f, 1.0f, 0.0f,
                                         -0.5f,  0.25f, 0.0f, 0.0f },
                            0, 16);
```

```
cannonVertices.setIndices(new short[] {0, 1, 2, 2, 3, 0}, 0, 6);

ballVertices = new Vertices(glGraphics, 4, 6, false, true);
ballVertices.setVertices(new float[] { -0.1f, -0.1f, 0.0f, 0.75f,
                                        0.1f, -0.1f, 0.25f, 0.75f,
                                        0.1f,  0.1f, 0.25f, 0.5f,
                                       -0.1f,  0.1f, 0.0f, 0.5f },
                                       0, 16);
ballVertices.setIndices(new short[] {0, 1, 2, 2, 3, 0}, 0, 6);

targetVertices = new Vertices(glGraphics, 4, 6, false, true);
targetVertices.setVertices(new float[] { -0.25f, -0.25f, 0.5f, 1.0f,
                                          0.25f, -0.25f, 1.0f, 1.0f,
                                          0.25f,  0.25f, 1.0f, 0.5f,
                                         -0.25f,  0.25f, 0.5f, 0.5f },
                                         0, 16);
targetVertices.setIndices(new short[] {0, 1, 2, 2, 3, 0}, 0, 6);
```

Each of our meshes is now composed of four vertices, each having a 2D position and texture coordinates. We added six indices to the mesh, specifying the two triangles we want to render. We also made the cannon a little smaller on the y-axis. It now has size of 1×0.5 meters instead of 1×1 meters. This is also reflected in the construction of the Cannon object earlier in the constructor:

```
cannon = new Cannon(0, 0, 1, 0.5f);
```

Since we don't do any collision detection with the cannon itself, it doesn't really matter what size we set in that constructor, though. We just do it for consistency.

The last thing we need to change is our render method. Here it is in its full glory:

```
@Override
public void present(float deltaTime) {
    GL10 gl = glGraphics.getGL();
    gl.glClear(GL10.GL_COLOR_BUFFER_BIT);
    camera.setViewportAndMatrices();

    gl.glEnable(GL10.GL_BLEND);
    gl.glBlendFunc(GL10.GL_SRC_ALPHA, GL10.GL_ONE_MINUS_SRC_ALPHA);
    gl.glEnable(GL10.GL_TEXTURE_2D);
    texture.bind();

    targetVertices.bind();
    int len = targets.size();
    for(int i = 0; i < len; i++) {
        GameObject target = targets.get(i);
        gl.glLoadIdentity();
        gl.glTranslatef(target.position.x, target.position.y, 0);
        targetVertices.draw(GL10.GL_TRIANGLES, 0, 6);
    }
    targetVertices.unbind();

    gl.glLoadIdentity();
    gl.glTranslatef(ball.position.x, ball.position.y, 0);
    ballVertices.bind();
    ballVertices.draw(GL10.GL_TRIANGLES, 0, 6);
    ballVertices.unbind();
```

```
        gl.glLoadIdentity();
        gl.glTranslatef(cannon.position.x, cannon.position.y, 0);
        gl.glRotatef(cannon.angle, 0, 0, 1);
        cannonVertices.bind();
        cannonVertices.draw(GL10.GL_TRIANGLES, 0, 6);
        cannonVertices.unbind();
}
```

Here, we enable blending and set a proper blending function, and enable texturing and bind our atlas texture. We also slightly adapt the cannonVertices.draw() call, which now renders two triangles instead of one. That's all there is to it. Figure 8–24 of our face-lifting operation.

Figure 8–24. *Beautifying the cannon example with a texture atlas*

There are a few more things we need to know about texture atlases:

- When we use GL_LINEAR as the minification and/or magnification filter, there might be artifacts when two images within the atlas are touching each other. This is due to the texture mapper actually fetching the four nearest texels from a texture for a pixel on the screen. When it does that for the border of an image, it will also fetch texels from the neighboring image in the atlas. We can eliminate this problem by introducing an empty border of 2 pixels between our images. Even better, we can duplicate the border pixel of each image. The first solution is of course easier—just make sure your texture stays a power of two.

- There's no need to lay out all the images in the atlas in a fixed grid. We could put arbitrarily sized images in the atlas as tightly as possible. All we need to know is where one image starts and ends in the atlas so we can calculate proper texture coordinates for it. Packing arbitrarily sized images is a nontrivial problem, however. There are a couple of tools on the Web that can help you with creating a texture atlas; just do a search and you'll be hit by a plethora of options.

- Often we cannot group all images of our game into a single texture. Remember that there's a maximum texture size that varies from device to device. We can safely assume that all devices support a texture size of 512×512 pixels (or even 1024×1024). So, we just have multiple texture atlases. You should try to group objects that will be seen on the screen together in one atlas, though—say, all the objects of level 1 in one atlas, all the objects of level 2 in another, all the UI elements in another, and so on. Think about the logical grouping before finalizing your art assets.

- Remember how we drew numbers dynamically in Mr. Nom? We used a texture atlas for that. In fact, we can perform all dynamic text rendering via a texture atlas. Just put all the characters you need for your game into an atlas and render them on demand via multiple rectangles mapping to the appropriate characters in the atlas. There are tools you can find on the Web that will generate such a so-called *bitmap font* for you. For our purposes in the coming chapters, we will stick to the approach we used in Mr. Nom, though: static text gets prerendered as a whole, and only dynamic text (e.g., numbers in high scores) will get rendered via an atlas.

You might have noticed that Bobs disappear a little before they are actually hit by the cannonball graphically. That's because our bounding shapes are a little too big. We have some whitespace around Bob and the cannonball in the border. What's the solution? We just make the bounding shapes a little smaller. I want you to get a feel for this, so manipulate the source until the collision feels right. You will often find such fine-tuning "opportunities" while developing a game. Fine tuning is probably one of the most crucial parts apart from good level design. Getting things to feel right can be hard, but is highly satisfactory once you achieved the level of perfection of Super Mario Brothers. Sadly, this is nothing I can teach you, as it is dependent on the look and feel of your game. Consider it the magic sauce that sets good and bad games apart.

NOTE: To handle the disappearance issue just mentioned, make the bounding rectangles a little smaller than their graphical representations to allow for some overlap before a collision is triggered.

Texture Regions, Sprites, and Batches: Hiding OpenGL ES

Our code so far for the cannon example is made up of a lot of boilerplate, some of which can be reduced. One such area is the definition of the Vertices instances. It's tedious to always have seven lines of code just to define a single textured rectangle. Another area we could improve is the manual calculation of texture coordinates for images in a texture atlas. Finally, there's a lot of code involved when we want to render our 2D rectangles that's highly repetitive. I also hinted at a better way of rendering many objects than having one draw call per object. We can solve all these issues by introducing a few new concepts:

- *Texture regions*: We worked with texture regions in the last example. A texture region is a rectangular area within a single texture (e.g., the area that contains the cannon in our atlas). We want a nice class that can encapsulate all the nasty calculations for translating pixel coordinates to texture coordinates.

- *Sprites*: A sprite is a lot like one of our game objects. It has a position (and possibly orientation and scale), as well as a graphical extent. We render a sprite via a rectangle, just as we render Bob or the cannon. In fact, the graphical representations of Bob and the other objects can and should be considered sprites. A sprite also maps to a region in a texture. That's where texture regions come into. While it is tempting to combine sprites with game directly, we keep them separated, following the Model-View-Controller pattern. This clean seperation between graphics and mode code makes for a better design.

- *Sprite batchers*: A sprite batcher is responsible for rendering multiple sprites in one go. To do this, the sprite batcher needs to know each sprite's position, size, and texture region. The sprite batcher will be our magic ingredient to get rid of multiple draw calls and matrix operations per object.

These concepts are highly interconnected; we'll discuss them next.

The TextureRegion Class

Since we've worked with texture regions already, it should be straightforward to figure out what we need. We know how to convert from pixel coordinates to texture coordinates. We want to have a class where we can specify pixel coordinates of an image in a texture atlas that then stores the corresponding texture coordinates for the atlas region for further processing (e.g., when we want to render a sprite). Without further ado, Listing 8–16 shows our TextureRegion class.

Listing 8–16. *TextureRegion.java: Converting Pixel Coordinates to Texture Coordinates*

```
package com.badlogic.androidgames.framework.gl;

public class TextureRegion {
    public final float u1, v1;
    public final float u2, v2;
    public final Texture texture;

    public TextureRegion(Texture texture, float x, float y, float width, float height) {
        this.u1 = x / texture.width;
        this.v1 = y / texture.height;
        this.u2 = this.u1 + width / texture.width;
        this.v2 = this.v1 + height / texture.height;
        this.texture = texture;
    }
}
```

The TextureRegion stores the texture coordinates of the top-left corner (u1,v1) and bottom-right corner (u2,v2) of the region in texture coordinates. The constructor takes a Texture and the top-left corner, as well as the width and height of the region, in pixel coordinates. To construct a texture region for the Cannon, we could do this:

```
TextureRegion cannonRegion = new TextureRegion(texture, 0, 0, 64, 32);
```

Similarly we could construct a region for Bob:

```
TextureRegion bobRegion = new TextureRegion(texture, 32, 32, 32, 32);
```

And so on and so forth. We could use this in the example code that we've already created, and use the TextureRegion.u1, v1, u2, and v2 members for specifying the texture coordinates of the vertices of our rectangles. But we won't do that, since we want to get rid of these tedious definitions altogether. That's what we'll use the sprite batcher for.

The SpriteBatcher Class

As already discussed, a sprite can be easily defined by its position, size, and texture region (and optionally, its rotation and scale). It is simply a graphical rectangle in our world space. To make things easier we'll stick to the conventions of the position being in the center of the sprite and the rectangle constructed around that center. Now, we could have a Sprite class and use it like this:

```
Sprite bobSprite = new Sprite(20, 20, 0.5f, 0.5f, bobRegion);
```

That would construct a new sprite with its center at (20,20) in the world, extending 0.25 meters to each side, and using the bobRegion TextureRegion. But we could do this instead:

```
spriteBatcher.drawSprite(bob.x, bob.y, BOB_WIDTH, BOB_HEIGHT, bobRegion);
```

Now that looks a lot better. We don't need to construct yet another object to represent the graphical side of our object. Instead we draw an instance of Bob on demand. We could also have an overloaded method:

```
spriteBatcher.drawSprite(cannon.x, cannon.y, CANNON_WIDTH, CANNON_HEIGHT, cannon.angle,
cannonRegion);
```

That would draw the cannon, rotated by its angle. So how can we implement the sprite batcher? Where are the `Vertices` instances? Let's think about how the batcher could work.

What is batching anyway? In the graphics community, batching is defined as collapsing multiple draw calls into a single draw call. This makes the GPU happy, as discussed in the previous chapter. A sprite batcher offers one way to make this happen. Here's how:

- The batcher has a buffer that is empty initially (or becomes empty after we signal it to be cleared). That buffer will hold vertices. It is a simple float array in our case.

- Each time we call the `SpriteBatcher.drawSprite()` method we add four vertices to the buffer, based on the position, size, orientation, and texture region that were specified as arguments. This also means that we have to manually rotate and translate the vertex positions without the help of OpenGL ES. Fear not, though, the code of our `Vector2` class will come in handy here. This is the key to eliminating all the draw calls.

- Once we have specified all the sprites we want to render, we tell the sprite batcher to actually submit the vertices for all the rectangles of the sprites to the GPU in one go, and then call the actual OpenGL ES drawing method to render all the rectangles. For this, we'll transfer the contents of the float array to a `Vertices` instance and use it to render the rectangles.

NOTE: We can only batch sprites that use the same texture. However, it's not a huge problem since we'll use texture atlases anyway.

The usual usage pattern of a sprite batcher looks like this:

```
batcher.beginBatch(texture);
// call batcher.drawSprite() as often as needed, referencing regions in the texture
batcher.endBatch();
```

The call to `SpriteBatcher.beginBatch()` will tell the batcher two things: it should clear its buffer and use the texture we pass in. We will bind the texture within this method for convenience.

Next we render as many sprites that reference regions within this texture as we need to. This will fill the buffer, adding four vertices per sprite.

The call to `SpriteBatcher.endBatch()` signals to the sprite batcher that we are done rendering the batch of sprites and that it should now upload the vertices to the GPU for actual rendering. We are going to use indexed rendering with a `Vertices` instance, so we'll also need to specify indices, in addition to the vertices in the float array buffer. However, since we are always rendering rectangles, we can generate the indices beforehand once in the constructor of the SpriteBatcher. For this we need to know how many sprites the batcher should be able to draw maximally per batch. By putting a hard limited on the number of sprites that can be rendered per batch, we don't need to grow any arrays of other buffers; we can just allocate these arrays and buffers once in the constructor.

The general mechanics are rather simple. The SpriteBatcher.drawSprite() method may seem like a mystery, but it's not a big problem (if we leave out rotation and scaling for a moment). All we need to do is calculate the vertex positions and texture coordinates as defined by the parameters. We have done this manually already in previous examples— for instance, when we defined the rectangles for the cannon, the cannonball, and Bob. We'll do more or less the same in the SpriteBatcher.drawSprite() method, only automatically based on the parameters of the method. So let's check out the SpriteBatcher. Listing 8–17 shows the code.

Listing 8–17. *Excerpt from SpriteBatcher.java, Without Rotation and Scaling*

```
package com.badlogic.androidgames.framework.gl;

import javax.microedition.khronos.opengles.GL10;

import android.util.FloatMath;

import com.badlogic.androidgames.framework.impl.GLGraphics;
import com.badlogic.androidgames.framework.math.Vector2;

public class SpriteBatcher {
    final float[] verticesBuffer;
    int bufferIndex;
    final Vertices vertices;
    int numSprites;
```

Let's look at the members first. The member verticesBuffer is the temporary float array we store the vertices of the sprites of the current batch in. The member bufferIndex indicates where in the float array we should start to write the next vertices. The member vertices is the Vertices instance is used to render the batch. It also stores the indices we'll define in a minute. The member numSprites holds the number drawn so far in the current batch.

```
    public SpriteBatcher(GLGraphics glGraphics, int maxSprites) {
        this.verticesBuffer = new float[maxSprites*4*4];
        this.vertices = new Vertices(glGraphics, maxSprites*4, maxSprites*6, false,
true);
        this.bufferIndex = 0;
        this.numSprites = 0;

        short[] indices = new short[maxSprites*6];
        int len = indices.length;
        short j = 0;
        for (int i = 0; i < len; i += 6, j += 4) {
                indices[i + 0] = (short)(j + 0);
                indices[i + 1] = (short)(j + 1);
                indices[i + 2] = (short)(j + 2);
```

```
            indices[i + 3] = (short)(j + 2);
            indices[i + 4] = (short)(j + 3);
            indices[i + 5] = (short)(j + 0);
        }
        vertices.setIndices(indices, 0, indices.length);
    }
```

Moving to the constructor, we see that we have two arguments: the GLGraphics instance we need for creating the Vertices instance, and the maximum number of sprites the batcher should be able to render in one batch. The first thing we do in the constructor is create the float array. We have four vertices per sprite, and each vertex takes up four floats (two for the x- and y-coordinates and another two for the texture coordinates). We can have maxSprites sprites maximally, so that's 4 × 4 × maxSprites floats that we need for the buffer. Next we create the Vertices instance. We need it to store maxSprites × 4 vertices and maxSprites × 6 indices at most. We also tell the Vertices instance that we have not only positional attributes, but also texture coordinates for each vertex. We then initialize the bufferIndex and numSprites members to zero. Then we create the indices for our Vertices instance. We need to do this only once, as the indices will never change. The first sprite in a batch will always have the indices 0, 1, 2, 2, 3, 0; the next sprite will have 4, 5, 6, 6, 7, 4; and so on. We can precompute those and store them in the Vertices instance. This way we only need to set them once, instead of once for each sprite.

```
    public void beginBatch(Texture texture) {
        texture.bind();
        numSprites = 0;
        bufferIndex = 0;
    }
```

Next up is the beginBatch() method. It binds the texture and resets the numSprites and bufferIndex members so the first sprite's vertices will get inserted at the front of the verticesBuffer float array.

```
    public void endBatch() {
        vertices.setVertices(verticesBuffer, 0, bufferIndex);
        vertices.bind();
        vertices.draw(GL10.GL_TRIANGLES, 0, numSprites * 6);
        vertices.unbind();
    }
```

The next method is endBatch(); we'll call it to finalize and draw the current batch. It first transfers the vertices defined for this batch from the float array to the Vertices instance. All that's left is binding the Vertices instance, drawing numSprites × 2 triangles, and unbinding the Vertices instance again. Since we use indexed rendering, we specify the number of indices to use—which is six indices per sprite times numSprites. That's all there is to rendering.

```
    public void drawSprite(float x, float y, float width, float height, TextureRegion
region) {
        float halfWidth = width / 2;
        float halfHeight = height / 2;
        float x1 = x - halfWidth;
        float y1 = y - halfHeight;
```

```
        float x2 = x + halfWidth;
        float y2 = y + halfHeight;

        verticesBuffer[bufferIndex++] = x1;
        verticesBuffer[bufferIndex++] = y1;
        verticesBuffer[bufferIndex++] = region.u1;
        verticesBuffer[bufferIndex++] = region.v2;

        verticesBuffer[bufferIndex++] = x2;
        verticesBuffer[bufferIndex++] = y1;
        verticesBuffer[bufferIndex++] = region.u2;
        verticesBuffer[bufferIndex++] = region.v2;

        verticesBuffer[bufferIndex++] = x2;
        verticesBuffer[bufferIndex++] = y2;
        verticesBuffer[bufferIndex++] = region.u2;
        verticesBuffer[bufferIndex++] = region.v1;

        verticesBuffer[bufferIndex++] = x1;
        verticesBuffer[bufferIndex++] = y2;
        verticesBuffer[bufferIndex++] = region.u1;
        verticesBuffer[bufferIndex++] = region.v1;

        numSprites++;
    }
```

The next method is the workhorse of the SpriteBatcher. It takes the x- and y-coordinates of the center of the sprite, its width and height, and the TextureRegion it maps to. The method's responsibility is to add four vertices to the float array starting at the current bufferIndex. These four vertices form a texture-mapped rectangle . We calculate the position of the bottom-left corner (x1,y1) and the top-right corner (x2,y2), and use these four variables to construct the vertices, together with the texture coordinates from the TextureRegion. The vertices are added in counterclockwise order, starting at the bottom-left vertex. Once they are added to the float array, we increment the numSprites counter and wait for either another sprite to be added or for the batch to be finalized.

And that is all there is to do. We just eliminated a lot of drawing methods by simply buffering pretransformed vertices in a float array and rendering them in one go. That will increase our 2D sprite-rendering performance considerably compared to the method we were using before. Fewer OpenGL ES state changes and fewer drawing calls make the GPU happy.

There's one more thing we need to implement: a SpriteBatcher.drawSprite() method that can draw a rotated sprite All we need to do is construct the four corner vertices without adding the position, rotate them around the origin, add the position of the sprite so that the vertices are placed in the world space, and then proceed as in the previous drawing method. We could use Vector2.rotate() for this, but that would mean some functional overhead. We therefore reproduce the code in Vector2.rotate() and optimize where possible. The final method of the SpriteBatcher looks like Listing 8–18.

Listing 8–18. *The Rest of SpriteBatcher.java: A Method to Draw Rotated Sprites*

```java
    public void drawSprite(float x, float y, float width, float height, float angle,
TextureRegion region) {
        float halfWidth = width / 2;
        float halfHeight = height / 2;

        float rad = angle * Vector2.TO_RADIANS;
        float cos = FloatMath.cos(rad);
        float sin = FloatMath.sin(rad);

        float x1 = -halfWidth * cos - (-halfHeight) * sin;
        float y1 = -halfWidth * sin + (-halfHeight) * cos;
        float x2 = halfWidth * cos - (-halfHeight) * sin;
        float y2 = halfWidth * sin + (-halfHeight) * cos;
        float x3 = halfWidth * cos - halfHeight * sin;
        float y3 = halfWidth * sin + halfHeight * cos;
        float x4 = -halfWidth * cos - halfHeight * sin;
        float y4 = -halfWidth * sin + halfHeight * cos;

        x1 += x;
        y1 += y;
        x2 += x;
        y2 += y;
        x3 += x;
        y3 += y;
        x4 += x;
        y4 += y;

        verticesBuffer[bufferIndex++] = x1;
        verticesBuffer[bufferIndex++] = y1;
        verticesBuffer[bufferIndex++] = region.u1;
        verticesBuffer[bufferIndex++] = region.v2;

        verticesBuffer[bufferIndex++] = x2;
        verticesBuffer[bufferIndex++] = y2;
        verticesBuffer[bufferIndex++] = region.u2;
        verticesBuffer[bufferIndex++] = region.v2;

        verticesBuffer[bufferIndex++] = x3;
        verticesBuffer[bufferIndex++] = y3;
        verticesBuffer[bufferIndex++] = region.u2;
        verticesBuffer[bufferIndex++] = region.v1;

        verticesBuffer[bufferIndex++] = x4;
        verticesBuffer[bufferIndex++] = y4;
        verticesBuffer[bufferIndex++] = region.u1;
        verticesBuffer[bufferIndex++] = region.v1;

        numSprites++;
    }
}
```

We do the same as in the simpler drawing method, except that we construct all four corner points instead of only the two opposite ones. This is needed for the rotation. The rest is the same as before.

What about scaling? We do not explicitly need another method, since scaling a sprite only requires scaling its width and height. We can do that outside the two drawing methods, so there's no need to have another bunch of methods for scaled drawing of sprites.

And that's the big secret behind lighting-fast sprite rendering with OpenGL ES.

Using the SpriteBatcher Class

Let's incorporate the TextureRegion and SpriteBatcher classes in our cannon example. I copied the TextureAtlas example and renamed it SpriteBatcherTest. The classes contained in it are called SpriteBatcherTest and SpriteBatcherScreen.

The first thing I did was get rid of the Vertices members in the screen class. We don't need them anymore, since the SpriteBatcher will do all the dirty work for us. Instead I added the following members:

```
TextureRegion cannonRegion;
TextureRegion ballRegion;
TextureRegion bobRegion;
SpriteBatcher batcher;
```

We now have a TextureRegion for each of the three objects in our atlas, as well as a SpriteBatcher.

Next I modified the constructor of the screen. I got rid of all the Vertices instantiation and initialization code, and replaced it with a single line of code:

```
batcher = new SpriteBatcher(glGraphics, 100);
```

That will set out batcher member to a fresh SpriteBatcher instance that can render 100 sprites in one batch.

The TextureRegions get initialized in the resume() method, as they depend on the Texture:

```
@Override
public void resume() {
    texture = new Texture(((GLGame)game), "atlas.png");
    cannonRegion = new TextureRegion(texture, 0, 0, 64, 32);
    ballRegion = new TextureRegion(texture, 0, 32, 16, 16);
    bobRegion = new TextureRegion(texture, 32, 32, 32, 32);
}
```

No surprises there. The last thing we need to change is the present() method. You'll be surprised how clean it's looking now. Here it is:

```
@Override
public void present(float deltaTime) {
    GL10 gl = glGraphics.getGL();
    gl.glClear(GL10.GL_COLOR_BUFFER_BIT);
    camera.setViewportAndMatrices();

    gl.glEnable(GL10.GL_BLEND);
    gl.glBlendFunc(GL10.GL_SRC_ALPHA, GL10.GL_ONE_MINUS_SRC_ALPHA);
```

```
gl.glEnable(GL10.GL_TEXTURE_2D);

batcher.beginBatch(texture);

int len = targets.size();
for(int i = 0; i < len; i++) {
    GameObject target = targets.get(i);
    batcher.drawSprite(target.position.x, target.position.y, 0.5f, 0.5f, bobRegion);
}

batcher.drawSprite(ball.position.x, ball.position.y, 0.2f, 0.2f, ballRegion);
batcher.drawSprite(cannon.position.x, cannon.position.y, 1, 0.5f, cannon.angle,
cannonRegion);
    batcher.endBatch();
}
```

That is super sweet. The only OpenGL ES calls we issue now are for clearing the screen, enabling blending and texturing, and setting the blend function. The rest is pure SpriteBatcher and Camera2D goodness. Since all our objects share the same texture atlas, we can render them in a single batch. We call batcher.beginBatch() with the atlas texture, render all the Bob targets using the simple drawing method, render the ball (again with the simple drawing method), and finally render the cannon using the drawing method that can rotate a sprite. We end the method by calling batcher.endBatch(), which will actually transfer the geometry of our sprites to the GPU and render everything.

Measuring Performance

So how much faster is the SpriteBatcher method than the method we used in BobTest? I added an FPSCounter to the code and timed it on a Hero, a Droid, and a Nexus One, as we did in the case of BobTest. I also increased the number of targets to 100 and set the maximum number of sprites the SpriteBatcher can render to 102, since we render 100 targets, 1 ball, and 1 cannon. Here are the results:

```
Hero (1.5):
12-27 23:51:09.400: DEBUG/FPSCounter(2169): fps: 31
12-27 23:51:10.440: DEBUG/FPSCounter(2169): fps: 31
12-27 23:51:11.470: DEBUG/FPSCounter(2169): fps: 32
12-27 23:51:12.500: DEBUG/FPSCounter(2169): fps: 32

Droid (2.1.1):
12-27 23:50:23.416: DEBUG/FPSCounter(8145): fps: 56
12-27 23:50:24.448: DEBUG/FPSCounter(8145): fps: 56
12-27 23:50:25.456: DEBUG/FPSCounter(8145): fps: 56
12-27 23:50:26.456: DEBUG/FPSCounter(8145): fps: 55

Nexus One (2.2.1):
12-27 23:46:57.162: DEBUG/FPSCounter(754): fps: 61
12-27 23:46:58.171: DEBUG/FPSCounter(754): fps: 61
12-27 23:46:59.181: DEBUG/FPSCounter(754): fps: 61
12-27 23:47:00.181: DEBUG/FPSCounter(754): fps: 60
```

Before we come to any conclusions, let's test the old method as well. Since our example is not equivalent to the old BobTest, I also modified the TextureAtlasTest, which is the same as our current example—the only difference being that it uses the old BobTest method for rendering. Here are the results:

```
Hero (1.5):
12-27 23:53:45.950: DEBUG/FPSCounter(2303): fps: 46
12-27 23:53:46.720: DEBUG/dalvikvm(2303): GC freed 21811 objects / 524280 bytes in 135ms
12-27 23:53:46.970: DEBUG/FPSCounter(2303): fps: 40
12-27 23:53:47.980: DEBUG/FPSCounter(2303): fps: 46
12-27 23:53:48.990: DEBUG/FPSCounter(2303): fps: 46

Droid (2.1.1):
12-28 00:03:13.004: DEBUG/FPSCounter(8277): fps: 52
12-28 00:03:14.004: DEBUG/FPSCounter(8277): fps: 52
12-28 00:03:15.027: DEBUG/FPSCounter(8277): fps: 53
12-28 00:03:16.027: DEBUG/FPSCounter(8277): fps: 53

Nexus One (2.2.1):
12-27 23:56:09.591: DEBUG/FPSCounter(873): fps: 61
12-27 23:56:10.591: DEBUG/FPSCounter(873): fps: 60
12-27 23:56:11.601: DEBUG/FPSCounter(873): fps: 61
12-27 23:56:12.601: DEBUG/FPSCounter(873): fps: 60
```

The Hero performs a lot worse with our new SpriteBatcher method as compared to the old way of using glTranslate() and similar methods. The Droid actually benefits from the new SpriteBatcher method, and the Nexus One doesn't really care what we use. If we'd increased the number of targets by another 100, you'd see that the SpriteBatcher method would also be faster on the Nexus One.

So what's up with the Hero? The problem in BobTest was that we called too many OpenGL ES methods, so why is it performing worse now that we're fewer OpenGL ES method calls?

Working Around a Bug in FloatBuffer

The reason for this isn't obvious at all. Our SpriteBatcher puts a float array into a direct ByteBuffer each frame when we call Vertices.setVertices(). The method boils down to calling FloatBuffer.put(float[]), and that's the culprit of our performance hit here. While desktop Java implements that FloatBuffer method via a real bulk memory move, the Harmony version calls FloatBuffer.put(float) for each element in the array. And that's extremely unfortunate, as that method is a JNI method, which has a lot of overhead (much like the OpenGL ES methods, which are also JNI methods).

There are a couple of solutions. IntBuffer.put(int[]) does not suffer from this problem, for example. We could replace the FloatBuffer in our Vertices class with an IntBuffer and modify Vertices.setVertices() so that it first transfers the floats from the float array to a temporary int array and then copies the contents of that int array to the IntBuffer. This solution was proposed by Ryan McNally, a fellow game developer, who also reported the bug on the Android bug tracker. It produces a five-times performance increase on the Hero, and a little less on other Android devices.

I modified the Vertices class to include this fix. For this I changed the vertices member to be an IntBuffer. I also added a new member called tmpBuffer, which is an int[] array. The tmpBuffer array is initialized in the constructor of Vertices as follows:

```
this.tmpBuffer = new int[maxVertices * vertexSize / 4];
```

We also get an IntBuffer view from the ByteBuffer in the constructor instead of a FloatBuffer:

```
vertices = buffer.asIntBuffer();
```

And the Vertices.setVertices() method looks like this now:

```
public void setVertices(float[] vertices, int offset, int length) {
    this.vertices.clear();
    int len = offset + length;
    for(int i=offset, j=0; i < len; i++, j++)
        tmpBuffer[j] = Float.floatToRawIntBits(vertices[i]);
    this.vertices.put(tmpBuffer, 0, length);
    this.vertices.flip();
}
```

So, all we do is first transfer the contents of the vertices parameter to the tmpBuffer. The static method Float.floatToRawIntBits() reinterprets the bit pattern of a float as an int. We then just need to copy the contents of the int array to the IntBuffer, formerly known as a FloatBuffer. Does it improve performance? Running the SpriteBatcherTest produces the following output now on the Hero, Droid, and Nexus One:

```
Hero (1.5):
12-28 00:24:54.770: DEBUG/FPSCounter(2538): fps: 61
12-28 00:24:54.770: DEBUG/FPSCounter(2538): fps: 61
12-28 00:24:55.790: DEBUG/FPSCounter(2538): fps: 62
12-28 00:24:55.790: DEBUG/FPSCounter(2538): fps: 62

Droid (2.1.1):
12-28 00:35:48.242: DEBUG/FPSCounter(1681): fps: 61
12-28 00:35:49.258: DEBUG/FPSCounter(1681): fps: 62
12-28 00:35:50.258: DEBUG/FPSCounter(1681): fps: 60
12-28 00:35:51.266: DEBUG/FPSCounter(1681): fps: 59

Nexus One (2.2.1):
12-28 00:27:39.642: DEBUG/FPSCounter(1006): fps: 61
12-28 00:27:40.652: DEBUG/FPSCounter(1006): fps: 61
12-28 00:27:41.662: DEBUG/FPSCounter(1006): fps: 61
12-28 00:27:42.662: DEBUG/FPSCounter(1006): fps: 61
```

Yes, I double-checked; this is not a typo. The Hero really achieves 60 FPS now. A workaround consisting of five lines of code increases our performance by 50 percent. The Droid also benefited from this fix a little.

The problem is fixed in the latest release of Android version 2.3. However, it will be quite some time before most phones run this version, so we should keep this workaround for the time being.

> **NOTE:** There's another, even faster workaround. It involves a custom JNI method that does the memory move in native code. You can find it if you search for the "Android Game Development Wiki" on the Net. I use this most of the time instead of the pure Java workaround. However, including JNI methods is a bit more complex, which is why I described the pure-Java workaround here.

Sprite Animation

If you've ever played a 2D video game, you know that we are still missing one vital component: sprite animation. The animation consists of so-called *keyframes*, which produce the illusion of movement. Figure 8–25 shows a nice animated sprite by Ari Feldmann (part of his royalty-free SpriteLib).

Figure 8–25. *A walking caveman, by Ari Feldmann (grid not in original)*

The image is 256×64 pixels in size, and each keyframe is 64×64 pixels. To produce animation, we just draw a sprite using the first keyframe for some amount of time—say, 0.25 seconds—then we switch to the next keyframe, and so on. When we reach the last frame we have two options: we can stay at the last keyframe or start at the beginning again (and perform what is called a *looping animation*).

We can easily do this with our `TextureRegion` and `SpriteBatcher` classes. Usually we'd not only have a single animation like in Figure 8–25, but many more in a single atlas. Besides the walk animation, we could have a jump animation, an attack animation, and so on. For each animation we need to know the frame duration, which tells us how long we keep using a single keyframe of the animation before we switch to the next frame.

The Animation Class

From this we can define the requirements for an Animation class, which stores the data for a single animation, such as the walk animation in Figure 8–25:

- An Animation holds a number of TextureRegions, which store where in the texture atlas each keyframe is located. The order of the TextureRegions is the same as that used for playing back the animation.

- The Animation also stores the frame duration that has to pass before we switch to the next frame.

- The Animation should provide us with a method to which we pass the time we've been in the state that the Animation represents (e.g., walking left), and that will return the appropriate TextureRegion. The method should take into consideration whether we want the Animation to loop or to stay at the last frame when the end is reached.

This last bullet point is important because it allows us to store a single Animation instance to be used by multiple objects in our world. An object just keeps track of its current state (e.g., whether it is walking, shooting, or jumping, and how long it has been in that state). When we render this object, we use the state to select the animation we want to play back, and the state time to get the correct TextureRegion from the Animation. Listing 8–19 shows the code of our new Animation class.

Listing 8–19. *Animation.java, a Simple Animation Class*

```java
package com.badlogic.androidgames.framework.gl;

public class Animation {
    public static final int ANIMATION_LOOPING = 0;
    public static final int ANIMATION_NONLOOPING = 1;

    final TextureRegion[] keyFrames;
    final float frameDuration;

    public Animation(float frameDuration, TextureRegion ... keyFrames) {
        this.frameDuration = frameDuration;
        this.keyFrames = keyFrames;
    }

    public TextureRegion getKeyFrame(float stateTime, int mode) {
        int frameNumber = (int)(stateTime / frameDuration);

        if(mode == ANIMATION_NONLOOPING) {
            frameNumber = Math.min(keyFrames.length-1, frameNumber);
        } else {
            frameNumber = frameNumber % keyFrames.length;
        }
        return keyFrames[frameNumber];
    }
}
```

We first define two constants to be used with the getKeyFrame() method. The first one says the animation should be looping, and the other one says that is should stop at the last frame.

Next we define two members: an array holding the TextureRegions and a float storing the frame duration.

We pass the frame duration and the TextureRegions that hold the keyframes to the constructor, which simply stores them. We could make a defensive copy of the keyFrames array, but that would allocate a new object, which would make the garbage collector a little mad.

The interesting piece is the getKeyFrame() method. We pass in the time that the object has been in the state that the animation represents, as well as the mode, either Animation.ANIMATION_LOOPING or Animation.NON_LOOPING. We first calculate how many frames have already been played for the given state based on the stateTime. In case the animation shouldn't be looping, we simply clamp the frameNumber to the last element in the TextureRegion array. Otherwise, we take the modulus, which will automatically create the looping effect we desire (e.g., 4 % 3 = 1). All that's left is returning the proper TextureRegion.

An Example

Let's create an example called AnimationTest with a corresponding screen called AnimationScreen. As always we'll only discuss the screen itself.

We want to render a number of cavemen, all walking to the left. Our world will be the same size as our view frustum, which has the size 4.8×3.2 meters (this is really arbitrary; we could use any size). A caveman is a DynamicGameObject with a size of 1×1 meters. We will derive from DynamicGameObject and create a new class called Caveman, which will store an additional member that keeps track of how long the caveman has been walking already. Each caveman will move 0.5 m/s either to the left or to the right. We'll also add an update() method to the Caveman class to update the caveman's position based on the delta time and his velocity. If a caveman reaches the left or right edge of our world, we set him to the other side of the world. We'll use the image in Figure 8–25 and create TextureRegions and an Animation instance accordingly. For rendering we'll use a Camera2D instance and a SpriteBatcher because they are fancy. Listing 8–20 shows the code of the Caveman class.

Listing 8–20. *Excerpt from AnimationTest, Showing the Inner Caveman Class.*

```
static final float WORLD_WIDTH = 4.8f;
static final float WORLD_HEIGHT = 3.2f;

static class Caveman extends DynamicGameObject {
    public float walkingTime = 0;

    public Caveman(float x, float y, float width, float height) {
        super(x, y, width, height);
        this.position.set((float)Math.random() * WORLD_WIDTH,
```

```
                                (float)Math.random() * WORLD_HEIGHT);
        this.velocity.set(Math.random() > 0.5f?-0.5f:0.5f, 0);
        this.walkingTime = (float)Math.random() * 10;
    }

    public void update(float deltaTime) {
        position.add(velocity.x * deltaTime, velocity.y * deltaTime);
        if(position.x < 0) position.x = WORLD_WIDTH;
        if(position.x > WORLD_WIDTH) position.x = 0;
        walkingTime += deltaTime;
    }
}
```

The two constants WORLD_WIDTH and WORLD_HEIGHT are part of the enclosing AnimationTest class and are used by the inner classes. Our world is 4.8×3.2 meters in size.

Next up is the inner Caveman class, which extends DynamicGameObject, since we will move cavemen based on velocity. We define an additional member that keeps track of how long the caveman is walking already. In the constructor we place the caveman at a random position and let him either walk left or right. We also initialize the walkingTime member to a number between 0 and 10; this way our cavemen won't walk in sync.

The update() method advances the caveman based on his velocity and the delta time. In case he leaves the world, we reset him to either the left or right edge. We also add the delta time to the walkingTime to keep track of how long he's been walking.

Listing 8–21 shows the AnimationScreen class.

Listing 8–21. *Excerpt from AnimationTest.java: The AnimationScreen Class*

```
class AnimationScreen extends Screen {
    static final int NUM_CAVEMEN = 10;
    GLGraphics glGraphics;
    Caveman[] cavemen;
    SpriteBatcher batcher;
    Camera2D camera;
    Texture texture;
    Animation walkAnim;
```

Our screen class has the usual suspects as members. We have a GLGraphics instance, a Caveman array, a SpriteBatcher, a Camera2D, the Texture containing the walking keyframes, and an Animation instance.

```
    public AnimationScreen(Game game) {
        super(game);
        glGraphics = ((GLGame)game).getGLGraphics();
        cavemen = new Caveman[NUM_CAVEMEN];
        for(int i = 0; i < NUM_CAVEMEN; i++) {
            cavemen[i] = new Caveman((float)Math.random(), (float)Math.random(), 1, 1);
        }
        batcher = new SpriteBatcher(glGraphics, NUM_CAVEMEN);
        camera = new Camera2D(glGraphics, WORLD_WIDTH, WORLD_HEIGHT);
    }
```

In the constructor we create the Caveman instances, as well as the SpriteBatcher and Camera2D.

```
@Override
public void resume() {
    texture = new Texture(((GLGame)game), "walkanim.png");
    walkAnim = new Animation( 0.2f,
                              new TextureRegion(texture, 0, 0, 64, 64),
                              new TextureRegion(texture, 64, 0, 64, 64),
                              new TextureRegion(texture, 128, 0, 64, 64),
                              new TextureRegion(texture, 192, 0, 64, 64));
}
```

In the resume() method we load the texture atlas containing the animation keyframes from the asset file walkanim.png, which is the same as in Figure 8–25. Afterward, we create the Animation instance, setting the frame duration to 0.2 seconds and passing in a TextureRegion for each of the keyframes in the texture atlas.

```
@Override
public void update(float deltaTime) {
    int len = cavemen.length;
    for(int i = 0; i < len; i++) {
        cavemen[i].update(deltaTime);
    }
}
```

The update() method just loops over all Caveman instances and calls their Caveman.update() method with the current delta time. This will make the cavemen move and update their walking times.

```
@Override
public void present(float deltaTime) {
    GL10 gl = glGraphics.getGL();
    gl.glClear(GL10.GL_COLOR_BUFFER_BIT);
    camera.setViewportAndMatrices();

    gl.glEnable(GL10.GL_BLEND);
    gl.glBlendFunc(GL10.GL_SRC_ALPHA, GL10.GL_ONE_MINUS_SRC_ALPHA);
    gl.glEnable(GL10.GL_TEXTURE_2D);

    batcher.beginBatch(texture);
    int len = cavemen.length;
    for(int i = 0; i < len; i++) {
        Caveman caveman = cavemen[i];
        TextureRegion keyFrame = walkAnim.getKeyFrame(caveman.walkingTime,
Animation.ANIMATION_LOOPING);
        batcher.drawSprite(caveman.position.x, caveman.position.y,
caveman.velocity.x < 0?1:-1, 1, keyFrame);
    }
    batcher.endBatch();
}

@Override
public void pause() {
}
```

```
    @Override
    public void dispose() {
    }
}
```

Finally we have the `present()` method. We start off by clearing the screen and setting the viewport and projection matrix via our camera. Next we enable blending and texture mapping, and set the blend function. We start rendering by telling the sprite batcher that we want to start a new batch using the animation texture atlas. Next we loop through all the cavemen and render them. For each caveman we first fetch the correct keyframe from the `Animation` instance based on the caveman's walking time. We specify that the animation should be looping. Then we draw the caveman with the correct texture region at his position.

But what do we do with the `width` parameter here? Remember that our animation texture only contains keyframes for the "walk left" animation. We want to flip the texture horizontally in case the caveman is walking to the right, which we can do by simply specifying a negative width. If you don't trust me, go back to the `SpriteBatcher` code and check whether this works. We essentially flip the rectangle of the sprite by specifying a negative width. We could do the same vertically as well by specifying a negative height.

Figure 8–26 shows our walking cavemen.

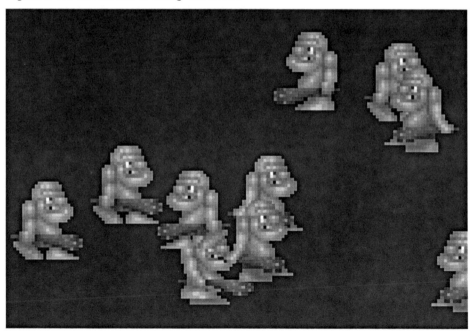

Figure 8–26. *Cavemen walking*

And that is all there is to know to produce a nice 2D game with OpenGL ES. Note how we still separate the game logic and the presentation from each other. A caveman does not need to know that he is actually being rendered. He therefore doesn't keep any rendering-related members, such as an `Animation` instance or a `Texture`. All we need to do is keep track of the state of the caveman and how long he's been in that state. Together with his position and size, we can then render him easily by using our little helper classes.

Summary

You should now be well equipped to create almost any 2D game you want. We discussed vectors and how to work with them, resulting in a nice, reusable `Vector2` class. We also looked into basic physics for creating things like ballistic cannonballs. Collision detection is also a vital part of most games, and you should now know how to do it correctly and efficiently via a `SpatialHashGrid`. We explored a way to keep our game logic and objects separated from the rendering by creating `GameObject` and `DynamicGameObject` classes that keep track of the state and shape of objects. We covered how easy it is to implement the concept of a 2D camera via OpenGL ES, all based on a single method called `glOrthof()`. We discussed texture atlases, why we need them, and how we can use them. We expanded on the concept by introducing texture regions, sprites, and how we can render them efficiently via a `SpriteBatcher`. Finally we looked into sprite animation, which turns out to be extremely simple to implement.

In the next chapter, we'll create a new game with all the new tools we have. You'll be surprised how easy that will be.

Chapter 9

Super Jumper: A 2D OpenGL ES Game

Time to put all we've learned together into a game. As discussed in Chapter 3, there are a couple of very popular genres in the mobile space we can choose from. For our next game I decided to go the more casual route. We'll implement a jump-'em-up game similar to Abduction or Doodle Jump. As with Mr. Nom, we start by defining our game mechanics.

Core Game Mechanics

I'd suggest you quickly install Abduction on your Android phone or look up videos of it on the Web. From this example we can condense the core game mechanics of our game, which will be called Super Jumper. Here are some details:

- The protagonist is constantly jumping upward, moving from platform to platform. The game world spans multiple screens vertically.

- Horizontal movement can be controlled by tilting the phone to the left or right.

- When the protagonist leaves one of the horizontal screen boundaries, he reenters the screen on the opposite side.

- Platforms can be static or moving horizontally.

- Some platforms will be pulverized randomly when the protagonist hits them.

- Along the way up, the protagonist can collect items to score points.

- Besides coins, there are also springs on some platforms that will make the protagonist jump higher.

- Evil forces populate the game world, moving horizontally. When our protagonist hits one of them, he dies and the game is over.

- When our protagonist falls below the bottom edge of the screen, the game is over as well.

- At the top of the level is some sort of goal. When the protagonist hits that goal, a new level begins.

While the list is longer than the one we created for Mr. Nom, it doesn't seem a lot more complex. Figure 9–1 shows an initial mock-up of the core principles. This time I went straight to Paint.NET for creating the mock-up. Let's come up with a backstory.

Figure 9–1. *Our initial game mechanics mock-up, showing the protagonist, platforms, coins, evil forces, and goal at the top of the level*

A Backstory and Art Style

We are going to be totally creative here and come up with the following unique story for our game.

Bob, our protagonist, suffers from chronic jumperitis. He is doomed to jump every time he touches the ground. Even worse, his beloved princess, which shall remain nameless, was kidnapped by an evil army of flying killer squirrels and placed in a castle in the sky.

Bob's condition proves beneficial after all, and he begins the hunt for his loved one, battling the evil squirrel forces.

This classic video game story lends itself well to an 8-bit graphics style that can be found in games such as the original Super Mario Brothers on the NES. The mock-up in Figure 9–1 shows the final game graphics for all the elements of our game. Bob, coins, squirrels, and pulverized platforms are of course animated. We'll also use music and sound effects that fit our visual style.

Screens and Transitions

We are now able to define our screens and transitions. We'll follow the same formula we used in Mr. Nom:

- We'll have a main screen with a logo; PLAY, HIGHSCORES, and HELP menu items; and a button to disable and enable sound.

- We'll have a game screen that will ask the player to get ready and handle running, paused, game-over, and next-level states gracefully. The only new addition to what we used in Mr. Nom will be the next-level state of the screen, which will be triggered once Bob hits the castle. In that case a new level will be generated, and Bob will start at the bottom of the world again, keeping his score.

- We'll have a high-scores screen that will show the top five scores the player has achieved so far.

- We'll have help screens that present the game mechanics and goals to the player. We'll be sneaky and leave out a description of how to control the player. Kids these days should be able to handle the complexity we faced back in the '80s and early '90s, when games didn't tell you how to play them.

That is more or less the same as what we had in Mr. Nom. Figure 9–2 shows all screens and transitions. Note that we don't have any buttons on the game screen or its subscreens, except for the pause button. Users will intuitively touch the screen when asked to be ready.

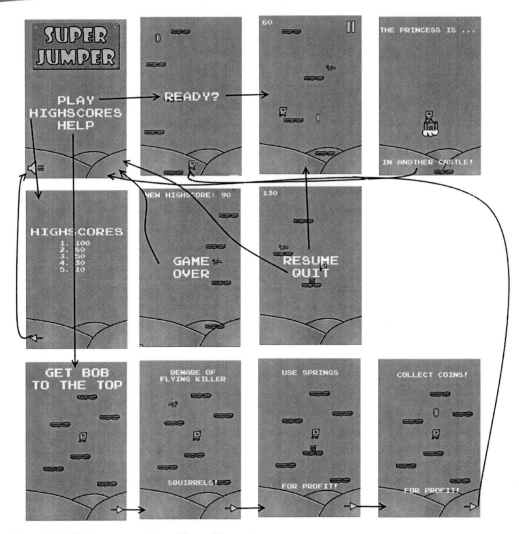

Figure 9–2. *All the screens and transitions of Super Jumper*

With that out of our way, we can now think about our world's size and units, as well as how that maps to the graphical assets.

Defining the Game World

The classic chicken-and-egg problem haunts us again. You learned in the last chapter that we have a correspondence between world units (e.g., meters) and pixels. Our objects are defined physically in world space. Bounding shapes and positions are given in meters, velocities are given in meters per second. The graphical representations of our objects are defined in pixels, though, so we have to have some sort of mapping. We overcome this problem by first defining a target resolution for our graphical assets. As with Mr. Nom we will use a target resolution of 320×480 pixels (aspect ratio of 1.5). The next thing we have to do is establish a correspondence between pixels and meters in our world. The mock-up in Figure 9–1 gives us a sense of how much screen space different objects use, as well as their proportions relative to each other. I usually choose a mapping of 32 pixels to 1 meter for 2D games. So let's overlay our mock-up, which is 320×380 pixels in size with a grid where each cell is 32×32 pixels. In our world space this would map to 1×1 meter cells. Figure 9–3 shows our mock-up and the grid.

Figure 9–3. *The mock-up overlaid with a grid. Each cell is 32×32 pixels and corresponds to a 1×1-meter area in the game world.*

Figure 9–3 is of course a little bit cheated. I arranged the graphics in a way so that they line up nicely with the grid cells. In the real game we'll place the objects at noninteger positions.

So what can we make of Figure 9–3? First of all we can directly estimate the width and height of each object in our world in meters. Here are the values we'll use for the bounding rectangles of our objects:

- Bob is 0.8×0.8 meters; he does not entirely span a complete cell.

- A platform is 2×0.5 meters, taking up two cells horizontally and half a cell vertically.

- A coin is 0.8×0.5 meters. It nearly spans a cell vertically and takes up roughly half a cell horizontally.

- A spring is 0.5×0.5 meters, talking up half a cell in each direction. The spring is actually a little bit taller than it is wide. We make its bounding shape square so that the collision testing is a little bit more forgiving.

- A squirrel is 1×0.8 meters.

- A castle is 0.8×0.8 meters.

With those sizes we also have the sizes of the bounding rectangles of our objects for collision detection. We can adjust them if they turn out to be a little too big or small depending on how the game plays out with those values.

Another thing we can derive from Figure 9–3 is the size of our view frustum. It will show us 10×15 meters of our world.

The only thing left to define are the velocities and accelerations we have in the game. This is highly dependent on how we want our game to feel. Usually you'd have to do some experimentation to get those values right. Here's what I came up with after a few iterations of tuning:

- The gravity acceleration vector is (0,–13) m/s², slightly more than what we have here on earth and what we used in our cannon example.

- Bob's initial jump velocity vector is (0,11) m/s. Note that the jump velocity only affects the movement on the y-axis. The horizontal movement will be defined by the current accelerometer readings.

- Bob's jump velocity vector will be 1.5 times his normal jump velocity when he hits a spring. That's equivalent to (0,16.5) m/s. Again, this value is purely derived from experimentation.

- Bob's horizontal movement speed is 20 m/s. Note that that's a directionless speed, not a vector. I'll explain in a minute how that works together with the accelerometer.

- The squirrels will patrol from the left to the right and back continuously. They'll have a constant movement speed of 3 m/s. Expressed as a vector that's either (–3,0) m/s if the squirrel moves to the left or (3,0) m/s if the squirrel moves to the right.

So how will Bob's horizontal movement work? The movement speed we defined before is actually Bob's maximum horizontal speed. Depending on how much the player tilts her phone, Bob's horizontal movement speed will be between 0 (no tilt) and 20 m/s (fully tilted to one side).

We'll use the value of the accelerometer's x-axis since our game will run in portrait mode. When the phone is not tilted, the axis will report an acceleration of 0 m/s². When fully tilted to the left so that the phone is in landscape orientation, the axis will report roughly –10 m/s². When fully tilted to the right the axis will report an acceleration of roughly 10 m/s². All we need to do is normalize the accelerometer reading by dividing it by the maximum absolute value (10) and then multiply Bob's maximum horizontal speed by that. Bob will thus travel 20 m/s to the left or right when the phone is fully tilted to one side and less if the phone is tilted less. Bob can move around the screen twice per second when the phone is fully tilted.

We'll update this horizontal movement velocity each frame based on the current accelerometer value on the x-axis, and combine it with Bob's vertical velocity, which is derived from the gravity acceleration and his current vertical velocity, as we did for the cannonball in the earlier examples.

One essential aspect of the world is the portion we see of it. Since Bob will die when he leaves the screen on the bottom edge, our camera also plays a role in the game mechanics. While we'll use a camera for rendering and move it upward when Bob jumps, we won't use it in our world simulation classes. Instead we record Bob's highest y-coordinate so far. If he's below that value minus half the view frustum height, we know he has left the screen. We thus don't have a completely clean separation between the model (our world simulation classes) and the view, since we need to know the view frustum's height to determine whether Bob is dead or not. We can live with this, I'd say.

Let's have a look at the assets we need.

Creating the Assets

Our new game has two types of graphical assets: UI elements and actual game, or world, elements. Let's start with the UI elements.

The UI Elements

The first thing to notice is that the UI elements (buttons, logos, etc.) do not depend on our pixel-to-world unit mapping. As in Mr. Nom we design them to fit a target resolution—in our case 320×480 pixels. Looking at Figure 9–2 we can determine which UI elements we have.

The first UI elements we create are the buttons we need for the different screens. Figure 9–4 shows all the buttons of our game.

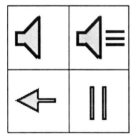

Figure 9–4. *Various buttons, each 64×64 pixels in size*

I always like to create all graphical assets in a grid with cells having sizes of 32×32 or 64×64 pixels. The buttons in Figure 9–4 are laid out in a grid with each cell having 64×64 pixels. The buttons in the top row are used on the main menu screen to signal whether sound is enabled or not. The arrow at the bottom left is used in a couple of screens to navigate to the next screen. The button in the bottom right is used in the game screen when the game is running to allow the user to pause the game.

You might wonder why there's no arrow pointing to the right. Remember that with our fancy sprite batcher we can easily flip things we draw by specifying negative width and/or height values. We'll use that trick for a couple of graphical assets to save some memory.

Next up are the elements we need on the main menu screen. There we have a logo, the menu entries, and the background. Figure 9–5 shows all those elements.

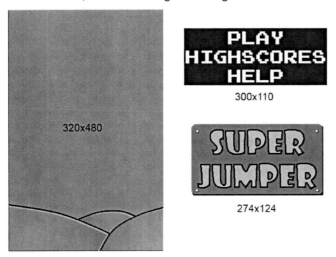

Figure 9–5. *The background image, the main menu entries, and the logo*

The background image is used not only on the main menu screen, but on all screens. It is the same size as our target resolution, 320×480 pixels. The main menu entries make up 300×110 pixels. The black background you see in Figure 9–5 is there since white on white wouldn't look all that good. In the actual image, the background is made up of transparent pixels, of course. The logo is 274×142 pixels with some transparent pixels at the corners.

Next up are the help screen images. Instead of compositing each of them with a couple of elements, I was lazy and made them all full-screen images of size 320×480 instead. That will reduce the size of our drawing code a little while not adding at lot to our program's size. You can see all of the help screens in Figure 9–2. The only thing we'll composite these images with is the arrow button.

For the high-scores screen we'll reuse the portion of the main menu entries image that says HIGHSCORES. The actual scores are rendered with a special technique we'll look into later on in this chapter. The rest of that screen is again composed of the background image and a button.

The game screen has a few more textual UI elements, namely the READY? label, the menu entries for the paused state (RESUME and QUIT), and the GAME OVER label. Figure 9–6 shows them in all their glory.

Figure 9–6. *The READY?, RESUME, QUIT, and GAME OVER labels*

Handling Text with Bitmap Fonts

So, how do we render the other textual elements in the game screen? With the same technique we used in Mr. Nom to render the scores. Instead of just having numbers, we also have characters now. We use an image atlas where each subimage represents on character (e.g., *0* or *a*). This image atlas is called a bitmap font. Figure 9–7 shows the bitmap font we'll use.

Figure 9–7. *A bitmap font*

The black background and the grid in figure 9–7 are of course not part of the actual image. Bitmap fonts are a very old technique to render text on the screen in a game. They usually contain images for a range of ASCII characters. One such character image is referred to as a *glyph*. ASCII is one of the predecessors of Unicode. There are 128 characters in the ASCII character set, as shown in Figure 9–8.

ASCII Table

Dec	Hex	Oct	Char	Dec	Hex	Oct	Char	Dec	Hex	Oct	Char	Dec	Hex	Oct	Char
0	0	0		32	20	40	[space]	64	40	100	@	96	60	140	`
1	1	1		33	21	41	!	65	41	101	A	97	61	141	a
2	2	2		34	22	42	"	66	42	102	B	98	62	142	b
3	3	3		35	23	43	#	67	43	103	C	99	63	143	c
4	4	4		36	24	44	$	68	44	104	D	100	64	144	d
5	5	5		37	25	45	%	69	45	105	E	101	65	145	e
6	6	6		38	26	46	&	70	46	106	F	102	66	146	f
7	7	7		39	27	47	'	71	47	107	G	103	67	147	g
8	8	10		40	28	50	(	72	48	110	H	104	68	150	h
9	9	11		41	29	51	)	73	49	111	I	105	69	151	i
10	A	12		42	2A	52	*	74	4A	112	J	106	6A	152	j
11	B	13		43	2B	53	+	75	4B	113	K	107	6B	153	k
12	C	14		44	2C	54	,	76	4C	114	L	108	6C	154	l
13	D	15		45	2D	55	-	77	4D	115	M	109	6D	155	m
14	E	16		46	2E	56	.	78	4E	116	N	110	6E	156	n
15	F	17		47	2F	57	/	79	4F	117	O	111	6F	157	o
16	10	20		48	30	60	0	80	50	120	P	112	70	160	p
17	11	21		49	31	61	1	81	51	121	Q	113	71	161	q
18	12	22		50	32	62	2	82	52	122	R	114	72	162	r
19	13	23		51	33	63	3	83	53	123	S	115	73	163	s
20	14	24		52	34	64	4	84	54	124	T	116	74	164	t
21	15	25		53	35	65	5	85	55	125	U	117	75	165	u
22	16	26		54	36	66	6	86	56	126	V	118	76	166	v
23	17	27		55	37	67	7	87	57	127	W	119	77	167	w
24	18	30		56	38	70	8	88	58	130	X	120	78	170	x
25	19	31		57	39	71	9	89	59	131	Y	121	79	171	y
26	1A	32		58	3A	72	:	90	5A	132	Z	122	7A	172	z
27	1B	33		59	3B	73	;	91	5B	133	[	123	7B	173	{
28	1C	34		60	3C	74	<	92	5C	134	\	124	7C	174		
29	1D	35		61	3D	75	=	93	5D	135	]	125	7D	175	}
30	1E	36		62	3E	76	>	94	5E	136	^	126	7E	176	~
31	1F	37		63	3F	77	?	95	5F	137	_	127	7F	177	

Figure 9–8. *ASCII characters and their decimal, hexadecimal, and octal values*

Out of those 128 characters, 96 are printable (characters 32 to 127). Our bitmap font only contains printable characters. The first row in the bitmap font contains the characters 32 to 47, the next row contains the characters 48 to 63, and so on. ASCII is only useful if you want to store and display text that uses the standard Latin alphabet. There's an extended ASCII format that uses the values 128 to 255 to encode other common characters of Western languages, such as ö or é. More expressive character sets (e.g., for Chinese or Arabic) are represented via Unicode, and can't be encoded via ASCII. For our game, the standard ASCII character set suffices, though.

So how do we render text with a bitmap font? That turns out to be really easy. First we create 96 texture regions, each mapping to a glyph in the bitmap font. We can store those texture regions in an array like this:

```
TextureRegion[] glyphs = new TextureRegion[96];
```

Java strings are encoded in 16-bit Unicode. Luckily for us, the ASCII characters we have in our bitmap font have the same values in ASCII and Unicode. To fetch the region for a character in a Java string, we just need to do this:

```
int index = string.charAt(i) - 32;
```

This gives us a direct index into the texture region array. We just subtract the value for the space character (32) from the current character in the string. If the index is smaller than zero or bigger than 95, we have a Unicode character that is not in our bitmap font. Usually we just ignore such a character.

To render multiple characters in a line, we need to know how much space there should be between characters. The bitmap font in Figure 9–7 is a so-called fixed-width font. That means that each glyph has the same width. Our bitmap font glyphs have a size of 16×20 pixels each. When we advance our rendering position from character to character in a string, we just need to add 20 pixels. The number of pixels we move the drawing position from character to character is called *advance*. For our bitmap font it is fixed, but in general it is variable depending on the character we draw. A more complex form of *advance* takes both the current character we are about to draw and the next character into consideration for calculating the advance. This technique is called *kerning*, if you want to look it up on the Web. We'll only use fixed-width bitmap fonts, as they make our lives considerably easier.

So, how did I generate that ASCII bitmap font? I used one of the many tools available on the Web for generating bitmap fonts. The one I used is called Codehead's Bitmap Font Generator and is freely available. You can select a font file on your hard drive and specify the height of the font, and the generator will produce an image from it for the ASCII character set. The tool has a lot more options I can't discuss here. I recommend checking it out yourself and playing around with it a little.

We'll draw all the remaining strings in our game with this technique. Later you'll see a concrete implementation of a bitmap font class. Let's get on with our assets.

With the bitmap font we now have assets for all our graphical UI elements. We will render them via a `SpriteBatcher` using a camera that sets up a view frustum that directly maps to our target resolution. This way we can specify all the coordinates in pixel coordinates.

The Game Elements

What's left are the actual game objects. Those are dependent on our pixel-to-world unit mappings, as discussed earlier. To make the creation of those as easy as possible, I used a little trick: I started each drawing with a grid of 32×32 pixels per cell. All the objects are centered in one or more such cells, so that they correspond easily with the physical sizes they have in our world. Let's start with Bob, depicted in Figure 9–9.

Figure 9–9. *Bob and his five animation frames.*

Figure 9–9 shows two frames for jumping, two frames for falling, and one frame for being dead. The image is 160×32 pixels in size, and each animation frame is 32×32 pixels in size. The background pixels are transparent.

Bob can be in three states: jumping, falling, and being dead. We have animation frames for each of these states. Granted, the difference between the two jumping frames is minor—only his forelock is wiggling. We'll create an `Animation` instance for each of the three animations of Bob and use them for rendering according to his current state. We also don't have duplicate frames for Bob heading left. As with the arrow button, we'll just specify a negative width with the SpriteBatcher.drawSprite() call to flip Bob's image horizontally.

Figure 9–10 depicts the evil squirrel. We have two animation frames again, so the squirrel appears to by flapping its evil wings.

Figure 9–10. *An evil flying squirrel and its two animation frames.*

The image in figure 9–10 is 64×32 pixels, and each frame is 32×32 pixels.

The coin animation in Figure 9–11 is special. Our keyframe sequence will not be 1, 2, 3, 1, but 1, 2, 3, 2, 1. Otherwise the coin would go from its collapsed state in frame 3 to its fully extended state in frame 1. We can conserve a little space by reusing the second frame.

Figure 9–11. *The coin and its animation frames.*

The image in figure 9–11 is 96×32 pixels, and each frame is 32×32 pixels.

Not a lot has to be said about the spring image in Figure 9–12. The spring just sits there happily in the center of the image.

Figure 9–12. *The spring. The image is 32×32 pixels.*

The castle in Figure 9–13 is also not animated. It is bigger than the other objects (64×64 pixels).

Figure 9–13. *The castle*

The platform in Figure 9–14 (64x64 pixels) has four animation frames. According to our game mechanics, some platforms will be pulverized when Bob hits them. We'll play back the full animation of the platform in that case once. For static platforms we'll just use the first frame.

Figure 9–14. *The platform and its animation frames.*

Texture Atlas to the Rescue

That's all the graphical assets we have in our game. Now, we already talked about how textures need to have power-of-two widths and heights. Our background image and all the help screens have a size of 320×480 pixels. We'll store those in 512×512-pixel images so we can load them as textures. That's already six textures.

Do we create separate textures for all the other images as well? No. We create a single texture atlas. It turns out that everything else fits nicely in a single 512×512 pixel atlas, which we can load as a single texture—something that will make the GPU really happy, since we only need to bind one texture for all game elements, except the background and help screen images. Figure 9–15 shows the atlas.

Figure 9–15. *The mighty texture atlas.*

The image in figure 9–15 is 512×512 pixels in size. The grids and red outlines are not part of the image, and the background pixels are transparent. This is also true for the black background pixels of the UI labels and the bitmap font. The grid cells are 32×32 pixels in size.

I placed all the images in the atlas at corners with coordinates that are multiples of 32. This makes creating TextureRegions easier.

Music and Sound

We also need sound effects and music. Since our game is an 8-bit retro-style game, it's fitting to use so-called *chip tunes*. Chip tunes are sound effects and music generated by a synthesizer. The most famous chip tunes were generated by Nintendo's NES, SNES and GameBoy. For the sound effects I used a tool called sfxr, by Tomas Pettersson (or rather the Flash version, called as3sfxr). It can be found at www.superflashbros.net/as3sfxr. Figure 9–16 shows its user interface.

Figure 9–16. *as3sfxr, a Flash port of sfxr, by Tomas Pettersson*

I created sound effects for jumping, hitting a spring, hitting a coin, and hitting a squirrel. I also created a sound effect for clicking UI elements. All I did was mash the buttons to the left of as3sfxr for each category until I found a fitting sound effect.

Music for games is usually a little bit harder to come by. There are a few sites on the Web that feature 8-bit chip tunes fitting for a game like Super Jumper. We'll use a single song called "New Song," by Geir Tjelta. The song can be found at www.freemusicarchive.org. It's licensed under the Creative Commons Attribution-NonCommercial-NoDerivatives (aka Music Sharing) license. This means we can use it in noncommercial projects such as our open source Super Jumper game as long as we give attribution to Geir and don't modify the original piece. When you scout the Web for music to be used in your games, always make sure that you adhere to the license. People put a lot of work into those songs. If the license doesn't fit your project (e.g., if it is a commercial one), then you can't use it.

Implementing Super Jumper

Implementing Super Jumper will be pretty easy. We can reuse our complete framework from the previous chapter and follow the architecture we had in Mr. Nom on a high level. This means we'll have a class for each screen, and each of these classes will implement the logic and presentation expected from that screen. Besides that, we'll also have our standard project setup with a proper manifest file, all our assets in the assets/ folder, an icon for our application, and so on. Let's start with our main Assets class.

The Assets Class

In Mr. Nom we already had an Assets class that consisted only of a metric ton of Pixmap and Sound references held in static member variables. We'll do the same in Super Jumper. This time we'll add a little loading logic, though. Listing 9–1 shows the code.

Listing 9–1. *Assets.java, Which Holds All Our Assets Except for the Help Screen Textures*

```java
package com.badlogic.androidgames.jumper;

import com.badlogic.androidgames.framework.Music;
import com.badlogic.androidgames.framework.Sound;
import com.badlogic.androidgames.framework.gl.Animation;
import com.badlogic.androidgames.framework.gl.Font;
import com.badlogic.androidgames.framework.gl.Texture;
import com.badlogic.androidgames.framework.gl.TextureRegion;
import com.badlogic.androidgames.framework.impl.GLGame;

public class Assets {
    public static Texture background;
    public static TextureRegion backgroundRegion;

    public static Texture items;
    public static TextureRegion mainMenu;
    public static TextureRegion pauseMenu;
    public static TextureRegion ready;
    public static TextureRegion gameOver;
    public static TextureRegion highScoresRegion;
    public static TextureRegion logo;
    public static TextureRegion soundOn;
    public static TextureRegion soundOff;
    public static TextureRegion arrow;
    public static TextureRegion pause;
    public static TextureRegion spring;
    public static TextureRegion castle;
    public static Animation coinAnim;
    public static Animation bobJump;
    public static Animation bobFall;
    public static TextureRegion bobHit;
    public static Animation squirrelFly;
    public static TextureRegion platform;
    public static Animation brakingPlatform;
    public static Font font;
```

```
public static Music music;
public static Sound jumpSound;
public static Sound highJumpSound;
public static Sound hitSound;
public static Sound coinSound;
public static Sound clickSound;
```

The class holds references to all the Texture, TextureRegion, Animation, Music, and Sound instances we need throughout our game. The only thing we don't load here are the images for the help screens.

```
public static void load(GLGame game) {
    background = new Texture(game, "background.png");
    backgroundRegion = new TextureRegion(background, 0, 0, 320, 480);

    items = new Texture(game, "items.png");
    mainMenu = new TextureRegion(items, 0, 224, 300, 110);
    pauseMenu = new TextureRegion(items, 224, 128, 192, 96);
    ready = new TextureRegion(items, 320, 224, 192, 32);
    gameOver = new TextureRegion(items, 352, 256, 160, 96);
    highScoresRegion = new TextureRegion(Assets.items, 0, 257, 300, 110 / 3);
    logo = new TextureRegion(items, 0, 352, 274, 142);
    soundOff = new TextureRegion(items, 0, 0, 64, 64);
    soundOn = new TextureRegion(items, 64, 0, 64, 64);
    arrow = new TextureRegion(items, 0, 64, 64, 64);
    pause = new TextureRegion(items, 64, 64, 64, 64);

    spring = new TextureRegion(items, 128, 0, 32, 32);
    castle = new TextureRegion(items, 128, 64, 64, 64);
    coinAnim = new Animation(0.2f,
                            new TextureRegion(items, 128, 32, 32, 32),
                            new TextureRegion(items, 160, 32, 32, 32),
                            new TextureRegion(items, 192, 32, 32, 32),
                            new TextureRegion(items, 160, 32, 32, 32));
    bobJump = new Animation(0.2f,
                            new TextureRegion(items, 0, 128, 32, 32),
                            new TextureRegion(items, 32, 128, 32, 32));
    bobFall = new Animation(0.2f,
                            new TextureRegion(items, 64, 128, 32, 32),
                            new TextureRegion(items, 96, 128, 32, 32));
    bobHit = new TextureRegion(items, 128, 128, 32, 32);
    squirrelFly = new Animation(0.2f,
                            new TextureRegion(items, 0, 160, 32, 32),
                            new TextureRegion(items, 32, 160, 32, 32));
    platform = new TextureRegion(items, 64, 160, 64, 16);
    brakingPlatform = new Animation(0.2f,
                            new TextureRegion(items, 64, 160, 64, 16),
                            new TextureRegion(items, 64, 176, 64, 16),
                            new TextureRegion(items, 64, 192, 64, 16),
                            new TextureRegion(items, 64, 208, 64, 16));

    font = new Font(items, 224, 0, 16, 16, 20);
```

```
            music = game.getAudio().newMusic("music.mp3");
            music.setLooping(true);
            music.setVolume(0.5f);
            if(Settings.soundEnabled)
                music.play();
            jumpSound = game.getAudio().newSound("jump.ogg");
            highJumpSound = game.getAudio().newSound("highjump.ogg");
            hitSound = game.getAudio().newSound("hit.ogg");
            coinSound = game.getAudio().newSound("coin.ogg");
            clickSound = game.getAudio().newSound("click.ogg");
        }
```

The load() method, which will be called once at the start of our game, is responsible for populating all the static members of the class. It loads the background image and creates a corresponding TextureRegion for it. Next it loads the texture atlas and creates all the necessary TextureRegions and Animations. Compare the code to Figure 9–15 and the other figures in the last section. The only noteworthy thing about the code for loading graphical assets is the creation of the coin Animation instance. As discussed, we reuse the second frame at the end of the animation frame sequence. All the animations use a frame time of 0.2 seconds.

We also create an instance of the Font class, which we have not discussed yet. It will implement the logic to render text with the bitmap font embedded in the atlas. The constructor takes the Texture, which contains the bitmap font glyphs, the pixel coordinates of the top-left corner of the area that contains the glyphs, the number of glyphs per row, and the size of each glyph in pixels.

We also load all the Music and Sound instances in that method. As you can see, we work with our old friend the Settings class again. We can reuse it from the Mr. Nom project pretty much as is, with one slight modification, as you'll see in a minute. Note that we set the Music instance to be looping and its volume to 0.5 so it is a little quieter than the sound effects. The music will only start playing if the user hasn't previously disabled the sound, which is stored in the Settings class, as in Mr. Nom.

```
        public static void reload() {
            background.reload();
            items.reload();
            if(Settings.soundEnabled)
                music.play();
        }
```

Next we have a mysterious method called reload(). Remember that the OpenGL ES context will get lost when our application is paused. We have to reload the textures when the application is resumed, and that's exactly what this method does. We also resume the music playback in case sound is enabled.

```
        public static void playSound(Sound sound) {
            if(Settings.soundEnabled)
                sound.play(1);
        }
    }
```

The final method of this class is a helper method we'll use in the rest of the code to play back audio. Instead of having to check whether sound is enabled everywhere, we encapsulate that check in this method.

Let's have a look at the modified Settings class.

The Settings Class

Not a lot has changed. Listing 9–2 shows the code of our slightly modified Settings class.

Listing 9–2. *Settings.java, Our Slightly Modified Settings Class, Stolen from Mr. Nom*

```java
package com.badlogic.androidgames.jumper;

import java.io.BufferedReader;
import java.io.BufferedWriter;
import java.io.IOException;
import java.io.InputStreamReader;
import java.io.OutputStreamWriter;

import com.badlogic.androidgames.framework.FileIO;

public class Settings {
    public static boolean soundEnabled = true;
    public final static int[] highscores = new int[] { 100, 80, 50, 30, 10 };
    public final static String file = ".superjumper";

    public static void load(FileIO files) {
        BufferedReader in = null;
        try {
            in = new BufferedReader(new InputStreamReader(files.readFile(file)));
            soundEnabled = Boolean.parseBoolean(in.readLine());
            for(int i = 0; i < 5; i++) {
                highscores[i] = Integer.parseInt(in.readLine());
            }
        } catch (IOException e) {
            // :( It's ok we have defaults
        } catch (NumberFormatException e) {
            // :/ It's ok, defaults save our day
        } finally {
            try {
                if (in != null)
                    in.close();
            } catch (IOException e) {
            }
        }
    }

    public static void save(FileIO files) {
        BufferedWriter out = null;
        try {
            out = new BufferedWriter(new OutputStreamWriter(
                    files.writeFile(file)));
```

```
                    out.write(Boolean.toString(soundEnabled));
                    out.write("\n");
                    for(int i = 0; i < 5; i++) {
                        out.write(Integer.toString(highscores[i]));
                        out.write("\n");
                    }

            } catch (IOException e) {
            } finally {
                try {
                    if (out != null)
                        out.close();
                } catch (IOException e) {
                }
            }
        }
    }

    public static void addScore(int score) {
        for(int i=0; i < 5; i++) {
            if(highscores[i] < score) {
                for(int j= 4; j > i; j--)
                    highscores[j] = highscores[j-1];
                highscores[i] = score;
                break;
            }
        }
    }
}
```

The only difference from the Mr. Nom version of this class is the file we read and write the settings from and to. Instead of .mrnom we now use the file .superjumper.

The Main Activity

We need an Activity as the main entry point of our game. We'll call it SuperJumper. Listing 9–3 shows its code.

Listing 9–3. *SuperJumper.java, the Main Entry Point Class*

```
package com.badlogic.androidgames.jumper;

import javax.microedition.khronos.egl.EGLConfig;
import javax.microedition.khronos.opengles.GL10;

import com.badlogic.androidgames.framework.Screen;
import com.badlogic.androidgames.framework.impl.GLGame;

public class SuperJumper extends GLGame {
    boolean firstTimeCreate = true;

    @Override
    public Screen getStartScreen() {
        return new MainMenuScreen(this);
    }
```

```java
    @Override
    public void onSurfaceCreated(GL10 gl, EGLConfig config) {
        super.onSurfaceCreated(gl, config);
        if(firstTimeCreate) {
            Settings.load(getFileIO());
            Assets.load(this);
            firstTimeCreate = false;
        } else {
            Assets.reload();
        }
    }

    @Override
    public void onPause() {
        super.onPause();
        if(Settings.soundEnabled)
            Assets.music.pause();
    }
}
```

We derive from GLGame and implement the getStartScreen() method, which returns a
MainMenuScreen instance. The other two methods are a little less obvious.

We override onSurfaceCreate(), which is called each time the OpenGL ES context is recreated (compare with the code of GLGame in Chapter 6). If the method is called for the
first time we use the Assets.load() method to load all assets for the first time, and also
load the settings from the settings file on the SD card, if available. Otherwise all we need
to do is reload the textures and start playback of the music via the Assets.reload()
method. We also override the onPause() method to pause the music in the case it is
playing.

We do both of these things so that we don't have to repeat them in the resume() and
pause() methods of our screens.

Before we dive into the screen implementations, let's have a look at our new Font class.

The Font Class

We are going to use bitmap fonts to render arbitrary (ASCII) text. We already discussed
how this works on a high level, so let's look at the code in Listing 9–4.

Listing 9–4. *Font.java, a Bitmap Font–Rendering Class*

```java
package com.badlogic.androidgames.framework.gl;

public class Font {
    public final Texture texture;
    public final int glyphWidth;
    public final int glyphHeight;
    public final TextureRegion[] glyphs = new TextureRegion[96];
```

The class stores the texture containing the font's glyph, the width and height of a single
glyph, and an array of TextureRegions—one for each glyph. The first element in the array
holds the region for the space glyph, the next one holds the region for the exclamation

mark glyph, and so on. In other words, the first element corresponds to the ASCII character with the code 32, and the last element corresponds to the ASCII character with the code 127.

```java
public Font(Texture texture,
            int offsetX, int offsetY,
            int glyphsPerRow, int glyphWidth, int glyphHeight) {
    this.texture = texture;
    this.glyphWidth = glyphWidth;
    this.glyphHeight = glyphHeight;
    int x = offsetX;
    int y = offsetY;
    for(int i = 0; i < 96; i++) {
        glyphs[i] = new TextureRegion(texture, x, y, glyphWidth, glyphHeight);
        x += glyphWidth;
        if(x == offsetX + glyphsPerRow * glyphWidth) {
            x = offsetX;
            y += glyphHeight;
        }
    }
}
```

In the constructor we store the configuration of the bitmap font and generate the glyph regions. The offsetX and offsetY parameters specify the top-left corner of the bitmap font area in the texture. In our texture atlas, that's the pixel at (224,0). The parameter glyphsPerRow tells us how many glyphs there are per row, and the parameters glyphWidth and glyphHeight specify the size of a single glyph. Since we use a fixed-width bitmap font, that size is the same for all glyphs. The glyphWidth is also the value by which we will advance when rendering multiple glyphs.

```java
public void drawText(SpriteBatcher batcher, String text, float x, float y) {
    int len = text.length();
    for(int i = 0; i < len; i++) {
        int c = text.charAt(i) - ' ';
        if(c < 0 || c > glyphs.length - 1)
            continue;

        TextureRegion glyph = glyphs[c];
        batcher.drawSprite(x, y, glyphWidth, glyphHeight, glyph);
        x += glyphWidth;
    }
}
```

The drawText() method takes a SpriteBatcher instance, a line of text, and the x and y positions to start drawing the text at. The x- and y-coordinates specify the center of the first glyph. All we do is get the index for each character in the string, check whether we have a glyph for it, and if so, render it via the SpriteBatcher. We then increment the x-coordinate by the glyphWidth so we can start rendering the next character in the string.

You might wonder why we don't need to bind the texture containing the glyphs. We assume that this is done before a call to drawText(). The reason is that the text rendering might be part of a batch, in which case the texture must already be bound.

Why unnecessarily bind it again in the drawText() method? Remember, OpenGL ES loves nothing more than minimal state changes.

Of course, we can only handle fixed-width fonts with this class. If we want to support more general fonts, we also need to have information about the advance of each character. One solution would be to use kerning as described in the section "Handling Text with Bitmap Fonts". We are happy with our simple solution, though.

GLScreen

In the examples in the last two chapters, we always got the reference to GLGraphics by casting. Let's fix this with a little helper class called GLScreen, which will do the dirty work for us and store the reference to GLGraphics in a member. Listing 9–5 shows the code.

Listing 9–5. *GLScreen.java, a Little Helper Class*

```java
package com.badlogic.androidgames.framework.impl;

import com.badlogic.androidgames.framework.Game;
import com.badlogic.androidgames.framework.Screen;

public abstract class GLScreen extends Screen {
    protected final GLGraphics glGraphics;
    protected final GLGame glGame;

    public GLScreen(Game game) {
        super(game);
        glGame = (GLGame)game;
        glGraphics = ((GLGame)game).getGLGraphics();
    }
}
```

We store the GLGraphics and GLGame instances. Of course, this will crash if the Game instance passed as a parameter to the constructor is not a GLGame. But we'll make sure it is. All the screens of Super Jumper will derive from this class.

The Main Menu Screen

This is the screen that is returned by SuperJumper.getStartScreen(), so it's the first screen the player will see. It renders the background and UI elements and simply waits there for us to touch any of the UI elements. Based on which element was hit, we either change the configuration (sound enabled/disabled) or transition to a new screen. Listing 9–6 shows the code.

Listing 9–6. *MainMenuScreen.java: The Main Menu Screen*

```java
package com.badlogic.androidgames.jumper;

import java.util.List;
```

```java
import javax.microedition.khronos.opengles.GL10;

import com.badlogic.androidgames.framework.Game;
import com.badlogic.androidgames.framework.Input.TouchEvent;
import com.badlogic.androidgames.framework.gl.Camera2D;
import com.badlogic.androidgames.framework.gl.SpriteBatcher;
import com.badlogic.androidgames.framework.impl.GLScreen;
import com.badlogic.androidgames.framework.math.OverlapTester;
import com.badlogic.androidgames.framework.math.Rectangle;
import com.badlogic.androidgames.framework.math.Vector2;

public class MainMenuScreen extends GLScreen {
    Camera2D guiCam;
    SpriteBatcher batcher;
    Rectangle soundBounds;
    Rectangle playBounds;
    Rectangle highscoresBounds;
    Rectangle helpBounds;
    Vector2 touchPoint;
```

The class derives from GLScreen so we can acess the GLGraphics instance more easily.

There are a couple of members in this class. The first one is a Camera2D instance called guiCam. We also need a SpriteBatcher to render our background and UI elements. We'll use Rectangles to determine if the user touched a UI element. Since we use a Camera2D, we also need a Vector2 instance to transform the touch coordinates to world coordinates.

```java
    public MainMenuScreen(Game game) {
        super(game);
        guiCam = new Camera2D(glGraphics, 320, 480);
        batcher = new SpriteBatcher(glGraphics, 100);
        soundBounds = new Rectangle(0, 0, 64, 64);
        playBounds = new Rectangle(160 - 150, 200 + 18, 300, 36);
        highscoresBounds = new Rectangle(160 - 150, 200 - 18, 300, 36);
        helpBounds = new Rectangle(160 - 150, 200 - 18 - 36, 300, 36);
        touchPoint = new Vector2();
    }
```

In the constructor we simply set up all the members. And here's a surprise. The Camera2D instance will allow us to work in our target resolution of 320×480 pixels. All we need to do is set the view frustum width and height to the proper values. The rest is done by OpenGL ES on the fly. Note, however, that the origin is still in the bottom-left corner and the y-axis is pointing upward. We'll use such a GUI camera in all screens that have UI elements so we can lay them out in pixels instead of world coordinates. Of course, we cheat a little on screens that are not 320×480 pixels wide, but we already did that in Mr. Nom, so we don't need to feel bad about it. The Rectangles we set up for each UI element are thus given in pixel coordinates.

```java
    @Override
    public void update(float deltaTime) {
        List<TouchEvent> touchEvents = game.getInput().getTouchEvents();
        game.getInput().getKeyEvents();
```

```
        int len = touchEvents.size();
        for(int i = 0; i < len; i++) {
            TouchEvent event = touchEvents.get(i);
            if(event.type == TouchEvent.TOUCH_UP) {
                touchPoint.set(event.x, event.y);
                guiCam.touchToWorld(touchPoint);

                if(OverlapTester.pointInRectangle(playBounds, touchPoint)) {
                    Assets.playSound(Assets.clickSound);
                    game.setScreen(new GameScreen(game));
                    return;
                }
                if(OverlapTester.pointInRectangle(highscoresBounds, touchPoint)) {
                    Assets.playSound(Assets.clickSound);
                    game.setScreen(new HighscoresScreen(game));
                    return;
                }
                if(OverlapTester.pointInRectangle(helpBounds, touchPoint)) {
                    Assets.playSound(Assets.clickSound);
                    game.setScreen(new HelpScreen(game));
                    return;
                }
                if(OverlapTester.pointInRectangle(soundBounds, touchPoint)) {
                    Assets.playSound(Assets.clickSound);
                    Settings.soundEnabled = !Settings.soundEnabled;
                    if(Settings.soundEnabled)
                        Assets.music.play();
                    else
                        Assets.music.pause();
                }
            }
        }
    }
```

Next is the update() method. We loop through the TouchEvents returned by our Input
instance and check for touch-up events. In case we have such an event we first
translate the touch coordinates to world coordinates. Since the camera is set up in a
way so that we work in our target resolution, this transformation boils down to simply
flipping the y-coordinate on a 320×480 pixel screen. On larger or smaller screens we just
transform the touch coordinates to the target resolution. Once we have our world touch
point, we can check it against the rectangles of the UI elements. If PLAY,
HIGHSCORES, or HELP was hit, we transition to the respective screen. In case the
sound button was pressed we change the setting and either resume or pause the music.
Also note that we play the click sound in case a UI element was pressed via the
Assets.playSound() method.

```
    @Override
    public void present(float deltaTime) {
        GL10 gl = glGraphics.getGL();
        gl.glClear(GL10.GL_COLOR_BUFFER_BIT);
        guiCam.setViewportAndMatrices();

        gl.glEnable(GL10.GL_TEXTURE_2D);
```

```
        batcher.beginBatch(Assets.background);
        batcher.drawSprite(160, 240, 320, 480, Assets.backgroundRegion);
        batcher.endBatch();

        gl.glEnable(GL10.GL_BLEND);
        gl.glBlendFunc(GL10.GL_SRC_ALPHA, GL10.GL_ONE_MINUS_SRC_ALPHA);

        batcher.beginBatch(Assets.items);

        batcher.drawSprite(160, 480 - 10 - 71, 274, 142, Assets.logo);
        batcher.drawSprite(160, 200, 300, 110, Assets.mainMenu);
        batcher.drawSprite(32, 32, 64, 64,
Settings.soundEnabled?Assets.soundOn:Assets.soundOff);

        batcher.endBatch();

        gl.glDisable(GL10.GL_BLEND);
    }
```

The present() method shouldn't really need any explanation at this point. We clear the screen, set up the projection matrices via the camera, and render the background and UI elements. Since the UI elements have transparent backgrounds, we enable blending temporarily to render them. The background does not need blending, so we don't use it to conserve some GPU cycles. Again, note that the UI elements are rendered in a coordinate system with the origin in the lower left of the screen and the y-axis pointing upward.

```
    @Override
    public void pause() {
        Settings.save(game.getFileIO());
    }

    @Override
    public void resume() {
    }

    @Override
    public void dispose() {
    }
}
```

The last method that actually does something is the pause() method. Here we make sure that the settings are saved to the SD card since the user can change the sound settings on this screen.

The Help Screens

We have a total of five help screens that all work the same: load the help screen image, render it along with the arrow button, and wait for a touch of the arrow button to move to the next screen. The only thing the screens differ in is the image they each load and the screen they transition to. For this reason I'll only present you with the code of the first help screen, which transitions to the second one. The image files for the help screens are named help1.png and so on, up to help5.png. The respective screen classes are called HelpScreen, Help2Screen, and so on. The last screen, Help5Screen, transitions to the MainMenuScreen again.

```
package com.badlogic.androidgames.jumper;

import java.util.List;

import javax.microedition.khronos.opengles.GL10;

import com.badlogic.androidgames.framework.Game;
import com.badlogic.androidgames.framework.Input.TouchEvent;
import com.badlogic.androidgames.framework.gl.Camera2D;
import com.badlogic.androidgames.framework.gl.SpriteBatcher;
import com.badlogic.androidgames.framework.gl.Texture;
import com.badlogic.androidgames.framework.gl.TextureRegion;
import com.badlogic.androidgames.framework.impl.GLScreen;
import com.badlogic.androidgames.framework.math.OverlapTester;
import com.badlogic.androidgames.framework.math.Rectangle;
import com.badlogic.androidgames.framework.math.Vector2;

public class HelpScreen extends GLScreen {
    Camera2D guiCam;
    SpriteBatcher batcher;
    Rectangle nextBounds;
    Vector2 touchPoint;
    Texture helpImage;
    TextureRegion helpRegion;
```

We have a couple of members, again holding a camera, a SpriteBatcher, the rectangle for the arrow button, a vector for the touch point, and a Texture and TextureRegion for the help image.

```
    public HelpScreen(Game game) {
        super(game);

        guiCam = new Camera2D(glGraphics, 320, 480);
        nextBounds = new Rectangle(320 - 64, 0, 64, 64);
        touchPoint = new Vector2();
        batcher = new SpriteBatcher(glGraphics, 1);
    }
```

In the constructor we set up all members pretty much the same way we did in the MainMenuScreen.

```
    @Override
    public void resume() {
        helpImage = new Texture(glGame, "help1.png" );
        helpRegion = new TextureRegion(helpImage, 0, 0, 320, 480);
    }

    @Override
    public void pause() {
        helpImage.dispose();
    }
```

In the `resume()` method we load the actual help screen texture and create a corresponding TextureRegion for rendering with the SpriteBatcher. We do the loading in this method, as the OpenGL ES context might be lost. The textures for the background and the UI elements are handled by the Assets and SuperJumper classes, as discussed before. We don't need to deal with them in any of our screens. Additionally we dispose of the help image texture in the pause() method again to clean up memory.

```java
@Override
public void update(float deltaTime) {
    List<TouchEvent> touchEvents = game.getInput().getTouchEvents();
    game.getInput().getKeyEvents();
    int len = touchEvents.size();
    for(int i = 0; i < len; i++) {
        TouchEvent event = touchEvents.get(i);
        touchPoint.set(event.x, event.y);
        guiCam.touchToWorld(touchPoint);

        if(event.type == TouchEvent.TOUCH_UP) {
            if(OverlapTester.pointInRectangle(nextBounds, touchPoint)) {
                Assets.playSound(Assets.clickSound);
                game.setScreen(new HelpScreen2(game));
                return;
            }
        }
    }
}
```

Next up is the update() method, which simply checks whether the arrow button was pressed, in which case we transition to the next help screen. We also play the click sound.

```java
@Override
public void present(float deltaTime) {
    GL10 gl = glGraphics.getGL();
    gl.glClear(GL10.GL_COLOR_BUFFER_BIT);
    guiCam.setViewportAndMatrices();

    gl.glEnable(GL10.GL_TEXTURE_2D);

    batcher.beginBatch(helpImage);
    batcher.drawSprite(160, 240, 320, 480, helpRegion);
    batcher.endBatch();

    gl.glEnable(GL10.GL_BLEND);
    gl.glBlendFunc(GL10.GL_SRC_ALPHA, GL10.GL_ONE_MINUS_SRC_ALPHA);

    batcher.beginBatch(Assets.items);
    batcher.drawSprite(320 - 32, 32, -64, 64, Assets.arrow);
    batcher.endBatch();

    gl.glDisable(GL10.GL_BLEND);
}

@Override
public void dispose() {
}
```

In the present() method we clear the screen, set up the matrices, render the help image in one batch, and then render the arrow button. Of course, we don't need to render the background image here, as the help image already contains that.

The other help screens are analogous as outlined before.

The High-Scores Screen

Next on our list is the high-scores screen. Here we'll use part of the main menu UI labels (the HIGHSCORES portion) and render the high scores stored in Settings via the Font instance we store in the Assets class. Of course, we have an arrow button so the player can get back to the main menu. Listing 9–7 shows the code.

Listing 9–7. *HighscoresScreen.java: The High-Scores Screen*

```java
package com.badlogic.androidgames.jumper;

import java.util.List;

import javax.microedition.khronos.opengles.GL10;

import com.badlogic.androidgames.framework.Game;
import com.badlogic.androidgames.framework.Input.TouchEvent;
import com.badlogic.androidgames.framework.gl.Camera2D;
import com.badlogic.androidgames.framework.gl.SpriteBatcher;
import com.badlogic.androidgames.framework.impl.GLScreen;
import com.badlogic.androidgames.framework.math.OverlapTester;
import com.badlogic.androidgames.framework.math.Rectangle;
import com.badlogic.androidgames.framework.math.Vector2;

public class HighscoreScreen extends GLScreen {
    Camera2D guiCam;
    SpriteBatcher batcher;
    Rectangle backBounds;
    Vector2 touchPoint;
    String[] highScores;
    float xOffset = 0;
```

As always, we have a couple of members for the camera, the SpriteBatcher, bounds for the arrow button, and so on. In the highscores array we store the formatted strings for each high score we present to the player. The xOffset member is a value we compute to offset the rendering of each line so that the lines are centered horizontally.

```java
    public HighscoreScreen(Game game) {
        super(game);

        guiCam = new Camera2D(glGraphics, 320, 480);
        backBounds = new Rectangle(0, 0, 64, 64);
        touchPoint = new Vector2();
        batcher = new SpriteBatcher(glGraphics, 100);
        highScores = new String[5];
        for(int i = 0; i < 5; i++) {
            highScores[i] = (i + 1) + ". " + Settings.highscores[i];
```

```
                xOffset = Math.max(highScores[i].length() * Assets.font.glyphWidth,
    xOffset);
            }
            xOffset = 160 - xOffset / 2;
    }
```

In the constructor we set up all members as usual and compute that xOffset value. We do so by evaluating the size of the longest string out of the five strings we create for the five high scores. Since our bitmap font is fixed-width, we can easily calculate the number of pixels needed for a single line of text by multiplying the number of characters with the glyph width. This will of course not account for nonprintable characters or characters outside of the ASCII character set. Since we know that we won't be using those, we can get away with this simple calculation. The last line in the constructor then subtracts half of the longest line width from 160 (the horizontal center of our target screen of 320×480 pixels) and adjusts it further by subtracting half of the glyph width. This is needed since the Font.drawText() method uses the glyph centers instead of one of the corner points.

```
    @Override
    public void update(float deltaTime) {
        List<TouchEvent> touchEvents = game.getInput().getTouchEvents();
        game.getInput().getKeyEvents();
        int len = touchEvents.size();
        for(int i = 0; i < len; i++) {
            TouchEvent event = touchEvents.get(i);
            touchPoint.set(event.x, event.y);
            guiCam.touchToWorld(touchPoint);

            if(event.type == TouchEvent.TOUCH_UP) {
                if(OverlapTester.pointInRectangle(backBounds, touchPoint)) {
                    game.setScreen(new MainMenu(game));
                    return;
                }
            }
        }
    }
```

The update() method just checks whether the arrow button was pressed, in which case it plays the click sound and transitions back to the main menu screen.

```
    @Override
    public void present(float deltaTime) {
        GL10 gl = glGraphics.getGL();
        gl.glClear(GL10.GL_COLOR_BUFFER_BIT);
        guiCam.setViewportAndMatrices();

        gl.glEnable(GL10.GL_TEXTURE_2D);

        batcher.beginBatch(Assets.background);
        batcher.drawSprite(160, 240, 320, 480, Assets.backgroundRegion);
        batcher.endBatch();

        gl.glEnable(GL10.GL_BLEND);
        gl.glBlendFunc(GL10.GL_SRC_ALPHA, GL10.GL_ONE_MINUS_SRC_ALPHA);
```

```
            batcher.beginBatch(Assets.items);
            batcher.drawSprite(160, 360, 300, 33, Assets.highScoresRegion);

            float y = 240;
            for(int i = 4; i >= 0; i--) {
                Assets.font.drawText(batcher, highScores[i], xOffset, y);
                y += Assets.font.glyphHeight;
            }

            batcher.drawSprite(32, 32, 64, 64, Assets.arrow);
            batcher.endBatch();

            gl.glDisable(GL10.GL_BLEND);
        }

    @Override
    public void resume() {
    }

    @Override
    public void pause() {
    }

    @Override
    public void dispose() {
    }
}
```

The present() method is again very straightforward. We clear the screen, set the matrices, render the background, render the highscores portion of the main menu labels, and then render the five high-score lines using the xOffset we calculated in the constructor. Now we can see why the Font does not do any texture binding: we can batch the five calls to Font.drawText(). Of course, we have to make sure that the SpriteBatcher instance can batch as many sprites (or glyphs in this case) as are needed for rendering our texts. We made sure it can when creating it in the constructor with a maximum batch size of 100 sprites (glyphs).

Time to look at the classes of our simulation.

The Simulation Classes

Before we can dive into the game screen we need to create our simulation classes. We'll follow the same pattern as in Mr. Nom, with a class for each game object and an all-knowing superclass called World that ties together the loose ends and makes our game world tick. We'll need classes for

- Bob
- Squirrels
- Springs
- Coins
- Platforms

Bob, squirrels, and platforms can move, so we'll base their classes on the DynamicGameObject we created in the last chapter. Springs and coins are static, so those will derive from the GameObject class. The tasks of each of our simulation classes are as follows:

- Store the position, velocity, and bounding shape of the object.

- Store the state and length of time that the object has been in that state (state time) if needed.

- Provide an update() method that will advance the object if needed according to its behavior.

- Provide methods to change an object's state (e.g., tell Bob he's dead or hit a spring).

The World class will then keep track of multiple instances of these objects, update them each frame, check collisions between objects and Bob, and carry out the collision responses (e.g., let Bob die, collect a coin, etc.). We will go through each class, from simplest to most complex.

The Spring Class

Let's start with the Spring class in Listing 9–8.

Listing 9–8. *Spring.java, the Spring Class*

```
package com.badlogic.androidgames.jumper;

import com.badlogic.androidgames.framework.GameObject;

public class Spring extends GameObject {
    public static float SPRING_WIDTH = 0.3f;
    public static float SPRING_HEIGHT = 0.3f;

    public Spring(float x, float y) {
        super(x, y, SPRING_WIDTH, SPRING_HEIGHT);
    }
}
```

The Spring class derives from the GameObject class: we only need a position and bounding shape since a spring does not move.

Next we define two constants that are publically accessible: the spring width and height in meters. We already estimated those values previously, and we just reuse them here.

The final piece is the constructor, which takes the x- and y-coordinates of the spring's center. With this we call the constructor of the superclass GameObject, which takes the position as well as the width and height of the object to construct a bounding shape from (a Rectangle centered around the given position). With this information our Spring is fully defined, having a position and bounding shape to collide against.

The Coin Class

Next up is the class for coins in Listing 9–9.

Listing 9–9. *Coin.java, the Coin Class*

```java
package com.badlogic.androidgames.jumper;

import com.badlogic.androidgames.framework.GameObject;

public class Coin extends GameObject {
    public static final float COIN_WIDTH = 0.5f;
    public static final float COIN_HEIGHT = 0.8f;
    public static final int COIN_SCORE = 10;

    float stateTime;
    public Coin(float x, float y) {
        super(x, y, COIN_WIDTH, COIN_HEIGHT);
        stateTime = 0;
    }

    public void update(float deltaTime) {
        stateTime += deltaTime;
    }
}
```

The Coin class is pretty much the same as the Spring class, with only one difference: we keep track of the duration the coin has been alive already. This information is needed when we want to render the coin later on, using an Animation. We did the same thing for our cavemen in the last example of the last chapter. It is a technique we'll use for all our simulation classes. Given a state and a state time, we can select an Animation, as well as which keyframe of that Animation to use for rendering. The coin only has a single state, so we only need to keep track of the state time. For that we have the update() method, which will increase the state time by the delta time passed to it.

The constants defined at the top of the class specify a coin's width and height as we defined it before, as well as the number of points Bob earns if he hits a coin.

The Castle Class

Next up we have a class for the castle at the top of our world. Listing 9–10 shows the code.

Listing 9–10. *Castle.java, the Castle Class*

```java
package com.badlogic.androidgames.jumper;

import com.badlogic.androidgames.framework.GameObject;

public class Castle extends GameObject {
    public static float CASTLE_WIDTH = 1.7f;
    public static float CASTLE_HEIGHT = 1.7f;

    public Castle(float x, float y) {
```

```
        super(x, y, CASTLE_WIDTH, CASTLE_HEIGHT);
    }
}
```

Not too complex. All we need to store is the position and bounds of the castle. The size of a castle is defined by the constants CASTLE_WIDTH and CASTLE_HEIGHT, using the values we discussed earlier.

The Squirrel Class

Next is the Squirrel class in Listing 9–11.

Listing 9–11. *Squirrel.java, the Squirrel Class*

```java
package com.badlogic.androidgames.jumper;

import com.badlogic.androidgames.framework.DynamicGameObject;

public class Squirrel extends DynamicGameObject {
    public static final float SQUIRREL_WIDTH = 1;
    public static final float SQUIRREL_HEIGHT = 0.6f;
    public static final float SQUIRREL_VELOCITY = 3f;

    float stateTime = 0;

    public Squirrel(float x, float y) {
        super(x, y, SQUIRREL_WIDTH, SQUIRREL_HEIGHT);
        velocity.set(SQUIRREL_VELOCITY, 0);
    }

    public void update(float deltaTime) {
        position.add(velocity.x * deltaTime, velocity.y * deltaTime);
        bounds.lowerLeft.set(position).sub(SQUIRREL_WIDTH / 2, SQUIRREL_HEIGHT / 2);

        if(position.x < SQUIRREL_WIDTH / 2 ) {
            position.x = SQUIRREL_WIDTH / 2;
            velocity.x = SQUIRREL_VELOCITY;
        }
        if(position.x > World.WORLD_WIDTH - SQUIRREL_WIDTH / 2) {
            position.x = World.WORLD_WIDTH - SQUIRREL_WIDTH / 2;
            velocity.x = -SQUIRREL_VELOCITY;
        }
        stateTime += deltaTime;
    }
}
```

Squirrels are moving objects so we let the class derive from DynamicGameObject, which gives us a velocity and acceleration vector as well. The first thing we do is define a squirrel's size, as well as its velocity. Since a squirrel is animated we also keep track of its state time. A squirrel has a single state, like a coin: moving horizontally. Whether it moves to the left or right can be decided based on the velocity vector's x-component, so we don't need to store a separate state member for that.

In the constructor we of course call the superclass's constructor with the initial position and size of the squirrel. We also set the velocity vector to (SQUIRREL_VELOCITY,0). All squirrels will thus move to the right in the beginning.

The update() method updates the position and bounding shape of the squirrel based on the velocity and delta time. It's our standard Euler integration step, which we talked about and used a lot in the last chapter. We also check whether the squirrel hit the left or right edge of the world. If that's the case we simply invert its velocity vector so it starts moving in the oposite direction. Our world's width is fixed at a value of 10 meters, as discussed earlier. The last thing we do is update the state time based on the delta time so that we can decide which of the two animation frames we need to use for rendering that squirrel later on.

The Platform Class

The Platform class is shown in Listing 9–12.

Listing 9–12. *Platform.java, the Platform Class*

```java
package com.badlogic.androidgames.jumper;

import com.badlogic.androidgames.framework.DynamicGameObject;

public class Platform extends DynamicGameObject {
    public static final float PLATFORM_WIDTH = 2;
    public static final float PLATFORM_HEIGHT = 0.5f;
    public static final int PLATFORM_TYPE_STATIC = 0;
    public static final int PLATFORM_TYPE_MOVING = 1;
    public static final int PLATFORM_STATE_NORMAL = 0;
    public static final int PLATFORM_STATE_PULVERIZING = 1;
    public static final float PLATFORM_PULVERIZE_TIME = 0.2f * 4;
    public static final float PLATFORM_VELOCITY = 2;
```

Platforms are a little bit more complex, of course. Let's go over the constants defined in the class. The first two constants define the width and height of a platform, as discussed earlier. A platform has a type; it can be either a static platform or a moving platform. We denote this via the constants PLATFORM_TYPE_STATIC and PLATFORM_TYPE_MOVING. A platform can also be in one of two states: it can be in a normal state—that is, either sitting there statically or moving—or it can be pulverized. The state is encoded via one of the constants PLATFORM_STATE_NORMAL or PLATFORM_STATE_PULVERIZING. Pulverization is of course a process limited in time. We therefore define the time it takes for a platform to be completely pulverized, which is 0.8 seconds. This value is simply derived from the number of frames in the Animation of the platform and the duration of each frame—one of the little quirks we have to accept while trying to follow the MVC pattern. Finally we define the speed of moving platforms to be 2 m/s, as discussed earlier. A moving platform will behave exactly like a squirrel in that it just travels in one direction until it hits the world's horizontal boundaries, in which case it just inverts its direction.

```java
    int type;
    int state;
    float stateTime;
```

```java
    public Platform(int type, float x, float y) {
        super(x, y, PLATFORM_WIDTH, PLATFORM_HEIGHT);
        this.type = type;
        this.state = PLATFORM_STATE_NORMAL;
        this.stateTime = 0;
        if(type == PLATFORM_TYPE_MOVING) {
            velocity.x = PLATFORM_VELOCITY;
        }
    }
```

To store the type, the state, and the state time of the Platform instance, we need three members. These get initialized in the constructor based on the type of the Platform, which is a parameter of the constructor, along with the platform center's position.

```java
    public void update(float deltaTime) {
        if(type == PLATFORM_TYPE_MOVING) {
            position.add(velocity.x * deltaTime, 0);
            bounds.lowerLeft.set(position).sub(PLATFORM_WIDTH / 2, PLATFORM_HEIGHT / 2);

            if(position.x < PLATFORM_WIDTH / 2) {
                velocity.x = -velocity.x;
                position.x = PLATFORM_WIDTH / 2;
            }
            if(position.x > World.WORLD_WIDTH - PLATFORM_WIDTH / 2) {
                velocity.x = -velocity.x;
                position.x = World.WORLD_WIDTH - PLATFORM_WIDTH / 2;
            }
        }

        stateTime += deltaTime;
    }
```

The update() method will move the platform and check for the out-of-world condition, acting accordingly by inverting the velocity vector. This is exactly the same thing we did in the Squirrel.update() method. We also update the state time at the end of the method.

```java
    public void pulverize() {
        state = PLATFORM_STATE_PULVERIZING;
        stateTime = 0;
        velocity.x = 0;
    }
}
```

The final method of this class is called pulverize(). It switches the state from PLATFORM_STATE_NORMAL to PLATFORM_STATE_PULVERIZING and resets the state time and velocity. This means that moving platforms will stop moving. The method will be called if the World class detects a collision between Bob and the Platform, and decides to pulverize the Platform based on a random number. We'll talk about that in a bit.

The Bob Class

First we need to talk about Bob. The Bob class is shown in Listing 9–13.

Listing 9–13. *Bob.java*

```java
package com.badlogic.androidgames.jumper;

import com.badlogic.androidgames.framework.DynamicGameObject;

public class Bob extends DynamicGameObject{
    public static final int BOB_STATE_JUMP = 0;
    public static final int BOB_STATE_FALL = 1;
    public static final int BOB_STATE_HIT = 2;
    public static final float BOB_JUMP_VELOCITY = 11;
    public static final float BOB_MOVE_VELOCITY = 20;
    public static final float BOB_WIDTH = 0.8f;
    public static final float BOB_HEIGHT = 0.8f;
```

We start with a couple of constants again. Bob can be in one of three states: jumping upward, falling downward, or being hit. He also has a vertical jump velocity, which is only applied on the y-axis, and a horizontal move velocity, which is only applied on the x-axis. The final two constants define Bob's width and height in the world. Of course, we also have to store Bob's state and state time.

```java
    int state;
    float stateTime;

    public Bob(float x, float y) {
        super(x, y, BOB_WIDTH, BOB_HEIGHT);
        state = BOB_STATE_FALL;
        stateTime = 0;
    }
```

The constructor just calls the superclass's constructor so that Bob's center position and bounding shape are initialized correctly, and the initializes the `state` and `stateTime` member variables.

```java
    public void update(float deltaTime) {
        velocity.add(World.gravity.x * deltaTime, World.gravity.y * deltaTime);
        position.add(velocity.x * deltaTime, velocity.y * deltaTime);
        bounds.lowerLeft.set(position).sub(bounds.width / 2, bounds.height / 2);

        if(velocity.y > 0 && state != BOB_STATE_HIT) {
            if(state != BOB_STATE_JUMP) {
                state = BOB_STATE_JUMP;
                stateTime = 0;
            }
        }

        if(velocity.y < 0 && state != BOB_STATE_HIT) {
            if(state != BOB_STATE_FALL) {
                state = BOB_STATE_FALL;
                stateTime = 0;
            }
        }
    }
```

```
        if(position.x < 0)
            position.x = World.WORLD_WIDTH;
        if(position.x > World.WORLD_WIDTH)
            position.x = 0;

        stateTime += deltaTime;
    }
```

The update() method starts off by updating Bob's position and bounding shape based on gravity and his current velocity. Note that the velocity is a composite of the gravity and Bob's own movement due to jumping and moving horizontally. The next two big conditional blocks set Bob's state to either BOB_STATE_JUMPING or BOB_STATE_FALLING, and reinitialize his state time depending on the y component of his velocity. If it is greater than zero Bob is jumping, and if it is smaller than zero Bob is falling. We only do this if Bob hasn't been hit and if he isn't already in the correct state. Otherwise we'd always reset the state time to zero, which wouldn't play nice with Bob's animation later on. We also wrap Bob from one edge of the world to the other if he leaves the world to the left or right. Finally we update the stateTime member again.

Where does Bob get his velocity from apart from gravity? That's where the other methods come in.

```
    public void hitSquirrel() {
        velocity.set(0,0);
        state = BOB_STATE_HIT;
        stateTime = 0;
    }

    public void hitPlatform() {
        velocity.y = BOB_JUMP_VELOCITY;
        state = BOB_STATE_JUMP;
        stateTime = 0;
    }

    public void hitSpring() {
        velocity.y = BOB_JUMP_VELOCITY * 1.5f;
        state = BOB_STATE_JUMP;
        stateTime = 0;
    }
}
```

The method hitSquirrel() is called by the World class in case Bob hit a squirrel. If that's the case Bob stops moving by himself and enters the BOB_STATE_HIT state. Only gravity will apply to Bob from this point on; the player can't control him anymore and he doesn't interact with platforms anymore. That's similar to the behavior Super Mario exhibits when he gets hit by an enemy. He just falls down.

The hitPlatform() method is also called by the World class. It will be invoked when Bob hits a platform while falling downward. If that's the case, then we set his y velocity to BOB_JUMP_VELOCITY, and we also set his state and state time accordingly. From this point on Bob will move upward until gravity wins again, making Bob fall down.

The last method, `hitSpring()`, is invoked by the `World` class if Bob hits a spring. It does the same as the `hitPlatform()` method, with one exception: the initial upward velocity is set to 1.5 times `BOB_JUMP_VELOCITY`. This means that Bob will jump a little higher when hitting a spring compared to when hitting a platform.

The World Class

The last class we have to discuss is the `World` class. It's a little longer, so we'll split it up. Listing 9–14 shows the first part of the code.

Listing 9–14. *Excerpt from World.java: Constants, Members, and Initialization*

```java
package com.badlogic.androidgames.jumper;

import java.util.ArrayList;
import java.util.List;
import java.util.Random;

import com.badlogic.androidgames.framework.math.OverlapTester;
import com.badlogic.androidgames.framework.math.Vector2;

public class World {
    public interface WorldListener {
        public void jump();
        public void highJump();
        public void hit();
        public void coin();
    }
```

The first thing we define is an interface called `WorldListener`. What does it do? We need it to solve a little MVC problem: when do we play sound effects? We could just add invocations of `Assets.playSound()` to the respective simulation classes, but that's not very clean. Instead we'll let a user of the `World` class register a `WorldListener`, which will be called when Bob jumps from a platform, jumps from a spring, gets hit by a squirrel, or collects a coin. We will later register a listener that plays back the proper sound effects for each of those events, keeping the simulation classes clean from any direct dependencies on rendering and audio playback.

```java
    public static final float WORLD_WIDTH = 10;
    public static final float WORLD_HEIGHT = 15 * 20;
    public static final int WORLD_STATE_RUNNING = 0;
    public static final int WORLD_STATE_NEXT_LEVEL = 1;
    public static final int WORLD_STATE_GAME_OVER = 2;
    public static final Vector2 gravity = new Vector2(0, -12);
```

Next we define a couple of constants. The `WORLD_WIDTH` and `WORLD_HEIGHT` specify the extents of our world horizontally and vertically. Remember that our view frustum will show a region of 10×15 meters of our world. Given the constants defined here, our world will span 20 view frustums or screens vertically. Again, that's a value I came up with by tuning. We'll get back to it when we discuss how we generate a level. The world can also be in one of three states: running, waiting for the next level to start, or the

game-over state—when Bob falls too far (outside of the view frustum). We also define
our gravity acceleration vector as a constant here.

```java
public final Bob bob;
public final List<Platform> platforms;
public final List<Spring> springs;
public final List<Squirrel> squirrels;
public final List<Coin> coins;
public Castle castle;
public final WorldListener listener;
public final Random rand;

public float heightSoFar;
public int score;
public int state;
```

Next up are all the members of the World class. It keeps track of Bob; all the Platforms,
Springs, Squirrels, and Coins; and the Castle. Additionally it has a reference to a
WorldListener and an instance of Random, which we'll use to generate random numbers
for various purposes. The last three members keep track of the highest height Bob has
reached so far, as well as the World's state and the score achieved.

```java
public World(WorldListener listener) {
    this.bob = new Bob(5, 1);
    this.platforms = new ArrayList<Platform>();
    this.springs = new ArrayList<Spring>();
    this.squirrels = new ArrayList<Squirrel>();
    this.coins = new ArrayList<Coin>();
    this.listener = listener;
    rand = new Random();
    generateLevel();

    this.heightSoFar = 0;
    this.score = 0;
    this.state = WORLD_STATE_RUNNING;
}
```

The constructor initializes all members and also stores the WorldListener passed as a
parameter. Bob is placed in the middle of the world horizontally and a little bit above the
ground at (5,1). The rest is pretty much self-explanatory, with one exception: the
generateLevel() method.

Generating the World

You might have wondered already how we actually create and place the objects in our
world. We use a method called procedural generation. We come up with a simple
algorithm that will generate a random level for us. Listing 9–15 shows the code.

Listing 9–15. *Exceprt from World.java: The generateLevel() Method*

```java
private void generateLevel() {
    float y = Platform.PLATFORM_HEIGHT / 2;
    float maxJumpHeight = Bob.BOB_JUMP_VELOCITY * Bob.BOB_JUMP_VELOCITY
            / (2 * -gravity.y);
```

```
    while (y < WORLD_HEIGHT - WORLD_WIDTH / 2) {
        int type = rand.nextFloat() > 0.8f ? Platform.PLATFORM_TYPE_MOVING
                : Platform.PLATFORM_TYPE_STATIC;
        float x = rand.nextFloat()
                * (WORLD_WIDTH - Platform.PLATFORM_WIDTH)
                + Platform.PLATFORM_WIDTH / 2;

        Platform platform = new Platform(type, x, y);
        platforms.add(platform);

        if (rand.nextFloat() > 0.9f
                && type != Platform.PLATFORM_TYPE_MOVING) {
            Spring spring = new Spring(platform.position.x,
                    platform.position.y + Platform.PLATFORM_HEIGHT / 2
                            + Spring.SPRING_HEIGHT / 2);
            springs.add(spring);
        }

        if (y > WORLD_HEIGHT / 3 && rand.nextFloat() > 0.8f) {
            Squirrel squirrel = new Squirrel(platform.position.x
                    + rand.nextFloat(), platform.position.y
                    + Squirrel.SQUIRREL_HEIGHT + rand.nextFloat() * 2);
            squirrels.add(squirrel);
        }

        if (rand.nextFloat() > 0.6f) {
            Coin coin = new Coin(platform.position.x + rand.nextFloat(),
                    platform.position.y + Coin.COIN_HEIGHT
                            + rand.nextFloat() * 3);
            coins.add(coin);
        }

        y += (maxJumpHeight - 0.5f);
        y -= rand.nextFloat() * (maxJumpHeight / 3);
    }

    castle = new Castle(WORLD_WIDTH / 2, y);
}
```

Let me outline the general idea of the algorithm in plain words:

1. Start at the bottom of the world at y = 0.

2. While we haven't reached the top of the world yet, do the following:

    a. Create a platform, either moving or stationary at the current y position with a random x position.

    b. Fetch a random number between 0 and 1, and if it is greater than 0.9 and if the platform is not moving, create a spring on top of the platform.

    c. If we are above the first third of the level, fetch a random number, and if it is above 0.8, create a squirrel offset randomly from the platform's position.

d. Fetch a random number, and if it is greater than 0.6, create a coin offset randomly from the platform's position.

e. Increase y by the maximum normal jump height of Bob, decrease it a tiny bit randomly—but only so far that it doesn't fall below the last y value—and goto 2

3. Place the castle at the last y position, centered horizontally.

The big secret of this procedure is how we increase the y position for the next platform in step 2e. We have to make sure that each subsequent platform is reachable by Bob by jumping from the current platform. Bob can only jump as high as gravity allows, given his initial jump velocity of 11 m/s vertically. How can we calculate how high Bob will jump? With the following formula:

```
height = velocity × velocity / (2 × gravity) = 11 × 11 / (2 × 13) ~= 4.6m
```

This means we should have a distance of 4.6 meters vertically between each platform so that Bob can still reach it. To make sure all platforms are reachable, we use a value that's a little bit less than the maximum jump height. This guarantees that Bob will always be able to jump from one platform to the next. The horizontal placement of platforms is random again. Given Bob's horizontal movement speed of 20 m/s, we can be more than sure that he will not only be able to reach a platform vertically but also horizontally.

The other objects are created based on chance. The method `Random.nextFloat()` returns a random number between 0 and 1 on each invocation, where each number has the same probability of occuring. Squirrels are only generated when the random number we fetch from Random is greater than 0.8. This means that we'll generate a squirrel with a probability of 20 percent (1 – 0.8). The same is true for all other randomly created objects. By tuning this values we can have more or fewer objects in our world.

Updating the World

Once we have generated our world we can update all objects in it and check for collisions. Listing 9–16 shows the update methods of the `World` class.

Listing 9–16. *Excerpt from World.java: The Update Methods*

```java
public void update(float deltaTime, float accelX) {
    updateBob(deltaTime, accelX);
    updatePlatforms(deltaTime);
    updateSquirrels(deltaTime);
    updateCoins(deltaTime);
    if (bob.state != Bob.BOB_STATE_HIT)
        checkCollisions();
    checkGameOver();
}
```

The method `update()` is the one called by our game screen later on. It receives the delta time and acceleration on the x-axis of the accelerometer as an argument. It is responsible for calling the other update methods as well as performing the collision checks and game-over check. We have an update method for each object type in our world.

```
private void updateBob(float deltaTime, float accelX) {
    if (bob.state != Bob.BOB_STATE_HIT && bob.position.y <= 0.5f)
        bob.hitPlatform();
    if (bob.state != Bob.BOB_STATE_HIT)
        bob.velocity.x = -accelX / 10 * Bob.BOB_MOVE_VELOCITY;
    bob.update(deltaTime);
    heightSoFar = Math.max(bob.position.y, heightSoFar);
}
```

The updateBob() method is responsible for updating Bob's state. The first thing it does is check whether Bob is hitting the bottom of the world, in which case Bob is instructed to jump. This means that at the start of each level Bob is allowed to jump off the ground of our world. As soon as the ground is out of sight, this won't work anymore, of course. Next we update Bob's horizontal velocity based on the value of the x-axis of the accelerometer we get as an argument. As discussed, we normalize this value from a range of –10 to 10 to a range of –1 to 1 (full left tilt to full right tilt), and the multiply it by Bob's standard movement velocity. Next we tell Bob to update himself by calling the Bob.update() method. The last thing we do is keep track of the highest y position Bob has reached so far. We need this to determine whether Bob has fallen too far later on.

```
private void updatePlatforms(float deltaTime) {
    int len = platforms.size();
    for (int i = 0; i < len; i++) {
        Platform platform = platforms.get(i);
        platform.update(deltaTime);
        if (platform.state == Platform.PLATFORM_STATE_PULVERIZING
                && platform.stateTime > Platform.PLATFORM_PULVERIZE_TIME) {
            platforms.remove(platform);
            len = platforms.size();
        }
    }
}
```

Next we update all the platforms in updatePlatforms(). We loop through the list of platforms and call each platform's update() method with the current delta time. In case the platform is in the process of pulverization, we check for how long that has been going on. If the platform is in the PLATFORM_STATE_PULVERIZING state for more than PLATFORM_PULVERIZE_TIME, we simply remove the platform from our list of platforms.

```
private void updateSquirrels(float deltaTime) {
    int len = squirrels.size();
    for (int i = 0; i < len; i++) {
        Squirrel squirrel = squirrels.get(i);
        squirrel.update(deltaTime);
    }
}

private void updateCoins(float deltaTime) {
    int len = coins.size();
    for (int i = 0; i < len; i++) {
        Coin coin = coins.get(i);
        coin.update(deltaTime);
    }
}
```

In the updateSquirrels() method we update each Squirrel instance via its update() method, passing in the current delta time. We do the same for coins in the updateCoins() method.

Collision Detection and Response

Looking back at our original World.update() method, we can see that the next thing we do is check for collisions between Bob and all the other objects he can collide with in the world. We only do this if Bob is in a state not equal to BOB_STATE_HIT, in which case he just continues to fall down due to gravity. Let's have a look at those collision-checking methods in Listing 9–17.

Listing 9–17. *Excerpt from World.java: The Collision-Checking Methods*

```java
private void checkCollisions() {
    checkPlatformCollisions();
    checkSquirrelCollisions();
    checkItemCollisions();
    checkCastleCollisions();
}
```

The checkCollisions() method is more or less another master method, which simply invokes all the other collision-checking methods. Bob can collide with a couple of things in the world: platforms, squirrels, coins, springs, and the castle. For each of those object types, we have a separate collision-checking method. Remember that we invoke this method and the slave methods after we have updated the positions and bounding shapes of all objects in our world. Think of it as a snapshot of the state of our world at the given point in time. All we do is observe this still image and see whether anything overlaps. We can then take action and make sure that the objects that collide react to those overlaps or collisions in the next frame by manipulating their states, positions, velocities, and so on.

```java
private void checkPlatformCollisions() {
    if (bob.velocity.y > 0)
        return;

    int len = platforms.size();
    for (int i = 0; i < len; i++) {
        Platform platform = platforms.get(i);
        if (bob.position.y > platform.position.y) {
            if (OverlapTester
                    .overlapRectangles(bob.bounds, platform.bounds)) {
                bob.hitPlatform();
                listener.jump();
                if (rand.nextFloat() > 0.5f) {
                    platform.pulverize();
                }
                break;
            }
        }
    }
}
```

In the checkPlatformCollisions() method we test for overlap between Bob and any of the platforms in our world. We break out of that method early in case Bob is currently on his way up. This way Bob can pass through platforms from below. For Super Jumper that's good behavior; in a game like Super Mario Brothers we'd probably want Bob to fall down if he hits a block from below. Next we loop through all platforms and check whether Bob is above the current platform. If he is, we test whether his bounding rectangle overlaps the bounding rectangle of the platform, in which case we tell Bob that he hit a platform via a call to Bob.hitPlatform(). Looking back at that method, we see that it will trigger a jump and set Bob's states accordingly. Next we call the WorldListener.jump() method to inform the listener that Bob has just started to jump again. We'll use this later on to play back a corresponding sound effect in the listener. The last thing we do is fetch a random number, and if it is above 0.5 we tell the platform to pulverize itself. It will be alive for another PLATFORM_PULVERIZE_TIME seconds (0.8) and will then be removed in the updatePlatforms() method shown earlier. When we render that platform, we'll use its state time to determine which of the platform animation keyframes to play back.

```
private void checkSquirrelCollisions() {
    int len = squirrels.size();
    for (int i = 0; i < len; i++) {
        Squirrel squirrel = squirrels.get(i);
        if (OverlapTester.overlapRectangles(squirrel.bounds, bob.bounds)) {
            bob.hitSquirrel();
            listener.hit();
        }
    }
}
```

The method checkSquirrelCollisions() tests Bob's bounding rectangle against the bounding rectangle of each squirrel. If Bob hits a squirrel, we tell him to enter the BOB_STATE_HIT state, which will make him fall down without the player being able to control him any further. We also tell the WorldListener about it so he can play back a sound effect, for example.

```
private void checkItemCollisions() {
    int len = coins.size();
    for (int i = 0; i < len; i++) {
        Coin coin = coins.get(i);
        if (OverlapTester.overlapRectangles(bob.bounds, coin.bounds)) {
            coins.remove(coin);
            len = coins.size();
            listener.coin();
            score += Coin.COIN_SCORE;
        }
    }

    if (bob.velocity.y > 0)
        return;

    len = springs.size();
    for (int i = 0; i < len; i++) {
        Spring spring = springs.get(i);
```

```
            if (bob.position.y > spring.position.y) {
                if (OverlapTester.overlapRectangles(bob.bounds, spring.bounds)) {
                    bob.hitSpring();
                    listener.highJump();
                }
            }
        }
    }
}
```

The checkItemCollisions() method checks Bob against all coins in the world and against all springs. In case Bob hits a coin we remove the coin from our world, tell the listener that a coin was collected, and increase the current score by COIN_SCORE. In case Bob is falling downward, we also check Bob against all springs in the world. In case he hit one we till him about it so that he'll perform a higher jump than usual. We also inform the listener of this event.

```
private void checkCastleCollisions() {
    if (OverlapTester.overlapRectangles(castle.bounds, bob.bounds)) {
        state = WORLD_STATE_NEXT_LEVEL;
    }
}
```

The final method checks Bob against the castle. If Bob hits it, we set the world's state to WORLD_STATE_NEXT_LEVEL, signaling any outside entity (such as our game screen) that we should transition to the next level, which will again be a randomly generated instance of World.

Game Over, Buddy!

The last method in the World class, which is invoked in the last line of the World.update() method, is shown in Listing 9–18.

Listing 9–18. *The Rest of World.java: The Game Over–Checking Method*

```
private void checkGameOver() {
    if (heightSoFar - 7.5f > bob.position.y) {
        state = WORLD_STATE_GAME_OVER;
    }
}
```

Remember how we defined the game-over state: Bob must leave the bottom of the view frustum. The view frustum is of course governed by a Camera2D instance, which has a position. The y-coordinate of that position is always equal to the biggest y-coordinate Bob has had so far, so the camera will somewhat follow Bob on his way upward. Since we want to keep the rendering and simulation code separate, we don't have a reference to the camera in our world, though. We thus keep track of Bob's highest y-coordinate in updateBob() and store that value in heightSoFar. We know that our view frustum will have a height of 15 meters. Thus we also know that if Bob's y-coordinate is below heightSoFar – 7.5, then he has left the view frustum on the bottom edge. That's when Bob is declared to be dead. Of course, this is a tiny bit hackish, as it is based on the assumption that the view frustum's height will always be 15 meters and that the camera will always be at the highest y-coordinate Bob has been able to reach so far. If we'd allowed zooming or used a different camera-following method, this would not hold true anymore. Instead of overcomplicating things, we'll just leave it as is, though. You will often face such decisions in game development, as it is hard at times to keep everything clean from a software engineering point of view (as evidenced by our overuse of public or package private members).

You may be wondering why we don't use the `SpatialHashGrid` class we developed in the last chapter. I'll show you the reason in a minute. Let's get our game done by implementing the `GameScreen` class first.

The Game Screen

We are nearing the completion of Super Jumper. The last thing we need to implement is the game screen, which will present the actual game world to the player and allow it to interact with it. The game screen consists of five subscreens, as shown in Figure 9–2. We have the ready screen, the normal running screen, the next-level screen, the game-over screen, and the pause screen. The game screen in Mr. Nom was similar to this; it only lacked a next-level screen, as there was only one level. We will use the same approach as in Mr. Nom: we'll have separate update and present methods for all subscreens that update and render the game world, as well as the UI elements that are part of the subscreens. Since the game screen code is a little longer, we'll split it up into multiple listings here. Listing 9–19 shows the first part of the game screen.

Listing 9–19. *Excerpt from GameScreen.java: Members and Constructor*

```java
package com.badlogic.androidgames.jumper;

import java.util.List;

import javax.microedition.khronos.opengles.GL10;

import com.badlogic.androidgames.framework.Game;
import com.badlogic.androidgames.framework.Input.TouchEvent;
import com.badlogic.androidgames.framework.gl.Camera2D;
import com.badlogic.androidgames.framework.gl.FPSCounter;
import com.badlogic.androidgames.framework.gl.SpriteBatcher;
import com.badlogic.androidgames.framework.impl.GLScreen;
import com.badlogic.androidgames.framework.math.OverlapTester;
import com.badlogic.androidgames.framework.math.Rectangle;
import com.badlogic.androidgames.framework.math.Vector2;
import com.badlogic.androidgames.jumper.World.WorldListener;

public class GameScreen extends GLScreen {
    static final int GAME_READY = 0;
    static final int GAME_RUNNING = 1;
    static final int GAME_PAUSED = 2;
    static final int GAME_LEVEL_END = 3;
    static final int GAME_OVER = 4;

    int state;
    Camera2D guiCam;
    Vector2 touchPoint;
```

```java
SpriteBatcher batcher;
World world;
WorldListener worldListener;
WorldRenderer renderer;
Rectangle pauseBounds;
Rectangle resumeBounds;
Rectangle quitBounds;
int lastScore;
String scoreString;
```

The class starts off with a couple of constants defining the five states that the screen can be in. Next we have the members. We have a camera for rendering the UI elements, as well as a vector so we can transform touch coordinates to world coordinates (as in the other screens, to a view frustum of 320×480 units, our target resolution). Next we have a SpriteBatcher, a World instance, and a WorldListener. The WorldRenderer class is something we'll look into in a minute. It basically just takes a World and renders it. Note that it takes a reference to the SpriteBatcher as well as the World as parameters of its constructors. This means we'll use the same SpriteBatcher to render the UI elements of the screen, as well as the game world. The rest of the members are Rectangles for different UI elements (such as the RESUME and QUIT menu entries on the paused subscreen) and two members for keeping track of the current score. We want to avoid creating a new string every frame when rendering the score so that we make the garbage collector happy.

```java
public GameScreen(Game game) {
    super(game);
    state = GAME_READY;
    guiCam = new Camera2D(glGraphics, 320, 480);
    touchPoint = new Vector2();
    batcher = new SpriteBatcher(glGraphics, 1000);
    worldListener = new WorldListener() {
        @Override
        public void jump() {
            Assets.playSound(Assets.jumpSound);
        }

        @Override
        public void highJump() {
            Assets.playSound(Assets.highJumpSound);
        }

        @Override
        public void hit() {
            Assets.playSound(Assets.hitSound);
        }

        @Override
        public void coin() {
            Assets.playSound(Assets.coinSound);
        }
    };
    world = new World(worldListener);
    renderer = new WorldRenderer(glGraphics, batcher, world);
    pauseBounds = new Rectangle(320- 64, 480- 64, 64, 64);
```

Rendering of the game screen is done in two steps. We first render the actual game world via the WorldRenderer class, and then render all the UI elements on top of the game world depending on the current state of the game screen. The render() method does just that. As with our update methods, we again have a separate rendering method for all the subscreens.

```
private void presentReady() {
    batcher.drawSprite(160, 240, 192, 32, Assets.ready);
}
```

The presentRunning() method just displays the pause button in the top-right corner, as well as the score string in the top-left corner.

```
private void presentRunning() {
    batcher.drawSprite(320 - 32, 480 - 32, 64, 64, Assets.pause);
    Assets.font.drawText(batcher, scoreString, 16, 480-20);
}
```

In the presentRunning() method we simply render the pause button and the current score string.

```
private void presentPaused() {
    batcher.drawSprite(160, 240, 192, 96, Assets.pauseMenu);
    Assets.font.drawText(batcher, scoreString, 16, 480-20);
}
```

The presentPaused() method displays the pause menu UI elements and the score again.

```
private void presentLevelEnd() {
    String topText = "the princess is ...";
    String bottomText = "in another castle!";
    float topWidth = Assets.font.glyphWidth * topText.length();
    float bottomWidth = Assets.font.glyphWidth * bottomText.length();
    Assets.font.drawText(batcher, topText, 160 - topWidth / 2, 480 - 40);
    Assets.font.drawText(batcher, bottomText, 160 - bottomWidth / 2, 40);
}
```

The presentLevelEnd() method renders the string THE PRINCESS IS ... at the top of the screen and the string IN ANOTHER CASTLE! at the bottom of the screen, as shown in Figure 9–2. We perform some calculations to center those strings horizontally.

```
private void presentGameOver() {
    batcher.drawSprite(160, 240, 160, 96, Assets.gameOver);
    float scoreWidth = Assets.font.glyphWidth * scoreString.length();
    Assets.font.drawText(batcher, scoreString, 160 - scoreWidth / 2, 480-20);
}
```

The presentGameOver() method displays the game-over UI element as well the score string. Remember that the score screen is set in the updateRunning() method to either score: #score or new highscore: #value.

Finishing Touches

That's basically our game screen class. The rest of its code is given in Listing 9–22.

Listing 9–22. *The Rest of GameScreen.java: The pause(), resume(), and dispose() Methods*

```java
    @Override
    public void pause() {
        if(state == GAME_RUNNING)
            state = GAME_PAUSED;
    }

    @Override
    public void resume() {
    }

    @Override
    public void dispose() {
    }
}
```

We just make sure our game screen is paused when the user decides to pause the application.

The last thing we have to implement is the WorldRenderer class.

The WorldRenderer Class

This class should be no surprise. It simply uses the SpriteBatcher we pass to it in the constructor and renders the world accordingly. Listing 9–23 shows the beginning of the code.

Listing 9–23. *Excerpt from WorldRenderer.java: Constants, Members, and Constructor*

```java
package com.badlogic.androidgames.jumper;

import javax.microedition.khronos.opengles.GL10;

import com.badlogic.androidgames.framework.gl.Animation;
import com.badlogic.androidgames.framework.gl.Camera2D;
import com.badlogic.androidgames.framework.gl.SpriteBatcher;
import com.badlogic.androidgames.framework.gl.TextureRegion;
import com.badlogic.androidgames.framework.impl.GLGraphics;

public class WorldRenderer {
    static final float FRUSTUM_WIDTH = 10;
    static final float FRUSTUM_HEIGHT = 15;
    GLGraphics glGraphics;
    World world;
    Camera2D cam;
```

```
SpriteBatcher batcher;

public WorldRenderer(GLGraphics glGraphics, SpriteBatcher batcher, World world) {
    this.glGraphics = glGraphics;
    this.world = world;
    this.cam = new Camera2D(glGraphics, FRUSTUM_WIDTH, FRUSTUM_HEIGHT);
    this.batcher = batcher;
}
```

As always we start off by defining some constants. In this case it's the view frustum's width and height, which we define as 10 and 15 meters. We also have a couple of members—namely a GLGraphics instance, a camera, and the SpriteBatcher reference we get from the game screen.

The constructor takes a GLGraphics instance, a SpriteBatcher, and the World the WorldRenderer should draw as parameters. We set up all members accordingly. Listing 9–24 shows the actual rendering code.

Listing 9–24. *The Rest of WorldRenderer.java: The Actual Rendering Code*

```
public void render() {
    if(world.bob.position.y > cam.position.y )
        cam.position.y = world.bob.position.y;
    cam.setViewportAndMatrices();
    renderBackground();
    renderObjects();
}
```

The render() method splits up rendering into two batches: one for the background image and another one for all the objects in the world. It also updates the camera position based on Bob's current y-coordinate. If he's above the camera's y-coordinate, the camera position is adjusted accordingly. Note that we use a camera that works in world units here. We only set up the matrices once for both the background and the objects.

```
public void renderBackground() {
    batcher.beginBatch(Assets.background);
    batcher.drawSprite(cam.position.x, cam.position.y,
                    FRUSTUM_WIDTH, FRUSTUM_HEIGHT,
                    Assets.backgroundRegion);
    batcher.endBatch();
}
```

The renderBackground() method simply renders the background so that it follows the camera. It does not scroll, but instead is always rendered so that it fills the complete screen. We also don't use any blending for rendering the background so we can squeeze out a little bit more performance.

```
public void renderObjects() {
    GL10 gl = glGraphics.getGL();
    gl.glEnable(GL10.GL_BLEND);
    gl.glBlendFunc(GL10.GL_SRC_ALPHA, GL10.GL_ONE_MINUS_SRC_ALPHA);

    batcher.beginBatch(Assets.items);
    renderBob();
    renderPlatforms();
```

```
        renderItems();
        renderSquirrels();
        renderCastle();
        batcher.endBatch();
        gl.glDisable(GL10.GL_BLEND);
    }
```

The renderObjects() method is responsible for rendering the second batch. This time we use blending, as all our objects have transparent background pixels. All the objects are rendered in a single batch. Looking back at the constructor of GameScreen, we see that the SpriteBatcher we use can cope with 1,000 sprites in a single batch—more than enough for our world. For each object type we have a separate rendering method.

```
    private void renderBob() {
        TextureRegion keyFrame;
        switch(world.bob.state) {
        case Bob.BOB_STATE_FALL:
            keyFrame = Assets.bobFall.getKeyFrame(world.bob.stateTime,
Animation.ANIMATION_LOOPING);
            break;
        case Bob.BOB_STATE_JUMP:
            keyFrame = Assets.bobJump.getKeyFrame(world.bob.stateTime,
Animation.ANIMATION_LOOPING);
            break;
        case Bob.BOB_STATE_HIT:
        default:
            keyFrame = Assets.bobHit;
        }

        float side = world.bob.velocity.x < 0? -1: 1;
        batcher.drawSprite(world.bob.position.x, world.bob.position.y, side * 1, 1,
keyFrame);
    }
```

The method renderBob() is responsible for rendering Bob. Based on Bob's state and state time, we select a keyframe out of the total of five keyframes we have for Bob (see Figure 9–9 earlier in the chapter). Based on Bob's velocity's x-component, we also determine which side Bob is facing. Based on that, we multiply his by with either 1 or –1 to flip the texture region accordingly. Remember, we only have keyframes for a Bob looking to the right. Note also that we don't use BOB_WIDTH or BOB_HEIGHT to specify the size of the rectangle we draw for Bob. Those sizes are the sizes of the bounding shapes, which are not necessarily the sizes of the rectangles we render. Instead we use our 1×1-meter-to-32×32-pixel mapping. That's something we'll do for all sprite rendering; we'll either use a 1×1 rectangle (Bob, coins, squirrels, springs), a 2×0.5 rectangle (platforms), or a 2×2 rectangle (castle).

```
    private void renderPlatforms() {
        int len = world.platforms.size();
        for(int i = 0; i < len; i++) {
            Platform platform = world.platforms.get(i);
            TextureRegion keyFrame = Assets.platform;
            if(platform.state == Platform.PLATFORM_STATE_PULVERIZING) {
                keyFrame = Assets.brakingPlatform.getKeyFrame(platform.stateTime,
Animation.ANIMATION_NONLOOPING);
```

```
            }
            batcher.drawSprite(platform.position.x, platform.position.y,
                            2, 0.5f, keyFrame);
        }
    }
```

The method `renderPlatforms()` loops through all the platforms in the world and selects a TextureRegion based on the platform's state. A platform can either be pulverized or not pulverized. In the latter case, we simply use the first keyframe, and in the former case we fetch a keyframe from the pulverization animation based on the platform's state time.

```
    private void renderItems() {
        int len = world.springs.size();
        for(int i = 0; i < len; i++) {
            Spring spring = world.springs.get(i);
            batcher.drawSprite(spring.position.x, spring.position.y, 1, 1,
Assets.spring);
        }

        len = world.coins.size();
        for(int i = 0; i < len; i++) {
            Coin coin = world.coins.get(i);
            TextureRegion keyFrame = Assets.coinAnim.getKeyFrame(coin.stateTime,
Animation.ANIMATION_LOOPING);
                batcher.drawSprite(coin.position.x, coin.position.y, 1, 1, keyFrame);
        }
    }
```

The method `renderItems()` renders springs and coins. For springs we just use the one TextureRegion we defined in Assets, and for coins we again select a keyframe from the animation based on a coin's state time.

```
    private void renderSquirrels() {
        int len = world.squirrels.size();
        for(int i = 0; i < len; i++) {
            Squirrel squirrel = world.squirrels.get(i);
            TextureRegion keyFrame = Assets.squirrelFly.getKeyFrame(squirrel.stateTime,
Animation.ANIMATION_LOOPING);
            float side = squirrel.velocity.x < 0?-1:1;
            batcher.drawSprite(squirrel.position.x, squirrel.position.y, side * 1, 1,
keyFrame);
        }
    }
```

The method `renderSquirrels()` renders squirrels. We again fetch a keyframe based on the squirrel's state time, figure out which direction it faces, and manipulate the width accordingly when rendering it with the `SpriteBatcher`. This is necessary since we only have a left-facing version of the squirrel in the texture atlas.

```
    private void renderCastle() {
        Castle castle = world.castle;
        batcher.drawSprite(castle.position.x, castle.position.y, 2, 2, Assets.castle);
    }
}
```

The last method is called renderCastle(), and simply draws the castle with the TextureRegion we defined in the Assets class.

That was pretty simple, wasn't it? We only have two batches to render: one for the background and one for the objects. Taking a step back we see that we render a third batch for all the UI elements of the game screen as well. That's three texture changes and three times uploading new vertices to the GPU. We could theoretically merge the UI and object batches, but that would be cumbersome and would introduce some hacks into our code. According to our optimization guidelines from Chapter 6, we should have lightning-fast rendering. Let's see whether that's true.

We are finally done. Our second game, Super Jumper, is now ready to be played.

To Optimize or Not to Optimize

It's time to benchmark our new game. The only place we really need to deal with speed is the game screen. I simply placed an FPSCounter instance in the GameScreen class and called its FPSCounter.logFrame() method at the end of the GameScreen.render() method. Here are the results on a Hero, a Droid, and a Nexus One:

```
Hero (1.5):
01-02 20:58:06.417: DEBUG/FPSCounter(8251): fps: 57
01-02 20:58:07.427: DEBUG/FPSCounter(8251): fps: 57
01-02 20:58:08.447: DEBUG/FPSCounter(8251): fps: 57
01-02 20:58:09.447: DEBUG/FPSCounter(8251): fps: 56

Droid (2.1.1):
01-02 21:03:59.643: DEBUG/FPSCounter(1676): fps: 61
01-02 21:04:00.659: DEBUG/FPSCounter(1676): fps: 59
01-02 21:04:01.659: DEBUG/FPSCounter(1676): fps: 60
01-02 21:04:02.666: DEBUG/FPSCounter(1676): fps: 60

Nexus One (2.2.1):
01-02 20:54:05.263: DEBUG/FPSCounter(1393): fps: 61
01-02 20:54:06.273: DEBUG/FPSCounter(1393): fps: 61
01-02 20:54:07.273: DEBUG/FPSCounter(1393): fps: 60
01-02 20:54:08.283: DEBUG/FPSCounter(1393): fps: 61
```

Sixty frames per second out of the box is pretty good, I'd say. The Hero struggles a little, of course, due to its less-than-stellar CPU. We could use the SpatialHashGrid to speed up the simulation of our world a little. I'll leave that as an exercise to you, dear reader. There's no real necessity for doing so, though, as the Hero will always be fraught with problems (as will any other 1.5 device, for that matter). What's worse is the hiccups due to garbage collection every now and then on the Hero. We know the reason (a bug in direct ByteBuffer), but we can't really do anything about it. Let's hope Android version 1.5 will die a quick death soon.

I took the preceding measurements with sound disabled in the main menu. Let's try again with audio playback turned on:

```
Hero (1.5):
01-02 21:01:22.437: DEBUG/FPSCounter(8251): fps: 43
```

```
01-02 21:01:23.457: DEBUG/FPSCounter(8251): fps: 48
01-02 21:01:24.467: DEBUG/FPSCounter(8251): fps: 49
01-02 21:01:25.487: DEBUG/FPSCounter(8251): fps: 49

Droid (2.1.1):
01-02 21:10:49.979: DEBUG/FPSCounter(1676): fps: 54
01-02 21:10:50.979: DEBUG/FPSCounter(1676): fps: 56
01-02 21:10:51.987: DEBUG/FPSCounter(1676): fps: 54
01-02 21:10:52.987: DEBUG/FPSCounter(1676): fps: 56

Nexus One (2.2.1):
01-02 21:06:06.144: DEBUG/FPSCounter(1470): fps: 61
01-02 21:06:07.153: DEBUG/FPSCounter(1470): fps: 61
01-02 21:06:08.173: DEBUG/FPSCounter(1470): fps: 62
01-02 21:06:09.183: DEBUG/FPSCounter(1470): fps: 61
```

Ouch. The Hero has significantly lower performance when we play back our background music. The audio also takes its toll on the Droid. The Nexus One doesn't really care, though. What can we do about it? Nothing really. The big culprit is not so much the sound effects but the background music. Streaming and decoding an MP3 or OGG file takes away CPU cycles from our game; that's just how the world works. Just remember to factor that into your performance measurements.

Summary

We've created our second game with the power of OpenGL ES. Due to our nice framework, it was actually a breeze to implement. The use of a texture atlas and the SpriteBatcher made for some very good performance. We also discussed how to render fixed-width ASCII bitmap fonts. Good initial design of our game mechanics and a clear definition of the relationship between world units and pixel units makes developing a game a lot easier. Imagine the nightmare we'd have if we tried to do everything in pixels. All our calculations would be riddled with divisions—something the CPUs of less-powerful Android devices don't like all that much. We also took great care to separate our logic from the presentation. All in all, I'd call Super Jumper a success.

Now it's time to turn the knobs to 11. Let's get our feet wet with some 3D graphics programming.

Chapter 10

OpenGL ES: Going 3D

Super Jumper worked out rather well with our 2D OpenGL ES rendering engine. Now it's time to go full 3D. We actually already worked in a 3D space when we defined our view frustum and the vertices of our sprites. In the latter case the z-coordinate of each vertex was simply set to zero by default. The difference from 2D rendering isn't all that big, really:

- Vertices not only have x- and y-coordinates, but also a z-coordinate.

- Instead of an orthographic projection, we use a perspective projection. Objects further away from the camera will appear smaller.

- Transformations, such as rotations, translations, and scales, have more degrees of freedom in 3D. Instead of just moving the vertices in the x-y plane we can now move them around freely on all 3 axes.

- We can define a camera with an arbitrary position and orientation in 3D space.

- The order we render the triangles of our objects with is now important. Objects further away from the camera must be overlapped by objects closer to the camera.

The best thing is that we have already laid the groundwork for all of this in our framework. We just need to adjust a couple classes slightly to go 3D.

Before We Begin

As always we'll write a couple of examples in this chapter. For this we'll follow the same route as before, by having a starter activity showing us a list of examples. We'll reuse all of the framework we created over the last couple of chapters, including the GLGame, GLScreen, Texture, and Vertices classes.

The starter activity of this chapter is called GL3DBasicsStarter. We can reuse the code of the GLBasicsStarter from Chapter 6, and just change the package name for the example classes we are going to run to com.badlogic.androidgames.gl3d. We also have to add each of the tests to the manifest in the form of <activity> elements again. All our tests will be run in fixed landscape orientation, which we will specify per <activity> element.

Each of the tests is an instance of the GLGame abstract class, and the actual test logic is implemented in the form of a GLScreen contained in the GLGame implementation of the test, as in previous chapters. I will only present the relevant portions of the GLScreen to conserve some pages. The naming conventions are again XXXTest and XXXScreen for the GLGame and GLScreen implementation of each test.

Vertices in 3D

In Chapter 7 you learned that a vertex has a few attributes:

- Position
- Color (optional)
- Texture coordinates (optional)

We created a helper class called Vertices, which handles all the dirty details for us. We limited the vertex positions to only have x- and y-coordinates. All we need to do to go 3D is modify the Vertices class so that it supports 3D vertex positions.

Vertices3: Storing 3D Positions

Let's write a new class called Vertices3 to handle 3D vertices based on our original Vertices class. Listing 10–1 shows the code.

Listing 10–1. *Vertices3.java, Now with More Coordinates*

```
package com.badlogic.androidgames.framework.gl;

import java.nio.ByteBuffer;
import java.nio.ByteOrder;
import java.nio.IntBuffer;
import java.nio.ShortBuffer;

import javax.microedition.khronos.opengles.GL10;

import com.badlogic.androidgames.framework.impl.GLGraphics;

public class Vertices3 {
    final GLGraphics glGraphics;
    final boolean hasColor;
    final boolean hasTexCoords;
    final int vertexSize;
    final IntBuffer vertices;
    final int[] tmpBuffer;
    final ShortBuffer indices;
```

```java
public Vertices3(GLGraphics glGraphics, int maxVertices, int maxIndices,
        boolean hasColor, boolean hasTexCoords) {
    this.glGraphics = glGraphics;
    this.hasColor = hasColor;
    this.hasTexCoords = hasTexCoords;
    this.vertexSize = (3 + (hasColor ? 4 : 0) + (hasTexCoords ? 2 : 0)) * 4;
    this.tmpBuffer = new int[maxVertices * vertexSize / 4];

    ByteBuffer buffer = ByteBuffer.allocateDirect(maxVertices * vertexSize);
    buffer.order(ByteOrder.nativeOrder());
    vertices = buffer.asIntBuffer();

    if (maxIndices > 0) {
        buffer = ByteBuffer.allocateDirect(maxIndices * Short.SIZE / 8);
        buffer.order(ByteOrder.nativeOrder());
        indices = buffer.asShortBuffer();
    } else {
        indices = null;
    }
}

public void setVertices(float[] vertices, int offset, int length) {
    this.vertices.clear();
    int len = offset + length;
    for (int i = offset, j = 0; i < len; i++, j++)
        tmpBuffer[j] = Float.floatToRawIntBits(vertices[i]);
    this.vertices.put(tmpBuffer, 0, length);
    this.vertices.flip();
}

public void setIndices(short[] indices, int offset, int length) {
    this.indices.clear();
    this.indices.put(indices, offset, length);
    this.indices.flip();
}

public void bind() {
    GL10 gl = glGraphics.getGL();

    gl.glEnableClientState(GL10.GL_VERTEX_ARRAY);
    vertices.position(0);
    gl.glVertexPointer(3, GL10.GL_FLOAT, vertexSize, vertices);

    if (hasColor) {
        gl.glEnableClientState(GL10.GL_COLOR_ARRAY);
        vertices.position(3);
        gl.glColorPointer(4, GL10.GL_FLOAT, vertexSize, vertices);
    }

    if (hasTexCoords) {
        gl.glEnableClientState(GL10.GL_TEXTURE_COORD_ARRAY);
        vertices.position(hasColor ? 7 : 3);
        gl.glTexCoordPointer(2, GL10.GL_FLOAT, vertexSize, vertices);
    }
}
```

```
    public void draw(int primitiveType, int offset, int numVertices) {
        GL10 gl = glGraphics.getGL();

        if (indices != null) {
            indices.position(offset);
            gl.glDrawElements(primitiveType, numVertices,
                    GL10.GL_UNSIGNED_SHORT, indices);
        } else {
            gl.glDrawArrays(primitiveType, offset, numVertices);
        }
    }

    public void unbind() {
        GL10 gl = glGraphics.getGL();
        if (hasTexCoords)
            gl.glDisableClientState(GL10.GL_TEXTURE_COORD_ARRAY);

        if (hasColor)
            gl.glDisableClientState(GL10.GL_COLOR_ARRAY);
    }
}
```

Everything stays the same compared to Vertices except for four little things. In the constructor we calculate vertexSize differently, since the vertex position takes three instead of two floats now.

In the bind() method we tell OpenGL ES that our vertices have three instead of two coordinates in the call to glVertexPointer() (first argument). We also have to adjust the offsets we set in the calls to vertices.position() for the optional color and texture coordinate components.

That's all we need to do. Using the Vertices3 class, we now have to specify the x-, y-, and z-coordinates for each vertex when we call the Vertices3.setVertices() method. Everything else stays the same usage-wise. We can have per-vertex colors, texture coordinates, indices, and so on.

An Example

Let's write a simple example called Vertices3Test. We want to draw two triangles, one with z being –3 for each vertex and one with z being –5 for each vertex. We'll also use per-vertex color. Since we haven't discussed how to use a perspective projection, we'll just use an orthographic projection with appropriate near and far clipping planes so that the triangles are in the view frustum (e.g., near is 10 and far is –10). Figure 10–1 shows the scene.

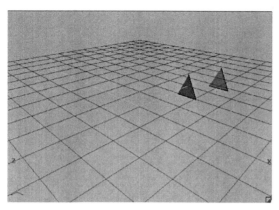

Figure 10–1. *A red triangle (front) and a green triangle (back) in 3D space*

The red triangle is in front of the green triangle. We can say "in front" because our camera is located at the origin looking down the negative z-axis by default in OpenGL ES (which actually doesn't have the notation of a camera). The green triangle is also shifted a little to the right so that we can see a portion of it when viewed from the front. It should be overlapped by the red triangle for the most part. Listing 10–2 shows the code for rendering this scene.

Listing 10–2. *Vertices3Test.java: Drawing Two Triangles*

```java
package com.badlogic.androidgames.gl3d;

import javax.microedition.khronos.opengles.GL10;

import com.badlogic.androidgames.framework.Game;
import com.badlogic.androidgames.framework.Screen;
import com.badlogic.androidgames.framework.gl.Vertices3;
import com.badlogic.androidgames.framework.impl.GLGame;
import com.badlogic.androidgames.framework.impl.GLScreen;

public class Vertices3Test extends GLGame {

    @Override
    public Screen getStartScreen() {
        return new Vertices3Screen(this);
    }

    class Vertices3Screen extends GLScreen {
        Vertices3 vertices;

        public Vertices3Screen(Game game) {
            super(game);

            vertices = new Vertices3(glGraphics, 6, 0, true, false);
            vertices.setVertices(new float[] { -0.5f, -0.5f, -3, 1, 0, 0, 1,
                                                0.5f, -0.5f, -3, 1, 0, 0, 1,
                                                0.0f,  0.5f, -3, 1, 0, 0, 1,

                                                0.0f,  -0.5f, -5, 0, 1, 0, 1,
```

```
                                                1.0f,  -0.5f, -5, 0, 1, 0, 1,
                                                0.5f,   0.5f, -5, 0, 1, 0, 1}, 0, 7 * 6);
    }

    @Override
    public void present(float deltaTime) {
        GL10 gl = glGraphics.getGL();
        gl.glClear(GL10.GL_COLOR_BUFFER_BIT);
        gl.glViewport(0, 0, glGraphics.getWidth(), glGraphics.getHeight());
        gl.glMatrixMode(GL10.GL_PROJECTION);
        gl.glLoadIdentity();
        gl.glOrthof(-1, 1, -1, 1, 10, -10);
        gl.glMatrixMode(GL10.GL_MODELVIEW);
        gl.glLoadIdentity();
        vertices.bind();
        vertices.draw(GL10.GL_TRIANGLES, 0, 6);
        vertices.unbind();
    }

    @Override
    public void update(float deltaTime) {
    }

    @Override
    public void pause() {
    }

    @Override
    public void resume() {
    }

    @Override
    public void dispose() {
    }
    }
}
```

This is the complete source file, as you can see. For the following examples we'll go back to only showing the relevant portions, since the rest stays mostly the same, apart from the class names.

We have a Vertices3 member in Vertices3Screen, which we initialize in the constructor. We have six vertices in total, a color per vertex, and no texture coordinates. Since neither triangle shares vertices with the other, we don't use indexed geometry. This information is passed to the Vertices3 constructor. Next we set the actual vertices with a call to Vertices3.setVertices(). The first three lines specify the red triangle in the front, and the other three lines specify the green triangle in the back, slightly offset to the right by 0.5 units. The third float on each line is the z-coordinate of the respective vertex.

In the present() method we first clear the screen and set the viewport, as always. Next we load an orthographic projection matrix, setting up a view frustum big enough to show all of our scene. Finally we just render the two triangles contained within the Vertices3 instance. Figure 10–2 shows the output of this program.

Figure 10-2. *The two triangles, but something's wrong*

Now that is strange. According to our theory, the red triangle (in the middle) should be in front of the green triangle. Our camera is located at the origin looking down the negative z-axis, and from Figure 10–1 we see that the red triangle is closer to the origin than the green triangle. What's happening here?

OpenGL ES will render the triangles in the order we specify them in the Vertices3 instance. Since we specified the red triangle first, it will get drawn first. We could change the order of the triangles to fix this. But what if our camera weren't looking down the negative z-axis, but from behind? We'd again have to sort the triangles before rendering according to their distance from the camera. That can't be the solution. And it isn't. We'll fix this in a minute. Let's first get rid of this orthographic projection and use a perspective one instead.

Perspective Projection: The Closer, the Bigger

Until now we have always used an orthographic projection, meaning that no matter how far an object is from the near clipping plane, it will always have the same size on the screen. Our eyes show us a different picture of the world. The further away an object is, the smaller it appears to us. This is called perspective projection, and we've already talked about it a little in Chapter 4.

The difference between an orthographic projection and a perspective projection can be explained by the shape of the view frustum. In an orthographic projection, we have a box. In a perspective projection, we have a pyramid with a cut off top as the near clipping plane; the pyramid's base as the far clipping plane; and its sides as the left, right, top, and bottom clipping planes. Figure 10–3 shows a perspective view frustum through which we can view our scene.

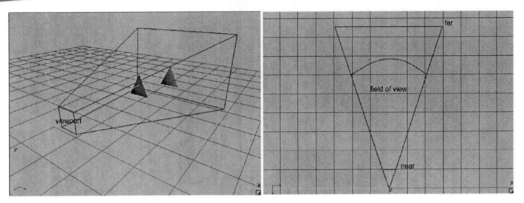

Figure 10–3. *A perspective view frustum containing our scene (left); the frustum viewed from above (right)*

The perspective view frustum is define by four parameters:

- The distance from the camera to the near clipping plane
- The distance from the camera to the far clipping plane
- The aspect ratio of the viewport, which is embedded in the near clipping plane given by viewport width divided by viewport height
- The field of view, specifying how wide the view frustum is and therefore how much of the scene it shows

While we've talked about a camera, there's no such concept involved here yet. We just pretend there is a camera sitting fixed at the origin looking down the negative z-axis, as in Figure 10–3.

The near and far clipping plane distances are no strangers to us. We just need to set them up so that the complete scene is contained in the view frustum. The field of view is also easily understandable when looking at the right image in Figure 10–3.

The aspect ratio of the viewport is a little less intuitive. Why is it needed? It makes sure that our world doesn't get stretched in case the screen we render to has an aspect ratio that's not equal to 1.

Previously we used glOrthof() to specify the orthographic view frustum in the form of a projection matrix. For the perspective view frustum we could use a method called glFrustumf(). However, there's an easier way.

Traditionally OpenGL comes with a utility library called GLU. It contains a couple of helper functions for things like setting up projection matrices and implementing camera systems. That library is also available on Android in the form of a class called GLU. It features a few static methods we can invoke without needing a GLU instance. The method we are interested in is called gluPerspective():

```
GLU.gluPerspective(GL10 gl, float fieldOfView, float aspectRatio, float near, float far);
```

This method will multiply the currently active matrix (e.g., projection or model-view matrix) with a perspective projection matrix, similar to glOrthof(). The first parameter is an instance of GL10, usually the one we use for all other OpenGL ES–related business. The second parameter is the field of view given in angles, the third parameter is the aspect ratio of the viewport, and the last two parameters specify the distance of the near and far clipping plane from the camera position. Since we don't have a camera yet, those values are given relative to the origin of the world, forcing us to look down the negative z-axis, as shown in Figure 10–3. That's totally fine for our purposes at the moment; we will make sure that all the objects we render stay within this fixed and immovable view frustum. As long as we only use gluPerspective(), we can't change the position or orientation of our virtual camera. We'll always only see a portion of the world looking down the negative z-axis.

Let's modify the last example so it uses perspective projection. I just copied over all code from Vertices3Test to a new class called PerspectiveTest, and also renamed Vertices3Screen to PerspectiveScreen. The only thing we need to change is the present() method. Listing 10–3 shows the code.

Listing 10–3. *Excerpt from PerspectiveTest.java: Perspective Projection*

```
@Override
public void present(float deltaTime) {
    GL10 gl = glGraphics.getGL();
    gl.glClear(GL10.GL_COLOR_BUFFER_BIT);
    gl.glViewport(0, 0, glGraphics.getWidth(), glGraphics.getHeight());
    gl.glMatrixMode(GL10.GL_PROJECTION);
    gl.glLoadIdentity();
    GLU.gluPerspective(gl, 67,
                       glGraphics.getWidth() / (float)glGraphics.getHeight(),
                       0.1f, 10f);
    gl.glMatrixMode(GL10.GL_MODELVIEW);
    gl.glLoadIdentity();
    vertices.bind();
    vertices.draw(GL10.GL_TRIANGLES, 0, 6);
    vertices.unbind();
}
```

The only difference from the previous present() method is that we are now using GLU.gluPerspective() instead of glOrtho(). We use a field of view of 67 degrees, which is close to the average human field of view. By increasing or decreasing this value, you can see more or less to the left and right. The next thing we specify is the aspect ratio, which is just the screen's width divided by its height. Note that this will be a floating-point number, so we have to cast one of the values to a float before dividing. The final arguments are the near and far clipping plane distance. Given that our virtual camera is located at the origin looking down the negative z-axis, anything with a z-value smaller than –0.1 and bigger than –10 will be between the near and far clipping planes, and thus be potentially visible. Figure 10–4 shows the output of this example.

Figure 10–4. *Perspective (mostly correct)*

Now we are actually doing proper 3D graphics. As you can see, we still have a problem with the rendering order of our triangles. Let's fix that by using the almighty z-buffer.

Z-buffer: Bringing Order into Chaos

What is a z-buffer? In Chapter 4 we discussed the framebuffer. It stores the color for each pixel on the screen. When OpenGL ES renders a triangle to the framebuffer, it just changes the color of the pixels that make up that triangle.

The z-buffer is very similar to the framebuffer in that it also has a storage location for each pixel on the screen. Instead of storing colors, it stores depth values, though. The depth value of a pixel is roughly the normalized distance of the corresponding point in 3D to the near clipping plane of the view frustum.

OpenGL ES will write a depth value for each pixel of a triangle to the z-buffer by default (if a z-buffer was created alongside the framebuffer). All we have to tell OpenGL ES is to use this information to decide whether a pixel being drawn is closer to the near clipping plane than the one that's currently there. For this we just need to call glEnable() with an appropriate parameter:

```
GL10.glEnable(GL10.GL_DEPTH_TEST);
```

That's all we need to do. OpenGL ES will then compare the incoming pixel depth with the pixel depth that's already in the z-buffer. If it is smaller, it is also closer to the near clipping plane and thus in front of the pixel that's already in the frame- and z-buffer.

Figure 10–5 illustrates the process. The z-buffer starts of with all values set to infinity (or a very high number). When we render our first triangle, we compare each of its pixels' depth value to the value of the pixel in the z-buffer. If the depth value of a pixel is smaller than the value in the z-buffer, it passes the so-called *depth test*, or *z-test*. The pixel's color will be written to the framebuffer and its depth will overwrite the corresponding value in the z-buffer. If it fails the test, neither the pixel's color nor the depth value will be written to the buffers. This is shown in Figure 10–5, where the second triangle is rendered. Some of the pixels have smaller depth values and thus get rendered; other pixels don't pass the test.

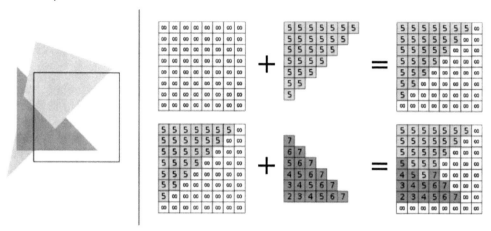

Figure 10–5. *Image in the framebuffer (left); z-buffer contents after rendering each of the two triangles (right)*

As with the framebuffer, we also have to clear the z-buffer each frame, otherwise the depth values from the last frame would still be in there. To do this we can call `glClear()`, like this:

```
gl.glClear(GL10.GL_COLOR_BUFFER_BIT | GL10.GL_DEPTH_BUFFER_BIT);
```

This will clear the framebuffer (or colorbuffer), as well as the z-buffer (or depthbuffer), all in one go.

Fixing the Last Example

Let's fix the last example's problems by using the z-buffer. I just copied all the code over to a new class called ZBufferTest and modified the present() method of the new ZBufferScreen class, as shown in Listing 10–4.

Listing 10–4. *Excerpt from ZBufferTest.java: Using the Z-buffer*

```java
@Override
public void present(float deltaTime) {
    GL10 gl = glGraphics.getGL();
    gl.glClear(GL10.GL_COLOR_BUFFER_BIT | GL10.GL_DEPTH_BUFFER_BIT);
    gl.glViewport(0, 0, glGraphics.getWidth(), glGraphics.getHeight());
    gl.glMatrixMode(GL10.GL_PROJECTION);
    gl.glLoadIdentity();
    GLU.gluPerspective(gl, 67,
            glGraphics.getWidth() / (float)glGraphics.getHeight(),
            0.1f, 10f);
    gl.glMatrixMode(GL10.GL_MODELVIEW);
    gl.glLoadIdentity();

    gl.glEnable(GL10.GL_DEPTH_TEST);

    vertices.bind();
```

```
    vertices.draw(GL10.GL_TRIANGLES, 0, 6);
    vertices.unbind();

    gl.glDisable(GL10.GL_DEPTH_TEST);
}
```

The first thing we changed is the arguments to the call to glClear(). We now clear both buffers instead of just the framebuffer.

We also enable depth-testing before we render our two triangles. After we are done with rendering all our 3D geometry, we disable depth-testing again. Why? Imagine that we want to render 2D UI elements on top of our 3D scene, like the current score or buttons. Since we'd use the SpriteBatcher for this, which only works in 2D, we wouldn't have any meaningful z-coordinates for the vertices of the 2D elements. We wouldn't need depth-testing either, since we would explicitly specify the order we want the vertices to be drawn to the screen.

The output of this example, shown in Figure 10–6, looks as expected now.

Figure 10–6. *The z-buffer in action, making our rendering order-independent*

Finally the green triangle in the middle is rendered correctly behind the red triangle, thanks to our new best friend, the z-buffer. But as with most friends, there are times when your friendship suffers a little from minor issues. Let's examine some caveats when using the z-buffer.

Blending: There's Nothing Behind You

Assume we want to enable blending for the red triangle at z = –3 in our scene. Say we set each vertex color's alpha component to 0.5f so that anything behind the triangle shines through. In our case the green triangle at z = –5 should shine through. Let's think about what OpenGL ES will do and what else will happen:

- OpenGL ES will render the first triangle to the z-buffer and colorbuffer.

- Next OpenGL ES will render the green triangle, because it comes after the red triangle in our Vertices3 instance.

```
                              -0.5f, -0.5f, -0.5f, 0, 1,
                              -0.5f, -0.5f,  0.5f, 1, 1,
                              -0.5f,  0.5f,  0.5f, 1, 0,
                              -0.5f,  0.5f, -0.5f, 0, 0,

                              -0.5f,  0.5f,  0.5f, 0, 1,
                               0.5f,  0.5f,  0.5f, 1, 1,
                               0.5f,  0.5f, -0.5f, 1, 0,
                              -0.5f,  0.5f, -0.5f, 0, 0,

                              -0.5f, -0.5f,  0.5f, 0, 1,
                               0.5f, -0.5f,  0.5f, 1, 1,
                               0.5f, -0.5f, -0.5f, 1, 0,
                              -0.5f, -0.5f, -0.5f, 0, 0
    };

    short[] indices = { 0,  1,  3,  1,  2,  3,
                        4,  5,  7,  5,  6,  7,
                        8,  9, 11,  9, 10, 11,
                       12, 13, 15, 13, 14, 15,
                       16, 17, 19, 17, 18, 19,
                       20, 21, 23, 21, 22, 23,
    };

    Vertices3 cube = new Vertices3(glGraphics, 24, 36, false, true);
    cube.setVertices(vertices, 0, vertices.length);
    cube.setIndices(indices, 0, indices.length);
    return cube;
}

@Override
public void resume() {
    texture.reload();
}

@Override
public void update(float deltaTime) {
    angle += 45 * deltaTime;
}

@Override
public void present(float deltaTime) {
    GL10 gl = glGraphics.getGL();
    gl.glViewport(0, 0, glGraphics.getWidth(), glGraphics.getHeight());
    gl.glClear(GL10.GL_COLOR_BUFFER_BIT | GL10.GL_DEPTH_BUFFER_BIT);
    gl.glMatrixMode(GL10.GL_PROJECTION);
    gl.glLoadIdentity();
    GLU.gluPerspective(gl, 67,
                       glGraphics.getWidth() / (float) glGraphics.getHeight(),
                       0.1f, 10.0f);
    gl.glMatrixMode(GL10.GL_MODELVIEW);
    gl.glLoadIdentity();

    gl.glEnable(GL10.GL_DEPTH_TEST);
    gl.glEnable(GL10.GL_TEXTURE_2D);
    texture.bind();
    cube.bind();
```

```
        gl.glTranslatef(0,0,-3);
        gl.glRotatef(angle, 0, 1, 0);
        cube.draw(GL10.GL_TRIANGLES, 0, 36);
        cube.unbind();
        gl.glDisable(GL10.GL_TEXTURE_2D);
        gl.glDisable(GL10.GL_DEPTH_TEST);
    }

    @Override
    public void pause() {
    }

    @Override
    public void dispose() {
    }
}
```

We have a field to store the cube's mesh, a Texture instance, and a float to store the current rotation angle in. In the constructor we create the cube mesh and load the texture from an asset file called crate.png, a 128×128-pixel image of one side of a crate.

The cube creation code is located in the createCube() method. It just sets up the vertices and indices, and creates a Vertices3 instance from them. Each vertex has a 3D position and texture coordinates.

The resume() method just tells the texture to reload it. Remember, textures must be reloaded after an OpenGL ES context loss.

The update() method just increases the rotation angle by which we'll rotate the cube around the y-axis.

The present() method first sets the viewport and clears the framebuffer and depthbuffer. Next we set up a perspective projection and load an identity matrix to the model-view matrix of OpenGL ES. We enable depth testing and texturing, and bind the texture, as well as the cube mesh. Then we use glTranslatef() to move the cube to the position (0,0,–3) in world space. With glRotatef() we rotate the cube in model space around the y-axis. Remember that the order in which these transformations get applied to the mesh is reversed. The cube will first be rotated (in model space), and then the rotated version will be positioned in world space. Finally we draw the cube, unbind the mesh, and disable depth-testing and texturing. We don't need to disable those states; I just put that in in case we are going to render 2D elements on top of the 3D scene. Figure 10–12 shows the output of our first real 3D program.

Figure 10–12. *A spinning texture cube in 3D*

Matrices and Transformations Again

In Chapter 6 we talked a little bit about matrices. Let's summarize some of their properties as a little refresher:

- A matrix translates points (or vertices in our case) to a new position. This is achieved by multiplying the matrix with the point's position.

- A matrix can translate points on each axis by some amount.

- A matrix can scale points, meaning that it multiplies each coordinate of a point by some constant.

- A matrix can rotate a point around an axis.

- Multiplying an identity matrix with a point has no effect on that point.

- Multiplying one matrix with another matrix results in a new matrix. Multiplying a point with this new matrix will apply both transformations encoded in the original matrices to that point.

- Multiplying a matrix with an identity matrix has no effect on the matrix.

OpenGL ES provides us with three types of matrices:

- *Projection matrix*: We use this to set up our view frustum's shape and size, which governs the type of projection and how much of our world is shown to us.

- *Model-view matrix*: We use this to transform our models in model space, and to place a model in world space.

- *Texture matrix*: We keep ignoring this, as it is broken on many devices.

Now that we are working in 3D we have more options at our disposal. We can, for example, not only rotate a model around the z-axis like we did with Bob, but around any arbitrary axis. The only thing that really changes, though, is the additional z-axis we can now use to place our objects. We were actually already working in 3D when we rendered Bob back in Chapter 6; we just ignored the z-axis. But there's more we can do.

The Matrix Stack

Up until now, we have used matrices like this with OpenGL ES:

```
gl.glMatrixMode(GL10.GL_PROJECTION);
gl.glLoadIdentity();
gl.glOrthof(-1, 1, -1, 1, -10, 10);
```

The first statement sets the currently active matrix. All subsequent matrix operations will be executed on that matrix. In this case, we set the active matrix to an identity matrix and then multiply it by an orthographic projection matrix. We did something similar with the model-view matrix:

```
gl.glMatrixMode(GL10.GL_MODELVIEW);
gl.glLoadIdentity();
gl.glTranslatef(0, 0, -10);
gl.glRotate(45, 0, 1, 0);
```

This snippet manipulates the model-view matrix. It first loads an identity matrix to clear whatever was in the model-view matrix before that call. Next it multiplies the matrix with a translation matrix and a rotation matrix. This order of multiplication is important, as it defines in what order these transformations get applied to the vertices of our meshes. The last transformation we specify will be the first to be applied to the vertices. In the preceding case, we first rotate each vertex by 45 degrees around the y-axis. Then we move each vertex by −10 units along the z-axis.

In both cases all the transformations are encoded in a single matrix, in either the OpenGL ES projection or model-view matrix. But it turns out that for each matrix type, there's actually a stack of matrices at our disposal.

For now we're only using a single slot in this stack: the top of the stack (TOS). The TOS of a matrix stack is the one actually used by OpenGL ES to transform our vertices, be it with the projection or model-view matrix. Any matrix below the TOS on the stack just sits there idly, waiting to become the new TOS. So how can we manipulate this stack?

OpenGL ES has two methods we can use to push and pop the current TOS:

```
GL10.glPushMatrix();
GL10.glPopMatrix();
```

Like glTranslatef() and consorts, these methods always work on the currently active matrix stack that we set via glMatrixMode().

The glPushMatrix() method takes the current TOS, makes a copy of it, and pushes it on the stack. The glPopMatrix() method takes the current TOS and pops it from the stack so that the element below it becomes the new TOS. Let's work through a little example:

```
gl.glMatrixMode(GL10.GL_MODELVIEW);
gl.glLoadIdentity();
gl.glTranslate(0,0,-10);
```

Up until this point, there has only been a single matrix on the model-view matrix stack. Let's "save" this matrix:

```
gl.glPushMatrix();
```

Now we've made a copy of the current TOS and pushed down the old TOS. We have two matrices on the stack now, each encoding a translation on the z-axis by –10 units.

```
gl.glRotatef(45, 0, 1, 0);
gl.glScalef(1, 2, 1);
```

Since matrix operations always work on the TOS, we now have a scaling operation, a rotation, and a translation encoded in the top matrix. The matrix we pushed still only contains a translation. When we now render a mesh given in model space, like our cube, it will first be scaled on the y-axis, then rotated around the y-axis, and then translated by –10 units on the z-axis. Let's pop the TOS:

```
gl.glPopMatrix();
```

This will remove the TOS and make the matrix below it the new TOS. In our example, that's the original translation matrix. After this call there's only one matrix on the stack again—the one we initialized in the beginning of the example. If we render an object now, it will only be translated by –10 units on the z-axis. The matrix containing the scaling, rotation, and translation is gone due to us popping it from the stack. Figure 10–13 shows what happens to the matrix stack when we execute the preceding code.

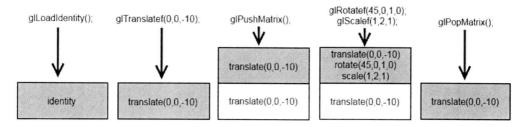

Figure 10–13. *Manipulating the matrix stack*

So what's this good for? The first thing we can use it for is to remember transformations that should be applied to all the objects in our world. Say we want all objects in our world to be offset by 10 units on each axis. We could do the following:

```
gl.glMatrixMode(GL10.GL_MODELVIEW);
gl.glLoadIdentity();
gl.glTranslatef(10, 10, 10);
for( MyObject obj: myObjects) {
    gl.glPushMatrix();
    gl.glTranslatef(obj.x, obj.y, obj.z);
    gl.glRotatef(obj.angle, 0, 1, 0);
    // render model of object given in model space, e.g., the cube
    gl.glPopMatrix();
}
```

We will use this pattern later on when we discuss how to create a camera system in 3D. The camera position and orientation is usually encoded as a matrix. We will load this camera matrix, which will transform all objects in such a way that we see them from the camera's point of view. There's something even better we can use the matrix stack for, though.

Hierarchical Systems with the Matrix Stack

What's a hierarchical system? Our solar system is an example of one. In the center we have the sun. Around the sun are the planets orbiting it at certain distances. Around some planets we find moons that orbit the planet itself. And the sun, the planets, and the moons each rotate around their own centers (sort of). We can build such a system with the matrix stack.

The sun has a position in our world and rotates around itself. All planets move with the sun, so if the sun changes position, the planets must change position as well. We can use glTranslatef() to position the sun and glRotatef() to let it rotate around itself.

The planets have a position relative to the sun and rotate around themselves, as well as around the sun. Rotating the planet around itself can be done via glRotatef(), and rotating it around the sun can be done using glTranslatef() and glRotatef(). Letting the planet move with the sun can be done by an additional glTranslatef().

The moons have a position relative to the planet they orbit and rotate around themselves, as well as around their planet. Rotating the moon around itself can be done via glRotatef(), and rotating it around the planet can be done by glTranslatef() and glRotatef(). Letting the moon move with the planet can be done by glTranslatef(). And since the planet moves with the sun, the moon also has to move with the sun, which can again be done via a call to glTranslatef().

We have so-called parent/child relationships here. The sun is a parent of each planet, and each planet is a parent of each moon. Each planet is a child of the sun, and each moon is a child of its planet. This means that the position of a child is always given relative to its parent, not relative to the world's origin.

The sun has no parent, so its position is indeed given relative to the world's origin. A planet is a child of the sun, so its position is given relative to the sun, and a moon is a child of a planet, so its position is given relative to the planet. You can think of each parent's center being the origin of the coordinate system that we specify a parent's children in.

The self-rotation of each of the objects in our system is independent of its parent. The same would be true if we wanted to scale an object. These things are given relative to their center. This is essentially the same as the model space.

A Simple Crate Solar System

Let's create a little example, a very simple crate solar system. We have one crate in the center of the system located at (0,0,5) in our world's coordinate system. Around this "sun" crate, we want to have "planet" crate orbiting that sun at a distance of 3 units. The planet crate should also be smaller than the sun crate; let's say we scale it down to 0.2

units. Around the planet crate we want to have a "moon" crate. The distance between the planet crate and the moon crate should be 1 unit, and the moon crate will also be scaled down, say to 0.1 units. All the objects rotate around their respective parent in the x-z plane and also around their own y-axes. Figure 10–14 shows the basic setup of our scene.

Figure 10–14. *Our crate system*

The HierarchicalObject Class

Let's define a simple class that can encode a generic solar system object with the following properties:

- A position relative to its parent's center
- A rotation angle around the parent
- A rotation angle around its own y-axis
- A scale
- A list of children
- A reference to a `Vertices3` instance to be rendered

Our `HierarchicalObject` should update its rotation angles and its children, and render itself and all its children. This is a recursive process since each child will render its own children. We will use `glPushMatrix()` and `glPopMatrix()` to save a parent's transformations so that children will move along with the parent. Listing 10–7 shows the code.

Listing 10–7. *HierarchicalObject.java, Representing an Object in Our Crate System*

```
package com.badlogic.androidgames.gl3d;

import java.util.ArrayList;
import java.util.List;
```

```
import javax.microedition.khronos.opengles.GL10;

import com.badlogic.androidgames.framework.gl.Vertices3;

public class HierarchicalObject {
    public float x, y, z;
    public float scale = 1;
    public float rotationY, rotationParent;
    public boolean hasParent;
    public final List<HierarchicalObject> children = new
ArrayList<HierarchicalObject>();
    public final Vertices3 mesh;
```

The first three members encode the position of the object relative to its parent (or
relative to the world's origin if the object has no parent). The next member stores the
scale of the object. The rotationY member stores the rotation of the object around itself,
and the rotationParent member stores the rotation angle around the parent's center.
The hasParent member indicates whether this object has a parent or not. In case it
doesn't, then we don't have to apply the rotation around the parent. This is true for the
"sun" in our system. Finally we have a list of children, as well as a reference to a
Vertices3 instance, which holds the mesh of the cube we use to render each object.

```
    public HierarchicalObject(Vertices3 mesh, boolean hasParent) {
        this.mesh = mesh;
        this.hasParent = hasParent;
    }
```

The constructor just takes a Vertices3 instance and a boolean indicating whether this
object has a parent or not.

```
    public void update(float deltaTime) {
        rotationY += 45 * deltaTime;
        rotationParent += 20 * deltaTime;
        int len = children.size();
        for (int i = 0; i < len; i++) {
            children.get(i).update(deltaTime);
        }
    }
```

In the update() method, we first update the rotationY and rotationParent members.
Each object will rotate by 45 degrees per second around itself, and by 20 degrees per
second around its parent. We also call the update() method recursively for each child of
the object.

```
    public void render(GL10 gl) {
        gl.glPushMatrix();
        if (hasParent)
            gl.glRotatef(rotationParent, 0, 1, 0);
        gl.glTranslatef(x, y, z);
        gl.glPushMatrix();
        gl.glRotatef(rotationY, 0, 1, 0);
        gl.glScalef(scale, scale, scale);
        mesh.draw(GL10.GL_TRIANGLES, 0, 36);
        gl.glPopMatrix();
```

```
        int len = children.size();
        for (int i = 0; i < len; i++) {
            children.get(i).render(gl);
        }
        gl.glPopMatrix();
    }
}
```

The render() method is where it gets interesting. The first thing we do is push the current TOS of the model-view matrix, which will be set active outside of the object. Since this method is recursive, we will save the parent's transformations by this.

Next we apply the transformations that rotate our object around the parent and place it relative to the parent's center. Remember that transformations are executed in reverse order, so we actually first place the object relative to the parent and then rotate it around the parent. The rotation is only executed in case the object actually has a parent. Our sun crate doesn't have a parent, so we don't rotate it. These are transformations that are relative to the parent of the object and will also apply to the children of the object. Moving a planet around the sun also moves the "attached" moon.

The next thing we do is push the TOS again. Up until this point, it has contained the parent's transformation and the object's transformation relative to the parent. We need to save this matrix since it's also going to be applied to the object's children. The self-rotation of the object and its scaling do not apply to the children, and that's why we perform this operations on a copy of the TOS (which we created by pushing the TOS). After we apply the self-rotation and the scaling transformation, we can render this object with the crate mesh it stores a reference to. Let's think about what will happen to the vertices given in model space due to the TOS matrix. Remember the order in which transformations are applied: last to first.

The crate will be scaled to the appropriate size first. The next transformation that gets applied is the self-rotation. These two transformations are applied to the vertices in model space. Next the vertices will be translated to the position relative to the object's parent. If this object has no parent, we'll effectively translate the vertices to the world space. If it has a parent, we'll translate them to the parent's space, with the parent being at the origin. We will also rotate the object around the parent if it has one in parent space. If you unroll the recursion, you will see that we also apply the transformations of this object's parent, and so on. Through this mechanism, a moon will first be placed in a parent's coordinate system, and then into the sun's coordinate system, which is equivalent to world space.

Once we are done rendering the current object, we pop the TOS so that the new TOS only contains the transformation and rotation of the object relative to its parent. We don't want the children to also have the "local" transformations of the object applied to them (i.e., rotation around the object's y-axis and object scale). All that's left is recursing into the children.

> **NOTE:** We should actually encode the position of the `HierarchicalObject` in the form of a vector so we can work with it more easily. However, we have yet to write a `Vector3` class. We'll do that in the next chapter.

Putting It All Together

Let's use this `HierarchicalObject` class in a proper program. For this I simply copied over the code from the `CubeTest`, which also contains the `createCube()` method that we'll reuse. I renamed the class `HierarchyTest` and also renamed the `CubeScreen` to `HierarchyScreen`. All we need to do is create our object hierarchy and call the `HierarchicalObject.update()` and `HierarchicalObject.render()` methods in the appropriate place. Listing 10–8 shows the portions of `HierarchyTest` that are relevant.

Listing 10–8. *Excerpt from HierarchyTest.java: Implementing a Simple Hierarchical System*

```
class HierarchyScreen extends GLScreen {
        Vertices3 cube;
        Texture texture;
        HierarchicalObject sun;
```

We only added a single new member to the class, called sun. It represents the root of our object hierarchy. Since all other objects are stored as children inside this sun object, we don't need to store them explicitly.

```
        public HierarchyScreen(Game game) {
            super(game);
            cube = createCube();
            texture = new Texture(glGame, "crate.png");

            sun = new HierarchicalObject(cube, false);
            sun.z = -5;

            HierarchicalObject planet = new HierarchicalObject(cube, true);
            planet.x = 3;
            planet.scale = 0.2f;
            sun.children.add(planet);

            HierarchicalObject moon = new HierarchicalObject(cube, true);
            moon.x = 1;
            moon.scale = 0.1f;
            planet.children.add(moon);
        }
```

In the constructor we set up our hierarchical system. First we load the texture and create the cube mesh to be used by all the objects. Next we create the sun. It does not have a parent, and is located at (0,0,–5) relative to the world's origin (where our virtual camera sits). Next we create the planet crate orbiting the sun. It's located at (0,0,3) relative to the sun and has a scale of 0.2. Since our crate has a side length of 1 in model space this scaling factor will make it render with a side length of 0.2 units. The crucial step here is that we add the planet to the sun as a child. For the moon we do something similar. It is located at (0,0,1) relative to the planet, and has a scale of 0.1 units. We also add it as a child to the planet. Refer to Figure 10–14, which uses the same unit system to get a picture of our setup.

```
@Override
public void update(float deltaTime) {
    sun.update(deltaTime);
}
```

In the update() method we simply tell the sun to update itself. It will recursively call the same methods of all its children, which in turn call the same methods of all their children, and so on. This will update the rotation angles of all objects in the hierarchy.

```
@Override
public void present(float deltaTime) {
    GL10 gl = glGraphics.getGL();
    gl.glViewport(0, 0, glGraphics.getWidth(), glGraphics.getHeight());
    gl.glClear(GL10.GL_COLOR_BUFFER_BIT | GL10.GL_DEPTH_BUFFER_BIT);
    gl.glMatrixMode(GL10.GL_PROJECTION);
    gl.glLoadIdentity();
    GLU.gluPerspective(gl, 67, glGraphics.getWidth()
            / (float) glGraphics.getHeight(), 0.1f, 10.0f);
    gl.glMatrixMode(GL10.GL_MODELVIEW);
    gl.glLoadIdentity();
    gl.glTranslatef(0, -2, 0);

    gl.glEnable(GL10.GL_DEPTH_TEST);
    gl.glEnable(GL10.GL_TEXTURE_2D);
    texture.bind();
    cube.bind();

    sun.render(gl);

    cube.unbind();
    gl.glDisable(GL10.GL_TEXTURE_2D);
    gl.glDisable(GL10.GL_DEPTH_TEST);
}
// rest as in CubeScreen
```

Finally we have the render() method. We start off with the usual setting of the viewport and clearing of the framebuffer and depthbuffer. We also set up a perspective projection matrix and load an identity matrix to the model-view matrix of OpenGL ES. The call to glTranslatef() afterward is interesting: it will push our solar system down by 2 units on the y-axis. This way we sort of look down on the system. We could think of this as actually moving the camera up by 2 units on the y-axis. This interpretation is actually the key to a proper camera system, which we'll investigate in the next chapter.

Once we have all our basics set up, we enable depth-testing and texturing, bind the texture and the cube mesh, and tell the sun to render itself. Since all the objects in the hierarchy use the same texture and mesh, we only need to bind these once. This call will render the sun and all its children recursively, as outlined in the last section. Finally we disable depth-testing and texturing just for fun. Figure 10–15 shows the output of our program.

Figure 10–15. *Our crate solar system in action*

Great, everything works as expected. Our sun is rotating only around itself. The planet is orbiting the sun at a distance of 3 units, also rotating around itself, and being 20 percent as big as the sun. The moon orbits the planet, but also moves along with it around the sun due to our use of the matrix stack. It also has local transformations in the form of self-rotation and scaling.

The HierarchicalObject class is generic enough so that you can play around with it. Add more planets and moons, and maybe even moons of moons. Go crazy with the matrix stack until you get the hang off it. It's again something you can get the hang of only by a lot of practice. You need to be able to visualize in your brain what's actually going on when combining all the transformations.

> **NOTE:** Don't go too crazy with the matrix stack. It has a maximum depth, usually between 16 and 32 entries depending on the GPU/driver. Four hierarchy levels are the most I've ever had to use in an application.

A Simple Camera System

In the last example we saw a hint of how we could implement a camera system in 3D. We used glTranslatef() to push down the complete world by 2 units on the y-axis. Since our camera is fixed to be at the origin, looking down the negative z-axis, this approach gives the impression that the camera itself was moved up by 2 units. All the objects are still defined with their y-coordinates set to zero.

It's like in the classic saying, "If the mountain will not come to the prophet, the prophet will go to the mountain." Instead of actually moving the camera, we move the world around. Say we want our camera to be at position (10,4,2). All we need to do is use glTranslatef() like this:

```
gl.glTranslatef(-10,-4,-2);
```

If we wanted our camera to be rotated around its y-axis by 45 degrees, we could do this:

```
gl.glRotatef(-45,0,1,0);
```

We can also combine these two steps, just as we do for "normal" objects:

```
gl.glTranslatef(-10,-4,-2);
gl.glRotatef(-45,0,1,0);
```

The secret is that we have to invert the arguments to the transformation methods. Let's think about it using the preceding example. We know that our "real" camera is doomed to sit at the origin of the world looking down the z-axis. By applying inverse camera transformations, we bring the world into the camera's fixed view. Using a virtual camera rotated around the y-axis by 45 degrees is the same as fixing the camera and rotating the world around the camera by –45 degrees. The same is true for translation. Our virtual camera could be placed at (10,4,2). But since our real camera is fixed at the origin of the world, we just need to translate all objects by the inverse of that position vector, which is (–10,–4,–2).

When we modify the following three lines of the last example's present() method:

```
gl.glMatrixMode(GL10.GL_MODELVIEW);
gl.glLoadIdentity();
gl.glTranslatef(0, -2, 0);
```

with these four lines:

```
gl.glMatrixMode(GL10.GL_MODELVIEW);
gl.glLoadIdentity();
gl.glTranslatef(0, -3, 0);
gl.glRotatef(45, 1, 0, 0);
```

We get the output in Figure 10–16.

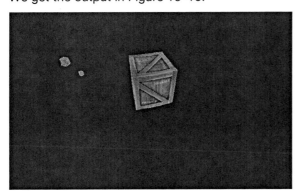

Figure 10–16. *Looking down at our world from (0,3,0)*

Conceptually, our camera is now located at (0,3,0), and looks down at our scene at a – 45 degree angle (which is the same as rotating the camera by –45 degrees around the x-axis. Figure 10–17 shows the setup of our scene with the camera.

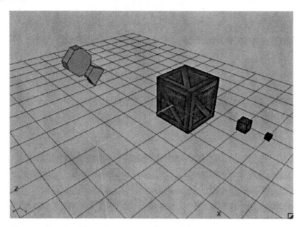

Figure 10–17. *How the camera is positioned and oriented in the scene*

We could actually specify a very simple camera with four attributes:

■ Its position in world space.

■ Its rotation around its x-axis (pitch). This is equivalent to tilting your head up and down.

■ Its rotation around its y-axis (yaw). This is equivalent to turning your head left and right.

■ Its rotation around its z-axis (roll). This is equivalent to tilting your head to the left and right.

Given these attributes we can use OpenGL ES methods to create a camera matrix. This is called an *Euler rotation* camera. Many first-person shooter games use this kind of camera to simulate the tilting of a head. Usually you'd leave out the roll and only apply the yaw and pitch . The order in which the rotations are applied is important. For a first-person shooter, you'd first apply the pitch rotation and then the yaw rotation:

```
gl.glTranslatef(-cam.x,- cam.y,-cam.z);
gl.glRotatef(cam.yaw, 0, 1, 0);
gl.glRotatef(cam.pitch, 1, 0, 0);
```

Many games still use this very simplistic camera model. If we had included the roll rotation, we might observe an effect called *gimbal lock*. This effect will cancel out one of the rotations given a certain configuration.

NOTE: Explaining gimbal lock with text or even images is very difficult. Since we'll only use yaw and pitch, we don't have this problem. To get an idea of what gimbal lock actually is, I suggest looking it up on your favorite video site on the Web. We can't solve this problem with Euler rotations. The actual solution is mathematically complex and we won't go into that in this book.

A second approach to a very simple camera system is the use of the GLU.glLookAt() method.

```
GLU.gluLookAt(GL10 gl,
              float eyeX, float eyeY, float eyeZ,
              float centerX, float centerY, float centerZ,
              float upX, float upY, float upZ);
```

Like the GLU.gluPerspective() method, it will multiply the currently active matrix with a transformation matrix. In this case it's a camera matrix, which will transform the world:

- gl is just the GL10 instance we use throughout our rendering.

- eyex, eyey, and eyez specify the camera's position in the world.

- centerx, centery, and centerz specify a point in the world that the camera looks at.

- upX, upY, and upZ specify the so-called *up vector*. Think of it as an arrow coming out at the top of your skull pointing upward. Tilt your head to the left or right and the arrow will point in the same direction the top of your head does.

The up vector is usually set to (0,1,0) even if that's not entirely correct. The gluLookAt() method can renormalize this up vector in most cases. Figure 10–18 shows our scene with the camera at (3,3,0) looking at (0,0,–5), as well as its "real" up vector.

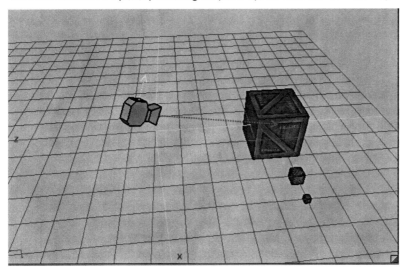

Figure 10–18. *A camera at position (3,3,0), looking at (0,0,–3)*

We can replace the code in the HierarchyScreen.present() method we changed before with the following code snippet:

```
gl.glMatrixMode(GL10.GL_MODELVIEW);
gl.glLoadIdentity();
GLU.gluLookAt(gl, 3, 3, 0, 0, 0, -5, 0, 1, 0);
```

This time I also commented out the call to `sun.update()`, so the hierarchy will look like in Figure 10–18. Figure 10–19 shows the result of using the camera.

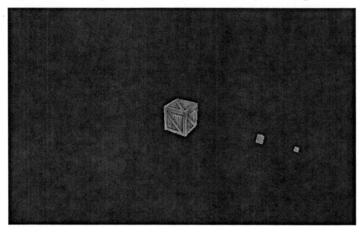

Figure 10–19. *The camera in action*

This kind of camera is great when we want to follow a character or want better control over how we view our scene by only specifying the camera's position and look-at point. For now that's all we need to know about cameras. In the next chapter we'll write two simple classes for a first-person shooter–type camera and a look-at camera that can follow an object.

Summary

You should now know the basics of 3D graphics programming with OpenGL ES. You learned how to set up a perspective view frustum, how to specify 3D vertex positions, and what the z-buffer is. You also saw how the z-buffer can both be friend and foe, depending on whether we use it correctly. We created our first 3D object: a texture cube, which turned out to be really easy. Finally we talked a little bit more about matrices and transformations, and created a hierarchical and very simple camera system. You'll be happy to know that this was not even the tip of the iceberg. In the next chapter we'll revisit a couple of topics from Chapter 7 in the context of 3D graphics programming. We'll also introduce a few new tricks that will come in handy when we write our final game. I highly recommend playing around with the examples in this chapter. Create new shapes and go crazy with transformations and the camera systems.

Chapter 11

3D Programming Tricks

3D programming is an incredibly complex and wide field. This chapter explores some topics that are the absolute minimum requirement to write a simple 3D game:

> We'll revisit our friend the vector and attach one more coordinate.

> Lighting is a vital part of any 3D game. We'll look at how to perform simple lighting with OpenGL ES.

> Defining objects programmatically is cumbersome. We'll look at a simple 3D file format so we can load and render 3D models created with 3D modeling software.

> In Chapter 8 we discussed object representation and collision detection. We'll look at how to go about that in 3D.

> We'll also briefly revisit some of the physics concepts we explored in Chapter 10[OK?], this time in a 3D context.

Let's start with 3D vectors.

Before We Begin

As always, we'll create a couple of simple example programs in this chapter. To do that we just create a new project and copy over all the source code of our framework we've developed so far.

As previous chapters we'll have a single test starter activity, which presents us the tests in form of a list. We'll call it GLAdvancedStarter and make it our default activity. Simply copy over the GL3DBasicsStarter and replace the class names of the tests. We also need to add each of the test activities to the manifest with a proper <activity> element.

Each of the tests will extend GLGame as usual; the actual code will be implemented as a GLScreen that we'll hook up with the GLGame instance. To conserve space I'll only present you with the relevant portions of the GLScreen implementations. All the tests and the starter activity reside in the package com.badlogic.androidgames.gladvanced Some of the classes will be part of our framework and go into the respective framework packages.

Vectors in 3D

In Chapter 8 we discussed vectors and their interpretation in 2D. As you might have guessed, all the things we discussed there hold in 3D space as well. All we do is add one more coordinate to our vector, namely the z-coordinate.

The operations we looked at with vectors in 2D can be easily transferred to 3D space. We specify vectors in 3D with a statement like this:

```
v = (x, y, z)
```

Addition in 3D is carried out as follows:

```
c = a + b = (a.x, a.y, b.z) + (b.x, b.y, b.z) = (a.x + b.x, a.y + b.y, a.z + b.z)
```

Subtraction works exactly the same way:

```
c = a - b = (a.x, a.y, b.z) - (b.x, b.y, b.z) = (a.x - b.x, a.y - b.y, a.z - b.z)
```

Multiplying a vector by a scalar works like this:

```
a' = a × scalar = (a.x × scalar, a.y × scalar, a.z × scalar)
```

Measuring the length of a vector in 3D is also quite simple; we just add the z-coordinate to the Pythagorean equation:

```
|a| = sqrt(a.x × a.x + a.y × a.y + a.z × a.z)
```

And based on this we can also normalize our vectors to unit length again:

```
a' = (a.x / |a|, a.y / |a|, a.z / |a|)
```

All the interpretations of vectors we talked about in Chapter 8 hold in 3D as well:

> Positions are just denoted by a normal vector's x-, y- and z-coordinate.

> Velocities and accelerations can also be represented as 3D vectors. Each component then represents a certain quantity of the attribute on one axis, such as meters per second in case of velocity or meters per second per second for acceleration.

> We can represent directions (or axes) as simple 3D unit vectors. We did that in Chapter 8 when we used the rotation facilities of OpenGL ES.

> We can measure distances by subtracting the starting vector from the end vector and measuring the resulting vector's length.

One more operation that can be rather useful is rotating a 3D vector around a 3D axis. We used this principle via the OpenGL ES glRotatef() method earlier. However, we can't use it to rotate one of the vectors that we'll use to store positions or directions of our game objects, because it only works on vertices we submit to the GPU. Luckily there's a Matrix class in the Android API that allows us to emulate what OpenGL ES does on the GPU. Let's write a Vector3 class that implements all of these features. Listing 11–1 shows you the code, which I'll again explain along the way.

Listing 11–1. *Vector3.java, a Vector in 3D*

```java
package com.badlogic.androidgames.framework.math;

import android.opengl.Matrix;
import android.util.FloatMath;

public class Vector3 {
    private static final float[] matrix = new float[16];
    private static final float[] inVec = new float[4];
    private static final float[] outVec = new float[4];
    public float x, y, z;
```

The class starts with a couple of private static final float arrays. We'll need them later on when we implement the new rotate() method of our Vector3 class. Just remember that the matrix member has 16 elements and the inVec and outVec each have 4 elements.

The x, y and z members defined next should be self-explanatory. They store the actual components of the vector:

```java
    public Vector3() {
    }

    public Vector3(float x, float y, float z) {
        this.x = x;
        this.y = y;
        this.z = z;
    }

    public Vector3(Vector3 other) {
        this.x = other.x;
        this.y = other.y;
        this.z = other.z;
    }

    public Vector3 cpy() {
    return new Vector3(x, y, z);
    }

    public Vector3 set(float x, float y, float z) {
        this.x = x;
        this.y = y;
        this.z = z;
        return this;
    }

    public Vector3 set(Vector3 other) {
        this.x = other.x;
        this.y = other.y;
        this.z = other.z;
        return this;
    }
```

Like Vector2, our Vector3 class has a couple of constructors and setters and a cpy() method, so we can easily clone vectors or set them from components calculated in our program.

```java
public Vector3 add(float x, float y, float z) {
    this.x += x;
    this.y += y;
    this.z += z;
    return this;
}

public Vector3 add(Vector3 other) {
    this.x += other.x;
    this.y += other.y;
    this.z += other.z;
    return this;
}

public Vector3 sub(float x, float y, float z) {
    this.x -= x;
    this.y -= y;
    this.z -= z;
    return this;
}

public Vector3 sub(Vector3 other) {
    this.x -= other.x;
    this.y -= other.y;
    this.z -= other.z;
    return this;
}

public Vector3 mul(float scalar) {
    this.x *= scalar;
    this.y *= scalar;
    this.z *= scalar;
    return this;
}
```

The various add(), sub() and mul() methods are just an extension of what we had in our Vector2 class with an additional z-coordinate. They implement what we discussed a few pages ago. Straightforward, right?

```java
public float len() {
    return FloatMath.sqrt(x * x + y * y + z * z);
}

public Vector3 nor() {
    float len = len();
    if (len != 0) {
        this.x /= len;
        this.y /= len;
        this.z /= len;
    }
    return this;
}
```

Usually we'll only set the diffuse and specular intensities of a light source and leave the other two at their defaults. We'll also use the same RGBA color for both the diffuse and specular intensity most of the time.

Materials

Every object in our world has a material. The material defines how the light that is hitting an object will be reflected and modify the color of the reflected light. OpenGL ES lets us specify the same four RGBA colors for a material as for a light source:

> **Ambient**: This is the color that's combined with the ambient color of any light source in the scene.

> **Diffuse**: This is the color that's combined with the diffuse color of any light source.

> **Specular**: This is the color that's combined with the specular color of any light source for specular highlight points on an objects surface.

> **Emissive**: We again ignore this as it has little use in our context.

Figure 11–3 illustrates the first three types of material/light source properties: ambient, diffuse, and specular.

Figure 11–3. *Different material/light types. Left: ambient only. Middle: diffuse only. Right: ambient and diffuse with specular highlight.*

In Figure 11–3 we can see the contributions of the different material and light properties. Ambient light illuminates the object uniformly. Diffuse light will be reflected depending on the angle the light rays hit the object; areas that directly face the light source will be brighter, and areas that can't be reached by light rays are dark. In the rightmost image we see the combination of ambient, diffuse, and specular light. The specular light manifests itself as a white highlight on the sphere.

How OpenGL ES Calculates Lighting: Vertex Normals

You know that the intensity of the reflected light bouncing back from an object depends on the angle it hits the surface of the object. OpenGL ES uses this fact to calculate lighting. It does so by using *vertex normals*, which we have to define in our code, just as we define texture coordinates or vertex colors. Figure 11–4 shows a sphere with its vertex normals.

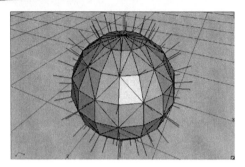

Figure 11–4:.*A sphere and its vertex normals*

Normals are simply unit-length vectors that point in the direction a surface is facing. In our case a surface is a triangle. Instead of specifying a surface normal, though, we have to specify a vertex normal. The difference between a surface normal and a vertex normal is that the vertex normal might not have to point in the same direction as the surface normal. We can clearly see this in Figure 11–4, where each vertex normal is actually the average of the normals of the triangles that vertex belongs to. This averaging makes for a smooth shading of the object.

When we render an object with vertex normals and lighting enabled, OpenGL ES will determine the angle between each vertex and light source. With this angle it can calculate the vertex's color based on the ambient, diffuse, and specular properties of the material of the object and the light source. The end result is a color for each vertex of an object that is then interpolated over each triangle in combination with the calculated colors of the other vertices. This interpolated color will then be combined with any texture maps we apply to the object.

This sounds scary but it really isn't that bad. All we need to do is enable lighting and specify the light sources, the material for the object we want to render, and the vertex normals, in addition to the other vertex attributes we usually specify, like position or texture coordinates. Let's have a look how to implement all that with OpenGL ES.

In Practice

We'll now go through all the necessary steps to get lighting to work with OpenGL ES. Along the way we'll create a few little helper classes that make working with light sources a bit easier. We'll put those in the com.badlogic.androidgames.framework.gl package.

Enabling and Disabling Lighting

As with all OpenGL ES states, we first have to enable the functionality in question. We do that with this:

```
gl.glEnable(GL10.GL_LIGHTING);
```

Once enabled, lighting will be applied to all objects we render. We'll have to specify the light sources and materials as well as the vertex normals to achieve meaningful results, of course. Once we are done with rendering all the objects that should be lit we can disable lighting again:

```
gl.glDisable(GL10.GL_LIGHTING);
```

Specifying Light Sources

OpenGL ES offers us four types of light sources: ambient lights, point lights, directional lights and spot lights. We'll take a look at how to define the first three. In order for spot lights to be effective and look good, we'd need to have a very high triangle count for each of our objects' models. That's prohibitive on most current mobile devices.

OpenGL ES lets us have eight light sources in a scene at most, plus a global ambient light. Each of the eight light sources has an identifier, from GL10.GL_LIGHT0 up to GL10.GL_LIGHT7. If we want to manipulate the properties of one of these light sources we do so by specifying the respective ID of that light source.

Light sources have to be enabled with this syntax:

```
gl.glEnable(GL10.GL_LIGHT0);
```

OpenGL ES will then take the properties of that light source with ID zero and apply it to all rendered objects accordingly. If we want to disable a light source we can do it with a statement like this:

```
gl.glDisable(GL10.GL_LIGHT0);
```

Ambient light is a special case as it does not have an identifier. There is only one ambient light ever in an OpenGL ES scene. Let's have a look at that.

Ambient Light

Ambient light is a special type of light, as I explained already. It has no position or direction but only a color by which all objects in the scene will be uniformly lit. OpenGL ES lets us specify the global ambient light as follows:

```
float[] ambientColor = { 0.2f, 0.2f, 0.2f, 1.0f };
gl.glLightModelfv(GL10.GL_LIGHT_MODEL_AMBIENT, color, 0);
```

The ambientColor array holds the RGBA values of the ambient light's color encoded as floats in the range 0 to 1. The glLightModelfv() method takes a constant as the first parameter specifying that we want to set the ambient light's color, the float array holding the color and an offset into the float array from which the method should start reading the RGBA values. Let's put this into a lovely little class. Listing 11–2 shows the code.

Listing 11–2. *AmbientLight.java, a Simple Abstraction of OpenGL ES Global Ambient Light*

```
package com.badlogic.androidgames.framework.gl;

import javax.microedition.khronos.opengles.GL10;
```

```java
public class AmbientLight {
    float[] color = {0.2f, 0.2f, 0.2f, 1};

    public void setColor(float r, float g, float b, float a) {
        color[0] = r;
        color[1] = g;
        color[2] = b;
        color[3] = a;
    }

    public void enable(GL10 gl) {
        gl.glLightModelfv(GL10.GL_LIGHT_MODEL_AMBIENT, color, 0);
    }
}
```

All we do is store the ambient light's color in a float array and provide two methods: one to set the color and another to make OpenGL ES use the ambient light color we defined. By default we use a gray ambient light color.

Point Lights

Point lights have a position as well as an ambient, diffuse, and specular color/intensity (we leave out the emissive color/intensity). To specify the different colors we can do the following:

```java
gl.glLightfv(GL10.GL_LIGHT3, GL10.GL_AMBIENT, ambientColor, 0);
gl.glLightfv(GL10.GL_LIGHT3, GL10.GL_DIFFUSE, diffuseColor, 0);
gl.glLightfv(GL10.GL_LIGHT3, GL10.GL_SPECULAR, specularColor, 0);
```

The first parameter is the light identifier; in this case we use the fourth light. The next parameter specifies the attribute of the light we want to modify. The third parameter is again a float array holding the RGBA values, and the final parameter is an offset into that array. Specifying the position is as easy:

```java
float[] position = {x, y, z, 1};
gl.glLightfv(GL10.GL_LIGHT3, GL10.GL_POSITION, position, 0);
```

We again specify the attribute we want to modify (in this case the position), along with a four-element array storing the x-, y- and z-coordinate of the light in our world. Note that the fourth element of the array must be set to 1 for a positional light source! Let's put this into a helper class. Listing 11–3 shows you the code.

Listing 11–3. *PointLight.java, a Simple Abstraction of OpenGL ES Point Lights*

```java
package com.badlogic.androidgames.framework.gl;

import javax.microedition.khronos.opengles.GL10;

public class PointLight {
    float[] ambient = { 0.2f, 0.2f, 0.2f, 1.0f };
    float[] diffuse = { 1.0f, 1.0f, 1.0f, 1.0f };
    float[] specular = { 0.0f, 0.0f, 0.0f, 1.0f };
    float[] position = { 0, 0, 0, 1 };
    int lastLightId = 0;
```

Figure 11–5. *Vertex normals for each vertex of our cube*

A vertex normal is just another vertex attribute, like position or color. In order to upload vertex normals, we have to modify our Vertices3 class one more time. To tell OpenGL ES where it can find the normals for each vertex we use the glNormalPointer() method, just like we used the glVertexPointer() or glColorPointer() methods previously. Listing 11–6 shows our final revised Vertices3 class.

Listing 11–6. *Vertices3.java, the Final Version with Support for Normals*

```
package com.badlogic.androidgames.framework.gl;

import java.nio.ByteBuffer;
import java.nio.ByteOrder;
import java.nio.IntBuffer;
import java.nio.ShortBuffer;

import javax.microedition.khronos.opengles.GL10;

import com.badlogic.androidgames.framework.impl.GLGraphics;

public class Vertices3 {
    final GLGraphics glGraphics;
    final boolean hasColor;
    final boolean hasTexCoords;
    final boolean hasNormals;
    final int vertexSize;
    final IntBuffer vertices;
    final int[] tmpBuffer;
    final ShortBuffer indices;
```

Among the members, the only new addition is the hasNormals boolean, which keeps track of whether the vertices have normals or not.

```
    public Vertices3(GLGraphics glGraphics, int maxVertices, int maxIndices,
            boolean hasColor, boolean hasTexCoords, boolean hasNormals) {
        this.glGraphics = glGraphics;
        this.hasColor = hasColor;
        this.hasTexCoords = hasTexCoords;
```

```
        this.hasNormals = hasNormals;
        this.vertexSize = (3 + (hasColor ? 4 : 0) + (hasTexCoords ? 2 : 0) + (hasNormals
? 3    : 0)) * 4;
        this.tmpBuffer = new int[maxVertices * vertexSize / 4];

        ByteBuffer buffer = ByteBuffer.allocateDirect(maxVertices * vertexSize);
        buffer.order(ByteOrder.nativeOrder());
        vertices = buffer.asIntBuffer();

        if (maxIndices > 0) {
            buffer = ByteBuffer.allocateDirect(maxIndices * Short.SIZE / 8);
            buffer.order(ByteOrder.nativeOrder());
            indices = buffer.asShortBuffer();
        } else {
            indices = null;
        }
    }
```

In the constructor we now also take a hasNormals parameter. We have to modify the
calculation of the vertexSize member as well, adding three floats per vertex if normals
are available.

```
    public void setVertices(float[] vertices, int offset, int length) {
        this.vertices.clear();
        int len = offset + length;
        for (int i = offset, j = 0; i < len; i++, j++)
            tmpBuffer[j] = Float.floatToRawIntBits(vertices[i]);
        this.vertices.put(tmpBuffer, 0, length);
        this.vertices.flip();
    }

    public void setIndices(short[] indices, int offset, int length) {
        this.indices.clear();
        this.indices.put(indices, offset, length);
        this.indices.flip();
    }
```

As you can see, the methods setVertices() and setIndices() stay the same.

```
    public void bind() {
        GL10 gl = glGraphics.getGL();

        gl.glEnableClientState(GL10.GL_VERTEX_ARRAY);
        vertices.position(0);
        gl.glVertexPointer(3, GL10.GL_FLOAT, vertexSize, vertices);

        if (hasColor) {
            gl.glEnableClientState(GL10.GL_COLOR_ARRAY);
            vertices.position(3);
            gl.glColorPointer(4, GL10.GL_FLOAT, vertexSize, vertices);
        }

        if (hasTexCoords) {
            gl.glEnableClientState(GL10.GL_TEXTURE_COORD_ARRAY);
            vertices.position(hasColor ? 7 : 3);
            gl.glTexCoordPointer(2, GL10.GL_FLOAT, vertexSize, vertices);
        }
```

```
        if (hasNormals) {
            gl.glEnableClientState(GL10.GL_NORMAL_ARRAY);
            int offset = 3;
            if (hasColor)
                offset += 4;
            if (hasTexCoords)
                offset += 2;
            vertices.position(offset);
            gl.glNormalPointer(GL10.GL_FLOAT, vertexSize, vertices);
        }
    }
```

In the bind() method just shown, we do the usual ByteBuffer tricks, this time
incorporating normals via the glNormalPointer() method as well. To calculate the offset
for the normal pointer we have to take into account whether colors and texture
coordinates are given.

```
    public void draw(int primitiveType, int offset, int numVertices) {
        GL10 gl = glGraphics.getGL();

        if (indices != null) {
            indices.position(offset);
            gl.glDrawElements(primitiveType, numVertices,
                    GL10.GL_UNSIGNED_SHORT, indices);
        } else {
            gl.glDrawArrays(primitiveType, offset, numVertices);
        }
    }
```

You can see that the draw() method is again unmodified; all the magic happens in the
bind() method.

```
    public void unbind() {
        GL10 gl = glGraphics.getGL();
        if (hasTexCoords)
            gl.glDisableClientState(GL10.GL_TEXTURE_COORD_ARRAY);

        if (hasColor)
            gl.glDisableClientState(GL10.GL_COLOR_ARRAY);

        if (hasNormals)
            gl.glDisableClientState(GL10.GL_NORMAL_ARRAY);
    }
}
```

Finally, we also modify the unbind() method a little bit. We disable the normal pointer if
normals have been, cleaning up the OpenGL ES state properly.

Using this modified Vertices3 version is as easy as before. Here's a small example:

```
float[] vertices = { -0.5f, -0.5f, 0, 0, 0, 1,
                      0.5f, -0.5f, 0, 0, 0, 1,
                      0.0f,  0.5f, 0, 0, 0, 1 };
Vertices3 vertices = new Vertices3(glGraphics, 3, 0, false, false, true);
vertices.setVertices(vertices);
```

We create a float array to hold three vertices, each having a position (the first three floats on each line) and a normal (the last three floats on each line). In this case we have a triangle in the x/y plane with its normals pointing in the direction of the positive z-axis. All that's left is creating the Vertices3 instance and setting the vertices. Easy, right? Binding, drawing, and unbinding work exactly the same as with the old version. We can, of course, also add vertex colors and texture coordinates as previously.

Putting it All Together

Let's put all this together. We want to draw a scene with a global ambient light, a point light, and a directional light all illuminating a cube centered at the origin. For good measure we'll also throw in a call to gluLookAt() to position our camera in the world. Figure 11–6 shows the setup of our world.

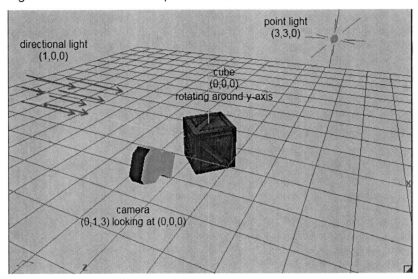

Figure 11–6. *Our first lit scene*

As with all of our examples, we create a class called LightTest, which extends GLGame as usual. It returns a new LightScreen instance from its getStartScreen() method. The LightScreen class extends GLScreen and is shown in Listing 11–7.

Listing 11–7. *Excerpt from LightTest.java, Lighting with OpenGL ES*

```
class LightScreen extends GLScreen {
    float angle;
    Vertices3 cube;
    Texture texture;
    AmbientLight ambientLight;
    PointLight pointLight;
    DirectionalLight directionalLight;
    Material material;
```

We start off with a couple of members. The angle member stores the current rotation of the cube around the y-axis. The Vertices3 member stores the vertices of the cube model, which we are going to define in a bit. Additionally, we store an AmbientLight, PointLight and DirectionalLight instance as well as a Material.

```
public LightScreen(Game game) {
    super(game);

    cube = createCube();
    texture = new Texture(glGame, "crate.png");
    ambientLight = new AmbientLight();
    ambientLight.setColor(0, 0.2f, 0, 1);
    pointLight = new PointLight();
    pointLight.setDiffuse(1, 0, 0, 1);
    pointLight.setPosition(3, 3, 0);
    directionalLight = new DirectionalLight();
    directionalLight.setDiffuse(0, 0, 1, 1);
    directionalLight.setDirection(1, 0, 0);
    material = new Material();
}
```

Next is the constructor. Here we create the cube model's vertices and load the crate texture, just as we did in the previous chapter. We also instantiate all the lights and the material and set their attributes. The ambient light color is a light green, and the point light is red and sits at (3,3,0) in our world. The directional light has a blue diffuse color and comes from the left. For the material we use the default values (a little ambient, white for diffuse, and black for specular).

```
@Override
public void resume() {
    texture.reload();
}
```

In the resume() method we make sure that our texture is (re)loaded in case of a context loss.

```
private Vertices3 createCube() {
    float[] vertices = { -0.5f, -0.5f,  0.5f, 0, 1,  0,  0,  1,
                          0.5f, -0.5f,  0.5f, 1, 1,  0,  0,  1,
                          0.5f,  0.5f,  0.5f, 1, 0,  0,  0,  1,
                         -0.5f,  0.5f,  0.5f, 0, 0,  0,  0,  1,

                          0.5f, -0.5f,  0.5f, 0, 1,  1,  0,  0,
                          0.5f, -0.5f, -0.5f, 1, 1,  1,  0,  0,
                          0.5f,  0.5f, -0.5f, 1, 0,  1,  0,  0,
                          0.5f,  0.5f,  0.5f, 0, 0,  1,  0,  0,

                          0.5f, -0.5f, -0.5f, 0, 1,  0,  0, -1,
                         -0.5f, -0.5f, -0.5f, 1, 1,  0,  0, -1,
                         -0.5f,  0.5f, -0.5f, 1, 0,  0,  0, -1,
                          0.5f,  0.5f, -0.5f, 0, 0,  0,  0, -1,

                         -0.5f, -0.5f, -0.5f, 0, 1, -1,  0,  0,
                         -0.5f, -0.5f,  0.5f, 1, 1, -1,  0,  0,
                         -0.5f,  0.5f,  0.5f, 1, 0, -1,  0,  0,
                         -0.5f,  0.5f, -0.5f, 0, 0, -1,  0,  0,

                         -0.5f,  0.5f,  0.5f, 0, 1,  0,  1,  0,
```

```
                        0.5f,   0.5f,   0.5f, 1, 1, 0, 1, 0,
                        0.5f,   0.5f,  -0.5f, 1, 0, 0, 1, 0,
                       -0.5f,   0.5f,  -0.5f, 0, 0, 0, 1, 0,

                       -0.5f,  -0.5f,  -0.5f, 0, 1, 0, -1, 0,
                        0.5f,  -0.5f,  -0.5f, 1, 1, 0, -1, 0,
                        0.5f,  -0.5f,   0.5f, 1, 0, 0, -1, 0,
                       -0.5f,  -0.5f,   0.5f, 0, 0, 0, -1, 0 };
        short[] indices = { 0, 1, 2, 2, 3, 0,
                            4, 5, 6, 6, 7, 4,
                            8, 9, 10, 10, 11, 8,
                            12, 13, 14, 14, 15, 12,
                            16, 17, 18, 18, 19, 16,
                            20, 21, 22, 22, 23, 20,
                            24, 25, 26, 26, 27, 24 };
        Vertices3 cube = new Vertices3(glGraphics, vertices.length / 8, indices.length,
false, true, true);
        cube.setVertices(vertices, 0, vertices.length);
        cube.setIndices(indices, 0, indices.length);
        return cube;
    }
```

The createCube() method is mostly the same as the one we used in previous examples. This time, however, we add normals to each vertex as shown in Figure 11–4. Apart from that nothing really changed.

```
    @Override
    public void update(float deltaTime) {
        angle += deltaTime * 20;
    }
```

In the update() method we simply increase the rotation angle of the cube.

```
    @Override
    public void present(float deltaTime) {
        GL10 gl = glGraphics.getGL();
        gl.glClearColor(0.2f, 0.2f, 0.2f, 1.0f);
        gl.glClear(GL10.GL_COLOR_BUFFER_BIT | GL10.GL_DEPTH_BUFFER_BIT);
        gl.glEnable(GL10.GL_DEPTH_TEST);
        gl.glViewport(0, 0, glGraphics.getWidth(), glGraphics.getHeight());

        gl.glMatrixMode(GL10.GL_PROJECTION);
        gl.glLoadIdentity();
        GLU.gluPerspective(gl, 67, glGraphics.getWidth()
                / (float) glGraphics.getHeight(), 0.1f, 10f);
        gl.glMatrixMode(GL10.GL_MODELVIEW);
        gl.glLoadIdentity();
        GLU.gluLookAt(gl, 0, 1, 3, 0, 0, 0, 0, 1, 0);

        gl.glEnable(GL10.GL_LIGHTING);

        ambientLight.enable(gl);
        pointLight.enable(gl, GL10.GL_LIGHT0);
        directionalLight.enable(gl, GL10.GL_LIGHT1);
        material.enable(gl);

        gl.glEnable(GL10.GL_TEXTURE_2D);
```

```
        texture.bind();

        gl.glRotatef(angle, 0, 1, 0);
        cube.bind();
        cube.draw(GL10.GL_TRIANGLES, 0, 6 * 2 * 3);
        cube.unbind();

        pointLight.disable(gl);
        directionalLight.disable(gl);

        gl.glDisable(GL10.GL_TEXTURE_2D);
        gl.glDisable(GL10.GL_DEPTH_TEST);
    }
```

And here it gets interesting. The first couple of lines are our boilerplate code for clearing the color and depth buffer, enabling depth testing, and setting the viewport.

Next we set the projection matrix to a perspective projection matrix via gluPerspective() and also use gluLookAt() for the model view matrix so that we have a camera set up as in Figure 11–6.

Next we enable lighting itself. At this point no lights are defined yet, so we do that in the next couple of lines by calling the enable() methods of the lights as well as the material.

As usual we also enable texturing and bind our crate texture. Finally, we call glRotatef() to rotate our cube and then render its vertices with well-placed calls to the Vertices3 instance.

To round off the method, we disable the point and directional lights (remember, the ambient light is a global state) as well as texturing and depth testing. And that's all there is to lighting in OpenGL ES!

```
    @Override
    public void pause() {
    }

    @Override
    public void dispose() {
    }
}
```

The rest of the class is just empty; we don't have to do anything special in case of a pause.

Figure 11–7 shows you the output of our example.

Figure 11–7. *Our scene from Figure 11–6 rendered with OpenGL ES*

Some Notes on Lighting in OpenGL ES

While lighting can add some nice eye candy, it has its limits and pitfalls. Here's a few things you should take to heart.

Lighting is expensive, especially on low-end devices. Use it with care. The more light sources you enable the more computational power is required to render the scene.

When specifying the position/direction of point/directional lights, you must do it after you have loaded the camera matrices and before you multiply the model-view matrix with any matrices to move and rotate objects around! This is crucial. If you don't follow this method, you will have some inexplicable lighting artifacts.

When you use glScalef() to change the size of a model, its normals will also be scaled. This is bad, because OpenGL ES expects unit-length normals. To work around this issue you can use the command glEnable(GL10.GL_NORMALIZE) or in some circumstances glEnable(GL10.GL_RESCALE_NORMAL). I'd suggest sticking to the former, as the later has some restrictions and caveats. The problem is that normalizing or rescaling normals is computationally heavy. Not scaling your lit objects is best for performance.

Mipmapping

If you've played around with our previous examples and let the cube move further away from the camera, you might have noticed that the texture starts to looks grainy and full of little artifacts the smaller the cube gets. This effect is called *aliasing*, a prominent effect in all types of signal processing. Figure 11–8 shows you the effect on the right side and the result of applying a technique called *mipmapping* on the left side.

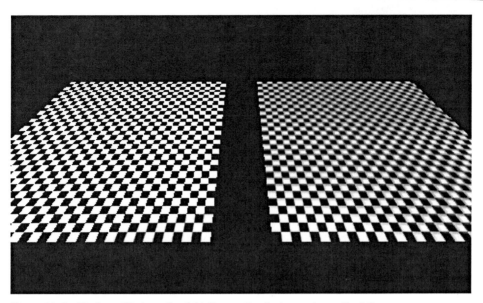

Figure 11–8. *Aliasing artifacts on the right; the results of mipmapping on the left*

I won't go into the details of why aliasing happens; all you need to know is how to make objects look better. That's where mipmapping comes in. [Au: OK? CE]

They key to fixing aliasing problems is to use lower-resolution images for parts of an object that are smaller on screen or further away from the view point. This is usually called a mipmap pyramid or chain. Given an image in its default resolution, say 256! 256 pixels, we create smaller versions of it, dividing the sides by two for each level of the mipmap pyramid. Figure 11–9 shows the crate texture with the various mipmap levels.

Figure 11–9. *A mipmap chain*

To make a texture mipmapped in OpenGL ES we have to do two things:

Set the minification filter to one of the GL_XXX_MIPMAP_XXX constants, usually GL_LINEAR_MIPMAP_NEAREST.

Create the images for each mipmap chain level by resizing the original image and upload them to OpenGL ES. The mipmap chain is attached to a single texture, not multiple textures.

To resize the base image for the mipmap chain we can simply use the Bitmap and Canvas classes the Android API provides us with. Let us modify the Texture class a little. Listing 11–8 shows you the code.

Listing 11–8. *Texture.java, Our Final Version of the Texture Class*

```
package com.badlogic.androidgames.framework.gl;

import java.io.IOException;
import java.io.InputStream;

import javax.microedition.khronos.opengles.GL10;

import android.graphics.Bitmap;
import android.graphics.BitmapFactory;
import android.graphics.Canvas;
import android.graphics.Rect;
import android.opengl.GLUtils;

import com.badlogic.androidgames.framework.FileIO;
import com.badlogic.androidgames.framework.impl.GLGame;
import com.badlogic.androidgames.framework.impl.GLGraphics;

public class Texture {
    GLGraphics glGraphics;
    FileIO fileIO;
    String fileName;
    int textureId;
    int minFilter;
    int magFilter;
    public int width;
    public int height;
    boolean mipmapped;
```

We add only one new member, called mipmapped, which stores whether the texture has a mipmap chain or not.

```
    public Texture(GLGame glGame, String fileName) {
        this(glGame, fileName, false);
    }

    public Texture(GLGame glGame, String fileName, boolean mipmapped) {
        this.glGraphics = glGame.getGLGraphics();
        this.fileIO = glGame.getFileIO();
        this.fileName = fileName;
        this.mipmapped = mipmapped;
        load();
    }
```

For compatibility we leave the old constructor in which calls the new constructor. The new constructor takes a third argument that lets us specify whether we want the texture to be mipmapped or not.

```
private void load() {
    GL10 gl = glGraphics.getGL();
    int[] textureIds = new int[1];
    gl.glGenTextures(1, textureIds, 0);
    textureId = textureIds[0];

    InputStream in = null;
    try {
        in = fileIO.readAsset(fileName);
        Bitmap bitmap = BitmapFactory.decodeStream(in);
        if (mipmapped) {
            createMipmaps(gl, bitmap);
        } else {
            gl.glBindTexture(GL10.GL_TEXTURE_2D, textureId);
            GLUtils.texImage2D(GL10.GL_TEXTURE_2D, 0, bitmap, 0);
            setFilters(GL10.GL_NEAREST, GL10.GL_NEAREST);
            gl.glBindTexture(GL10.GL_TEXTURE_2D, 0);
            width = bitmap.getWidth();
            height = bitmap.getHeight();
            bitmap.recycle();
        }
    } catch (IOException e) {
        throw new RuntimeException("Couldn't load texture '" + fileName
                + "'", e);
    } finally {
        if (in != null)
            try {
                in.close();
            } catch (IOException e) {
            }
    }
}
```

The load() method stays pretty much the same as well. The only addition is the call to createMipmaps() in case the texture should be mipmapped. Non-mipmapped Texture instances are created as before.

```
private void createMipmaps(GL10 gl, Bitmap bitmap) {
    gl.glBindTexture(GL10.GL_TEXTURE_2D, textureId);
    width = bitmap.getWidth();
    height = bitmap.getHeight();
    setFilters(GL10.GL_LINEAR_MIPMAP_NEAREST, GL10.GL_LINEAR);

    int level = 0;
    int newWidth = width;
    int newHeight = height;
    while (true) {
        GLUtils.texImage2D(GL10.GL_TEXTURE_2D, level, bitmap, 0);
        newWidth = newWidth / 2;
        newHeight = newHeight / 2;
        if (newWidth <= 0)
            break;
```

```
            Bitmap newBitmap = Bitmap.createBitmap(newWidth, newHeight,
                    bitmap.getConfig());
            Canvas canvas = new Canvas(newBitmap);
            canvas.drawBitmap(bitmap,
                    new Rect(0, 0, bitmap.getWidth(), bitmap.getHeight()),
                    new Rect(0, 0, newWidth, newHeight), null);
            bitmap.recycle();
            bitmap = newBitmap;
            level++;
        }

        gl.glBindTexture(GL10.GL_TEXTURE_2D, 0);
        bitmap.recycle();
    }
```

The createMipmaps() method is pretty straightforward. We start off by binding the texture so that we can manipulate its attributes. The first thing we do is to keep track of the bitmap's width and height and set the filters. Note that we use GL_LINEAR_MIPMAP_NEAREST for the minification filter. If we don't use that filter mipmapping will not work, and OpenGL ES will fall back to normal filtering, only using the base image.

The while loop is straightforward. We upload the current bitmap as the image for the current level. We start at level 0, the base level with the original image. Once the image for the current level is uploaded we create a smaller version of it, dividing its width and height by 2. If the new width is less than or equal to zero we can break out of the infinite loop as we have uploaded an image for each mipmap level (the last image has a size of 1! 1 pixels). We use the Canvas class to resize the image and store the result in newBitmap. We then recycle the old bitmap so we clean up any memory it used and set the newBitmap as the current bitmap. This process is repeated until the image is smaller than 1! 1 pixels.

Finally we unbind the texture and recycle the last bitmap that got created in the loop.

```
    public void reload() {
        load();
        bind();
        setFilters(minFilter, magFilter);
        glGraphics.getGL().glBindTexture(GL10.GL_TEXTURE_2D, 0);
    }

    public void setFilters(int minFilter, int magFilter) {
        this.minFilter = minFilter;
        this.magFilter = magFilter;
        GL10 gl = glGraphics.getGL();
        gl.glTexParameterf(GL10.GL_TEXTURE_2D, GL10.GL_TEXTURE_MIN_FILTER,
                minFilter);
        gl.glTexParameterf(GL10.GL_TEXTURE_2D, GL10.GL_TEXTURE_MAG_FILTER,
                magFilter);
    }

    public void bind() {
        GL10 gl = glGraphics.getGL();
        gl.glBindTexture(GL10.GL_TEXTURE_2D, textureId);
    }
```

```
    public void dispose() {
        GL10 gl = glGraphics.getGL();
        gl.glBindTexture(GL10.GL_TEXTURE_2D, textureId);
        int[] textureIds = { textureId };
        gl.glDeleteTextures(1, textureIds, 0);
    }
}
```

The rest of the class is the same as in the previous version. The only difference in usage is how we call the constructor. And since that is perfectly simple, we won't write an example just for mipmapping. We'll use mipmapping on all our textures used for 3D objects. In 2D mipmapping has less use. A few final notes on mipmapping:

> Mipmapping can increase performance quite a bit if the objects you draw using a mipmapped texture are small. The reason for this is that the GPU has to fetch fewer texels from smaller images in the mipmap pyramid. It's therefore wise to always use mipmapped textures on object that might get small.

> A mipmapped texture takes up 33% more memory than an equivalent non-mipmapped version. This trade-off is usually fine.

> Mipmapping works only with square textures in OpenGL ES 1.x. This is crucial to remember. If your objects stay white even though they are textured with a nice image you can be pretty sure that you forgot about this limitation.

> **NOTE** Once again, because this is really important. Mipmapping will only work with square textures! A 512×256 pixel image will not work.

Simple Cameras

In the previous chapter we talked about two ways to create a camera. The first one, the Euler camera, was similar to what is used in first-person shooters. The second one, the look-at camera, is used for cinematic camera work or for following an object. Let's create two helper classes that we can use in our games.

The First-Person or Euler Camera

The first-person or Euler camera is defined by the following attributes:

> The field of view in degrees.

> The viewport aspect ratio.

> The near and far clipping planes.

> A position in 3D space.

An angle around the y-axis (yaw).

An angle around the x-axis (pitch). This is limited to the range –90 to +90 degrees. Think how far you can tilt your own head and try to go beyond those angles! I'm not responsible for any injuries.

The first three attributes are used to define the perspective projection matrix. We did this already with calls to gluPerspective() in all of your 3D examples.

The other three attributes define the position and orientation of the camera in our world. We will construct a matrix from this as outlined in the previous chapter. Let's put all this together into a simple class. Listing 11–9 shows you the code.

Additionally we want to be able to move the camera in the direction it is heading. For this we need a unit length direction vector, which we can add to the position vector of the camera. We can create such a vector with the help of the Matrix class the Android API offers us. Let's think about this for a moment.

In its default configuration our camera will look down the negative z-axis. So its direction vector is (0, 0,–1). When we specify a yaw or pitch angle, this direction vector will be rotated accordingly. To figure out the direction vector we just need to multiply it with a matrix that will rotate the default direction vector just as OpenGL ES will rotate the vertices of our models.

Let's have a look at how all this works in code. Listing 11–9 shows you the EulerCamera class.

Listing 11–9. *EulerCamera.java, a Simple First Person Camera Based on Euler Angles Around the x- and y-Axes*

```
package com.badlogic.androidgames.framework.gl;

import javax.microedition.khronos.opengles.GL10;

import android.opengl.GLU;
import android.opengl.Matrix;

import com.badlogic.androidgames.framework.math.Vector3;

public class EulerCamera {
    final Vector3 position = new Vector3();
    float yaw;
    float pitch;
    float fieldOfView;
    float aspectRatio;
    float near;
    float far;
```

The first three members hold the position and rotation angles of the camera. The other four members hold the parameters used for calculating the perspective projection matrix. By default our camera is located at the origin of the world, looking down the negative z-axis.

```
    public EulerCamera(float fieldOfView, float aspectRatio, float near, float far){
        this.fieldOfView = fieldOfView;
```

```
        this.aspectRatio = aspectRatio;
        this.near = near;
        this.far = far;
    }
```

The constructor takes four parameters that define the perspective projection. We leave the camera position and rotation angles as they are.

```
    public Vector3 getPosition() {
        return position;
    }
    public float getYaw() {
        return yaw;
    }

    public float getPitch() {
        return pitch;
    }
```

The getter methods just return the camera orientation and position.

```
    public void setAngles(float yaw, float pitch) {
        if (pitch < -90)
            pitch = -90;
        if (pitch > 90)
            pitch = 90;
        this.yaw = yaw;
        this.pitch = pitch;
    }

    public void rotate(float yawInc, float pitchInc) {
        this.yaw += yawInc;
        this.pitch += pitchInc;
        if (pitch < -90)
            pitch = -90;
        if (pitch > 90)
            pitch = 90;
    }
```

The setAngles() method allows us to directly specify the yaw and pitch of the camera. Note that we limit the pitch to be in the range –90 to 90. We can't rotate our own head further than that, so our camera shouldn't be able to do that either.

The rotate() method is nearly identical to the setAngles() method. Instead of setting the angles it increases them by the parameters. This will be useful when we implement a little touchscreen-based control scheme in the next example.

```
    public void setMatrices(GL10 gl) {
        gl.glMatrixMode(GL10.GL_PROJECTION);
        gl.glLoadIdentity();
        GLU.gluPerspective(gl, fieldOfView, aspectRatio, near, far);
        gl.glMatrixMode(GL10.GL_MODELVIEW);
        gl.glLoadIdentity();
        gl.glRotatef(-pitch, 1, 0, 0);
        gl.glRotatef(-yaw, 0, 1, 0);
        gl.glTranslatef(-position.x, -position.y, -position.z);
    }
```

The setMatrices() method just sets the projection and model-view matrices as discussed earlier. The projection matrix is set via gluPerspective() based on the parameters given to the camera in the constructor. The model-view matrix performs the "prophet-mountain" trick by applying a rotation around the x- and y-axes as well as a translation. All involved factors are negated to achieve the effect that the camera remains at the origin of the world looking down the negative z-axis. We thus rotate and translate the objects around the camera, not the other way around.

```
final float[] matrix = new float[16];
    final float[] inVec = { 0, 0, -1, 1 };
    final float[] outVec = new float[4];
    final Vector3 direction = new Vector3();

    public Vector3 getDirection() {
        Matrix.setIdentityM(matrix, 0);
        Matrix.rotateM(matrix, 0, yaw, 0, 1, 0);
        Matrix.rotateM(matrix, 0, pitch, 1, 0, 0);
        Matrix.multiplyMV(outVec, 0, matrix, 0, inVec, 0);
        direction.set(outVec[0], outVec[1], outVec[2]);
        return direction;
    }
}
```

Finally we have the mysterious getDirection() method. It is accompanied by a couple of final members that we use for the calculations inside the method. We do this so that we don't allocate new float arrays and Vector3 instances each time the method is called. Consider those members to be temporary working variables.

Inside the method we first set up a transformation matrix that contains the rotation around the x- and y-axes. We don't need to include the translation, since we only want a direction vector, not a position vector. The direction of the camera is independent of its location in the world. The Matrix methods we invoke should be self-explanatory. The only strange thing is that we actually apply them in reverse order without negating the arguments. We do the opposite in the setMatrices() method. That's because we are now actually transforming a point the same way we'd transform our virtual camera, which does not have to be located at the origin and oriented so that it looks down the negative z-axis. The vector we rotate is (0,0,–1), stored in inVec. That's the default direction of our camera if not rotation is applied. All the matrix multiplications do is rotate this direction vector by the camera's pitch and roll so that it points in the direction the camera is heading toward. The last thing we do is set a Vector3 instance based on the result of the matrix-vector multiplication and return that to the caller. We can use this unit-length direction vector later on to move the camera in the direction it is heading.

Equipped with this little helper class we can write a tiny example program that allows us to move through a world of crates.

An Euler Camera Example

We now want to use the EulerCamera class in a little program. We want to be able to rotate it up and down and left and right based on swiping the touchscreen with a finger.

We also want it to move forward when a button is pressed. Our world should be populated by a couple of crates. Figure 11–10 shows you the initial setup of our scene.

Figure 11–10. *A simple scene with 25 crates, a point light, and an Euler camera in its initial position and orientation*

The camera will be located at (0,1,3). We also have a white point light at (3,3,-3). The crates are positioned in a grid from -4 to 4 on the x-axis and 0 to -8 on the z-axis, with a 2-unit distance between the centers.

How will we rotate the camera via swipes? We want the camera to rotate around the y-axis when we swipe horizontally. That is equivalent to turning our head left and right. We also want the camera to rotate around the x-axis when we swipe vertically. That's equivalent to tilting our head up and down. We also want to be able to combine these two swipe motions. The most straightforward way to achieve this is to check for whether a finger is on the screen, and if so measure the difference on each axis to the last known position of that finger on the screen. We can then derive a change in rotation on both axes by using the difference in x for the y-axis rotation and the difference in y for the x-axis rotation.

We also want the camera to be able to move forward by pressing an on-screen button. That's simple; we just need to call `EulerCamera.getDirection()` and multiply its result[OK?] by the speed we want the camera to move with and the delta time, so that we once again perform time-based movement. The only thing that we need to do is draw the button (I decided to draw a 64! 64 button in the bottom-left corner of the screen) and check whether it is currently touched by a finger.

To simplify our implementation we'll only allow the user to either swipe-rotate or move. We could use the multitouch facilities for this but that would complicate our implementation quite a bit.

With this plan of attack let us look at `EulerCameraScreen`, a `GLScreen` implementation contained in a `GLGame` implementation called `EulerCameraTest` (just the usual test structure). Listing 11–10 shows the code.

Listing 11–10. *Excerpt from EulerCameraTest.java, the EulerCameraScreen*

```java
class EulerCameraScreen extends GLScreen {
    Texture crateTexture;
    Vertices3 cube;
    PointLight light;
    EulerCamera camera;
    Texture buttonTexture;
    SpriteBatcher batcher;
    Camera2D guiCamera;
    TextureRegion buttonRegion;
    Vector2 touchPos;
    float lastX = -1;
    float lastY = -1;
```

We start off with a couple of members. The first two store the texture for the crate as well as the vertices of the texture cube. We'll generate the vertices with the createCube() method from the last example.

The next member is a PointLight, which we are already familiar with, as well as an instance of our new EulerCamera class.

Next up are a couple of members we need to render the button. We use a separate 64! 64 image called button.png for that button. To render it we also need a SpriteBatcher as well as a Camera2D instance and a TextureRegion. This means that we are going to combine 3D and 2D rendering in this example! The last three members are used to keep track of the current touchPos in the UI coordinate system (which is fixed to 480! 320) as well as store the last known touch positions. We'll use the value –1 for lastX and lastY to indicate that no valid last touch position is known yet.

```java
    public EulerCameraScreen(Game game) {
        super(game);

        crateTexture = new Texture(glGame, "crate.png", true);
        cube = createCube();
        light = new PointLight();
        light.setPosition(3, 3, -3);
        camera = new EulerCamera(67, glGraphics.getWidth() /
(float)glGraphics.getHeight(), 1, 100);
        camera.getPosition().set(0, 1, 3);

        buttonTexture = new Texture(glGame, "button.png");
        batcher = new SpriteBatcher(glGraphics, 1);
        guiCamera = new Camera2D(glGraphics, 480, 320);
        buttonRegion = new TextureRegion(buttonTexture, 0, 0, 64, 64);
        touchPos = new Vector2();
    }
```

In the constructor we load the crate texture and create the cube vertices as we did in the last example. We also create a PointLight and set its position to (3,3,–3). The EulerCamera is created with the standard parameters, a 67-degree field of view, the aspect ratio of the current screen resolution, a near clipping plane distance of 1, and a far clipping plane distance of 100. Finally we set the camera position to (0,1,3) as shown in Figure 11–10.

In the rest of the constructor we just load the button texture and create a `SpriteBatcher`, a `Camera2D`, and `TextureRegion` instance needed for rendering the button. Finally we create a `Vector2` instance so that we can transform real touch coordinates to the coordinate system of the `Camera2D` we use for UI rendering, just as we did in Super Jumper in Chapter 9.

```
private Vertices3 createCube() {
    // same as in previous example
}

@Override
public void resume() {
    crateTexture.reload();
}
```

The `createCube()` and `resume()` methods are exactly the same as in the previous example, so I don't repeat all the code here.

```
@Override
public void update(float deltaTime) {
    game.getInput().getTouchEvents();
    float x = game.getInput().getTouchX(0);
    float y = game.getInput().getTouchY(0);
    guiCamera.touchToWorld(touchPos.set(x, y));

    if(game.getInput().isTouchDown(0)) {
        if(touchPos.x < 64 && touchPos.y < 64) {
            Vector3 direction = camera.getDirection();
            camera.getPosition().add(direction.mul(deltaTime));
        } else {
            if(lastX == -1) {
                lastX = x;
                lastY = y;
            } else {
                camera.rotate((x - lastX) / 10, (y - lastY) / 10);
                lastX = x;
                lastY = y;
            }
        }
    } else {
        lastX = -1;
        lastY = -1;
    }
}
```

The `update()` method is where all the swipe rotation and movement happens, based on touch events. The first thing we do is empty the touch event buffer via a call to `Input.getTouchEvents()`. Next we fetch the current touch coordinates for the first finger on the screen. Note that if no finger is currently touching the screen, the methods we invoke will return the last known position of the finger with index zero. We also transform the real touch coordinates to the coordinate system of our 2D UI so that we can easily check whether the button in the bottom left corner is pressed.

Equipped with all these values, we then check whether a finger is actually touching the screen. If so, we first check whether it is touching the button, which spans the coordinates (0,0) to (64,64) in the 2D UI system. If that is the case, we fetch the current direction of the camera and add it to its position, multiplied by the current delta time. Since the direction vector is a unit-length vector, this means that the camera will move one unit per second.

If the button is not touched, we interpret the touch as a swipe gesture. For this to work we need to have a valid last known touch coordinate. The first time the user puts his finger down the lastX and lastY members will have a value of –1, indicating that we can't create a difference between the last and current touch coordinates, since we only have a single data point. So we just store the current touch coordinates and return from the update() method. If we recorded touch coordinates the last time update() was invoked, we simply take the difference on the x- and y-axes between the current and the last touch coordinates. We directly translate these into increments of the rotation angles. To make the rotation a little slower we divide the differences by 10. The only thing left is calling the EulerCamera.rotate() method, which will adjust the rotation angles accordingly.

Finally, if no finger is currently touching the screen we set the lastX and lastY members to –1 to indicate that we have to await the first touch event before we can do any swipe gesture processing.

```java
@Override
public void present(float deltaTime) {
    GL10 gl = glGraphics.getGL();
    gl.glClear(GL10.GL_COLOR_BUFFER_BIT | GL10.GL_DEPTH_BUFFER_BIT);
    gl.glViewport(0, 0, glGraphics.getWidth(), glGraphics.getHeight());

    camera.setMatrices(gl);

    gl.glEnable(GL10.GL_DEPTH_TEST);
    gl.glEnable(GL10.GL_TEXTURE_2D);
    gl.glEnable(GL10.GL_LIGHTING);

    crateTexture.bind();
    cube.bind();
    light.enable(gl, GL10.GL_LIGHT0);

    for(int z = 0; z >= -8; z-=2) {
        for(int x = -4; x <=4; x+=2 ) {
            gl.glPushMatrix();
            gl.glTranslatef(x, 0, z);
            cube.draw(GL10.GL_TRIANGLES, 0, 6 * 2 * 3);
            gl.glPopMatrix();
        }
    }

    cube.unbind();

    gl.glDisable(GL10.GL_LIGHTING);
    gl.glDisable(GL10.GL_DEPTH_TEST);

    gl.glEnable(GL10.GL_BLEND);
```

```
        gl.glBlendFunc(GL10.GL_SRC_ALPHA, GL10.GL_ONE_MINUS_SRC_ALPHA);

        guiCamera.setViewportAndMatrices();
        batcher.beginBatch(buttonTexture);
        batcher.drawSprite(32, 32, 64, 64, buttonRegion);
        batcher.endBatch();

        gl.glDisable(GL10.GL_BLEND);
        gl.glDisable(GL10.GL_TEXTURE_2D);
    }
```

The present() method is surprisingly simple, thanks to the work we put into all those little helper classes. We start off with the usual things like clearing the screen and setting the viewport. Next we tell the EulerCamera to set the projection and model-view matrix. From this point on we can render anything that should be 3D on screen. Before we do that, we enable depth testing, texturing, and lighting. Next we bind the crate texture and the cube vertices and also enable the point light. Note that we bind the texture and cube vertices only once, since we are going to reuse them for all the crates we render. That's the same trick we used in our BobTest in Chapter 8 to speed up rendering by reducing state changes.

The next piece of code just draws the 25 cubes in the grid formation via a simple nested for loop. Since we have to multiply the model-view matrix with a translation matrix to put the cube vertices at a specific position, we must also use glPushMatrix() and glPopMatrix() so that we don't destroy the camera matrix that's also stored in the model-view matrix.

Once we are done with rendering our cubes, we unbind the cube vertices and disable lighting and depth testing. This is crucial since we are now going to render the 2D UI overlay with the button. Since the button is actually circular, we also enable blending to make the edges of the texture transparent.

Rendering the button works the same as when we rendered the UI elements in Super Jumper. We tell the Camera2D to set the viewport and matrices (we wouldn't really need to set the viewport here again; feel free to "optimize" this method) and tell the SpriteBatcher that we are going to render a sprite. We render the complete button texture at (32,32) in our 480! 320 coordinate system that we set up via the guiCamera.

Finally, we just disable the last few states we enabled previously, blending and texturing.

```
    @Override
    public void pause() {

    }

    @Override
    public void dispose() {
    }
}
```

The rest of the class is again just some stub methods for pause() and dispose(). Figure 11–11 shows the output of this little program.

Figure 11–11. *A simple example of first-person-shooter controls, without multitouch for simplicity*

Pretty nice, right? It also doesn't take a lot of code, either, thanks to the wonderful job our helper classes do for us. Now, adding multi-touch support would be awesome of course. Here's a hint: instead of using polling, as in the example just seen, use the actual touch events. On a "touch down" event, check whether the button was hit. If so, mark the pointer ID associated with it as not being able to produce swipe gestures until a corresponding "touch up" event is signaled. Touch events from all other pointer IDs can be interpreted as swipe gestures!

A Look-At Camera

The second type of camera usually found in games is a simple look-at camera. It is defined by the following:

> A position in space.

> An up vector. Think of this as an arrow coming out of the top of your skull, pointing in the direction of the top of your skull.

> A look-at position in space or alternatively a direction vector. We'll use the former.

> A field of view in degrees.

> A viewport aspect ratio.

> A near and far clipping plane distance.

The only difference from the Euler camera is the way we encode the orientation of the camera. In this case we specify the orientation by the up vector and the look-at position. Let's write a helper class for this type of camera. Listing 11–11 shows you the code.

Listing 11–11. *LookAtCamera.java, a Simple Look-At Camera Without Bells and Whistles*

```java
package com.badlogic.androidgames.framework.gl;

import javax.microedition.khronos.opengles.GL10;

import android.opengl.GLU;

import com.badlogic.androidgames.framework.math.Vector3;

public class LookAtCamera {
    final Vector3 position;
    final Vector3 up;
    final Vector3 lookAt;
    float fieldOfView;
    float aspectRatio;
    float near;
    float far;

    public LookAtCamera(float fieldOfView, float aspectRatio, float near, float far) {
        this.fieldOfView = fieldOfView;
        this.aspectRatio = aspectRatio;
        this.near = near;
        this.far = far;

        position = new Vector3();
        up = new Vector3(0, 1, 0);
        lookAt = new Vector3(0,0,-1);
    }

    public Vector3 getPosition() {
        return position;
    }

    public Vector3 getUp() {
        return up;
    }

    public Vector3 getLookAt() {
        return lookAt;
    }

    public void setMatrices(GL10 gl) {
        gl.glMatrixMode(GL10.GL_PROJECTION);
        gl.glLoadIdentity();
        GLU.gluPerspective(gl, fieldOfView, aspectRatio, near, far);
        gl.glMatrixMode(GL10.GL_MODELVIEW);
        gl.glLoadIdentity();
        GLU.gluLookAt(gl, position.x, position.y, position.z, lookAt.x, lookAt.y,
lookAt.z, up.x, up.y, up.z);
    }
}
```

No real surprises here. We just store the position, up, and lookAt values as Vector3 instances along with the perspective projection parameters we also had in the EulerCamera. Additionally, we provide a couple of getters so we can modify the attributes of the camera. The only interesting method is setMatrices(). But even that is an old hat for us. We first set the projection matrix to a perspective projection matrix, based on the field of view, aspect ratio, and near and far clipping plane distances. Then we set the model-view matrix to contain the camera position and orientation matrix via gluLookAt() as discussed in the previous chapter. This will actually produce a matrix very similar to the matrix we "handcrafted" in the EulerCamera example. It will also rotate the objects around the camera instead of the other way around. However, the nice interface of the gluLookAt() method shields us from all those silly things like inverting positions or angles.

We could in fact use this camera just like an EulerCamera. All we need to do is create a direction vector by subtracting the camera's position from its look-at point and normalizing it. Then we just rotate this direction vector by the yaw and pitch angles. Finally we set the new look-at to the position of the camera and add the direction vector. Both methods would produce exactly the same transformation matrix. It's just two different ways to handle camera orientation.

We'll refrain from writing an explicit example for the LookAtCamera, as the interface is perfectly simple. We'll use it in our last game in this book, were we let it follow a neat little space ship! If you want to play around with it a little, add it to the LightTest we wrote earlier or modify the EulerCameraTest in such a way that the LookAtCamera can be used like a first-person-shooter camera, as outlined in the previous paragraph.

Loading Models

Defining models like our cube in code is very cumbersome to say the least. A better way to create such models is to use special software that allows WYSIWYG creation of complex forms and objects. There's a plethora of software available for that task:

> Blender, an open source project used in many game and movie productions. Very capable and flexible but also a little bit intimidating.

> Wings3D, my weapon of choice and also open-source. I use it for simple low-poly (read: not many triangles) modeling of static objects. It's very simplistic but gets the job done.

> 3D Studio Max, one of the *de facto* standards in the industry. It's a commercial product but there are student versions available.

> Maya, another industry favorite. It's also a commercial product but has some pricing options that might fit smaller purses.

That's just a selection of the more popular options out in the wild. Teaching you how to use one of these is well outside the scope of this book. However, no matter what software you use, at some point you will save your work to some kind of format. One such format is Wavefront OBJ, a very old plain-text format that can be easily parsed and translated to one of our Vertices3 instances.

The Wavefront OBJ Format

We will implement a loader for a subset of this format. Our loader will support models that are composed of triangles only and optionally may contain texture coordinates and normals. The OBJ format also supports storing arbitrary convex polygons, but we won't go into that. Whether you simply find an OBJ model, or create your own, just make sure that it is triangulated, meaning that it's composed of triangles only.

The OBJ format is-line based. Here are the parts of the syntax we are going to process:

> v x y z: The v indicates that the line encodes a vertex position, while x, y, and z are the coordinates encoded as floating-point numbers.

> vn i j k: The n indicates that the line encodes a vertex normal, with i, j, and k being the x-, y- and z-components of the vertex normal.

> vt u v: The vt indicates that the line encodes a texture coordinate pair, with u and v being the texture coordinates.

> f v1/vt1/vn1 v2/vt2/vn2 v3/vt3/vn3: The f indicates that the line encodes a triangle. Each of the v/vt/vn blocks contains the indices of the position, texture coordinates, and vertex normal of a single vertex of the triangle. The indices are relative to the vertex positions, texture coordinates, and vertex normal defined previously by the other three line formats. The vt and vn indices can be left out, indicating that there are no texture coordinates or normal for a specific vertex of a triangle.

We will ignore any line that does not start with v, vn, vt, or f; we will also output an error if any of the permissible lines don't follow the formatting just described. Items within a single line are delimited by whitespaces, which can include spaces, tabs, and so on.

> **NOTE** The OBJ format can store a lot more information that we are going to parse her. We can get away with only parsing the syntax shown here and ignoring anything else as long as the models are triangulated and have normal and texture coordinates.

Here's a very simple example, a texture triangle with normals in OBJ format:

```
v -0.5 -0.5 0
v 0.5 -0.5 0
v 0 0.5 0
vn 0 0 1
vn 0 0 1
vn 0 0 1
vt 0 1
vt 1 1
vt 0.5 0
f 1/1/1 2/2/2 3/3/3
```

Note that the vertex positions, texture coordinates and normals do not have to be defined in such a nice order. They could be intertwined if the software that saved the file chose to do so.

The indices given in an f statement are one based, rather than zero-based (as in the case of a Java array). Some software even outputs negative indices at times. This is permitted by the OBJ format specification but is a major pain. We have to keep track how many vertex positions, texture coordinates, or vertex normals we have loaded so far and then add that negative index to the respective number of positions, vertex coordinates, or normals depending on what vertex attribute that index points at.

Implementing an OBJ Loader

Our plan of attack will be to load the file completely into memory and create a string per line. We will also create temporary float arrays for all the vertex positions, texture coordinates and normals we are going to load. Their size will be equal to the number of lines in the OBJ file times the number of components per attribute; that is, two for texture coordinates or three for normals. By this we overshoot the necessary amount of memory needed to store the data, but that's still better than allocating new arrays every time we have filled them up.

We also do the same for the indices that define each triangle. While the OBJ format is indeed an indexed format, we can't use those indices directly with our Vertices3 class. The reason for this is that a vertex attribute might be reused by multiple vertices, so there's a one-to-many relationship that is not allowed in OpenGL ES. Therefore we'll use a non-indexed Vertices3 instance and simply duplicate vertices. For our needs that's OK.

Let's see how we can implement all this. Listing 11–12 shows the code.

Listing 11–12. *ObjLoader.java, a Simple Class for Loading a Subset of the OBJ Format*

```
package com.badlogic.androidgames.framework.gl;

import java.io.BufferedReader;
import java.io.IOException;
import java.io.InputStream;
import java.io.InputStreamReader;
import java.util.ArrayList;
import java.util.List;

import com.badlogic.androidgames.framework.impl.GLGame;

public class ObjLoader {
    public static Vertices3 load(GLGame game, String file) {
        InputStream in = null;
        try {
            in = game.getFileIO().readAsset(file);
            List<String> lines = readLines(in);

            float[] vertices = new float[lines.size() * 3];
            float[] normals = new float[lines.size() * 3];
            float[] uv = new float[lines.size() * 2];

            int numVertices = 0;
            int numNormals = 0;
            int numUV = 0;
            int numFaces = 0;
```

The first thing we do is open an InputStream to the asset file specified by the file parameter. We then read in all lines of that file in a method called readLines() (defined in the code that follows). Based on the number of lines, we allocate float arrays that will store the x-, y- and z-coordinates of each vertex's position, the x-, y- and z-component of each vertex's normal, and the u- and v-components of each vertex's texture coordinates. Since we don't know how many vertices there are in the file, we just allocate more space than needed for the arrays. Each vertex attribute is stored in subsequent elements of the three arrays. The position of the first read vertex is in vertices[0], vertices[1], and vertices[2], and so on. We also keep track of the indices in the triangle definitions for each of the three attributes of a vertex. Additionally we have a couple of counters to keep track of how many things we have already loaded.

```
for (int i = 0; i < lines.size(); i++) {
    String line = lines.get(i);
```

Next we have a for loop that iterates through all the lines in the files.

```
if (line.startsWith("v ")) {
    String[] tokens = line.split("[ ]+");
    vertices[vertexIndex] = Float.parseFloat(tokens[1]);
    vertices[vertexIndex + 1] = Float.parseFloat(tokens[2]);
    vertices[vertexIndex + 2] = Float.parseFloat(tokens[3]);
    vertexIndex += 3;
    numVertices++;
    continue;
}
```

If the current line is a vertex position definition, we split the line by whitespaces, read the x-, y- and z-coordinate, and store it in the vertices array:

```
if (line.startsWith("vn ")) {
    String[] tokens = line.split("[ ]+");
    normals[normalIndex] = Float.parseFloat(tokens[1]);
    normals[normalIndex + 1] = Float.parseFloat(tokens[2]);
    normals[normalIndex + 2] = Float.parseFloat(tokens[3]);
    normalIndex += 3;
    numNormals++;
    continue;
}

if (line.startsWith("vt")) {
    String[] tokens = line.split("[ ]+");
    uv[uvIndex] = Float.parseFloat(tokens[1]);
    uv[uvIndex + 1] = Float.parseFloat(tokens[2]);
    uvIndex += 2;
    numUV++;
    continue;
}
```

We do the same for normals and texture coordinates:

```
if (line.startsWith("f ")) {
    String[] tokens = line.split("[ ]+");

    String[] parts = tokens[1].split("/");
    facesVerts[faceIndex] = getIndex(parts[0], numVertices);
```

```
        if (parts.length > 2)
            facesNormals[faceIndex] = getIndex(parts[2], numNormals);
        if (parts.length > 1)
            facesUV[faceIndex] = getIndex(parts[1], numUV);
        faceIndex++;

        parts = tokens[2].split("/");
        facesVerts[faceIndex] = getIndex(parts[0], numVertices);
        if (parts.length > 2)
            facesNormals[faceIndex] = getIndex(parts[2], numNormals);
        if (parts.length > 1)
            facesUV[faceIndex] = getIndex(parts[1], numUV);
        faceIndex++;

        parts = tokens[3].split("/");
        facesVerts[faceIndex] = getIndex(parts[0], numVertices);
        if (parts.length > 2)
            facesNormals[faceIndex] = getIndex(parts[2], numNormals);
        if (parts.length > 1)
            facesUV[faceIndex] = getIndex(parts[1], numUV);
        faceIndex++;
        numFaces++;
        continue;
    }
}
```

In this code, each vertex of a triangle (here called a *face*, as that is the term used in the OBJ format) is defined by a triplet of indices into the vertex position, texture coordinate, and normal arrays. The texture coordinate and normal indices can be omitted, so we keep track of this. The indices can also be negative, in which case we have to add them to the number of positions/texture coordinates/normals loaded so far. That's what the getIndex() method does for us.

```
float[] verts = new float[(numFaces * 3)
        * (3 + (numNormals > 0 ? 3 : 0) + (numUV > 0 ? 2 : 0))];
```

Once we have loaded all vertex positions, texture coordinates, normals, and triangles we can start assembling a float array holding the vertices in the format expected by a Vertices3 instance. The number of floats needed to store these vertices can be easily derived from the number of triangles we loaded and whether normal and texture coordinates are given.

```
for (int i = 0, vi = 0; i < numFaces * 3; i++) {
    int vertexIdx = facesVerts[i] * 3;
    verts[vi++] = vertices[vertexIdx];
    verts[vi++] = vertices[vertexIdx + 1];
    verts[vi++] = vertices[vertexIdx + 2];

    if (numUV > 0) {
        int uvIdx = facesUV[i] * 2;
        verts[vi++] = uv[uvIdx];
        verts[vi++] = 1 - uv[uvIdx + 1];
    }

    if (numNormals > 0) {
```

```
            int normalIdx = facesNormals[i] * 3;
            verts[vi++] = normals[normalIdx];
            verts[vi++] = normals[normalIdx + 1];
            verts[vi++] = normals[normalIdx + 2];
        }
    }
```

To fill the verts array we just loop over all the triangles, fetch the vertex attribute for each vertex of a triangle and put them into the verts array in the layout we usually use for a Vertices3 instance.

```
    Vertices3 model = new Vertices3(game.getGLGraphics(), numFaces * 3,
            0, false, numUV > 0, numNormals > 0);
    model.setVertices(verts, 0, verts.length);
    return model;
```

The last thing we do is instantiate the Vertices3 instance and set the vertices.

```
    } catch (Exception ex) {
        throw new RuntimeException("couldn't load '" + file + "'", ex);
    } finally {
        if (in != null)
            try {
                in.close();
            } catch (Exception ex) {

            }
    }
}
```

The rest of the method just does some exception handling and closing of the InputStream.

```
static int getIndex(String index, int size) {
    int idx = Integer.parseInt(index);
    if (idx < 0)
        return size + idx;
    else
        return idx - 1;
}
```

The getIndex() method takes one of the indices given for an attribute of a vertex in a triangle definition, as well as the number of attributes loaded so far, and returns an index suitable to reference the attribute in one of our working arrays.

```
static List<String> readLines(InputStream in) throws IOException {
    List<String> lines = new ArrayList<String>();

    BufferedReader reader = new BufferedReader(new InputStreamReader(in));
    String line = null;
    while ((line = reader.readLine()) != null)
        lines.add(line);
    return lines;
}
}
```

Finally there's the readLines() method, which just reads in each line of a file and returns all these lines as a List of strings.

To load a OBJ file from an asset we can use the ObjLoader as follows:

```
Vertices3 model = ObjLoader.load(game, "mymodel.obj");
```

Pretty straightforward after all this index juggling, right? To render this Vertices3 instance we need to know how many vertices it has, though. Let's extend the Vertices3 class one more time, adding two methods to return the number of vertices as well as the number of indices currently defined in the instance. Listing 11–13 shows you the code.

Listing 11–13. *An excerpt from Vertices3.java, Fetching the Number of Vertices and Indices*

```
public int getNumIndices() {
    return indices.limit();
}

public int getNumVertices() {
    return vertices.limit() / (vertexSize / 4);
}
```

For the number of indices we just return the limit of the ShortBuffer storing the indices. For the number of vertices we do the same. However, since the limit is reported in the number of floats defined in the FloatBuffer, we have to divide it by the vertex size. Since we store that in number of bytes in vertexSize, we divide that member by 4.

Using the OBJ Loader

To demonstrate the OBJ loader, I've rewritten the last example and created a new test called ObjTest along with an ObjScreen. I copied over all the code from the previous example and only changed a single line in the constructor of ObjScreen:

```
cube = ObjLoader.load(glGame, "cube.obj");
```

So, instead of using the createCube() method (which I removed), we are now directly loading a model from an OBJ file called cube.obj. I created a replica of the cube we previously specified programmatically in createCube() in Wings3D. It has the same vertex positions, texture coordinates and normals as the handcrafted version. It should come as no surprise that when you run ObjTest it will look exactly like our EulerCameraTest. I'll therefore spare you the obligatory screenshot.

Some Notes on Loading Models

For the game we are going to write in the next chapter[OK?] our loader is sufficient, but it is far from robust. There are some caveats:

String processing in Android is inherently slow. The OBJ format is a plain-text format and as such needs a lot of parsing. This will have a negative influence on load times. You can work around this issue by converting your OBJ models to a custom binary format. You could for example just serialize the verts array that we fill in the ObjLoader.load() method.

The OBJ format has a lot more features that we don't exploit. If you want to extend our simple loader look up the format specification on the web. It should be easy to add additional functionality.

An OBJ file is usually accompanied by what's called a *material file*. This file defines the colors and textures to be used by groups of vertices in the OBJ file. We will not need this functionality as we know which texture to use for a specific OBJ file. For a more robust loader you'll want to look into the material file specification as well.

A Little Physics in 3D

In Chapter 8 we developed a very simple point-mass-based physics model in 2D. Here's the good news: everything works the same in 3D!

Positions are now 3D vectors instead of 2D vectors. We just add a z-coordinate.

Velocities are still expressed in meters per second on each axis. We just add one more component for the z-axis!

Accelerations are also still expressed in meters per second per second on each axis. Again, we just add another coordinate.

The pseudocode in Chapter 8 describing a physics simulation update looked like this:

```
Vector2 position = new Vector2();
Vector2 velocity = new Vector2();
Vector2 acceleration = new Vector2(0, -10);
while(simulationRuns) {
    float deltaTime = getDeltaTime();
    velocity.add(acceleration.x * deltaTime, acceleration.y * deltaTime);
    position.add(velocity.x * deltaTime, velocity.y * deltaTime);
}
```

We can translate this into 3D space by simply exchanging the Vector2 instances with Vector3 instances:

```
Vector3 position = new Vector3();
Vector3 velocity = new Vector3();
```

```
Vector3 acceleration = new Vector3(0, -10, 0);
while(simulationRuns) {
    float deltaTime = getDeltaTime();
    velocity.add(acceleration.x * deltaTime, acceleration.y * deltaTime, acceleration.z *
deltaTime);
    position.add(velocity.x * deltaTime, velocity.y * deltaTime, velocity.z * deltaTime);
}
```

And that is all there is to it. This simple physics model is again sufficient for many simple 3D games. In the final game of this book we will not even use any acceleration, because of the nature of the objects in the game.

More complex physics in 3D (and 2D) are, of course, harder to implement. For this purpose you'd usually use a third-party library instead of reinventing the wheel yourself. The problem on Android is that Java-based solutions will be much too slow due to the heavy computations involved. There are some solutions for 2D physics for Android that wrap native C++ libraries like Box2D via the Java Native Interface (JNI), providing the native API to a Java application. For 3D physics there's a library called Bullet. However, there don't exist any usable JNI bindings for this library yet. Those topics are well outside of the scope of this book, though, and in many cases we don't need any sophisticated rigid-body physics.

Collision Detection and Object Representation in 3D

In Chapter 8 we discussed the relation between object representation and collision detection. We strive to make our game-world objects as independent from their graphical representation as possible. Instead we'd like to define them in terms of their bounding shape, position, and orientation. Position and orientation are not much of a problem: we can express the former as a Vector3 and the later as the rotation around the x-, y- and z-axes (minding the potential gimbal lock problem mentioned in the last chapter. Let's take a look at bounding shapes.

Bounding Shapes in 3D

In terms of bounding shapes we again have a ton of options. Figure 11–12 shows some of the more popular bounding shapes in 3D programming.

Figure 11–12. *Various bounding shapes. From left to right: triangle mesh, axis aligned bounding box, bounding sphere*

Triangle Mesh: This bounds the object as tightly as possible. However, colliding two objects based on their triangle meshes is computationally heave.

Axis Aligned Bounding Box: This bounds the object loosely. It is a lot less computationally intensive than a triangle mesh.

Bounding Sphere: This bounds the object even less well. It is the fastest way to check for collisions.

Another problem with triangle meshes and bounding boxes is that we have to reorient them whenever we rotate or scale the object, just as in 2D. Bounding spheres on the other hand don't need any modification if we rotate an object. If we scale an object, we just need to scale the radius of the sphere, which is a simple multiplication.

Bounding Sphere Overlap Testing

The mathematics of triangle mesh and bounding box collision detection can be pretty involved. For our next game, bounding spheres will do just fine. There's also a little trick we can apply which we already used in Super Jumper: to make the bounding sphere fit a little better we make it smaller than the graphical representation. Figure 11–13 shows you how that could look in case of the space ship.

Figure 11–13. *Making the bounding sphere smaller to better fit an object*

That's of course a very cheap trick, but it turns out that in many situations it is more than sufficient to keep up the illusion of mostly correct collision detection.

So how do we collide two spheres with each other? Or rather, how do we test for overlap? It works exactly the same as in the case of circles! All we need to do is measure the distance from the center of one sphere to the center of the other sphere. If that distance is smaller than the two radii of the spheres added together, then we have a collision. Let's create a simple Sphere class. Listing 11–13 shows you the code.

Listing 11–13. *Sphere.java, a Simple Bounding Sphere*

```java
package com.badlogic.androidgames.framework.math;

public class Sphere {
    public final Vector3 center = new Vector3();
    public float radius;

    public Sphere(float x, float y, float z, float radius) {
        this.center.set(x,y,z);
        this.radius = radius;
    }
}
```

That's the same code as in the Circle class. All we changed is the vector holding the center, which is now a Vector3 instead of a Vector2.

Let's also extend our OverlapTester class with methods to check for overlap of two spheres and to test whether a point is inside a sphere. Listing 11–14 shows the code.

Listing 11–14. *Excerpt from OverlapTester.java, Adding Sphere-Testing Methods*

```java
public static boolean overlapSpheres(Sphere s1, Sphere s2) {
    float distance = s1.center.distSquared(s2.center);
    float radiusSum = s1.radius + s2.radius;
    return distance <= radiusSum * radiusSum;
}

public static boolean pointInSphere(Sphere c, Vector3 p) {
    return c.center.distSquared(p) < c.radius * c.radius;
}

public static boolean pointInSphere(Sphere c, float x, float y, float z) {
    return c.center.distSquared(x, y, z) < c.radius * c.radius;
}
```

That's again exactly the same code as in the case of Circle overlap testing. We just use the center of the spheres, which is a Vector3 instead of a Vector2 as in the case of a Circle.

> **NOTE** Entire books have been filled on the topic of 3D collision detection. If you want to dive deep into that rather interesting world, I suggest the book *Real-time Collision Detection* by Christer Ericson (Morgan Kaufmann, 2005). It should be on the shelf of any self-respecting game developer!

GameObject3D and DynamicGameObject3D

Now that we have a nice bounding shape for our 3D objects, we can easily write the equivalent of the GameObject and DynamicGameObject classes we used in 2D. We just replace any Vector2 with a Vector3 instance and use the Sphere class instead of the Rectangle class. Listing 11–15 shows you the GameObject3D class.

Listing 11–15. *GameObject3D, Representing a Simple Object with a Position and Bounds*

```
package com.badlogic.androidgames.framework;

import com.badlogic.androidgames.framework.math.Sphere;
import com.badlogic.androidgames.framework.math.Vector3;

public class GameObject3D {
    public final Vector3 position;
    public final Sphere bounds;

    public GameObject3D(float x, float y, float z, float radius) {
        this.position = new Vector3(x,y,z);
        this.bounds = new Sphere(x, y, z, radius);
    }
}
```

This code is so trivial, you probably don't need any explanation. The only hitch is that we have to store the same position twice: once as the position member in the GameObject3D class, and again within the position member of the Sphere instance that's contained in the GameObject3D class. That's a tiny bit ugly, but for the sake of clarity we'll stick to this.

Deriving a DynamicGameObject3D class from this class is simple as well. Listing 11–16 shows you the code.

Listing 11–16. *DynamicGameObject3D.java, the Dynamic Equivalent to GameObject3D*

```
package com.badlogic.androidgames.framework;

import com.badlogic.androidgames.framework.math.Vector3;

public class DynamicGameObject3D extends GameObject {
    public final Vector3 velocity;
    public final Vector3 accel;

    public DynamicGameObject3D(float x, float y, float z, float radius) {
        super(x, y, z, radius);
        velocity = new Vector3();
        accel = new Vector3();
    }
}
```

We again just replace any Vector2 with a Vector3 and smile happily.

In 2D we had to think hard about the relationship between the graphical representation of our objects (given in pixels) and the units used within the model of our world. In 3D we can break free from this! The vertices of our 3D models that we load from, say, an OBJ file can be defined in whatever unit system we want. We no longer need to transform pixels to world units and vice versa. This makes working in 3D a little. We just need to train our artist so that she provides us with models that are properly scaled to the unit system of our world.

Summary

Again we uncovered a lot of mysteries in the world of game programming. We talked a little bit about vectors in 3D, which turned out to be as simple to use as their 2D counterparts. The general theme: we just add a z-coordinate! We also took a look at lighting in OpenGL ES. With the helper classes we wrote to represent materials and light sources, it is pretty simple to set up the lighting in a scene. For better performance and fewer graphical artifacts we also implemented simple mipmapping as part of our Texture class. We also explored implementing simple Euler and look-at cameras with very little code and a little help from the Matrix class. Since creating 3D meshes by hand in code is tedious, we also looked at one of the most simple and popular 3D file formats: Wavefront OBJ. We revisited our simple physics model and transferred it to the realm of 3D, which turned out to be as simple as creating 3D vectors. The last point on our agenda was to figure out how to cope with bounding shapes and object representation in 3D. Given our modest needs we arrived at very simple solutions for both problems, which are very similar or even identical to those we used in 2D.

While there is a lot more to 3D programming than I can present here, you now have a pretty good idea about what is needed to write a 3D game. The big realization is that there is indeed not a lot of difference between a 2D game and a 3D game (up to a certain degree of complexity, of course). We don't have to be afraid of 3D anymore! In Chapter 12 we'll use our new knowledge to write the final game of this book: Droid Invaders!

Droid Invaders: the Grand Finale

We are finally ready to create the last game of this book. This time we are going to develop a simple action/arcade game. We'll adapt an old classic and give it a nice 3D look, using the techniques we talked about in the last two chapters.

Core Game Mechanics

As you might have guessed from the title of this chapter we are about to implement a variation of Space Invaders, a 2D game in its original form (illustrated in Figure 12–1).

Figure 12–1. *The original Space Invaders arcade game*

Here's a little surprise: we'll stay in 2D as well for the most part. All our objects will have 3D bounds in the form of bounding spheres and positions in 3D space. However, movement will only happen in the x/z plane, which makes some things a little easier. Figure 12–2 shows you our adapted 3D Space Invaders world. The mock-up was created with Wings3D.

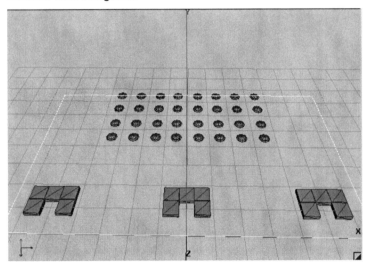

Figure 12–2. *Our 3D game field mock-up*

Let's define the game mechanics:

- We have a ship flying in the bottom of the playfield capable of navigating on the x-axis only.

- The movement is limited to the boundaries of the playfield. When the ship reaches the left or right boundary of the game field, it simply stops moving.

- We want to give the player the option of either using the accelerometer to navigate the ship or on-screen buttons for left and right movement.

- The ship can fire one shot per second. The player shoots by pressing an on-screen button.

- At the bottom of the game field there are three shields, each composed of five cubes.

- Invaders start off with the configuration shown in Figure 12–2, and then move to the left for some distance, then some distance in the positive z-direction, and then to the right for some distance. There will be 32 invaders in total, making up four rows of eight invaders.

- Invaders will shoot randomly.

- When a shot hits the ship, the ship explodes and loses one life.

- When a shot hits a shield, the shield disappears permanently.

- When a shot hits an invader, it explodes. The score is increased by 10 points.

- When all invaders are destroyed a new wave of invaders appears, moving slightly faster than the last wave.

- When an invader directly collides with a ship the game is over.

- When the ship has lost all its lives the game is over.

That's not an overwhelming list, is it? All operations can essentially be performed in 2D (in the x/z instead of the x/y plane). We'll still use 3D bounding spheres though. Maybe you want to extend the game to real 3D after we are done with its first iteration. Let's move on to the back story.

A Backstory and Art Style

We'll call the game Droid Invaders in reference to Android and Space Invaders. That's cheap, but we don't plan on producing an AAA title for now. In the tradition of classic shooters like Doom, the backstory will be minimal. It goes like this:

> *Invaders from outer space attack Earth. You are the sole person capable of fending off the evil forces.*

That was good enough for Doom and Quake, so it's good enough for Droid Invaders as well.

The art style will be a little retro when it comes to the GUI, using the same old-fashioned font we used in Chapter 9 for Super Jumper. The game world itself will be displayed in fancy 3D with textured and lighted 3D models. Figure 12–3 shows what the game screen will look like.

Figure 12–3. *The Droid Invaders mockup. Fancy!*

The music will be a rock/metal mixture, and sound effects will match the scenario.

Screens and Transitions

Since we have already implemented help screens and high-score screens twice, in Chapter 6's Mr. Nom and in Chapter 9's Super Jumper, we'll refrain from doing so for Droid Invaders; it's always the same principle, and a player should immediately know what to do once presented with the game screen, anyway. Instead, we'll add a settings screen that allows the player to select the type of input (multitouch or accelerometer) and disable or enable sound. Here's the list of screens of Droid Invaders:

- A main screen with a logoand Play and Settings options.

- A game screen that will immediately start with the game (no more ready signal!) and also handle paused states as well as display a "Game Over" text once the ship has no more lives.

- A settings screen that displays three icons representing the configuration options (multitouch, accelerometer, and sound).

That's again very similar to what we had in the previous two games. Figure 12–4 shows all the screens and transitions.

Figure 12–4. *Screens and transitions of Droid Invaders*

Defining the Game World

One of the joys of working in 3D is that we are free from the shackles of pixels. We can define our world in whatever units we want. The game mechanics we outlined dictate a limited playing field, so let's start by defining that field. Figure 12–5 shows you the playing field area in our game's world.

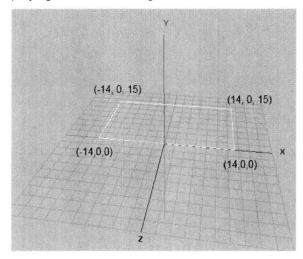

Figure 12–5. *The playing field*

Everything in our world will happen inside this boundary in the x/z plane. Coordinates will be limited on the x-axis from −14 to 14 and on the z-axis from 0 to −15. The ship will be able to move along the bottom edge of the playing field, from (−14,0,0) to (14,0,0).

Next we should define the sizes of all objects in our world:

- The ship will have a radius of 0.5 units.
- The invaders have a slightly bigger radius of 0.75 units. This makes them easier to hit.
- The shield blocks each have a radius of 0.5 units.
- The shots each have a radius of 0.1 units.

How did I arrive at those values? I simply divided the game world up in cells of 1 unit by 1 unit and thought about how big each game element has to be in relation to the size of the playing field. Usually you arrive at those measures through a little experimentation or by taking real-world units like meters. In Droid Invaders we don't use meters but nameless units.

The radii we just defined can be directly translated to bounding spheres of course. In case of the shield blocks and ship we cheat a little, as those are clearly not spherical. Thanks to the 2D properties of our world we get away with this little trick, though. In case of the invaders the sphere is actually a pretty good approximation.

We also have to define the velocities of our moving objects:

- The ship can move with a maximum velocity of 20 units per second. As in Super Jumper, we'll usually have a lower velocity as it is dependent on the phone's tilt.

- The invaders move with 1 unit per second initially. Each wave will increase this speed slightly.

- The shots move with 10 units per second.

With these definitions we can already start implementing the logic of our game world. It turns out, however, that creating the assets is directly related to the units we defined here.

Creating the Assets

As in the previous games we have two kinds of graphical assets: UI elements such as logos or buttons, and the models of the different types of objects of our game.

The UI Assets

We'll again create our UI assets relative to some target resolution. Our game will be run in landscape mode, so we simply choose a target resolution of 480×320 pixels. The screens in Figure 12–4 already show all the elements we have in our UI: a logo, different menu items, a couple of buttons, and some text. For the text we'll reuse the font we used in Super Jumper. We've already done the compositing of all these things in previous games, and you've learned that putting them into a texture atlas can be rather beneficial for performance. So here is the texture atlas we'll use for Droid Invaders, containing all the UI elements as well as the font we'll use for all the screens in the game, shown in Figure 12–6.

Figure 12–6. *The UI element atlas with buttons, the logo, and our font. It is stored in the file items.png, 512×512 pixels*

It's essentially the same concept as we used in Super Jumper. We also have a background that will be rendered in all screens. Figure 12–7 shows the image.

Figure 12–7. *The background, stored in background.jpg. 512×512 pixels*

As you can see back in Figure 12–4, we'll only use the top-left region of this image to render a full frame (480×320 pixels).

That's all the UI elements we need. Let's look at our 3D models and their textures.

The Game Assets

As I said in Chapter 11, this book can't possibly go into detail how to create 3D models with software like Wings3D. If you want to create your own models, you'll have to choose an application to work with and plow through some tutorials, often freely available on the net. For the models of Droid Invaders I used Wings3D and simply exported them to the OBJ format we can load with our framework. All models are composed of triangles only and have texture coordinates and normals. For some of them we don't need texture coordinates, but it doesn't hurt to have them.

The ship model and its texture are illustrated in Figure 12–8.

Figure 12–8. *The ship model in Wings3D (ship.obj) and its texture (ship.png, 256×256 pixels)*

The crucial thing is that the ship in Figure 12–8 does roughly have the "radius" we outlined in the previous section. We don't need to scale anything or transform sizes and positions from one coordinate system to the other. The ship's model is defined with the same units as its bounding sphere!

Figure 12–9 shows you the invader model and its texture.

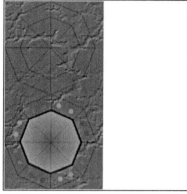

Figure 12–9. *The invader model (invader.obj) and its texture (invader.png, 256×256 pixels)*

The invader model follows the same principles as the ship model. We have one OBJ file storing the vertex positions, texture coordinates, normals and faces, and a texture image.

The shield blocks and shots are modeled as cubes and are stored in the files shield.obj and shot.obj. Although they have texture coordinates assigned, we don't actually use texture mapping when rendering them. We just draw them as (translucent) objects with a specific color (blue in the case of the shield blocks, yellow for the shots).

Finally there are the explosions (see Figure 12–3 again). How do we model those? We don't. We'll do what we did in 2D and simply draw a rectangle with a proper z-position in our 3D world, texture mapping it with one frame from a texture image containing an explosion animation. It's the same principle we used for the animated objects in Super Jumper. The only difference is that we will draw the rectangle at a z-position smaller than zero (wherever the exploding object is located). We can even abuse the SpriteBatcher class to do this! Hurray for OpenGL ES. Figure 12–10 shows you the texture.

Figure 12–10. *The explosion animation texture (explode.png, 256×256 pixels)*

Each frame of the animation is 64×64 pixels in size. All we need to do is generate
TextureRegions for each frame and put them into an Animation instance we can use to
fetch the correct frame for a given animation time, just as we did for the squirrels or Bob
in Super Jumper.

Sound and Music

For the sound effects I used sfxr again. The explosion sound effect I found on the web.
It's a public domain sound effect so we can use it in Droid Invaders. The music I
recorded myself. With real instruments. Yes, I'm that old-school. Here's the list of audio
files of Droid Invaders.

- ▨ click.ogg, a click sound used for the menu items/buttons

- ▨ shot.ogg, a shot sound

- ▨ explosion.ogg, an explosion

- ▨ music.mp3, the rock/metal song I wrote for Droid Invaders

Plan of Attack

With our game mechanics, design, and assets in place we can start coding. As usual we'll create a new project, copy over all of our framework code, make sure we have a proper manifest and icons, and so on. By now you should have a pretty good grasp of how to set things up. All the code of Droid Invaders will be placed in the package com.badlogic.androidgames.droidinvaders. The assets are stored in the assets/ directory of the Android project. We'll use the exact same general structure that we used in Super Jumper: a default activity deriving from GLGame, a couple of GLScreen instances implementing the different screens and transitions as shown in Figure 12–4, classes for loading assets and storing settings as well as the classes for our game objects and a rendering class that can draw our game world in 3D. Let's start with the Assets class.

The Assets Class

Well, we've done this before, so don't expect any surprises. Listing 12–1 shows you the code of the Assets class.

Listing 12–1. *Assets.java, Loading and Storing Assets as Always*

```java
package com.badlogic.androidgames.droidinvaders;

import com.badlogic.androidgames.framework.Music;
import com.badlogic.androidgames.framework.Sound;
import com.badlogic.androidgames.framework.gl.Animation;
import com.badlogic.androidgames.framework.gl.Font;
import com.badlogic.androidgames.framework.gl.ObjLoader;
import com.badlogic.androidgames.framework.gl.Texture;
import com.badlogic.androidgames.framework.gl.TextureRegion;
import com.badlogic.androidgames.framework.gl.Vertices3;
import com.badlogic.androidgames.framework.impl.GLGame;

public class Assets {
    public static Texture background;
    public static TextureRegion backgroundRegion;
    public static Texture items;
    public static TextureRegion logoRegion;
    public static TextureRegion menuRegion;
    public static TextureRegion gameOverRegion;
    public static TextureRegion pauseRegion;
    public static TextureRegion settingsRegion;
    public static TextureRegion touchRegion;
    public static TextureRegion accelRegion;
    public static TextureRegion touchEnabledRegion;
    public static TextureRegion accelEnabledRegion;
    public static TextureRegion soundRegion;
    public static TextureRegion soundEnabledRegion;
    public static TextureRegion leftRegion;
    public static TextureRegion rightRegion;
```

```
public static TextureRegion fireRegion;
public static TextureRegion pauseButtonRegion;
public static Font font;
```

We have a couple of members storing the texture of the UI elements as well as the background image. We also store a couple of TextureRegions as well as a Font. This covers all our UI needs.

```
public static Texture explosionTexture;
public static Animation explosionAnim;
public static Vertices3 shipModel;
public static Texture shipTexture;
public static Vertices3 invaderModel;
public static Texture invaderTexture;
public static Vertices3 shotModel;
public static Vertices3 shieldModel;
```

We also have textures and Vertices3 instances that store the models and textures of our game's objects. We also have an Animation instance that holds the frames of the explosion animation.

```
public static Music music;
public static Sound clickSound;
public static Sound explosionSound;
public static Sound shotSound;
```

Finally we have a couple of Music and Sound instances storing the game's audio.

```
public static void load(GLGame game) {
    background = new Texture(game, "background.jpg", true);
    backgroundRegion = new TextureRegion(background, 0, 0, 480, 320);
    items = new Texture(game, "items.png", true);
    logoRegion = new TextureRegion(items, 0, 256, 384, 128);
    menuRegion = new TextureRegion(items, 0, 128, 224, 64);
    gameOverRegion = new TextureRegion(items, 224, 128, 128, 64);
    pauseRegion = new TextureRegion(items, 0, 192, 160, 64);
    settingsRegion = new TextureRegion(items, 0, 160, 224, 32);
    touchRegion = new TextureRegion(items, 0, 384, 64, 64);
    accelRegion = new TextureRegion(items, 64, 384, 64, 64);
    touchEnabledRegion = new TextureRegion(items, 0, 448, 64, 64);
    accelEnabledRegion = new TextureRegion(items, 64, 448, 64, 64);
    soundRegion = new TextureRegion(items, 128, 384, 64, 64);
    soundEnabledRegion = new TextureRegion(items, 190, 384, 64, 64);
    leftRegion = new TextureRegion(items, 0, 0, 64, 64);
    rightRegion = new TextureRegion(items, 64, 0, 64, 64);
    fireRegion = new TextureRegion(items, 128, 0, 64, 64);
    pauseButtonRegion = new TextureRegion(items, 0, 64, 64, 64);
    font = new Font(items, 224, 0, 16, 16, 20);
```

The load() method starts of by creating the UI-related stuff. It's just some texture loading and region creation as usual.

```
    explosionTexture = new Texture(game, "explode.png", true);
    TextureRegion[] keyFrames = new TextureRegion[16];
    int frame = 0;
    for (int y = 0; y < 256; y += 64) {
```

Listing 12–4. *MainMenuScreen.java, the Main Menu Screen*

```java
package com.badlogic.androidgames.droidinvaders;

import java.util.List;

import javax.microedition.khronos.opengles.GL10;

import com.badlogic.androidgames.framework.Game;
import com.badlogic.androidgames.framework.Input.TouchEvent;
import com.badlogic.androidgames.framework.gl.Camera2D;
import com.badlogic.androidgames.framework.gl.SpriteBatcher;
import com.badlogic.androidgames.framework.impl.GLScreen;
import com.badlogic.androidgames.framework.math.OverlapTester;
import com.badlogic.androidgames.framework.math.Rectangle;
import com.badlogic.androidgames.framework.math.Vector2;

public class MainMenuScreen extends GLScreen {
    Camera2D guiCam;
    SpriteBatcher batcher;
    Vector2 touchPoint;
    Rectangle playBounds;
    Rectangle settingsBounds;
```

As usual we need a camera to set up our viewport and virtual target resolution of 480×320 pixels. We use a SpriteBatcher to render the UI elements and background image. The Vector2 and Rectangle instances will help us to decide whether a touch hit a button or not.

```java
    public MainMenuScreen(Game game) {
        super(game);

        guiCam = new Camera2D(glGraphics, 480, 320);
        batcher = new SpriteBatcher(glGraphics, 10);
        touchPoint = new Vector2();
        playBounds = new Rectangle(240 - 112, 100, 224, 32);
        settingsBounds = new Rectangle(240 - 112, 100 - 32, 224, 32);
    }
```

In the constructor we setup the camera and SpriteBatcher as we always do. We also instantiate the Vector2 and the Rectangles, using the position and width and height of the two elements on screen in our 480×320 target resolution.

```java
    @Override
    public void update(float deltaTime) {
        List<TouchEvent> events = game.getInput().getTouchEvents();
        int len = events.size();
        for(int i = 0; i < len; i++) {
            TouchEvent event = events.get(i);
            if(event.type != TouchEvent.TOUCH_UP)
                continue;

            guiCam.touchToWorld(touchPoint.set(event.x, event.y));
            if(OverlapTester.pointInRectangle(playBounds, touchPoint)) {
                Assets.playSound(Assets.clickSound);
                game.setScreen(new GameScreen(game));
```

```
            }
            if(OverlapTester.pointInRectangle(settingsBounds, touchPoint)) {
                Assets.playSound(Assets.clickSound);
                game.setScreen(new SettingsScreen(game));
            }
        }
    }
```

In the update() method we fetch the touch events and check for "touch-up" events. If there is such an event we transform its real coordinates to the coordinate system the camera sets up. All that's left is checking the touch point against the two rectangles bounding the menu entries. If one of them is hit we play the click sound and transition to the respective screen.

```
    @Override
    public void present(float deltaTime) {
        GL10 gl = glGraphics.getGL();
        gl.glClear(GL10.GL_COLOR_BUFFER_BIT);
        guiCam.setViewportAndMatrices();

        gl.glEnable(GL10.GL_TEXTURE_2D);

        batcher.beginBatch(Assets.background);
        batcher.drawSprite(240, 160, 480, 320, Assets.backgroundRegion);
        batcher.endBatch();

        gl.glEnable(GL10.GL_BLEND);
        gl.glBlendFunc(GL10.GL_SRC_ALPHA, GL10.GL_ONE_MINUS_SRC_ALPHA);

        batcher.beginBatch(Assets.items);
        batcher.drawSprite(240, 240, 384, 128, Assets.logoRegion);
        batcher.drawSprite(240, 100, 224, 64, Assets.menuRegion);
        batcher.endBatch();

        gl.glDisable(GL10.GL_BLEND);
        gl.glDisable(GL10.GL_TEXTURE_2D);
    }
```

The present() method does the same thing we did in most screens of Super Jumper. We clear the screen and set up the projection matrix via our camera. We enable texturing and then immediately render the background via the SpriteBatcher and TextureRegion defined in the Assets class. The menu items have translucent areas, so we enable blending before we render them.

```
    @Override
    public void pause() {
    }

    @Override
    public void resume() {
    }

    @Override
    public void dispose() {
    }
}
```

The rest of the class consists of boilerplate methods that don't do anything. Texture reloading is done in the DroidInvaders activity, so there isn't anything left to take care of in the MainMenuScreen.

The Settings Screen

The settings screen offers the player to change the input method as well as enable or disable audio. We indicate this by three different icons (see Figure 12–4). Touching either the hand or the tilted phone will enable the respective input method. The icon for the currently active input method will have a gold color. For the audio icon we do the same as in the previous games.

The choices of the user are reflected by setting the respective boolean values in the Settings class. We also make sure that these settings are instantly saved to the SD card each time on of them changes via a call to Settings.save(). Listing 12–5 shows you the code.

Listing 12–5. *SettingsScreen.java, the Settings Screen*

```
package com.badlogic.androidgames.droidinvaders;

import java.util.List;

import javax.microedition.khronos.opengles.GL10;

import com.badlogic.androidgames.framework.Game;
import com.badlogic.androidgames.framework.Input.TouchEvent;
import com.badlogic.androidgames.framework.gl.Camera2D;
import com.badlogic.androidgames.framework.gl.SpriteBatcher;
import com.badlogic.androidgames.framework.impl.GLScreen;
import com.badlogic.androidgames.framework.math.OverlapTester;
import com.badlogic.androidgames.framework.math.Rectangle;
import com.badlogic.androidgames.framework.math.Vector2;

public class SettingsScreen extends GLScreen {
    Camera2D guiCam;
    SpriteBatcher batcher;
    Vector2 touchPoint;
    Rectangle touchBounds;
    Rectangle accelBounds;
    Rectangle soundBounds;
    Rectangle backBounds;
```

As usual we have a camera and SpriteBatcher to render our UI elements and the background. For checking whether a touch event hit a button, we also store a vector and rectangles for the three buttons on screen.

```
    public SettingsScreen(Game game) {
        super(game);
        guiCam = new Camera2D(glGraphics, 480, 320);
        batcher = new SpriteBatcher(glGraphics, 10);
        touchPoint = new Vector2();
```

```
        touchBounds = new Rectangle(120 - 32, 160 - 32, 64, 64);
        accelBounds = new Rectangle(240 - 32, 160 - 32, 64, 64);
        soundBounds = new Rectangle(360 - 32, 160 - 32, 64, 64);
        backBounds = new Rectangle(32, 32, 64, 64);
    }
```

In the constructor we again just set up all the members of the screen. No rocket surgery involved here.

```
    @Override
    public void update(float deltaTime) {
        List<TouchEvent> events = game.getInput().getTouchEvents();
        int len = events.size();
        for (int i = 0; i < len; i++) {
            TouchEvent event = events.get(i);
            if (event.type != TouchEvent.TOUCH_UP)
                continue;

            guiCam.touchToWorld(touchPoint.set(event.x, event.y));
            if (OverlapTester.pointInRectangle(touchBounds, touchPoint)) {
                Assets.playSound(Assets.clickSound);
                Settings.touchEnabled = true;
                Settings.save(game.getFileIO());
            }
            if (OverlapTester.pointInRectangle(accelBounds, touchPoint)) {
                Assets.playSound(Assets.clickSound);
                Settings.touchEnabled = false;
                Settings.save(game.getFileIO());
            }
            if (OverlapTester.pointInRectangle(soundBounds, touchPoint)) {
                Assets.playSound(Assets.clickSound);
                Settings.soundEnabled = !Settings.soundEnabled;
                if (Settings.soundEnabled) {
                    Assets.music.play();
                } else {
                    Assets.music.pause();
                }
                Settings.save(game.getFileIO());
            }
            if (OverlapTester.pointInRectangle(backBounds, touchPoint)) {
                Assets.playSound(Assets.clickSound);
                game.setScreen(new MainMenuScreen(game));
            }
        }
    }
```

The update() method fetches the touch events and checks whether a "touch-up" event has been registered. If so, it transforms the touch coordinates to the camera's coordinate system. With these coordinates it tests the various rectangles to decide what action to take.

```
    @Override
    public void present(float deltaTime) {
        GL10 gl = glGraphics.getGL();
        gl.glClear(GL10.GL_COLOR_BUFFER_BIT);
        guiCam.setViewportAndMatrices();
```

```
        gl.glEnable(GL10.GL_TEXTURE_2D);

        batcher.beginBatch(Assets.background);
        batcher.drawSprite(240, 160, 480, 320, Assets.backgroundRegion);
        batcher.endBatch();

        gl.glEnable(GL10.GL_BLEND);
        gl.glBlendFunc(GL10.GL_SRC_ALPHA, GL10.GL_ONE_MINUS_SRC_ALPHA);

        batcher.beginBatch(Assets.items);
        batcher.drawSprite(240, 280, 224, 32, Assets.settingsRegion);
        batcher.drawSprite(120, 160, 64, 64,
                Settings.touchEnabled ? Assets.touchEnabledRegion : Assets.touchRegion);
        batcher.drawSprite(240, 160, 64, 64,
                Settings.touchEnabled ? Assets.accelRegion
                    : Assets.accelEnabledRegion);
        batcher.drawSprite(360, 160, 64, 64,
                Settings.soundEnabled ? Assets.soundEnabledRegion : Assets.soundRegion);
        batcher.drawSprite(32, 32, 64, 64, Assets.leftRegion);
        batcher.endBatch();

        gl.glDisable(GL10.GL_BLEND);
        gl.glDisable(GL10.GL_TEXTURE_2D);
    }
```

The render() method also does the same thing as the MainMenuScreen.render() method. We render the background and buttons with texturing and blending where needed. Based on the current settings we decide which TextureRegion to use to render the three settings buttons.

```
    @Override
    public void pause() {
    }

    @Override
    public void resume() {
    }

    @Override
    public void dispose() {
    }
}
```

The rest of the class is again composed of a few boilerplate methods with no functionality whatsoever.

Before we can create the GameScreen we have to first implement the logic and rendering of our world. Model-View-Controller to the rescue.

The Simulation Classes

As usual we'll create a single class for each object in our world. We have the following:

- A ship
- Invaders
- Shots
- Shield Blocks

The orchestration is performed by an all-knowing World class. As you saw in the last chapter, there's really not such a huge difference between 2D and 3D when it comes to object representation. Instead of GameObject and DynamicObject, we'll now use GameObject3D and DynamicObject3D. The only difference is that we use Vector3 instances instead of Vector2 instances to store positions, velocities, and accelerations, and that we use bounding spheres instead of bounding rectangles to represent the shapes of our objects. All that's left to do is implement the behavior of the different objects in our world.

The Shield Class

From our game mechanics definition we know the size and behavior of our shield blocks. They just sit there in our world at some location, waiting to be annihilated by a shot either from our ship or an invader. There's not a lot of logic in them, so the code is rather concise. Listing 12–6 shows you a shield block's internals.

Listing 12–6. *Shield.java, the Shield Block Class*

```
package com.badlogic.androidgames.droidinvaders;

import com.badlogic.androidgames.framework.GameObject3D;

public class Shield extends GameObject3D {
    static float SHIELD_RADIUS = 0.5f;

    public Shield(float x, float y, float z) {
        super(x, y, z, SHIELD_RADIUS);
    }
}
```

We defined the shield's radius and initialize its position and bounding sphere according to the constructor parameters. That's all there is to it!

The Shot Class

The shot class is equally simplistic. It derives from DynamicGameObject3D, as it is actually moving. Listing 12–7 shows you the code.

Listing 12–7. *Shot.java, the Shot Class*

```java
package com.badlogic.androidgames.droidinvaders;

import com.badlogic.androidgames.framework.DynamicGameObject3D;

public class Shot extends DynamicGameObject3D {
    static float SHOT_VELOCITY = 10f;
    static float SHOT_RADIUS = 0.1f;

    public Shot(float x, float y, float z, float velocityZ) {
        super(x, y, z, SHOT_RADIUS);
        velocity.z = velocityZ;
    }

    public void update(float deltaTime) {
        position.z += velocity.z * deltaTime;
        bounds.center.set(position);
    }
}
```

We again define some constants, namely the shot velocity and its radius. The constructor takes a shot's initial position as well as its velocity on the z-axis. Wait, didn't we just define the velocity as a constant? Yes, but that would let our shot travel in the direction of the positive z-axis only. That's OK for shots fired by the invaders, but the shots of our ship must travel in the opposite direction. When we create a shot (outside of this class) we know which direction the shot should travel in. So the shot has its velocity set by its creator.

The update() method just does the usual point-mass physics. We don't have any acceleration involved and thus only need to add the constant velocity multiplied by the delta time to the shot's position. The crucial part is that we also update the position of the bounding sphere's center in accordance with the shot's position. Otherwise the bounding sphere would not move along with our shot.

The Ship Class

The Ship class is responsible for updating the ship's position, keeping it within the bounds of the game field and keeping track of the state it is in. It can either be alive or exploding. In both cases we keep track of the amount of time the ship has been in that state. This state time can then be later used to do animations, for example, just as we did it in Super Jumper and its WorldRenderer class. The ship will get its current velocity from the outside based on the user input, either accelerometer readings as we did it for Bob, or based on a constant depending on what on-screen buttons are being pressed. Additionally, the ship will keep track of the number of lives it has and offer us a way to tell it that it has been killed. Listing 12–8 shows you the code.

Listing 12–8. *Ship.java, the Ship Class*

```java
package com.badlogic.androidgames.droidinvaders;

import com.badlogic.androidgames.framework.DynamicGameObject3D;
```

```
public class Ship extends DynamicGameObject3D {
    static float SHIP_VELOCITY = 20f;
    static int SHIP_ALIVE = 0;
    static int SHIP_EXPLODING = 1;
    static float SHIP_EXPLOSION_TIME = 1.6f;
    static float SHIP_RADIUS = 0.5f;
```

We start off with a couple of constants defining the maximum ship velocity, two states (alive and exploding), the amount of time it takes the ship to fully explode, and the ship's bounding sphere radius. We also let the class derive from DynamicGameObject3D since it has a position and bounding sphere as well as a velocity. The acceleration vector stores in a DynamicGameObject3D will again be unused.

```
    int lives;
    int state;
    float stateTime = 0;
```

Next we have the members, consisting of two integers to keep track of the number of lives the ship has and its states (either SHIP_ALIVE or SHIP_EXPLODING). The last member keeps track of how many seconds the ship has been in its current state.

```
    public Ship(float x, float y, float z) {
        super(x, y, z, SHIP_RADIUS);
        lives = 3;
        state = SHIP_ALIVE;
    }
```

The constructor performs the usual super class constructor call and initializes some of the members. Our ship will have a total of three lives.

```
    public void update(float deltaTime, float accelY) {
        if (state == SHIP_ALIVE) {
            velocity.set(accelY / 10 * SHIP_VELOCITY, 0, 0);
            position.add(velocity.x * deltaTime, 0, 0);
            if (position.x < World.WORLD_MIN_X)
                position.x = World.WORLD_MIN_X;
            if (position.x > World.WORLD_MAX_X)
                position.x = World.WORLD_MAX_X;
            bounds.center.set(position);
        } else {
            if (stateTime >= SHIP_EXPLOSION_TIME) {
                lives--;
                stateTime = 0;
                state = SHIP_ALIVE;
            }
        }
        stateTime += deltaTime;
    }
```

The update() method is pretty simple. It takes the delta time as well as the current accelerometer reading on the y-axis of the device (remember, we are in landscape mode, so the accelerometer y-axis is our screen's x-axis). If the ship is alive, we set its velocity based on the accelerometer value (which will be in the range −10 to 10) just as we did for Bob in Super Jumper. Additionally, we update its position based on the current velocity. Next we check whether the ship has left the boundaries of the playing field, using two constants we'll define in our World class later on. When the position is fixed up we can finally update the center of the bounding sphere of the ship.

In case the ship is exploding we check for how long that's been the case. After 1.6 seconds in the exploding state the ship is finished exploding, loses one life, and goes back to the alive state.

Finally we just update the stateTime member based on the given delta time.

```
    public void kill() {
        state = SHIP_EXPLODING;
        stateTime = 0;
        velocity.x = 0;
    }
}
```

The last kill() method will be called by the World class if it determines a collision between the ship and a shot or an invader. It will set the state to exploding, reset the state time and make sure that the ship's velocity is zero on all axes (we never set the y- and z-component of the velocity vector, since we only move on the x-axis).

The Invader Class

Invaders are just floating in space according to a predefined pattern. Figure 12–11 shows you this pattern.

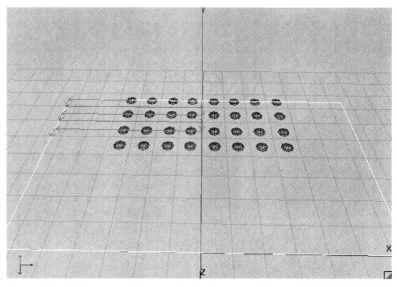

Figure 12–11. *Movement of the invaders. Left, down, right, down, left, down, right, down...*

An invader follows an extremely simplistic movement pattern. From its initial position it first moves to the right for some distance. Next it moves downward (which means in the direction of the positive z-axis on our playing field), again for a specified distance. Once done with that it will start moving to the right, basically backtracking to the same x-coordinate it was before it started moving left.

The left and right movement distances are always the same, except in the beginning. Figure 12–11 illustrates the movement of the top-left invader. Its first left movement is shorter than all subsequent movements to the left or right. The horizontal movement distance is half the playing field width, 14 units in our case. For the first horizontal movement the distance an invader has to travel is half of that, 7 units.

What we have to do is keep track of the direction an invader is moving in and how far he has moved in that direction already. If he reaches the movement distance for the given movement state (14 units for horizontal movement, 1 unit for vertical movement) it switches to the next movement state. All invaders will have their movement distance set to half the playing field's width initially. Look again at Figure 12–11 to make sure why that works! This will make the invaders sort of bounce off the edges of the playing field to the left and right.

Invaders also have a constant velocity. Well, actually the velocity will increase each time we generate a new wave of invaders in case all invaders of the current wave are dead. We can achieve this by simply multiplying this default velocity by some constant which is set from outside, namely the World class responsible for updating all invaders.

Finally, we also have to keep track of the state of the invader, which can again be either alive or exploding. We'll use the same mechanism as in case of the ship, with a state and a state time. Listing 12–9 shows you the code.

Listing 12–9. *Invader.java, the Invader Class*

```
package com.badlogic.androidgames.droidinvaders;

import com.badlogic.androidgames.framework.DynamicGameObject3D;

public class Invader extends DynamicGameObject3D {
    static final int INVADER_ALIVE = 0;
    static final int INVADER_DEAD = 1;
    static final float INVADER_EXPLOSION_TIME = 1.6f;
    static final float INVADER_RADIUS = 0.75f;
    static final float INVADER_VELOCITY = 1;
    static final int MOVE_LEFT = 0;
    static final int MOVE_DOWN = 1;
    static final int MOVE_RIGHT = 2;
```

We start with some constants, defining the state of an invader, the duration of its explosion, its radius and default velocity, as well as three constants that allow us to keep track of what direction the invader is currently moving in.

```
    int state = INVADER_ALIVE;
    float stateTime = 0;
    int move = MOVE_LEFT;
    boolean wasLastStateLeft = true;
    float movedDistance = World.WORLD_MAX_X / 2;
```

We keep track of an invader's state, state time, movement direction, and movement distance, which we set to half the playing field width initially. We also keep track of whether the last horizontal movement was to the left or not. This allows us to decide which direction the invader should go once it has finished its vertical movement on the z-axis.

```java
public Invader(float x, float y, float z) {
    super(x, y, z, INVADER_RADIUS);
}
```

The constructor just performs the usual setup of the invader's position and bounding ship via the super class constructor.

```java
public void update(float deltaTime, float speedMultiplier) {
    if (state == INVADER_ALIVE) {
        movedDistance += deltaTime * INVADER_VELOCITY * speedMultiplier;
        if (move == MOVE_LEFT) {
            position.x -= deltaTime * INVADER_VELOCITY * speedMultiplier;
            if (movedDistance > World.WORLD_MAX_X) {
                move = MOVE_DOWN;
                movedDistance = 0;
                wasLastStateLeft = true;
            }
        }
        if (move == MOVE_RIGHT) {
            position.x += deltaTime * INVADER_VELOCITY * speedMultiplier;
            if (movedDistance > World.WORLD_MAX_X) {
                move = MOVE_DOWN;
                movedDistance = 0;
                wasLastStateLeft = false;
            }
        }
        if (move == MOVE_DOWN) {
            position.z += deltaTime * INVADER_VELOCITY * speedMultiplier;
            if (movedDistance > 1) {
                if (wasLastStateLeft)
                    move = MOVE_RIGHT;
                else
                    move = MOVE_LEFT;
                movedDistance = 0;
            }
        }

        bounds.center.set(position);
    }

    stateTime += deltaTime;
}
```

The update() method takes the current delta time and speed multiplier used to make new waves of invaders move faster. We only perform the movement if the invader is alive, of course.

We start off by calculating how many units the invader will travel in this update and increase the movedDistance member accordingly. If it moves to the left we update the position directly by subtracting the movement velocity to the x-coordinate of the position multiplied by the delta time and speed multiplier. If it has moved far enough we tell it to start moving vertically, by setting the move member to MOVE_DOWN. We also set the wasLastStateLeft to true so that we know that after the down movement is finished we have to move to the right.

We do exactly the same for handling movement to the right. The only difference is that we subtract the movement velocity from the position's x-coordinate and set the wasLastStateLeft to false once the movement distance has been reached.

If we move downward we manipulate the z-coordinate of the invader's position and again check how far we've been moving in that direction. If we reached the movement distance for downward movement we switch the movement state to either MOVE_LEFT or MOVE_RIGHT depending on the last horizontal movement direction encoded in wasLastStateLeft member. Once we are done updating the invaders position we can set the position of the bounding sphere, as we did for the ship. Finally we update the current state time and consider the update to be done.

```java
    public void kill() {
        state = INVADER_DEAD;
        stateTime = 0;
    }
}
```

The kill() method serves the same purpose as the kill() method of the Ship class. It allows us to tell the invader that it should start dying now. All we do is set its state to INVADER_DEAD and reset its state time. The invader will then not move anymore but only update its state time based on the current delta time.

The World Class

The World class is the mastermind in all of this. It stores the ship, the invaders, and the shots and is responsible for updating them and checking collisions. It's exactly the same thing as in Super Jumper with some minor differences. The initial placement of the shield blocks as well as the invaders is also a responsibility of the World class. We also create a WorldListener interface to inform any outside parties of events within the world, such as an explosion or a shot that's been fired. This will allow us to play sound effects, just like in Super Jumper. Let's go through its code one method at a time. Listing 12–10 shows you the code.

Listing 12–10. *World.java, the World Class, Tying Everything Together*

```java
package com.badlogic.androidgames.droidinvaders;

import java.util.ArrayList;
import java.util.List;
import java.util.Random;

import com.badlogic.androidgames.framework.math.OverlapTester;

public class World {
```

```
public interface WorldListener {
    public void explosion();

    public void shot();
}
```

We want outside parties to know when an explosion took place or a shot was fired. For this we define a listener interface, which we can implement and register with a World instance that will be called when one of these events happen. Exactly like in Super Jumper, just with different events.

```
final static float WORLD_MIN_X = -14;
final static float WORLD_MAX_X = 14;
final static float WORLD_MIN_Z = -15;
```

We also have a couple of constants that define the extents of our world, as discussed in the "Defining the Game World" section.

```
WorldListener listener;
int waves = 1;
int score = 0;
float speedMultiplier = 1;
final List<Shot> shots = new ArrayList<Shot>();
final List<Invader> invaders = new ArrayList<Invader>();
final List<Shield> shields = new ArrayList<Shield>();
final Ship ship;
long lastShotTime;
Random random;
```

The world keeps track of a couple of things. We have a listener that we'll invoke when an explosion happens or a shot is fired. We also keep track of how many waves of invaders the player already has destroyed. The score member keeps track of the current score, and the speedMultiplier allows us to speed up the movement of the invaders (remember the Invaders.update() method). We also store lists of shots, invaders, and shield blocks currently alive in our world. Finally we have an instance of a Ship and also store the last time a shot was fired by the ship. We will store this time in nanoseconds as returned by System.nanoTime(), hence the long data type. The Random instance will come in handy when we want to decide whether an invader should fire a shot or not.

```
public World() {
    ship = new Ship(0, 0, 0);
    generateInvaders();
    generateShields();
    lastShotTime = System.nanoTime();
    random = new Random();
}
```

In the constructor we create the Ship at its initial position, generate the invaders and shields, and initialize the rest of the members.

```
private void generateInvaders() {
    for (int row = 0; row < 4; row++) {
        for (int column = 0; column < 8; column++) {
            Invader invader = new Invader(-WORLD_MAX_X / 2 + column * 2f,
                0, WORLD_MIN_Z + row * 2f);
```

```
            invaders.add(invader);
        }
    }
}
```

The generateInvaders() method just creates a grid of eight by four invaders, arranged as in Figure 12–11.

```
    private void generateShields() {
        for (int shield = 0; shield < 3; shield++) {
            shields.add(new Shield(-10 + shield * 10 - 1, 0, -3));
            shields.add(new Shield(-10 + shield * 10 + 0, 0, -3));
            shields.add(new Shield(-10 + shield * 10 + 1, 0, -3));
            shields.add(new Shield(-10 + shield * 10 - 1, 0, -2));
            shields.add(new Shield(-10 + shield * 10 + 1, 0, -2));
        }
    }
```

The generateShields() class does pretty much the same: instantiating three shields composed of five shield blocks each, laid out as in Figure 12–2.

```
    public void setWorldListener(WorldListener worldListener) {
        this.listener = worldListener;
    }
```

We also have a setter method to set the listener of the World.

```
    public void update(float deltaTime, float accelX) {
        ship.update(deltaTime, accelX);
        updateInvaders(deltaTime);
        updateShots(deltaTime);

        checkShotCollisions();
        checkInvaderCollisions();

        if (invaders.size() == 0) {
            generateInvaders();
            waves++;
            speedMultiplier += 0.5f;
        }
    }
```

The update() method is surprisingly simple. It takes the current delta time as well as the reading on the accelerometer's y-axis, which we'll pass to Ship.update(). Once the ship has updated we call updateInvaders() and updateShots(), which are responsible for updating those two types of objects. After all objects in the world have been updated we can start checking for a collision. The checkShotCollision() method [??] will check collisions between any shots and the ship and/or invaders.

Finally, we check whether all invaders are dead, in which case we regenerate a new wave of invaders. For the love of the garbage collector we could have reused the old Invader instances, for example via a Pool. However, to keep it simple we just create new instances. The same is true for shots as well, by the way. Given the small number of objects we create in one game session, the GC is unlikely to fire. If you want to make the

GC really happy, just use a Pool to reuse dead invaders and shots. Also note that we increase the speed multiplier here!

```
private void updateInvaders(float deltaTime) {
    int len = invaders.size();
    for (int i = 0; i < len; i++) {
        Invader invader = invaders.get(i);
        invader.update(deltaTime, speedMultiplier);

        if (invader.state == Invader.INVADER_ALIVE) {
            if (random.nextFloat() < 0.001f) {
                Shot shot = new Shot(invader.position.x,
                            invader.position.y,
                                            invader.position.z,
                            Shot.SHOT_VELOCITY);
                shots.add(shot);
                listener.shot();
            }
        }

        if (invader.state == Invader.INVADER_DEAD &&
                    invader.stateTime > Invader.INVADER_EXPLOSION_TIME) {
            invaders.remove(i);
            i--;
            len--;
        }
    }
}
```

The updateInvaders() method has a couple of responsibilities. It loops through all invaders and calls their update() method. Once an Invader instance is updated we check whether it is alive. In that case we give it a chance to fire a shot by generating a random number. If that number is below 0.001 a shot is fired. This means that each invader has a 0.1% change of firing a shot each frame. If that happens we instantiate a new shot, set its velocity so that it moves in the direction of the positive z-axis, and inform that listener of that event. If the Invader is dead and is done exploding, we simply remove it from our current list of invaders.

```
private void updateShots(float deltaTime) {
    int len = shots.size();
    for (int i = 0; i < len; i++) {
        Shot shot = shots.get(i);
        shot.update(deltaTime);
        if (shot.position.z < WORLD_MIN_Z ||
            shot.position.z > 0) {
            shots.remove(i);
            i--;
            len--;
        }
    }
}
```

The updateShots() method is simple as well. We loop through all shots, update them and check whether each one has left the playing field, in which case we remove it from our shots list.

```java
private void checkInvaderCollisions() {
    if (ship.state == Ship.SHIP_EXPLODING)
        return;

    int len = invaders.size();
    for (int i = 0; i < len; i++) {
        Invader invader = invaders.get(i);
        if (OverlapTester.overlapSpheres(ship.bounds, invader.bounds)) {
            ship.lives = 1;
            ship.kill();
            return;
        }
    }
}
```

In the checkInvaderCollisions() method we check whether any of the invaders has collided with the ship. That's a pretty simple affair since all we need to do is loop through all invaders and check for overlap between each one's bounding sphere and the ship's bounding sphere. According to our game mechanics definition, the game ends if the ship collides with an invader. That's why we set the ship's lives to 1 before we call the Ship.kill() method. After that call the ship's live member is set to 0, which we'll use in another method to check for the game-over state.

```java
private void checkShotCollisions() {
    int len = shots.size();
    for (int i = 0; i < len; i++) {
        Shot shot = shots.get(i);
        boolean shotRemoved = false;

        int len2 = shields.size();
        for (int j = 0; j < len2; j++) {
            Shield shield = shields.get(j);
            if (OverlapTester.overlapSpheres(shield.bounds, shot.bounds)) {
                shields.remove(j);
                shots.remove(i);
                i--;
                len--;
                shotRemoved = true;
                break;
            }
        }
        if (shotRemoved)
            continue;

        if (shot.velocity.z < 0) {
            len2 = invaders.size();
            for (int j = 0; j < len2; j++) {
                Invader invader = invaders.get(j);
                if (OverlapTester.overlapSpheres(invader.bounds,
                        shot.bounds)
                        && invader.state == Invader.INVADER_ALIVE) {
                    invader.kill();
                    listener.explosion();
                    score += 10;
                    shots.remove(i);
```

```
                            i--;
                            len--;
                            break;
                        }
                    }
                } else {
                    if (OverlapTester.overlapSpheres(shot.bounds, ship.bounds)
                            && ship.state == Ship.SHIP_ALIVE) {
                        ship.kill();
                        listener.explosion();
                        shots.remove(i);
                        i--;
                        len--;
                    }
                }
            }
        }
    }
```

The checkShotCollisions() method is a little bit more complex. It loops through each Shot instance and checks for overlap between it and a shield block, an invader or the ship. Shield blocks can be hit by shots either fired by the ship or an invader. An invader can only be hit by a shot fired by the ship. And the ship can only be hit by a shot fired by an invader. To distinguish whether a shot was fired by a ship or invader, all we need to do is look at its z-velocity. If it is positive it moves toward the ship and was therefore fired by an invader. If it is negative it was fired by the ship.

```
    public boolean isGameOver() {
        return ship.lives == 0;
    }
```

The isGameOver() method just tells an outside party if the ship has lost all its lives.

```
    public void shoot() {
        if (ship.state == Ship.SHIP_EXPLODING)
            return;

        int friendlyShots = 0;
        int len = shots.size();
        for (int i = 0; i < len; i++) {
            if (shots.get(i).velocity.z < 0)
                friendlyShots++;
        }

        if (System.nanoTime() - lastShotTime > 1000000000 || friendlyShots == 0) {
            shots.add(new Shot(ship.position.x, ship.position.y,
                    ship.position.z, -Shot.SHOT_VELOCITY));
            lastShotTime = System.nanoTime();
            listener.shot();
        }
    }
}
```

Finally there's the shoot() method. It will be called from outside each time the Fire button is pressed by the user. In the game mechanics section we said that a shot can be fired by the ship every second or if there's no ship shot on the field yet. The ship can't fire if it explodes of course so that's the first thing we check. Next we run through all the Shots and check if one of them is a ship shot. If that's not the case we can immediately shoot. Otherwise we check when the last shot was fired. If more than a second has passed since the last shot, we fire a new one. This time we set the velocity to − Shot.SHOT_VELOCITY so that the shot moves in the direction of the negative z-axis toward the invaders. As always we also invoke the listener to inform it of the event.

And that's all the classes making up our game world! Compare that to what we had in Super Jumper. The principles are nearly the same and the code looks quite similar. Droid Invaders is of course a very simple game so we can get away with simple solutions like using bounding spheres for everything. For many simple 3D games that's all we need, though. On to the last two bits of our game: the GameScreen and the WorldRenderer class!

The GameScreen Class

Once the game transitions to the GameScreen class the player can immediately start playing without having to state that she is ready. The only states we have to care for are tthese:

- The running state where we render the background, the world, and the UI elements as in Figure 12–4.

- The paused state where we render the background, the world, and the paused menu, again as in Figure 12–4.

- The game-over state, where we render pretty much the same thing.

We'll again follow the same method we used in Super Jumper and have different update() and present() methods for each of the three states.

The only interesting part of this class is how we handle the user input to move the ship. We want our player to be able to control the ship with either on-screen buttons or the accelerometer. We can read the Settings.touchEnabled field to figure out what the user wants in that regard. Depending on which input method is active, we either render the on-screen buttons or not and also have to pass the proper accelerometer values to the World.update() method for the ship to move.

With the on-screen buttons we of course don't use the accelerometer values but instead just pass a constant artificial acceleration value to the World.update() method. It has to be in the range −10 (left) to 10 (right). After a little experimentation I arrived at a value of − 5 for left movement and 5 for right movement via the on-screen buttons.

The last interesting bit of this class is the way we combine rendering the 3D game world and the 2D UI elements. Let's take a look at the code of the GameScreen class in Listing 12–11.

Listing 12–11. *GameScreen.java, the Game Screen*

```java
package com.badlogic.androidgames.droidinvaders;

import java.util.List;

import javax.microedition.khronos.opengles.GL10;

import com.badlogic.androidgames.droidinvaders.World.WorldListener;
import com.badlogic.androidgames.framework.Game;
import com.badlogic.androidgames.framework.Input.TouchEvent;
import com.badlogic.androidgames.framework.gl.Camera2D;
import com.badlogic.androidgames.framework.gl.FPSCounter;
import com.badlogic.androidgames.framework.gl.SpriteBatcher;
import com.badlogic.androidgames.framework.impl.GLScreen;
import com.badlogic.androidgames.framework.math.OverlapTester;
import com.badlogic.androidgames.framework.math.Rectangle;
import com.badlogic.androidgames.framework.math.Vector2;

public class GameScreen extends GLScreen {
    static final int GAME_RUNNING = 0;
    static final int GAME_PAUSED = 1;
    static final int GAME_OVER = 2;
```

As usual we have a couple of constants encoding the screen's current state.

```java
    int state;
    Camera2D guiCam;
    Vector2 touchPoint;
    SpriteBatcher batcher;
    World world;
    WorldListener worldListener;
    WorldRenderer renderer;
    Rectangle pauseBounds;
    Rectangle resumeBounds;
    Rectangle quitBounds;
    Rectangle leftBounds;
    Rectangle rightBounds;
    Rectangle shotBounds;
    int lastScore;
    int lastLives;
    int lastWaves;
    String scoreString;
    FPSCounter fpsCounter;
```

The members of the GameScreen are also business as usual. We have a member keeping track of the state, a camera, a vector for the touch point, a SpriteBatcher for rendering the 2D UI elements, the World instance along with the WorldListener, the WorldRenderer (which we are going to write in a minute), and a couple of Rectangles for checking whether a UI element was touched. In addition, three integers keep track of the last number of lives, waves, and score, so that we don't have to update the scoreString each time to reduce GC activity. Finally, there is an FPSCounter so we can later figure out how well our game performs.

```java
    public GameScreen(Game game) {
        super(game);
```

```
                state = GAME_RUNNING;
                guiCam = new Camera2D(glGraphics, 480, 320);
                touchPoint = new Vector2();
                batcher = new SpriteBatcher(glGraphics, 100);
                world = new World();
                worldListener = new WorldListener() {
                    @Override
                    public void shot() {
                        Assets.playSound(Assets.shotSound);
                    }

                    @Override
                    public void explosion() {
                        Assets.playSound(Assets.explosionSound);
                    }
                };
                world.setWorldListener(worldListener);
                renderer = new WorldRenderer(glGraphics);
                pauseBounds = new Rectangle(480 - 64, 320 - 64, 64, 64);
                resumeBounds = new Rectangle(240 - 80, 160, 160, 32);
                quitBounds = new Rectangle(240 - 80, 160 - 32, 160, 32);
                shotBounds = new Rectangle(480 - 64, 0, 64, 64);
                leftBounds = new Rectangle(0, 0, 64, 64);
                rightBounds = new Rectangle(64, 0, 64, 64);
                lastScore = 0;
                lastLives = world.ship.lives;
                lastWaves = world.waves;
                scoreString = "lives:" + lastLives + " waves:" + lastWaves + " score:"
                        + lastScore;
                fpsCounter = new FPSCounter();
        }
```

In the constructor we just set up all those members as we are accustomed to doing. The
WorldListener is responsible for playing the correct sound in case of an event in our
world. The rest is exactly the same as in Super Jumper, just slightly adapted to the
somewhat different UI elements of course.

```
        @Override
        public void update(float deltaTime) {
            switch (state) {
            case GAME_PAUSED:
                updatePaused();
                break;
            case GAME_RUNNING:
                updateRunning(deltaTime);
                break;
            case GAME_OVER:
                updateGameOver();
                break;
            }
        }
```

The update() method delegates the real updating to one of the other three update
methods, depending on the current state of the screen.

```java
    private void updatePaused() {
        List<TouchEvent> events = game.getInput().getTouchEvents();
        int len = events.size();
        for (int i = 0; i < len; i++) {
            TouchEvent event = events.get(i);
            if (event.type != TouchEvent.TOUCH_UP)
                continue;

            guiCam.touchToWorld(touchPoint.set(event.x, event.y));
            if (OverlapTester.pointInRectangle(resumeBounds, touchPoint)) {
                Assets.playSound(Assets.clickSound);
                state = GAME_RUNNING;
            }

            if (OverlapTester.pointInRectangle(quitBounds, touchPoint)) {
                Assets.playSound(Assets.clickSound);
                game.setScreen(new MainMenuScreen(game));
            }
        }
    }
```

The updatePaused() method loops through any available touch events and checks
whether one of the two menu entries was pressed (**Resume** or **Quit**). In each case we play
the click sound. Nothing new here.

```java
    private void updateRunning(float deltaTime) {
        List<TouchEvent> events = game.getInput().getTouchEvents();
        int len = events.size();
        for (int i = 0; i < len; i++) {
            TouchEvent event = events.get(i);
            if (event.type != TouchEvent.TOUCH_DOWN)
                continue;

            guiCam.touchToWorld(touchPoint.set(event.x, event.y));

            if (OverlapTester.pointInRectangle(pauseBounds, touchPoint)) {
                Assets.playSound(Assets.clickSound);
                state = GAME_PAUSED;
            }
            if (OverlapTester.pointInRectangle(shotBounds, touchPoint)) {
                world.shot();
            }
        }

        world.update(deltaTime, calculateInputAcceleration());
        if (world.ship.lives != lastLives || world.score != lastScore
                || world.waves != lastWaves) {
            lastLives = world.ship.lives;
            lastScore = world.score;
            lastWaves = world.waves;
            scoreString = "lives:" + lastLives + " waves:" + lastWaves
                    + " score:" + lastScore;
        }
        if (world.isGameOver()) {
            state = GAME_OVER;
        }
    }
```

The updateRunning() method is responsible for two things: to check whether the pause button was pressed and react accordingly, and to update the world based on the user input. The first piece of the puzzle is trivial, so let's look at the world updating mechanism. As you can see we delegate the acceleration value calculation to a method called calculateInputAcceleration(). Once the world is updated we check whether any of the three states (lives, waves, or score) have changed and update the scoreString accordingly. Finally we check whether the game is over, in which case we enter the GameOver state.

```java
private float calculateInputAcceleration() {
    float accelX = 0;
    if (Settings.touchEnabled) {
        for (int i = 0; i < 2; i++) {
            if (game.getInput().isTouchDown(i)) {
                guiCam.touchToWorld(touchPoint.set(game.getInput()
                        .getTouchX(i), game.getInput().getTouchY(i)));
                if (OverlapTester.pointInRectangle(leftBounds, touchPoint)) {
                    accelX = -Ship.SHIP_VELOCITY / 5;
                }
                if (OverlapTester.pointInRectangle(rightBounds, touchPoint)) {
                    accelX = Ship.SHIP_VELOCITY / 5;
                }
            }
        }
    } else {
        accelX = game.getInput().getAccelY();
    }
    return accelX;
}
```

The calculateInputAcceleration() is where we actually interpret the user input. If touch is enabled we check whether the left or right on-screen movement buttons were pressed and set the acceleration value accordingly to either –5 (left) or 5. If the accelerometer is used we simply return its current value on the y-axis (remember, we are in landscape mode).

```java
private void updateGameOver() {
    List<TouchEvent> events = game.getInput().getTouchEvents();
    int len = events.size();
    for (int i = 0; i < len; i++) {
        TouchEvent event = events.get(i);
        if (event.type == TouchEvent.TOUCH_UP) {
            Assets.playSound(Assets.clickSound);
            game.setScreen(new MainMenuScreen(game));
        }
    }
}
```

The updateGameOver() method is again trivial and just checks for a touch event, in which case we transition to the MainMenuScreen.

```java
@Override
public void present(float deltaTime) {
    GL10 gl = glGraphics.getGL();
    gl.glClear(GL10.GL_COLOR_BUFFER_BIT | GL10.GL_DEPTH_BUFFER_BIT);
```

```
        guiCam.setViewportAndMatrices();

        gl.glEnable(GL10.GL_TEXTURE_2D);
        batcher.beginBatch(Assets.background);
        batcher.drawSprite(240, 160, 480, 320, Assets.backgroundRegion);
        batcher.endBatch();
        gl.glDisable(GL10.GL_TEXTURE_2D);

        renderer.render(world, deltaTime);

        switch (state) {
        case GAME_RUNNING:
            presentRunning();
            break;
        case GAME_PAUSED:
            presentPaused();
            break;
        case GAME_OVER:
            presentGameOver();
        }

        fpsCounter.logFrame();
    }
```

The present() method is actually pretty simple as well. As always we start off by clearing the framebuffer. We also clear the z-buffer since we are going to render some 3D objects for which we need z-testing. Next we set up the projection matrix so that we can render our 2D background image, just as we did in the MainMenuScreen or SettingsScreen. Once that is done, we tell the WorldRenderer to render our game world. Finally we delegate the rendering of the UI elements depending on the current state. Note that the WorldRenderer.render() method is responsible for setting up all things needed to render the 3D world!

```
    private void presentPaused() {
        GL10 gl = glGraphics.getGL();
        guiCam.setViewportAndMatrices();
        gl.glEnable(GL10.GL_BLEND);
        gl.glBlendFunc(GL10.GL_SRC_ALPHA, GL10.GL_ONE_MINUS_SRC_ALPHA);
        gl.glEnable(GL10.GL_TEXTURE_2D);

        batcher.beginBatch(Assets.items);
        Assets.font.drawText(batcher, scoreString, 10, 320-20);
        batcher.drawSprite(240, 160, 160, 64, Assets.pauseRegion);
        batcher.endBatch();

        gl.glDisable(GL10.GL_TEXTURE_2D);
        gl.glDisable(GL10.GL_BLEND);
    }
```

The presentPaused() method just renders the scoreString via the Font instance we store in the Assets as well as the Pause menu. Note that at this point we have already rendered the background image as well as the 3D world. All the UI elements will thus overlay the 3D world.

```
    private void presentRunning() {
        GL10 gl = glGraphics.getGL();
```

```
        guiCam.setViewportAndMatrices();
        gl.glEnable(GL10.GL_BLEND);
        gl.glBlendFunc(GL10.GL_SRC_ALPHA, GL10.GL_ONE_MINUS_SRC_ALPHA);
        gl.glEnable(GL10.GL_TEXTURE_2D);

        batcher.beginBatch(Assets.items);
        batcher.drawSprite(480- 32, 320 - 32, 64, 64, Assets.pauseButtonRegion);
        Assets.font.drawText(batcher, scoreString, 10, 320-20);
        if(Settings.touchEnabled) {
            batcher.drawSprite(32, 32, 64, 64, Assets.leftRegion);
            batcher.drawSprite(96, 32, 64, 64, Assets.rightRegion);
        }
        batcher.drawSprite(480 - 40, 32, 64, 64, Assets.fireRegion);
        batcher.endBatch();

        gl.glDisable(GL10.GL_TEXTURE_2D);
        gl.glDisable(GL10.GL_BLEND);
    }
```

The presentRunning() method is also pretty straightforward. We render the scoreString first. If touch input is enabled we then render the left and right movement buttons. Finally we render the Fire button and reset any OpenGL ES states we've changed (texturing and blending).

```
    private void presentGameOver() {
        GL10 gl = glGraphics.getGL();
        guiCam.setViewportAndMatrices();
        gl.glEnable(GL10.GL_BLEND);
        gl.glBlendFunc(GL10.GL_SRC_ALPHA, GL10.GL_ONE_MINUS_SRC_ALPHA);
        gl.glEnable(GL10.GL_TEXTURE_2D);

        batcher.beginBatch(Assets.items);
        batcher.drawSprite(240, 160, 128, 64, Assets.gameOverRegion);
        Assets.font.drawText(batcher, scoreString, 10, 320-20);
        batcher.endBatch();

        gl.glDisable(GL10.GL_TEXTURE_2D);
        gl.glDisable(GL10.GL_BLEND);
    }
```

The presentGameOver() method is more of the same. Just some string and UI rendering.

```
    @Override
    public void pause() {
        state = GAME_PAUSED;
    }
```

Finally we have the pause() method, which simply puts the GameScreen into the paused state.

```
    @Override
    public void resume() {

    }

    @Override
    public void dispose() {
```

```
        }
}
```

The rest is again just some empty stubs so that we fulfill the GLGame interface definition. On to our final class: the WorldRenderer!

The WorldRender Class

Let's recall what we have to render in 3D:

- Our ship, using the ship model and texture and applying lighting.

- The invaders, using the invader model and texture, again with lighting.

- Any shots on the playfield, based on the shot model, this time without texturing but with lighting.

- The shield blocks, based on the shield block model, again without texturing but with lighting and transparency (see Figure 12–3).

- Explosions instead of the ship or invader model in case the ship or an invader is exploding. The explosion is not lit, of course.

We know how to code the first four items on this list. But what about the explosions?

It turns out that we can abuse the SpriteBatcher. Based on the state time of the exploding ship or invader, we can fetch a TextureRegion from the Animation instance holding the explosion animation (see Assets class). The SpriteBatcher can only render textured rectangles in the x/y plane, so we have to find a way to move such a rectangle to an arbitrary position in space (where the exploding ship or invader is). We can easily achieve this by using glTranslatef() on the model-view matrix before rendering the rectangle via the SpriteBatcher!

The rendering setup for the other objects is pretty straightforward. We have a directional light coming from the top right and an ambient light to light all objects a little bit no matter their orientation. The camera is located a little bit above and behind the ship and will look at a point a little bit ahead of the ship. We'll use our LookAtCamera for this. To let the camera follow the ship we just need to keep the x-coordinate of its position and look-at point in sync with the ship's x-coordinate.

For some extra eye-candy we'll rotate the invaders around the y-axis. We'll also rotate the ship around the z-axis based on its current velocity so that it appears to be leaning to the side it moves toward.

Let's put this into code! Listing 12–12 shows you the final class of Droid Invaders.

Listing 12–12. *WorldRenderer.java, the World Renderer*

```java
package com.badlogic.androidgames.droidinvaders;

import java.util.List;

import javax.microedition.khronos.opengles.GL10;
```

```java
import com.badlogic.androidgames.framework.gl.AmbientLight;
import com.badlogic.androidgames.framework.gl.Animation;
import com.badlogic.androidgames.framework.gl.DirectionalLight;
import com.badlogic.androidgames.framework.gl.LookAtCamera;
import com.badlogic.androidgames.framework.gl.SpriteBatcher;
import com.badlogic.androidgames.framework.gl.TextureRegion;
import com.badlogic.androidgames.framework.impl.GLGraphics;
import com.badlogic.androidgames.framework.math.Vector3;

public class WorldRenderer {
    GLGraphics glGraphics;
    LookAtCamera camera;
    AmbientLight ambientLight;
    DirectionalLight directionalLight;
    SpriteBatcher batcher;
    float invaderAngle = 0;
```

The WorldRenderer keeps track of a GLGraphics instance from which we'll fetch the GL10 instance. We also have a LookAtCamera, an AmbientLight, and a DirectionLight and a SpriteBatcher. Finally, we have a member to keep track of the current rotation angle we'll use for all invaders.

```java
    public WorldRenderer(GLGraphics glGraphics) {
        this.glGraphics = glGraphics;
        camera = new LookAtCamera(67, glGraphics.getWidth()
                / (float) glGraphics.getHeight(), 0.1f, 100);
        camera.getPosition().set(0, 6, 2);
        camera.getLookAt().set(0, 0, -4);
        ambientLight = new AmbientLight();
        ambientLight.setColor(0.2f, 0.2f, 0.2f, 1.0f);
        directionalLight = new DirectionalLight();
        directionalLight.setDirection(-1, -0.5f, 0);
        batcher = new SpriteBatcher(glGraphics, 10);
    }
```

In the constructor we set up all members as usual. The camera has a field of view of 67 degrees, a near clipping plane distance of 0.1 units, and a far clipping plane distance of 100 units. The view frustum will thus easily contain all of our game world. We position it above and behind the ship and let it look at (0,0,−4). The ambient light is just a faint gray, and the directional light is white and comes from the top-right side. Finally, we instantiate the SpriteBatcher so that we can render the explosion rectangles.

```java
    public void render(World world, float deltaTime) {
        GL10 gl = glGraphics.getGL();
        camera.getPosition().x = world.ship.position.x;
        camera.getLookAt().x = world.ship.position.x;
        camera.setMatrices(gl);

        gl.glEnable(GL10.GL_DEPTH_TEST);
        gl.glEnable(GL10.GL_TEXTURE_2D);
        gl.glEnable(GL10.GL_LIGHTING);
        gl.glEnable(GL10.GL_COLOR_MATERIAL);
        ambientLight.enable(gl);
        directionalLight.enable(gl, GL10.GL_LIGHT0);
```

```
            renderShip(gl, world.ship);
            renderInvaders(gl, world.invaders, deltaTime);

            gl.glDisable(GL10.GL_TEXTURE_2D);

            renderShields(gl, world.shields);
            renderShots(gl, world.shots);

            gl.glDisable(GL10.GL_COLOR_MATERIAL);
            gl.glDisable(GL10.GL_LIGHTING);
            gl.glDisable(GL10.GL_DEPTH_TEST);
    }
```

In the render() method we start off by setting the camera's x-coordinate to the ship's x-coordinate. We of course also set the x-coordinate of the camera's look-at point accordingly. This way, the camera will follow the ship. Once the position and look-at point are updated we can set the projection and model-view matrix via a call to LookAtCamera.setMatrices().

Next we set up all the states we need for rendering. We'll need depth-testing, texturing, lighting, and the color material functionality so that we don't have to specify a material for the objects via glMaterial(). The next two statements activate the ambient and directional light. With these calls we have everything set up so that we can start rendering our objects.

The first thing we render is the ship, via a call to renderShip(). Next we render the invaders with a call to renderInvaders().

Since the shield blocks and shots don't need texturing we simply disable that to save some computations. Once texturing is turned off, we render the shots and shields via calls to renderShots() and renderShields().

Finally we disable the other states we set so that we return a clean OpenGL ES state to whoever called us.

```
    private void renderShip(GL10 gl, Ship ship) {
        if (ship.state == Ship.SHIP_EXPLODING) {
            gl.glDisable(GL10.GL_LIGHTING);
            renderExplosion(gl, ship.position, ship.stateTime);
            gl.glEnable(GL10.GL_LIGHTING);
        } else {
            Assets.shipTexture.bind();
            Assets.shipModel.bind();
            gl.glPushMatrix();
            gl.glTranslatef(ship.position.x, ship.position.y, ship.position.z);
            gl.glRotatef(ship.velocity.x / Ship.SHIP_VELOCITY * 90, 0, 0, -1);
            Assets.shipModel.draw(GL10.GL_TRIANGLES, 0,
                    Assets.shipModel.getNumVertices());
            gl.glPopMatrix();
            Assets.shipModel.unbind();
        }
    }
```

The renderShip() method starts off by checking the state of the ship. If it is exploding we disable lighting, call renderExplosion() to render an explosion at the position of the ship, and enable lighting again.

If the ship is alive we bind its texture and model, push the model-view matrix, move it to its position and rotate it around the z-axis based on its velocity, and draw its model. Finally, we pop the model-view matrix again (leaving only the camera's view) and unbind the ship model's vertices.

```
private void renderInvaders(GL10 gl, List<Invader> invaders, float deltaTime) {
    invaderAngle += 45 * deltaTime;

    Assets.invaderTexture.bind();
    Assets.invaderModel.bind();
    int len = invaders.size();
    for (int i = 0; i < len; i++) {
        Invader invader = invaders.get(i);
        if (invader.state == Invader.INVADER_DEAD) {
            gl.glDisable(GL10.GL_LIGHTING);
            Assets.invaderModel.unbind();
            renderExplosion(gl, invader.position, invader.stateTime);
            Assets.invaderTexture.bind();
            Assets.invaderModel.bind();
            gl.glEnable(GL10.GL_LIGHTING);
        } else {
            gl.glPushMatrix();
            gl.glTranslatef(invader.position.x, invader.position.y,
                    invader.position.z);
            gl.glRotatef(invaderAngle, 0, 1, 0);
            Assets.invaderModel.draw(GL10.GL_TRIANGLES, 0,
                    Assets.invaderModel.getNumVertices());
            gl.glPopMatrix();
        }
    }
    Assets.invaderModel.unbind();
}
```

The renderInvaders() method is pretty much the same as the renderShip() method. The only difference is that we loop through the list of invaders and bind the texture and mesh before we do so. This reduces the number of binds considerably and speeds up the rendering a little. For each invader we then check its state again and render either an explosion or the normal invader model. Since we bind the model and texture outside the for loop, we have to unbind and rebind them before we can render an explosion instead of an invader.

```
private void renderShields(GL10 gl, List<Shield> shields) {
    gl.glEnable(GL10.GL_BLEND);
    gl.glBlendFunc(GL10.GL_SRC_ALPHA, GL10.GL_ONE_MINUS_SRC_ALPHA);
    gl.glColor4f(0, 0, 1, 0.4f);
    Assets.shieldModel.bind();
    int len = shields.size();
    for (int i = 0; i < len; i++) {
        Shield shield = shields.get(i);
        gl.glPushMatrix();
        gl.glTranslatef(shield.position.x, shield.position.y,
```

```
                    shield.position.z);
            Assets.shieldModel.draw(GL10.GL_TRIANGLES, 0,
                    Assets.shieldModel.getNumVertices());
            gl.glPopMatrix();
        }
        Assets.shieldModel.unbind();
        gl.glColor4f(1, 1, 1, 1f);
        gl.glDisable(GL10.GL_BLEND);
    }
```

The renderShields() method renders, you guessed it, the shield blocks. We apply the same principle as in the case of rendering the invaders. We only bind the model once. Since we have no texture we don't need to bind one. However, we need to enable blending. Another thing we do is set the global vertex color to blue, with the alpha component set to 0.4. This will make the shield blocks a little transparent.

```
    private void renderShots(GL10 gl, List<Shot> shots) {
        gl.glColor4f(1, 1, 0, 1);
        Assets.shotModel.bind();
        int len = shots.size();
        for (int i = 0; i < len; i++) {
            Shot shot = shots.get(i);
            gl.glPushMatrix();
            gl.glTranslatef(shot.position.x, shot.position.y, shot.position.z);
            Assets.shotModel.draw(GL10.GL_TRIANGLES, 0,
                    Assets.shotModel.getNumVertices());
            gl.glPopMatrix();
        }
        Assets.shotModel.unbind();
        gl.glColor4f(1, 1, 1, 1);
    }
```

Rendering the shots in renderShots() is the same as rendering the shields, except that we don't use blending and use a different vertex color (yellow).

```
    private void renderExplosion(GL10 gl, Vector3 position, float stateTime) {
        TextureRegion frame = Assets.explosionAnim.getKeyFrame(stateTime,
                Animation.ANIMATION_NONLOOPING);

        gl.glEnable(GL10.GL_BLEND);
        gl.glPushMatrix();
        gl.glTranslatef(position.x, position.y, position.z);
        batcher.beginBatch(Assets.explosionTexture);
        batcher.drawSprite(0, 0, 2, 2, frame);
        batcher.endBatch();
        gl.glPopMatrix();
        gl.glDisable(GL10.GL_BLEND);
    }
}
```

Finally we have the mysterious renderExplosion() method. We get the position at which we want to render the explosion as well as the state time of the object that is exploding. The latter is used to fetch the correct TextureRegion from the explosion Animation, just as we did for Bob in Super Jumper.

The first thing we do is fetch the explosion animation frame based on the state time. Next we enable blending, since the explosion has transparent pixels we don't want to render. We push the current model-view matrix and call glTranslatef() so that anything we render after that call will be positioned at the given location. Then we tell the SpriteBatcher that we are about to render a rectangle using the explosion texture.

The next call is where the magic happens. We tell the SpriteBatcher to render a rectangle at (0,0,0) (the z-coordinate is not given but implicitly zero, remember?), with a width and height of 2 units. Because we used glTranslatef(), that rectangle will not be centered around the origin but instead be centered around the position we specified to glTranslatef(), which is exactly the position of the ship or invader that exploded. Finally we pop the model-view matrix and disable blending again.

That's it. Twelve classes forming a full 3D game parroting the classic Space Invaders. Try it out. When you come back we'll have a look at the performance characteristics.

Optimizations

Before we think about optimizing the game we have to evaluate how well it performs. We put an FPSCounter in the GameScreen class, so let's look at its output on a Hero, a Droid, and a Nexus One.

```
Hero (Android 1.5):
02-17 00:59:04.180: DEBUG/FPSCounter(457): fps: 25
02-17 00:59:05.220: DEBUG/FPSCounter(457): fps: 26
02-17 00:59:06.260: DEBUG/FPSCounter(457): fps: 26
02-17 00:59:07.280: DEBUG/FPSCounter(457): fps: 26

Nexus One (Android 2.2.1):
02-17 01:05:40.679: DEBUG/FPSCounter(577): fps: 41
02-17 01:05:41.699: DEBUG/FPSCounter(577): fps: 41
02-17 01:05:42.729: DEBUG/FPSCounter(577): fps: 41
02-17 01:05:43.729: DEBUG/FPSCounter(577): fps: 40

Droid (Android 2.1.1):
02-17 01:47:44.096: DEBUG/FPSCounter(1758): fps: 47
02-17 01:47:45.112: DEBUG/FPSCounter(1758): fps: 47
02-17 01:47:46.127: DEBUG/FPSCounter(1758): fps: 47
02-17 01:47:47.135: DEBUG/FPSCounter(1758): fps: 46
```

The Hero struggles quite a bit, but the game is playable at 25fps. The Nexus One achieves around 47 frames per second, and the Droid also reaches 47, which is pretty playable. Can we do better?

In terms of state changes we are not all that bad. We could reduce some redundant changes here and there, for example some glEnable()/glDisable() calls. But from previous optimization attempts we know that that won't shave off a lot of overhead.

On the Hero there's one thing we could do: disable lighting. Once we remove the respective glEnable()/glDisable() calls in WorldRenderer.render() as well as WorldRenderer.renderShip() and WorldRenderer.renderInvaders(), the Hero achieves the following frame rate:

```
Hero (Android 1.5):
02-17 01:14:44.580: DEBUG/FPSCounter(618): fps: 31
02-17 01:14:45.600: DEBUG/FPSCounter(618): fps: 31
02-17 01:14:46.610: DEBUG/FPSCounter(618): fps: 31
02-17 01:14:47.630: DEBUG/FPSCounter(618): fps: 31
```

That's quite a bit of improvement and all we had to do is turn off lighting. Special-casing the rendering code for a certain device is possible but we'd like to avoid that. Is there anything else we can do?

The way we render explosions is a little bit suboptimal in the case of an exploding invader. We change the model and texture bindings in the middle of rendering all invaders, which will make the graphics pipeline a little unhappy. However, explosions don't happen often and don't take a long time (1.6 seconds). The measurements just shown were taking without any explosions on screen, so that's not the culprit.

The truth is that we render too many objects per frame, causing significant call-overhead and stalling the pipeline a little. With our current knowledge of OpenGL ES there's nothing we can really do about that. However, given that the game "feels" rather playable on all devices, it is not an absolute must to try to achieve 60 frames per second. The Droid and Nexus One notoriously have a hard time rendering even mildly complex 3D scenes at 60 frames per second. So the last lesson to take away from this is: do not get crazy if your game does not run at 60 frames per second. If it is smooth visually and plays well, you can do even with 30 frames per second.

> **NOTE** Common other optimization strategies involve using culling, vertex buffer objects, and other more advanced topics we won't look into. I tried adding these as well to our Droid Invaders. The effect: zero. None of the devices could benefit from those optimizations. That does not mean these techniques are useless. That depends on a lot of factors and their side-effects, and it's hard to predict how certain configurations will behave. If you are interested, just search for those terms on the web and try the techniques out yourself!

Summary

In this chapter we completed our third game, a full-blown 3D Space Invaders clone. We employed all the nice little techniques and tricks we learned along our way through this book, and the final outcome was rather satisfying. Of course, those are not AAA games. In fact, none of them is enjoyable for a long time. That's where you come in. Get creative, extend those games, and make them fun! You have the tools at your disposal.

Chapter 13

Publishing Your Game

The last step in becoming an Android game developer is getting your game to your players. There are two possible routes:

- Take the APK file from your project's bin/ folder, put it up on the web, and tell your friends to download and install it on their devices.
- Publish your application on the Android Market, like a real pro.

The first option is a great way to let other people test your application before you throw it on the market. All they need to do is get a hold of the APK file and install it on their devices. The real fun starts once your game is ready for prime time.

A Word on Testing

As we've seen in the previous chapters there are differences between devices in various areas. Before you publish your application, make sure it runs well on a couple of common devices and Android versions. Sadly, there's no easy way to do that at this point. I was lucky enough to get a couple of phones, covering different device classes and generations. Depending on your budget, though, that might not be an option. You might have to rely on the emulator (but not too much, as it is indeed unreliable) or preferably on a couple of friends to help you out there.

Another way to test your application is to put a beta versionon the Android Market. You can clearly mark your application as beta in its title so that users know what to expect. Some users will gladly ignore all warnings and still complain about the quality of your potentially unfinished application. That's just how life is, and you have to learn to deal with negative and maybe unjustified comments. Remember, though, your users are king. Don't get angry at them but try to figure out how to improve your application instead.

Here's my current setup for testing applications, which has served me well:

- Samsung Galaxy Leo/I5801, 320×240 pixel screen
- HTC Hero with Android 1.5, 480×320 pixel screen
- Motorola Milestone/Droid with Android 2.1, 854×480 pixel screen

- HTC Desire HD with Android 2.2, 800×480 pixel screen

- Nexus One with Android 2.3, 800×480 pixel screen

As you can see, I cover quite a range of screen sizes/resolutions and device generations. If you look for outside testers, make sure you get coverage of most of the device generations outlined here. Newer devices like the Samsung Galaxy S or Motorola Atrix should, of course, also be on your list, but less for performance testing than for compatibility testing.

Another domain of devices that is just starting to gain traction is Android tablets. At the time of writing this book the Samsung Galaxy Tab was pretty much the only tablet on the market, and the Android Xoom was just announced. With tablets you have to prepare for a larger screen size and resolution, of course. The techniques we discussed should scale very well. If you want to get fancy, you can even try to use the methods that take screen density and physical size into account, as we discussed in Chapter 5.

Finally, you have to live with the fact that you can't test your application on all devices out there. You are likely to receive error reports that are inexplicable and might well stem from the fact that a user has a custom ROM running that doesn't behave as expected. In any case, don't panic; this is to be expected to some extent. If it goes overboard, though, you'll have to try to come up with a scheme to battle it. Luckily the Android Market helps us out in that regard. We'll see how that works in a bit.

> **NOTE** Apart from the Android Market's error reporting there's another nice solution, called Acra, which is an open source library specifically designed to report crashes of your Android application. It's available at `http://code.google.com/p/acra/` and very easy to use. Just follow the guide on the Google Code page to integrate it in your application.

Becoming a Registered Developer

Android makes it really easy to publish your application on the official Android Market. All you have to do is register as a developer for a one-time fee of $US25. Depending on the country you live in, this developer account will allow you to put up free and/or paid applications (see Chapter 1 for a list of countries you can sell applications from). Google is working hard to expand the number of countries you can sell applications to and from.

To register an account, visit `https://market.android.com/publish/signup` and follow the instructions given there.

In addition to your Android developer account, you will also need to register for a Google Checkout merchant account if you want to sell applications. This option is offered to you during the sign-up process. I'm not a lawyer, so I cannot give you any legal advice at this point. Make sure you understand the legal implications of selling an application before you do so. If in doubt, consider consulting an expert on the matter. I don't mean to scare you off by this, as the process is pretty streamlined in general.

However, the tax department of your government might want to know about what you are doing.

Google will take 30% from your hard earned money for distributing your app and providing the infrastructure. That seems to be pretty much standard for all the application stores on the various platforms.

Sign Your Game's APK

After you have successfully registered as an official Android developer it's time to prepare your application for publishing. In order to publish your application you have to sign the APK file. Before we do that we should make sure everything is in place. Here's a laundry list of things to do before signing the application:

- Remove the `android:debuggable` attribute from the `<application>` tag in your manifest file.

- In the `<manifest>` tag you'll find the `android:versionCode` and `android:versionName` attributes. If you have already published a previous version of your application, you have to increase the `versionCode` attribute and should also change the `versionName`. The `versionCode` attribute has to be an integer; the `versionName` can be anything you like.

- If your build target is equal to or higher than SDK level 8 (Android 2.2), you should also make sure the `<manifest>` tag has the `android:installLocation` attribute set to `preferExternal` or `auto`. This will ensure that your application is stored on the external storage if possible and make your users happy.

- Make sure you only specify the permissions your game really needs. Users don't like to install applications that seem to need unnecessary permissions. Check the `<uses-permission>` tags in your manifest file.

- Double-check that you set the `android:minSdkVersion` and `android:targetSdkVersion` correctly. Your application will only be visible on the Android Market to phones that run a version of Android equal to or higher than the specified SDK version.

Double-check all of those items. Once you are done you can finally export a signed APK file ready to be uploaded to the market:

1. For this you have to right-click your project in the package explorer view and select **Android Tools ➤ Export Signed Application Package**. You'll be greeted with the dialog shown in Figure 13–1.

Figure 13–1. *The signed export dialog*

 2. Click the Next button to bring up the dialog in Figure 13–2.

Figure 13–2. *Choosing or creating the keystore*

3. A *keystore* is a file that is password-protected and stores keys you sign your APK files with. Since we haven't created one yet, we do so now in this dialog. Just provide the location of the keystore along with a password that you will use to secure it. If you have already created a keystore (for example, if you're publishing a second version of your application) you can check the "Use existing keystore" radio button and just provide the dialog with the location of the key store file. Click the Next button to bring up the dialog shown in Figure 13–3.

Figure 13–3. *Creating the key for signing the APK*

4. For a valid key you have to fill out the alias, password, and validity in years as well as a name in the First and Last Name text box. The rest is optional but I tend to fill that out as well. Another click on Next and we are shown the final dialog (Figure 13–4).

Figure 13–4. *Specifying the destination file*

5.   And we are basically done. Just specify where the exported APK file should be stored and remember that path. We'll need it later when we want to upload that APK to the market.

When you want to publish a new version of a previously published application, you can just reuse the keystore/key you created the first time you went through that dialog. In the dialog in Figure 13–2, just select the keystore file you created previously and provide the password for the keystore. You'll then be shown the dialog in Figure 13–5.

Figure 13–5. *Reusing a key*

Just select the key you created previously, provide the password for it, and proceed as before. In both cases you get a signed APK file that is ready for upload to the Android Market.

NOTE Once you upload a signed APK you have to use the same key for signing any subsequent versions of the same application.

Putting Your Game on the Market

It's time to log in to our developer account on the Android Market website. Just go to http://market.android.com/publish and sign in. You'll be greeted with the interface shown in Figure 13–6.

Figure 13–6. *Welcome to the Android Market, developer!*

That's what Android calls the *developer console*, which we'll talk about in a minute. For now let us concentrate on publishing our app. The Upload Application button will let us do that Let us go through all the sections of the uploading page.

Uploading Assets

The first thing you have to specify is the APK file you just signed and exported. Just choose the file and click the Upload button. You can proceed with uploading the rest of the assets in the meantime, as the APK will be uploaded in the background. Once uploaded, the APK is checked by the system and will report any errors to you on the same page.

You must also provide at least two screenshots of your application. They must be of a certain format (JPEG or PNG) and size (320x×480, 480×800, or 480×854). These will be shown when a user views the details of your application on the Android Market (on the device and on the official website at http://market.android.com).

Next you have to upload a 512×512, high-resolution PNG or JPEG of your application's icon. At the moment this is only used on the Android Market website when a user views your application there. Make it fancy.

The promo graphic (180×120, PNG or JPEG) and feature graphic (1024×500) are shown on the Android Market if your game is featured. Being featured is a huge deal, as it means that your application will be the first thing users see when the open up the Android Market on the device or website. Who gets featured is up to Google, and only they know on what they base this decision.

Finally, you can provide a link to a promotional YouTube video of your application. This will be shown on the Android Market website.

Listing Details

In the Listing Details section you can specify the title (30 characters maximum) and the description of your app (4000 characters maximum) optionally [?]in multiple languages that will be shown to the users on the Android Market.

An additional 500 characters are available to notify users of recent changes in the latest version of your application. The promo text will be used if your application gets featured.

Next you have to specify your application's type and category. For each application type there's a range of categories you can choose from. For games you can specify Arcade & Action, Brain & Puzzle, Cards & Casino, Casual, and Racing and Sports Games. The categories are a bit of a bummer (racing is not a sport?) and don't seem to be well thought out. Here's hoping for some changes in the future.

Finally, you have to decide whether users have to pay for your game or not. This decision is final. Once you select one of the two options you can't change it unless you publish your game anew, with a different key. You'll lose any user reviews and you'll also alienate your users a little. Think about the route you want to go with your game. I won't give you tips on pricing your game, as that depends on a lot of factors. A price of US$0.99 seems to be the standard for most games, and users somewhat expect it. However, there's nothing keeping you from experimenting a little here.

If you sell your game make sure that you understand the legal issues involved in doing so.

Publishing Options

The Publishing Options panel lets you specify whether you want to copy-protect your application, its content rating, and the locations where you want to publish your game.

The copy-protection feature is pretty much useless as it can be easily circumnavigated by following a couple of guides on the Internet. Google is going to deprecate this type of copy-protection, which should prevent the user from copying your APK file from the device and offering it for free on the web. Instead, Google now offers an API to integrate a licensing service in your application. This service is supposed to make it harder for users to pirate your game. Evaluating this is a little bit out of scope of this book; I suggest heading over to the Android developer site if you are paranoid about pirates. As with many digital rights management (DRM) schemes there have been problems reported by users who can't run or install an app that uses the licensing service. Take this with a grain of salt, of course. It's the best option you have for DRM at the moment if you need it.

The content rating allows you to specify what your target audience is. There are guidelines for rating your own application, which you can find out about by clicking the Learn More link on the publishing page. Your application will be filtered by the market based on the content rating you give it. So evaluate carefully what's fitting for your game.

Finally you can choose the locations where your application will be available. Usually you want it to be available everywhere, of course. There might be scenarios where you might want to publish your application only in a selection of locations, possibly for legal reasons. Normally, that's nothing that would get in your way, though.

Publish!

The last few things to specify on the publishing page are your contact information, your agreement to the Android Content Guidelines (also linked to on the same page, read them), and that you agree with US export laws, which you usually do. With all that information provided, it's time to click the huge Publish button at the bottom of the page!

Your game will be instantaneously available to millions of people around the globe. On the Android Market your application will enter the Just In category, making it discoverable for users for as long as it doesn't get pushed down the list by other new applications. Do not try to game the Just I" mechanism; it won't work. Uploading a "new" version of your application every few hours will not result in your application bubbling up the Just In list.

Marketing

While it's way out of my area of expertise, here are a few thoughts on marketing. There's a healthy ecosystem around the Android platform on the web, consisting of news sites, blogs, forums, and so on. Most blogs and news sites are happy to report on new games, so try to get in touch with as many of them as possible. There are also game-specific Android sites, like http://www.droidgamers.com, that should be your number-one target for getting the word out. Without a little marketing your game is unlikely to get noticed, as the Just In list is highly dynamic. Marketing is part of the success of your game. Whole books have been written on the topic, but I assume there's no magic formula. Make a great game and make people know about it.

The Developer Console

Once your game is on the market you want to keep track of its status. How many people have downloaded it so far? Have there been crashes? What are the users saying? You can check all this in the developer console (see Figure 13–6).

For each of your published applications you can get a few pieces of information.

- The overall rating of your game and the number of ratings
- The comments by users (just click the "Comments" link for the respective application)
- The number of times your application has been installed so far
- The number of active installs of your application
- Error reports

The error reports are of special interest to us. Figure 13–7 shows you the error reports I got for my game Newton.

Figure 13–7. *Error reports overview*

There have been a total of eight freezes and two crashes. Newton has been on the market for more than a year, so that's not bad. You can further drill down into the specific errors, of course. The error reporting feature of the developer console will provide you with detailed information about the crashes and freezes such as the device model the problem appeared on, full stack traces and so on. This can be of immense help when you're trying to figure out what's actually going wrong. Comments on the market won't help as much.

> **NOTE** The error reporting is a device-side feature that is not supported on older Android versions. If you want to have full confidence that you are catching all problems, I suggest giving Acra a look as mentioned earlier.

Summary

Publishing your game on the market is a breeze and has a very low barrier of entry. The hard part is making people aware of your game, a task I sadly can't help you with. You now have all the knowledge necessary to design, implement, and publish your first game on Android. May the force be with you.

Chapter 14

What's Next?

We talked about a ton of stuff in this book, and still there's so much more to learn. If you feel comfortable with all the material in here, you'll probably want to dig deeper. Here are a couple of ideas and directions for your journey.

Getting Social

One of the biggest trends in gaming in the last couple of years has been the integration with social media and services. Twitter, Facebook, and Reddit have become a part of many people's lives. And those people want to have their friends and family with them in their games as well. What's cooler than having your Dad beat you in the latest iteration of Zombie Shooter 13, right?

Both Twitter and Facebook provide APIs that let you interact with their services. Want to give the user a way to tweet their latest high score in your game? No problem—integrate the Twitter API and away you go.

On a related note, there are two big services in the mobile space that make it their goal to connect gamers and let them discover new games easily: Scoreloop and OpenFeint. Both provide an API for Android that lets players easily keep online high scores, compare their achievements, and so on. Both APIs are pretty straightforward and come with good examples and documentation. I prefer Scoreloop, for what it's worth.

Location Awareness

We only briefly touched on this in Chapters 1 and 4 and didn't exploit it in any of our games. All Android devices come with some type of sensor that lets you determine a user's location. That in itself is interesting already, but using it in a game can make for some innovative and never-before-seen game mechanics. It's still a hardly used feature in most Android games. Can you think of a fun way to use the GPS sensor?

Multiplayer Functionality

This being a beginner's book, we haven't talked about how to create multiplayer games. Suffice it to say that Android provides you with the APIs to do just that. Depending on the type of game, the difficulty of implementing multiplayer functionality varies. Turn-based games, such as chess or card games, are pretty simple to implement. Fast-paced action games or real-time strategy games are a different matter altogether. In both cases, you need to have an understanding of network programming, a topic for which a lot of materials exist on the Web.

OpenGL ES 2.0 and More

So far, you've seen only half of OpenGL ES, so to speak. We used OpenGL ES 1.0 exclusively, because it is the most widely supported version on Android at this point. Its fixed-function nature lends itself well to getting into 3D graphics programming. However, there's a newer, shinier version of OpenGL ES that enables you to directly code on the GPU. It's very different from what you have seen in this book, in that you are responsible for all the nitty-gritty details such as fetching a single texel from a texture or manually transforming the coordinates of a vertex, all directly on the GPU.

OpenGL ES 2.0 has a so-called shader-based, or programmable, pipeline as opposed to the fixed-function pipeline of OpenGL ES 1.0 and 1.1. For many 3D (and 2D) games, OpenGL ES 1.x is more than sufficient. If you want to get fancy, you might want to consider checking out OpenGL ES 2.0, though! Don't be afraid—all the concepts you learned in this book will be easily transferable to the programmable pipeline.

We also haven't touched on topics such as animated 3D models and some more-advanced OpenGL ES 1.x concepts such as vertex buffer objects. As with OpenGL ES 2.0, you can find many resources on the Web as well as in book form. You know the basics. Now it's time to learn even more!

Frameworks and Engines

If you bought this book with a little prior game development knowledge, you may have wondered why I didn't choose to use one of the many frameworks available for Android game development. Reinventing the wheel is bad, right? I want you to firmly understand the principles. Although this may be tedious at times, it will pay off in the end. With the knowledge you gained here, it will be so much easier to pick up any precanned solution out there, and it is my hope that you'll recognize the advantage that gives you.

For Android, a couple of commercial and noncommercial, open source frameworks and engines exist. What's the difference between a framework and an engine?

A framework will give you control over every aspect of your game development environment. This comes at the price of having to figure out your own way of doing things (for example, how you organize your game world, how you handle screens and transitions, and so on). In this book, we developed a (very simple) framework upon which we build our games.

An engine, on the other hand, is more streamlined for specific tasks. It dictates how you should do things, giving you easy-to-use modules for common tasks and a general architecture for your game. The downside is that your game might not fit the precanned solutions the engine offers you. Often times, you'll have to modify the engine itself to achieve your goals, which might or might not be possible, depending on whether the source is available. Engines can greatly speed up initial development time but might slow it to a grinding halt if you encounter a problem that the engine was not made for.

In the end, it's a matter of personal taste, budget, and goals. As an independent developer, I prefer frameworks because those are usually easier for me to understand and because they let me do things in the exact way I want them to be done.

With that being said, choose your poison. Here's a list of frameworks and engines that can speed up your development process:

- *Unreal Development Kit* (`www.udk.com`): A commercial game engine running on a multitude of platforms and developed by Epic Games. Those guys made games such as Unreal Tournament, so this engine is quality stuff. Uses its own scripting language.

- *Unity* (`www.unity3d.com`): Another commercial game engine with great tools and functionality. It too works on a multitude of platforms, including iOS and Android, or in the browser and is easy to learn. Allows a couple of languages for coding the game logic; Java is not among them.

- *jPCT-AE* (`www.jpct.net/jpct-ae/`): A port of the Java-based jPCT engine for Android, this has some great features with regard to 3D programming. Works on the desktop and on Android. Closed source.

- *Ardor3D* (`www.ardor3d.com`): A very powerful Java-based 3D engine. Works on Android and on the desktop, and is open source with great documentation.

- *libgdx* (`code.google.com/p/libgdx/`): An open source Java-based game development framework by yours truly, for 2D and 3D games. Works on Windows, Linux, Mac OS X, and of course Android without any code modifications. You can develop and test on the desktop without the need for an attached device or the slow emulator (or waiting a minute until your APK file is uploaded to the device). You'll probably feel right at home after having read this book—my evil plan. Did you notice that this bullet-point is only slightly bigger than the rest?

- *Slick-AE* (`http://slick.cokeandcode.com`): A port of the Java-based Slick framework to Android, built on top of libgdx. Tons of functionality and easy-to-use API for 2D game development. Cross-platform and open source, of course.

■ *AndEngine* (www.andengine.org): A nice, Java-based Android-only 2D engine, partially based on libgdx code (open source for the win). Similar in concept to the famous cocos2d game development engine for iOS.

I suggest giving those options a try at some point. They can help you speed up your game development quite a bit.

Resources on the Web

The Web is full of game development resources. In general, Google will be your best friend, but there are some special places that you should check out, including these:

■ www.gamedev.net: One of the oldest game development sites on the Web, with a huge treasure chest of articles on all sorts of game development topics.

■ www.gamasutra.com: Another old Goliath of game development. More industry orientated, with lots of postmortems and insight into the professional game development world.

■ http://wiki.gamedev.net: A big wiki on game development, chock full of articles on game programming for different platforms, languages, and so on.

■ www.flipcode.com/archives/: The archives of the now defunct flipcode site. Some pearls can be found here. Although slightly outdated at times, it is still an incredibly good resource.

■ www.java-gaming.org: The -number one go-to place for Java game developers. People such as Markus Persson of Minecraft fame frequent this place (well, Markus doesn't that much anymore, given his current lifestyle).

Closing Words

It's 2:20 a.m. and I'm sitting at my kitchen table with my trusty netbook in front of me. That's been my default pose for the last couple of months at night. I hope I can change my sleeping pattern back to normal.

Writing this book was a joy (the mornings not so much), and I hope I gave you what you came here for. There's so much more to discover, so many more techniques, algorithms, and ideas to explore. This is just the beginning for you. There's more ahead to learn.

I feel confident that with the material we dissected and discussed, you have a solid foundation to build upon that will enable you to grasp new ideas and concepts faster. There's no need to fall into the trap of copying and pasting code anymore. Even better, almost all the things we discussed will translate well to any other platform (give or take some language or API differences). I hope you can see the big picture and that it will enable you to start building the games of your dreams.

Index

■H

N

O

■ S